FOUNDATION PRESS

LABOR LAW STORIES

Edited By

LAURA J. COOPER
J. Stewart & Mario Thomas McClendon Professor
in Law and Alternative Dispute Resolution
University of Minnesota Law School

and

CATHERINE L. FISK
Professor of Law
Duke University School of Law

For
The Labor Law Group

FOUNDATION PRESS
New York, New York
2005

The artwork on the cover was created by Kathleen Farrell for the United Brotherhood of Carpenters and Joiners of America. Ms Farrell is a member of the United Scenic Artists Union Local #829. She frequently works for regional and national labor unions. She is the president and founder of Friends of Community Public Art (FCPA) headquartered in Joliet, Illinois. To see more of her work visit the web site <FCPAonline.org>.

395 Hudson Street
New York, NY 10014
Phone Toll Free 1–877–888–1330
Fax (212) 367–6799
fdpress.com
Printed in the United States of America

ISBN 1–58778–875–6

LABOR LAW STORIES

FOUNDATION PRESS

LABOR LAW STORIES

*

Introduction

Laura J. Cooper and Catherine L. Fisk

The Enduring Power of Collective Rights

In 1935, in the depths of the Great Depression when prospects for American workers and businesses seemed bleak, Congress sought to improve both the lives of workers and the economy by enacting the National Labor Relations Act (NLRA). While some pieces of New Deal legislation, such as the Social Security Act and the Fair Labor Standards Act, decreed specific rights for workers and obligations for employers to address specific workplace problems, the vision reflected in the NLRA, named after its principal sponsor Robert Wagner, was radically different. Rather than dictating substantive rights and obligations, the Wagner Act instead established a process under which firms and their employees could define their own rights and obligations. Even more radically, the process it created was not one in which workers, as individuals, could, for the most part, assert their rights. Instead it was a process in which workers would have to channel their efforts into a collective voice in order to advance their interests. Workers could gain substantive rights under the NLRA only by joining together in labor organizations and using their collective economic power to persuade employers to grant employees rights in collective bargaining agreements. Unions of workers were granted rights that they could exercise collectively on behalf of their members. Individual employees were granted some rights—the rights to join unions and to engage in other concerted activity for mutual aid and protection—but the individual rights were granted to facilitate group activity. The government would police the process, but it would not define the terms of employment. The entire regime of individual and group rights is premised on assumptions about the social and economic importance of collective action. The chapters in *Labor Law Stories* consider the endurance of this collective model as the American workplace has evolved in the seventy years since enactment of the NLRA.

The text of the NLRA was brief. Congress created an administrative agency, the National Labor Relations Board (NLRB), and entrusted it further to define the meaning of the statute and to implement its provisions. In the beginning, the agency was fragile. Statutes similar to the NLRA had recently been held unconstitutional by the Supreme Court. Some labor relations experts were so sure that the NLRA would meet the same fate that would-be appointees were reluctant to assume positions at the agency and many employers felt confident in ignoring its directives.

Congress' decision to entrust enforcement of the National Labor Relations Act to an expert agency was animated by several concerns. Some were the same concerns that inspired the creation during the New Deal of expert administrative agencies in many areas of government, and some were unique to the field of labor relations. Congress distrusted the capacity and willingness of federal judges to resolve labor disputes because the federal courts had, in the view of Progressive supporters of labor legislation, completely disgraced themselves in the late nineteenth and early twentieth centuries by enjoining all manner of worker action. A politically accountable agency staffed with labor lawyers seemed infinitely preferable to federal courts. In addition, the New Deal was the high water mark of faith in the power of experts to resolve disputes in a way that could transcend politics. The NLRB was supposed to be staffed with expert labor economists, sociologists, and lawyers who would design a legal regime that would be the best it could be. The notion that the legal issues that emerged from the great contest of capital and labor could be resolved by the application of expertise has in retrospect come to seem hopelessly naive. Congress' early faith in experts never enjoyed the chance to be tested, as an early effort to purge the agency of suspected communists led to the elimination of the labor economists and sociologists. Yet the argument for judicial deference to the agency's expertise has persisted over time, if only because the Board and its staff examine thousands of labor disputes every year whereas any particular court sees only a handful. That labor policy should be made by a politically accountable agency remains a plausible justification for judicial deference to NLRB decisionmaking. But in labor law as elsewhere, courts find it extremely difficult to defer to the political judgments of an agency with which they strenuously disagree. In short, the dance between the agency and the judiciary—a dance that is done throughout the modern administrative state—is particularly elaborate and has an especially interesting and well-documented history in the field of labor relations, and its development over time merits study by anyone interested in modern American law and government.

Also underlying Congress' decision to trust labor relations to an expert agency was the Progressive-era conviction that an accurate understanding of the facts of a dispute was absolutely crucial to appropriate application of law. In one respect, labor is no different than any other field in the importance of facts. The facts of the case are crucial to the success of the litigants in many cases. Obviously that is true in the trial court or administrative agency where the facts are found, established, developed, or invented, depending on your point of view. Even in the appellate courts, where facts are conventionally thought to take a back seat to the law, facts matter. An eminent federal appellate judge once confessed that the most important part of a brief, the part most likely to persuade the court of appeals—after the names of the lawyers on the cover—was the statement of facts. A well-written statement of facts, in his view, could tell the court what the legal issues were and how they should be decided. Yet facts are given short shrift in most law school casebooks, and in most appellate opinions. Students learn to read facts in order to engage in common law reasoning, to distinguish the instant case from precedent, and they endure the recitation of old adages about facts ("hard cases make bad law" or "when the facts are in your favor, argue the facts; when the law is in your favor, argue the law, and when neither is in your favor, argue policy"). But students are sometimes not told much about how perceptions of facts shape the perceived need for legal rules. Nowhere is the importance of facts greater than in the area of labor law. Lawyers know, and young lawyers must learn, the importance of developing a solid factual record. In more than one case discussed in this book, the most important "facts" recited in the Supreme Court's opinion may not have been facts at all. The supposed facts became part of the administrative or lower court record and were not challenged on appeal. Law students are ill-served by training that teaches them to be blind to the importance of facts in shaping perceptions of justice, and to the necessity of and techniques for establishing a desirable factual record on which to base their legal arguments.

The chapters in this book tell the story of the development of labor law over the course of nearly seventy years, beginning with one of the earliest of the Supreme Court's cases under the NLRA and ending with one of its most recent. The first story we present is that of *Mackay*, where the employer believed it could avoid any liability for its actions by challenging the constitutionality of the Act. The case reached the Supreme Court in 1938, only one year after the constitutionality of the Act was established, and although the employer's constitutional challenge to the statute failed, the case found the Court and the NLRB still very cautious about the power of Congress to regulate the workplace. The case offered the Court an opportunity to address one of the fundamental questions that the brief statutory language had failed to answer. If the design of the Act called for employees to gain rights through the use of economic force—going on strike—was the employer free to give their jobs to others if they did so? In dicta that eventually proved to be far more powerful than the case's holding, the Court said that employers had the right permanently to replace striking workers. To contemporary ears, the conclusion seems profoundly at odds with the statute's express protection of the right to strike. Economic power, as exercised in a strike, was to be the catalyst that would produce collective bargaining agreements—the source of employee rights. The chapter by Julius G. Getman and Thomas C. Kohler on *Mackay Radio* explains the puzzle of how such a basic principle of American labor law could appear to be established so casually. It also explains why the power permanently to replace striking workers was not exercised frequently enough for the Court's conclusion to seem controversial until decades after the case was decided. The chapter also examines the devastating impact of the recent widespread use of permanent replacements in a legal regime that rests on the ability of workers to exercise economic power through strikes.

When the NLRA was first enacted, Congress is generally thought to have assumed that the process of collective bargaining could be advanced simply by protecting the right of employees to organize and by directing employers to bargain once their employees had chosen a labor organization as their representative. Economic power, demonstrated, if necessary, through strikes and lockouts, would determine the nature and results of the collective bargaining process. In 1947, however, with the Republican Party in control of Congress and the post-war wave of strikes testing the limits of legislative patience with laissez faire, Congress enacted the Taft–Hartley Act, which significantly modified the Wagner Act regime. While limiting the right of employees to use all sorts of economic weapons by adding union unfair labor practices to the statute for the first time, Congress also recognized that it would be necessary to establish legally-enforceable rules for bargaining to prevent union and employer behaviors that could make a mockery of the process. Although Congress in 1947 mandated that the parties bargain in good faith, again it left the details to the NLRB. Would collective bargaining be a rational process in which results arose from equal access to information and reflected the parties' mutual best interests? Or would it be an economic power struggle in which the stronger party, whether employer or union, would impose its will on the weaker? The chapter by Kenneth G. Dau–Schmidt on *Truitt Manufacturing Company* (1956) and *Insurance Agents' International Union* (1960) describes the struggle between the NLRB and the Supreme Court to define the duty to bargain in good faith. The chapter examines, from the perspective of economic analysis, the two cases, which seem paradoxically to expect collective bargaining to be both a process of rational decisionmaking and a battle of economic power.

While Congress' answer to workplace regulation in 1935 had been to establish a collective bargaining process, it had surprisingly little to say about the enforcement of the agreements reached through collective bargaining until it enacted the Taft–Hartley Act in 1947. In an effort to make unions and firms accountable for the agreements that they reached, Congress for the first time made unions subject to suit as entities and provided that collective bargaining agreements would be enforceable in federal court. Once again, though, its language was extraordinarily modest. Section 301 of the Taft–Hartley Act simply gave federal courts jurisdiction to hear actions for enforcement of collective bargaining agreements without saying a word about the substantive law that would govern such actions. Union lawyers who remembered the hostility of federal courts to unions in the years before Congress eliminated federal court jurisdiction over labor disputes were skeptical about the prospects of judicial enforcement of collective bargaining agreements. Katherine V. W. Stone's chapter on the *Steelworkers Trilogy* (1960) tells how a determined group of union attorneys conceived a vision of collective bargaining agreement enforcement in which courts would direct disputants to private arbitrators whose decisions would be final. The chapter explains how these lawyers persuaded the Supreme Court to adopt their vision even though it required courts to refrain from overruling arbitral awards with which they fundamentally disagreed. She also tells how the union lawyers' success in keeping the courts out of the arbitration process ironically facilitated greater judicial intrusion into union internal affairs and exacerbated labor's isolation from other social movements.

Although the central theme of the NLRA initially had been protection of workers' right to organize, the brief and deliberately vague language of the statute left many basic principles of the organizing process to be defined by the NLRB and the courts even decades later. In *Gissel Packing* (1969), the Supreme Court addressed two such issues. First, did the First Amendment permit the NLRB to preclude employers from making negative predictions about the effect of unionization on their businesses? Second, was the agency permitted to conclude that in some cases an employer's misconduct during an organizing campaign so intimidated workers that the agency could order the employer to bargain with the union as the exclusive representative of its employees even though the union never won a representation election? The chapter on *Gissel Packing* by Laura J. Cooper and Dennis R. Nolan describes how the Supreme Court accepted the agency's paternalistic image of worker vulnerability and answered both questions affirmatively but explains why that case's holdings seem to have had so limited an effect.

No story of American law or history, especially labor history, can be told without acknowledging the powerful legacy of slavery and the persistence of race discrimination. Not surprisingly, the law of labor relations struggled with issues of race over the course of the twentieth century. In the 1930's, a group of talented black lawyers began a litigation campaign to challenge segregation in schools, places of public transportation, and the workplace. One of the cases they brought, *Steele v. Louisville and Nashville Railroad,* challenged the racial segregation on Southern railroads maintained by the all-white railroad workers' unions. During World War II, when blacks were conscripted to fight and die along with whites, and when America professed to the world its moral superiority to the Nazi regime, the black workers finally found a sympathetic forum in the U.S. Supreme Court when the legal system could no longer afford to ignore blatant race discrimination on the home front. Deborah Malamud's chapter on *Steele v. Louisville and Nashville Railroad Company* (1944) describes how a careful litigation strategy led the Court to find that when law permits a union to be the exclusive representative of workers at a firm it also imposes upon the union an implicit obligation to represent all workers fairly. More broadly, the chapter informs the longstanding debate about the relationship between litigation and social change.

As the civil rights movement gained strength and a particularly forceful voice in the Black Power movement of the late 1960's, the fight over persistent racial inequality in employment continued. In *Emporium Capwell* (1975), a group of black department store employees in San Francisco were fired for picketing and demanding that the Emporium cease discriminating. The rule that the union is the *exclusive* representative of the workers—the very principle that had given rise to rights of black workers in *Steele*—now condemned the black department store workers for seeking to negotiate with their employer outside the collective bargaining process. Justice Thurgood Marshall, the first African–American to sit on the Supreme Court and a principal architect of the litigation strategy that struck down racial segregation, wrote the Court's opinion denying these workers the right to protest. In this chapter, Professors Calvin William Sharpe, Marion Crain and Reuel E. Schiller explore the painful dilemma posed by the principles of exclusive representation and majority rule upon which the labor law system rests. They offer diverse perspectives on whether the Supreme Court in *Emporium Capwell* properly balanced individual and collective rights.

The NLRA's vision that a process of collective bargaining, rather than legislated substantive rights, could best protect workers was again tested later in the twentieth century when American businesses found new ways to structure their operations in an effort to drive down labor costs. The Supreme Court concluded in *First National Maintenance* (1981) that the duty to bargain does not apply to the decision whether to eliminate unionized jobs by closing a part of a company's operations, at least in some situations. Of what value is collective bargaining if fundamental restructuring decisions that cost unionized workers their jobs can be made in the absence of an obligation to bargain? In the chapter on

First National, Alan Hyde reveals the peculiar path that brought the case before the Supreme Court and the courtyard negotiations between Supreme Court law clerks that produced Justice Blackmun's bewildering answer to the question.

As American businesses faced the challenge of global economic competition in the late 1980's they looked abroad to Japan and elsewhere and saw models of employee involvement in workplace decision-making that they thought enabled their foreign competitors to outdistance American productivity. Business owners asserted that a little-noticed provision of the NLRA, thought fundamental to prohibit employer-dominated "company unions" in the 1930's, was outdated and now prevented American firms from enjoying the benefits of worker participation. Unions feared a change in the law that had always prohibited employer domination of employee participation programs would pave the way for a resurgence of company unions to forestall employee demands for an independent union and full collective bargaining. In the chapter on *Electromation* (1992), Robert B. Moberly describes how employers and their lawyers organized a challenge to this provision before the NLRB and in Congress. Their argument that the NLRA's 1935 adversarial model of employer-union relationships could not meet the challenges of the twentieth century failed to persuade either the Board or Congress. The Act's mandate that worker-employer negotiations had to be channeled into a structure of collective bargaining and exclusive representation endured in the face of this powerful assault.

Now, in the twenty-first century, the Act's language and vision are facing new questions as the structure and composition of the American workforce change. Virtually every piece of protective labor legislation reflects major policy judgments about the scope of legal protection for workers in its definition of which workers are covered by it. The NLRA is no different. Particularly in the last two decades, as union organizing has spread into sectors of the economy where union density historically has been low—health care, white collar work, and low-wage workplaces dominated by recent immigrants—there have been pitched legal battles over which workers are to be protected. Two of the most controversial areas have been the exclusion of nominally supervisory workers and undocumented immigrant workers from the protections of the NLRA. The final two chapters deal with these issues, addressing the particular issue in each case in the context of the much broader legal and social dispute about the need and prospects for unions in the evolving globalized American labor market and in unconventional managerial structures where even relatively low-level employees have some responsibility to direct the work of others.

As the lines between employee and supervisor blur, will the result be that large proportions of the workforce become classified as supervisors with no protection from an Act that affords rights only to non-supervisory employees? Marley Weiss' chapter on *Kentucky River Community Care* (2001) addresses that question in the context of the growing health care industry. *Kentucky River* is the second of two cases decided by the Supreme Court within the space of a relatively few years that addressed the question of the circumstances in which nurses are exempt from labor law protections because they are "supervisors" rather than ordinary professional employees. The chapter examines the role of union organizing in the health care industry and the vexing question of how the exempt category of "supervisor" should be defined in an era of increasingly flat hierarchies.

Another profound change in the twenty-first century workforce is the growing number of foreign-born workers. Much union organizing today is occurring in low-wage workplaces dominated by immigrant workers, many of whom are undocumented. While the NLRB seeks to protect the NLRA rights of all workers, both documented and undocumented, immigration laws seek to discourage illegal immigration by prohibiting employers from hiring undocumented workers. Should the objectives of the immigration laws preclude the NLRB from providing remedies to a worker, denied work in violation of the NLRA, when doing that work was unlawful under immigration statutes? Or would denying remedies to undocumented aliens under the NLRA increase incentives to employ undocumented workers by making them less risky to hire and cheaper to fire? Catherine L. Fisk and Michael J. Wishnie in their chapter on *Hoffman Plastic Compounds* (2002) show how immigration law enforcement won the battle with labor rights enforcement, leaving an ever-expanding proportion of the workforce beyond the basic protections of the law.

While the chapters describe the doctrinal evolution of law under the NLRA in the seventy years since its enactment, the fundamental purpose of this book is to tell the stories of the cases in which these doctrines emerged. The authors have interviewed dozens of participants in these cases—representatives of unions and management, union organizers, lawyers for unions, companies and the NLRB, members of the NLRB and Supreme Court law clerks. They have pored over archival records of the NLRB and the papers of lawyers and Supreme Court justices. They have read transcripts of agency hearings and Supreme Court arguments. They bring to this volume quite remarkable stories of how law gets made, how this process of law-making by litigation affects the lives of the people involved and their advocates, and how the law they make sometimes has an impact on others, and sometimes does not.

Readers familiar with labor law may be charmed by some of the previously unknown anecdotes about these cases we discovered in our research. A worker's birth certificate dramatically thrown in the wastebasket in the midst of a hearing before an administrative law judge became the crucial evidence that led the case to the Supreme Court. An NLRB lawyer falsely represented the agency's law to the Supreme Court because he thought it would help the case. A lawyer who won his case in the Supreme Court later served time in prison for arson. A lawyer tried to tell a judge what a Senator meant by language in the statute, only to have the judge reply that he'd been the Senator's staff member at the time and knew exactly what the Senator meant.

There is more to knowing the story behind the leading labor law cases than the delight of surprise. This book resolves some of the mysteries that have puzzled generations of students and teachers. Few people who know Justice Thurgood Marshall's career as one of the pioneering lawyers who established the modern civil rights regime can read his opinion in *Emporium Capwell*, which paves the way to uphold the firing of black civil rights protesters *precisely because of* their civil rights protest, without wondering whether he felt any heartache about his decision. The chapters on *Steele* and *Emporium Capwell* make clear that his views on the benefits of unionization for black workers were strong and longstanding. Ever since employers began in the 1980's to invoke in earnest the right established in *Mackay Radio* permanently to replace striking workers, labor law students have wondered why such a major limitation on the right to strike was so casually engrafted onto the statute by the Supreme Court in 1938, and whether it was considered at the time to be nearly the death blow to the labor relations regime that later critics believed it to have been. Why did the employer in *First National Maintenance* expend the funds necessary for Board, appellate court, and Supreme Court review when it could have instead just bargained to impasse with the union at seemingly little cost?

The benefit of knowing the full story behind these cases is greater even than being charmed by stories or satisfied by the resolution of mysteries. The law of work shapes the life stories of real people. Work is central to every aspect of our society. It is where we spend most of our waking hours. It is how we support ourselves and our families. It is the origin of much of society's wealth. Personal identity is often defined in significant part by our workplace role. We bring to the workplace our basic values of freedom, democracy, autonomy, and fairness. The stories we tell here are the stories of people from many walks of life—railroad firemen, nurses, factory workers, insurance agents, janitors, retail clerks and radio operators—who sought by collaborating with fellow workers to control their destinies. Some, like William Steele, succeeded. Winning a case worked a significant improvement in his life. Some failed, like the anonymous undocumented worker whose unsuccessful union organizing effort became *Hoffman Plastic*. These are also the stories of those whom they challenged—employers in a variety of industries who sought recognition of their rights as owners of capital to manage their businesses in the interests of owners and stockholders. For almost all of them, the case was not about the arcana of legal doctrine; it was about how the law and lawyers would treat their aspirations and fears.

The ten chapters here present the story of fourteen decisions of the Supreme Court and one from the National Labor Relations Board that never made it to the Supreme Court. The cases were identified as the most important labor law decisions from a survey of professors who regularly discuss these cases in their labor law courses. The stories behind the cases show the great variety of ways in which landmark cases become landmarks. By itself, that process can be intriguing. To law students, it may help when wading through the darker moments of law school to realize that one day, sooner than you might think, it might be your case that makes it to the Supreme Court or that is reported in the newspaper or on TV. Some of these cases were planned to be landmarks from the very beginning. *Steele,* for example, was part of the decades-long legal strategy developed and implemented by African–American lawyers to challenge race discrimination in society. In this respect, the story of *Steele,* like the story of *Brown v. Board of Education,* is a story of the calculated use of law to effect radical social change. But other cases in this volume wound up as landmarks by fortuity, by the lawyer stumbling upon the right argument on the right facts in front of the right judge at the right time. Sometimes a case achieves prominence despite the parties' desires to the contrary, as in the unsuccessful effort of counsel on both sides to try to preclude oral argument before the NLRB in *Electromation*. More often, though, as with most of the cases in this book, routine cases that appear undifferentiated from the thousands of cases decided by the NLRB each year, by happenstance get selected for Supreme Court review, thrusting ordinary lawyers into the national legal spotlight. In some cases, the spotlight proved irresistible. In *Gissel*, a management lawyer argued the case in the Supreme Court without compensation from the client, not revealing to the Court that the case was moot, because he so desired the experience. In *First National Maintenance*, the company's lawyer insisted on arguing in the Supreme Court himself although the U.S. Chamber of Commerce reportedly offered him tens of thousands of dollars to let its lawyer present the argument instead.

While the cases were selected because of professors' perceptions that they were the most important in the labor law canon for their doctrinal holdings, our deeper research into the actual effects of these cases revealed the sometimes limited effect of Supreme Court decisionmaking to change the conduct of real parties in labor relations. The Court's decision in *First National Maintenance* articulated a rule for a set of circumstances so unlikely that even that case did not really manifest them. Neither of *Gissel*'s holdings ended up truly governing union elections because lower courts proved so resistant to its directives. *Truitt* set the ground rules for employer disclosure of financial information so clearly that the case provided a script for avoiding disclosure, wholly undermining what the decision sought to achieve.

To scholars, reading these chapters may shed light on the old question of the extent to which law changes because society changes and to what extent law changes because of debates internal to the law. All agree that the relationship between legal change and social change is extremely complex, and the last generation of legal scholarship has more or less established that no single theory can explain all cases. These stories confirm the multiple ways in which law and other social and economic forces contribute to change. The chapter on *Steele*, for example, shows that the multi-faceted litigation and political strategy that, eventually, dismantled the thorough-going racial segregation of so many aspects of life played a major role in changing the lives of black workers. The reductionist position that litigation by itself dismantled Jim Crow is proven false, as is the equally reductionist position that litigation did nothing that would not have been achieved by social protest or lobbying. The interesting story is the complex mix of deliberate choices and luck, the differences that litigation made, and the significant limits on what litigation achieved.

We hope that reading the stories behind these cases will deepen both your understanding of and your affection for labor law. Labor law is special because, unlike nearly all other legal doctrines, it prioritizes group collective rights above individual rights. It gives us the opportunity to examine law-making in a high-volume administrative agency that struggles to maintain uniform national application of the law while depending for ultimate enforcement on appellate courts that sometimes, despite Supreme Court insistence on deference, cannot resist effectuating their own notions of how the law should be interpreted and applied. While other courses about the law of the workplace sometimes seem an incoherent collection of independent doctrines, labor law offers a comprehensive and consistent vision of workplace organization and decision-making, whose success can be tested against a constantly changing variety of issues.

The collective model that captured Congress' vision of workplace governance in 1935 also is the organizational principle for the authors of this book. This book was written by the Labor Law Group, a non-profit organization created from the 1946 observation of W. Willard Wirtz, then a law professor at Northwestern University, that labor law professors, working collectively without individual compensation, could best bring to the law school classroom labor law teaching materials that truly reflected the real lives of employees and employers. The Labor Law

Group, composed of approximately fifty professors in the U.S., Canada, Europe and Israel, today have in print six books on labor and employment law. All royalties generated by Group publications are held in trust for educational purposes and none inure to the benefit of any individual. This book, like the statute that gave rise to its subject, is inspired by the belief that people working together can achieve objectives that those working alone cannot.

1

Julius G. Getman and Thomas C. Kohler

The Story of *NLRB v. Mackay Radio & Telegraph Co.*: The High Cost of Solidarity

Few cases in the labor law canon have generated more vigorous debate or sparked more heated criticism than the Supreme Court's 1938 *Mackay* opinion.[1] The decision represents one of the Court's earliest interpretations of the provisions of the National Labor Relations Act. On its way to holding that an employer may not discriminate on the basis of union activity in reinstating employees at the end of a strike, the *Mackay* Court also instructed that an employer enjoys the unrestricted right under the statute permanently to replace strikers.

Although stated as dictum, the latter proposition, which quickly became known to lawyers and scholars as the "*Mackay* doctrine," has remained an important, if highly controversial, aspect of American labor law. After nearly seven decades, the doctrine continues to provoke the notice and the nearly universal condemnation of scholars. Commentary on the case in the classroom and in the literature tends to run from bewilderment ("Why did the Court reach for an issue not properly before it?") to the more darkly suggestive ("*Mackay* seems to represent the triumph of entrenched property rights thinking on the part of the justices over new notions of workers' rights"), to the flatly condemnatory ("The case stands as a prime example of the judicial de-radicalization of the Wagner Act"). The criticism is understandable.

The *Mackay* doctrine, as it has emerged, effectively hollows out the protections the Act affords strikers. The rule forbids employers to discharge workers who engage in a legal strike. At the same time, it allows employers to hire other workers to take their jobs. The replaced

[1] NLRB v. Mackay Radio & Telegraph Co., 304 U.S. 333 (1938).

striker remains an employee, but one who enjoys only a preferential claim to the prior position, if and when it becomes vacant, and only if the former striker has been unable to find comparable work. This distinction between discharge and replacement, critics charge, is the sort that only a lawyer could love—or even have imagined. To most contemporary observers, the doctrine undermines the right to strike, a right given special acknowledgment in the Act. *Mackay,* they note, makes it a peculiar right, the exercise of which may lead to the loss of one's job. Critics also point out that by weakening the right to strike, *Mackay* inadvertently undermines the institution of collective bargaining. As the Supreme Court has observed, the strike is "part and parcel of the system" the NLRA established, and constitutes "a prime motive power for agreements in free collective bargaining."[2] Critics also argue that the rule upsets the neutrality toward the parties that the Act's framers intended the statute to embody.

Although the majority of contemporary commentators denounce *Mackay,* in 1938 it was heralded as a great victory for the National Labor Relations Board.[3] The Board's General Counsel, Charles Fahy, described it as a "gratifying" result which settled crucial constitutional and statutory interpretation issues, while the Union's President, Mervyn Rathborne, hailed it as a "complete vindication of the three-year fight of the union for reinstatement of the locked-out workers involved."[4] End-of-the-Court-Term assessments of the opinion by newspaper analysts[5] and the relatively small amount of law review commentary the case produced regarded *Mackay* as an important victory for the Wagner Act and for workers' rights.

As surprising as it may seem to us, the decision's striker-replacement language received little notice from observers at the time. The first piece critical of *Mackay* did not appear until 1941, three years after the decision was announced.[6] It would remain the sole critical piece for some

---

[2] NLRB v. Insurance Agents' International Union, 361 U.S. 477 (1960).

[3] *E.g., Decision Protects American Workers,* The Boston Evening Globe, May 16, 1938, at 1; *Court Backs Strike Right—Labor Board Scores in Mackay Case—Job Not Forfeit by Walk Out,* The Boston Morning Globe, May 17, 1938, at 1; *The Shape of Things,* The Nation, May 21, 1938, at 573.

[4] Lauren D. Lyman, *High Court Upholds NLRB in Mackay Radio Strike; Reopens Republic Case,* N.Y. Times, May 17, 1938, at 1, 12.

[5] Dean Dinwoodey, *Labor Law Wins High Court Tests,* N.Y. Times, May 22, 1938, at 62; Lewis Wood, *Court Again Helps New Deal,* N.Y. Times, May 29, 1938, at 40.

[6] Leonard B. Boudin, *The Rights of Strikers,* 35 Ill. L.Rev. 817 (1941) (The author of this piece would become one of the best-known civil rights lawyers of the 1960's, who represented, among others, Paul Robeson, Benjamin Spock, Daniel Ellsberg and the Cuban government. He was the great-nephew of Louis Boudin, a prominent labor lawyer and Karl

time. Serious and sustained criticism of the *Mackay* rule did not appear in the literature until the 1960's.

What accounts for this? If it is of such moment, why was so little mention made initially of *Mackay's* striker-replacement rule? Why does the case hold such different significance for us than it did for our predecessors? Why was it accepted at a time when the cause of labor was a primary concern of academics and liberals, but not today, a time when organized labor is in disarray and has far less support from intellectuals? The answers lie partly in the history of the case, but more significantly in the development of labor law and industrial relations in the years since *Mackay* was decided.

The holding of the case is relatively straightforward. Its history, however, takes some surprising turns and recounting it may reveal some of the basic problems and tensions that underlie the scheme of the National Labor Relations Act and the social understandings on which the statute rests.

Social and Legal Background

1. The Status of Strikers at Common Law

The NLRA became law on July 5, 1935. Now a mature statute with its basic principles well-established, one easily can forget the difficult choices its drafters confronted in framing its language, and the number of unforeseen problems that were left to be worked out through the process of what Justice Frankfurter called "elucidating litigation." It is also easy to forget that concepts very familiar to us had to be puzzled out over time by workers, their employers, the courts and other actors. Among these concepts are some that today hardly seem problematic at all: the definition and significance of a strike, the legal status of strikers, and the determination of when a strike ends.[7] We can best comprehend the problems the drafters faced concerning these issues by looking briefly at the basic common law doctrines that informed their thinking.

Any discussion of basic principles of American labor and employment law must take the employment at-will rule into account. That rule exerts a deep and often unnoticed gravitational pull on every aspect of

Marx scholar, and the father of two children who took rather different paths with regard to the law. His daughter, Kathy Boudin, was a member of the radical Weather Underground group that was implicated in a series of bombings across the U.S., including the Pentagon, the Capitol building, and the headquarters of the New York Police Department. She served twenty years for the robbery of an armored truck during which a police officer was killed. Louis' son, Michael, became a prominent conservative jurist and a judge of the United States Court of Appeals for the First Circuit.)

[7] For two examples of cases where such determinations were legally significant, see West Allis Foundry Co. v. State, 186 Wis. 24, 202 N.W. 302 (1925); Dail–Overland Co. v. Willys–Overland, Inc., 263 F. 171 (N.D. Ohio 1919).

the structure and operation of our employment regulatory schemes. It also conditions our ideas about the status and rights of strikers and their relationship with their employer.

Without doubt the most famous statement of the at-will rule comes from the Tennessee Supreme Court's 1884 opinion in *Payne v. The Western and Atlantic R.R. Co.*[8] There, the defendant railroad, presumably to protect its company-owned stores from competition, threatened to discharge any of its employees who bought goods from an independent merchant. The merchant, whose highly successful business was thereby destroyed, brought an action in tort against the railroad. The railroad, arguing in part that it "had the right to discharge employees because they traded with plaintiff, or for any other cause," successfully moved the trial court to dismiss the complaint.

The Tennessee Supreme Court affirmed the trial court's conclusion that the merchant's complaint stated no cause of action. If a master can direct his domestic servant not to trade with a merchant, the court reasoned, how could it be censurable if a master forbade a greater number from doing so? And if the law permits a master to withdraw his trade from a firm, how could it be unlawful for that master to order his servants to cease their trade, even if doing so will result in the failure of the company's business? The railroad's threat to discharge employees who continued to shop at the plaintiff's stores, the court concluded, also constituted no wrong. Employers, the court stated, "may dismiss their employees at will, be they many or few, for good cause, for no cause or even for cause morally wrong, without being thereby guilty of a legal wrong."

Notions of mutuality justified this rule. The right the employer enjoys "is a right which an employee may exercise in the same way, to the same extent, for the same cause or want of cause as the employer. He may refuse to work for a man or company, that trades with any obnoxious person, or does other things which he dislikes. He may persuade his fellows, and the employer may lose all his hands and be compelled to close his doors...." In this way, the Court declared,

> The great and rich and powerful are guaranteed the same liberty and privilege as the poor and weak. All may buy and sell when they choose; they may refuse to employ or dismiss whom they choose, without being thereby guilty of a legal wrong, though it may seriously injure and even ruin others.

The writer Anatole France parodied such formalized notions of even-handedness in his 1894 book, *The Red Lily,* as the "majestic equality" of

---

[8] 81 Tenn. 507 (1884). (The spelling of the word "employee" in quotes from the opinion has been modernized.)

the law "which forbid rich and poor alike to sleep under the bridges, to beg in the streets, and to steal their bread."[9] Adam Smith expressed a similar skepticism about the law's symmetry. In contests between masters and servants, he observed,

> It is not . . . difficult to foresee which of the two parties must, upon all ordinary occasions, have the advantage in the dispute, and force the other into compliance with their terms. . . . In all such disputes the masters can hold out much longer. . . . Many workmen could not subsist a week, few could subsist a month, and scarce any a year without employment. In the long-run the workman may be as necessary to his master as his master is to him; but the necessity is not so immediate.[10]

Unions soon would temper the rigors of the at-will rule through the inclusion of language in collective bargaining agreements that required an employer to have just cause to discharge an employee. Clauses limiting an employer's ability to discharge employees began to appear in collective agreements during the 1880's.[11] But the court in *Payne* did not elaborate on the rights of employees who accepted the invitation and withheld their work as a group to protest their employer's decisions. Had they not voluntarily quit their jobs? Could not the employer offer to others the positions the strikers had surrendered?

By the beginning of the twentieth century, common law courts largely had settled these issues. In his frequently cited concurrence in the 1908 case of *Iron Molders' Union v. Allis–Chalmers Co.*, for example, Judge Grosscup instructed that

> A strike is cessation of work by employees in an effort to get for the employees more desirable terms. A lock out is a cessation of the furnishing of work to employees in an effort to get for the employer more desirable terms. Neither strike nor lock out completely terminates, when this is its purpose, the relationship between the parties.[12]

As the Seventh Circuit subsequently would observe in *Michaelson v. United States*, when workers strike, "[t]hey are no longer working and receiving wages; but in the absence of any action other than . . . looking to a termination of the relationship, they are entitled to rank as

[9] Anatole France, *The Red Lily* 91 (Winifred Stephens, trans., Wm. H. Wise & Co. 1930).

[10] Adam Smith, 1 *An Inquiry into the Nature and Causes of the Wealth of Nations* 83–84 (R. H. Campbell and A. S. Skinner, eds., Oxford Univ. Press 1976).

[11] Sanford M. Jacoby, *The Duration of Indefinite Employment Contracts in the United States and England: An Historical Analysis,* 5 Comp. Lab. Law 85, 121–22 (1982).

[12] 166 F. 45, 52 (7th Cir. 1908) (Grosscup, J., concurring).

'employees,' with the adjective 'striking' defining their immediate status."[13]

The discussions of the status of strikers in the *Iron Molders'* and *Michaelson* cases, like that in other court decisions dealing with the issue, were incidental to appeals testing the granting or the limits of a labor injunction. The question of the employment status of the strikers was crucial to the question of their legally-protected right to picket and to engage in other activities seeking to persuade others not to take jobs with the struck employer. As employees, strikers had the right to make such appeals because the end sought—the betterment of their wages and working conditions—was lawful. In contrast, strangers with no employment-related interests to protect would be presumed to be acting out of malevolent and hence legally actionable motives.

The *Iron Molders'* opinion well illustrates these points. While enjoining threats of violence, the use of abusive or vile language and like acts, the court permitted the union to picket all the foundries in the city and county of Milwaukee in furtherance of a dispute over wages and working conditions. It also refused to enjoin striking members of the union from following work that had been transferred from the struck employers to foundries in other cities. As the court explained,

> [i]f appellee [the struck employers] had the right (and we think the right was perfect) to seek the aid of fellow foundrymen to the end that the necessary element of labor should enter into appellee's product, appellant [the union members] had the reciprocal right of seeking the aid of fellow molders to prevent that end. To whatever extent employers may lawfully combine and co-operate to control the supply and the conditions of work to be done, to the same extent should be recognized the right of workmen to combine and co-operate to control the supply and the conditions of the labor that is necessary to the doing of the work.[14]

The formal equality of the parties under the law, and their equal freedom to act in pursuit of their self-interest, governs the rationale and outcomes of these cases. As the *Michaelson* court explained, "In the industrial combat the two sides must have equal and reciprocal rights in exerting economic pressure . . . the strike was only tolerated as a weapon on one side because the other side was armed with an equivalent weapon." The "mutual freedom" of employers and employees to bring economic pressure on one another, the court instructed, "is the vitals of 'collective bargaining' or any bargaining."[15]

[13] 291 F. 940, 943 (7th Cir. 1923).

[14] 166 F. at 52.

[15] 291 F. at 943–44.

The formal equality of the law did not require effective equality. The common law did not seek to limit employer exercise of its economic power. The at-will rule, then-regnant concepts of contractual freedom, and formalized ideas of equality permitted employers to use devices such as yellow-dog contracts, by which employees agreed, as a condition of their employment, not to join a union or to attempt to organize fellow employees. Employers also remained free to discriminate against or discharge employees suspected of union activity, to use spies and to maintain blacklists, to establish company unions and representation plans to frustrate attempts at unionization and to employ other tactics designed to undermine strikes and to thwart other self-help efforts undertaken by their employees.

Commenting on the state of the law as it existed on the eve of the New Deal and the passage of the National Industrial Recovery Act of 1933, the labor historian Irving Bernstein noted that

> It was not true, however, as sometimes charged, that the law was tilted in the favor of employers. Labor relations law, statutory and, to a lesser extent, decisional, was characterized by a spirit of toleration. In theory there was essential equality. Workers might lawfully organize and bargain collectively, while employers with equal legality might frustrate freedom of association and refuse to bargain. In the realities of the market place this hypothetical balance gave the employer the advantage.[16]

Labor economist William Leiserson, who among many other activities in a very busy life was an arbitrator; the Executive Secretary of the National Labor Board (1933); the Chairman of the NLRB (1939–1943); a professor of economics at several schools including Johns Hopkins; and an advisor to Senator Robert Wagner, characterized the equality of the parties' rights under the law somewhat more pungently. "The law," Leiserson said, "recognized the equal freedom of the employers to destroy labor organizations and to deny the right of employees to join trade unions.... All that the employees had," Leiserson continued, "was a right to try to organize if they could get away with it; and whether they could or not depended on the relative economic strength of the employers' and employees' organizations."[17]

The short-lived National Industrial Recovery Act (NIRA) was passed in June 1933, a few months after the Roosevelt administration assumed office. The NIRA had many goals: its labor provisions were intended to promote effective equality under law between employers and employees

---

[16] Irving Bernstein, *The New Deal Collective Bargaining Policy* 7–8 (1950).

[17] William M. Leiserson, *Right and Wrong in Labor Relations* 26–27, *quoted in* Bernstein, *The New Deal Collective Bargaining Policy* at 8.

by protecting the right of workers to organize and "to engage in concerted activities for the purpose of collective bargaining or other mutual aid or protection." These provisions, set forth in § 7(a) of the NIRA,[18] anticipate the language of § 7 of the NLRA. The construction given the NIRA's labor provisions would establish important "common law" principles that would be carried over to the framing and administration of the terms of the NLRA.

2. Strikers, Striker Replacements, and the NIRA

When enacted by Congress, the NIRA established no procedures for enforcement of its labor provisions. To remedy this problem, President Roosevelt authorized the creation of the National Labor Board (NLB) on August 5, 1933, which had the duty to investigate and mediate industrial disputes, and later to conduct representation elections. The following year, Congress passed Public Resolution No. 44 authorizing the President to create a three-member National Labor Relations Board. The President subsequently issued the Executive Order establishing the NLRB on June 29, 1934. The Order gave the Board the power to investigate controversies, to hold hearings and make findings regarding complaints of discrimination or discharge of employees under § 7(a), to conduct elections, and to arbitrate disputes when requested. The Order also empowered the NLRB to establish regional offices throughout the United States, staffed with examiners and labor mediators and headed by regional directors, to assist the Board members in administering the NIRA.

The NLB and NLRB were unencumbered by any body of precedent save that they established for themselves, and their decisions have a certain inventively ad hoc quality about them. On issues involving the status of strikers and striker replacements, however, the NLB and the NLRB quickly adopted a familiar set of rules. When a strike occurred in reaction to an employer's breach of the terms of § 7(a), the NLB and the NLRB would order the reinstatement of the strikers, if necessary,

---

18 Section 7(a) provided that:

> Every code of fair competition, agreement, and license approved, prescribed, or issued under this title shall contain the following conditions: (1) That employees shall have the right to organize and bargain collectively through representatives of their own choosing, and shall be free from the interference, restraint, or coercion of employers of labor, or their agents, in the designation of such representatives or in self-organization or in other concerted activities for the purpose of collective bargaining or other mutual aid or protection; (2) that no employee and no one seeking employment shall be required as a condition of employment to join any company union or to refrain from joining, organizing, or assisting a labor organization of his own choosing; and (3) that employers shall comply with the maximum hours of labor, minimum rates of pay, and other conditions of employment, approved or prescribed by the President.

displacing workers hired as their replacements.[19] In its decision in *L. Mundet & Sons, Inc.*, for example, the NLRB explained that, "Where violations of Section 7(a) have provoked a strike, the appropriate restitution is reinstatement of all the strikers in preference to men hired during the strike."[20] In contrast, where the strike was economically-based, the strikers had no claim to reinstatement at the close of their job action. As the NLRB observed in its *Fischer–Jones Co.* decision, "We have held on a number of occasions that in the absence of a violation of Section 7(a) the company is under no obligation to discharge employees taken on during the course of a strike to replace striking employees."[21]

The Board's *Century Electric Co.* case provides a good illustration of these principles. There, discrimination charges were filed on behalf of strikers who were not reinstated following the end of a strike over wage rates. The Board found no evidence of bad faith bargaining on the company's part or of any discrimination practiced by it against any individuals, including members of the strike committee. The Board also noted that the company continued to reinstate strikers as the need for employees arose. "The case for the employees," the Board observed, "seems reduced to the contention that the ... [replacements] who were hired during the strike should be dismissed to make way for ... strikers who have not been reinstated." Such a complaint was legally insufficient. "In the absence of persuasive evidence that a violation of Section 7(a) by the company has caused all or some of ... [the replaced employees] to be out of work, there is no legal basis for requiring the company to make room for them by discharging other employees."[22]

Like the opinions of courts in civil law countries, Board decisions of this era appeared without dissents. The view of the NLRB about the reinstatement rights of economic strikers, however, may not have been unanimous. Board member Edwin S. Smith seems to have taken a stance that diverged from that of his colleagues, Harry A. Millis (a University of Chicago economist) and Lloyd Garrison (the Dean of the University of Wisconsin Law School).[23] A former newspaper reporter, researcher for the Russell Sage Foundation, personnel director for Filene's Department Store (a famously progressive Boston employer) and Commissioner of Labor and Industries in Massachusetts, Smith quickly gained a reputation as the most pro-labor NLRB member.

---

[19] *E.g.*, A. Roth & Co., 1 N.L.B. 75 (1934); Eagle Rubber Co., 2 N.L.B. 31 (1934).

[20] 2 N.L.R.B. 198, 199 (1935).

[21] 2 N.L.R.B. 236, 239 (1935).

[22] Century Electric Co., 1 N.L.R.B. 79, 81 (1934).

[23] Garrison remained on the Board only for a short period, and was replaced as Chairman by Francis Biddle, a Philadelphia lawyer with a background in corporate law.

In a memorandum he circulated to the other NLRB members, Smith put forth the position that replaced economic strikers should be entitled to reinstatement at the end of a strike. The threat of a strike and the strike itself, Smith maintained, "are properly included within the bargaining process." A striker "must therefore be regarded still as an employee who is attempting by voluntary abstention from work ... to influence the employer to broaden the terms of the bargain." It follows, Smith argued:

> If at any time during the progress of the strike a worker, or group of workers, go to the employer and state they are willing to resume their working relationship ... the employer must receive them back, displacing if necessary other workers who may have been hired during the period of the strikers' absence from work.... When strikers have declared their willingness to return to work on the employer's own terms, the utility of the strike breaker to the employer has ended. As a tool the strike breaker can be discarded—as an employee, dismissed.[24]

Smith failed to convince his colleagues to depart from the established doctrine regarding the rights of replaced economic strikers. Early versions of a bill that would evolve into the National Labor Relations Act, however, would for a time reflect his viewpoint.[25]

3. "Employee," Striker Replacements, and the Labor Disputes Bill of 1934

At the urging of the American Federation of Labor, Senator Robert Wagner took up the issue of the recall rights of economic strikers in his doomed labor disputes bill of 1934. The direct precursor of the National Labor Relations Act, the bill intended "[t]o equalize the bargaining power of employers and employees" and "to encourage the amicable settlement of disputes" between them. The bill addressed the issue of the recall rights of strikers in an indirect fashion, by providing that the term "employee" as used in the statute "shall not include an individual who has replaced a striking employee."[26]

---

[24] Edwin S. Smith, The Status of Strikers as Employees, National Archives, RG 25 (Records of the National Labor Relations Board) *quoted in,* John A. Logan, *The Striker Replacement Doctrine and State Intervention in Labor Relations, 1933–38,* Industrial Relations Research Association Series, 1 *Proceedings of the Fiftieth Annual Meeting* 347, 349–50 (1998).

[25] For accounts of the shortcomings of the NIRA's labor provisions and the many problems confronted by the first NLRB in enforcing the terms of § 7(a) of the NIRA, see Section 1 under Prior Proceedings *infra.*

[26] Labor Disputes Act, S. 2926, 73d Cong. § 3(3) (1934).

Not surprisingly, the exclusion of strikebreakers from the protections the bill afforded employees drew a torrent of criticism from employer groups. The exclusion, they argued, would lead to a variety of problems. For example, striker replacements, no matter how long they might work for an employer, could never gain employee status under the bill's terms. Consequently, it appeared that they would be permanently barred from enjoying the legally-protected right to bargain collectively with their employer.[27] Likewise, replacements could never participate in a union election, while those whom they replaced seemingly would retain an indefinite right to vote, even if they long since had gone to work for a different employer.[28] James Emery of the National Association of Manufacturers complained that the bill made the replacement worker "a legal cipher" and that this was done "by those who express profound interest in human right [sic]."[29]

Academic advisors to Wagner made similar points concerning the limbo to which the bill's definition of employee consigned replacement workers. Professor John Fitch of the New York School of Social Work, for example, noted that the bill would cause someone taking a job as a strikebreaker "to retain his non-employee status permanently." Fitch advised Wagner that no "harm would be done by dropping ... [the] reference to strike-breakers altogether." Wagner replied that Fitch's criticisms were "exceptionally well taken" and that they "will be invaluable to me when I attempt to iron out this legislation."[30]

The discrimination practiced against black workers by many unions further muddled the striker-replacement issue. T. Arnold Hill of the National Urban League, who wrote to Wagner expressing the League's "unqualified approval of any measure that seeks to equalize the bargaining power of employers and employees," nevertheless objected to the labor disputes bill because its language would permit labor organizations to exclude African–Americans from membership and it failed to protect them from acts of racial discrimination by labor unions. The bill also would deny to African–American "workers the status of 'employees' when they are engaged as strike-breakers in occupational fields where they are prohibited from joining the striking union." To remedy this

27 1 NLRB *Legislative History of the National Labor Relations Act, 1935* at 535 (Henry I. Harriman, President, United States Chamber of Commerce) (hereinafter *Legislative History*).

28 *Id.* at 721 (Leslie Vickers, American Transit Association).

29 *Id.* at 406.

30 John A. Logan, *The Striker Replacement Doctrine and State Intervention in Labor Relations, 1933–38,* Industrial Relations Research Association Series, 1 *Proceedings of the Fiftieth Annual Meeting* 352 (1998).

wrong, Hill recommended that the bill's definition of employee be revised to read:

> The term "employee" shall not include an individual who has replaced a striking employee, except when the labor organization either by direct constitutional or ritualistic regulation and/or by practices traceable to discriminatory policies bars an individual from joining such labor organization or restricts rights, privileges, and practices usually accorded members of such labor organizations.[31]

In an internal Urban League memorandum, Hill warned that if Wagner's labor disputes bill "passes in its present form, the power and influence of the labor movement will be greatly enhanced with the consequent danger of greater restrictions being practiced against Negro workers by organized labor." As presently framed, Hill continued, "the bill favors labor organizations, but does not benefit employees who replace striking employees." The discriminatory practices of unions, Hill observed, forced African–Americans "to work as strikebreakers when strikes are called by unions that bar them. As strikebreakers, they have no rights under the proposed" statute. Consequently, their "position will be made worse as that of other workers is enhanced."[32]

In response to their arguments, Wagner promised the leadership of the League that he would give "sympathetic consideration" to their concerns and that he remained "very receptive" to any language that would assist the League in accomplishing its objectives. Wagner professed that he was shocked "to find a measure which I have introduced to protect all working men [might be] used as an instrument to discriminate against some of them, and I shall examine my bill with the utmost care to prevent any such eventualities."[33]

The criticisms had effect. When Wagner introduced a revised version of the bill, the striker replacement exclusionary language was gone. It would not reappear, nor would any further reference be made concerning the status of striker replacements in Wagner's National Labor Relations Act, legislation he introduced in the next session of Congress in February 1935.

---

[31] 1 *Legislative History* at 1058–59.

[32] T. Arnold Hill, Acting Executive Secretary, National Urban League, April 3, 1934, Memorandum to all Coworkers, Library of Congress, NAACP Papers, Group 1, C–257, *quoted in* John A. Logan, *The Striker Replacement Doctrine and State Intervention in Labor Relations, 1933–38,* Industrial Relations Research Association Series, 1 *Proceedings of the Fiftieth Annual Meeting* 352 (1998).

[33] Letter of Robert F. Wagner to Lloyd Garrison, April 14, 1934; letter of Robert F. Wagner to Dr. D. Witherspoon, *quoted in* John A. Logan, *The Striker Replacement Doctrine and State Intervention in Labor Relations, 1933–38,* Industrial Relations Research Association Series, 1 *Proceedings of the Fiftieth Annual Meeting* 353 (1998).

4. Striker Replacements and the NLRA

By the time Wagner introduced S. 1958 in the 74th Congress, the bill that would become the National Labor Relations Act, § 2(3) of the statute, which defines the term "employee," had assumed its present form.[34] It reads, in pertinent part: "The term 'employee' shall include ... any individual whose work has ceased as a consequence of, or in connection with, any current labor dispute or because of any unfair labor practice, and who has not obtained any other regular and substantially equivalent employment." William Leiserson, who in 1934 had become the first Chairman of the National Mediation Board, was among those who submitted suggested amendments to the Senate Committee on Education and Labor concerning the language of the proposed statute. Leiserson also had prepared for the Committee an exhaustive analytical comparison of the terms of the failed labor disputes bill and the language of S. 1958. The memorandum dwelt at some length on the provisions of § 2(3).

Leiserson noted that some "extremely important changes" had been made in the new bill's definition of the term "employee" to bring within the proposed Act's coverage "employees whose work has ceased under particular circumstances." These changes were intended to conform the language of the bill to existing law. Consequently, Leiserson explained, the revisions embodied in § 2(3) included within the definition of employee "one whose work has ceased because of any unfair labor practice." The new language also ensured that economic strikers would be treated as employees and receive the Act's protections. The language of a previous committee draft, Leiserson pointed out, may have left economic strikers with no protections against "interference, restraint, or coercion," and would likely have left them without the "protection of the act if certain of their members, the strike leaders, for example, were discriminated against in reinstatement after all had agreed to return to work on the employer's terms." Such a result would contradict established doctrine. "The Textile Board ... and the National Labor Relations Board have both ruled that discrimination against particular strikers under the above circumstances is a violation of the present Section 7(a)."

Leiserson's memorandum reviewed the case law to assure the lawmakers that the language of § 2(3) broke no new ground. The courts, he noted, long had recognized both the legitimacy of the use of strikes as an economic weapon and that a strike did not terminate the employer-employee relationship. This case law, Leiserson admitted, did raise "the problem of when a strike is 'terminated' or 'lost,' " but, he continued,

---

34 The 1947 Taft–Hartley Amendments did not change the existing wording of § 2(3), but did add language specifically excluding supervisors and independent contractors from the definition of employee.

"S. 1958 provides that the labor dispute shall be 'current,' and the employer is free to hasten its end by hiring a new permanent crew of workers and running the plant on a normal basis." Leiserson further explained that:

> The broader definition of "employee" in S. 1958 does not lead to the conclusion that no strike may be lost or that all strikers must be restored to their jobs, or that an employer may not hire new workers, temporary or permanent, at will. All that is protected here is the right of those in a current labor dispute or strike to participate in elections, to be free from discrimination in reinstatement after they have agreed to return on the employer's terms, to collective bargaining, to freedom from interference, restraint, or coercion, etc.[35]

Although desultory comments on various parts of the language of § 2(3) can be found sprinkled throughout the legislative history of the Act, the status of strikers and their reinstatement rights generated neither discussion nor debate during the hearings over the Act. Leiserson's memorandum provided the Committee and Congress with the only comprehensive and substantive review of significance of the section's terms.

Determined to get his legislation enacted, Senator Wagner planned the course of his bill through the Congress with considerable care.[36] In keeping with his strategy, the hearings over the terms of S. 1958 occurred during a compact period of time—March 11 to April 2, 1935—and took place chiefly before the Senate Labor Committee. The debate before the full Senate over the bill's terms absorbed only a day, and took place on May 15, 1935. The following day, on a vote of 63 to 12, with 19 abstentions, S. 1958 was passed by the Senate. Throughout the discussions on the Act's terms, Wagner constantly reiterated that the bill simply restated or in some cases extended concepts already established in the law.

Wagner's Act went to conference on June 20, 1935. A week later, the House accepted the conference report on a 132 to 42 vote and the Senate adopted it the same day. After some failed attempts to find a convenient date, President Roosevelt signed the Act on Friday, July 5, 1935, using two pens that he presented, respectively, to Senator Wagner and to William Green, the President of the American Federation of Labor. Congress had embedded the striker replacement problem into the terms of the Act. A case presenting the issue would not be long in arriving.

[35] 1 *Legislative History* at 1346.

[36] On Wagner's legislative strategy and for details of the bill's progress through the Congress, see Irving Bernstein, *The New Deal Collective Bargaining Policy* 100–128 (1950).

Factual Background

In the mid-1930's, the Mackay Radio and Telegraph Company constituted a not insignificant presence in the international wireless telecommunications industry. The company, a part of what was known as the Mackay system, traced its beginnings to 1883 when John Mackay, an Irish immigrant who had made a fortune in silver mining in the Comstock Lode in Nevada, entered into a partnership with James Gordon Bennett, the publisher of the *New York Herald*, to form a telegraph company to compete with the transatlantic service of Western Union Company, then controlled by Jay Gould.[37] The company the two formed began laying transatlantic cable[38] and it built up its North–American system in part by buying and merging bankrupt firms. One of the Mackay system's companies, Commercial Cable, also participated in a joint-venture to lay the first transpacific telegraph cable, which became operative in 1904.[39] The Mackay-owned Postal Telegraph Company represented the Western Union Company's only significant competitor, but by the late 1920's, it held only about a fifth of the domestic market for telegraphic services.

---

[37] Bennett's interest in cable is easy to explain. At the time, Western Union held a monopoly on transatlantic cable transmissions and charged $2.50 per word, making the telegraphic transmission of news reports from Europe prohibitively expensive. At various times, Mackay unsuccessfully attempted to gain control of its much larger rival, Western Union and of the American Telephone and Telegraph Company (AT&T). On the history of Mackay, see Interview by Frank Polkinghorn with Ellery W. Stone, retired Vice–President of International Telephone and Telegraph Company, IEEE History Center, Rutgers University, *available at* <http://www.ieee.org/organizations/history_center/oral_ histories/transcripts/stone9.html>; Timothy W. Sturgeon, *How Silicon Valley Came to Be* in *Understanding Silicon Valley: Anatomy of an Entrepreneurial Region* (Martin Kenney, ed., 2000); Robert Sobel, *ITT: The Management of Opportunity*, 58–61 (1982).

[38] Mackay system companies eventually would lay and operate seven transatlantic cables. A Mackay-owned cable-laying ship, the Mackay–Bennett, sailing out of Halifax, Nova Scotia was chartered by the White Star Lines and employed in the effort to recover bodies from the sinking of its ship, the Titanic, in April, 1912. The Mackay–Bennett's crew eventually retrieved the remains of 306 victims.

[39] American Telephone and Telegraph (AT&T), which until the 1980's was the dominant provider of telephone service in the U.S., began providing transatlantic telephone service in 1927, and transpacific telephone service (initially between the U.S. and Japan) in 1934. Such service was carried by radio signal, its sound quality was dependent upon atmospheric conditions, and it was quite expensive. In 1927, a transatlantic call cost $75.00 for the first three minutes. Seven years later, a call to Japan cost $39.00 for the first three minutes. The transmission of telephone conversations by cable presents considerably greater technical challenges than those posed by the transmission of telegraphic signals. The first transatlantic telephone cable was not laid until 1956, while the first transpacific telephone cable did not go into service until 1964. In 1962, AT&T launched Telstar I, the first active communications satellite. Today, because of their lower cost and longer lifespan, lightweight submarine fibre-optic cables largely have displaced satellites as the carriers of communications traffic of all sorts.

Although the telegraph industry enjoyed substantial growth throughout the 1920's, it was by then in the process of becoming a dated technology, and by 1928, even the mighty Western Union Company found itself in trouble. Rates for long distance telephone use were declining and technical innovations had improved service. Moreover, new devices had entered the market, like the teletypewriter that used telephone lines to transmit written messages on leased equipment housed in the customer's own facilities, which made its debut in 1931.

Wireless communication by radio also posed a growing challenge to communication by conventional telegraph. This was particularly true for trans-oceanic communication, which could be accomplished by radio without the need of expensive submarine cable.[40] Guglielmo Marconi had transmitted the first radio telegraph signals in 1895, and the first transatlantic signals in 1901, but the radio industry remained in its infancy until after the First World War.[41] Complicated patent and licensing arrangements for the technology made entry into the wireless telegraphy market difficult, but by the mid-1920's, the Mackay Radio & Telegraph Company had been organized. Along with competitors like Globe Wireless and the giant Radio Corporation of America (RCA), Mackay Radio became an important provider of wireless communication services with Pacific Rim countries.

In addition to furnishing "point-to-point" communications between land-based wireless-sending facilities, like RCA, Mackay Radio also played a prominent role in supplying wireless marine radio service. Commercial vessels leased radio service and the equipment to provide it from Mackay or one of its competing service providers. The equipment was operated by the service providers' own employees, who sailed as radio officers on the vessels leasing the service. Mackay radios quickly became a familiar fixture on ships, and Mackay radio officers manned crews on vessels around the world.

By the mid-1930's, Mackay Radio's principal West Coast office was in San Francisco, and it had other sending facilities in several cities along the coast, as well as in Hawaii and Manila. These facilities transmitted and received both telegraph and radio messages. From the San Francisco facility, the company maintained point-to-point radio

---

40 Static and other technical difficulties made wireless telegraphy over land a less financially attractive alternative to communication by conventional telegraph, as did opposition from established telegraphic firms.

41 An almost unanticipated development, commercial radio broadcasting exploded as an industry in the post-war period. In the U.S., the number of in-home radio receivers increased from a mere 5,000 units in 1920 to 25 million sets only four years later, while the number of commercial broadcasters grew from eight in 1921 to 564 the following year. A holder of many of the key patents for this technology, RCA benefitted greatly from this development.

circuits with Los Angeles, Seattle, New York, Honolulu, Tokyo, and Shanghai, among other cities. Despite its extensive network, however, the Mackay system long had been in weak financial condition and by the mid-1930's, its corporate parent stood under considerable strain.[42] Disturbed by cutbacks in their working conditions and changes in employment policies, among other things, the radio operators in Mackay's San Francisco office quietly began a union-organizing effort in the early part of 1934. Their efforts mirrored those undertaken by Mackay employees at other facilities.

* * *

At about 8:30 p.m. on the evening of Friday, October 4, 1935, Leo K. Bash, an employee of Mackay Radio and Telegraph and the acting chairman of San Francisco Local 3 of the American Radio Telegraphists' Association (ARTA), called to order a meeting of the organization's membership.[43] The ARTA had initiated contract discussions with Mackay Radio in June, hoping to obtain its first system-wide agreement with the company.[44] Bash announced to the twenty-one members in attendance that the news was not good. Mackay's representatives had stalled and the Local now should be prepared to strike. During these talks, the union acquiesced to a company request to "let the agreement slide for a little while," because the parent corporation of Mackay had been contemplating the filing of a bankruptcy petition. In early September, the union once again presented Mackay with contract demands, eager to have the company agree to terms similar to those the union recently had concluded with RCA. The Local, which represented Mackay's San Fran-

[42] Wooed by many investors during late 1920's, Clarence Mackay, the son of the company's founder (and, incidentally, the father-in-law of Irving Berlin), sold the Mackay companies to the newly-organized International Telephone and Telegraph Company (IT&T) in 1928. A fast-expanding conglomerate, IT&T had become over-extended and was by the mid-1930's in rather precarious condition.

[43] Unless otherwise identified, this account of the strike is drawn from the testimony and exhibits from the hearing before the Trial Examiner contained in the Transcript of Record in NLRB v. Mackay Radio & Telegraph Co., October Term 1937, No. 706, and the Board's decision, reported at 1 NLRB 201 (1936).

[44] This agreement was to cover all of the land-based, or "point-to-point" operators in the Mackay Radio system. In the meantime, the ARTA also had been attempting to negotiate an agreement to apply to Mackay's marine radio operators serving on ships at sea. In September 1935, the marine and point-to-point operators agreed to unite for joint action, resolving that Mackay would have to settle both agreements for either to be effective. Local 3 had been organized in early 1934 and divided into two divisions, which represented marine radio operators and land, or point-to-point operators respectively. The point-to-point division itself was divided into three groups, one for the operators employed by the three large cable and wireless companies operating on the West Coast: Mackay Radio, Globe Wireless, and RCA. Only Local 3's Mackay Radio group was involved in the matter described here.

cisco based operators, had authorized a strike against the company should their demands not be met by September 23.[45] The deadline had passed. The men were resolute. The meeting was brief.

The job action against Mackay was to be nation-wide, and Bash told the membership that the walk-out was scheduled to begin at midnight, San Francisco time. After a short exchange, the members elected a strike committee and adjourned the meeting. Many of those not in attendance received telephone calls informing them of the situation. At the stroke of midnight, the entire operating force on duty in Mackay's San Francisco office abandoned their stations and began picketing, leaving a single supervisor to attempt to continue service. For the duration of the strike, only three of the San Francisco office's sixty-three operators continued to work.

Unfortunately for the members of the San Francisco Local, and particularly for their leadership, the solidarity they demonstrated did not display itself nationally. The strike at Mackay's Seattle office lasted but a few hours, while in Los Angeles, only one radio operator left work. At Mackay's offices in Washington, D.C., in New Orleans, in West Palm Beach, and in Rockville, Maine, the strike call went entirely unheeded. In Chicago, a few operators left their stations, but their number proved too small to have any effect on the office's ability to handle communications traffic. Meanwhile, the operators at Mackay's New York City office walked out when the strike began at 3:00 a.m. on Saturday, but before the day was out, most had returned. Portland, Oregon proved to be the only Mackay facility where dedication to the strike matched that demonstrated by the operators employed at the company's San Francisco office.

According to a report published in the Sunday, October 6th edition of *The New York Times*, union officials "asserted that the strike was so effective at some stations that it had paralyzed communications across both the Atlantic and Pacific." These officials also "estimated that 200 out of 300 radio operators had walked out." Service at the company's offices on Long Island, the union officials told the paper, was being maintained only because supervisors were working twenty-four hours a day, and because the company had resorted to the use of non-licensed operators. Company officials dismissed the union's claims as "gross exaggerations." "The strike is a washout," Ellery W. Stone,[46] Mackay's

---

[45] The union, The New York Times reported, was demanding "recognition, a contractual wage and working hours agreement, a forty-eight-hour week, and an average increase of $24 a month for radio operators now averaging $165 a month, according to the union." *Radio Operators Begin Walkout: Union Asserts that Pacific and Atlantic Traffic is Paralyzed by its Strike*, N.Y. Times, Oct. 6, 1935, at 45.

[46] Stone had been the President of the Federal Telegraph Company, the firm that had sold Mackay rights to patents that allowed it to enter the radio telegraphy business. During

vice president and chief negotiator told *The Times.* "The boys are licked and they know it. . . . The union was all set to strike yesterday afternoon without notice, but we were prepared for it. The men are coming back faster than we can put them to work."[47]

Mackay was as ready for the strike as the union was unprepared to conduct it. While Mackay's transcontinental traffic could be maintained by transferring San Francisco communications to its Los Angeles office, San Francisco was crucial because it handled the company's trans-Pacific circuits. Desperate to keep them in service, Mackay flew two operators from its Los Angeles office who arrived in San Francisco on the morning of Saturday, October 5. On Monday, October 7, another plane arrived carrying seven operators from Mackay's New York office and two others from its Chicago facility.

Morale remained strong among the San Francisco strikers throughout the weekend. By Monday, however, it had started to flag. Rumors were circulating that the company planned to abandon its circuits along the coast; that eighty-four operators in New York had returned to work along with seventy to eighty percent of the strikers in Portland, Oregon; and that the plane from New York carrying more replacements soon would arrive.

Late on Monday afternoon, a number of the strikers met informally at the union hall where one of the operators and a supervisor, both union members, exhorted the men to save their jobs and return to work. Others, sensing a spreading panic, counseled against bolting from the strike. One member, seeking to calm his fellows, plaintively observed that the "Wagner bill" required the company to recognize and bargain with the union. Supporters of the job action narrowly succeeded in convincing the others not to abandon the strike that evening and to postpone any decisions until the regularly scheduled morning strike meeting.

Local 3's leadership had planned to telephone New York late Monday evening to get an update on the status of the negotiations and of the job action on the East Coast. Several Local 3 members, including Robert Hatch, the chief electrician for Mackay's San Francisco facility, and Charles Burtz, one of the radio operators, had filtered back to the union hall to learn the latest. The news was not good, and the men listened dispiritedly as they heard the Local's leadership recommend to the union's New York negotiating team that they contact Mackay officials

---

an eventful career, Stone achieved the rank of Admiral in the U.S. Navy and became Vice-President of IT&T.

[47] *Radio Operators Begin Walkout: Union Asserts that Pacific and Atlantic Traffic is Paralyzed by its Strike*, N.Y. Times, Oct. 6, 1935, at 45.

the following morning and arrange for the striking operators to return to work pending further negotiations.

As they left the hall at about ten o'clock that evening, Hatch dejectedly told Burtz that he believed the strike had been lost and suggested that they call Andrew Jorgeson, the traffic manager of the company's San Francisco office immediately and ask to return to work. In response to their call, Jorgeson conferred with H.L. Rodman, Mackay's general superintendent, who instructed him to reinstate the strikers. "But remember," he told Jorgeson, "you are to take care of the men from New York and Los Angeles, but handle that your own way." This direction left Jorgeson with eleven extra operators should the nine replacements from New York and Chicago and the two from Los Angeles elect to stay in San Francisco. Uncertain how many of the group might ultimately choose to remain, Jorgeson quickly drew up a list of eleven strikers whom he thought the least desirable candidates for reinstatement. Once the replacements had made their decisions, Jorgeson planned to fill any remaining positions by selecting from among the eleven on "an all things being considered" basis.

As arranged, Jorgeson arrived at Hatch's apartment about half an hour after their telephone conversation, bringing with him a list of employee addresses and telephone numbers. He told Hatch and Burtz that eleven of the men would have to re-apply for employment, and that their applications would be subject to the approval of Ellery Stone at Mackay's headquarters in New York. Hatch and Burtz then proceeded to contact as many of the other San Francisco operating employees as possible, directing them to meet at a downtown hotel where Jorgeson would explain the company's position. Meanwhile, Jorgeson arranged for a two-room suite in which to hold the meeting and for a police detail to remain in discreet reserve in case the need for intervention arose. The invitees understood that Local 3 had neither called nor sanctioned the assembly.

At about 4:30 on the morning of Tuesday, October 8, with thirty-six operators present, the meeting began. After some initial discussion, Jorgeson entered the meeting from the second room of the suite. The company, Jorgeson assured the assembly, would forget the strike and that all but eleven of the employees could return to work. The excluded group, he said, would have to reapply for employment, and their applications would be forwarded to New York for review by company vice-president Stone. The names of the eleven then were read twice, and a rather tense discussion followed.

Some among the eleven had learned of the meeting and were in attendance, including Alonzo B. Loudermilk. One of the most active members of Local 3, Loudermilk had played a major role in organizing the operators in Mackay's San Francisco and New York offices, and he had engaged in numerous discussions with company officials over the operators' terms and conditions in New York and Chicago. A strike leader, Loudermilk also was one of the San Francisco office's most skilled and highly paid operators.

Loudermilk pointedly told the men that they should consider the question on which they were about to vote in the following terms: "Are you prepared to go back to work immediately and leave eleven men out on a limb?" After some wrangling, the attendees concluded that a two-thirds vote should decide the issue and that operators whose names appeared on the list could cast a ballot. The results revealed twenty-two votes to return to work, six votes against the proposal, and eight abstentions. Loudermilk later testified that when the results were announced, Robert Hatch excitedly shouted, "Hooray! Let's all go down and get our names on the pay roll." The meeting, and with it Local 3's strike against Mackay, came to a close at about 6:00 a.m. Later that day, at one o'clock local time, the ARTA's vice president in New York telephoned Ellery Stone and informed him that the nationwide job action against the company had ended.

By late Tuesday afternoon, only four of the San Francisco operators who participated in the strike had yet to be reinstated: Leo Bash, Alonzo Loudermilk, Glenn Palmer, and Lon Rone. All four had played important roles in organizing the union, all had held leadership positions in Local 3, and all had figured prominently in the strike. All four also were "Class A" operators and paid at the top of the company's pay scale.

The four also were the last of the strikers to apply for reinstatement. After some difficulties in gaining a meeting with H.L. Rodman, the general superintendent of the San Francisco office, Loudermilk and Palmer made their applications late on Tuesday, while Rone and Bash filed their requests the following day. At the time they applied, each was told that no vacancies then existed, but that their applications would be forwarded to New York for Stone's consideration. When Loudermilk asked about his chances for approval, Rodman replied that they were not "very good," and reminded him that he had "a national reputation for causing us trouble."

Stone returned the applications at the end of October, noting as to each of them that "there is no objection to favorable consideration being given this application when a vacancy occurs at San Francisco." Jorgeson told one of the men that he did not believe any openings would exist until the following summer. At the time the NLRB issued its decision in the case in February 1936, none of the men had been reinstated.

Prior Proceedings

1. Constitutional Uncertainty and Statutory Novelty: The New NLRB and Its Inaugural Cases

The ARTA filed charges against Mackay Radio on October 15, 1935, and the Board's regional office in San Francisco issued a complaint on November 9, alleging that the company's refusal to reinstate the four operators, as well as the manager of its downtown branch office,[48] constituted violations of §§ 8(1) and (3) of the Act.[49] In considering *Mackay,* it helps to keep in mind the context in which the case arose. *Mackay* was among the first matters that the fledgling NLRB handled. At the time the Board tried and argued it, the Agency's procedures were novel and untested and every decision the Board issued made new law. When regarded from the perspective of an observer in 1935, neither the prospects for the Act's passage nor for its survival at the hands of the Supreme Court exactly appeared to be lead-pipe cinches.

To begin with, the Roosevelt Administration did not regard the Wagner Act as a central part of its New Deal programs.[50] Despite appeals by Senator Wagner and the AFL, Roosevelt had declined to back the NLRA in Congress and did so only at the very last moment, when developments gave him little other choice. Frances Perkins, his Secretary of Labor, also showed at best a cool detachment toward the bill. The statute owed its existence to Wagner's stubborn determination to get it passed, and not to any prestige or support lent by the Administration. A contemporary observer summed up the situation by noting that "We who believed in the Act were dizzy with watching a 200–to–1 shot come up from the outside."[51]

---

[48] The manager, P.D. Phelps, was a member of the union but not an activist. The Board would conclude that the company discriminated against Phelps by refusing to reinstate him based in part on the admission of the general superintendent that "we did not approve of a commercial man, in charge of an office, becoming a member of an organization such as ARTA."

[49] The complaint also alleged a violation of Section 8(2), which the Board dismissed.

[50] For President Roosevelt, labor law reform was never a priority among his New Deal initiatives. Moreover, he feared that labor legislation would incur Supreme Court challenges and also threaten his coalition with business interests necessary to support his agenda of social and economic legislation. The information in the following paragraphs about the early days of the NLRB are drawn from accounts and quotations in Peter H. Irons, *The New Deal Lawyers,* 203–53 (1982); James A. Gross, 1 *The Making of the National Labor Relations Board: A Study in Economics, Politics, and the Law* (1933–1937), 109–88 (1974); and Irving Bernstein, *The New Deal Collective Bargaining Policy* 84–128 (1950).

[51] Malcolm Ross, *Death of a Yale Man* 170 (1939), *quoted in* Irving Bernstein, *The New Deal Collective Bargaining Policy* 1 (1950).

The executive branch's lukewarm attitude toward the statute did not represent its only source of difficulty. Less than a month before Congress acted on the NLRA, the Supreme Court decided *Schechter Poultry Corp. v. United States*,[52] which cast grave doubt in the minds of many on the constitutionality of the proposed Act's terms. The case hung like a pall over the NLRA both during its consideration by Congress and during the period between its passage and the Court's declaration of its constitutionality two years later in *NLRB v. Jones & Laughlin Steel Corp.*[53] Wagner and his legislative assistants were forced to redraft portions of the statute to respond to concerns raised by *Schechter,* and, especially during the first year of the Act's existence, the Board spent many of its resources litigating employer requests for injunctions to restrain the agency from enforcing its terms. It is one of history's little ironies that *Schechter,* actually may have assisted the Act's passage. The case permitted congressional opponents of the NLRA quietly to drop their opposition to it, thereby allowing them to gain credit with constituents who supported the statute while being privately convinced that the Court would void the law at the first opportunity.

The widespread belief that the Court would find the Act's terms unconstitutional also made it difficult to find individuals willing to serve as members of the new NLRB. Nearly two months passed between the signing of the Act and the Senate's confirmation of the first three NLRB members who would make initial rulings under the new law. Confirmed on August 24th, the new members assumed their offices three days later.

---

[52] 295 U.S. 495 (1935). (In *Schechter,* the Court invalidated the terms of the NIRA, ruling in part that the application of the Act to intrastate activities exceeded the powers of Congress under the commerce clause. *Schechter* involved convictions for violation of the wage, hour, and trade practice regulations contained in the Code of Fair Competition for the Live Poultry Industry for the New York City metropolitan area, which had been promulgated pursuant to the terms of the NIRA. The Court concluded that Schechter's business, which involved the slaughter and sale of poultry to retailers and butcher shops in New York City, did not constitute interstate commerce even though nearly all the poultry Schechter handled came from out-of-state. Rejecting "stream of commerce" and "affecting commerce" arguments, the Court, through Chief Justice Hughes, stated that the interstate character of the transactions ended when the live poultry reached Schechter's slaughterhouse. Neither the slaughtering nor the subsequent sale of the poultry, the Court stated, were transactions in interstate commerce. To accept the argument that hours and wages affect prices and commerce generally, Justice Hughes warned, would allow Congress to reach nearly all aspects of business transactions. The Court dismissed arguments that "efforts to enact state legislation establishing high labor standards have been impeded by the belief that unless similar action is taken generally, commerce will be diverted" to states without such regulation. "It is not the province of the Court to consider the economic advantages or disadvantages of such a centralized system," Hughes wrote, and the "Federal Constitution does not provide for it." A year later, in *Carter v. Carter Coal Co.,* 298 U.S. 238 (1936), the Court invalidated the Bituminous Coal Conservation Act of 1935, which established a scheme for wage and hour regulation in mining.)

[53] 301 U.S. 1 (1937).

Commenting on their appointments, *Business Week* magazine observed that "the feeling is that the President had to hunt a long time and drop down below the upper bracket to find anyone who would take a chance, the past history of labor boards being what it is." The three willing to take the risk were J. Warren Madden, a law professor from the University of Pittsburgh, who became the Chairman; John M. Carmody, an industrial engineer who at the time of his appointment was a member of the National Mediation Board; and Edwin S. Smith, a holdover from the old NLRB, who soon would become a highly controversial figure.

They were a diverse lot. A torts and property teacher, Madden came to the Board with scant experience in labor relations. A series of chance connections brought him to the Administration's attention as a candidate for the position. In 1933, the Governor of Pennsylvania, Gifford Pinchot, appointed Madden to a commission to study the use of private police forces by coal and steel companies. There, Madden became well-acquainted with Francis Biddle, a Philadelphia corporate law specialist who in late 1934 became Chairman of the old NLRB. Biddle, in turn, had been recruited for the Board position by his predecessor, Lloyd K. Garrison, who, eager to return to academic life, had told Roosevelt that he would serve in the post no longer than four months. Madden had developed a friendly relationship with Garrison during the summer of 1933 when they served as visiting faculty at Stanford Law School. Madden's third recommender was Charlton Ogburn, counsel for the AFL, who had been impressed with Madden when he arbitrated a wage dispute for the Pittsburgh street railway. During his pre-appointment interview with Frances Perkins, Madden rather disarmingly confessed that he "just didn't know anything about labor law" or "anything really about this board and the statute." Perkins was unfazed. "Well, that is fine," she reassuringly replied. "You will not have any preconceptions about it and you can just start it from the ground up and learn it as you go."

Despite his slim labor relations background, Madden quickly established himself as the intellectual and moral leader of the Board. Nathan Witt, a Frankfurter protégé and an assistant to Charles Fahy, the Board's first General Counsel, characterized Madden as "basically a conservative man ... certainly a liberal as far as civil liberties are concerned and certainly a conservative as far as basic economic issues are concerned." Madden would remain Chairman until 1940, guiding the Agency through some of its most dramatic and tumultuous years.

Carmody's appointment came at the recommendation of Senator Wagner, who described him "as a solid man who had his feet on the ground and had a lot of experience in labor relations." Prior to his service on the National Mediation Board, Carmody had chaired the National Bituminous Coal Labor Board under the NIRA and served as chief engineer of the Civil Works Administration. Committed to mediation rather than litigation, Carmody quickly became frustrated with "what he regarded as a lot of legal rigmarole." Witt described Carmody as "impatient" with legal issues and said that he "just wasn't the kind of personality who belonged on the Board." Evidently, Carmody agreed. He participated in the Board's *Mackay* decision, but resigned his post after a year and took an appointment with the Rural Electrification Administration.

The third member of the Board, Edwin Smith, was the sole holdover from the old NLRB. Like Carmody, he was not a lawyer, but unlike him, Smith enjoyed discussing legal issues and litigation strategy. Smith's positions and his "intemperate, radical, public utterances" quickly made him the Board's most controversial member and served to instigate considerable criticism of the Agency and its rulings, especially from the business community. Madden much later told an interviewer that Smith "quite certainly was a communist," although subsequent congressional investigations failed to substantiate such charges.

The new NLRB assumed the staffs and regional offices that the old NLRB had assembled. This, however, did not leave the new agency fully prepared to undertake its tasks under the NLRA. The old NLRB's regional staffs spent much of their time investigating and mediating disputes. In contrast, Congress intended the new agency to fulfill its now familiar prosecutorial and quasi-judicial roles. As of September 1, 1935, the agency had only thirteen lawyers in the Washington, D.C. office, and only one assigned to any of the Board's regional offices. Nathan Witt noted that the Board encountered "a hell of a time building up staff and getting qualified people" because potential applicants were "convinced that [the Board would] be put out of business by the Supreme Court" and because the pay scale was low. Fahy delegated the recruiting and hiring of lawyers to Witt and to Thomas Emerson, another Frankfurter protégé who later would become a law professor at Yale and one of the best-known civil rights lawyers of his era. Both Witt and Emerson had served on the staff of the old NLRB.

By October 14, 1935, sufficient staff had been assembled to permit Fahy to direct his lawyers to "start sending in their cases." To assist the regional offices in getting established, nearly all of the Board's Washington legal staff had been dispersed to the field. In conducting their work, Nathan Witt later explained, "we were under special instructions to look for test cases, since we knew that we were headed for the Supreme Court." Circumstances provided them with much from which to choose. By March 1936, the Board had handled 729 cases involving 165,792 employees.

Until January 1936, the Board prohibited regional directors from issuing a complaint in any matter until the General Counsel's office had reviewed and approved it. The Board also took care in timing the issuance of its decisions. Benedict Wolf, the Board's Secretary, justified the policy to a frustrated regional director. "The delay in issuing decisions," he explained, "is not caused solely by the inability to issue them at a particular time. It was extremely important that the Board be able to control to some extent the test cases which would first get to the Circuit Courts and the Supreme Court." It is better to contend with the parties' restiveness, Wolf continued, than to have the Board "find itself in the Supreme Court with a case which is not particularly strong on interstate commerce and involves a company so small that the courts would be disinclined to believe that company's business could possibly affect interstate commerce."

2. *Mackay Radio* as Supreme Court Litigation Vehicle: The Board's Decision

Because it so clearly involved interstate commerce, the *Mackay* case quickly came to the Board's attention. A complaint in the matter issued on November 9, 1935, and the Board conducted hearings in San Francisco before a trial examiner from the second to the twentieth of December. The day before the hearings concluded, the Board, on its own motion, transferred the proceedings to itself. Several weeks later, on February 20, 1936, the Board issued its decision in *Mackay*. Within days, the Board filed a petition for enforcement of its order with the Ninth Circuit and the court set the case for argument on April 16.

The Board's decision in *Mackay* was straightforward—the company had discriminated against the employees named in the complaint. The Board ordered their reinstatement with backpay. In so doing, it dismissed the company's contentions that the employees had not been reinstated because their positions were no longer available, having been filled by replacements brought by the company to San Francisco from other locations. The replacements, the Board observed, "were really strikebreakers." The company "is therefore contending that such strikebreakers are entitled to the four positions in question in preference to the men who held them at the time the strike had commenced and who because of union activity had temporarily severed their active work on those jobs but not their status as employees." "It might be argued by these four operators," the Board admitted, "that the granting of such a preference to the strikebreakers" constituted forbidden discrimination. "However," the Board continued, "since we find that a decision on the point is not necessary to the final judgment in this case, we will not decide the matter."[54]

In defending itself against the charge of discrimination, the company asserted that it was completely fortuitous that the only four operators not reinstated happened to be union leaders. The four simply were the last to apply for reinstatement, and they did so after all the positions had been filled. The results would have been different, the company insisted, had they been among the first to request reinstatement.

"The difficulty with this contention," the Board stated, "is that it was the respondent who chose the standard of time." Moreover, the company "chose that standard on Tuesday afternoon at a time when the four leaders had not as yet reapplied but it deliberately shifted to that standard at that point." Jorgeson himself, the Board noted, had testified that the reinstatement of the employees named on the list "was not to be a case of 'first come, first served.' " Instead, "Jorgeson and not time was to do the selecting." The company only shifted to that standard "on Tuesday afternoon coincident with the realization that the full quota had been reached" and the union leaders had not yet formally applied for reinstatement. Company officials, the Board concluded, "perceived that circumstances had provided them with an excellent opportunity to rid the respondent of the leaders of the Local which had just caused it to pass through a costly strike, and it did not fail to make the most of the opportunity." By taking advantage of that chance, the Board ruled, the company violated the Act.

Additionally, the company had induced each of the four to understand that he would not be reinstated. Believing that they were blacklisted, the Board found that it was not surprising that the four "would delay their request for reinstatement." In these circumstances, the application of a "first come, first served" principle to determine reinstatements constituted a violation of the statute.

The exquisite care with which the Board handled *Mackay* and the lengths to which it went in explaining its reasoning reflect the value the Agency put on the case as a means for testing the constitutionality of the Act. As the reader will have noticed, however, the point for which we know *Mackay*—the right it grants employers permanently to replace strikers—represents an issue the Board specifically declined to address. Rather, it treated the case as a discrimination matter. So, how did the issue of an employer's right to respond to an economic strike find its way into the Supreme Court's opinion in *Mackay*?

3. The Best Laid Plans: Frustration Before the Ninth Circuit

Although the Ninth Circuit heard the case in mid-April 1936, it did not render its decision denying enforcement of the Board's order until

[54] 1 NLRB at 216.

the following January. This confounded an assessment made by General Counsel Charles Fahy who, in deciding to proceed with the case, thought that the court would not "unreasonably delay this decision," thereby allowing it quickly to reach the Supreme Court.[55]

The three deeply divergent and at times confusing opinions the Ninth Circuit eventually produced may explain why deliberations in *Mackay* dragged on so long.[56] Judge Curtis D. Wilbur, who had presided as the Chief Justice of the California Supreme Court and as the Secretary of the Navy under Calvin Coolidge, wrote the lead opinion. He found that the Act was not wholly unconstitutional and that the strikers were employees for the purposes of the statute. Nevertheless, relying on *Adair v. United States*[57] and *Coppage v. Kansas,*[58] he concluded that the order to reinstate them violated the due process clause of the Fifth Amendment because it required the company to employ persons with whom it chose not to deal, thereby interfering with the employer's constitutionally-protected freedom of contract. Wilbur also found that the Act offended the guarantees of the Seventh Amendment insofar as it authorized the Board to assess damages without a jury trial.

Judge Clifton Mathews, a Roosevelt appointee to the Ninth Circuit, concurred in the result. However, unlike Wilbur, he concluded that the Board had not shown that the strikers were employees within the meaning of the Act. In Mathews' view, the discriminatees had not been discharged through the company's failure to reinstate them. Instead, he found that they had quit their jobs voluntarily when they went out on strike. In light of this, he found it unnecessary to consider Mackay's contention that the § 2(3) definition of employee as including strikers was unconstitutional or to make any rulings on the additional constitutional issues raised by the company.

Another Roosevelt appointee, Francis A. Garrecht, dissented. Noting that many lower courts and some of the circuit courts of appeals had sustained the constitutionality of the Act, he stated that "it cannot be said that there exists between the Constitution and this law and beyond all reasonable doubt a clear and unmistakable conflict." He also disagreed with Mathews' view that the strikers were not employees for the purposes of the Act. "[T]o reach such a conclusion," he said of Mathews' construction of § 2(3) of the statute, "is to ignore the declaration of the act itself that employees on a strike are to be considered still as employees." Congress had the power under the commerce clause to pass

55 Peter H. Irons, *The New Deal Lawyers* 263 (1982).

56 Reported at 87 F.2d 611 (9th Cir. 1937).

57 208 U.S. 161 (1908).

58 236 U.S. 1 (1915).

the Act, Garrecht wrote, and nothing in the Board's actions or its order in *Mackay* offended the Constitution.

In mid-April 1937, a few months after the Ninth Circuit decided *Mackay*, the Supreme Court handed down its landmark decision in *NLRB v. Jones & Laughlin Steel Corp.*, in which it upheld the constitutionality of the NLRA.[59] The Ninth Circuit granted the Board's petition for rehearing in *Mackay*, but in a decision issued in October, the court again refused enforcement of the Board's order. Judges Mathews and Garrecht adhered to the views they previously had expressed. In his opinion, however, Judge Wilbur retreated from his conclusion that strikers retained their status as employees under the Act. He now asserted that the Constitution permitted the Board to order reinstatement of employees only when they had ceased work by reason of an unfair labor practice. Employees who voluntarily went on strike quit their positions, and consistent with the constitutionally-protected liberty of contract, Congress has no power to compel parties to enter into new contracts of employment. Accordingly, he ruled, the Board lacked the power to order the reinstatement of the Mackay strikers. This view of the Act, Judge Garrecht retorted in his dissent, represented "a strained construction designed to nullify the National Labor Relations Act in an important field of its operations."

The Board agreed with Judge Garrecht's characterization of the matter. As it argued in seeking a writ of certiorari in *Mackay*, the NLRB, as well as its predecessors, "have uniformly ruled that discrimination in reinstatement of striking employees must be remedied by restoring the victims to their jobs."[60]

The Supreme Court Decision

Because it had languished on appeal, *Mackay* was not among the first cases employed by the Board to test the Act's constitutionality. Nevertheless, *Mackay* involved critically important issues concerning the Board's remedial powers. The Supreme Court granted the Board's petition for a writ of certiorari in February 1938, and heard arguments in early April. The following month, it handed down its opinion.

Charles Fahy, the Board's general counsel and its chief legal tactician, participated in briefing and arguing the case before the Court. Fahy came to the Board in August 1935 from the Department of the Interior, where he had served as Chairman of the NIRA-established Petroleum Administrative Board. He was recommended for the post by Calvert

---

[59] 301 U.S. 1 (1937).

[60] Petition for a Writ of Certiorari to the United States Circuit Court of Appeals for the Ninth Circuit at 25–26, NLRB v. Mackay Radio & Telegraph Co., 304 U.S. 333 (1938) (No. 37–706).

Magruder, the general counsel of the old NLRB, who had been eager to leave Washington to resume his position at Harvard Law School. Stanley Surrey, a young Board lawyer who later would become a leading tax law scholar and law professor at Harvard, characterized Fahy as "liberal in a rugged, fundamentalist sense, a very cautious lawyer, a very careful and methodical type." Fahy and Board Chairman J. Warren Madden became close friends, and one Board lawyer later stated that Madden "was certainly more swayed by Charlie Fahy's views than that of any other single person." Like Madden, Fahy remained at the Board during its first five years, and was responsible for shaping the Agency's crucial litigation strategy. He later served as Solicitor General and as a member of the U.S. Court of Appeals for the District of Columbia Circuit.[61]

As framed by the Board, *Mackay* presented the Court with several issues: whether economic strikers are employees within the meaning of the Act; whether discrimination in reinstatement of economic strikers because of their union activities constitutes an unfair labor practice, and whether the Act authorizes the Board to order the reinstatement of such discriminatees; and finally, whether the Act, construed to permit the Board to order reinstatements, violates the Fifth Amendment. In addition, Mackay contended that the evidence did not support the Board's factual findings, and its petition for review was not timely filed.

In a terse and business-like opinion, Justice Owen Roberts, writing for a unanimous Court, quickly disposed of all of Mackay's jurisdictional arguments and its objections to the Board's decision. Holding that "the Board's order is within its competence and does not contravene any provision of the Constitution," the Court ruled in the Agency's favor on all the issues it raised on appeal.[62]

The language in *Mackay* best known to us appears in a portion of the decision where the Court answers the company's contention that because it had not committed any unfair labor practices, the Board lacked jurisdiction in the case altogether. The Court started with a quote from § 8(3) and then proceeded with a serial review of the events leading up to the charge of discrimination. "There is no evidence and no finding," the Court said, "of any unfair labor practice in connection with the negotiations in New York." Rather, the company did negotiate with representatives of the union. "Nor," the opinion continued, "was it an unfair labor practice to replace the striking employees with others in an effort to carry on the business." Noting that § 13 of the Act provides

---

[61] *See* Peter H. Irons, *The New Deal Lawyers* 234, 235 (1982); James A. Gross, 1 *The Making of the National Labor Relations Board: A Study in Economics, Politics, and the Law* (1933–1937), 170–71 (1974).

[62] 304 U.S. at 343.

that nothing in the statute should be construed to impede or diminish the right to strike, the Court stated that:

> it does not follow that an employer, guilty of no act denounced by the statute, has lost the right to protect and continue his business by supplying places left vacant by strikers. And he is not bound to discharge those hired to fill the places of strikers, upon the election of the latter to resume their employment, in order to create places for them. The assurance by respondent to those who accepted employment during the strike that if they so desired their places might be permanent was not an unfair labor practice nor was it such to reinstate only so many of the strikers as there were vacant places to be filled.[63]

In contrast, the Court observed that Mackay had engaged in unlawful discrimination by refusing to reinstate certain strikers on the basis of their union activity. Because strikers retain the status of employees, "[a]ny such discrimination in putting them back to work is, therefore, prohibited" by the Act.

It is noteworthy that in denying reinstatement rights to strikers, the Court ignores the language of both § 2(3), which defines employees as including strikers, and § 13, which states that nothing in the Act "shall be construed so as either to interfere with or impede or diminish in any way the right to strike." Additionally, the Court does not analyze the employer's conduct in terms of the unfair labor practice provisions of the Act. Instead it simply restates doctrines developed by common law courts and adopted by the NLRB's predecessor labor boards.

It is true that the Board itself did not reach the question of whether an employer engages in unlawful discrimination by permanently replacing strikers. The Board, however, conceded the point in its reply brief. In answering Mackay's assertion that the Agency's construction of the Act "guarantees the striker his job whenever he wants it," the Board responded that the company's "argument rests upon a gross misstatement of the Board's position and the issues involved here." "The Board," the brief declared,

> has never contended, in this case or any other, that an employer who has neither caused nor prolonged a strike through unfair labor practices, cannot take full advantage of economic forces working for his victory in a labor dispute. The Act clearly does not forbid him, in the absence of such unfair labor practices, to replace the striking employees with new employees or authorize an order directing that

[63] *Id.* at 345–46, *citing* NLRB v. Bell Oil & Gas Co., 91 F.2d 509 (1937).

> all the strikers be reinstated and new employees discharged. Admittedly the strikers are not "guaranteed" reinstatement by the Act.[64]

As the Board further noted, citing several recent cases that had been enforced by various circuit courts, where a "strike is not caused by an unfair labor practice, but where, during the strike, the employer commits an unfair labor practice," the Board has ordered reinstatement "only to the extent that the strikers had not been replaced at the time of the unfair labor practice." The other replaced strikers are placed on a preferential hiring list, and "the employer is not required to discharge any new employees hired prior to the commission" of the unlawful act.

The Supreme Court's *Mackay* opinion squared on all fours with the Board's argument in the case, and it authoritatively restated for the law under the NLRA the doctrine governing the rights of economic strikers that common law courts and earlier labor boards had developed. It is also entirely consistent with the typically restrained approach taken by Madden and Fahy to the construction of the Act, an approach dictated not only by attitudes of lawyerly caution and reticence that characterized both men, but by a deeply shared concern that an assertive reading and application of the statute would provoke the Court into finding it unconstitutional. It also is consistent with the intent of the drafters of the Act insofar as such intent can be divined from William Leiserson's analytical memorandum that compared the terms of Wagner's failed 1934 labor disputes bill with the provisions of the NLRA. Nevertheless, does an employer's ability to grant permanent status to replacements discriminate against strikers by discouraging employees from engaging in protected activities? Does the *Mackay* doctrine actually undermine the collective bargaining system its framers intended to establish through the Act?

The Impact of Mackay

REEVALUATING THE *MACKAY* DOCTRINE

The *Mackay* doctrine was not a judicial effort to minimize the pro-labor goals of the original Wagner Act. It was, in fact, consistent with the law as understood by its framers, by the Board and by organized labor itself. The goal of the law was to promote free collective bargaining and all of the major players understood collective bargaining to be a system of private ordering in which the government's role would be minimal. The natural play of economic forces would regulate its operation and limit the extent to which either side could ignore the interests of the other. Both labor and management wanted to avoid a system in which the state and political actors chose collective bargaining outcomes. The

---

[64] Reply Brief for NLRB at 15, NLRB v. Mackay Radio & Telegraph Co., 304 U.S. 333 (1938) (No. 37–706).

state was to provide a framework for private ordering, but not the substance of that order.

State intervention was thought to be the opponent of free collective bargaining. Thus, Mary van Kleeck, a leading industrial relations scholar and a strong proponent of collective bargaining, opposed Wagner's 1934 labor disputes bill. She thought attempts to equalize the bargaining power of the parties were doomed to failure, and she presciently feared that government intervention into the process of collective bargaining would lead to the regulation of unions.[65]

Of course, collective bargaining under the Act never was intended to be entirely a laissez-faire system. State regulation was understood as necessary to protect the integrity of the system. It was obvious that the goal of protecting the integrity of the bargaining process without influencing its substantive results presented the Board and the courts with a difficult and subtle task. But it was not surprising that they concluded that the employer's ability to hire permanent replacements did not threaten the basic integrity of the system.

The basic rights of workers were protected by the definition of unfair labor practices in the Act. The section of the Act that was intended to protect job rights of union workers was § 8(3), which was violated only when the employer engaged in "discrimination ... to discourage union membership." The language was far from self-explanatory, but to make out a violation of its terms, it seemed to require that the employer treat union members and supporters differently from other employees and that it do so for the purpose of discouraging union membership. Neither of these conditions was obviously met in the hiring of replacements. The employer in *Mackay* was seeking to continue its business, not discourage union membership. And as already noted, *Mackay* was decided at a time when even minor limitations on an employer's right to hire and fire were thought to stretch the limits of government power.

It was not as if unions lacked effective techniques for making the hiring of permanent replacements costly. In basic industries unions were strong and both sides understood that they would become stronger. This gave employers a strong motive for avoiding no-holds-barred battles. The Act did not prevent unions from coming to the support of each other. Hiring permanent replacements not only meant the loss of top quality union workers but it was likely to prolong and spread the scope of a strike. It was also bound to lead to at least minor acts of violence and prolonged antipathy from those not replaced. And if the strike was caused by an unfair labor practice, something often difficult to determine, the workers would be reinstated with back pay by the Board.

[65] *See* Irving Bernstein, *The New Deal Collective Bargaining Policy* 67 (1950).

Thus in the presence of a strong labor movement with a broad right to strike one might conclude that using permanent replacements would be an employer threat but not a major feature of collective bargaining. And for many years this was true. But the National Labor Relations Act and reality have both changed significantly since the *Mackay* doctrine was first announced and today it constitutes an anomaly in the law, an invitation to employers to bargain in bad faith, and a danger to workers and unions.

Mackay and the Development of the NLRA

By the mid 1960's, the *Mackay* doctrine had become obviously inconsistent with the interpretation of § 8(a)(3) developed by the Board and the courts. Very early on, the Supreme Court announced two important basic principles about the goal of the section. First, it articulated the policy of free choice that lay behind the language of the subsection—"to allow employees to freely exercise their right to join unions, be good, bad, or indifferent members, or abstain from joining any union without imperiling their livelihood."[66] Second, it held that to "encourage or discourage membership" as used in the Act means also to encourage or discourage participation in union activities or fulfillment of union obligations.[67]

Similarly, the Court, early in the Act's development, made clear that discrimination could occur even when an employer did not treat union members and non-union members differently. The key case was *Republic Aviation v. NLRB,*[68] in which employees were discharged for violating a company rule against solicitation. The company argued that it did not discriminate against union members because it would have discharged any employee who violated its rule for whatever purpose. The Court rejected the argument, and in effect concluded that the discrimination consisted of treating these employees differently from the way the company would have treated them had they not engaged in union solicitation.[69]

The key issue in developing a consistent theory of § 8(a)(3), however, was whether the section required that the employer act for the specific purpose of discouraging union membership or activity. Although most cases alleging violations of § 8(a)(3) claim that employers have acted to discourage union activity, the first full discussion by the Court

---

[66] Radio Officers' Union v. NLRB, 347 U.S. 17, 40 (1954).

[67] *Id.* at 39–42.

[68] 324 U.S. 793 (1945).

[69] For analysis of this position, see Julius Getman, *Section 8(a)(3) of the NLRA and the Effort to Insulate Free Employee Choice*, 32 U. Chi. L. Rev. 735 (1965).

of the requirement of motive under § 8(a)(3) was in *Radio Officers' Union v. NLRB*,[70] where one of the consolidated cases alleged that an employer had reduced an employee's seniority for his failure to pay union dues, thereby acting to encourage union membership. The Court rejected the employer's defense that it had no purpose to encourage union membership. Although the Court reaffirmed the requirement of proof of motive and quoted approvingly from statements made in other contexts concerning the importance of motive, it said that no proof of specific intent was required where "employer conduct inherently encourages or discourages union membership." It approved the position of the NLRB and the appellate courts that had found that proof of "certain types of discrimination satisfies the intent requirement." Unfortunately, the basis for the Court's holding was not made clear.

The Court's language was bound to lead to confusion in subsequent cases. The *Radio Officers'* decision was cited both for the proposition that a finding of improper motive is necessary under § 8(a)(3) and for the proposition that it is not. The Court largely cleared up the confusion in *NLRB v. Erie Resistor Corp.*,[71] in which it upheld the Board's determination that the grant of superseniority to strike replacements violated § 8(a)(3). The employer argued, *inter alia*, that because it was not motivated by a desire to discourage union membership, its action was privileged. The Court rejected this argument in language which foretold the end of any motive requirement under the section.

> [A]s often happens, the employer may counter by claiming that his actions were taken in the pursuit of legitimate business ends and that his dominant purpose was not to discriminate or to invade union rights but to accomplish business objectives acceptable under the Act. ... [W]hatever the claimed overriding justification may be, [the employer's conduct] ... carries with it unavoidable consequences which the employer not only foresaw but which he must have intended. As is not uncommon in human experience, such situations present a complex of motives and preferring one motive to another is in reality the far more delicate task, reflected in part in decisions of this Court, of weighing the interests of employees in concerted activity against the interest of the employer in operating his business in a particular manner and of balancing in the light of the Act and its policy the intended consequences upon employee rights against the business ends to be served by the employer's conduct. This essentially is the teaching of the Court's prior cases.[72]

---

[70] 347 U.S. 17 (1954).

[71] 373 U.S. 221 (1963).

[72] *Id.* at 228–30.

The Court in *Erie Resistor* summed up its conclusion in language which would have been at least equally applicable had it been analyzing the legitimacy of hiring permanent replacements: "[S]uper-seniority by its very terms operates to discriminate between strikers and nonstrikers, both during and after a strike, and its destructive impact upon the strike and union activity cannot be doubted."[73]

The Court reaffirmed the conclusion that impact alone may justify a finding of violation in *NLRB v. Great Dane Trailers, Inc.*[74] In that case, the employer granted vacation pay to non-strikers but not to strikers. The employer argued that it was motivated by business concerns in so doing, not the desire to punish employees who engaged in concerted activity. The Court rejected this argument because the action was inherently destructive of the employees' rights under the statute.

The same method of analysis was subsequently used to conclude that replaced strikers are entitled to reinstatement when the employer increases its workforce after a strike.[75] And in *Laidlaw Corp. v. NLRB*[76] the Court refused to review the Board's conclusion that replaced economic strikers are entitled to priority in rehiring. Thus, the application of § 8(a)(3) today involves balancing employer rights and interests against the impact of the employer's conduct on employee statutory rights.

The law has changed significantly since the time that Congress framed the Act and the Court announced its decision in *Mackay.* Union economic pressure then unregulated is now subject to severe and complex regulation. The passage of the Taft–Hartley[77] and Landrum–Griffin amendments[78] seriously restrict the ability of unions to call upon one another for assistance in putting economic pressure on an employer or in making common cause to improve workers' terms and conditions generally. When it outlawed secondary activity by unions Congress significantly altered the balance of power between labor and management—the

---

[73] Although Justice White, who wrote the opinion in *Erie Resistor*, emphasized balancing, he recognized that motive plays an important role in the balancing process. The basic premise of the opinion is that existence of a legitimate business purpose, though relevant, is not necessarily dispositive if achieving such purpose would require serious interference with union rights. Moreover, as the opinion makes clear, if an employer is motivated by anti-union animus his action will be held to violate § 8(a)(3) even though it serves a valid business purpose and would otherwise have been permissible.

[74] 388 U.S. 26 (1967).

[75] NLRB v. Fleetwood Trailer Co., 389 U.S. 375 (1967).

[76] 397 U.S. 920 (1970), *declining to review*, 414 F.2d 99 (7th Cir. 1969).

[77] 61 Stat. 136 (1947).

[78] Pub. L. No. 86–257 (1959).

balance that made the *Mackay* decision acceptable to labor and its supporters.

The Continuing Importance of Mackay

MACKAY'S IMPACT ON FREEDOM OF CHOICE

The *Mackay* doctrine gives employers a powerful argument against unionization. In almost every union organizing election conducted by the NLRB, the employer mounts a campaign against representation in which it makes two points. Firstly, it will emphasize that it will bargain hard in the event of unionization, and that the only way for the union to force it to give benefits is through the strike. Secondly, the employer will point out that in the event of a strike, it has the right—which it is likely to use—permanently to replace the strikers. This is an argument that many employees interested in unions would be well advised to take seriously.

In addition, the hiring of replacement workers will often mean and will always threaten the termination of the union representation desired by the replaced employees. Under the Act, the replacement workers will be able to vote in a decertification election on whether they wish to continue representation. Such elections almost always lead to union decertification. *Mackay* thus provides employers with an incentive to seek a strike as a union-avoidance technique. There is reason to believe that this tactic was widely employed during the 1980's in several major industries, papermaking in particular.

MACKAY AND UNION POWER

The Supreme Court intimated in *Mackay* that employers need the right to permanently replace employees in order to continue operations during a strike. If that were ever true, it is no longer. The ability of employers in general to cope with a strike without hiring permanent replacements has significantly improved since the time of the *Mackay* decision.[79] The weakened state of the labor movement has made strike breaking more socially acceptable so that temporary replacements are easier to obtain. Provisions of the Act outlawing secondary union activity

---

[79] Contemporary commentators are not unanimous on how or, in some cases, whether the *Mackay* rule should be modified. For one proposal that also summarizes other positions, *see* Samuel Estreicher, *Collective Bargaining or "Collective Begging"?: Reflections on Antistrikebreaker Legislation,* 93 Mich. L. Rev. 577 (1994). Professor Estreicher suggests that employers must in some circumstances have an opportunity to replace strikers to provide "a market-based check on unreasonable union demands at the bargaining table." *Id.* at 599. He, however, proposes that employers be permitted to use permanent replacements after a strike has continued for more than six months and an employer can demonstrate business necessity. For a sense of the debate among economists over whether the holding of *Mackay* is efficient, see Seth D. Harris, *Coase's Paradox and the Inefficiency of Permanent Strike Replacements*, 80 Wash. U. L.Q. 1185 (2002).

and increased automation have all weakened the position of unions in economic strikes. There are now companies that specialize in providing replacement workers temporarily or permanently to struck companies.

The policies favoring free collective bargaining and freedom of choice are overlapping and mutually dependent. Successful collective bargaining is the culmination of the decision to unionize, and employees must feel free to support the union for collective bargaining to be successful. That employees who participate in the process in the manner contemplated by the law do so at the risk of their jobs seems contradictory and indifferent to the interests of the employees whose rights are supposedly at the heart of our labor relations laws.

There is little doubt that if the balancing of interests now called for under § 8(a)(3) were applied to the hiring of permanent replacements, the *Mackay* doctrine would be overturned. However, to this day, the Court has never analyzed the *Mackay* doctrine under contemporary standards. And despite the critical assessments to which the rule has been subjected, the Court has shown not the slightest inclination to moderate its effects.[80] The *Mackay* rule remains every bit as authoritative as the day the Court announced it.

The Impact of *Mackay* When Used

There have been few detailed studies of the impact of the *Mackay* doctrine. But what information we have paints a sad picture of human misery and community destruction. One of the most carefully studied strikes in this regard is the strike of 1200 replaced papermakers at the Androscoggin Mill of International Paper Company in Jay, Maine, from June of 1987 to October of 1988.[81] The strike lasted sixteen months before the union capitulated. The story of the Jay strike is a cautionary tale about the *Mackay* doctrine in the contemporary economy. In the aftermath of the strike, the hostility between former strikers, company management, and replacement workers harmed the quality of the paper produced. The former strikers, once exemplary paper workers, continued to see the company as the enemy and the quality of their work inevitably deteriorated. As one of the former strikers stated, "I go in every day with the same thought, just because I've got my job doesn't mean it's over. I've still got 600–800 friends on the outside and until they're back I

[80] One effort to overturn *Mackay* legislatively nearly succeeded. In 1990, the President of the paperworkers union local whose members had been replaced during its strike in Jay, Maine, persuaded a local congressman to introduce a bill that would have required employers to wait sixty days before hiring replacements. The bill was embraced by organized labor and passed overwhelmingly in the House of Representatives, but defeated by a filibuster in the Senate. Subsequent efforts to revive the legislation during the Clinton Administration also failed. Julius Getman, *The Betrayal of Local 14* 102–04 (1998).

[81] *Id.* All subsequent quotes about the strikers and the community are contained therein.

refuse to be friendly with these people." Remaining loyal to those on the outside was crucial to the self-respect of those who returned to the mill. Bruce Moran, a millwright, stated, "every time you see a brother or sister that hasn't got their job back you feel a very sick feeling knowing the only way they will get their job is if a scab dies or quits."

Concern with loyalty meant that scabs were not to be helped. Brent Gay, a senior machine operator, explained:

> Some of them come ask you about problems. "What do you think the problem is?" I tell them, "I don't know." Finally told one guy, "I could tell you how to solve that. I'm not gonna. Every time I do that, I'm cutting a guy's throat on the outside, and I'm not gonna do that." "Oh, I understand." He never asked me again after that.

The greatest anger continued to be directed at "crossovers," strikers who had abandoned the strike and crossed over the picket line. Five years after the strike ended, one of the crossovers explained his bitter view of the strike and its outcome.

> Some people won't speak to me that I've known for twenty years. I can meet them face to face and they still don't speak. That's their choice. A lot of times, I wave or I'll say hi, and that doesn't matter if it is on the street or if it's in the mill. I will ask them how their day's going or say good morning to 'em and they'll answer you back. But there is a few that to this day, they don't speak at all. I see two, a company, and the union that has spent millions of dollars. They both lost the battle. Nobody won. There's like a spirit of hatred and bitterness in this valley. There's no peace in this valley.
>
> And things are just not improving, and I'm looking for other opportunities. I've been praying about it, and I think the Lord's gonna tell me what's gonna happen, but he said the first thing I had to do was sell my house, and I got it up for sale and I'll sell it. And after that's sold, I'll work . . . something out.

A short time later he moved to Alaska.

Laurier Poulin, who was the last person to walk the picket line, left the mill in 1993. One of the scabs said, "You gonna shake my hand before you leave?" And I said "No, I didn't shake your hand when I came here, and I sure as hell am not gonna do it on the way out." He said, "What are you gonna do, carry it to the grave?" I says, "Yep, I told my wife to put it right in the paper, in the obituaries. I want it in my obituary that I'm not a scab."

Ray Pineau, a former striker, who testified before the Maine Legislature's labor committee, stated that being permanently replaced was more upsetting than walking into an ambush in Vietnam. Pineau's statement was made six years after the strike ended. The hiring of permanent replacements fundamentally changed the once cohesive mill community both inside and outside the plant. Six years after the strike ended, a former mill worker stated: "It has put brother against brother, friend against friend, and neighbor versus neighbor. It will take many generations before the hurt and anger will heal." Another former striker stated that the impact of the strike has been "devastation, break up of families and friendships. This generation will never see a complete healing."

Ken Finley, the town undertaker, described how the continued division affected the funeral of a woman whose son Norman was a supervisor at odds with his brothers, who were strikers.

> It was a large family, and totally divided. Norm was very supportive of the scabs, to the point where he got punched out a couple of times. And when the funeral was happening, he basically was in one area and the other family members were in another area. Not one of the strikers went to see him. You could see the demarcation. It's not unique; you see the bitterness, even in death.

When asked if the passage of time was easing the bitterness he was emphatic. "No, in five years it hasn't changed . . . it'll go a hundred years. The only change is people moving in and moving out."

The papermakers were used to thinking of themselves as helpful, cooperative, decent people, and productive members of the community. The aftermath of the strike put this comfortable self-image into serious doubt. One former striker was surprised by his own reaction to the death of one of the replacement workers as the result of an accident, six years after the strike ended. "Normally I am a compassionate man with sympathy for those with misfortune. However, after reading the article, my remark to my wife was, 'I guess there'll be one less scab in the mill.' Not that I rejoice in the man's death but sympathy for a scab comes hard." Another senior papermaker described the change in himself in this regard as "unbelievable."

> I was the type of person that anybody needed help I'm there. Two years ago a car drove over the road up here, on the bank. The guy was still in the car, upside down. He had to tell me who he was, where he was from and where he worked before I'd touch him. If he'd given the wrong answers I'd walked back over the bank and done nothing. That's bitter. That's damn bitter. That's what they created.

The stress involved in learning to deal with the world in a new way caused illnesses, divorce, alcoholism and even death. In 1994, six years after the strike ended, Ken Finley, the town undertaker, stated sarcastically, "The strike is still creating business for me."

Town residents and former strikers agree that the strike was responsible for increases in alcoholism and divorces. Henry Lerette stated that:

> All during the strike and since its end, I drank with increasing regularity.... My wife threatened to leave me if I refused to seek help. I am now in therapy and attend AA meetings frequently. At one recent AA meeting there were five other former strikers present.... I hesitate to blame the strike for my drinking problems, but it sure didn't help. I still harbor intense hatred for [International Paper] and the scabs that descended like rats to steal our jobs when we left the mill. I will take that hatred to my grave.

The devastating impact of the strike on the community was inevitably linked to the *Mackay* doctrine. Charles Noonan, the former city manager made it the central point of his congressional testimony in favor of the bill seeking to overturn *Mackay.*

> Christmas, birthdays, and other family occasions will never be the same for many families in Jay.... I suggest that before you pronounce the permanent replacement issue "not broke" and working well, you journey to Jay.[82]

> I don't have a lot of experience with strikes, and I certainly hope I never have to go through another one—but I have been talking to a number of town managers who have seen strikes, and the difference appears to be when you add that element of the permanent replacement worker that the level of violence, the bitterness, the desperation on those picket lines goes up considerably because every one of those replacement workers who goes in is taking someone's job.

Conclusion

One point about *Mackay* is clear. Despite what many of its critics have maintained, the rule the case announced is one intended by its framers and for which the Board itself argued. A deeper problem that any consideration of *Mackay* raises is the one that caused the strike in that case to founder: the need for solidarity. The willingness of individuals prudently and responsibly to make cause with others, to make some personal sacrifice for the common good even when they may not directly benefit from it, is the *sine qua non* for the labor movement. Such habits also are central to the survival of any democracy. No change in the law and no judicially-developed doctrine can instill those attitudes or act as a facile replacement for them. They require discipline and must come from the people themselves. But the Jay strike demonstrates that, even with remarkable solidarity and willingness to sacrifice, unions may be defeated by a combination of vast employer economic power and use of the *Mackay* doctrine.

---

[82] The "not broke" comment was a response to a previous witnesses' testimony, who had argued against changing the law on the grounds that "if it's not broke don't fix it."

*

2

Deborah C. Malamud

The Story of *Steele v. Louisville & Nashville Railroad*: White Unions, Black Unions, and the Struggle for Racial Justice on the Rails

By the time William Bestor Steele became a railroad fireman on the Louisville & Nashville Railroad (the "L & N") in February 1910, the unions representing firemen, engineers, brakemen and other operational railroad workers (often referred to as the "Big Four" unions) were already among the oldest and strongest labor organizations in the country. Organized on a craft basis, they had successfully negotiated collective bargaining agreements since the 1880's. By World War I, they "had virtually complete control of their respective crafts throughout the country." Among them was the Brotherhood of Locomotive Firemen and Engineers (the "BLFE" or the "Brotherhood"), established in 1873. Within the troubled history of labor unionism in the South, the railroad brotherhoods were uniquely successful in organizing workers. The success was, in part, because railroads were regulated by the federal government, which itself had recognized early that stable collective bargaining had benefits for labor peace on the rails. But one suspects that another cause for their success in the South was the role of race on the Southern railroads.[1]

[1] In this and the following section, the most helpful source is the superb history of black railroad worker unionism, Eric Arnesen, *Brotherhoods of Color: Black Railroad Workers and the Struggle for Equality* (2001). Also helpful for background on the best-known black railroad workers' union is Larry Tye, *Rising From the Rails: Pullman Porters and the Making of the Black Middle Class* (2004). For a critique of the New Deal's race

The fact that *Steele v. Louisville and Nashville Railroad Co.* is not simply a labor law case, but also an employment discrimination case, is obvious on the surface of the Supreme Court's opinion.[2] What is less obvious is that *Steele* is not simply a dispute between a labor union and unorganized black railroad employees, nor simply a dispute between private parties, nor simply a case raising questions of domestic race policy. The *Steele* case arose in the infancy of American labor law, at a time when the roles of courts and agencies were not yet well defined. It arose before federal employment discrimination law was even imaginable. And it arose on the eve of America's entry into World War II, a time when America's war against racism in Europe drew unfriendly foreign attention to America's racist practices at home. Against this background of uncertain law, the case illustrates the heroic, and in this case, successful efforts of black workers to use the collective strength of their own unions to seek legal redress. It also illuminates the often-futile efforts of the administration of Franklin D. Roosevelt and his chosen Supreme Court to ensure that the New Deal, which often bypassed minority workers, would at least defend the rights of the small minority among them with contractual rights worth defending.

Social and Legal Background

The Fireman's Job as Locus of Racial Conflict

The "Big Four" railroad brotherhoods only accepted white railroad workers as members. Racial exclusion was the norm for many reasons, one of which was the original role of the brotherhoods as fraternal orders and benevolent associations: admission of blacks would have suggested social equality, which was rejected by whites even more than was economic equality. But as the brotherhoods evolved into their role as labor unions, one of the services they provided to their white members was leadership in their fight against Southern railroad employment

policies and their long-term negative impact on black workers, *see* David Bernstein, *Only One Place of Redress: African–Americans, Labor Regulations, and the Courts from Reconstruction to the New Deal* (2001). *See also* Herbert R. Northrup, *The Negro in the Railway Unions*, 5 Phylon 159 (1944) (excerpts from Northrup's testimony before the Fair Employment Relations Authority, February 1943) (hereinafter "Northrup Testimony") (for the full hearings, see volume 2 of President's Committee on Fair Employment Practice, *A Hearing to Hear Evidence on Complaints of Racial Discrimination on Certain Railroads of the United States* (Alderson Pub. Co. 1943); and Howard W. Risher, *The Negro in the Railroad Industry* (1971)) (I use all three here without specific citation.) On southern organizing, *see* F. Ray Marshall, *Labor in the South* 50 (1967). On the BLFE's history, *see* George R. Horton & H. Ellsworth Steele, *The Unity Issue Among Railroad Engineers and Firemen*, 10 Indus. & Lab. Rel. Rev. 48 (1956). For a general history of federal railroad labor regulation, *see* Frank N. Wilner, *The Railway Labor Act and the Dilemma of Labor Relations* (1991).

[2] 323 U.S. 192 (1944).

practices that had, as early as 1875, brought black workers into "white jobs" (that is, job classifications within the jurisdiction of the white unions), a practice unique to the South. The situation created a classic conflict between the financial and dignitary needs of Southern white workers: if blacks were paid the same as whites, white supremacy would be threatened, but the availability of blacks to work at lower wages threatened white wages and job security. Ultimately, the unions would resolve the conflict by seeking total exclusion of blacks from "white jobs." Indeed, as early as 1910 white unions succeeded, through strikes and collective bargaining, in barring blacks from certain jobs and limiting their number in others—including the job of railroad fireman.

The job of fireman was a unique site of conflict between black and white railroad workers. Most firemen in the North were white, but blacks were well-represented among Southern firemen for fifty years before the *Steele* case was filed. The reason was largely the nature of the work: the job was physical, dirty, hard, and dangerous—just the kind of work Southern whites left to blacks. According to Steele himself, on a typical round-trip from Nashville to Birmingham on a hand-fired engine, he would shovel about thirty tons of coal, using a shovel that held 141 pounds, at a pace of something like four to six shovels-full per minute. The round-trip would take about fourteen hours, with only one fireman assigned to the engine for the whole trip. Steele said the fireman would become "very weak from perspiration [and] extreme exertion because of the amount of coal handled on the trip."[3]

Despite these working conditions, the job of fireman was desirable to Southern black men. One reason was financial. Firemen were paid far better than common laborers, especially after World War I, when, during a period of federal takeover of the railroads, the federal government equalized the pay of blacks and whites doing identical jobs. (Prior to the takeover, it was the railroads' practice for white firemen to be paid fifty percent of the going rate for engineers, while black firemen would be paid only forty percent of that rate.) Black firemen's pay was high not merely compared to the pay of black laborers but also compared to the pay of the struggling white-collar black middle class. As Charles Hamilton Houston, who was later to represent Steele all the way to the Supreme Court, explained to a black white-collar audience: "White collar or professional workers often look down on the Negro fireman and brakemen without realizing the strategic role they play in the struggle to democratize the industrial structure of the U.S.... Hour for hour of

[3] Birmingham Civil Rights Institute, Arthur D. Shores Papers, "Railroads" (hereinafter "Shores Papers"); Trial Transcript, at 86–89, Steele v. Louisville & Nashville Railroad, June 28, 1951, Jefferson County Circuit Court (hereinafter "Trial Transcript"). The Shores Papers are not yet catalogued, and folders and files within them are neither named nor numbered. I am extremely grateful to the Institute for giving me access to them.

service the firemen and brakemen make more money than most white collar and professional workers." Indeed, in Louisville, where the L & N had its headquarters, the good pay of black railroad workers put them just below the black white-collar elite in social status.[4]

Equalization of wages was a boost to black firemen's dignity, but it carried risks for long-term job security. If black workers were now as expensive as whites, and whites were believed superior, the railroads' economic incentive to hire blacks would disappear. As the already-employed black firemen would learn, no new black hiring meant that blacks would become a shrinking minority in the workforce with diminishing power to protect themselves. The need for self-protection was urgent. The period immediately following World War I saw a general backlash against blacks' claims to improved economic opportunity, of which a revival of Ku Klux Klan activity in the South was but one manifestation. White railroad workers, in what seemed to be a coordinated effort, used violence to terrorize blacks to leave the jobs whites now coveted. In 1921 and 1922, numerous black railroad workers were murdered, beaten, or threatened with violence if they were ever seen again doing "white men's jobs." The NAACP failed to have these acts declared federal crimes, just as it persistently failed to convince Congress to enact anti-lynching legislation. Of course, the threat and reality of violence meant that even employers otherwise inclined to hire blacks were "persuaded" not to. Indeed, for these and other reasons, including strike threats from the Brotherhood, 1926 was the last time (prior to the filing of the *Steele* lawsuit) that the L & N hired a black fireman, and all of the largest American railroads had stopped hiring black firemen—in the North and the South—by about 1928. Indeed, across the Southern railroad industry, blacks were 41.3 percent of all firemen in 1910, but only 33.1 percent in 1930.[5]

Ironically, those black firemen who were able to hold onto their jobs through the violent early 1920's came to acquire a second advantage over most black workers: job security through seniority. The Brotherhood secured seniority rights in its 1929 agreement with the L & N. These included the right to accumulate seniority and to use competitive seniority to bid for choice runs and (where racially permissible) promotions. The L & N accorded blacks seniority rights at the same time as

[4] Trial Transcript at 64; Charles Hamilton Houston, *Foul Employment Practice on the Rails*, 56 Crisis 269 (1949); *Victory for Firemen in FEPC Case Seen by Porters Committee*, Birmingham World, Sept. 10, 1943 (the *Birmingham World* was the leading black newspaper in Birmingham). On Louisville, *see* Russell Thomas Wigginton, *Both Sides of the Tracks: Louisville and Nashville Railroad's African–American Workers in Louisville, Kentucky, 1915–1945*, 209, 215 (2001) (unpublished Ph.D. dissertation, Univ. of Ill.).

[5] F. Ray Marshall, *Labor in the South* 55 (1967); Kenneth Robert Janken, *White: The Biography of Walter White, Mr. NAACP* 40, 226, 234 (2003).

whites gained them—although blacks, who by "tradition" were never allowed to serve as engineers, remained unable to do so regardless of seniority. Nonetheless, the seniority system was race-blind in one important respect: senior blacks could oust junior white firemen from their jobs through "rolling" (competitive bidding). Allowing black men to keep their jobs in direct competition with whites was an even greater challenge to principles of white racial monopoly than was pay equalization.

Although the work of the black fireman was arduous, being a firemen put black men in a unique position to develop a close working relationship based on mutual respect with their immediate white superiors: trainmasters, master mechanics, road foremen, and, especially, engineers. Engineers came to trust black firemen and to be "loyal" to them. Furthermore, given the likelihood that competent white firemen would be routinely promoted to engineer after only a short time working as a firemen, engineers (and railroad management) could not help but observe that many of their best firemen were senior blacks. Here, too, the pride of black firemen in their skills, and the recognition of those skills by whites up through the railroad job hierarchy, exacerbated the resentment of whites who remained firemen.[6]

White opposition to the presence of blacks in skilled railroad jobs became stronger during the Depression because the decline in industrial activity meant a steep loss of business for the railroad, and mass layoffs of railroad workers—many of them white—who had insufficient seniority to protect their jobs. The scarcer jobs became, the more white railroaders turned to violence to drive blacks out of the jobs to which seniority entitled them. Between 1931 and 1934, approximately ten black firemen and trainmen were killed and twenty-one wounded in a "reign of terror" in the lower Mississippi Valley. Even though the war effort reversed job losses for a while, there was an irreversible pattern of competition (from automotive transport) and technological change that was well understood to threaten firemen's job security. There would be fewer jobs for firemen, and those jobs that remained would be more attractive to whites. As Milton Webster, Vice President of the Brotherhood of Sleeping Car Porters, observed in 1941, "with stokerized engines and Diesel engines, the fireman now instead of shoveling 15 or 20 tons of coal per trip, now has what may be classified as a white collar job, and it naturally is attractive to the white man." Once again, the better the job,

---

[6] For the facts in this and the following paragraph, *see* George R. Horton & H. Ellsworth Steele, *The Unity Issue Among Railroad Engineers and Firemen*, 10 Indus. & Lab. Rel. Rev. 48, 49 (1956); Alexa B. Henderson, *FEPC and the Southern Railway Case: An Investigation Into the Discriminatory Practices of Railroads During World War II*, 61 J. Negro Hist. 173, 175 (1976); Howard University, Moorland–Spingarn Research Center, Papers of Charles Hamilton Houston (hereinafter "Houston Papers") box 163–23, folder 7, box 163–22, folder 22; Trial Transcript at 75.

the greater the resentment against blacks whose seniority permitted them to keep it.

Exclusivity and Racial Monopoly

By the mid–1930's, the law itself became the white brotherhoods' most important weapon against skilled black workers. Since 1898, a series of federal statutes had governed railroad labor relations, the most important of which, the Railway Labor Act (RLA), was passed in 1926. The RLA essentially codified the existing bargaining pattern in the industry. A set of amendments to the Railway Labor Act, enacted at the brotherhoods' initiative in 1934, gave the brotherhoods the most critical tool in their efforts to use collective bargaining itself as a means of displacing black workers.[7]

Under the Railway Labor Act as amended, union elections could be held only for the entire "craft or class" of employees working on the "carrier" as a whole. The flexibility eventually given to the National Labor Relations Board to determine "appropriate bargaining units" did not exist under the Railway Labor Act. Unit size was determined by law, because the unions that shaped the law had customarily operated on a whole-carrier, whole-craft basis and did not want their power diluted by insurgencies that might prevail were smaller bargaining units deemed acceptable. The National Mediation Board (the "NMB"), the body authorized by the Act to certify bargaining representatives, understood itself to be required to close its doors to any smaller group that sought union representation, regardless of the reasons for seeking separate representation.

Furthermore, the union elected by a majority of a craft or class of employees in a carrier-wide election became the exclusive bargaining representative for that craft or class. This meant that dissenting groups within the represented workforce—even groups excluded from union membership, as were blacks—could no longer represent themselves in negotiations with their employer, and would be bound by whatever deal the union imposed on them. And, to make matters worse, the National Railroad Adjustment Board ("NRAB"), which was the grievance-resolution mechanism established by the Act, understood itself as empowered to adjudicate only grievances brought by the exclusive representative. Also, the NRAB was not independent. Its members were officials of railroads and the well-established railroad unions, and their shared understanding of the requirements of the statute simply gave legal cover to their perceived self-interest in keeping their relationships stable. Well-

---

[7] David Bernstein, *Racism, Railroad Unions, and Labor Regulations*, 5 Indep. Rev. 237 (2000); Herbert Northrup, *The Railway Labor Act: A Critical Reappraisal,* 25 Indus. & L. Rel. Rev. 3 (1971); Edward B. Shils, *Union Fragmentation: A Major Cause of Transportation Labor Crisis*, 25 Indus. & L. Rel. Rev. 32 (1971).

informed critics understood at the time that neither the NMB nor the NRAB was impartial, consistently favoring the Big Four against black worker demands.[8]

Black union and civil rights leaders were among those who saw the damage the 1934 amendments might cause. The Independent Association of Railroad Employees (the "IARE")—Steele's union, which was founded in 1934—tried to secure an amendment making discriminatory contracts illegal, but failed. So did the National Urban League and the NAACP the following year, when they were soundly defeated in their efforts to amend the Wagner Act, which also used the principle of exclusivity, to render discrimination against racial minorities unlawful.[9]

For several years after the 1934 amendments, efforts of black railroad unions to use RLA administrative mechanisms to secure black railroad workers' rights were consistently rebuffed by the agencies on jurisdictional grounds. In particular, one of the NMB's rulings was that "a craft or class of employees may not be divided into two or more on the basis of race or color for the purpose of choosing representatives. All those employed in the craft or class, regardless of race, creed, or color must be given the opportunity to vote for the representatives of the whole craft or class." That opportunity was worth little when blacks were a minority within the craft or class and the majority's union was determined to undermine them.[10]

Black Railroad Unions and Their Turn to Litigation

Two black railroad unions (which eventually merged), the Association of Colored Railway Trainmen and Locomotive Firemen ("ACRT") and the IARE, responded to this worsening situation by initiating a program of litigation. For this purpose, first the ACRT and then the

---

[8] Federal railroad authorities had followed a majority-rule approach during the World War I federal takeover of the railroads, see Pennsylvania R.R. Co. v. United States R.R. Labor Bd., 261 U.S. 72 (1923), and many railroads continued the practice, but it was only under the RLA amendments of 1934 that majority rule and exclusivity became legally binding. *See* Brief of the United States Steele v. Louisville & Nashville Railroad, Case No. 45, Oct. Term 1944, 323 U.S. 192 (1944) and Tunstall v. Louisville and Nashville Railroad, Case No. 37, Oct. Term 1944, 323 U.S. 210 (1944) (hereinafter "SG Brief"). The RLA was different in this regard from the National Recovery Act, the labor provisions of which were interpreted by NRA officials as precluding exclusivity. Thomas E. Vadney, *Wayward Liberal: A Political Biography of Donald Richberg* (1970). For lack of independence at NRAB and NMB, *see* Howard W. Risher, *The Negro in the Railroad Industry* 143 (1971); Northrup Testimony at 164.

[9] Eric Arnesen, *Brotherhoods of Color: Black Railroad Workers and the Struggle for Equality* 137 (2001); Paul Frymer, *Acting When Elected Officials Won't: Federal Courts and Civil Rights Enforcement in U.S. Labor Unions, 1935–85*, 97 Am. Pol. Sci. Rev. 483, 484 (2003).

[10] J. Michael Eisner, *William Morris Leiserson: A Biography* 62 (1967).

IARE retained Charles Hamilton Houston, former head of the NAACP's legal department, as their general counsel.

Charles Hamilton Houston, a son of Washington D.C.'s black elite, graduated magna cum laude from Amherst College, and obtained both a law degree cum laude and a doctorate in law from Harvard Law School. He was the first black member of the editorial board of the *Harvard Law Review*. Roscoe Pound and Felix Frankfurter, the latter of whom was on the Supreme Court by the time Houston argued *Steele*, were his enthusiastic mentors at Harvard. Houston was a "man of striking self-possession" who became lead counsel at the NAACP, dean of Howard University Law School, and a much-respected advocate before the Supreme Court while at the same time continuing to face the daily humiliations blacks suffered in Southern public life. For example, after arguing a case before the Supreme Court—most often a civil rights case—Houston "would be denied the simple right to sit down in a public restaurant to eat his lunch." Houston's father, with whom he practiced for many years, kept urging him to be practical and abandon civil rights work for a more lucrative practice. Houston did consider financial issues when giving up his post at the NAACP and returning to his father's practice, but he continued to ignore his father's advice. Much of his "paying" work was civil rights litigation on behalf of blacks who could just barely afford the low fees he charged them.[11]

The case that introduced Houston to the ACRT and the IARE, and to the plight of black firemen, was that of Ed Teague. Teague was a black fireman who was deprived of a position on a mechanically-stoked engine, one which he was entitled to on the basis of seniority. The reason was an agreement between the BLFE and the railroad that gave junior white firemen preference over senior black firemen on mechanically-stoked engines. The union did not give the black firemen notice of the agreement or an opportunity to have their views heard. As became the pattern, they learned of the agreement only when their jobs were taken away.

After the railroad labor agencies both rejected Teague's claim on jurisdictional grounds, the black firemen brought their predicament to the NAACP, and Houston agreed to take it on. In 1940, Houston, working closely with J.T. Settle, a Memphis lawyer, filed suit in federal court in Tennessee in the case of *Teague v. Gulf, Mobile & Northern Railroad Company*. The complaint alleged that the 1938 agreement violated the vested seniority rights of Teague and other black firemen,

[11] Facts on Houston in this and following paragraphs are drawn from Genna Rae McNeil, *Groundwork: Charles Hamilton Houston and the Struggle for Civil Rights* (1983). *See also* Richard Kluger, *Simple Justice* 195 (1975); William J. Coleman, Jr., *Tribute to Charles Hamilton Houston,* 111 Harv. L. Rev. 1255 (1998); Robert L. Carter, *In Tribute: Charles Hamilton Houston*, 111 Harv. L. Rev. 2149 (1998).

their Fifth Amendment rights to due process, and the union's fiduciary duty to them. As radical as the complaint might seem, it was in many ways quite conservative. The complaint did not challenge the Brotherhood's practice of excluding blacks from membership or the railroad's refusal to hire new black firemen or to promote blacks to engineer. These choices did not signal an acceptance of these limiting practices, either by the black firemen or by their lawyers. It represented, instead, a strategic decision to proceed incrementally, to make it seem possible that the black firemen's needs could be met by remedying small injustices while leaving large ones for another day.

The Brotherhood, headquartered in Cleveland, was represented by Harold Heiss, a Cleveland lawyer who represented the BLFE throughout the *Steele* litigation, and continued to represent white brotherhoods until 1969. Heiss argued that the case raised only state-law issues and should be dismissed on jurisdictional grounds. The district court agreed, and ruled against Teague in March 1941.[12]

A. Philip Randolph and the Political Route

A. Philip Randolph, president of the most powerful black railroad union in the country, the Brotherhood of Sleeping Car Porters (the "BSCP"), understood that the fact that America's defense industries were gearing up to supply the British with arms and supplies in their defense against Hitler created the perfect opportunity for the kind of social protest he believed necessary to create real change. In mid-January 1941, Randolph began to promote a March on Washington Movement aimed at opening armed services and defense industry jobs to black Americans.[13]

As a railroad union president, Randolph paid close attention to the black firemen's situation, and sought to convince the firemen that the ACRT and IARE's litigation strategy was not the best black union response to the tightening of the Brotherhood's vise. Randolph convened a Conference for Colored Locomotive Firemen, which was held on March 28–29, 1941 in Washington, D.C. The conference goal was to bring all black firemen under the umbrella of a single large nationwide union, called the Provisional Committee to Organize Colored Locomotive Fire-

[12] The district court decision is unpublished; the description of the court's holding is drawn from the opinion of the Sixth Circuit, 127 F.2d 53 (6th Cir. 1942). For news coverage, *see* Microfilm Edition of Tuskegee Institute News Clippings File, "Labor" (hereinafter "Tuskegee Clippings"), 1939.

[13] On Randolph, *see* Eric Arnesen, *Brotherhoods of Color: Black Railroad Workers and the Struggle for Equality* (2001), Kenneth Robert Janken, *White: The Biography of Walter White, Mr. NAACP* (2003), and Larry Tye, *Rising From the Rails: Pullman Porters and the Making of the Black Middle Class* (2004). A transcript of the conference is in the Houston Papers, box 163–22, folder 22.

men, under BSCP leadership, and to launch a program of public protest against discrimination by the white brotherhoods and the railroads.

In his opening comments, Randolph noted the pending *Teague* litigation and said that, while a victory in the case would certainly "have favorable repercussions," litigation as a strategy had its limits:

> It cannot change the existing numerical relationship between black and white locomotive firemen on the railroad. It cannot compel railroads to employ a Negro to fill the place of a Negro fireman who dies, is retired or discharged.... It cannot take away or nullify the collective bargaining rights and power of the [Brotherhood].... Unless the colored firemen organize into a bona fide labor union, which embraces the majority of the colored firemen, their power to improve their lot will remain unchanged.

Invoking the tragedy of the white abandonment of Reconstruction, Randolph insisted that "the power of the colored firemen ... does not inhere in the law, but in their self organization.... Rights granted by the law may be nullified by power." Noting that even favorable decisions by the Supreme Court were being defied in the South, Milton Webster, Vice President of the Brotherhood of Sleeping Car Porters, reiterated that "Supreme Court decisions, while helpful, by no means solve the problem" and that "if prejudice and discrimination [are] to be eliminated in the labor movement ... it must be eliminated by Negroes themselves through strong organization."

Although Randolph and Webster did not expressly condemn the *Teague* litigation (after heated debate, they accepted a resolution supporting it "morally and financially"), the IARE and ACRT men present at the conference took umbrage at what seemed to be the disparaging of their litigation efforts in favor of an organizing strategy which, Randolph acknowledged, would still leave black firemen excluded from the bargaining table. "What's going to happen to our jobs," IARE officer Arthur Lewis asked, while the new organization was being built?

By May 1941, with the support of other civil rights leaders, Randolph announced that he would turn out 100,000 blacks to march down Pennsylvania Avenue on July 1 to protest the federal government's failure to use black labor in support of the war effort. Randolph's threat of a march on Washington prompted President Roosevelt to negotiate with Randolph, using New York mayor Fiorello LaGuardia as a go-between. The result of these negotiations was Executive Order 8802, signed on June 25, 1941. Part of the compromise was to create a "Fair Employment Practice Committee" ("FEPC") to address claims of employment discrimination in defense industries, including the railroads.

Milton Webster, "the most defiant of Randolph's chief lieutenants," was appointed a member of the FEPC.[14]

Houston himself understood the importance of politics. His strategy was litigation, but his audience went well beyond the courts. Houston urged his clients to move quickly, for political reasons: "It looks as if we may be in war before any of us realize. And the first thing the Government will do will be to take over the railroads as it did in the last war.... [I]f you have your protests in, and some cases started in court, when the government takes over you will be in position to ask the government to correct the wrongs done you." Here, Houston would be proven wrong: the railroads remained in private hands throughout World War II, robbing him of the opportunity to operate quietly behind the scenes to leverage his litigation into change on the ground. But Randolph was also proven wrong. The FEPC hearings on discrimination on the railroads—including, prominently, the problem of black firemen—only served to turn the situation of the black firemen into a political hot potato, tossed back and forth between Roosevelt and the courts.

Factual Background

On March 31, 1941—just one day after the end of Randolph's Washington conference—the IARE learned of another secret agreement that threatened all black firemen in the southeastern states. That agreement became the basis for the *Steele* litigation—and the source of considerable attention in the FEPC railroad hearings.

The Southeastern Carriers Agreement

Under the Railway Labor Act, collective bargaining agreements run for an indefinite term, and a party seeking to renegotiate part or all of the agreement must serve notice on the other party. On March 28, 1940, the Brotherhood gave notice to the Southeastern Carriers Association of its desire to negotiate over a proposal to alter the racial composition of the fireman's craft. The railroads rejected the proposal, and the dispute came before the National Mediation Board. A modified version of the proposal was brokered by the NMB and signed by the parties and the NMB on February 18, 1941. Pursuant to the agreement, more than fifty percent of fireman positions in each class of service in each seniority district would be reserved for whites, and until whites reached that percentage, all vacancies were to be filled by whites and, even more important, any white could "roll" (displace) any black fireman regardless

[14] Larry Tye, *Rising From the Rails: Pullman Porters and the Making of the Black Middle Class* 209 (2004); Merl E. Reed, *Seedtime for the Modern Civil Rights Movement: The President's Committee on Fair Employment Practice, 1941–1946* (1991); Alexa B. Henderson, *FEPC and the Southern Railway Case: An Investigation Into the Discriminatory Practices of Railroads during World War II*, 61 J. Negro Hist. 173, 177 (1976).

of their relative seniority. The Brotherhood and the carriers referred to the amendment as the Southeastern Carriers Agreement or the Washington Agreement. The black firemen—when they eventually learned of it—came to refer to it as "the Hitler agreement."

On March 31, 1941, the L & N gave notice to its firemen that all current pool assignments would be discontinued, and that the seniority of black firemen would not be honored in the re-bidding process. Steele was "rolled" (displaced) from his assignment the next day, and it was only when he appealed the decision to the L & N's Birmingham assistant superintendent that he learned of the Southeastern Agreement. He was told that the reason for the agreement was that the L & N needed to free up fireman slots so that whites could be trained as future engineers. Steele didn't buy it. And thus began the *Steele* case.[15]

By this time, Steele, a lifelong resident of Birmingham, had been working for the L & N as a locomotive firemen for just over thirty-one years. The job supported him well: he was married, owned a home, and raised six children. Steele was a well-respected member of the Birmingham black community and was involved in local civil rights activities. Steele served as General Chairman of the local of the IARE that included Birmingham.

Steele's connection to the L & N and to the fireman's craft went back even further. As Steele later testified, "my father before me were a fireman and stayed in the service of the Louisville & Nashville Railroad Company the biggest part of his life." Steele had tremendous pride in his railroad, his craft, and his work performance (he had not received a demerit in well over a decade). But he was especially proud of his seniority, which dated back to March 5, 1910. His seniority earned him a prized schedule on the southbound passenger run from Birmingham, a run which was (for a fireman) relatively easy (because of the grade of the track and the quality of the engines), paid well, and allowed him to spend most weekends at home with his family. But if he could be displaced by junior white firemen, his job would become far more burdensome. More important to him, he would be stripped of a hard-earned source of dignity available to very few black men in the South.

Looking back on his reactions to the announced Southeastern Agreement, Steele later testified:

---

[15] Most of the details in the following account of the history of the *Steele* case (and related cases) are drawn from the Shores Papers; Trial Transcript; Houston Papers, boxes 163–22 and 163–23; and the Joint Appendix in Steele v. Louisville and Nashville Railroad, U.S. Supreme Court. In letters and in trial testimony, Steele spoke and wrote clearly and persuasively, but idiomatically. I leave his statements as they appear, without editing for grammar or spelling.

> As my father before me were a fireman and stayed in the service of the L & NRR Co the biggest part of his life, and his job were not taken, I really feel that it was inconsistent for my job to be taken under the head that engineers were to be made. The L & NRR Co, as far as I know of, hasn't ever suffered for engineers so much until they couldn't get them, they always have for these 40 years that I have been in the service. . . . They have always sent North on the Northern Division and sent engineers down here when they didn't have nothing in service but negro firemens.

To stand by and allow his seniority rights to be taken away would be to take a major step backwards from the heritage his father had left him. He would not let it happen without a fight, and he was prepared to take it all the way to the top. His union's search for a lawyer was resolved quickly: Charles Hamilton Houston agreed to take the case, with the IARE as his paying client.

Preparations for Litigation

Houston explained to the IARE leadership that under the RLA, the position of the NMB would be that only the Brotherhood, as majority representative, has standing before the agency. He advised them that in order to "make a perfect case," they should carefully write letters, as individuals, to lay out their complaint to the local and national offices of the Brotherhood and to L & N. It was important that they proceed as individuals for reasons Houston knew but did not spell out: the last thing they would want to do was to suggest that this case was about a rivalry between two unions, because the Supreme Court had no interest whatsoever in involving the federal courts in inter-union disputes. In fact, nothing in pleadings or in any of the opinions in *Steele* and the related cases would reveal the existence of a black union or its status not only as the paying client, but also as an active player in framing the case.

In order to file one or more lawsuits in Alabama, the men would need local counsel in Birmingham. There was only one black attorney in the entire state of Alabama in 1941; his name was Arthur Shores. When Houston consulted with Thurgood Marshall about Shores, Marshall gave Shores "a fine rating as a lawyer," and said that "he has integrity and plenty of courage." On the assumption (later proven false) that Shores would take the leading oar, Houston said that he would be "glad to help him all I can on the cases." Houston and Shores would have to be paid—this was not pro bono litigation—and Houston warned the IARE "not to overreach yourselves and get more cases underway than you can finance."[16]

---

[16] Except as otherwise noted, sources on the preparation for litigation are Houston Papers, box 163–22, box 163–23, folders 1, 2, 3, 22. Marshall was not speaking lightly when

It took three more months for the IARE to file a complaint. But even before a complaint was filed, the L & N firemen's protests yielded results in Birmingham. The L & N had a relatively benign (albeit paternalistic) policy towards black employees, and prided itself on Louisville's relative freedom from Klan violence. As Steele later informed Lewis, news about discussions between the black firemen and the L & N in Louisville had spread "just like wildfire," and engineers, who sometimes sided with the black firemen, began to "call the Agreement into question." IARE officers wrote Houston on June 19 that the protests had "to some extent changed the minds of L & N officers as to acceptance of application" of the Agreement. They also noted with pleasure that the IARE protests had given their union an edge in the competition against Randolph's organizing efforts; 177 of the 230 black L & N firemen had signed IARE union authorization cards.[17]

The IARE leaders called a meeting in Birmingham in June aimed at pulling its litigation strategy together. Officers of the international and the Birmingham local, along with some other local members, met in advance to lay out questions to ask Shores. It is quite remarkable how much these union officials already knew about relevant procedural and substantive law. Shores explained that Alabama law now permitted class suits, and advocated filing suit in state court in Birmingham. Arthur Lewis of the IARE noted the Kentucky Supreme Court's 1923 decision in *Piercy v. Louisville & Nashville R. Co.*,[18] which treated vested seniority rights as inviolable by later contracts, suggesting Kentucky might be a more favorable forum.

On July 23, while Joseph Waddy, Houston's law partner, was interviewing firemen from the L & N's Pensacola division to explore the possibility of bringing a suit there, Shores and Steele went to Knoxville for a meeting of the legal team. At that meeting, Steele was interviewed to see whether he would be a good plaintiff. The lawyers were impressed that he had been disciplined only once in his thirty-two years of service

---

stating that courage was a requirement for doing civil rights work in the South: in the course his his long career as a civil rights lawyer, Shores' life was threatened numerous times, and several times shots were fired into his home. *See* Editorial, *A Pioneer Passes,* N.Y. Times, Dec. 21, 1996 ("All across the South, in towns small and large, there was a generation of obscure black heroes who prepared the ground and planted the seeds and never minded the peril."); Eric Pace, *Arthur D. Shores, 92, Lawyer and Advocate For Civil Rights,* N.Y. Times, Dec. 18, 1996; *In Memoriam, Arthur D. Shores, 1904–1996,* J. of Blacks in Higher Educ. 5 (1997).

[17] On the L & N and Louisville, *see* Russell Thomas Wigginton, *Both Sides of the Tracks: Louisville and Nashville Railroad's African–American Workers in Louisville, Kentucky, 1915–1945* (2001) (unpublished Ph.D. dissertation, Univ. of Ill.).

[18] 248 S.W. 1042 (Ky.1923).

and that he gave a good oral presentation of the facts of the case thus far, both of which weighed in favor of using him as a plaintiff.

On August 6, Houston and Lewis reported their decision not to bring suit in Pensacola, but to hold open that possibility for the future. "In all these cases," they reported, "we are treading new ground, and it is well to use no more ammunition than necessary until we find we are on target and treading on a solid foundation." Mistakes made in one case could be corrected in subsequent cases. As to whether Steele's case should be brought in Kentucky or in Alabama, Houston expressed a preference for Kentucky because of the favorable *Piercy* decision. Shores later did some legal research which suggested that Alabama procedure would be hospitable to the suit and reported (incorrectly it turned out) that "there is no doubt that we could get a full hearing on the merits of the case within sixty days." Houston's research on Kentucky law revealed suit could not be filed against an unincorporated association such as the Brotherhood. That proved to be determinative. Houston chose Alabama, notwithstanding the greater value of *Piercy* in Kentucky.

Meanwhile, the IARE local leaders were expressing concern that the L & N would retaliate against them if they brought suit. Houston urged them not to worry: under the union contract, Steele could be fired only for just cause and, given his excellent safety record, he should have no trouble performing his job "from now on with such perfection that the company will not have a chance to get any just cause against him." There was no sign of retaliation for their complaints thus far. Indeed, Shores reported that by the beginning of August, "negro Firemen have been given the type of consideration they received prior to the February agreement." But this did not assuage the men's anxiety. They saw the improvement as L & N trying to "quiet them hoping they will let the matter rest," and didn't expect their good fortune to last.

Concerned about the issue of Steele's job security, Houston met first with the general counsel for the L & N and then with W.B. Porter, assistant director of personnel at the L & N, to get an answer to the question of "what would be the attitude of the company if Steele sued for establishment of his seniority right." Porter, Houston reported, "talked quite freely." Porter complimented Steele's service record, said that "the white engineers were very fond of their negro firemen and very loyal to them," and that "the railroad had been much troubled by this contract." Indeed, Porter said that the only reason black firemen were not promoted to engineer was that "the public was not willing to accept Negroes as engineers," but that they "could probably drive the engines just as well as anybody else." As to Steele himself, Porter said that he would not dismiss Steele for bringing a suit to challenge the Agreement "if there was no effort to get a lot of back pay out of the railroad company." Porter also explained to Houston that the railroad would not be pleased with a litigation strategy relying on the *Piercy* rule that seniority rights are inviolable. This, he explained, would take away the railroad's operational flexibility even in cases in which no race discrimination was alleged. But he left it up to Houston whether to pursue that argument, without threat of retaliation against Steele if he chose to do so.

After that meeting, Shores and Houston filed a complaint in August 1941 in the Jefferson County Circuit Court in Birmingham. Following Porter's advice, they were careful not to ask for damages against the railroad. They did, however, argue for the inviolability of vested seniority rights. At the time of filing the complaint, Houston did not forget the ongoing organizing battle between the IARE and Randolph's Provisional Committee. He planned to release a copy of the complaint "to the press to offset the publicity which the Brotherhood of Sleeping Car Porters is getting" for the creation, just a month earlier, of the FEPC.

In the months after the suit was filed, Steele found himself working runs with longer hours and harder conditions for lower pay. This was not because he was being retaliated against for filing suit. Indeed, it would seem the opposite was the case. The L & N offered Steele any number of better opportunities, all of which he refused. As he explained years later at trial, he rejected offered runs "because the hours were not suitable, knowing that I were the oldest in point of seniority and seniority rights would place me anywhere that I wanted to go." He rejected seemingly attractive passenger runs from Birmingham to Nashville because he preferred his existing runs: he already knew those runs, there were fewer men senior to him on the southern runs (giving him more bidding power), and he didn't want to "wrong" the younger black men whose runs he would be taking.

Steele's main reason for objecting to what might have seemed to others to be reasonable solutions was one of principle. "Under that I would not have been exercising seniority.... I knew it wasn't right, ... I knew it shouldn't have been handled this way. I believed I were entitled to the job that I had been on for all those number of years [nineteen years] on the South end passenger pool." When, years later, he was mocked for that position at trial, he reaffirmed it. He said that "to go in a different direction to that I had been, yes, sir," would be "an injustice," if the reason was a substitution of gratuity for seniority. "Seniority is for the specific purpose of obtaining the choice runs or jobs; that is what it is exercised for, and there was nothing choice that I wanted on the North end."

Prior Proceedings

The Trial Court

The complaint brought by Steele, on his own behalf and as representative of a class of black firemen on the L & N, alleged a conspiracy between the Brotherhood and L & N to violate the seniority provisions of each black fireman's individual contract with the L & N. The source of these rights was alleged to be Article 26 of the March 1, 1929 Locomotive Firemen and Hostlers Schedule, as "embodied" in each black fireman's individual contract. The complaint, without specifics, alleged that the BLFE had made efforts over fifteen years, while functioning as the "sole and exclusive representative" of all the firemen under the RLA, to secure a "monopoly for its own members" and "force them out of employment and destroy their vested property rights," in violation of its "statutory and fiduciary duty to each locomotive fireman" (including Steele and the class). The complaint then alleged that the Southeastern Carriers Agreement was, in violation of that fiduciary duty, a "secret, fraudulent agreement to impair and destroy plaintiff's vested seniority rights" and those of the class, and that the Brotherhood used its "coercive power" over the L & N to force it to break the black firemen's individual contracts. The complaint requested $50,000 in damages against the Brotherhood (no damages were requested of the L & N), reversal of the Southeastern Carriers Agreement, and a permanent injunction against the Brotherhood purporting to represent the black firemen "so long as or if they refuse to give plaintiff and the other Negro firemen notice, opportunity to be heard, and a voice on all matters affecting them individually or in common with the other locomotive firemen on Defendant's railroad as a class."

Just as was the case in *Teague*, the *Steele* complaint did not challenge the Brotherhood's racially-exclusive membership policy, insisting only upon notice and "voice"—without explaining what form "voice" should take or why it would have made a difference, given the very history of discrimination the complaint recited. Nor did the complaint challenge the railroad's policy of not promoting black firemen to engineer.

The failure to challenge non-promotability made perfect sense under Houston's incrementalist approach to the litigation, but it did open up an area of vulnerability. The L & N routinely trained future white engineers by having them serve first as firemen, preferably on the same runs on which they would later serve as engineers. If senior black firemen were free to use their seniority rights to roll junior white firemen, they would routinely fill the slots the railroad might otherwise fill with white future engineers. By challenging the Southeastern Carrier's Agreement without challenging black non-promotability, Steele's complaint was vulnerable to the defense that it was operational necessity, not race, that motivated the Agreement.

Then again, it may have been realism that caused Houston to stop short of challenging black non-promotability. When Porter of the L & N said to Houston that he thought blacks had the skills to be engineers,

Houston was thrilled and spent some time talking to Porter about how the L & N might overcome supposed public opposition and take the lead in promoting blacks. The senior black firemen quickly developed new skills and mastery of new technologies. But promotion to engineer was governed by a pencil-and-paper test that the poorly-educated black firemen, never given formal training by the railroads, would likely all fail. A push by Houston for promoting blacks to engineer was hardly the way to protect the jobs of his current clients.[19]

The filing of the complaint had an immediate positive effect for black firemen in Birmingham. Lewis reported just three days after the complaint was filed, "it seems that all action towards changing the policy of displacing colored firemen was abandoned," and that the L & N was now allowing black firemen full seniority rights in bidding for new runs. It took longer for the black firemen to regain the positions they had lost on already-established runs, but Steele reported in October 1941 that jobs were being restored in Birmingham. As Porter had suggested, it seemed that the L & N liked the old order and was prepared to stand up to the Brotherhood's demands on the ground even as it defended the Agreement in litigation.[20]

The L & N and the Brotherhood responded to the complaint by challenging the court's jurisdiction, asserting that it was rogue individuals, not the Brotherhood itself, that negotiated the Southeastern Carriers Agreement, and denying that the black firemen each had an individual contract with seniority rights. The L & N also disclaimed any conspiracy, alleging instead that the RLA imposed on it the obligation to negotiate with the Brotherhood as exclusive representative of the firemen.

As the defendants stalled, the Birmingham men began to get nervous about how the case was being handled. Steele and one of his fellow IARE officers began to question whether the union's legal team could do the job. They agreed that because (in Steele's words) "Alabama is a Little White State and uphold white supremacy," they ought to have a white lawyer on the team. They consulted Houston first, however. One suspects that his written response tones down the fury he must have felt at the suggestion: "I am opposed to associating with a white lawyer unless he knows more than I do. I am glad to associate with any lawyer

---

[19] It would only be with the Supreme Court's decision in Griggs v. Duke Power Co., 401 U.S. 424 (1971), that the "disparate impact" theory under which such a test could itself be legally challenged as discriminatory would enter the law. The NAACP, in its own approach to employment litigation, stayed clear of any cases that required defining "discrimination" as anything other than failing to treat blacks exactly like whites. *See* Risa L. Goluboff, *"We Live's in a Free House Such As It Is": Class and the Creation of Modern Civil Rights*, 151 U. Pa. L. Rev. 1977 (2003).

[20] Discussion of the pretrial process is drawn from materials in the Houston Papers, box 163–23, folders 4, 6, 7, and 10.

who knows more than I do. But I do not propose to do all the work for practically nothing and then let some white lawyer get a large fee just because he is white.''

Steele was also worried that the case's slow progress was adversely affecting the IARE in its competition with Randolph. He reported rumors that Randolph intended to come to Birmingham to lure black firemen away from the IARE and into his Provisional Committee. Although Randolph reassured Houston that he intended to organize all the black firemen in the country into one union, but that he had no intention of interfering with the lawsuit, his response begged the question: Steele wasn't claiming that Randolph's purpose was to threaten the suit. Rather, he feared that Randolph ''would weaken our number,'' thus starving the IARE of the dues that funded the litigation, and that the suit would be threatened politically by any showing by Randolph of lack of support for the IARE.

Argument was held on both motions on November 12, 1941 before Judge Creel. First, Houston denied the Brotherhood's legal right, as a matter of agency law, to alter the black firemen's previously-established contractual rights. Choosing evocative language, he said that if the rule were otherwise, ''the Brotherhood [would be] walking in just like masters, just the same as if they dominated and owned the contract.'' Then, arguing in the alternative, Houston argued that, in negotiating to alter the black firemen's seniority rights, the Brotherhood violated the ''fiduciary and statutory duty'' it owes as a ''statutory bargaining agent under the RLA'' to all the firemen, including non-members. Houston closed with a political analogy between a union and the president: the president is president of all of the people, not just members of his own party; a Democrat, once elected president, must fairly represent Republicans as well. Of course, this political analogy was not transparently helpful. Unless positive law or political force stands in the way, Democrats in office are free to do all kinds of things to weaken the Republican Party, and vice-versa. But the basic insight that principles of democratic governance might be as powerful as common law principles of fiduciary duty was a valuable one, and would be refined by Houston and others in the course of the litigation.

On January 21, 1942, Judge Creel rejected the Brotherhood's argument that the court had no jurisdiction over unincorporated associations, but sustained the L & N's and Brotherhood's claims in all other respects, saying only that they were ''well taken.'' Houston received more bad news on April 9, 1942. The Sixth Circuit concluded in *Teague* that there was no federal jurisdiction over the challenge to the railroad collective bargaining agreements. This made success in state court in *Steele* all the more important.[21] So did another disappointing development. In early December 1941, the Japanese attacked the American fleet at Pearl Harbor and the United States declared war on Japan. But the government made no move—then or at any other time during World War II—to take over operation of the railroads and set things right for black railroad workers, as it had done in World War I and as Houston thought it would do this time around.

But for Steele himself, the news was far better. On January 3, 1942, the L & N restored Steele to his original passenger runs, and he remained on those runs from that point forward. He continued to be involved in the litigation, though, both as lead plaintiff and as active strategist. Steele reported later in 1942 that he was working on diesel engines, and that "other Negroes are taking their turns on Diesels on the L & NRR as well." The grapevine, Steele said, "has it that the railroad is afraid of our litigation."

With leave of court, Houston filed an amended complaint on August 14, 1942. But even strengthened by amendment, the *Steele* complaint had unresolved problems. There was significant legal uncertainty about the source of Steele's seniority rights and their inviolability through subsequent collective bargaining. The amended complaint still failed to deal with arguments of "operational necessity" that flowed from the unchallenged non-promotability of black firemen. There remained the oddity of presenting notice, hearing, and a vote as a solution to problems of a despised black minority that would likely—if not surely—lose out to the racial self-interests of the white firemen in any carrier-wide vote. And there remained the issue of how little monetary loss Steele himself had suffered, and how much less he would have suffered had he mitigated his losses by accepting runs offered to him that would have come close to making him whole.

Houston had no intention of putting all of his eggs in one basket. In April 1942, while Houston was fine-tuning his amended complaint in *Steele*, Houston and his partner Waddy filed suit to challenge the Southeastern Agreement in federal district court in Norfolk, Virginia, with Tom Tunstall, another IARE man, as named plaintiff. The legal team had to prevail on the issue on which they had lost in *Teague*—that the duty the Brotherhood breached arose not out of general state agency law, but out of the RLA itself. They would also have to persuade the court that this duty is subject to judicial enforcement. The federal district court recognized that the suit arose under federal law (the RLA), but interpreted the RLA as denying courts the power to decide cases

---

[21] Houston Papers, box 163–23, folder 10.

regarding representation, and dismissed the *Tunstall* complaint in April 1943.[22]

A few days later, the Alabama state trial court dismissed *Steele*. The opinion gave no indication of the court's reasoning. But again making the best of a bad situation, Houston expressed satisfaction that, given the substantive nature of the defendants' demurrers, at least the judge "did not throw us out on any ground of technical pleading. He has thrown us out on the flat proposition that the BLF & E had the right to make the contract it did." In this posture, he said, the case would make for a good, clean vehicle for making law on appeal.[23]

Ever aware of the fact that the litigation was still having good effects for the firemen on the ground, Houston urged his clients and his legal team that the very pendency of the cases had benefits: "We must show by vigorously appealing that we intend to fight all the way through, otherwise the [Brotherhood] will force the railroad to backtrack on all the advances our men have made." Those gains were steadily increasing. Indeed, the L & N was even hiring additional black firemen, something it had not done since 1926. Lewis responded to Houston's call for support by saying that "the spirit of the men is still high and their faith unshaken, so let us take the fight on as we have in the past." While Houston was not counting on victory on appeal, he and Shores both expressed the view that they had a "good chance of reversal in Montgomery" before the Alabama Supreme Court "and, thinking further ahead, that the proper groundwork was now laid for certiorari to the U.S. Supreme Court."

Steele and *Tunstall* on Appeal

Houston argued *Steele* before the Alabama Supreme Court on November 24, 1943. He was the first black lawyer ever to argue a case before that court, a fact noted at the hearing by Chief Justice Lucien D. Gardner. Immediate feedback from the appellate argument was positive. Shores reported to Houston that "there were numerous comments on your argument to the Court. One lawyer called me the following morning before eight o'clock stating that your argument was one of the best he had ever heard." During argument, the Alabama Supreme Court expressed concern with the relative roles of courts and administrative agencies under the RLA. The U.S. Supreme Court had held years earlier

---

22 The district court opinion is unpublished, but is reprinted in the Joint Appendix in Tunstall v. Brotherhood of Locomotive Firemen, U.S. Supreme Court.

23 The discussion of the appeal is drawn from Houston Papers, box 163–23, folders 12, 13, Shores Papers, and *Alabama Justices Hear First Negro Lawyer*, Birmingham World, Nov. 26, 1943. *See also* Fair Employment Practices Committee, Records of the Committee on Fair Employment Practices, 1941–1946 (Microfilm) (hereinafter "FEPC Papers") roll 12 (on L & N hiring).

that the agency charged with enforcing a pre-RLA statute had the power to make representation decisions, and that those decisions are not subject to judicial review. While the Railway Labor Act of 1926 was described by the Supreme Court as "a fresh start," elements of this earlier jurisprudence, which emphasized that the resolution of labor disputes requires the practical expertise of administrative bodies rather than the rights-orientation of courts, might survive.[24] Therefore, Houston emphasized a decision of the United States District Court of Appeals for the District of Columbia that left an opening for judicial review of representation issues raising issues of racial justice. That case, which involved the efforts of black "red-caps" to get out from under the thumb of the racially-exclusionary Brotherhood of Railway Clerks and organize themselves as a local of a union that permitted blacks to become members, held that "the employer's refusal in this case to deal with the only labor organization these employees could join ... certainly violates both the spirit and the letter" of the RLA.[25]

Unfortunately for Houston, that precedent was cut out from under him at the very moment he was relying on it. Two days before Houston argued *Steele*, the U.S. Supreme Court handed down a trilogy of RLA decisions that articulated a rule of deference to the NMB in representation cases. In that RLA Trilogy, the Court, by Justice Douglas, took it to be Congress' judgment that these are "explosive" issues and said that "if Congress had desired to implicate the federal judiciary and to place on the federal courts the burden of having the final say on any aspect of the problem, it would have made its desire plain." Shortly thereafter, the Supreme Court summarily reversed the District of Columbia court's decision in the red-caps case on the authority of the RLA Trilogy.[26]

The appellate courts in *Tunstall* and *Steele* came down with their decisions a few days apart in January 1944. The IARE lost both. In *Tunstall*, the court concluded there was no federal question jurisdiction and that the RLA itself denied the courts jurisdiction in representation cases.[27] In *Steele*, the court, in an opinion by Chief Justice Gardner, rejected Houston's arguments across the board. The court held that Steele had no "vested property right" because his seniority rights were

---

24 Pennsylvania R.R. Co. v. United States R.R. Labor Bd., 261 U.S. 72 (1923). "Fresh start" is from Texas & N.O.R. Co. v. Bhd. of Ry. & S.S. Clerks, 281 U.S. 548 (1930).

25 Bhd. of Ry. & S.S. Clerks v. United Transport Serv. Employees, 137 F.2d 817 (D.C. Cir. 1943).

26 The Trilogy consists of Switchmen's Union v. Nat'l Mediation Bd., 320 U.S. 297 (1943); Gen. Comm. v. Missouri–Kansas–Texas R.R. Co., 320 U.S. 323 (1943); and Gen. Comm. v. S. Pac. R.R. Co., 320 U.S. 338 (1943). The quote is from Switchmen's Union.

27 Steele v. Louisville & Nashville R.R., 16 So.2d 416 (Ala. 1944); Tunstall v. Bhd. of Locomotive Firemen, 140 F.2d 35 (4th Cir. 1944).

the creature of the 1929 agreement which is, by its terms, subject to modification through subsequent collective bargaining. It held that because the RLA did not contemplate "the notion of [union] liability to the individual," there was no cognizable agency relationship as a matter of state law, and thus no basis for applying fiduciary standards to unions. The court understood Steele to "assert no seniority rights by virtue of any individual contract," which suggests either that Houston had abandoned that theory in argument or that the court missed it. The court found no conspiracy, and no wrongdoing whatsoever on the part of the L & N. Indeed, it held that limiting the seniority rights of black firemen because of the railroad's policy of "having only white engineers" was reasonable. As to the whites-only policy for engineers, which Houston had not challenged, the court quoted extensively from the Supreme Court's infamous decision in *Plessy v. Ferguson* in defending the railroad's right to "act with reference to the established usages, customs and traditions of the people" with respect to race. The black press, taking note of the Court's reliance on *Plessy*, accused it of having "grabbed at a ghost in order to throw its weight on the side of the jim crow trade unions."[28]

The next month, on February 28, 1944, another legal development took place that should have been cause for some concern. On February 28, the Supreme Court decided *J.I. Case Co. v. National Labor Relations Board*.[29] There the Court, in an opinion by Justice Jackson, held that collective bargaining agreements largely supersede inconsistent terms in individual labor contracts between the employer and members of the bargaining unit. Elements of the Court's reasoning in *J.I. Case* echoed arguments that the lower courts and the Brotherhood had already used against the black firemen. The Court stated that in administering the NLRA, "the Board asserts a public right vested in it as a public body, charged in the public interest.... Wherever private contracts conflict with its function, they obviously must yield or the Act would be reduced to futility." This reinforced the theory of the RLA Trilogy, by saying that in all of federal labor law, the enforcement of private "rights" is less important than implementation of public policy in favor of orderly collective bargaining. The Court further emphasized that "advantages to individuals" under prior individual contracts "might prove as disruptive of industrial peace as disadvantages," and that once a majority chooses representation, "individual advantages or favors will generally in practice go in as a contribution to the collective result." This echoed the Brotherhood's constant refrain that the black firemen had received

[28] Plessy v. Ferguson, 163 U.S. 537 (1896); *Alabama Court "Evades Real Issue" in Firemen Ruling, Writer Charges*, Birmingham World, Jan. 18, 1944.

[29] 321 U.S. 332 (1944).

advantages from the existence of a collective bargaining agreement, and could not then complain about the burden of disadvantages imposed on them through collective bargaining.

By early 1944, then, things were looking bad on the litigation front. There was little reason to think that the same Supreme Court that failed to see any difference between the Trilogy and the red-caps case would choose to wade into the questions of union representation that *Steele* and *Tunstall* presented.

The FEPC

At the same time, the black firemen failed to secure relief through the political route. Although Houston had been involved with the FEPC from the beginning, others involved in shaping FEPC strategy seem to have become aware of the *Steele* litigation only in February 1942, noting that "this case opens a wholly new line of endeavor for us." In March 1942, Houston and Waddy filed with the FEPC a full-blown, closely-argued complaint on behalf of the ACRT and IARE, which discussed the underlying facts and procedural postures of the firemen's cases. From that point forward, the IARE and the *Steele* litigation team became actively involved in preparing the FEPC's case against the railroads. From April 1942 to July 1942, the IARE men, first by themselves and then with the assistance of Maceo Hubbard, a field representative for the FEPC, collected evidence for use in the upcoming FEPC hearings.[30]

After Democrats lost ground in the November 1942 mid-term congressional elections, the Roosevelt Administration was not at all pleased with holding railroad hearings. These were to be the FEPC's first industry-wide investigation of discrimination, and it was known that FEPC investigators had "sensational findings" of rampant discrimination. Roosevelt delayed and then cancelled the railroad hearings—a move that resulted in the highly-publicized resignations of several staff members and commissioners, including Houston and Webster. The stalled FEPC process received tremendous attention in the black community, with Walter White, head of the NAACP, urging ministers to "preach and pray" for a successful FEPC process. Thus, despite the efforts the black firemen invested in the FEPC process, by April 1943, the month in which the trial courts in both *Tunstall* and *Steele* announced their decisions, it was looking all the more likely that the black firemen would get no relief from the political process and that their fate would, in the end, be decided in the courts.[31] But in May 1943, Roosevelt recovered his

---

[30] FEPC Papers, Roll 10.

[31] For the 1942 election, *see* Alan Brinkley, *The End of Reform: New Deal Liberalism in Recession and War* (1995). For press quotes, *see FDR Orders McNutt to Reschedule Hearings on Rail Discrimination*, Birmingham World, Feb. 9, 1943; *Act Now or FEPC Is*

nerve and breathed new life into the FEPC railroad investigation by issuing a new executive order reconstituting the FEPC. Houston resumed his role as special counsel. Although his schedule did not allow him to work full-time on his FEPC duties, he was consulted by key FEPC staff as they developed their case against the railroads.[32]

The much-awaited railroad hearings were finally held in September 1943. Particularly significant was the testimony of Herbert Northrup, a Cornell University economist and noted expert on black railroad labor in the South. Northrup reportedly testified that "Dr. William M. Leiserson, chairman of the National Mediation Board, and the late James W. Carmalt, former member, had aided and advised white labor unions in methods to deny negro workers fair representation in collective bargaining." Letters from Leiserson and Carmalt were read into the record. The hearings thus not only impugned the race policies of the unions and railroads. They made it clear that the RLA administrative agencies—the same agencies to which the courts routinely deferred—were part of the problem.[33]

In late November 1943, just as Houston was arguing the *Steele* case before the Alabama Supreme Court, the FEPC issued directives ordering the railroads to cease their discriminatory practices. The directives against the L & N and the other southeastern carriers were a powerful indictment of the railroad's racial policies across the board. The FEPC received support in important newspaper editorials. The *Washington Post*, picking up on the wartime need not to permit "prejudices or monopolies to keep skilled and willing workers out of essential jobs," came out in support of the directives. Indeed, Houston had enough confidence in the FEPC process at this point to accept an appointment as a member of the commission.[34]

Most of the railroads (including the L & N) and all of the Brotherhoods simply defied the directives. In the face of that defiance, the FEPC certified the case to the President for action. Roosevelt followed the FEPC's advice to form a committee to urge compliance. One of those recommended was Walter P. Stacey of North Carolina, and the group, appointed in January 1944, came to be known as the Stacey Commit-

---

Doomed, White Warns, Birmingham World, Mar. 9, 1943; *Victory for Firemen in FEPC Case Seen by Porter's Committee*, Birmingham World, Sept. 10, 1943.

32 See FEPC Papers, Roll 10.

33 Tuskegee Clippings, Wash. Post, Sept. 6, 1943 (headline missing).

34 The *Washington Post* is quoted in Tuskegee Clippings, *Railway Job Jim Crow Attacked by Daily Press*, Chicago Defender, Dec. 25, 1943. For Houston, *see* Genna Rae McNeil, *Groundwork: Charles Hamilton Houston and the Struggle for Civil Rights* 166 (1983).

tee.[35] But by May 18, 1944, all the Stacey Committee had done was to hold two days of conferences with the Brotherhoods and the railroads, and to urge the railroads to try to resolve the situation. Of course, the railroads and the Brotherhood could have reached accommodations with black railroad men long before, had they chosen to do so.

To make matters worse, congressional opponents of the FEPC acted independently to undermine the efficacy of the directives. In March 1944, before the Stacey Committee had taken any action, the House of Representatives held hearings, headed by Rep. Howard Smith, to review the legality of the FEPC and other agencies Roosevelt had created by executive order. The House hearings made clear—in part based on Houston's own testimony—that the FEPC's directives were "nothing but recommendations" without "binding legal effect" or "implications of penalty." The implication was clear. If Roosevelt himself was unpersuaded by the FEPC's directives—or if he was unwilling to take action on them for political reasons—the directives would go nowhere.[36]

By early May 1944, nothing had gone right for the black firemen. In Houston's view, the FEPC process had not been a total loss. Houston thought that the FEPC was to be commended for being the first federal agency to "deal with a problem like slavery that isn't going to be put off." Even if no action was taken, the FEPC had served its real purpose. It had informed the public about the intensity of discrimination on the railroads. But, just as the IARE men had argued to Randolph years earlier, publicity did nothing to protect jobs in the here and now.

On the litigation front, Houston filed petitions for certiorari with the United States Supreme Court in both cases in March. But there was no particular reason to think that the Supreme Court would voluntarily enter the fray, let alone rule in the black firemen's favor, in light of its recent decisions. At the same time, Houston's first son was born and the U.S. Army drafted Houston's law partner and co-counsel on the black firemen's cases, Joseph Waddy. Houston would have to present his case to the Supreme Court under enormous personal and professional strain.[37]

Proceedings in the Supreme Court

In deciding on certiorari petitions in individual cases, the justices are always aware of the cases they have already decided to hear. The

---

[35] FEPC Records, Roll 10.

[36] All quotes are from Houston's testimony. See Tuskegee Clippings, *Ten Railroads Balk at Hiring Negroes*, N.Y. Times, Mar. 3, 1944; *Agency is Powerless to Enforce Edicts*, Birmingham World, Mar. 7, 1944.

[37] *See* Genna Rae McNeil, *Groundwork: Charles Hamilton Houston and the Struggle for Civil Rights* 169 (1983); Shores Papers.

context for *Steele* and *Tunstall* in the Supreme Court was more than just the arcana of labor law. The war was an important part of the decisional environment, even more so once the cases reached the Court. The issue of race and the war was already before the Court. The previous term, in a case called *Hirabayashi v. United States*, the Court had upheld a military curfew order applied to persons of Japanese ancestry, citizen and non-citizen alike, throughout the Pacific Coast states (and some other areas). On March 27, 1943, the Supreme Court granted certiorari in two related cases, each involving aspects of Japanese internment. The more famous of the two was *Korematsu v. United States*—the controversial case in which the Supreme Court articulated the rule of "strict scrutiny" for racial classifications, but refused to see the internment of Japanese–Americans as an issue of race. The other was the less-known case of *In re Mitsuye Endo*, which concerned the appropriate circumstances for releasing individual Japanese–Americans from internment. A Supreme Court faced with issues of racial justice might prefer to show its race-liberal face in cases in which private racism on the railroads was alleged to be hurting the war effort than in cases in which public racism (if that is what it was) was alleged to be necessary for the war effort.[38]

Another significant constitutional law issue, one central to racial justice in the political process, was before the Court when the *Steele* and *Tunstall* certiorari petitions were pending. That case was *Smith v. Allwright*, in which the NAACP was challenging Texas' all-white political primary system. The route to overturning the white primary was to convince the Court that the technically "private" Texas Democratic Party should be viewed as a "state actor" subject to the equal protection clause of the Fourteenth Amendment. The Court was able to muster a majority to strike down the white primary only by reassuring Justices Black and Jackson that the case could be limited to its facts—in the face of their concern that the opinion would subject many private associations to constitutional scrutiny. The case was still in the drafting process when the *Steele* and *Tunstall* petitions were filed, and the application of equal protection standards to private conduct was controversial.[39]

Even the labor law context for the consideration of the *Steele* and *Tunstall* certiorari petitions was complex. The RLA Trilogy and the redcaps case were still within recent memory. In addition, the Court already had under consideration the case of *Wallace Corp. v. National Labor Relations Board*, a case from the United States Court of Appeals for the

---

[38] Hirabayashi v. United States, 320 U.S. 81 (1943); Korematsu v. United States, 319 U.S. 432 (1943) (reviewability), 323 U.S. 214 (1944) (merits); Ex Parte Endo, 323 U.S. 283 (1944).

[39] Smith v. Allwright, 321 U.S. 649 (1944). For conference deliberations, *see* Mark Tushnet, *Making Civil Rights Law: Thurgood Marshall and the Supreme Court, 1936–1961* 106 (1994).

Fourth Circuit dealing with a representation question arising under the National Labor Relations Act. *Wallace* also raised related issues of conflicts of interest between unions and non-members whose employment was adversely affected by union action.[40]

The petitions came up for consideration by the Court on May 29, 1944. Four votes for certiorari were needed for the Court to accept the cases. In *Steele* and *Tunstall*, only three justices, Murphy, Rutledge, and Frankfurter, voted to grant.[41] Murphy, former mayor of Detroit, had significant expertise (and concern) about issues of race, labor, and civil liberties. Insiders would joke, in early 1944, that "the Supreme Court tempers justice with Murphy." Murphy had begun the 1943 term by telling his law clerk that he wanted to stay "to the left of Douglas and Black." Murphy was particularly concerned with the need for the Court to address issues of racism. In *Hirabayashi*, the predecessor case to *Korematsu* and *Endo*, Murphy had been persuaded by Justices Reed and Frankfurter to refrain from publishing a dissenting opinion that would have denounced the curfew on Japanese–Americans as unconstitutionally racist, and he instead concurred, characterizing the curfew as reaching "the very brink" of unconstitutionality. Murphy came to view backing down in *Hirabayashi* as a mistake.[42] Rutledge was a new appointee to the Court, and he was close to Murphy, both personally and ideologically. While a lower court judge he had developed some expertise in the administrative law issues presented by the RLA. As a Supreme Court justice, he dissented from the denial of the red-caps petition for rehearing despite having been with the majority in the RLA Trilogy—suggesting a willingness to permit judicial review where race discrimination was at issue.

The presence of the internment cases on the docket might also have pointed towards a grant of certiorari in the railroad cases. Rutledge had gone along with the curfew in *Hirabayashi*, but the early draft of the

---

40 Wallace Corp. v. NLRB, 141 F.2d 87 (4th Cir.), *aff'd*, 323 U.S. 248 (1944); *see also* Robert E. Cushman, *Constitutional Law in 1944–45: The Constitutional Decisions of the Supreme Court of the United States in the October Term, 1944*, 40 Am. Pol. Sci. Rev. 231, 246 (1946).

41 For the votes, *see* Library of Congress, William O. Douglas Papers (hereinafter "Douglas Papers"), Box 93, 1943 Docket Book, at 207; docket notes on *Steele* and *Tunstall* continue in Box 107, 1944 Docket Book, at 376–377. I am assuming that Douglas recorded votes correctly. Douglas' records were not the official records of the Court, but there are, in fact, no official records of conference deliberations.

42 *See* Mark Tushnet, *Making Civil Rights Law: Thurgood Marshall and the Supreme Court, 1936–1961* 69 (1994) (Rutledge and Murphy were "devoted liberals, consistently among the strongest supporters" for the NAACP Legal Defense Fund); Sidney Fine, *Frank Murphy: The Washington Years* 236, 249, 256, 341, 441–42 (1984); *see also* John M. Ferren, *Salt of the Earth: Conscience of the Court: The Story of Justice Wiley Rutledge* 244 (2004).

concurrence he eventually published included language, deleted in the final version, expressing "strong sympathy" with Murphy's concerns and calling the internment order "a racial discrimination" which "approaches the ultimate stain on democratic institutions constitutionally established." Some of the anguish he felt about *Hirabayashi* must have remained. Rutledge may indeed have felt a greater pull towards the firemen's cases than did Murphy as an opportunity to do something right on the question of race because, unlike Murphy, Rutledge later felt that his vote in *Hirabayashi* required him to join the majority in *Korematsu*. Given his general liberalism on issues of race, Rutledge might well have seen *Steele* and *Tunstall* as the best opportunity to act on his anti-racist concerns.[43]

Frankfurter's vote, on the other hand, was a surprise. Frankfurter was known to be hesitant to bring the Court into race issues, which he saw as very sensitive, almost too hot to handle. He also was strongly in favor of giving Congress broad authority to delegate decisionmaking to administrative agencies without triggering searching judicial review; he was particularly inclined to keep the courts out of labor matters. These concerns pointed towards a vote to deny certiorari in *Steele* and *Tunstall*. Perhaps for this reason, Frankfurter's law clerk recommended a denial of certiorari, arguing that the "dispute is fundamentally economic ... and should be resolved by the usual methods of adjusting such conflicts." The clerk said, "To drag in the courts would be futile. Courts would find it impossible to ensure fair representation; every bargaining contract which classifies workers would be open to attack."[44] But Frankfurter voted to grant certiorari. He would have noticed that it was Houston seeking certiorari, and had reasons his clerk would be unaware of to take Houston's arguments very seriously. Frankfurter had been one of Houston's professors and mentors at Harvard, and Frankfurter considered him one of the best doctoral students he had ever taught. Houston's petition took an approach for which Frankfurter had great sympathy. One of Houston's arguments was that Congress must have intended that

[43] On Rutledge's reluctant conclusion that he was constrained in *Korematsu*, *see* University of Michigan, Bentley Historical Library, Frank Murphy Papers (hereinafter "Murphy Papers"), Roll 130 (statement by Rutledge at conference, as noted by Murphy).

[44] For Frankfurter on race, *see* Mark Tushnet, *Making Civil Rights Law: Thurgood Marshall and the Supreme Court, 1936–1961* 68–69 (1994); on Frankfurter's opposition to judicial interference, see Felix Frankfurter & Nathan Greene, *The Labor Injunction* (1930). A particularly clear statement of Frankfurter's application of that view to railroad labor appears in a memorandum regarding the November 1943 Trilogy cases. Harvard Law Library, Papers of Felix Frankfurter (hereinafter "Frankfurter Papers"), part III reel 10, 215–21 (for example, he wrote "the reasons for excluding the courts from labor controversies ... are manifoldly more relevant in keeping courts out of railway labor controversies"). For his clerk's recommendation and the quote in text, *see* Frankfurter Papers, Part III Reel 8, 582–86.

the "exclusive representative" actually represent the interests of minorities within the bargaining unit, rather than trouncing minority rights in the interest of the majority, particularly where that union excluded the minority from membership solely on the basis of race. Frankfurter was a great fan of interpreting statutes to avoid constitutional questions. Doing so here would allow the Court to make a modest but significant statement against racism, all the while speaking in Congress' voice rather than attracting controversy by speaking in its own. This would have given Frankfurter the two things he most sought in race cases: "austerity of speech" and "eloquence of action"[45]

There are no conference notes to explain why the justices took a second round of votes in *Steele* and *Tunstall* and decided, by a comfortable margin, to hear the cases. Of the three who voted to hear the case in the first round, Frankfurter was the most likely to "proselytize" in conference. That it was Frankfurter who prompted the second go-round is also suggested by the fact that, on re-vote, it was Justices Jackson, Roberts, and Stone who changed their votes, and they were more likely than the other justices to have been open to persuasion by Frankfurter.[46]

At the certiorari stage, then, *Steele* presented itself to the Court as a chance to weigh its deferential stance towards administrative agencies in the field of railroad labor against its growing (and perhaps tortured) concern with issues of race. Justice Frankfurter seems to have been the pivotal vote and voice in the process, despite the fact that he ultimately did not write an opinion in the case. Without Houston at the helm, and without Houston's incremental approach to achieving racial justice, the Court might never have taken the case.

Just six days after the Court granted certiorari, the United States armed forces staged D–Day, the mass landing on the beaches of Normandy that marked the United States' official entrance into the war in Europe. Even before that point, it had been apparent to the FEPC that rampant racism against blacks in the United States made for bad publicity: the Japanese were featuring it in anti-U.S. propaganda. The issue of race became all the more important when the enemy was Hitler's Germany.[47]

---

[45] Mark Tushnet, *Making Civil Rights Law: Thurgood Marshall and the Supreme Court, 1936–1961* 68–69 (1994).

[46] For revote results, *see* Douglas Papers, Docket Book 1943; for Frankfurter as proselytizer, *see* William O. Douglas, *The Court Years* 18 (1980); for ideological closeness among Black, Murphy, Rutledge, and Douglas, *see id.* at 243 and Sidney Fine, *Frank Murphy: The Washington Years* 243–44 (1984); for strains among the justices in 1943–1944, *see generally id.* at 248–254 (note that Fine's chapter title is "Den of Discord").

[47] For increased salience of race, *see* Mark Tushnet, *Making Civil Rights Law: Thurgood Marshall and the Supreme Court, 1936–1961* 70 (1994) ("[T]he justices were

Months after the Court granted review, Houston confided to Shores that he had not yet written the brief on the merits in *Steele* and *Tunstall*; he confidently stated that "we can stand on our brief supporting the petition for certiorari." Houston may never have filed briefs on the merits. Had Houston had any idea how close he came to having certiorari denied, he would not have had such confidence in the persuasiveness of the briefs he filed at the certiorari stage.[48]

Houston was rescued by the decision of U.S. Solicitor General Charles Fahy to file an amicus curiae brief in support of the black firemen. The Office of the Solicitor General ("SG"), which represents the United States in the Supreme Court, has a special history and role in Supreme Court litigation. At its best, the Solicitor General's office views itself not only as a representative of the federal government but also as an officer of the Court, with an ethical obligation to engage in scrupulously honest advocacy. Douglas wrote in 1980 that Fahy excelled in the role. "[Fahy's] virtue was not only clarity and precision, reflecting a sharp-edged mind, but complete honesty." Douglas continued, "He never overstated his case; he never stretched a finding of fact to serve his end; he was . . . meticulous in pointing out the factual weaknesses in the record so far as the merits of his case were concerned." The briefs filed by the United States under his leadership were, to Douglas, "completely reliable."[49]

When the Court itself wanted to hear the views of the United States on a federal statutory or constitutional issue, its practice was to ask the Solicitor General ("SG") to file a brief and, usually, to present oral argument. The Court had in fact done so quite recently in RLA cases, including in the lead case in the RLA Trilogy. But it did not do so here. Lawyers representing parties to Supreme Court cases often try to persuade the Solicitor General to file a brief on their clients' side of the

acutely aware of the relation between racism and totalitarianism, represented by the Nazi government in Germany.").

[48] *See* Shores Papers. According to the microfilm set of briefs in Supreme Court cases held by the Court and by many academic libraries, Houston never did file a merits brief on behalf of Steele or Tunstall in the Supreme Court. I have encountered two references to such a brief, in J. Smith Clay & E. Desmond Hogan, *Remembered Hero, Forgotten Contribution: Charles Hamilton Houston, Legal Realism, and Labor Law*, 14 Harv. BlackLetter L.J. 1 (1998), and in Karl E. Klare, *The Quest for Industrial Democracy and the Struggle Against Racism: Perspectives from Labor Law and Civil Rights Law*, 61 Or. L. Rev. 157, 189 n.127 (1982) (describing the brief as "difficult to obtain"). Perhaps Houston wrote a brief that the Supreme Court did not accept for filing. In any event, there was no reference to Houston's brief at conference, while the SG's Brief was influential both in conference and in the Court's opinion. *See* Herbert Hill, *Black Labor and the American Legal System: Race, Work and the Law* 107–08 (1985).

[49] Lincoln Caplan, *The Tenth Justice: The Solicitor General and the Rule of Law* (1987); William O. Douglas, *The Court Years* 183 (1980).

case, but there is no evidence Houston did so. Instead, it seems that the Solicitor General entered the case on his own, as he is always permitted to do on questions of federal law, without first seeking consent of the parties.

One reason the SG may have entered the case was that Fahy had a guilty conscience about the internment cases. Many years after the *Steele* case was decided, the federal Commission on Wartime Relocation and Internment of Civilians, created by Congress to re-examine the factual predicate for the Roosevelt Administration's internment policy, discovered that, with Fahy's knowledge and participation, the Justice Department had withheld information from the Supreme Court that would have cast serious doubt on the factual basis for the government report that had recommended internment. Absent that factual misrepresentation, the Court in *Korematsu* might have seen racism at work. The suspect revisions in the SG's brief were made in September 1944, and Fahy had come under fire from Justice Frankfurter in oral argument in October over precisely the question of the accuracy of the internment report. Having been complicit in hiding racism from the Court in the internment cases, Fahy must have welcomed the opportunity to fight racism in *Steele* and *Tunstall*.[50]

Fahy also had experience in the field of labor relations—he had been the General Counsel of the NLRB—and the NLRB had reasons of its own to participate in the shaping of the RLA cases. While the NLRB was just as interested in avoiding excessive judicial supervision as the NMB, its substantive policies on questions of representation were sharply different from those of the NMB. The NLRA was—quite controversially—using its power to contest traditional craft unions, in significant part precisely because of the racist practices they had in common with railroad brotherhoods. The NLRB was apparently willing to create an exception to the non-justiciability of representation questions where race discrimination was concerned.[51] An NLRB case, *Wallace Corporation,* was pending that also involved a union using its statutory powers to discriminate against a disfavored group. In *Wallace*, the disfavored group was composed of employees who had voted against the union in an election. The NLRB's position in *Wallace* was that the NLRA prohibited

[50] *See* Koramatsu v. United States, 584 F.Supp. 1406 (N.D. Cal. 1984); *see also* Greg Robinson, *By Order of the President: FDR and the Internment of Japanese Americans* 210 (2001); Peter Irons, *Justice at War* 278–92 (1983). These facts were only revealed after Justice Douglas published his glowing evaluation of Fahy's performance as Solicitor General.

[51] For a fascinating account of the schism between the NMB and NLRB approaches, portrayed as stemming from a philosophical divide between Wisconsin-school pluralist and Columbia legal-realist approaches to the New Deal, *see* Daniel Ernst, *Common Laborers? Industrial Pluralists, Legal Realists, and the Law of Industrial Disputes, 1915–1943*, 11 L. & Hist. Rev. 59 (1993).

employers from giving force to such discriminatory behavior by unions. Fahy's office was preparing its *Steele* and *Tunstall* brief with NLRB lawyers in November; all concerned knew by that point that argument in *Wallace* would follow the arguments in *Steele* and *Tunstall* by only a day. The NLRB would have wanted to bolster its position that unions cannot act with hostility towards the interests of political minorities by making the analogy to racial minorities perfectly clear.

The Solicitor General is not totally free to decide which side to take or which arguments to make. He is ultimately accountable to the Attorney General, whose job it is to resolve conflicts among federal agencies in pursuing a single administration policy. In this instance, the Attorney General, Francis Biddle, had himself been chairman of the NLRB's predecessor under the 1933 National Industrial Recovery Act. A supporter of majority rule, he might well have been inclined to agree with, or at least defer to, the NLRB's view of the need to buffer majority rule with fairness to minorities. Although the Roosevelt Administration had backed off from the FEPC's recommendations, it was apparently prepared to voice its critique of railroad racism before the Supreme Court so long as Biddle endorsed it as sound labor policy.[52]

The SG's brief in *Steele* and *Tunstall* argued two points: that the RLA must be interpreted to impose a duty of fair representation on unions, and that the courts have jurisdiction to enforce this duty.[53] In defending its interpretation of the term "representative" as implicitly including a duty of fair representation, the brief emphasized the principle, newly established in the NLRB context in *J.I. Case*, that federal labor laws prohibit disgruntled employees from negotiating with employers on their own behalf. Particularly where the union bars blacks from membership, "clearly Congress would not have so incapacitated them from advancing their own interests without imposing on the craft representative a duty to serve on behalf of the craft as a whole, and not merely for the well-being of certain portions it favored as a result of discrimination against others in the craft." Furthermore, the SG argued, there must be a remedy for breach, one which the RLA administrative agencies lack the jurisdiction to provide. Of course, it would have been far more consistent with the general policy preferences of Congress, discerned in the RLA Trilogy, for the Court to extend the jurisdiction of

[52] For Biddle and the importance of his pro-majority-rule stance, *see* James A. Gross, 1 *The Making of the National Labor Relations Act* 96–101 (1974); for NLRB attorneys' failed efforts to persuade the Justice Department to take a more radical stand, *see* Herbert Hill, *Black Labor and the American Legal System: Race, Work and the Law* 107–08 n.* (1985).

[53] The SG Brief, captioned for both *Steele* and *Tunstall*, is found in the Supreme Court microfilm series for the *Tunstall* case. Unless otherwise noted, quotes in these paragraphs are from the briefs discussed in the text and are in the Supreme Court records for the cases.

the agencies as opposed to extending its own. But thanks to the FEPC process, the evidence was clear that the NMB and the NRAB had been part of the problem. They could not be expected fairly to implement the solution.

The NAACP, by Thurgood Marshall and William Hastie, also filed a brief on behalf of Steele and Tunstall, one that followed an honest if risky strategy. The NAACP explained that, under present practices and conditions not being challenged in the litigation, blacks would lose out on railroad fireman's jobs regardless of how the Court ruled. The NAACP argued that "it is impossible for the Brotherhood to represent the Negro firemen fairly and impartially so long as they are barred from membership." Black minorities in unions could not protect themselves by pleas for white altruism. They could only protect themselves by being players in repeat rounds of coalition politics on issues that did not, on their face, concern race. If blacks failed at coalition building, so be it. But nothing short of membership could create the conditions in which coalition-building could occur.

It is odd indeed to argue that the relief you are seeking is, in the end, incapable of doing much to change the situation on the ground. The risk of the NAACP's strategy was that the Court, unwilling to embrace the more radical theories required for a more powerful remedy, would choose to do nothing at all. This suggests that a real division of labor between Houston and the NAACP was taking place in these cases. Houston served his clients' immediate interests as best he could. The NAACP's main goal was to encourage the Court to use the black firemen's cases to make sweeping new law. But even the NAACP was extremely careful to make clear that labor unions were not themselves the problem and that the solution was not generally to weaken their power. Marshall and Hastie took the position that blacks need the unified power given to unions by the exclusivity principle as much as, indeed, more than whites do. It was only the anomalous combination of the history of railroad unions and the partisan structure of the RLA's grievance system that robbed blacks of the usual benefits of exclusivity. To be pro-black, Marshall argued, was not to be anti-union—and vice-versa.[54]

The Court heard oral argument in *Steele* and *Tunstall* together on November 14, 1944. This was Houston's third Supreme Court oral argument. The most significant and most recent of his two prior arguments was *State of Missouri ex rel. Gaines*, argued and decided in late 1938, in which he won a black student admission into the University of

---

54 Readers should here think forward in time to Justice Thurgood Marshall's opinion in Emporium Capwell Co. v. Western Addition Community Organization, 420 U.S. 50 (1975). See Chapter Six of *Labor Law Stories* on *Emporium Capwell*.

Missouri's law school. Three of the justices who heard that case (Stone, Roberts, and Black) remained on the Court, and Houston had gotten all of their votes. Frankfurter, as noted, had been his teacher and mentor at Harvard. But most of the justices (Douglas, Reed, Jackson, Murphy, and Rutledge) were new to him.[55]

No transcript of the oral argument is available, but there was some press coverage. The justices asked: Why couldn't the claim be brought before the Adjustment Board? Was the case solely about race, or could there be other grounds for invoking this duty? Was non-promotability solely because of race? Oral arguments do not often decide cases, but Houston's clearly helped his cause. Douglas later commented that Houston "was a veritable dynamo of energy guided by a mind that had as sharp a cutting edge as any I have known," and that his argument in *Steele* was "one of his best." He grouped Houston with "the top ten of any group of advocates at the appellate level in the country"—not bad praise, coming from a justice who voted against even hearing his case.[56]

The Court discussed the cases in conference on November 20. At this point, draft opinions had been circulated in the internment cases, and those cases were being intensively discussed in the halls. It would have been impossible for the justices to consider *Steele* and *Tunstall* without thinking of the issue of race more generally.[57] Chief Justice Stone had the practice of speaking first—and, often, of arguing on behalf of his position rather than listening to what others had to say. Despite not having been one of the initial supporters of certiorari, Stone came into conference with intense interest in the cases. Douglas wrote in his conference notes that Stone "assumes there was gross discrimination between white and black" and that the question is whether there is a "remedy where there is established bargaining agency but it ignores minority—blacks are not members of union and cannot get hearing." After noting that the court of appeals in *Tunstall* had held that the "Labor Act is silent and imposes no duty which we can enforce," Stone then stated that the Solicitor General's brief was "persuasive" in its argument that "we are entitled to interpret" the RLA "so as to impose" a duty. Stone may well have been particularly open to persuasion where that approach was concerned. Stone had quite recently, in *Endo*, recommended in conference the "ingenious argument" that the case raises no

---

[55] Missouri ex rel. Gaines, 305 U.S. 337 (1938).

[56] Tuskegee Clippings, (untitled) The People's Voice (New York), Nov. 25, 1944. For Douglas quote, *see* William O. Douglas, *The Court Years* 185 (1980).

[57] On the Court's practices in this era and the discussion of the cases in the next several paragraphs, *see* Roger K. Newman, *Hugo Black: A Biography* 677 n.4 (1994); Sidney Fine, *Frank Murphy: The Washington Years* 243, 394–95, 451 (1984). For conference quotes *see* Douglas Papers, Box 108.

constitutional issue because Congress never authorized confinement, though he also said that it would be "a large order to sustain the assertion." Douglas, in writing an opinion for the Court in *Endo*, did precisely that. Saying that "here is gross wrong," Stone nonetheless worried that "we have been shy in finding judicial remedies in view of other remedies under the Act." He raised the possibility that the RLA could be interpreted to give the NMB jurisdiction to hear cases like these, and that the "administrative remedy should go there first," subject to court review.

Exercising the prerogative of the Chief Justice when in the majority, Stone assigned the opinions in *Steele* and *Tunstall* to himself. He treated *Steele* as the lead case and set forth the reasoning relevant to both cases in it. Stone circulated a draft opinion on November 30, only two weeks after the argument; the draft was in most respects identical to the published opinion.

In the memoranda circulated among the justices, most of the issues raised concerned the task of fitting the judicial remedy into the existing scheme of administrative agency remedies.[58] The draft opinion said "the Adjustment Board has consistently declined in more than 400 cases to entertain grievance complaints by individual members of a craft represented by a labor organization." It then quoted from a Senate report that said, "The only way that an individual may prevail is by taking his case to the union and causing the union to carry it through to the Board." The draft continued, "We cannot say that there is an administrative remedy available to petitioner...." The draft opinion also noted that the members of the NRAB are selected by unions and carriers and that Congress could not have intended individual employees to have to plead for relief before a biased tribunal: "the Negro firemen would be

---

[58] For all of the quotations that follow, *see* Library of Congress, Papers of Harlan Fiske Stone, Box 72, File on Steele (hereinafter "Stone Papers"). It is unclear why *Steele* became the lead case, given that certiorari was granted in *Tunstall* before it was granted in *Steele*. While one might have expected considerable discussion among the justices about the nature of the constitutional problem its statutory interpretation was avoiding, there was in fact none. Stone's draft said very little on that subject—a fact which itself is quite interesting as a matter of the history of American constitutional theory. Justice Stone was the author of the Supreme Court's decision in United States v. Carolene Products, 304 U.S. 144 (1938), with its famous "footnote four" which laid out a new theory of the role and limits of constitutional judicial review. *See generally* Matthew Perry, *Justice Stone and Footnote 4,* 6 C.R. L.J. 35 (1996). Much in footnote four would have been relevant to the fair representation issue in *Steele*, and Stone was known for his propensity for citing his own prior opinions. *See* William O. Douglas, *The Court Years* 171 (1980) ("Frankfurter and I labeled Stone's passion for citing his own opinions 'Stone's disease'."). His reluctance suggests that the footnote four approach had not yet gained sufficient acceptance to be part of the obvious background for considering questions of representation and discrimination—all the more reason for the Court's posture of avoiding the constitutional question in *Steele*.

required to appear before a group which is in large part chosen by the respondents against whom their real complaint is made."

Several justices took issue with these passages. Justice Reed thought that this was an oversimplification. Cases like *Steele*, he argued, "are primarily" disputes "between the railroad and the negro firemen," plainly within the grievance-handling jurisdiction of the NRAB. After all, he argued, "Steele seeks an injunction against the railroad's action and restoration of seniority rights." "Wouldn't it be better," he wrote, to admit that there were elements of the dispute that the NRAB could not resolve (meaning, perhaps, that it could not order the union to pay damages to the complainant) and that the "makeup of the Board (railroad and brotherhood) was interested in the outcome" making futile to ask the "single employee" to seek redress there? He ended with "I leave it to you," suggesting that his vote did not turn on Stone accepting this modification of his draft. In response to Reed, Stone bolstered his Adjustment Board argument by saying that, while the case could be brought before the Adjustment Board, that body could not provide an adequate remedy. It could not, Stone added, "settle the entire controversy which is involved in this dispute." It also could not be objective. The firemen would be "required to appear before a group which is in part chosen by the representative against whom their real complaint is made."

Frankfurter had already joined the opinion with great enthusiasm, both for its result and its reasoning. He wrote again, however, to weigh in on the Adjustment Board question. Frankfurter asked Stone to make clear that the question of whether a case like this was within the jurisdiction of the Adjustment Board was a matter "as to which we express no opinion." He also said that he was "very dubious" about the paragraph on the likely bias of the Adjustment Board, and would prefer that it be left out. Justice Rutledge, too, had problems with this question of NRAB jurisdiction, but, unlike Frankfurter, had no doubt about NRAB bias. Rutledge argued that the Adjustment Board's interpretation of the statute was in error: to Rutledge, the statute expressly permits "employees individually affected" by contract disputes to go to the Adjustment Board, whether or not the union chose to pursue their claim. He saw the Adjustment Board as engaged in "nullification" of that right "in practice," but urged that its practice "does not nullify the law." Stone responded with a phrase that made clear that the Court was not endorsing the Adjustment Board's interpretation of the statute. Before the phrase, "we cannot say that there is an administrative remedy available to the petitioner," he added "Whether or not judicial power might be exerted to require the Adjustment Board to consider individual grievances, as to which we express no opinion."

Rutledge also objected to two other passages in which he though Stone gave away too much. First, he took issue with the draft opinion's statement that "Unless the labor union representing a craft owes some duty to represent non-union members of the craft, at least to the extent of not discriminating against them as such in the contracts which it makes as their representative, the minority would be left with no means of protecting their interests...." Rutledge thought the Court should at least leave open the possibility that the minority might have an alternative remedy. "I am not convinced," he wrote, "we have to decide in this case whether a representative chosen by the majority and entitled to represent the class may not forfeit that right, and thus free the minority to choose their own representative, by a consistent course of conduct which ignores or violates the minority's rights. Exclusion from membership is not, or may not be enough. But that, plus something more, may be. And I do not think we should imply or state, if you do, the contrary." Here Stone made no changes in response.

Second, Rutledge objected to a passage in which the draft opinion gave examples of situations in which the representative would be permitted to "mak[e] contracts which may have unfavorable effects on some of the members the craft represented." The draft opinion specified "relevant differences" that the representative could use as the basis for imposing contractual disadvantages on members of the craft. These were "differences relevant to the authorized purposes of the contract in conditions to which they are to applied, such as differences in seniority, the type of work performed, [and] the competence and skill with which it is performed." The draft also stated that all members of the craft "are not identical in their interest or merit." Rutledge raised the concern that "I am not sure it is wise to specify quite so much as to possibly permissible discriminations and thus encourage their use to achieve indirectly others not explicitly avowed. I think that the paragraph would be better with only a general reservation if any is needed, without specific instances." Rutledge had good reason to be concerned here. After all, there remained unresolved on the facts of *Steele* and *Tunstall* the operational-efficiency claim that non-promotable firemen were standing in the way of training future engineers. Again, Stone made no changes in response.

Jackson wrote Stone that "I agree with all you have said and am delighted at the way you have said it," but he raised one concern, about a possible inconsistency between the draft opinion and the position that he and Stone were taking in dissent in *Wallace* (joined by Justices Roberts and Frankfurter). Their dissenting position in *Wallace* was that when two unions vie for the right to represent a bargaining unit, nothing in the NLRA prohibits the victorious union from excluding supporters of the rival union from membership and then excluding them from employment by negotiating a closed shop agreement. Jackson stated his concern as follows:

> There may be to superficial readers, who constitute the greater number, an apparent conflict between your position in this case that the minority is entitled to representation and to jobs and the position we take in [*Wallace*] that the Labor Board cannot punish the employer for joining in a contract which denies them. Of course we are not dealing in this case with any question of the closed shop. The NLRA authorizes a closed shop, and that is the distinction. I merely mention this in the thought that you might want to insert a saving clause somewhere. I am satisfied as it is, if you are.

Stone responded to Jackson by saying that he had considered saying something about *Wallace*, but had decided against it, with the hope that Jackson would do the reconciling in his *Wallace* dissent.

By December 13, all justices except Murphy and Black had joined Stone's final version of the draft opinion. Justice Black, in the end, concurred in the result, without opinion and without ever having stated his objections to Stone's opinion. Justice Murphy circulated and then published a passionate concurring opinion, which appeared to accept the statutory-interpretation route Stone followed but to reject the tone of his opinion:

> No statutory interpretation can erase this ugly example of economic cruelty against colored citizens of the United States. Nothing can destroy the fact that the accident of birth has been used as the basis to abuse individual rights by an organization purporting to act in conformity with its Congressional mandate.... Racism is far too virulent today to permit the slightest refusal, in the light of a Constitution that abhors it, to expose and condemn it wherever it appears in the course of a statutory interpretation.

It is quite clear that Frankfurter, who may have been the justice responsible for the grant of certiorari in these cases, was very pleased with the gradualism of the final opinion. In private correspondence, Frankfurter criticized Murphy for having "failed to heed the strong reasons for gradualism in breaking new ground." To Frankfurter, it was "inadmissible to say that in a case in which judicial protection is accorded[,] one must say that it would be unconstitutional not to accord it."[59] Also, given Frankfurter's overarching concern with the explosiveness of race as an issue, Frankfurter expressed disapproval of Murphy for making it appear that Congress had intended to leave black workers without a remedy against racially-exclusive unfair representation. Far better to depict a fantasy Congress that had the interests of black

[59] Sidney Fine, Frank Murphy: *The Washington Years* 394–95 (1984).

railroad workers front and center when it enacted legislation essentially rubber-stamping the railroad brotherhoods' move to increase their own power.

Looking at the justices' interaction in the opinion-writing process thus reveals that there was no debate about the central question in the case—race discrimination of the sort practiced by the BLFE was inconsistent with federal labor policy. But protecting minority rights within a framework of deference to administrative agencies was not an easy task. The justices resolved their differences by leaving open the question of whether other remedies—administrative or judicial—were available to redress race discrimination in railroad unions. They acknowledged that under the agencies' own practices, no remedy was available. Whether the agencies were acting lawfully in refusing a remedy was a question left for another day.

The Court's decisions in *Steele* and *Tunstall* were announced on December 18, 1944.[60] It held in *Steele* that "the language of the [Railway Labor] Act ..., read in light of the purposes of the Act, expresses the aim of Congress to impose on the bargaining representative of a craft or class of employees the duty to exercise fairly the power conferred upon it in behalf of all those for whom it acts, without hostile discrimination against them." The union must act "fairly, impartially, and in good faith," and must, "wherever necessary to that end, ... consider requests of non-union members of the craft and expressions of their views with respect to collective bargaining with the employer and give to them notice of and opportunity for hearing upon its proposed action."

In *Tunstall*, which raised the question of federal jurisdiction, the Court held that "the right asserted by petitioner ... is a federal right implied from the statute and the policy which it has adopted.... The case is therefore one arising under a law regulating commerce of which the federal courts are given jurisdiction" under a provision of the Judicial Code.

In both cases, the Court remanded to the lower courts for further proceedings. In *Steele*, the order called for "further proceedings not inconsistent with this opinion." As interpreted by the Alabama courts, these proceedings would include a trial to determine whether the BLFE violated its federal duty of fair representation with respect to Steele, and to determine damages. In *Tunstall*, the order instructed the lower courts to resolve "other jurisdictional questions [that] were raised in the courts below which have not been considered by the Court of Appeals." Neither case, then, would end with the Supreme Court's favorable decisions. There was more to be done.

---

[60] Steele v. Louisville & Nashville R.R. Co., 323 U.S. 192 (1944); Tunstall v. Bhd. of Locomotive, Firemen & Engine Men, Ocean Lodge No. 76, 323 U.S. 210 (1944).

As it happened, the Court announced *Wallace*, *Korematsu*, and *Endo* on the same day as *Steele* and *Tunstall*. Needless to say, the internment cases got most of the attention in the general press. But the black press featured *Steele*, lauding the result and quoting, with great satisfaction, the language of Justice Murphy's ringing concurrence. After all of the FEPC struggles and years of waiting, the Court had finally understood their world and done something to set it right.

The Immediate Impact of Steele

Only two days after the Supreme Court's decision in *Steele* and *Tunstall*, Houston wrote a memo to the two black firemen's unions, Steele, Tunstall, Shores, and Thurgood Marshall celebrating the Court's decision, discussing its limitations, assessing how to proceed on remand, and evaluating the likelihood that litigation alone would solve the problems underlying *Steele*. Houston wrote that "every single proposition we have advocated for five years was adopted" by the Supreme Court.[61] For a document written a mere two days after an astonishing victory, Houston's memorandum showed admirable objectivity. That being said, Houston read some specifics into the Court's opinion that were not there, or that proved over time not to be.

Houston was right that the Court accepted and built upon the analogy between the work of railroad unions and the work of legislatures, thereby imposing some sort of analogous equal protection obligation on the unions. Houston saw in the opinion a robust acceptance of his proceduralist understanding of a duty of fair representation, but Houston exaggerated when he said that the Court agreed with his position that "where the union wanted to put through a collective bargaining agreement, it first had to come out of its union hall into open convention and give the non-members notice and an opportunity to be heard." The Court did, in fact, require the union to give non-union members of the craft an "opportunity for hearing upon its proposed action." But the Court did not say what "hearing" was, and certainly did not hold that an "open convention" would be required. Nor did it place this kind of procedural approach at the center of its new doctrine. What the Court seemed to have in mind, instead, was a substantive review of the union's decision, judging the justifications for what it did rather than the openness of its decisionmaking process. It was never clear why Houston was so sure that white unions would stop discriminating against blacks if "notice" and "opportunity to be heard" were provided. The Court, at least in this respect, may have been influenced by the NAACP's view that no "procedural" change short of full membership

[61] Houston Papers, box 163–23, folder 14.

could be counted on to make a difference, and may have chosen the substantive route for this reason.

Turning to substance, Houston concluded in his memorandum that as a result of the Court's opinion, the Southeastern Carrier's Agreement was now "substantially knocked out." As a legal matter, Houston was certainly right that the Court was exceedingly suspicious of the Agreement, suggesting a willingness to see it as the product of union race discrimination. But "substantially knocked out" was an overstatement. The Supreme Court had held that unions that represent non-members have a duty to represent them without racial prejudice, but stopped short of invalidating the Southeastern Carrier's Agreement. As Houston himself recognized, the Court had left open the possibility that circumstances might justify such an agreement—so long as those circumstances did not turn on race. The union, with support from management, had claimed throughout that operational necessity was the reason behind the Agreement. It was by no means clear that a decision to exclude blacks from their seniority-based firemen's positions to make room for engineers-in-training would be viewed as "racial" if the decision were in fact made for that operational reason—even though the black firemen's status as unpromotable was itself racially-based, under tradition unchallenged in Steele. It would take a factual hearing on remand, and the lower court's interpretation of what issues remained open for determination on remand, as well as a hearing on damages, to turn the Supreme Court victory into a complete legal victory.

As a practical matter, too, Houston was overly optimistic in thinking the Southeastern Agreement was "substantially knocked out." Indeed, the Brotherhood continued to act as if the Supreme Court had never decided *Steele*. It continued to enforce the Southeastern Agreement on every railroad but the Louisville & Nashville, taking the position that it would stop only on railroads whose black firemen brought successful lawsuits against it. In defending litigation brought against it in the context of other railroads, the Brotherhood used procedural challenges to keep the status quo in place as long as possible. One such case reached the Supreme Court in 1949 on the issue of venue; the Court ruled against the Brotherhood.[62]

Without specifying the work still to be done on remand in Steele's case, Houston expressed a continuing mistrust of the Alabama courts and a desire to find some way to move Steele's case out of the state courts and out of Alabama. "I am afraid," he wrote, "that state courts would be under the influence of the local people to the end that even though we win on principle, we would always be thrown out of court on some technicality." He expressed certainty that the Alabama Supreme

[62] Graham v. BLFE, 338 U.S. 232 (1949).

Court would have gone off on technicalities and refused to reach the merits "if for one moment it thought it might be reversed. We cannot expect it to make the same mistake again." Houston said that "the smart thing to do would probably be to abandon further action in the Alabama state courts and transfer the case to the United States District Court in Kentucky at the home of the Louisville and Nashville Railroad." He later abandoned this view upon closer examination.

Houston recognized, too, that the strategy of the *Steele* litigation kept important questions from being addressed by the Supreme Court. He noted that the Court did not deal with whether a union that discriminates in membership can serve as a statutory representative. That is an understatement: the Court held that the duty of fair representation had to be a part of the statutory scheme because, clearly, unions were free to set their own membership standards and their statutory authority as representatives was not undermined by discriminatory membership policies. Here, Houston remained hesitant to raise that question too soon, but thought the *Steele* victory pointed in the right direction: "It may be best that we do not bite off too much at one time but it seems to me that the ground work has now been laid" for such a challenge. Here, again, he was unduly optimistic about the course of the law—at least under the Railway Labor Act.

Despite the victory, Houston remained doubtful about whether litigation was the right strategy for the long term. He saw the opinion as vindicating the work of the FEPC with regard to the Southeastern Agreement, and also as "do[ing] a great deal toward supporting the justification for a permanent FEPC because all these questions cannot be fought out in the courts because the courts are too slow and litigation is too expensive. What is needed now is some sort of administrative body which can move quickly and cheaply and instead of moving in an atmosphere of contention and fighting, try to get the parties together to work out the differences in an amicable way."

After the Supreme Court remanded *Steele* to the Alabama Supreme Court, and that court remanded the case back to the Jefferson County Circuit Court, matters stalled. In fact, very little happened in Steele's case until the trial judge wrote to the parties in mid-January of 1948 requesting that they set a date for trial.

This does not mean, however, that things were quiet between the Brotherhood and Houston's clients. While *Steele* was inactive, Tunstall's case moved forward. On remand from the Supreme Court the district court ruled in Tunstall's favor on all legal issues, reserving the question of damages. During the hearing on damages, Houston and Heiss, the Brotherhood's lawyer, agreed to begin settlement discussions on a number of cases, including *Steele* and *Tunstall*. They met, with no success, in

February and March of 1947. The Brotherhood then appealed the district court's decision in *Tunstall* and that decision was sustained. The Brotherhood sought certiorari, and its petition was quickly denied by the Supreme Court in mid-September.[63]

One might have thought that the Brotherhood, chastised by the Supreme Court, would at least have abandoned the practice of negotiating new secret agreements prejudicing the interests of black firemen. One would have been wrong. While negotiations were taking place on the Southeastern Agreement court cases, the Brotherhood developed a proposal which gleefully took the black firemen's pursuit of racial justice and turned it on its head. Under this proposal, the ban on promoting black firemen to engineer would be eliminated, and all black firemen eligible to become engineers on the basis of seniority would be required to take the engineers' qualifying examination. The new rule would be "up or out." The Brotherhood would have known that even the best of the black firemen would fail this paper-and-pencil test. The black firemen, almost all of whom had been hired in the 1920's, had very little formal education. Many of them had in fact done the work of an engineer in emergency circumstances with little difficulty, and they were proud of their skills. But proving their skills on paper was not something they could reasonably be expected to do. Formal equality would mean substantive inequality, as it so often does in American race relations.[64]

The Brotherhood submitted this proposal to the southeastern railroads on January 9, 1948, requesting negotiations to include the proposal in its collective bargaining agreement. The black firemen were told about it on January 26, 1948, only after it had been agreed to by the railroads and the Brotherhood's southeastern locals. This was just one week after the parties in *Steele* were notified by the trial court that it was time to set a trial date. On February 15, Houston wrote to the Brotherhood objecting to the proposals, and soon thereafter filed two lawsuits, on the IARE's behalf, to enjoin the Brotherhood from negotiating about the proposal. Houston got a preliminary injunction against enforcement of this new agreement, but the ultimate issue of whether this new proposal violated the duty articulated in *Steele* remained to be decided.

Clearly, then, the trial in Steele's case would not be about just the Southeastern Agreement; it would take place in the shadow of this new up-or-out contract proposal. If the up-or-out policy were permitted, Steele could win at trial but lose his job. In late June of 1948, the first evidentiary hearing in *Steele* was finally held; before a judge without a

[63] The discussion in the next several paragraphs is drawn from the Trial Transcript at 142.

[64] This history is recited in Rolax v. Atl. Coast Line, 91 F.Supp. 585 (E.D. Va. 1950).

jury. Available transcripts cover only the first two days of the trial, during which Steele was the most important witness. The Brotherhood's lawyers sought to demonstrate that the railroad did, in fact, have an operational need to use the job of fireman to train engineers, that black firemen were displaced not because they were black but because they were "unpromotable," and that black firemen were less skilled than white firemen and were not capable of running diesel engines at the required level of efficiency. In addition, the Brotherhood argued that seniority is not an absolute, but must yield when the common good requires; that without the Brotherhood, there would be no seniority for black or white firemen alike; and that the black firemen were merely free-riding on the work of the Brotherhood, taking all the benefits of unionization but paying none of the costs, personal or financial, of the collectivization of the workplace. As to Steele himself, their position was that Steele was not displaced for very long, and could have mitigated his losses by displacing less senior blacks from other runs.

Steele held up well (very well, in fact) through Brotherhood cross-examination. He came across as a bright, witty and principled man, proud of his own career and of the work of railroad firemen in general. He was sharply protective of his rights and dignity as a senior member of his craft, and unperturbed by the efforts of opposing counsel to belittle him or his sense of entitlement to justice.

After the trial, the pattern of delay in *Steele* continued. In the meantime, the black firemen saw mixed results in the up-or-out litigation. The federal court in Virginia bought the Brotherhood's "operational necessity" argument hook, line, and sinker. The court essentially ignored the Supreme Court's opinion in *Steele* and its description of the Brotherhood's discrimination. Using the Brotherhood's old rhetoric of portraying the black firemen as wanting rights but eschewing responsibilities, the court viewed the black firemen as barred from equitable relief because they themselves were acting inequitably: "they insist upon full equality in reaping the benefits of seniority while resisting any effort to place upon their shoulders the responsibilities which accompany that right."[65]

On April 22, 1950, with no further action having taken place in *Steele*, and with litigation against the up-or-out rule proceeding in multiple courts, Houston died of acute coronary thrombosis. Just before his death, it must have looked to Houston as if all he had fought for in *Steele* would be of naught to the black firemen. But less than two weeks after Houston's death, the black firemen received a better result from the federal district court in—of all places—Alabama. There, the court rejected the operational necessity defense, and also rejected any charac-

[65] Rolax v. Atl. Coast Line, 91 F.Supp. 585 (E.D. Va. 1950).

terization of the black firemen as failing to "do equity." The district judge said:

> I cannot censure Negro firemen for going into court.... This is merely an act of self-defense on their part. These Negro firemen are old and will soon pass out of the picture.... They were hired with the understanding that they could not become engineers, and have never been afforded an opportunity or given any incentive to study and train themselves to be engineers.... They are entitled to have the courts protect their seniority rights as firemen ... during the last few years they will remain in railroad service.

This conclusion precisely mirrored testimony by Gulf, Mobile & Ohio Railroad management in this case: "Most of these firemen have been in our service for twenty, thirty, forty years, and to dismiss them now, after this long service, solely because they are not qualified for promotion which they never anticipated, would be an inequity."[66]

With Houston's death, Shores took charge of the *Steele* litigation, with the assistance of Houston's partner Joseph Waddy. Finally, with no action having been taken by the trial court, the parties reached a settlement in *Steele* and a number of other cases on November 26, 1951. Five months later, on April 10, 1952, Waddy received a check from the Brotherhood for $27,500. He sent $17,333 to the IARE. The funds went to the union, not to Steele as an individual, despite the fact that the union was not officially a party to the litigation. But it had been the IARE's case all along. Steele remained active in the IARE, launching grievances against the Brotherhood on other issues of race discrimination.

On February 6, 1954, Steele died. Unlike Houston, he had the satisfaction of seeing his case through to the end.[67]

The Continuing Importance of Steele

By the mid-1950's, in the aftermath of *Brown v. Board of Education*,[68] supporters of the black firemen's cause came to recognize that separate could never be equal, and that it was time to sue for the right to be members of the Brotherhood. Joseph Rauh brought a lawsuit in federal district court in Cleveland aimed at forcing the Brotherhood to

---

66 Mitchell v. Gulf, Mobile & Ohio R.R. Co., 91 F.Supp. 175, 182 (N.D. Ala. 1950), *aff'd in relevant part*, BLFE v. Mitchell, 190 F.2d 308 (5th Cir. 1951). Regarding Houston, it appears that he had previously suffered a heart attack, in 1949. Roger A. Fairfax, Jr., *Wielding the Double-Edged Sword: Charles Hamilton Houston and Judicial Activism in the Age of Legal Realism*, 14 Harv. Black-Letter L.J. 17 (1998).

67 For Steele's death, see Alabama State Archives, Death Record Index, Reel 6, Frame 00-003191. For remainder, see Shores Papers.

68 347 U.S. 483 (1954).

admit black firemen to membership. After years of disappointing experience under *Steele*, it was clear that the only assurance of fair representation was full membership. Rauh therefore argued that the Railway Labor Act should be read to have contemplated a requirement of open membership since, as the Court had already held in *Steele*, Congress must be presumed to have intended that blacks receive fair representation.[69]

The district court rejected this argument, saying that "it is impossible to interpret the legislative intent" in this fashion. Indeed, it held just the opposite: "Apparently the Act itself would not have been acceptable to the Congress if Negro membership in the agent had been required." The court also expressed doubt that membership would do the black firemen any good, not because they would remain a minority and the majority could still work against their interests, but because, in the court's view, the Brotherhood wasn't the problem. Unbelievably, in light of everything that was then known about the Brotherhood, the court said, "there can be no real assurance that membership in the [Brotherhood] would prevent discrimination, since it is my opinion under the evidence here that the effective discrimination is by the railroad employer, rather than by the Brotherhood."

The black firemen lost on appeal as well. "Although these proceedings have been punctuated by accusations of racial discrimination, it would seem that we are really concerned only with ascertaining the rights of any person who, for any reason, finds himself in a minority or out-voted status." So far as the court of appeals was concerned, all that was at issue here was the basic principle of labor law that the majority rules, and "individual advantages or favors will generally in practice go in as a contribution to the collective result." In *Steele*, the principle of majority rule required an implied duty of fair representation. In Rauh's case, the principle of majority rule was the reason for denying a claim that there could be no fairness without truly fair representation. The longstanding, well-documented context of discrimination by the Brotherhood against the black firemen disappeared altogether. Harold Heiss, who had been counsel for the Brotherhood in most of the cases since the 1930's, must have been gratified indeed to see how much courts could be induced to forget.[70]

In 1964, Congress finally acted in the sphere of civil rights, and, in Title VII of the Civil Rights Act of 1964, made it illegal for labor unions and employers to discriminate on the basis of race. Shores lived to see that change, and many others, in the civil rights environment. Shores lived to the age of ninety-two and died half a century after the Supreme Court's decision in *Steele*. By then, he had built a distinguished career in

---

[69] Oliphant v. BLFE, 156 F.Supp. 89 (N.D. Ohio 1957).

[70] Oliphant v. BLFE, 262 F.2d 359, 362 (6th Cir. 1958).

Birmingham as a leader on both the legal and political sides of the civil rights struggle. Indeed, his political career started just three days after Steele's death, when he was deemed qualified to run for office in Birmingham. By the time of Shores' death, Birmingham—and the American law of civil rights—had changed for the better. But few if any would give the duty of fair representation much of the credit.

Did the Court really believe that the new duty it had found in the Railway Labor Act would be adequate to protect the interests of the black workers represented by racially-exclusive unions? Certainly the *Steele* opinion expressed no doubts, but did the message of the NAACP's brief fail to register at all?[71] Exactly six months after its decision in *Steele*, a unanimous Supreme Court upheld the constitutionality of a New York statute requiring unions representing workers in the state to admit workers into membership regardless of race.[72] Holding that the Fourteenth Amendment does not bar the states from exercising their police power to enact prohibitions of race discrimination "beyond that which the Constitution itself exacts," the Court found it necessary to explain why the barring of racially-exclusive membership was a justifiable state measure. The Court, by Justice Reed, observed:

> To deny a fellow-employee membership because of race, color or creed may operate to prevent that employee from having any part in the determination of labor policies to be promoted and adopted in the industry and deprive him of all means of protection from unfair treatment arising out of the fact that the terms imposed by a dominant union apply to all employees, whether union members or not.

If the Court saw the duty it created in *Steele* as efficacious, and if it saw that duty as sufficiently inherent in statutory grants of exclusivity to be necessarily implied by all such grants, then it was plainly inaccurate to say that blacks barred from membership in white unions were "deprived of all means of protection." The Court had not forgotten *Steele* and *Tunstall*. Indeed, it cited both cases in the paragraph immediately before the quoted passage. But no one on the Court was prepared to suggest that the "means of protection" the Court had just created was powerful enough to solve the problem of unfair representation.

[71] Some black commentators expressed regret that the Court had not required the brotherhoods to admit blacks into membership. *See* C.A. Chick, *Some Recent United States Supreme Court Decisions Affecting the Rights of Negro Workers*, 16 J. Negro Educ. 172, 176 (1947) ("many of us were hoping that it would make such a ruling"). Some NLRB attorneys involved in drafting the SG Brief expressed regret, once they read the Court's opinion, that their brief had stopped short of asking the Court to do so. Herbert Hill, *Black Labor and the American Legal System: Race, Work and the Law* 107–08 n.* (1985).

[72] Ry. Mail Ass'n v. Corsi, 326 U.S. 88, 94, 98 (1945).

In the end, it wasn't. Real progress required courts, administrative agencies, and national politics to line up together on the side of equality for black workers and to do so at a time of economic growth in industries that had the potential to hire and promote black workers. The most rapid and pervasive change happened when the Equal Employment Opportunity Commission, provoked by political opportunity and financial constraints, creatively developed disparate impact and affirmative action strategies to avoid the need to prove intentional discrimination in individual cases.[73] The Supreme Court went along, and, at least for now, these legal innovations have survived. So long as they do, civil rights statutes, not the duty of fair representation, will do the bulk of the work of protecting the interests of blacks in unions.[74]

What, then, is the continuing significance of the duty of fair representation?

In its brief on the merits to the Supreme Court in *Steele,* the BLFE made the prediction that a duty of fair representation would not merely apply in race cases, but would become a general basis for disgruntled workers to attack their unions. Workers would sue any time they thought their "rights were sacrificed unjustly to the interests of others." Courts would look behind the circumstances of the collective bargaining process, "the economic pressures involved, the public policy involved, and the element of human judgment involved" in order to judge whether the union had adequately protected workers' interests. The threat of suit would "intimidate bargaining representatives in the discharge of their duties." Some union leaders (and lawyers) might say, today, that the BLFE's dire predictions were entirely correct.[75] This overstates the case. The reason is that the Supreme Court—perhaps to foil precisely those predictions—has articulated a standard of review that is decidedly deferential to union decisionmaking.

Both in contract enforcement and in contract negotiation, the Supreme Court has said that unions cannot depart from a "wide range of reasonableness"; their conduct cannot be wholly "irrational" or "arbitrary" or "illogical" or "in bad faith." The level of judicial review must be "similar to that between the courts and the legislature" (meaning "rationality review," the most deferential standard in the Court's arse-

---

[73] *See* John David Skrentny, *The Ironies of Affirmative Action* (1996). The Labor Management Reporting and Disclosure Act of 1959 also increased accountability of unions to their members, including racial minorities.

[74] The NLRB eventually held, in Miranda Fuel Co., 140 NLRB 181 (1962), that a violation of the duty of fair representation constituted an unfair labor practice. But when Title VII of the Civil Rights Act of 1964 was passed, it took center stage.

[75] *See* Michael J. Goldberg, *The Duty of Fair Representation: What The Courts Do In Fact*, 34 Buff. L. Rev. 89, 92 (1985).

nal), and the courts must "recogniz[e] the wide latitude that negotiators need for the effective performance of their bargaining responsibilities."[76] Given this standard, and given the many procedural hurdles that stand in the way of plaintiffs in duty of fair representation cases, it should come as no surprise that many duty of fair representation claims are filed but few are won.[77]

The Supreme Court has yet to make clear the extent to which the duty of fair representation bars unions from putting the interests of the collective ahead of the interests of the individual in cases where the union has no "hostility" towards those individuals. The Court has stated that "a union must, in good faith and in a nonarbitrary manner, make decisions as to the merits of particular grievances."[78] But what if the union concludes that it would be in the workers' best interests to hold off on taking new grievances to arbitration during the pendency of a delicate round of collective bargaining? May it do so even with respect to grievances it deems meritorious? The Seventh Circuit has articulated a vision of the duty of fair representation in which unions are permitted to make collective judgments that compromise individuals' interests in securing proper contract enforcement. Other circuits hold to a more individualistic view of "fairness" in the context of the duty of fair representation. Questions such as these have serious implications for how we envision the very nature and role of labor unions—just as *Steele* did in the 1940's.[79] It is surprising how few have been definitively answered.

Conclusion

Steele and the duty of fair representation grew out of two decisions by black railroad firemen: to unionize to protect their rights, and to seek cutting-edge civil rights counsel to take their fight to the courts. The fact that the *Steele* decision produced no dissent does not mean that the fight was easy or the conclusion obvious. As the Court's internal deliberations demonstrate, it took delicate work to convince the Court that it could take a small step towards a liberal position on the question of racism in unions without undermining its liberal position on administrative agency

---

[76] Air Line Pilots Ass'n v. O'Neill, 499 U.S. 65 (1991); Vaca v. Sipes, 386 U.S. 171 (1967).

[77] *See generally* Michael J. Goldberg, *The Duty of Fair Representation: What The Courts Do In Fact*, 34 Buff. L. Rev. 89 (1985).

[78] Vaca v. Sipes, 386 U.S. 171 (1967).

[79] For the Seventh Circuit's approach, *see, e.g.*, Camacho v. Ritz–Carlton Water Towers, 786 F.2d 242, 244, 245 (7th Cir. 1986). For a recent discussion of the conflict, *see* Robert Gorman & Matthew Finkin, *Basic Text on Labor Law: Unionization and Collective Bargaining* 1006–08 (2d ed. 2004).

discretion on questions of labor law. That the *Steele* doctrine was not itself enough to make a place for black workers in racist unions should come as no surprise. But for the twenty years between *Steele* and the passage of the Civil Rights Act of 1964, that case stood as the federal government's best and most conspicuous effort to make room for racial minorities in white-dominated unions. The underlying problem of *labor union* policy—the problem of how to keep unions both open and strong—will remain as long as America has labor unions and American employers resist them.[80]

---

[80] *See, e.g.*, Chapter Six of *Labor Law Stories* on *Emporium Capwell*; Paul Frymer, *Acting When Elected Officials Won't: Federal Courts and Civil Rights Enforcement in U.S. Labor Unions, 1935–85*, 97 Am. Pol. Sci. Rev. 483 (2003).

*

3

Kenneth G. Dau-Schmidt

The Story of *NLRB v. Truitt Manufacturing Co.* and *NLRB v. Insurance Agents' International Union:* The Duty to Bargain in Good Faith

Introduction

The process of collective bargaining contains an inherent conflict between the individual interests of the parties in acting strategically to gain an advantage at the expense of the other, and their collective interest in cooperating and dividing the fruits of their joint enterprise without industrial strife. By being stubborn, lying, refusing to meet, committing to a favorable position or otherwise "bargaining hard," each party can hope to gain an advantage over the other in the ultimate bargain that is struck, but if both sides engage in such recalcitrant behavior the negotiations are more likely to devolve into industrial warfare and a strike. By bargaining cooperatively, not only can the parties avoid the lost wages and lost profits of a strike, but they can also constructively explore new ways in which both sides might benefit through improved production or more efficient contract terms.[1]

Of course, one can't solve this dilemma by simply outlawing strikes. The exercise of economic weapons is essential to any system for the private determination of disputes through collective bargaining. Without

[1] Kenneth G. Dau-Schmidt, *A Bargaining Theory of American Labor Law and the Search for Bargaining Equity and Industrial Peace,* 91 Mich. L. Rev. 419, 431–34 (1992).

the possibility of resort to economic pressure, neither side would have an incentive to make concessions nor reach agreement. In public sector bargaining where strikes are prohibited, the parties adjudicate disputes before a neutral arbitrator in interest arbitration.[2] Unless we want to replace our system of private determination of terms and conditions of employment by the parties through collective bargaining with a system in which the parties appeal to a neutral arbitrator to determine employment terms, the parties need at least some reasonable prospect of resort to economic weapons. Moreover, strikes sometimes serve other purposes. They communicate employer resolve or poverty to the union and union resolve and ability to conduct a strike to the employer, and they build (or destroy) political consensus within the union.[3] Because of the essential motivating role strikes play, they might be described as the "engine" that drives collective bargaining.[4]

The solution to this dilemma is to regulate the conduct of collective bargaining so as to prohibit outright acts of strategic behavior and to formulate the problem of collective bargaining in such a way as to promote the parties' ability to act on their collective interest in cooperation, rather than their individual interest in being recalcitrant. By following this strategy, the law might be used to promote the resolution of industrial disputes by the parties themselves through collective bargaining, while minimizing the number of strikes and thus promoting "industrial peace." One objective of labor law is to produce an efficient industrial relations system that needs only a small amount of industrial strife to drive the parties' private decisionmaking.[5]

To help achieve this solution, Congress required in the National Labor Relations Act (NLRA) that employers and unions bargain in "good faith." Section 8(a)(5) of the NLRA makes it an unfair labor practice for an employer "to refuse to bargain collectively with the representatives of his employees" and § 8(b)(3) places a reciprocal obligation on the union.[6] Section 8(d) of the NLRA specifies that "to bargain collectively" is the "mutual obligation of the employer and the representative of the employees to meet at reasonable times and confer in good faith with respect

---

[2] Alvin L. Goldman, *Labor and Employment Law in the United States*, ¶ 118 (1996).

[3] Sir John Richard Hicks, *The Theory of Wages* 146–47 (2d ed. 1963); Orley Ashenfelter & George E. Johnson, *Bargaining Theory, Trade Unions and Industrial Strike Activity*, 59 Am. Econ. Rev. 35, 36–37 (1969).

[4] George W. Taylor, *Government Regulation of Industrial Relations* 18 (1948); Archibald Cox, *The Duty to Bargain in Good Faith*, 71 Harv. L. Rev. 1401, 1409 (1958).

[5] Kenneth G. Dau–Schmidt, *A Bargaining Analysis of American Labor Law*, 91 Mich. L. Rev. 419, 487–88 (1992).

[6] 29 U.S.C. §§ 158(a)(5), 158(b)(3).

to wages, hours, and other terms and conditions of employment."[7] But what does it mean to bargain in "good faith"? What behavior does this obligation prohibit, and what behavior does it require, in order to promote cooperation between the parties while still allowing recourse to economic weapons that may ultimately decide the dispute?

This chapter discusses two classic Supreme Court cases from the 1950's that explore the contours of the obligation to bargain in good faith. In the first, *NLRB v. Truitt Manufacturing Co.*,[8] the Supreme Court addressed the question whether the obligation to bargain in good faith requires an employer to open its books to the union when the employer refuses a union request for a larger wage increase on the basis that such an increase will drive the employer out of business. What is the extent of the employer's obligation to provide the union with information? In the second, *NLRB v. Insurance Agents' International Union*,[9] the Supreme Court addressed the question whether union tactics to slow down work to put pressure on the employer in negotiations, tactics which are not protected by the NLRA, were consistent with the union's obligation to bargain in good faith. Does the obligation to bargain in good faith limit the parties' recourse to economic warfare? These two cases are considered together in this chapter, because their seemingly inconsistent holdings illustrate the tension in the NLRA between regulating the conduct of collective bargaining to promote the parties' ability to bargain cooperatively in industrial peace, while still allowing the recourse to economic weapons that is necessary for the process of collective bargaining. This chapter offers the stories behind these two great cases, the arguments the lawyers made on behalf of their clients, how these cases were resolved by the Board and the courts, and some of the theory behind what it means to "bargain in good faith."

Social, Economic and Political Background

Perhaps it was inevitable that the Board and courts would define the boundaries of the concept of good faith bargaining during the 1950's. The core of the NLRA, the Wagner Act, had been passed just two decades earlier in 1935, while major substantive amendments, including the union's obligation to bargain collectively and the § 8(d) specification that "to bargain collectively" meant to bargain "in good faith," were added in the 1947 Taft–Hartley amendments. Although the obligation to bargain in good faith had a jurisprudential history under the pre-Wagner Act National Labor Board and the pre-Taft–Hartley amendments National Labor Relations Board, it is not surprising that seminal cases

[7] 29 U.S.C. § 158(d).

[8] 351 U.S. 149 (1956).

[9] 361 U.S. 477 (1960).

regarding the meaning of the language in these statutes would develop during the two decades immediately following their enactment.[10]

Moreover, in America during the 1950's, collective bargaining was generally undertaken between healthy and prosperous employers and relatively strong and powerful labor organizations. The production required to win World War II purged the last vestiges of the Great Depression from the American economy and made even marginally productive firms profitable. Moreover, the destruction wreaked on Europe and Asia by the war left the United States as one of the few industrialized nations with an intact industrial plant and infrastructure. American industry emerged from the war stronger than when it entered, and with few international competitors until the late 1960's.[11] The American labor movement prospered during this period of economic expansion and shelter from international trade. Fired with idealism born of the Great Depression, and armed with the new labor law, unions successfully organized an ever larger share of the American workforce throughout the 1940's and 50's, reaching their zenith in 1954 of thirty-nine percent of private non-agricultural employees organized.[12] Although initially split into two competing organizations, the older craft-oriented American Federation of Labor (AFL) and the upstart industrial-based Congress of Industrial Organizations (CIO), these two organizations merged in 1955 to form the AFL–CIO.[13] Strong employers faced by strong unions made for many important contests, both in the process of collective bargaining, and before the courts.

Despite economic prosperity at home, the 1940's and 50's saw a significant change in the American political landscape. The Democrats, under the leadership of Franklin Delano Roosevelt and Harry S Truman, controlled both the presidency and Congress throughout the recovery from the Great Depression and the victory in World War II. Although tremendous diversity of political perspective existed within the Democratic Party, especially between northern and southern politicians, Democrats generally favored the interests of unions and were responsible for passage of the Wagner Act. However, with the election of a Republican-majority House and Senate in 1946, and President Eisenhower in 1952, control of the federal government became mixed, or passed back and

[10] 1 *The Developing Labor Law*, 763–70 (Patrick Hardin & John E. Higgins, Jr. eds. 4th ed. 2001).

[11] Kenneth G. Dau–Schmidt, *Employment in the New Age of Trade and Technology: Implications for Labor and Employment Law*, 76 Ind. L. J. 1, 9 (2001).

[12] U.S. Bureau of Labor Statistics, *Handbook of Labor Statistics*, Bulletin 2070 (1980), tables 72, 162 and 165. Although the percentage of workers organized in the private sector fluctuated after 1954, it did not begin its precipitous decline until the 1960's.

[13] Foster Rhea Dulles, *Labor in America: A History* 373 (3d ed. 1966).

forth between the Democrats and the Republicans, who were generally more inclined toward employer interests. Indeed, the Republicans gained control of Congress in 1946 at least in part due to public unease over a series of postwar strikes by major unions, in particular the United Mine Workers and the United Steelworkers.

The Republican Congress passed the Taft–Hartley amendments to the NLRA in 1947, over President Truman's veto, as a check on union power. The election of Republicans also meant that appointees to the NLRB and courts would more likely favor employer interests. The replacement of Democrat Paul Herzog with Republican Guy Farmer as Chair of the National Labor Relations Board in June of 1953 marked a passing of the torch from a pro-union to a pro-employer Board.[14] Although Eisenhower's policies were fairly moderate, some more conservative elements of the Republican Party used the Cold–War competition after World War II between the United States and the Soviet Union as an excuse to persecute communists, socialists and leftists in the United States, particularly within the motion picture industry, the academy and the labor movement. Even within the labor movement itself, alleged communists were ferreted out and the AFL–CIO expelled several allegedly communist-controlled unions and created competing labor organizations to raid their members.[15] In the 1950's, unions also came under increased scrutiny for corruption. In 1959 Congress passed the Landrum–Griffin Act in response to a congressional hearing that showed some union leaders had misappropriated union funds, accepted bribes from management, failed to maintain records and interfered with members' rights within the union.[16]

Legal Background

The parties' legal obligation to bargain in good faith is set forth in several provisions of the National Labor Relations Act. The original Wagner Act established the employer's obligation to bargain collectively in what is now § 8(a)(5):

> It shall be an unfair labor practice for an employer—
>
> to refuse to bargain collectively with the representatives of his employees....[17]

---

[14] James A. Gross, *The NLRB: An Historical Perspective, in A Guide to Sources of Information on the National Labor Relations Board* 14, 16 (Gordon T. Law, Jr. ed., 2002).

[15] Henry Pelling, *American Labor* 192–96 (1960).

[16] Foster Rhea Dulles, *Labor in America: A History* 382–89 (3d ed. 1966).

[17] 29 U.S.C. § 158(a)(5).

Later, in the 1947 Taft–Hartley amendments, Congress added an obligation on the part of the union to bargain collectively in § 8(b)(3),[18] and a definition of what it meant to "collectively bargain" in § 8(d):

> For the purposes of this section, to bargain collectively is the performance of the mutual obligation of the employer and the representatives of the employees to meet at reasonable times and confer in good faith with respect to wages, hours, and other terms and conditions of employment, or the negotiation of an agreement, or any question arising thereunder, and the execution of a written contract incorporating any agreement reached if requested by either party, but such obligation does not compel either party to agree to a proposal or require the making of a concession. . . .[19]

Taken together, these statutory provisions have been interpreted to impose on both the employer and the union an obligation to "bargain in good faith" concerning wages, hours and other terms and conditions of employment in collective negotiations. However, none of these provisions expressly answers the questions raised in the two cases addressed in this chapter—the employer's obligation to supply information consistent with good faith bargaining raised in *Truitt*, and the question whether partial work-stoppages and other "harassing tactics" are consistent with good faith bargaining posed by *Insurance Agents'*. The precedents relevant to the *Truitt* case will be discussed here, while *Textile Workers Union of America*,[20] the case that most influenced *Insurance Agents'*, will be discussed later in the chapter.

Several precedents influenced the actions and arguments of the parties in *Truitt*. Board and court decisions had established that an employer's obligation to bargain in good faith included the obligation to supply the union with data on the wage rates and hours worked by unit members.[21] Such information was necessary for the union to compute the cost of its bargaining proposals and intelligently to discuss those proposals with management. However, it was unclear whether good faith included an obligation to share financial data on the firm's economic health.

The Board first addressed the question of the employer's obligation to supply financial information in *Southern Saddlery*.[22] In that case, the

---

[18] 29 U.S.C. § 158(b)(3).

[19] 29 U.S.C. § 158(d).

[20] 108 NLRB 743 (1954).

[21] *See, e.g.*, Boston Herald-Traveler Corp. v. NLRB, 223 F.2d 58 (1st Cir. 1955); NLRB v. Yawman & Erbe Mfg. Co., 187 F.2d 947 (2d Cir. 1951); NLRB v. Whitin Machine Works, 217 F.2d 593 (4th Cir. 1954).

[22] Southern Saddlery Company, 90 NLRB 1205 (1950).

employer rejected union demands for even a nominal wage increase on the basis that the firm's financial condition would not allow one. Moreover, the employer refused to make any counterproposal on wages or provide information substantiating its repeated claims of poverty. The Board held that it was necessary for the company to provide sufficient information to enable the union to understand and intelligently discuss all the issues relating to negotiations and that, by repeatedly rejecting the union's wage demands and refusing to provide information substantiating its claims of poverty, the company had impermissibly "erected an insurmountable barrier to successful conclusion of the bargaining." No appeal was taken from the order of the Board that the employer end its refusals to provide substantiating information and bargain in good faith.

The Board affirmed *Southern Saddlery* in *The Jacobs Manufacturing Co.*[23] In *Jacobs*, the employer rejected the union's request for a wage increase, stating that a wage increase would require a product price increase and that the decrease in demand for the firm's product that would result made this "infeasible." When the union requested information to substantiate the company's claim, the company refused, stating that the decision whether to grant a wage increase was purely one of "business judgment." The Board unanimously held that under *Southern Saddlery* the company was required to provide the union with information to substantiate its claim that a wage increase would lead to substantial economic harm. The employer's refusal to provide any substantiating information whatsoever constituted bad faith bargaining. Accordingly, the Board ordered the company to bargain in good faith and supply the union with "such statistical and other information as will substantiate the Respondent's position in bargaining with the union." The Second Circuit enforced the Board's order, holding that the employer was required to produce "whatever relevant information it has to indicate whether it can or cannot afford to comply with the union's demands."[24] However, the employer was not required to "produce proof that he is right in his business decision as to what he can, or cannot afford to do," nor to produce any specific books and records.

Factual Background of Truitt

The Truitt Manufacturing Company was founded in 1941 by twin brothers William and Wallace Truitt. The twins made the down payment on a small manufacturing plant in Greensboro, North Carolina using money their father, William Brooks ("W. B.") Truitt, had saved for their college tuition, but which had been left unused due to scholarships. Soon after the founding, the twins invited W. B. to leave his job at Carolina

---

[23] 94 NLRB 1214 (1951).

[24] 196 F.2d 680, 684 (2d Cir. 1952).

Steel and join the Truitt Company as its President. In 1942 W. B. and the twins invited the twins' younger brother, John, to join the firm's management to help with war production. The Truitts were all engineers trained at North Carolina State University. Like many professionals, the Truitts delighted more in the professional challenges of their enterprise—designing and constructing sophisticated projects in structural steel—rather than the day-to-day running of the business.[25]

The Truitt Manufacturing Company produced rolled and structural steel. Projects ranged from mundane high-volume work (simple brackets and braces, metal containers on rollers for use in other manufacturing concerns and metal stands to display quarts of oil in gas stations) to very sophisticated one-of-a-kind projects (structural steel towers used in early implosion experiments in the development of the atom bomb and a supersonic wind tunnel used by the National Advisory Commission on Aeronautics—a precursor of NASA). The timing of the firm's founding allowed the company to flourish on World War II production and the Truitts were able largely to retire the debt from the purchase and construction of the firm with war production profits. From the firm's founding in 1941 to the height of war production in 1945, the firm grew from 9,000 square feet of production space and twenty employees to 90,000 square feet of production space and 300 employees. After the war, the firm's size declined to about 150 employees, but the Truitts still had plenty of business with private and government contracts and were doing about $1.5 million in annual sales by the mid–1950's.[26]

The employees of Truitt Manufacturing Company began organizing in the late 1940's. The primary motive appears to have been a desire to attain wages comparable to those of union workers in the North.[27] Both the International Association of Bridge, Structural and Ornamental Iron Workers (AFL) (Iron Workers) and the United Steelworkers (CIO) made organizing efforts. At first the campaigns were subtle, and just "snuck-up" on management, but soon they escalated into organizational picketing and strikes.[28] On the first day of picketing, W. B. Truitt called Robert Dick Douglas, Jr. ("Dick Douglas"), the attorney who handled Truitt's general legal matters, and asked him to represent the company in the organizing campaign. Although Douglas professed no expertise in labor

---

[25] Interview with John Truitt, March 15, 2004.

[26] Interview with John Truitt, March 15, 2004; Greensboro Record, Aug. 16, 1957, at 1; Truitt Manufacturing Co., 110 NLRB 856, 859 (1954).

[27] Some management practices may have also been at issue. John Truitt said: "They say that good management doesn't get organized, there may be some truth to that in our case." Interview with John Truitt, March 15, 2004.

[28] Interview with John Truitt, March 15, 2004.

The Truitt brothers, William, John and Wallace, inspect a supersonic wind tunnel the Truitt Co. built for the NACA, 1946. The picture first appeared in the December 1946 issue of PIC Magazine and is used with the permission of John Truitt.

law, W. B. prevailed on him to represent the firm because W. B. trusted Douglas and Douglas was cheaper than a labor relations specialist. At the time, Douglas had no idea that acceptance of this assignment would lead to an appearance in the United States Supreme Court and a thirty-year career in labor law.[29] The organizing campaign continued for several years and included two union electoral defeats (one by only two votes) and a "long-planned" peremptory raise in base pay from sixty-five to eighty cents an hour.[30] Finally, on October 27, 1950, the Iron Workers Local 729 won an election and the right to represent all production and maintenance employees at Truitt. Shortly after that, the union successfully negotiated a two-year contract.[31]

29 Robert Dick Douglas, Jr., *The Best 90 Years of My Life* 219–36 (2003); Interview with Robert Dick Douglas, Jr., March 15, 2004.

30 Interview with Robert Dick Douglas, Jr., March 15, 2004; Greensboro Record, Feb. 25, 1953, at 1.

31 Truitt Manufacturing Co., 110 NLRB 856, 859 (1954).

Truitt Co. employees in the plate steel manufactory in the early 1950's. Photograph from a company brochure used with the permission of John Truitt.

In the summer of 1953, the Truitt Company and the Iron Workers undertook negotiations for a second collective bargaining agreement. In these negotiations the company was represented by Dick Douglas, W. B. Truitt and the Truitt brothers. The employees were represented by Henry D. Cole, George F. Beck, John W. Sandlin and a representative of the international union, Julian F. Head. The Iron Workers opened negotiations for a new contract on August 4, 1953, with a demand for a ten cent an hour wage increase, citing prevailing rates for similar workers in the Pittsburgh area. The company responded that the average wage of Truitt workers was already higher than the average wage of its competitors in the Greensboro area and countered with an offer of a two and a half cent an hour wage increase. Because of the recent Board decision in *Southern Saddlery*, both Mr. Douglas and Mr. Head knew that the Board was looking for a "plead poverty" case to test the new doctrine. Douglas had cautioned the company bargaining committee to let him talk and not to plead poverty. However, after being worn down by the union's repeated demands for a ten cent an hour wage increase, and perhaps short on insulin, W. B. rose to his feet, cited the "undercapitalization" of the firm asserting that they "had never paid dividends" and angrily told the union bargaining committee: "If we give you that raise, we will go broke!" Dick Douglas recalled that, after W. B.'s outburst, the union representatives looked at each other and smiled.[32]

The bargaining committees continued to meet throughout August, but made no progress on the question of a wage increase. On August 10, 1953, the employees went on strike, but returned to work five days later without moving the company on its offer of a two and a half cent an hour wage increase. Perhaps seeking to lay a firm evidentiary basis for an unfair labor practice charge based on *Southern Saddlery*, in early September, Julian Head wrote to the company stating that the union had rejected the company's offer based on its belief that the company could meet the union's demand of a ten cent an hour wage increase, and stating that the union "respectfully requests permission to have a certified public accountant examine such books, records, financial data, etc. to ascertain or substantiate the Company's position or claim of being unable to meet the Union's proposal . . . of a wage increase in excess of two and one-half cents . . . per hour."[33] Dick Douglas responded that "the Company takes the position that confidential financial information . . . of this Company is not a matter of bargaining or discussing with the Union. The Company's position throughout the recent negotiations and in previous sessions with you and the Union, has been that the question of granting a wage increase concerns our competitive bidding for jobs to keep the plant operating."[34] Douglas also offered to share data on the wages the employees were paid, but noted that he thought the union already had that information.

Mr. Head made one more effort to gain access to the firm's financial information through a letter, perhaps drafted by a union attorney, that specifically cited *Southern Saddlery* and used some of the language from that opinion:

> The Union does not contend that financial affairs of the Company are subject to collective bargaining. It does contend, however, that the Company should submit full and complete information with respect to its financial standing and profits . . . in order that the Committee, as well as the other members of the Union . . ., can intelligently decide whether or not they should continue to press their request of ten (10) cents per hour. Such financial information is pertinent to collective bargaining. *Failure on the part of the*

[32] *Id*; Interview with Robert Dick Douglas, Jr., March 15, 2004. John Truitt's recollection of his father's outburst was that it was precipitated by the union representatives' dogged commitment to their bargaining position. The explanation that his father was short on insulin was merely creative lawyering on the part of Mr. Douglas. Interview with John Truitt, March 15, 2004.

[33] Records and Briefs of Cases Decided by the Supreme Court of the United States, Volume 351, Transcript of Record at 1–2, NLRB v. Truitt Manufacturing Co.

[34] *Id*. at 3–4.

Company to furnish such information has the effect of erecting an insurmountable barrier to a successful conclusion of the bargaining.[35]

Dick Douglas responded for the company that he was aware of *Southern Saddlery* but still did not believe the union had a right to the information it had requested. The union filed an unfair labor practice charge alleging that the company had failed to bargain in good faith. In January 1954, the NLRB Regional Director issued a complaint against the Truitt Company for its refusal to supply the requested information.[36]

Prior Proceedings in Truitt

Before the Board and the court of appeals, the parties disputed both precedent and policy. Dick Douglas labored mightily to distinguish the facts in *Truitt* from those of *Southern Saddlery,* arguing that in *Truitt* the company had not said it could not afford a wage increase, but had instead merely told the union that the requested wage increase would make the company uncompetitive. Douglas also argued that, unlike in *Jacobs*, the Truitt Company had not refused to discuss a wage increase based on inability to pay, but had instead offered a wage increase of two and a half cents an hour. Board Attorney Duane Beeson argued that Truitt had claimed inability to pay and that, under *Southern Saddlery* and *Jacobs,* Truitt was obliged to supply information to verify this claim.[37] Before the Fourth Circuit, Douglas also assailed the inconsistency of *Southern Saddlery* and *Jacobs* with the language and purposes of the NLRA. Douglas argued that § 8(d) of the NLRA specified that the duty to bargain in good faith did not require the making of a concession—including the concession of financial information. On behalf of the NLRB, Beeson also cited the larger policies of the NLRA, arguing that disclosure of information was necessary to reasoned bargaining and the promotion of industrial peace.[38] As will be discussed later, this larger policy framework of promoting industrial peace within our system of private collective bargaining is ultimately the best basis for understanding the importance of the *Truitt* case and reconciling it with the Supreme Court's later decision in *Insurance Agents'*.

The Board affirmed the holding of the Trial Examiner that the company had violated its obligation to bargain in good faith by refusing to substantiate its plea of poverty. Rejecting as mere semantics Truitt's distinction between a claim of "lack of competitiveness" and "inability

---

[35] *Id.* at 4–6 (emphasis supplied). The language in italics is taken almost directly from the Board's opinion in Southern Saddlery Company, 90 NLRB 1205 (1950).

[36] Truitt Manufacturing Co., 110 NLRB 856, 859 (1954).

[37] *Id.* at 868–69.

[38] NLRB v. Truitt Manufacturing Co., 224 F.2d 869, 870 (4th Cir. 1955).

to pay,'' the Trial Examiner found that W. B. Truitt's assertions—that the company had never paid dividends, was undercapitalized and would be driven out of business by the union's wage demands—to be precisely the kind of economic conclusions that required documentation. Thus, the facts of the *Truitt* case fell squarely within the precedents of *Southern Saddlery* and *Jacobs*.[39] Despite recent Republican appointments to the Board,[40] the Board unanimously agreed that the Truitt Company had violated its duty to bargain in good faith. Citing *Jacobs*, the Board stated that "it is settled law, that when an employer seeks to justify the refusal of a wage increase upon economic basis . . . , good-faith bargaining under the Act requires that upon request the employer attempt to substantiate its economic position by reasonable proof."[41] Accordingly, the Board ordered Truitt to bargain in good faith and provide the necessary documentation to the union. The company refused to comply and the Board sought enforcement in the Fourth Circuit.

The Fourth Circuit denied enforcement. The court's opinion was written by Chief Judge John J. Parker, whose 1930 nomination to the United States Supreme Court by President Herbert Hoover had been rejected by the Senate thirty-nine to forty-one because of his racist and anti-labor views.[42] Parker cited the language of Taft–Hartley, noting that the Act's definition of good faith bargaining in § 8(d) expressly disavowed a requirement of agreement or the making of any concessions. The panel said:

> We do not think that merely because the company has objected to a proposed wage rate on the ground that it cannot afford to pay it, good faith bargaining requires it to open up its books to the union. . . . To bargain in good faith does not mean that the bargainer must substantiate by proof statements made by him in the course of bargaining. It means merely that he bargain in sincere desire to reach agreement.[43]

Chief Judge Parker stood the application of the NLRA's purpose of promoting industrial peace on its head in the case and stated that, if

[39] Truitt Manufacturing Co., 110 NLRB 856, 868–69 (1954).

[40] Republican appointees Ivar Peterson, Guy Farmer, Philip Rogers and Albert Breeson had recently been added to Abe Murdock, the only remaining Democratic appointee to the Board. James A. Gross, *The NLRB: An Historical Perspective in A Guide to Sources of Information on the National Labor Relations Board* 14–16 (Gordon T. Law, Jr. ed., 2002).

[41] Truitt Manufacturing Co., 110 NLRB 856 (1954).

[42] <http://www.senate.gov/artandhistory/history/minute/Judicial_Tempest.htm>.

[43] NLRB v. Truitt Manufacturing Co., 224 F.2d 869, 874 (4th Cir. 1955). Also on the Board's brief were Solicitor General Simon E. Sobeloff, General Counsel Theophil Kammholz, Assistant General Counsel Dominick L. Manoli and Attorney Frederick U. Reel.

employers were required to disclose financial information, unions' demands for such information "could be used as a club to force employers to agree to an unjustified wage rate rather than disclose their financial condition ... which could conceivably be used to their great damage." The court's opinion largely ignored *Southern Saddlery* and read *Jacobs* extremely narrowly. The Board sought and the Supreme Court granted a writ of certiorari based on the division between the Second Circuit's decision in *Jacobs* and the Fourth Circuit's decision in *Truitt*.

The Supreme Court Decision in Truitt

The Supreme Court argument was assigned to NLRB Associate General Counsel David P. Findling, a seasoned attorney who had already represented the Board several times before the Supreme Court.[44] The National Association of Manufacturers prevailed upon W. B. Truitt to retain the services of Whiteford S. Blakeney, a nationally known labor law expert from Charlotte, North Carolina, for the argument before the Supreme Court. Although Blakeney helped with the Supreme Court brief, Dick Douglas represented Truitt in the oral argument before the Supreme Court because it was felt that Douglas knew the case best and had been doing pretty well on his own.[45]

The parties' Supreme Court briefs fleshed out the basic arguments they had made before the court of appeals. In its brief, the Board asserted that the duty to bargain in good faith had been uniformly held to embrace the duty to supply information relevant to bargaining issues. In support of this proposition, the Board cited appellate court opinions requiring employers to supply unions with wage data in bargaining, and the Supreme Court's opinion in *NLRB v. American National Insurance Co.* for the proposition that good faith bargaining required the exchange of relevant information.[46] Citing *Southern Saddlery* and *Jacobs*, the Board argued that if an employer can plead financial inability and withhold relevant information upon which it relies, the employer can erect a virtually insurmountable barrier to successful conclusion of bargaining. Returning once again to the fundamental purposes of the NLRA, the Board argued that the experience of the Board and students of labor relations demonstrated that the production of such information furthers good faith negotiations and industrial peace. The Board con-

[44] Findling had represented the Board in Universal Camera Corp. v. NLRB, 340 U.S. 474 (1951), Bus Employees v. Wisconsin Board, 340 U.S. 416 (1951), and Brooks v. Labor Board, 348 U.S. 96 (1954).

[45] Interview with Robert Dick Douglas, Jr., March 15, 2004.

[46] 343 U.S. 395 (1952). Records and Briefs of Cases Decided by the Supreme Court of the United States, Volume 351, Brief for the NLRB at 12, NLRB v. Truitt Manufacturing Co.

tended that the employer's distinction between pleading "lack of competitiveness" and "inability to pay" was mere semantics and that the employer had not demonstrated any harm it would suffer as a result of sharing information with the union to demonstrate that it was undercapitalized, had never paid dividends and could not afford a ten cent an hour wage increase.

The company's brief argued that the obligation to bargain in good faith required only that the parties approach bargaining "with a fair mind and a sincere purpose to reach agreement" and that the Taft–Hartley definition of the duty to bargain expressly disavowed any requirement that an employer make a concession or reach an agreement.[47] From this the company deduced that an employer negotiating in a genuine effort to reach agreement may not be required to agree to any particular proposal or request, including a request for information. The company characterized the Board's rule as a per se violation of the duty to bargain. Moreover, asserted the company, the Board's rule could be easily evaded: employers who did not want to disclose financial information could simply avoid any plea of poverty. The disclosure obligation was also difficult to administer: Did the employer need to document all of its financial obligations and all the obligations of its competitors?

The Supreme Court heard oral argument on March 29, 1956. Associate General Counsel Findling barely finished his recitation of the facts and outline of the Board's basic argument when he was interrupted by Justice Felix Frankfurter concerning the breadth of the Board's remedy. Justice Frankfurter, an FDR appointment and expert on labor law who had been a Harvard law professor, wanted to know if the employer really had to open its books in order to bargain in good faith. "I don't see how you can say that failure to open the books is a failure to bargain in good faith," exclaimed Frankfurter.[48] Findling responded that the Board's rule did not require the employer to make all books available, but merely to offer "reasonable proof" of an asserted inability to pay. "The Board held that the employer failed its good faith obligation in this case when it refused to supply *any* supporting information.... Otherwise the union is just bargaining in the dark"[49] To allow an employer to "merely sit back and say 'I can't afford to pay,' without proof," would "stagnate bargaining," Findling maintained.[50] Justice Sherman Minton, a Truman appointee and former Senator from Indiana, wanted to know who was to

47 Records and Briefs of Cases Decided by the Supreme Court of the United States, Volume 351, Brief of the Respondent at 2, NLRB v. Truitt Manufacturing Co.

48 Greensboro Daily News, Mar. 29, 1956, at 1, 4.

49 Tape of Supreme Court Oral Argument in the Truitt Case, on File with the U.S. Supreme Court.

50 Greensboro Daily News, Mar. 29, 1956, at 1, 4.

determine what was "reasonable proof" and how. Findling responded that the Board would decide on the basis of the negotiations in each case. "No unreasonable burden is required.... The employer must disclose merely the information that is the basis for his assertions of inability to pay." Findling also argued that the appellate court's finding that the union could use a demand for information as a "club" was unfounded. "The company has never asserted that disclosure would do it harm, only that this information was none of the union's business.... If harm to the business from disclosure can be shown, that is a different case than the one before you."[51] If the Board's arguments had any friends among the six Democrats and three Republicans sitting on the bench that day, it was not apparent in the questioning of Findling.[52]

The Court's treatment of Dick Douglas was much more cordial. In a homily some observers described as a "fireside chat," Douglas tried to persuade and charm the Justices by mixing his attack on the Board's arguments with a discussion of North Carolina basketball. Douglas began by taking exception to Findling's assertion that the Board order did not require Truitt to open its books. In support of this position, Douglas cited the letters from the union requesting information including a broad breakdown of costs and sales. Chief Justice Warren asked if such an extensive disclosure was required by the Board's order, to which Douglas replied "No sir. But I contend that these things—costs, price structure and other full and complete information ... is what they are going to point us to if you send us back to the NLRB." The Chief Justice then asked Dick Douglas to read the language of the order which required the company to "furnish such statistical and financial information as to substantiate their stand." Justice Frankfurter asked attorney Douglas whether a basic picture of company conditions could be given to the union without opening the books and without harming the company. Douglas conceded that an employer needed to give the union some information necessary to conduct labor negotiations, "But I don't think the Government should order us to give them our books." In outlining the potential costs that the Board's order would require the company to justify, Douglas mentioned Truitt's sponsorship of radio broadcasts of basketball games. This led to an informal exchange on various aspects of

[51] Tape of Supreme Court Oral Argument in the Truitt Case, on File with the U.S. Supreme Court.

[52] Actually, the politics of the Supreme Court at this time were a little complicated. Justices Hugo Black, Stanley Reed, Felix Frankfurter, William O. Douglas, Harold Burton, Tom Clark and Sherman Minton were Democratic appointees, but Burton had been a Republican Senator from Ohio. Chief Justice Earl Warren and Justice John Marshall Harlan were Eisenhower appointees, but Warren was of such political stature that he had been both the Republican and the Democratic candidate for Governor of California in 1946. Peter Irons, *A People's History of the Supreme Court* 327–94 (1999).

North Carolina basketball including a description of what was a "free-throw." In the end, the Justices were charmed enough by Douglas' down-home style that they granted him an additional four minutes to finish his argument.[53]

The Supreme Court overturned the Fourth Circuit, and upheld the Board's decision in the case, by a six to three vote. On May 7, 1956, in an opinion that covered a mere five pages, Justice Hugo Black, joined by Chief Justice Warren and Justices Reed, Douglas, Clark and Minton, decided that "in determining whether the obligation of good-faith bargaining has been met the Board has a right to consider an employer's refusal to give information about its financial status. . . ."[54] To support this finding, the Court noted the relevance of the employer's financial status on the facts of the case and the importance of accurate information to collective bargaining:

> In their effort to reach agreement here both the union and the company treated the company's ability to pay increased wages as highly relevant. . . . Good-faith bargaining necessarily requires that claims made by either bargainer should be honest claims. . . . If such an argument is important enough to present in the give and take of bargaining, it is important enough to require some sort of proof of its accuracy.

The Court's reasoning about the importance of accuracy in collective bargaining drew on the Board's argument that exchanges of information served the NLRA's fundamental purpose of promoting industrial peace. Just as exchanges of accurate information promote trust and cooperation in bargaining, substantial inaccuracies or deceptions in negotiations produce industrial strife.[55] The Court strengthened its rationale with the idea from *Southern Saddlery* that unsubstantiated claims can pose an obstacle to bargaining:

> And it would certainly not be far fetched for a trier of fact to reach the conclusion that bargaining lacks good faith when an employer mechanically repeats a claim of inability to pay without making the slightest effort to substantiate the claim. . . .[56]

---

[53] Greensboro Daily News, Mar. 29, 1956, at 1, 4; Tape of Supreme Court Oral Argument in the Truitt Case, on File with the U.S. Supreme Court; Robert Dick Douglas, Jr., *The Best 90 Years of My Life* 223–24 (2003).

[54] NLRB v. Truitt Manufacturing Co., 351 U.S. 149, 152–53 (1956).

[55] Kenneth G. Dau–Schmidt, *A Bargaining Analysis of American Labor Law*, 91 Mich. L. Rev. 419, 485 (1992).

[56] NLRB v. Truitt Manufacturing Co., 351 U.S. 149, 152–3 (1956).

The Court then concluded "that a refusal to attempt to substantiate a claim of inability to pay increased wages may support a finding of a failure to bargain in good faith."[57]

The Court gave only modest direction about the breadth and application of the new rule. As to the extent of the burden an employer must bear in providing financial information, the Court noted that Truitt had not complained that disclosure would be burdensome or injurious, but instead merely "that the requested information was irrelevant to the bargaining process and related to matters exclusively within the province of management." Accordingly, the Court did not define the level of burden that would relieve an employer of the obligation to provide information, but noted that it was the Board's position that it required only "reasonable proof" "made available in a manner not so burdensome or time-consuming as to impede the process of bargaining." As to the application of its holding in future cases, the Court stated: "Each case must turn upon its particular facts. The inquiry must always be whether or not under the circumstances of the particular case the statutory obligation to bargain in good faith has been met."

Justice Frankfurter wrote a minority opinion, joined by Justices Clark and Harlan, concurring in part and dissenting in part. In Frankfurter's opinion, the Board was not necessarily wrong in its determination that Truitt had failed to bargain in good faith, but it had applied the wrong standard by focusing merely on the question of whether the employer had failed to substantiate its claim of poverty rather than on examining the employer's conduct as a whole: "The totality of the conduct of the negotiation was apparently deemed irrelevant to the question; one fact alone disposed of the case.... This is to make a rule of law out of one item—even if a weighty item—of the evidence. There is no warrant for this."[58] Frankfurter would have remanded the case to the Board to apply the appropriate legal standard, examining the company's conduct as a whole.

The Immediate Impact of Truitt

The immediate impact of the Supreme Court's decision on the parties was slight. Truitt and the Iron Workers had already agreed to a contract including an immediate two and a half cent an hour wage increase, followed by another two and a half cent increase a year later. As a result, the issue of the company's ability to pay was moot and the company never actually had to open the books.[59] As to what they would

---

[57] *Id.*

[58] *Id.* at 155 (opinion of Justice Frankfurter).

[59] Interview with Robert Dick Douglas, Jr., March 15, 2004.

have found if they had gotten a look at the books, John Truitt maintains that, although the company was not then at risk of bankruptcy, his father's representations were largely correct.[60]

Although Dick Douglas had lost in the Supreme Court, he had acquitted himself well and the publicity the case brought led to many more years representing the interests of employers in labor relations. In future negotiations on behalf of Truitt and other employers, Douglas was very careful that the company would not characterize its position as an inability to pay so as to avoid the constraints of the Supreme Court ruling. Although Douglas lost the battle of the *Truitt* case, his side ultimately won the war. In the 1980's the demand for employer representation in contests with unions declined so that Douglas adopted a more general practice with an emphasis on employment law. At the age of ninety-two, in 2004, Dick Douglas was still practicing in Greensboro, North Carolina, largely in the area of trusts and estates.[61]

The Truitt Manufacturing Company continued in operation for a little more than a year after the Supreme Court decision and was sold to Robert Edmonds on August 16, 1957, with 115 employees, 90,000 square feet of manufacturing space and annual sales of $2 million.[62] W. B. Truitt remained Chairman of the Board of Directors while the Truitt brothers also stayed on in various managerial positions. Explaining the reason for the sale, John Truitt later said "people don't sell profitable businesses." Nevertheless, he attributed the sale more to the Truitts' interest in engineering over running a business rather than to the influence of the union.[63]

At the time, the members of the bar and the academy recognized *Truitt* as an important decision; however, they did not yet know whether its theory would be broadly applied by the Board and courts or whether it would prove a narrow precedent limited largely to its facts. The *Washington Post* and *New York Times* ran stories implicitly recognizing the extraordinary nature of the remedy of ordering union access to company books within the context of American labor relations. Both stories pointed out, however, that the opinion stated that the existence or extent of the duty to disclose would depend on the facts of each case.[64]

Among lawyers, there was initially some discussion of how to use or avoid the doctrine, and whether the Court's action in the case was consistent with its words. Much was made of the apparent ease with

---

[60] Interview with John Truitt, March 15, 2004.

[61] Interview with Robert Dick Douglas, Jr., March 15, 2004.

[62] Greensboro Record, Aug. 16, 1957, at 1.

[63] Interview with John Truitt, March 15, 2004.

[64] Wash. Post & Times Herald, May 8, 1956, at 30; N.Y. Times, May 8, 1956, at 42.

which employers could avoid disclosure by merely avoiding any claims that smacked of inability to pay.[65] Whether the opinion had broader implications, or was limited merely to cases in which the employer used the "magic words" of inability to pay, remained to be seen. Archibald Cox ventured the opinion that the doctrine would have little effect on employer practices because "employers accustomed to labor negotiations seldom balk at giving the modicum of financial information required by the NLRB."[66] Others suggested that unions would not ask for information that would damage their firm, since they also had an interest in the firm's success.[67]

Even though most experts saw the substance of the holding as innocuous, they sometimes worried about its impact on the procedure of collective bargaining. Cox and others worried that *Truitt* would result in the damaging insinuation of courts into the process of collective bargaining.[68] One negative result might be posturing by the parties, in anticipation of unfair labor practice charges, that would detract from or have a negative impact on collective negotiations.[69] A lot of ink was spilled over the question whether the Supreme Court's apparent application of the doctrine as a per se rule was consistent with the opinion's closing admonition that good faith had to be determined on a case-by-case basis. The consensus was that the Court's failure to remand for a factual determination meant that it had in effect announced a per se rule against employers pleading poverty without documentation.[70] There was no discussion of the implications of the larger themes of *Truitt* on the importance of truthfulness and exchanges of information to the success of collective bargaining.

Factual Background of Insurance Agents'

The Prudential Insurance Company of America was founded by insurance agent John F. Dryden in Newark, New Jersey in 1875 as the

[65] Note, *Union Requests for Information in the Collective Bargaining Process*, 105 U. Pa. L. Rev. 90 (1956); Archibald Cox, *The Duty to Bargain in Good Faith,* 71 Harv. L. Rev. 1401 (1958).

[66] Archibald Cox, *The Duty to Bargain in Good Faith,* 71 Harv. L. Rev. at 1437.

[67] *Union Requests for Information in the Collective Bargaining Process,* 105 U. Pa. L. Rev. 90, 102–103 (1956).

[68] Archibald Cox, *The Duty to Bargain in Good Faith,* 71 Harv. L. Rev. 1401, 1437 (1958). *See also The Supreme Court Term, 1955 Term,* 70 Harv. L. Rev. 95, 177–79 (1956); Archibald Cox & John T. Dunlop, *Regulation of Collective Bargaining by the National Labor Relations Board,* 63 Harv. L. Rev. 389, 390 (1950).

[69] Archibald Cox, *The Duty to Bargain in Good Faith,* 71 Harv. L. Rev. 1401, 1437 (1958).

[70] Brent Robbins, *Rethinking Financial Information Disclosure Under the National Labor Relations Act,* 47 Vand. L. Rev. 1905, 1914 (1994).

"Prudential Friendly Society." It was one of the first companies to make insurance available to people of modest means, selling "Industrial Insurance" that provided funeral and burial expenses for weekly premiums as low as three cents. The company's sales quickly grew as its area of operations expanded to New York and Philadelphia and, by 1885, company assets had reached $1 million. Shortly afterward, the company adopted the Rock of Gibraltar as its symbol, one of the most identifiable corporate logos in American business. Despite bank failures and mortgage delinquencies during the Great Depression, Prudential sales continued to grow.[71]

Prudential enjoyed a self-proclaimed "Golden Period" during the 1940's and 50's providing insurance to employees and employers of the prospering American economy. Monetary assets grew sixfold during the 1940's, and the company's prosperity continued into the 1950's. For 1955, the year before the insurance agents' job actions, Prudential reported record life insurance sales of $6.4 billion, record life insurance in force of $51.5 billion and record assets of $12.5 billion. The company expanded its sales area in North America, opening regional offices in Los Angeles, Chicago, Minneapolis, Jacksonville, Houston, Boston, northern New Jersey and Toronto.[72]

Prudential's methods of motivating and organizing its sales force had much to do with both Prudential's success and its agents' motivations for organizing. Prudential's methods, along with the nature of the insurance industry itself, also determined the means by which the agents would take collective action. First, to motivate sales, the company paid insurance agents on a strict commission basis dependent on the premiums for new or existing business attributable to the agent. In addition to commissions, agents received only a small fixed payment, amounting to roughly $4.50 per week, to cover expenses. Second, the company assigned each of its insurance agents to a district office run by a district manager. The district manager received a share of all sales commissions earned in the office. To increase sales, the district manager might require motivational sales meetings, sponsor sales contests or set sales quotas. District managers rewarded agents who succeeded and chastised or fired agents who did not meet sales objectives. These mercenary working conditions, combined with the constant pressure of commission sales, fed agents' desire to organize.[73] Finally, Prudential believed that

---

[71] William H. A. Carr, *From Three Cents a Week: The Story of the Prudential Insurance Company of America* (1975).

[72] *Id.*; N.Y. Times, Mar. 14, 1956, at 51.

[73] My grandfather, Carl Algot Bloom, sold insurance all of his life and deeply impressed upon me the need to avoid being in the situation where feeding my family depended on getting a commission.

success in selling insurance depended on the development of a personal relationship between agents and the insured. Accordingly, each agent was assigned a sales territory or "debit" in which he had sole responsibility to make sales, process paperwork and collect premiums. For agents, the size of their debit represented income and potential income, and the reassignment of areas from one salesman to another, either because of retirement or because the company was not satisfied with an agent's performance, was a hotly contested issue in contract negotiations. Government regulations designed to ensure that those who purchased insurance actually received it required that agents report all sales and payments and turn in all premiums in a timely fashion. Agents who failed to comply with these regulations would lose their license and ability to sell insurance. As a result, agents could not lawfully participate in a full work stoppage in which they failed to report on or turn in premiums for existing business, and their alternative was to fail to cooperate with the hated district sales policies and cease soliciting new business.[74]

Prudential agents in New York, Pennsylvania, and Wisconsin began to organize in 1937. The organizing campaigns were contests between the Insurance Agents' International Union (AFL) and the United Office and Professional Workers of America (CIO). Prudential fought tooth and nail against organization, arguing first that its agents were independent contractors exempt from the Act, and then contesting the appropriate bargaining unit.[75] The first union contract, which covered Prudential agents in New York, was signed in 1942. By 1949, the Insurance Agents' International Union had won out and represented agents across thirty-five states and the District of Columbia. Early experiences under the new contracts led to friction between the company and the union. On January 5, 1951, as one disagreement came to a head, Prudential found it "necessary" to suspend a group of union agents in Pittsburgh. Within a week, 2,300 agents had called in sick and 1,600 agents had staged a wildcat demonstration outside the Corporate Home Office in Newark to protest the suspensions. Normalcy returned to the company when the union helped calm the wildcat action. However, the next winter contract negotiations led to a union-sanctioned eighty-one-day "strike" from December 1, 1951 to February 20, 1952. The Labor Department reported that the strike was then the longest in American history by white collar workers. Of course, one reason the strike may have lasted so long was that the agents had to continue servicing existing customers during the work stoppage.[76]

---

[74] Telephone Interview with Isaac N. Groner, June 22, 2004.

[75] *Id.*

[76] William H. A. Carr, *From Three Cents a Week: The Story of Prudential Insurance Company of America*, 191–92 (1975).

The Supreme Court case arose out of the negotiations that began January 16, 1956, to replace the collective agreement that would expire March 18, 1956. Prudential's President was Carrol M. Shanks, a man who had supported New Deal legislation, but who was also confrontational enough to have his chauffeur drop him off a block or two from the company's front door so that he could walk past picketing agents. Within the company, Shanks was known as a take-charge man who accomplished objectives by shaking up entrenched bureaucracy and cutting through red tape.[77] Shank's Vice President in charge of district agencies, the vice president with primary responsibility for labor relations, was Paul B. Palmer. The company's legal counsel throughout the dispute were Nahum A. Bernstein and Donald R. Seawell of the New York firm of Silver & Bernstein. The President of the International Insurance Agents' Union was George L. Russ, the man who had led the union's successful organization of Prudential and who eventually negotiated the merger of his union with the competing Insurance Workers of America union in 1959. Russ began his work life as an insurance agent in Virginia where he began organizing for the union. However, his ability as a motivator and his devotion to the interests of the insurance agents soon propelled him to the union presidency.[78] The union's legal counsel was Isaac N. Groner, a Yale law graduate, former law clerk to United States Chief Justice Vinson, and solo practitioner from Washington, D.C.[79]

As the March 18 expiration date for the existing collective bargaining agreement neared, the union negotiating committee became dissatisfied with the progress of negotiations. On February 28, 1956, the union President George Russ sent a letter to all local presidents advising them that there had been "some progress" toward a "satisfactory contract" but that the "attitude of the Company" necessitated that they be prepared to "take action" after the expiration of the existing agreement.[80] The primary issues in dispute were the company's insistence on contract language guaranteeing it the power to determine the size of an agent's "debits" or sales territory, differences about the appropriate grievance procedure, and a disagreement over the appropriate contract length, with the union favoring two years and the company favoring five.[81] On March 13, 1956, the President of Prudential, Carrol Shanks,

[77] *Id.* at 192–93.

[78] Telephone Interview with Isaac N. Groner, June 22, 2004.

[79] *Id.*

[80] Records and Briefs of Cases Decided by the Supreme Court of the United States, Volume 361, Transcript of Record at 66–67, NLRB v. Insurance Agents' Int'l Union.

[81] Newark Star–Ledger, Mar. 24, 1956, at 3; *Id.*, Mar. 28, 1956, at 4; *Id.*, Mar. 30, 1956, at 7.

announced that Prudential had enjoyed record insurance sales of $6.4 billion for 1955.[82] The same day, union President Russ wrote another letter to the local presidents directing them to take a "strike vote" and to carry out a "work without a contract program" beginning March 19 if no satisfactory contract had been reached by then. The "work without a contract program" involved abstaining from writing new business and demonstrating and distributing leaflets in front of district offices on March 21 and 23. The same letter said: "During this period the union shall continue its negotiations with the Company and make every effort to reach a satisfactory agreement. . . . Your participation is necessary to the success of this effort."[83] Some days later, union members voted by a margin of three to one in favor of a job action.[84]

On March 19, 1956, the old collective bargaining agreement expired without agreement on a new contract. As planned, on March 21 and 23, the agents undertook the "work without a contract program" and picketed their district and home offices. An estimated three thousand insurance agents demonstrated in front of Prudential's headquarters in Newark.[85] Still dissatisfied with the progress of negotiations, union President George Russ and the union bargaining committee determined to continue the "work without a contract program." George Russ orchestrated the offensive through a series of letters directing the agents to engage in further acts of defiance. Between March 23 and about June 26, 1956, the insurance agents intermittently refused to write new insurance, reported late for work, engaged in "sit-in mornings" by staying in the office "doing what comes naturally" rather than going out to pursue sales, and refused to work after 4:30 p.m. They also picketed and demonstrated in front of company offices, leafleted policyholders and solicited their signatures on petitions supporting the insurance agents, boycotted company sales meetings and sales campaigns, and refused to file company paperwork.[86] Of course, all of these activities were designed to impose financial losses on the company and pressure it into making concessions at the bargaining table. The General Counsel later computed that the union's activities cost Prudential approximately $62 million in

---

[82] N.Y. Times, Mar. 14, 1956, at 53.

[83] Records and Briefs of Cases Decided by the Supreme Court of the United States, Volume 361, Transcript of Record at 66–67, NLRB v. Insurance Agents' Int'l Union.

[84] N.Y. Times, Mar. 24, 1956, at 41.

[85] Newark Evening News, Mar. 23, 1956, at 1; Newark Star–Ledger, Mar. 24, 1956, at 3.

[86] Records and Briefs of Cases Decided by the Supreme Court of the United States, Volume 361, Transcript of Record at 63–104, NLRB v. Insurance Agents' Int'l Union; Insurance Agents' Int'l Union, 119 NLRB 768, 769–70 (1957).

new sales over the course of the seven weeks most affected by the "work without a contract program."[87]

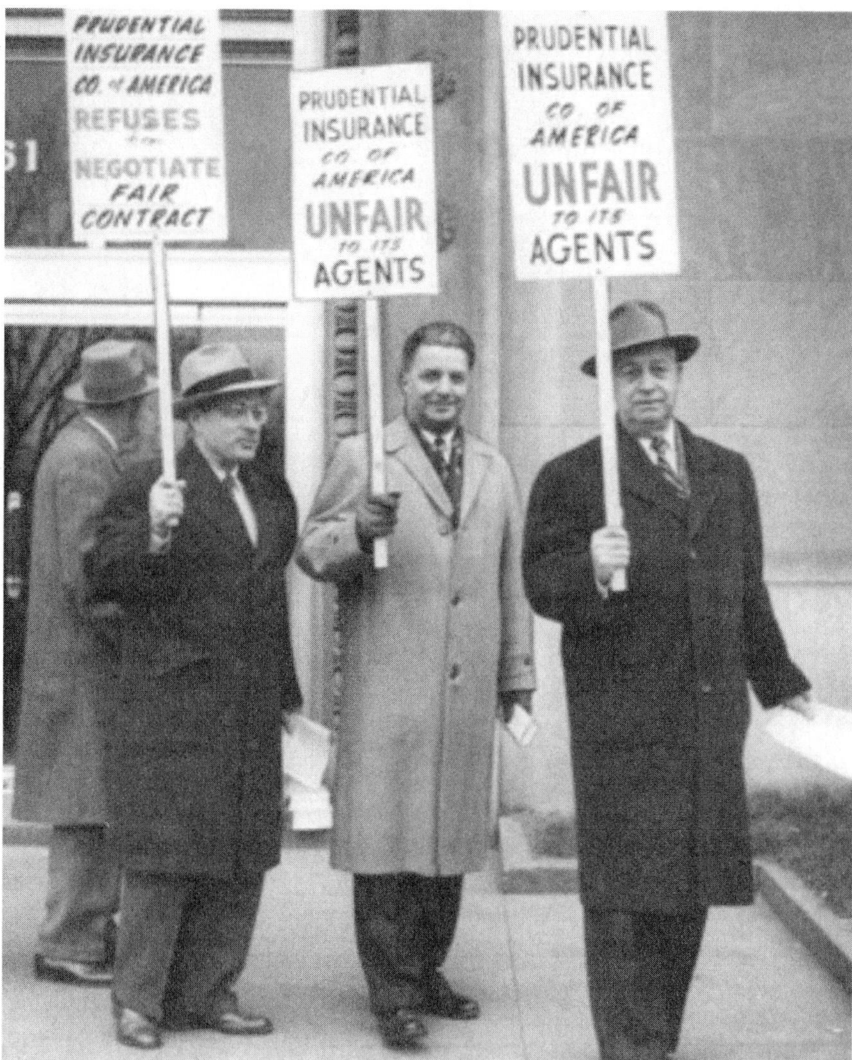

From left, Insurance Agents' Secretary-Treasurer Max Shine, Vice President Charles G. Heisel and President George L. Russ picket the Newark Prudential headquarters, 1956. Photograph used with the permission of the George Meany Memorial Archives.

---

[87] Records and Briefs of Cases Decided by the Supreme Court of the United States, Volume 361, Transcript of Record at 136, NLRB v. Insurance Agents' Int'l Union.

Prudential Vice President Paul Palmer condemned the union's tactics of "harassment" in a March 29 letter to agents.[88] Palmer told the agents that these tactics were not in their, or the company's, best interests and were self-destructive. Palmer's choice of the word "harassment" was well advised. The Board had previously held in *Textile Workers Union of America*[89] that partial work stoppages were unlawful "harassment" in contravention of the union's obligation to bargain in good faith under § 8(b)(3) of the NLRA. Palmer's use of the term

Insurance Agents' Vice President Charles G. Heisel leads picketing Prudential agents in Newark, 1956. Photograph used with the permission of the George Meany Memorial Archives.

[88] Newark Star–Ledger, Mar. 30, 1956, at 7.

[89] 108 NLRB 743 (1954). The *Textile Workers* case is also sometimes referred to as the *Personal Products* case, a reference to the company involved in the dispute, in an effort to distinguish this case from other Board decisions involving the Textile Workers Union.

"harassment" was undoubtedly an attempt to set the stage for an unfair labor practice charge against the Insurance Agents' to prohibit the "work without a contract program." The *Textile Workers* precedent was weak, however, since the D.C. Circuit had refused enforcement of the Board's order there, reasoning that if the union could lawfully call a complete strike consistent with its obligation to bargain in good faith it could also call lesser partial work stoppages.[90] Nevertheless, on April 9, 1956, Prudential filed a charge with the NLRB alleging that the union's "work without a contract program" amounted to a failure to bargain in good faith. After investigation, the New York Regional Director of the NLRB, Charles T. Douds, filed a complaint on June 5, 1956. At the request of the union, the Board proceeding against it was recessed for a brief period so that a new collective bargaining agreement between the company and the union could be reached on July 17, 1956.[91]

Prior Proceedings in Insurance Agents'

Counsel for the Board and the Insurance Agents' Union honed their arguments in the initial proceedings before the Board and the court of appeals. The Board was represented by Regional Attorney Samuel K. Kaynard and Associate General Counsel Frederick U. Reel, both long-time Board attorneys. Kaynard and Reel argued that the union's partial work stoppages were inconsistent with the reasoned deliberations necessary for good faith bargaining and were unprotected by the National Labor Relations Act as a form of "harassing tactics" that the Board had already determined were an unfair labor practice in *Textile Workers*.[92]

The union was represented throughout the dispute by Isaac N. Groner, a solo practitioner from Washington, D.C. Groner served as the union's General Counsel from 1952 until the union's merger with the United Food and Commercial Workers in 1983. Even after the merger, Groner served as union Special Counsel handling Insurance Agents' legal matters until he retired in 2000.[93] Groner argued that the plain language of § 13 of the NLRA and § 501 (2) of the Labor Management Relations Act (LMRA) prohibited the Board from diminishing the right to strike. Moreover, within the unique circumstances of the insurance industry, with its lack of a set workplace and hours and the regulation of existing business, such tactics were the only realistic recourse for insurance agents in collective bargaining. For the Board to determine which economic weapons the parties could, and could not, use would entangle the Board too deeply in the process of collective bargaining. He also argued that the union could strike without violating the requirements of good faith bargaining, and therefore they could undertake lesser econom-

[90] Textile Workers Union v. NLRB, 227 F.2d 409, 410 (D.C. Cir. 1955).

[91] Insurance Agents' Int'l Union, 119 NLRB 768, 777 (1957).

[92] *Id.* at 780–84.

[93] Telephone Interview with Isaac N. Groner, June 22, 2004.

ic actions while still bargaining in good faith. Groner argued that the Board's decision in *Textile Workers* was not of much significance since the Court of Appeals for the D.C. Circuit had refused to enforce the Board's order in that case.[94]

The Board, in a three-member panel consisting of Boyd Leedom, Abe Murdock and Joseph Alton Jenkins,[95] overturned the ruling of the Trial Examiner, and found that the union had failed to bargain in good faith. The Trial Examiner had found that, although the union's "slowdown" was "unprotected" activity, it was not "unlawful."[96] The Trial Examiner noted that § 13 of the NLRA expressly stated that the NLRA should not be construed to diminish the right to strike, which was defined to include "slowdowns" in § 501 of the LMRA.[97] The Board, however, concluded that the Insurance Agents' "harassing" activities were inconsistent with the Act's requirement of "reasoned discussions ... upon which good-faith bargaining must rest."[98] The Board analogized the union's slowdown at Prudential to employer unilateral action and other unfair labor practices. Ignoring the union's arguments about the unique attributes of the insurance industry that impeded full work stoppages, the Board concluded that the facts of this case were governed by its prior decision in *Textile Workers* and constituted a failure to bargain in good faith.[99] With affected members in thirty-five states and the District of Columbia, Mr. Groner chose to take the union's appeal to the D.C. Circuit, where the Board had already lost the *Textile Workers* case.

The Court of Appeals for the D.C. Circuit rewarded Mr. Groner's choice of venue. On October 23, 1958, in a one-paragraph, per curiam opinion, Judges Elijah Prettyman, Wilbur Miller and George Washington, all Truman appointees, denied enforcement of the Board's order. The panel stated:

> This case involves the same question of law presented in *Textile Workers* ... we find no critical difference between the two cases. On

---

[94] Insurance Agents' Int'l Union, 119 NLRB 768, 771, 780–84 (1957).

[95] All three of these members had been appointed or reappointed by Eisenhower, although Murdock was a Democrat who had originally been appointed by Truman and Jenkins was also a Democrat. James A. Gross, *The NLRB: An Historical Perspective in A Guide to Sources of Information on the National Labor Relations Board* at 14–16 (Gordon T. Law, Jr., ed. 2002).

[96] Well-settled Board doctrine established that, unlike a full strike, slowdowns are not protected concerted activity under § 7 of the NLRA. Insurance Agents' Int'l Union, 119 NLRB 768, 779 (1957); Phelps Dodge Copper Products Corp., 101 NLRB 360, 368 (1952).

[97] Insurance Agents' Int'l Union, 119 NLRB 768, 779–82 (1957).

[98] *Id.* at 772.

[99] *Id.*

> the authority of that case, the order of the Board here under review must be set aside. One panel of this court will not attempt to overrule a recent precedent set by another panel, even though one or more of its members may disagree with the ruling.[100]

The Board petitioned the United States Supreme Court for a writ of certiorari. The writ was granted on January 26, 1959.

The Supreme Court Decision in Insurance Agents'

The Board was represented in the Supreme Court by Dominick ("Dom") L. Manoli. Manoli was born in Lentini, Italy, raised in Omaha, Nebraska, and educated at Harvard Law School. He began his career in private practice, but became a Board Attorney in 1941. Manoli rose rapidly through the ranks at the Board, becoming Supervisory Attorney in 1945, Assistant General Counsel in Charge of Supreme Court Litigation in 1953 and Associate General Counsel in Charge of the Litigation Division in 1960. His work for the Board included work on several important Supreme Court cases including *Truitt*, *Borg-Warner* and *Mastro Plastics*.[101]

In its brief before the Supreme Court, the Board recognized the importance of economic sanctions to the process of collective bargaining, but argued that good faith bargaining included resort only to the "traditional" strike weapon. The Board argued that slowdowns were repugnant to the statute's purposes of promoting equity in bargaining power and industrial peace, and so could properly be found to be a failure to bargain in good faith.[102] The Board described on-the-job pressure such as slowdowns or intermittent strikes as "foul blows" and "diseases of collective bargaining" which "cost one party little or nothing in relation to the disadvantage imposed on the other." "With the economic pressure largely one-sided," the Board argued, "these tactics

---

100 Insurance Agents' Int'l Union v. NLRB, 260 F.2d 736 (D.C. Cir. 1958).

101 NLRB Bulletin, Division of Information, Washington, D.C., July 25, 1980. NLRB v. Borg–Warner, 356 U.S. 342 (1958) (determining the scope of mandatory collective bargaining under the Act); Mastro Plastics v. NLRB, 350 U.S. 270 (1956) (determining the applicability of a "cooling-off period" to unfair labor practice strikes). Other significant Supreme Court cases Mr. Manoli participated in were NLRB v. Truck Drivers Local 449, 353 U.S. 87 (1957) (testing the legality of employer lock-outs in response to union "whipsawing" tactics); and Local 1976, Carpenters v. NLRB, 357 U.S. 93 (1958) (determining the legality of "hot-cargo" agreements as a defense to secondary boycott charges). Manoli's surprising representations to the Supreme Court in his oral argument in NLRB v. Gissel Packing Co., 395 U.S. 575 (1969), are discussed in the chapter on that case in *Labor Law Stories*.

102 Records and Briefs of Cases Decided by the Supreme Court of the United States, Volume 361, Brief for the NLRB at 10–11, NLRB v. Insurance Agents' Int'l Union.

take on more the character of coercion than collective bargaining."[103] According to the Board, the one-sidedness of the harm imposed by slowdowns justified their being both unprotected by the Act and evidence of a party's failure to bargain in good faith. In the Board's view, "a reading of the Statute which leaves the employer ... with only the choice of dismissing those employees who engage in improper tactics would fail to give full effect to Section 8(b)(3), which seeks to preserve and enhance the stability of the bargaining relationship."[104] The Board argued that slowdowns were included in the definition of strikes in § 501(2) of the LMRA, not to bring them within the protections of § 13 of the NLRA, but instead to bring them within the penalties and prohibitions of §§ 8(b)(4) and 8(d) of the NLRA and §§ 303 and 305 of the LMRA.[105]

The union, represented by its stalwart lawyer, Isaac Groner, argued in its brief that private resolution of bargaining disputes was essential to the system of bargaining under the NLRA. Mr. Groner argued that to allow the Board to regulate bargaining power would be to allow the Board to determine the resolution of collective bargaining issues—a proposition expressly disallowed by the definition of good faith bargaining in § 8(d) of the NLRA.[106] Citing legislative history from the Wagner Act, Groner argued that the obligation to bargain in good faith allowed the Board to regulate merely the "process" of negotiations, not the parties' substantive bargaining "powers." He contended that the Board's pronouncements that the union's activities were "foul blows" or "diseases of collective bargaining" had no basis in the statute and were too general to produce a workable standard. "If the Board can take action on the basis of such judgments, it literally can do anything in the field of collective bargaining."[107] The union also emphasized the plain words of the statute defining the right to strike and the obligation to bargain in good faith. Section 13 of the NLRA safeguards "the right to strike" from Board interference or diminution "except as specifically provided for herein." Section 501(2) of the LMRA expressly defines the term "strike" to include "any concerted slowdown or other concerted interruption of operations by employees."[108] In the union's view, the Board's decision

---

[103] *Id.* at 13 (quoting NLRB v. Electrical Workers, 346 U.S. 464, 477 (1953)).

[104] *Id.* at 14.

[105] *Id.* at 35.

[106] Records and Briefs of Cases Decided by the Supreme Court of the United States, Volume 361, Brief for Insurance Agents' International Union at 23–25, NLRB v. Insurance Agents' Int'l Union.

[107] *Id.* at 21.

[108] *Id.* at 22.

made illegal what § 13 protected. Finally, Mr. Groner cited the unique characteristics of the insurance industry and their effect on the agents' ability to undertake a full work-stoppage, but did not make this a central theme of the brief.

Insurance Agents' was argued before the Supreme Court on December 7 and 8, 1959. For the Board, Assistant General Counsel Manoli began with a recitation of the relevant statutory provisions, facts and history of the case. Manoli then expounded upon the view articulated in the Board's brief that good faith bargaining, under the NLRA, was a system of reasoned discussion, subject to resort to economic sanctions that were consistent with the purposes of the Act. He asserted that good faith bargaining required more than simply a desire to reach agreement and that the language of the Act established several substantive requirements, such as those to meet and to reduce agreements to writing. Traditional strikes were a necessary cost of collective bargaining and were consistent with the purposes of the NLRA. Such work stoppages imposed costs on both sides, encouraging them to negotiate in good faith and avoid costly breaches of industrial peace. On the other hand, slowdowns and harassing tactics imposed costs disproportionately on only one side and amounted to coercion which the perpetrator had no reason to avoid. Accordingly, the Board's determination that such "foul blows" amounted to a failure to bargain in good faith was consistent with the basic purposes of the Act of promoting good faith bargaining and industrial peace. About three-fourths of the way through Manoli's presentation, Justices Black and Douglas in turn pressed him on the consistency of his position with the protection of the right to strike in § 13 of the NLRA and the express inclusion of slowdowns in the definition of strike in § 501(2) of the LMRA. Although Mr. Manoli twice walked the justices through his argument that the definition of a strike in the LMRA was relevant only to that statute and the prohibitions and penalties against secondary boycotts under the NLRA, they seemed to remain unconvinced at the end of his presentation.[109]

Mr. Groner's argument on behalf of the union commenced at the end of the day, and had to be completed the next day. Groner, as a former clerk for Chief Justice Vinson, knew most of the justices and what to expect in their questioning even though it was his first Supreme Court argument. Groner would appear before the Supreme Court many more times, including an appearance on behalf of the Amalgamated Transit Workers and several appointments by the Court itself on behalf of individual litigants.[110] Groner began with his basic argument that the

[109] Tape of Supreme Court Oral Argument in the Insurance Agents' Case, on file with the U.S. Supreme Court.

[110] Telephone Interview with Isaac N. Groner, June 22, 2004.

Board had no authority for its ruling. According to Groner, at the expiration of the contract on March 18, the union had the choice of either capitulating on the issue of the company's control of the assignment of debits—an issue touching the fundamental economic security of its members—or to take economic action. The unique characteristics of the insurance industry made a traditional strike impossible. Accordingly, the agents determined that the only way they could exert effective pressure on their employer over this matter of vital concern was to undertake the "no new business" and picketing exercises in which they engaged. Both the agents and the company suffered from the refusal to take new business, Groner pointed out, and the picketing activities were protected by § 8(c) of the NLRA. Moreover, the union had been willing to meet with the company, engaged in "give-and-take" negotiations and was ultimately successful in reaching an agreement. How could this be bargaining in bad faith? Groner also insisted that the Board did not have the authority to consider the exercise of economic power in determining whether there had been a failure to bargain in good faith because to enable the Board to create a balance of power between the parties would enable the Board effectively to determine the terms and conditions of employment. Mr. Groner closed by arguing that if the Court sustained the Board's position, the Board could intrude into collective bargaining based on nothing more than the Board's characterization of an activity as "harassing."[111]

Groner expected some tough questioning by the Court—especially Justice Frankfurter. He knew that Justice Frankfurter was one of the most active questioners on the Court, and was particularly tenacious in his questioning of former Supreme Court clerks. He was not disappointed. When Groner described the union's activities as merely picketing, Frankfurter asked whether it wasn't the combination of the union's activities to which the Board objected. Groner responded that under the Board's decision all of the union's individual activities were harassment and bargaining in bad faith, but that in fact many of those activities were expressly protected by § 8(c). After more discussion of § 8(c), Justice Frankfurter quipped "But why did the Board bring this case? Why did we take it on certiorari? If your characterization of the dispute is correct, there would seem to be nothing to this case." In an effort to head off more grilling, Mr. Groner responded "There *is* nothing to the case. I *am* right. There is no authority or basis for the Board's decision.... Don't assume that just because the Board brings a dispute before you that they have a case!" In a backhanded slap at the Board (and perhaps the former clerk) that smoothed over the situation, Justice

[111] Tape of Supreme Court Oral Argument in the Insurance Agents' Case, on file with the U.S. Supreme Court.

Frankfurter responded "I can only speak for myself, but I wouldn't think that *anyone* would make such a rash assumption."[112]

In an opinion by Justice William J. Brennan, announced on February 23, 1960, the Supreme Court upheld the decision of the court of appeals and rejected the position of the Board. Joining Justice Brennan's opinion were Chief Justice Earl Warren and Justices Black, Douglas, Clark and Stewart. Justice Frankfurter, joined by Justices Harlan and Whittaker, wrote a separate opinion preferring that the case be remanded to the Board to apply the correct legal standard. Justice Brennan's opinion is remarkable for the sophistication and clarity with which it treats a very complex question. Justice Brennan, the son of Irish immigrants, showed obvious potential in his studies at the University of Pennsylvania and Harvard. Although his father was a labor leader, Brennan represented employer interests during his years in private practice. Despite the fact that Brennan was a Democrat, President Eisenhower appointed him to the Supreme Court to fill the "Catholic seat" and to demonstrate that his appointments were above political partisanship. Brennan's personal warmth and brilliance combined to make him one of the most successful facilitators and consensus builders in the history of the Court.[113] Working among some of the most independent and egotistical legal minds in the country, Brennan articulated clear and soundly reasoned public policy, on complicated questions, consistent with the legislative pronouncements of elected representatives. Brennan's opinion in *Insurance Agents'* outlines much of our modern theory of the obligation to bargain in good faith under the NLRA.

Justice Brennan's opinion first recounted the relevant language and legislative history of the NLRA. The NLRA's duty to bargain collectively, the opinion observed, was first imposed upon employers in § 8(5) of the original Wagner Act. This obligation was narrowly conceived. Senator Walsh, Chair of the Senate Labor Committee, described the obligation imposed by the Act as follows:

> When the employees have chosen their ... representatives, all the bill proposes to do is to escort them to the door of their employer and say "Here they are, the legal representatives of your employee." What happens behind those doors is not inquired into, and the bill does not seek to inquire into it.[114]

---

[112] *Id.*; Telephone Interview with Isaac N. Groner, June 22, 2004.

[113] Eisenhower is said to have expressed regret about appointing Brennan and Chief Justice Earl Warren to the Supreme Court. Peter Irons, *A People's History of the Supreme Court* 402–03 (1999); <http://www.michaelariens.com/ConLaw/justices/brennan.htm>.

[114] NLRB v. Insurance Agents' Int'l Union, 361 U.S. at 484 (citing Senator Walsh at 79 Cong. Rec. 7660).

However, as Brennan explained, this narrow formulation carries a broader and essential purpose of the obligation to bargain in good faith. "That purpose is the making effective of the duty of management to extend recognition to the union; the duty of management to bargain in good faith is essentially a corollary of its duty to recognize the union." Although, as Walsh's quote makes clear, in passing the NLRA Congress was generally not concerned with the substantive terms of collective bargaining agreements, and believed such matters should be left up to the parties, realization of the fundamental purpose of the obligation to bargain in good faith "necessarily led beyond the door . . . , and into the conference room." "For example, an employer's unilateral wage increase during the bargaining process tends to subvert the union's position as the representative of the employees . . . , and hence is violative of [the obligation to bargain in good faith]."

Justice Brennan noted that "[o]bviously there is tension between the principle that the parties need not contract on any specific terms and a practical enforcement of the principle that they are bound to deal with each other in a serious attempt to resolve differences and reach a common ground." In the Board's efforts in the 1940's to address this tension, Congress became concerned that the Board had strayed too far into the approval of various substantive terms in its determination of what constituted employers' good faith bargaining. Accordingly, the 1947 Taft–Hartley amendments to the NLRA defined the obligation to bargain collectively in § 8(d). Moreover, Congress had become more concerned with abuses of union power. As a result, said the Court, Congress enacted § 8(b)(3) to impose the obligation to bargain in good faith on unions. As Brennan asserted: "It is apparent from the legislative history of the whole Act that the policy of Congress is to impose a mutual duty upon the parties to confer in good faith with a desire to reach agreement, in the belief that such an approach from both sides of the table promotes the overall design [of the Act] of achieving industrial peace."

Addressing the case at hand, Justice Brennan described the Board's position as based on "an erroneous view of collective bargaining:"

> It must be realized that collective bargaining, under a system where the Government does not attempt to control the results of negotiations, cannot be equated with an academic collective search for truth—or even with what might be thought to be an ideal one. . . . The presence of economic weapons in reserve, and their actual exercise on occasion by the parties, is part and parcel of the system that the Wagner and Taft–Hartley Acts have recognized. . . . [T]he truth of the matter is that at the present statutory stage of our national labor relations policy, the two factors—necessity of good faith bargaining between the parties, and the availability of econom-

> ic pressure devices ... to make the other party incline to agree to one's terms—exist side by side.

The Board's approach—evaluating the economic weapons employed by the parties as indicia of good faith bargaining—involved an intrusion into the substance of collective bargaining that was not authorized by Congress in the NLRA:

> [I]f the Board could regulate the choice of economic weapons that may be used as part of collective bargaining, it would be in a position to exercise considerable influence upon the substantive terms on which the parties contract. As the parties' own devices became more limited, the Government might have to enter even more directly into the negotiation of collective agreements. Our policy is not presently erected on a foundation of government control of the results of negotiations.

As a result, the Supreme Court found that the Board had exceeded its authority in holding that the union had failed to bargain in good faith, and upheld the decision of the D.C. Circuit Court of Appeals.

The Immediate Impact of Insurance Agents'

Isaac Groner was thrilled with the Court's decision. He recalled that the union experienced the exhilaration that can only be felt when one is shot at but missed. Because of the peculiar characteristics of the insurance industry and the legal requirements to maintain service to existing customers, had the Board won the case and the union's partial work stoppage strategies been held unlawful, the employees' bargaining power in the insurance industry would have been severely undermined. As the case turned out, the insurance agents were able to resort to similar slowdown and picketing strategies in later negotiations, and maintained their bargaining relationship with the Prudential Insurance Company into the twenty-first century. However, this strategy is not quite so effective or cost free for the workers as the Board's argument in the case might suggest. Participating agents forego commissions they could have earned on unsolicited business and of course Prudential could fire agents who participated in slowdowns or failed to follow company rules.[115]

The bar and the academy recognized *Insurance Agents'* as an important case with potentially far ranging implications for interpretation of the NLRA. No one anticipated any major change in strategy by the labor movement on the basis of the Court's limited endorsement of the slowdown in *Insurance Agents'*, and none occurred.[116] However, there was a general recognition that the analysis of the case would have a

---

[115] Telephone Interview with Isaac N. Groner, June 22, 2004.

[116] *Id.*

significant impact on the way future bargaining cases were decided. *The New York Times* described the Court's ruling as "important" and having "far reaching implications."[117] Academic authors identified larger themes in the case concerning the obligation to bargain in good faith. The Court's analysis in *Insurance Agents'* was seen as a step back from the per se analysis that had seemed implicit in recent good faith cases, including *Truitt*, and a return to an analysis that considered the facts of the case as a whole.[118] Furthermore, the opinion was seen as an important check on the encroachment of the Board into the process of collective bargaining.[119] Although some authors rejoiced in this, others wondered what the implications of the ruling would be for employer actions against unions. The Court's gloves-off "freedom of contract" philosophy in *Insurance Agents'* and other cases would benefit the stronger party in collective bargaining, and some realized that the stronger party would often be the employer. Just four years after it was decided, Harry H. Wellington cited *Insurance Agents'* as "perhaps the high watermark for freedom of contract in modern labor-management relations."[120]

The Continuing Importance of Truitt and Insurance Agents' Today

The *Truitt* and *Insurance Agents'* cases stand today as landmarks resolving important questions and establishing important principles in the interpretation of the NLRA's obligation to "bargain in good faith." Over the years, the specific holding of the *Truitt* case has been narrowed at the hands of the Board and the courts. Despite the fact that similar arguments were ably made by Dick Douglas in the original case, and either ignored or rejected by the Court, several Board and court opinions have distinguished employer claims of inability to pay from those of competitive disadvantage and applied the financial disclosure requirements of *Truitt* only to the former and not the later.[121] Thus, although it seems doubtful that this is the best interpretation of the Supreme

[117] N.Y. Times, Feb. 24, 1960, at 22; Wash. Post Times Herald, Feb. 24, 1960, at B3; Newark Evening News, Feb. 23, 1960, at 1.

[118] Recent Case, *NLRB May Not Equate Partial Strike to Harass Employer with Failure to Bargain in Good Faith*, 109 U. Pa. L. Rev. 134, 139 (1960).

[119] *The Supreme Court, 1959 Term*, 74 Harv. L. Rev. 97 (1960).

[120] Harry H. Wellington, *Freedom of Contract and the Collective Bargaining Agreement*, 112 U. Pa. L. Rev. 467, 477 (1964).

[121] *See, e.g.*, Nielson Lithographing Co., 305 NLRB 697 (1991), *enforced sub nom.* Graphic Communications Local 508 v. NLRB, 977 F.2d 1168 (7th Cir. 1992); NLRB v. Harvstone Manufacturing Corp., 785 F.2d 570 (7th Cir. 1986); AMF Trucking & Warehousing, Inc., 342 NLRB No. 116, 2004 WL 2138194 (2004) (no *Truitt* obligation where the company merely claims that it is "in distress").

Court's opinion, most commentators acknowledge that, in practice, *Truitt* has been narrowed and the employer's claim of "inability to pay" has taken on the aura of the "magic words" necessary to trigger the employers obligation to share financial data on the firm.[122] This narrowing of *Truitt* is undoubtedly a product of shifts of the judiciary and the Board under successive Republican administrations.

Despite this narrowing in interpretation, *Truitt* still stands for the important propositions that good faith bargaining requires truthful representations and that the union has the right to relevant information. These principles reaffirmed the basis for the doctrine of good faith bargaining requiring employers to provide the union with sufficient information or "wage data" to enable its representatives to understand and intelligently discuss the issues raised in bargaining.[123] Moreover, the Supreme Court has extended the principles applied to collective bargaining in *Truitt* to information that is relevant to the enforcement of the collective agreement. In *NLRB v. Acme Industrial Co.*,[124] the Supreme Court used *Truitt* to establish a right to discovery in our system of industrial jurisprudence, allowing unions to gain the information they need to evaluate the merit of grievances, prepare for arbitration and enforce any award. *Truitt* and its progeny establish that the union and employer both have a right to all information that is relevant to performing their responsibilities in negotiating and enforcing collective bargaining agreements.[125] It is recognized that the sharing of relevant information in negotiations and contract enforcement helps to achieve the NLRA's purposes of promoting productive collective bargaining and industrial peace.[126]

Unlike the holding of *Truitt*, the "hands-off" approach of *Insurance Agents'* has fared well in the current conservative judicial environment. Although the *Insurance Agents'* case itself was a union victory, the

---

122 *See, e.g.*, Brent Robbins, *Rethinking Financial Disclosure Under the National Labor Relations Act*, 47 Vand. L. Rev. 1905 (1994); Amy Gladstein, *It's All in the Phrasing: When Does A Demand for Concessions Require the Provision of Information to the Union?*, 470 PLI/Lit. 31 (1993); Christopher T. Hexter, *Duty to Supply Information Nielson Lithographing Co. Revisited: The Board's Retreat from Collective Bargaining as a Rational Process Leading to Agreement*, 8 Lab. Law. 831 (1992).

123 *See, e.g.*, Boston Herald-Traveler Corp. v. NLRB, 223 F.2d 58 (1st Cir. 1955); NLRB v. Yawman & Erbe Mfg. Co., 187 F.2d 947 (2d Cir. 1951); NLRB v. Whitin Machine Works, 217 F.2d 593 (4th Cir. 1954); Industrial Welding Co., 175 NLRB 477 (1969).

124 385 U.S. 432 (1967).

125 Julius G. Getman, Bertrand B. Pogrebin & David L. Gregory, *Labor Management Relations and the Law* 150–54 (2d ed. 1999).

126 Neil W. Chamberlain & James W. Kuhn, *Collective Bargaining* 78 (2d ed. 1965); Lavania Hall, *Negotiation: Strategies for Mutual Gain* (1993).

hands-off approach to the use of economic weapons has probably benefitted employers much more than unions. Since the 1980's, American employers have become more aggressive about exercising economic weapons in collective bargaining. Although the use of strike replacements was fairly rare in the 1950's, American employers have resorted to this strategy more often since President Reagan fired and replaced the striking air traffic controllers in the early 1980's.[127] Also, since 1965 and the *American Ship Building* case,[128] the Board and courts have accepted employers' use of the lock-out as an offensive weapon in collective bargaining.[129] Although *Insurance Agents'* establishes that, consistent with good faith bargaining, employees may use unprotected and non-traditional economic weapons in collective bargaining, the logical corollary, of course, is that employers may do the same.

Beyond the particular holdings and principles they establish, *Truitt* and *Insurance Agents'* are useful for understanding the concept of good faith bargaining because they illustrate a fundamental tension in the concept of good faith bargaining identified by Justice Brennan. At first the cases seem irreconcilable. *Truitt*'s requirements of honesty and the duty to divulge information are consistent with a model of "rational bargaining." The *Truitt* Court seemed to promote exactly the vision of collective bargaining as a "collective academic search for truth" that it later expressly rejected in *Insurance Agents'*. Moreover, the Court promoted this vision in a fairly intrusive manner, requiring employers to open their books to the union under an almost per se rule based on a plea of poverty. On the other hand, *Insurance Agents'* promotes the idea of collective bargaining as an economic contest or struggle. At least with respect to the choice of economic weapons, this struggle is to be free from interference by the Board or courts lest the government, rather than the parties, have the power to determine the outcome of the negotiations. The Court's approach in *Insurance Agents'* seemed to eschew per se rules concerning the parties' behavior in favor of "consideration of the facts of the case as a whole." Yet, as Justice Brennan made clear in his opinion in *Insurance Agents'*, neither of these conceptions of collective bargaining can be strictly true and both must exist within our understanding of good faith bargaining.

The problem of requiring good faith bargaining to promote industrial peace can be analyzed using a simple game theoretic model of

---

[127] Paul C. Weiler, *Governing the Workplace: The Future of Labor and Employment Law* 109, 112–13 (1990). The use of strike replacements is discussed in Chapter One of *Labor Law Stories* on NLRB v. Mackay Radio & Telegraph Co., 304 U.S. 333 (1938).

[128] 380 U.S. 300 (1965).

[129] William B. Gould IV, *A Primer on American Labor Law* 109–11 (4th ed. 2004).

collective bargaining.[130] In this model, we examine how the employer and the union might agree to divide $10 in profits that will be earned over the life of the collective bargaining agreement.[131] It is assumed that the parties each adopt a strategy of either intransigence or cooperation in bargaining and that each party's success in bargaining depends on how "hard" it bargains relative to the other party. If one side is intransigent while the other is cooperative, the intransigent party will gain at the other's expense. However, if both sides are intransigent, the result is a strike in which the parties waste a portion of the $10 they could have earned because the parties forego profits and wages during the strike.[132] A plausible schedule for the division of the $10 in this bargaining game is as follows: if both parties are cooperative, they each get $5; if one side is intransigent while the other is cooperative, the intransigent party will get $8 while the cooperative party will get $2; and if both sides are

Matrix 1

Union and Employer Expected Payoffs for the Negotiations Game

		Employer	
		Cooperative Bargaining	Intransigent Bargaining
Union	Cooperative Bargaining	5 \ 5	2 \ 8
	Intransigent Bargaining	8 \ 2	3 \ 3

130 This model borrows from my analysis in Kenneth G. Dau–Schmidt, *A Bargaining Analysis of American Labor Law and The Search for Bargaining Equity and Industrial Peace*, 91 Mich. L. Rev. 419, 444–50 (1992).

131 In game theory, the value of a contract that is subject to negotiations is referred to as the "cooperative surplus." In collective bargaining, the cooperative surplus is the amount by which the profits of the firm over the life of the collective agreement exceed the amount each input to production must be paid in a competitive market. Robert Cooter & Thomas Ulen, *Law and Economics* 93–94 (1988).

132 In economics, the costs of intransigence in this bargaining problem are characterized as a "positional externality" in that the parties are rewarded based on their relative performance in being intransigent, and the costs of such intransigence is experienced by, or externalized on, the other party. Robert H. Frank, *Microeconomics and Behavior* 629–38 (1991).

intransigent, the result is a strike that wastes $4, after which the parties agree to divide the remaining profits at $3 each. These payoffs are shown in Matrix 1, with the union's payoff for each cell given below the diagonal and the employer's payoff for each cell given above the diagonal.

The divergence of the parties' individual and collective interests in collective bargaining can be seen by examining Matrix 1. In the negotiations, each party has an individual incentive to be intransigent and attempt to gain at the other's expense. Examining the problem from the union's perspective, if the company decides to be cooperative, the union does better by being intransigent ($8) than by being cooperative ($5) and if the company decides to be intransigent, the union still does better by being intransigent ($3) than by being cooperative ($2). Similarly, from the company's perspective, intransigence is also individually the best strategy.[133] However, if both parties follow their individual interest in being intransigent, the result will be a strike that wastes a portion of the company's profit and yields a low payoff for both parties ($3). The parties' collective interest is to cooperate so that they can avoid the strike and divide the profits with a higher payoff for both parties ($5). In game theory, a problem that poses such a divergence between individual and collective interests is referred to as a "dilemma game" because it poses a dilemma between individual and collective interests in the parties' choice of strategies.[134]

This divergence between individual and collective interests poses an opportunity for regulation to avoid industrial strife and waste of potential profits and wages. From the perspective of avoiding strikes, the simplest solution would be to direct the parties to submit the entire dispute to an arbitrator who would find that the company would earn $10 in profits over the term of the collective agreement and that the parties should split those profits at $5 each. Of course, there may be substantial costs from deriving and enforcing such a solution, not to mention the infringement on the parties' autonomy. Short of such an intrusive solution, what can the government do?

An alternative regulatory strategy to promote cooperative bargaining and minimize industrial strife would be for the government to prohibit and punish clear cases of intransigent behavior. If the government could identify intransigence or other opportunistic behavior in the above bargaining game, and punish it with an expected fine of $4, the payoffs for each party would change so that it would always pay to cooperate.[135] Unfortunately, it may not always be possible to identify

---

[133] In game theory, a strategy that is the best regardless of what the other side does is referred to as a "dominant" strategy. Eric Rasmusen, *Games and Information: An Introduction to Game Theory* 38 (1989).

[134] Martin Shubik, *Game Theory in the Social Sciences* 240 (1989).

[135] In Matrix 1, adding a $4 penalty for intransigence changes the $8 payoffs to $4, and the $3 payoffs to -$1. With such a payoff structure, cooperation dominates for both the union and the employer.

intransigence or other opportunistic behavior in bargaining. Is the employer bargaining hard because it's being intransigent, or because it really can't afford to pay? Taken to an extreme, this solution requires only slightly less of a herculean effort on the part of the adjudicator, and only slightly less an infringement of the parties' individual autonomy, than just arbitrating to the $5 solution.

Fortunately, one last regulatory strategy remains for the government to promote cooperative bargaining and industrial peace. The government can try to formulate the context for collective bargaining in such a way as to increase the parties' chances of acting on their collective interest in cooperating, rather than their individual interest in being intransigent. In experiments with dilemma games, researchers have found that people are more likely to act on their collective interests and cooperate if (a) the parties have good information so they know when they are being treated fairly; (b) there is a limited number of parties to the game so that there is no free-riding on cooperation; (c) there is a community of interests with the other people on their side of the table so that it is easy to identify the cooperative solution; and (d) there is a reasonable prospect of repeat future bargaining so that intransigence now can be punished in the future.[136]

This analysis suggests that an optimal regulatory strategy for encouraging cooperative or "good faith" bargaining will be a mixed strategy. The government should adopt some per se rules to prohibit clearly intransigent or strategic behavior, such as lying or refusing to bargain, as bargaining in "bad faith."[137] The government should also regulate the context of collective bargaining to promote the parties' ability to see and act on their collective interest in cooperation by requiring exchanges of information, promoting organization among employees with similar interests in "appropriate bargaining units" and creating a "presumption of continuing majority status" so that there is a reasonable expectation of future collective negotiations between the parties.[138] Accordingly, it is consistent with the purpose of promoting industrial peace to require that

---

136 Kenneth G. Dau-Schmidt, *A Bargaining Analysis of American Labor Law,* 91 Mich. L. Rev. 419, 484–86 (1992); Henry Hamburger, *Games as Models of Social Phenomena* 177–92 (1979).

137 Although "puffing" is allowed in bargaining, outright misrepresentations are generally found to be a violation of the duty to bargain in good faith. Neil Lloyd, *Management's Duty to Back Up Competitive Disadvantage Claims*, 61 U. Chi. L. Rev. 675, 679 (1994). The strategies of lying and refusing to bargain, along with the strategy of committing to third parties, can be analyzed graphically using a game theory model similar to the one presented in this chapter. Henry Hamburger, *Games as Models of Social Phenomena* 117–22 (1979).

138 Kenneth G. Dau-Schmidt, *A Bargaining Analysis of American Labor Law,* 91 Mich. L. Rev. 419, 492–504 (1992).

the parties exchange relevant information in collective bargaining, as part of "good faith" bargaining, as a means of engendering trust and cooperation between the parties.[139] However, unless the government wants to intercede in the relationship of the parties and adjudicate the cooperative solution through arbitration, at some point the government must leave the resolution of the dispute to the parties with their skill, knowledge—and economic weapons—trusting that the best interests of the parties and the context of the negotiations the government has created will minimize industrial strife. This seems to approximate the doctrine of good faith bargaining that Congress intended by enacting the NLRA, and that the Supreme Court has developed through cases like *Truitt* and *Insurance Agents'*.

Conclusion

The doctrine of good faith bargaining under the NLRA is a careful balance between regulating the conduct and context of collective bargaining to promote the parties' ability to act on their collective interest in cooperation, while still maintaining private determination of terms and conditions of employment through negotiation and possible resort to economic weapons. The *Truitt* and *Insurance Agents'* cases represent two distinct observation points in the Supreme Court's development of the contours of this doctrine. *Truitt* stands for the proposition that the Board and courts must regulate certain behavior of the parties in order to promote their ability to reach productive agreements and avoid industrial strife. The general principle announced in *Truitt* that the union has the right to information that is relevant to the performance of its duties as the exclusive representative of the employees is consistent with this proposition and the Act's purpose of promoting industrial peace. The Supreme Court's opinion in *Insurance Agents'* astutely outlines the tension implicit in the balancing of these objectives in our doctrine of good faith bargaining. The Court's holding in *Insurance Agents'*, that the Board and courts must not regulate the economic weapons of collective bargaining for fear of determining the substance of collective agreements, is consistent with the national labor policy of maintaining a system for the private determination of the terms and conditions of employment.

---

[139] Indeed, under the presented analysis one could reasonably ask why employers aren't *always* required to share financial information with their employees, at least where such sharing can be done without substantial burden or harm to the employer. Absent burden or harm, the only reason for the employer to keep such information silent is to trick the employees into accepting less than they otherwise would, at the risk of industrial strife. This strategy would seem at odds with both of the fundamental purposes of the NLRA—promoting equity in bargaining power and industrial peace.

4

Katherine V.W. Stone

The *Steelworkers' Trilogy*: The Evolution of Labor Arbitration

On November 9, 1955, James Sparks began working at the Plating Department of the American Manufacturing Company's metal stamping and wire manufacturing plant in Chattanooga, Tennessee. Sparks' job involved hoisting heavy frames from waist level to overhead racks, pushing loaded trucks up and over ramps, and bending at the waist to empty bins into vats of hot, acidic chemicals. After less than four months on the job, Sparks had an accident in which he ruptured an intervertebral disc. He took some time off to recover and then returned to work. A year later, on March 29, 1957, Sparks suffered another accident, aggravating the earlier injury and requiring surgery. He then filed a workers' compensation claim. Sparks' physician stated that Sparks could not lift over thirty pounds without incurring further injury. The company admitted the accident but contested the extent of his disability. The parties reached a settlement in September 1957 in which they agreed that Sparks had suffered a permanent partial disability of twenty-five percent. The company gave Sparks a monetary award of $3006 for the partial disability and reimbursement for his medical expenses.

Within a week of the settlement, Sparks sought to return to work, armed with a letter from his physician stating he was capable of performing all his job duties. The company was skeptical, and arranged for its doctor to examine Sparks. The company's physician concluded that Sparks remained twenty-five percent disabled and said Sparks should not be placed in work requiring heavy lifting, prolonged stooping, or bending. On the basis of its doctor's report and Sparks' admission, in the workers' compensation settlement, that he was twenty-five percent disabled, the company refused to re-employ Sparks. It claimed that if

Sparks returned to the job, he would pose a danger not only to himself but also to others because he might drop heavy frames in the vats and splash acids and other chemicals.

Sparks complained to his union, which filed a grievance. When the company continued to refuse to reinstate Sparks, the union sought to bring the case before an impartial arbitrator to determine whether Sparks had been fired for just cause. The company refused to arbitrate.[1]

Sparks' dispute is not unlike thousands that arise every day in the multitude of factories, mills, offices, and other American workplaces. These disputes about injuries, accidents, ability to perform work and the like have been present for over a hundred years. However, due more to an accident of fate rather than an accident at work, Sparks' case became one of the most important cases in all of U.S. labor law. Initially, Sparks' case was about his right to return to work, but as a result of the historical moment in which it arose, it came to be about something more. By the time it reached the Supreme Court, Sparks' case posed the question of whether and how a union could enforce rights in a collective bargaining agreement. Sparks' case, together with two other cases involving the same union, was decided by the Supreme Court in 1960 in a trilogy of decisions that defined the role of arbitration in the U.S. system of collective bargaining. Those cases, known as the *Steelworkers' Trilogy,* defined the legal status of collective bargaining agreements and the circumstances and manner in which their provisions would be enforced.[2]

Social and Legal Background

The Problem of Enforcing Collective Agreements in the Early Twentieth Century

Today we assume that collective bargaining is the core activity of labor unions. However, this was not always the case. For over 200 years, American workers organized to improve their position in society using a variety of tactics and for a wide range of objectives. For most of the nineteenth century, workers organized by city, by trade, by employer, and by political objective, sometimes seeking to form political parties, sometimes trying to achieve specific legislative gains. At times, workers formed producer cooperatives or mutual benefit societies. It was not until the end of the nineteenth century that collective bargaining emerged as organized labor's primary goal.

---

1 *See* Transcript of Record, United Steelworkers of America v. American Manufacturing Co., Supreme Court of the United States, No. 360, Oct. Term, 1959 [hereinafter cited as *American Manufacturing* Record].

2 United Steelworkers of America v. American Manufacturing Co., 363 U.S. 564 (1960); United Steelworkers of America v. Warrior & Gulf Navigation Co., 363 U.S. 574 (1960); United Steelworkers of America v. Enterprise Wheel & Car Corp., 363 U.S. 593 (1960).

Negotiations and trade agreements in the late nineteenth century were quite different from collective bargaining today.[3] Writing in 1905, John R. Commons, the leading industrial relations theorist of the day, described one process of negotiating trade agreements. Great Lakes longshoremen and the dock managers met twice a year to negotiate terms and conditions of employment.[4] At these meetings, the managers constituted themselves as a House of Lords, delegates of the longshoremen as a House of Commons, and the two assemblies met in halls on opposite sides of the same street. Each appointed members to a conference committee which met in joint sessions to set a wage scale and working conditions for all ports in the Great Lakes. The conferees referred back to their respective full Houses from time to time for instructions, as they presented demands and counter-demands. Over a period of ten to fifteen days, the conferees reached an agreement which they took back to their respective constituencies for consent. Once there was ratification, the agreement became "law."[5]

Turn-of-the-century collective bargaining agreements were brief documents, setting wage rates and a few working conditions such as hours of employment. They usually included a promise by the employer not to employ nonunion workers. They typically said nothing of such matters as seniority rules, grievance procedures, benefits, holidays, and layoff and recall procedures. And they did not specify an enforcement mechanism. Because they were negotiated frequently, each side constantly had to mobilize its supporters to apply economic pressure both to enforce past agreements and to secure new ones.

Although American unions fought valiantly to establish collective bargaining, they were not in favor of making collective agreements

---

[3] The term "trade agreement" is used here, as it was at the time, to describe agreements between unions and employers governing working conditions of union members. Trade agreements are to be distinguished from "collective bargaining agreements" negotiated after enactment of the National Labor Relations Act and the Railway Labor Act. Those statutes permit unions to become the exclusive representatives of workers within a defined bargaining unit and to negotiate collective bargaining agreements that establish terms and conditions for all members of the bargaining unit.

[4] John R. Commons, *Trade Unionism and Labor Problems*, 1–2 (1905).

[5] Commons also described a similar form of bargaining in the coal industry. In the Central Competitive Field of Illinois, Indiana, Ohio, and Pennsylvania, a system of negotiations evolved over a twenty-five-year period between miners and coal operators that resulted in an Interstate Bituminous Coal Agreement. As with the Longshoremen, the United Mine Workers officials and representatives of the coal operators association met for a week's "Parliament" every year. The coal industry had a more complex structure than the dock industry for ensuring each side's representation in the joint conference, but the result was the same. The miners and the operators each had an equal number of votes in joint conferences, out of which a wage scale and certain working conditions were agreed to unanimously. *Id.* at 2–6.

legally enforceable. The president of the American Federation of Labor (AFL) in the late-nineteenth and early-twentieth century, Sam Gompers, believed that trade agreements should be enforced by the same mechanism by which they were initially obtained—economic weapons. He was opposed to legal enforcement of collective agreements because he feared it would insert the government into the otherwise private world of free contract. Gompers and other labor leaders of the era were suspicious of government due to the hostile treatment unions had received at the hands of the courts. Courts in the early twentieth century did not hesitate to issue injunctions against peaceful strikes on the basis of ex parte petitions from employers. They jailed union leaders who refused to obey strike injunctions, interpreted anti-trust laws to make labor boycotts unlawful, and used the power of judicial review to nullify labor's hard-won legislative gains.[6] As a result of these experiences with the courts, Gompers was determined to avoid government involvement in labor-management affairs.[7]

In addition to the unions' reluctance to subject collective agreements to judicial enforcement, early twentieth century courts refused to treat such agreements as enforceable legal obligations. Most courts refused to permit unions to sue to enforce collective agreements because unions were not incorporated and hence had no juridical personality under the common law.[8] Without legal personality, they could not bring an action in their own name in a court of law. Courts also refused to permit individual members to enforce particular terms and conditions contained in trade agreements on the ground that the agreements were not employment contracts in a conventional sense. Trade agreements, said the courts, did not guarantee any particular worker the right to a job nor did they obligate any particular worker, or the union, to work for an employer. Trade agreements thus lacked "mutuality of obligation," and therefore courts refused to enforce them.[9] Further, when unions sought equitable remedies to enforce closed shop clauses, they were rebuffed on the ground that the individual union members had an adequate remedy at law.[10]

---

[6] Felix Frankfurther & Nathan Greene, *The Labor Injunction* (1930); Victoria Hattam, *Labor Visions and State Power* (1993); William Forbath, *Law and the Shaping of the American Labor Movement* (1991).

[7] Samuel Gompers, *Seventy Years of Life and Labor* 26 (Nick Salvatore, ed., 1984); Harold C. Livesay, *Samuel Gompers and Organized Labor in America* 132–33 (1978).

[8] *See, e.g.*, Burnetta v. Marceline Coal Co., 180 Mo. 241, 79 S.W. 136 (1904). *See generally* William G. Rice, Jr., *Collective Labor Agreements,* 44 Harv. L. Rev. 572, 607 (1931). *See also* Edward H. Warne, *Corporate Advantages Without Incorporation* 668 (1920), and cases cited therein.

[9] *See, e.g.*, St. Louis, Iron Mountain & So. Ry. v. Mathews, 64 Ark. 398 (1897).

[10] *See* Stone Cleaning & Pointing Union v. Russell, 77 N.Y.S. 1049, 1050 (S. Ct., Spec. Term, N.Y. Co. 1902) (refusing to enjoin employer breach of closed shop provision because

The non-enforceability of collective agreements had both a positive and a negative aspect for unions. On the positive side, unions could not be liable when they breached collective agreements by going on strike in the face of a no-strike clause. On the other hand, unions could not turn to a court for enforcement of provisions that benefitted them as institutions, such as clauses requiring employers to use union labels or maintain closed shops. These clauses were important because in industries composed of many small employers, successful maintenance of closed shops and union labels was critical to union growth. Non-enforceability deprived unions of these organizational protections.[11] Non-enforceability also meant that individual workers were unable to sue employers to collect wages or other benefits that were promised in their collective agreements.

Lacking legal channels for the enforcement of trade agreements, some unions attempted to create enforcement mechanisms in the trade agreements themselves, such as by requiring the employer to pay a performance bond which would be forfeited in the event of breach. However, courts usually refused to enforce the bonds, holding that the underlying trade agreements were obtained under duress or were otherwise unenforceable.[12]

Some agreements set up primitive arbitration mechanisms, but those mechanisms also did not solve the enforcement problem. Arbitration systems at the turn of the century did not involve neutral decisionmakers but rather were mechanisms for the principals in a dispute to meet and confer to discuss a disputed matter. They looked more like

employment in question was neither unique nor extraordinary, so that plaintiff, "if it has any cause of action, will have an adequate remedy at law, just as would any other employe wrongfully discharged"); Schwartz v. Driscoll, 186 N.W. 522 (Mich. 1922) (refusing to issue injunction to enforce union's closed shop clause on the ground that, "an injunction will not lie to compel [an employer] to refrain from breaking his contract with his employee and to retain the latter in his service when he is not acceptable to him for service of that character, as a court of equity will not by means of an injunction compel the affirmative acceptance by the employer of the personal services of his employee from day to day; besides the remedy of the employee at law for damages is adequate and complete").

[11] *See, e.g.*, Curran v. Galen, 46 N.E. 297 (N.Y.1897) (closed shop agreement unlawful as violative of public policy); accord, Berry v. Donavan, 74 N.E. 603 (Mass. 1905); Master Horseshoer's Protective Ass'n v. Quinlivan, 82 N.Y.S. 288 (App. Div. 1st Dept. 1903) (enjoining strike by union attempting to force employers to utilize union label).

[12] *See, e.g.*, Statement of Henry White, General Secretary of United Garment Workers of America, 1 National Civic Federation Monthly Review, at 4–5 (1903) (courts would not enforce performance bonds when employers breached because trade agreements were obtained under duress). *See also* Davis v. Bonn, 37 N.Y.S. 688 (S. Ct., App. Term, 1st Dept. 1896) (union could not collect on performance bond because union breached collective agreement first); Jacobs v. Cohen, 90 N.Y.S. 854 (App. Div., 2d. Dept. 1904) (refusing to enforce employer's performance bond to secure enforcement of closed shop because closed shop clause violates public policy).

negotiation than arbitration and on serious issues, they almost invariably deadlocked.[13] In addition, courts in that period would not compel parties to arbitrate against their wishes. Rather, they espoused the view that an agreement to arbitrate was revocable by either party prior to the time an arbitral award was rendered.[14]

The Three-Cornered Dilemma of the Collective Bargaining Agreement

The problematic nature of enforcement of collective bargaining agreements at common law reflected a deeper problem that had very specific practical consequences. A collective bargaining agreement is a three-cornered contract, negotiated between a union and an employer, yet specifying rights and obligations of the employer, the union, and individual employees. A union often is the party seeking to enforce the agreement, but most of the obligations in a typical collective agreement flow from the employer to the individual employee. Yet if a union cannot enforce an agreement, its role in the workplace is severely limited. At the same time, individual workers usually lack the means to enforce provisions bargained for their benefit.

Since the beginning of the twentieth century, courts have searched for an analogy that would clarify which party has obligations and which party can sue to enforce provisions in a collective bargaining agreement. Beginning about 1910, some state courts adopted the view that the collective bargaining agreement created a custom or a usage which individual union members then incorporated into their individual contracts of hire. Under this theory, an individual worker could sue on the basis of a provision in a collective agreement, but only if he could show that he knew of the custom or usage and had incorporated it into his employment agreement.[15] The usage approach did not enable unions to enforce provisions designed for the benefit of all, such as a union label or closed shop provision.

By the 1920's, some courts permitted individuals to sue to enforce collective agreements on a different theory, one that overcame limitations of the usage approach. The new theory held that unions negotiated agreements for the benefit of individual workers, so that the individuals

---

[13] *See* John R. Commons, *Herman Justi, in* 8 Encycl. Soc. Sci. 507–08 (1932) (describing turn-of-the-century coal agreements, in which differences over contract interpretation were referred to, and resolved by, union officials).

[14] *See, e.g.*, Tobey v. County of Bristol, 23 F. Cas. 1313, 1321 (C.C.D.Mass. 1845) (Story, J.). *See also* Katherine V.W. Stone, *Rustic Justice: Community and Coercion Under the Federal Arbitration Act,* 77 N.C. L. Rev. 931(1999) (recounting history of revocability doctrine).

[15] *See, e.g.*, Hudson v. Cincinnati, N.O. & T.P. Ry. Co., 152 Ky. 711, 154 S.W. 47, 48–50 (1913); Yazoo & M.V.R. Co. v. Webb, 64 F.2d 902 (5th Cir. 1933).

were third-party beneficiaries of the contract. These courts permitted individuals to enforce rights negotiated for their benefit.[16] However, the third-party beneficiary theory made it impossible for a union to renegotiate any term for which the beneficiaries' rights had "vested."[17] This theory afforded unions no role in administering contracts and settling grievances.

Some courts adopted a different theory, holding that unions acted as agents of the individual members when they negotiated collective agreements. Under the agency theory, a union had no independent interest in enforcing the agreement, and any member could modify the agreement by revoking the agency and agreeing to inconsistent or substandard terms.[18]

None of the prevailing theories of collective agreements provided a basis for a union to enforce an agreement on behalf of and yet independently of individual members.

In the 1920's, a few state courts broke with the prevailing common law approaches and permitted unions to enforce terms in collective agreements that dealt with the collective rights of union members. In 1922, in *Schlesinger v. Quinto,* a New York court granted a union an injunction to prevent the garment makers' association from restoring piece-rates, raising hours and reducing wages.[19] A few years later, the Supreme Court of Washington enjoined a laundry establishment from using a union label on its sales slips after its contract with the union had expired.[20] Similarly, in *Goldman v. Cohen,* the New York court issued an injunction preventing a company from moving its plant and operating with nonunion workers in violation of the closed shop clause of its collective bargaining agreement.[21] All of these suits upheld the right of unions to sue to enforce clauses in a collective agreement that benefitted the union itself or the collective rights of employees. Very few states in that decade permitted unions to sue to enforce contractual rights of individual members. Rather, even among courts that permitted unions to enforce collective rights in collective agreements, most took the view that individual rights could only be enforced by individual employees.[22] By the

---

[16] *See, e.g.*, Schlesinger v. Quinto, 201 A.D. 487, 194 N.Y.S. 401 (1st Dept. 1922).

[17] *See, e.g.*, Huston v. Washington Wood & Coal Co., 103 P.2d 1095, 1097 (Wash. 1940).

[18] *See, e.g.*, Mueller v. Chicago & N.W. Ry. Co., 194 Minn. 83 (1935).

[19] 201 A.D. 487, 194 N.Y.S. 401 (1922).

[20] Wetzel v. Clise, 148 Wash. 75 (1928).

[21] 222 A.D. 631 (1928). *Accord* Harper v. Int'l Bhd. of Electrical Workers, 48 S.W.2d 1033 (Tex. Civ. App. 1932) (enjoining employer to comply with closed shop provision in its labor contract).

[22] *See* James E. Pfander, *Judicial Purpose and the Scholarly Process: The* Lincoln Mills *Case,* 69 Wash. Univ. L.Q. 243, 286–87 (1991). *See also* Katherine Van Wezel Stone, *The Postwar Paradigm in American Labor Law*, 90 Yale L. J. 1509, 1518–21 (1981).

time the Wagner Act was passed in 1935,[23] there was still no widespread reliable mechanism for unions to enforce collective bargaining agreements.

The Wagner Act gave unions a right to organize and imposed on employers a duty to bargain with the majority representative. Because the statute was silent on the subject of enforcement of collective agreements, the matter remained in the state courts. Most state courts continued to treat individual rights in collective agreements as matters for individual, not union, enforcement throughout the 1930's and 40's.[24] Congress did not address the issue of the enforcement of collective bargaining agreements until 1947, when it enacted the Taft-Hartley Act.

The Use of Private Arbitration as a Substitute for Judicial Enforcement

Because of the difficulty of enforcing collective agreements in courts, some unions in the first half of the century turned to private arbitration. Arbitration today refers to dispute resolution systems designed by private parties in which they agree to designate a third-party neutral, or panel of neutrals, to hear and decide their dispute. The decision of the arbitrator, or arbitral panel, is final and binding. In the labor-management field, the parties have constructed many different types of arbitration systems to decide disputes over the interpretation and application of their collective agreements. They have also devised many different methods of selecting an arbitrator. Sometimes the third party is an outsider, selected for an absence of ties to either side. But sometimes the decisionmaker is a panel made up of representatives of the two sides, the union and the company, who then select a neutral. In arbitration, parties have the freedom to design their own procedures. Generally, evidence is presented without restriction by the rules of evidence or civil procedure. In the hearings, parties are given wide leeway to tell their stories. There is usually no discovery or motion practice. Cases are heard and decided in an informal setting.

Grievance arbitration was introduced into American labor relations in the 1910's and 20's in the garment industries, but was slow to spread to other industries.[25] Under then-existing law, arbitration did not ensure

---

[23] 49 Stat. 449 (1935).

[24] *See, e.g.*, Hall v. St. Louis–S.F. Ry, 224 Mo. App. 431 (1930) (denying union enforcement for individual wrongful discharge); Christiansen v. Local 680, Milk Drivers & Dairy Employees, 126 N.J. Eq. 508 (1940) (denying enforcement of severance pay for individuals). *See generally* James E. Pfander, *Judicial Purpose and the Scholarly Process: The* Lincoln Mills *Case,* 69 Wash. Univ. L.Q. 243, 287 (1991).

[25] *See* William Leiserson, *Constitutional Government in Industry*, 12 Am. Econ. Rev. 56 (Supp. 1922); Julius Cohen, *Law and Order in Industry* 61 (1916). *See also* Katherine Van

enforcement because common law courts at that time refused to enforce executory agreements to arbitrate.[26] Also, many unions were wary of empowering outsiders to decide disputes about the meaning of their contracts.[27] As a result, arbitration was not widely embraced by the labor movement in the early years of the century.

During World War II, the attitude of courts and unions toward grievance arbitration changed. The War Labor Board (WLB), intent on maintaining labor peace to ensure stable wartime production, made arbitration the preferred method for resolving workplace disputes. The WLB encouraged parties to include arbitration clauses in their collective bargaining agreements and accorded arbitration awards substantial deference. After the war, many WLB staff members became professional labor arbitrators and encouraged widespread adoption of arbitration to resolve collective bargaining disputes.[28]

In 1947, Congress enacted § 301 of the Labor Management Relations Act (LMRA), which provided:

> Suits for violation of contracts between an employer and a labor organization . . . may be brought in any district court of the United States having jurisdiction of the parties, without respect to the amount in controversy or without regard to the citizenship of the parties.[29]

On its face, this provision appeared to give federal courts jurisdiction to hear and decide disputes over the enforcement of collective bargaining agreements without indicating the substantive law to be applied. It was drafted by Senator Taft in order to give unions collective legal personality, to promote uniformity in enforcement, and to reject the individual employment contract theories that existed in the state courts.[30] Organized labor opposed it, fearing the law would make it easier for corporations to sue unions for breach of contract. A number of labor law

---

Wezel Stone, *The Postwar Paradigm in American Labor Law*, 90 Yale L. J. 1509, 1514 & n. 24 (1981).

26 *See* Kulukundis Shipping v. Amtorg Trading Corp., 126 F.2d 978 (2d Cir. 1942); *see also* Julius H. Cohen & Kenneth Dayton, *The New Federal Arbitration Law*, 12 Va. L. Rev. 265 (1926).

27 Steven Fraser, *Labor Will Rule: Sidney Hillman and the Rise of American Labor* (1991).

28 *See* James Atleson, *Labor and the Wartime State: The Continuing Impact of Labor Relations During World War II* 97–103 (1998); Dennis R. Nolan & Roger I. Abrams, *American Labor Arbitration: The Maturing Years*, 35 U. Fla. L. Rev. 557, 564–69 (1983).

29 29 U.S.C. § 185(a) (2000).

30 James E. Pfander, *Judicial Purpose and the Scholarly Process: The* Lincoln Mills *Case,* 69 Wash. Univ. L.Q. 243, 287, 287–304 (1991).

scholars also objected to judicial enforcement of collective agreements, fearing that it would supplant the emerging role of arbitration in resolving contractual disputes.[31] These scholars viewed collective bargaining under the NLRA as a system of self-regulation, by which management and labor devised rules for their mutual governance. They wanted the self-regulatory regime to function with a minimum of external interference.[32]

Section 301 in the Courts

Section 301(a) provided that contracts between an employer and a labor organization representing employees were enforceable in federal courts. Soon after its enactment, federal courts divided over whether the provision meant that unions could enforce all the provisions in collective bargaining agreements or merely those that benefitted unions as such. That is, some courts held that provisions in collective bargaining agreements that benefitted individual employees were not "contracts between an employer and a labor organization" but rather were individual contracts of employment and thus not covered by the statute.[33] To resolve this controversy, courts had to address the metaphysical debates about the essential nature of the three-cornered collective bargaining agreement.

Association of Westinghouse Employees v. Westinghouse Corporation was one case that posed the question.[34] The company had withheld one day's pay from some 4000 salaried workers who were represented by the plaintiff union. The union sued in a federal district court under § 301. It lost on the merits because the court found that the employer did not owe any wages. But on appeal, the court of appeals dismissed the case on jurisdictional grounds without reaching the merits. The appellate court said that for there to be jurisdiction under § 301, suit had to be brought on a contract between "an employer and a labor organization." The court considered whether the employer's obligation to pay wages to individual workers grew out of the employer's contract with the union. It

---

[31] *See, e.g.,* Harry Shulman, *Reason, Contract, and Law in Labor Relations,* 72 Harv. L. Rev. 999 (1955); Joseph Rosenfarb, *The Court and Arbitration*, Proc. of N.Y.U. Sixth Ann. Conf. on Labor Law 161 (1953). *But see* Archibald Cox, *Current Problems in the Law of Grievance Arbitration*, 30 Rocky Mtn. L. Rev. 247 (1958); Archibald Cox, *The Legal Nature of Collective Bargaining Agreements*, 57 Mich. L. Rev. 1 (1958); Archibald Cox, *Reflections upon Labor Arbitration*, 72 Harv. L. Rev. 1483 (1959) (arguing that courts should interpret § 301 in a manner that is respectful of the special role of labor arbitration).

[32] *See generally* Katherine V.W. Stone, *The Post–War Paradigm in American Labor Law,* 90 Yale L. J. 1509 (1981) (describing ideology of pro-arbitration labor law scholars).

[33] *See, e.g.*, Ass'n of Westinghouse Salaried Employees v. Westinghouse Corp., 210 F.2d 623 (3d Cir. 1954).

[34] *Id.*

reviewed the usage, agency and third-party beneficiary theories of collective agreements but ultimately adopted what it termed an "eclectic" view in which provisions in collective agreements that redounded directly to the benefit of workers were part of individual contracts of employment and provisions that benefitted unions, such as dues checkoff and union security provisions, were "contracts between an employer and a labor organization." According to the court, unions could sue under § 301 to enforce provisions that benefitted unions, but could not sue under § 301 to enforce unpaid wage claims or other individual matters. An employer who failed to pay a worker the negotiated wage "breached, not its collective contract with the union, but its contract of hire with that individual employee." Accordingly, the court dismissed the case for lack of jurisdiction and held that § 301 did not confer jurisdiction for unions to enforce wage provisions in collective bargaining agreements.

The Vision and Strategy of Arthur Goldberg

Arthur Goldberg, then General Counsel for the Congress of Industrial Organization (CIO) and the United Steelworkers of America (USWA), followed the § 301 cases closely.[35] Goldberg, a Harvard Law School graduate, practiced labor law in Chicago in the late 1930's, representing CIO unions. During the war he worked with the Office of Strategic Services, the precursor to the CIA, assisting trade unionists in Europe organize resistance to the Nazi regime. After the war, Goldberg joined labor circles in Washington, and in March, 1948 was selected by CIO President Philip Murray to be the CIO and USWA General Counsel. Goldberg was hired to replace Lee Pressman, who had been dismissed from his position as General Counsel for his communist affiliations.[36]

At the CIO, Goldberg hired three associates—Tom Harris, David Feller, and Elliot Bredhoff—and together they were given a free hand to select labor cases to take to the Supreme Court and to file amicus briefs in cases already scheduled for Supreme Court review. Tom Harris had been chief of litigation at the Office of Alien Property Custodian, then an important department within the Department of Justice. Harris recommended Goldberg also hire one of his former colleagues at the Justice Department, David Feller. Feller was a Harvard law school graduate who had been an editor of the Harvard Law Review and a clerk to Supreme Court Justice Fred Vinson. Feller recommended that Goldberg hire Elliot Bredhoff, a new Yale Law School graduate who had been editor of the Yale Law Journal.

---

[35] Arthur Goldberg later served as U.S. Secretary of Labor in 1961, Associate Justice of the Supreme Court from 1962 to 1965, and U.S. Representative to the United Nations from 1965 to 1968.

[36] David Stebenne, *Arthur J. Goldberg: New Deal Liberal* (1996).

Goldberg interpreted his mandate from the CIO as safeguarding the interests of the entire labor movement and, indeed, the public interest generally. Goldberg had developed an ardent faith in arbitration as a result of his work with the USWA, a union whose members were deeply concerned about issues of work rules and shop floor governance. In 1947, before Arthur Goldberg joined the USWA, the union had negotiated a master agreement with U.S. Steel and several other steel companies that placed severe restrictions on management's right to set or revise work rules. In the 1952 contract negotiations, U.S. Steel demanded changes in the work rules provisions of the agreement and asked that management be given the right to change job assignments, work schedules, and incentive pay rates at will. Goldberg, as chief negotiator, refused to concede on work rules because he viewed management's demand as an effort to dilute union power on the shop floor and thus potentially undermine union member support. The union struck for a month over the issue of work rules and ultimately won the right to retain its work rule restrictions.[37] The USWA's focus on work rules and its determination to limit management's prerogatives over shop floor decisions made arbitration essential because arbitration was the only practical method the union had to enforce whatever power it negotiated over shop floor governance.

In 1959 the steel companies again tried to reassert management prerogatives and limit the union's input into work rules, and again the union resisted. Union President, David MacDonald, contended that the company was trying to turn the union into a company union. He believed that a union that could only negotiate wages and benefits was not a real union; to be a real union, a union had to have a role in workplace governance.[38] The issue of work rules proved to be an important issue in the four-month steel strike that ensued. Although the union again prevailed in its efforts to retain its power over work rules, it became apparent to Goldberg and his associates that the only way to realize that power was to have an effective enforcement mechanism for shop floor grievances. Hence it was important to defend the autonomy of labor arbitration.

The Westinghouse Employees and Lincoln Mills Cases

As General Counsel of the CIO, Goldberg asked his newly formed legal staff to watch the lower federal courts for issues of importance to the labor movement as a whole and assist in those cases in every possible way. The Third Circuit opinion in *Westinghouse Employees* caught the attention of David Feller, who understood that the issue at stake was

---

[37] *Id.* at 89–95.

[38] *Id.* at 203.

whether § 301 could be used by unions to enforce their members' rights contained in collective bargaining agreements.[39] The court of appeals decision ruled out such a possibility, so Feller sought and obtained the consent of the local union to petition the Supreme Court for certiorari review.

In his brief to the Supreme Court, Feller advanced a comprehensive theory of collective bargaining agreements. He argued that the collective bargaining agreement was a unique institution that did not fit into conventional legal categories, even the "eclectic" one the court of appeals espoused. Rather, Feller argued, a collective bargaining agreement is but one part of a continuing relationship that includes the negotiation of the agreement and its on-going administration through grievance processing. The court of appeals, he claimed, had incorrectly concluded that the union's role in an agreement ceased once a formal contract was signed, and that the further relationship between the employer and the employees was governed by individual contracts of hire. To the contrary, Feller argued:

> Once we accept, as we must, the proposition that collective bargaining is a continuing process, and that the settlement of grievances is part of that process, then the legal requirement that in collective bargaining the union chosen by the majority is the exclusive representative of all necessarily excludes the view that the individual employee owns, and owns exclusively, the right to bring suit upon a grievance. For a suit for breach of contract is, in essence, the same thing as a grievance.... A legal theory that excludes the collective group—the union—from the suit at law is, we believe, incompatible with a system in which the collective group participates, and indeed controls, the processing of a grievance.[40]

To bolster his argument, Feller appended to his brief a scholarly essay, written by labor economist Jack Barbash, on the nature of the collective bargaining agreement. Barbash stressed the continuous nature of collective bargaining and the union's central role in negotiating, administering, and enforcing collective bargaining agreements.[41]

The Court, in a plurality opinion, rejected Feller's argument. Justice Frankfurter, writing for Justices Burton, Minton and himself, opined that if the union were correct, § 301 might pose constitutional questions because it appeared to be a bare grant of jurisdiction without creating a

---

[39] David E. Feller, *How the Trilogy Was Made*, Proc. of the 47th Ann. Mtg., Nat'l Acad. of Arbitrators 329, 334 (1995).

[40] Brief for Petitioner at 40, Ass'n of Westinghouse Salaried Employees v. Westinghouse Electric Corp., 348 U.S. 437 (1955).

[41] *Id.* at 49–90.

new substantive law. As such, § 301 would violate Article III because it would create federal jurisdiction for cases that did not pose a federal question or have diversity of citizenship. To duck the constitutional issue, Frankfurter found that each individual worker had a cause of action for breach of contract in state court, and on that basis, he upheld the court of appeals' dismissal for lack of jurisdiction.

Arthur Goldberg and David Feller were intent on reversing the *Westinghouse Employees* decision. They found an opportunity in *Textile Workers v. Lincoln Mills*, in the Fifth Circuit.[42] There the union brought a § 301 action in a federal court to force an employer to comply with a promise to arbitrate grievances over work assignments. *Lincoln Mills*, unlike *Westinghouse Employees*, involved a union's suit to enforce a contractual provision that benefitted the union rather than the individual union members. On the basis of that distinction, the district court had upheld the union's cause of action and granted it an injunction compelling arbitration. However, the court of appeals reversed. It found that there was jurisdiction under § 301, but it applied the common law rule against granting specific enforcement of promises to arbitrate in commercial contexts, and held that the union was not entitled to equitable relief.[43]

Goldberg and Feller appealed the decision in *Lincoln Mills* to the Supreme Court. In their brief, they stressed that labor arbitration should not be subject to the same restrictive common law treatment as commercial arbitration, because "[l]abor arbitration, unlike commercial arbitration, is not a substitute for litigation. It is a substitute for a strike."[44] With labor arbitration, they argued, the "traditional rule against the enforcement of commercial arbitration agreements [is] inapplicable," and hence the Court had both jurisdiction and power to grant the union's requested relief.[45] They also addressed the lurking constitutional question of § 301 raised by Frankfurter in *Westinghouse*. They argued that § 301(a) was substantive because it provided for substantive enforceability of an agreement to arbitrate.[46] They also distinguished

---

42 230 F.2d 81 (5th Cir. 1956).

43 The court invoked a rule, well established in the commercial context, that executory agreements to arbitrate could not be specifically enforced. It further held that a collective bargaining agreement is a contract of employment for purposes of the United States Arbitration Act, 9 U.S.C. § 1 (2000), and was thus excluded from the operation of that statute. It also found that there was no substantive law in § 301 that would change these common law and statutory principles. Having found no right to relief under § 301 or the law of arbitration, the court held that there was no enforceable right to specific performance of the promise to arbitrate.

44 Brief for Petitioner at 8, Textile Workers v. Lincoln Mills.

45 *Id.* at 8–9.

46 *Id.* at 10.

Westinghouse on the ground that it involved individual wage claims whereas *Lincoln Mills* involved "a claim [that] is peculiarly a union claim."[47]

The union won *Lincoln Mills*. Justice Douglas, writing for the majority, drew much of his reasoning from the Goldberg–Feller brief. He held that § 301 was constitutional and that it gave unions the right to injunctive relief to enforce contractual promises to arbitrate.[48] The Court also stated that the substantive law to be applied in § 301 cases could be derived from the congressional intent to promote arbitration of disputes under collective bargaining agreements. While the *Lincoln Mills* Court upheld the constitutionality of § 301, Douglas avoided the difficult conceptual questions about the nature of collective bargaining agreements. Instead, he wrote that federal courts should fashion a judicial common law of collective bargaining agreements in subsequent cases, looking to analogous state and federal law for guidance.

Although *Lincoln Mills* was a victory for the union, the outcome distressed many in the labor relations community. The National Academy of Arbitrators devoted a day to a discussion of the case in its 1959 annual meeting, where a number of prominent speakers predicted that *Lincoln Mills* would prove to be a "disaster for the labor arbitration process." Benjamin Aaron expressed the prevailing sentiment when he stated that the decision was "almost certain to be disruptive ... [because] judges are poorly informed about industrial relations at the plant level [and therefore would] apply principles or attitudes that are generally inimical to the arbitration process and to the best interests of the parties."[49] He said that the present trend toward increased judicial enforcement of collective bargaining agreements would nullify the system of self-government the parties erected through the collective bargaining relationship. Other scholars and practitioners at the meeting seconded Aaron's view that it was dangerous for unions to involve courts in enforcing collective agreements because courts had proven themselves for decades to be unsympathetic to labor's concerns.

Archibald Cox shared his colleagues' concern about the dangers of judicial involvement in arbitration, but cautioned that such involvement was now inevitable. He thus urged the National Academy to articulate a view of the role of arbitration in collective bargaining that would educate courts about the danger of interference and convince courts to defer all substantive issues to arbitration. To illustrate his point, he discussed a

---

[47] *Id.* at 60.

[48] 353 U.S. 547 (1957).

[49] Benjamin Aaron, *On First Looking in the* Lincoln Mills *Decision*, Proc. of the 12th Ann. Mtg., Nat'l Acad. of Arbitrators 1 (1959).

case in which a court refused to order a company to arbitrate a grievance that it claimed was frivolous. He said, in a point later adopted by Justice Douglas in the *Steelworkers' Trilogy*, that

> [b]randing a claim as frivolous is hardly more than an expression of the strength of one's own conviction. What one man considers frivolous another may find meritorious. Frivolous cases, more often, are taken, and are often expected to be taken, to arbitration. The cathartic value of arbitrating even a frivolous grievance on which employees place value balances the inconvenience and cost.[50]

David Feller was in attendance at the meeting and responded to criticisms of the *Lincoln Mills* decision. He acknowledged that he had pursued the case because he believed it was in unions' best interest to make collective agreements enforceable in the federal courts under § 301. The alternatives, he admonished, were either non-enforcement or enforcement in state courts, neither of which was preferable. He also informed the gathered experts that he and Arthur Goldberg had already embarked on a litigation strategy that would affirm unions' use of § 301 as a tool for enforcing collective bargaining agreements and at the same time would keep courts out.[51] Their strategy was to make arbitration, not courts, the primary forum for hearing and deciding disputes arising under collective bargaining agreements. They achieved this objective three years after *Lincoln Mills,* in the *Steelworkers' Trilogy.*

Factual Background and Prior Proceedings

After their victory in *Lincoln Mills,* Goldberg and Feller wanted to solidify the status of labor arbitration as the primary institution for the enforcement of collective agreements. Goldberg and his associates found three cases in the lower courts that posed issues key to their objective of expanding *Lincoln Mills* and bolstering the autonomy of arbitration. It was fortuitous that the three cases all came from the United Steelworkers' Union, Goldberg's original and primary union client.

United Steelworkers v. American Manufacturing Company

The first case in the *Trilogy* was that of James Sparks, discussed above, who was injured on the job and who agreed, in a workers' compensation settlement, that he was twenty-five percent disabled.[52] When Sparks attempted to return to work, the company refused to

---

[50] Archibald Cox, *Reflections Upon Labor Arbitration in the Light of the* Lincoln Mills *Case*, Proc. of the 12th Ann. Mtg., Nat'l Acad. of Arbitrators 24, 63 (1959).

[51] Remarks of David Feller, Proc. of the 12th Ann. Mtg., Nat'l Acad. of Arbitrators 14, 21–22 (1959).

[52] *American Manufacturing* Record. The facts of the case are described in the opening paragraphs of this chapter.

permit it. The union filed a grievance claiming that the company's refusal to reinstate Sparks was a violation of his seniority rights under the collective bargaining agreement. The company denied the grievance and refused to arbitrate, even though the collective agreement contained a clause that provided:

> Any disputes, misunderstandings, differences or grievances arising between the parties as to the meaning, interpretation and application of the provisions of this agreement, which are not adjusted as herein provided, may be submitted to the Board of Arbitration for decision.[53]

The company argued that the management rights clause of the collective agreement gave it the right to make unilateral decisions about hiring, suspending, transferring, or discharging employees on any ground that might affect plant efficiency. It further argued that by accepting the workers' compensation settlement, Sparks admitted that he was not able to perform the job and so should be estopped from making any contrary arguments. The company asserted that the grievance was patently frivolous and hence it had no obligation to arbitrate.

Sparks' grievance posed a simple question: Could he return to work after admitting that the prior accident left him twenty-five percent disabled? The grievance provoked a prolonged lawsuit not about Sparks' ability to do his job, but about who should make that decision. If there had been no union, the company would have an unchallenged right to make such determinations. But once there was a union with a contract containing a seniority clause, a just-cause-for-dismissal clause, a management rights clause, and an arbitration clause, the issue became more complicated. The company contended that whether Sparks had the ability to perform his work was a matter for unilateral management decision pursuant to the management rights clause. The union could have countered that the company breached either the seniority or the just-cause-for-dismissal clause of the contract, and that a court should decide that question on the merits under its authority in § 301. The union did not do so, however. Instead it argued that the contract gave Sparks, and the union, a contractual right to have the issue heard by an arbitrator, and the arbitrator rather than a court should decide whether Sparks could return to work.

The district court granted the employer's motion for summary judgment. It held that because Sparks had admitted to being twenty-five percent disabled, he was estopped to claim that he was fully capable of performing his work. On appeal, the Sixth Circuit affirmed, but for a different reason. The appellate court reviewed evidence of Sparks' medical condition and photographs showing the dangerous nature of the work

---

[53] Collective Bargaining Agreement, *American Manufacturing* Record at 7–8.

and concluded that the evidence cast serious doubt on Sparks' claim that he was able to work at his former position. Accordingly it held that his grievance was "frivolous, patently baseless" and thus "not subject to arbitration under the collective bargaining agreement between the parties."[54] Goldberg and Feller, on behalf of the USWA, sought certiorari in the Supreme Court.

United Steelworkers of America v. Warrior & Gulf Navigation

In *United Steelworkers of America v. Warrior & Gulf Navigation*, the issue was also whether the court should order the employer to arbitrate a grievance. The grievance concerned the company's contracting out of maintenance work from its Chicksaw, Alabama, plant to a nonunion dry dock firm. The grievance was filed on behalf of several workers who were laid off, and who contended that they would have been employed and retained their seniority rights if the company had not subcontracted their work. The grievance alleged that the subcontract violated the no-lockout and nondiscrimination provisions in the collective bargaining agreement, and was subject to the arbitration clause.

In *Warrior & Gulf*, the arbitration clause was not as broad as the clause in *American Manufacturing*. Rather the *Warrior & Gulf* arbitration clause provided:

> [M]atters which are strictly a function of management shall not be subject to arbitration under this section.
>
> Should differences arise between the Company and the Union or its members employed by the Company as to the meaning and application of the provisions of this Agreement, or should any local trouble of any kind arise, there shall be no suspension of work on account of such differences, but an earnest effort shall be made to settle such differences immediately in the following manner. . . .

The agreement then set forth a five-step grievance procedure, culminating in arbitration before an impartial umpire and provided that "[t]he decision of the umpire shall be final."[55]

The company refused to arbitrate so, in October 1958, the union brought suit under § 301 to compel arbitration of the subcontracting dispute. The union made several arguments. First, it asserted that the arbitration clause made the dispute arbitrable because it extended the arbitration obligation to "any local trouble." It maintained that subcontracting of bargaining unit work was "local trouble" and thus arbitrable.

---

[54] 264 F.2d 624, 628 (6th Cir. 1959).

[55] Section 10 of Collective Bargaining Agreement Between Warrior & Gulf Navigation Co. and United Steelworkers of America, quoted in Petition for a Writ of Certiorari at 3–4 from the Fifth Circuit Court of Appeals, No. 360 (October Term 1959).

Second, the union claimed that contracting out was not "strictly a function of management" under this agreement because the contract contained limits on management's right to subcontract. Specifically, it contended that the no-lockout and nondiscrimination provisions operated as limitations on management's right to subcontract bargaining unit work to nonunion enterprises.

The company moved to dismiss the complaint. It claimed that the contracting-out dispute was "strictly a function of management," and therefore grievances about contracting out were contractually excluded from arbitration. It also alleged that it had engaged in subcontracting of maintenance work continually, without any grievance being filed, so its right to do so was established by past practice. It further argued that the union had attempted to restrict the company's subcontracting practices during negotiations and had failed to achieve a limitation on management's pre-existing right to engage in unfettered subcontracting. It accused the union of attempting, through the lawsuit, to "have the contract 'judicially' amended to give it a benefit which it voluntarily traded away for other benefits in collective bargaining negotiations."[56]

The case came before U.S. District Judge Daniel Thomas on October 30, 1958. The judge reserved ruling on the company's motion to dismiss and held a hearing on the merits. The union called as witnesses several employees from Warrior & Gulf who had been laid off for lack of work when the company transferred maintenance work to Harrison Brothers Dry Dock Company. One laid off employee testified that since his layoff he had been working at Harrison Dry Dock on the same barges that he had worked on at Warrior & Gulf, doing the same tasks under the supervision of the same foreman who had directed his work at Warrior & Gulf. The employee testified that because Harrison was nonunion, it did not pay him the benefits he would have received from Warrior & Gulf.

At that point and on several instances thereafter, Judge Thomas interrupted the testimony to inquire whether the testimony had anything to do with the case. The judge stated that he understood the sole issue to be whether the parties were required to arbitrate. Ironically, it was the company, not the union, which defended the line of testimony. The company's attorney argued that such facts were important to its defense that there had been a continuous practice of subcontracting to which the union had acquiesced. The judge permitted the testimony to continue, and on cross-examination, the employee-witness admitted that he had seen the company subcontract a considerable portion of repair work from time to time during his eight years at the company. Several other witnesses for the union offered similar testimony. Even the presi-

[56] Defendant's Answer, Third Defense, in Record in the United States Supreme Court, United Steelworkers of America v. Warrior & Gulf, Case No. 443 (October Term 1959).

dent of the union testified that subcontracting repair work had been a continuous practice during his twelve years at the company.

When it was the company's turn to present its case, its first witness was its vice president, who gave a detailed account of the Chicksaw plant's fluctuating workforce and a history of its subcontracting. The vice president also described the negotiations for the current collective bargaining agreement. He said that the company had, in negotiations, rejected the union's demand that the firm discontinue its subcontracting practice. The vice president also said that the issue had also been raised in 1952, and then too the company had refused to restrict its right to subcontract.

At the end of the testimony, the court took the matter under advisement without benefit of closing argument or briefs. Shortly thereafter, the court ruled for the company on the basis of the factual evidence from the hearing. The judge made findings of fact concerning the company's continuous contracting-out practices and the union's knowledge of those practices. He also found that the union had sought in negotiations to limit the company's right to subcontract but had not succeeded. The court concluded that "[t]he labor contract does not prohibit, and is not susceptible to being interpreted to require that defendant is prohibited from contracting out work." He further held that the contract did not give the union or its members a right to have the issue arbitrated. He opined that "[t]he right to contract out work is an inherent, traditional right of management which may not be questioned or subjected to arbitration in the absence of an ... express limitation thereof set forth in the labor contract."

On appeal to the Fifth Circuit, Judge Tuttle affirmed the district court. He relied on the district's court findings concerning the history of the negotiations and the company's subcontracting practices to conclude that subcontracting was not subject to arbitration under the agreement. Judge Rives dissented. He contended that the dispute turned on the meaning of the term "lock-out" under the agreement, and thus it was a "local dispute" that should be arbitrated under the arbitration clause in the contract. He also accused the district court of making findings of fact which, while perhaps relevant to the merits of the grievance, did not bear on the issue of the case—the issue of arbitrability.

United Steelworkers of America v. Enterprise Wheel and Car Corp.

The third case in the *Trilogy* grew out of a dispute between the Steelworkers' Union and the Enterprise Wheel and Car Corp. in West Virginia. It began January 17, 1957, when William Slone and ten other employees walked off their jobs to protest the treatment of a fellow employee who had been dismissed for unauthorized absences. The company dismissed the ten, claiming they had quit their jobs when they engaged in a wildcat strike. The collective bargaining agreement had a grievance procedure, culminating in arbitration, that applied to all disputes about the meaning or application of the agreement. It also had a provision that made disputes about discharge explicitly subject to the grievance procedure.

The union brought a grievance about the dismissal of all eleven employees, but the company refused to arbitrate. The union successfully brought an action in court to compel the employer to arbitrate the employees' discharges. Arbitration was held on April 6. However, in the arbitration hearing, the company argued that the grievance was moot because the collective agreement had expired on April 4, 1957, and no new one had been negotiated.

The union prevailed in arbitration. The arbitrator ruled that although the walk-out was not justified, the employer had violated its contractual obligation to suspend prior to discharge. Therefore he found the discharge to be without good cause. He ordered the employees reinstated with back pay, but imposed a disciplinary penalty of ten days.[57] The arbitrator rejected the company's mootness argument by stating:

> Not only was the Agreement effective during and for several months after the grievance arose, but, even after that, the Union continued as the representative and collective bargaining agent for the grievants and all other employees in the unit. Their status as employees continued, during the subsequent period of negotiations for contract renewal. They were protected by the law from improper discrimination or termination of their employment without good cause.[58]

The company refused to comply with the arbitrator's award, so the union returned to district court to enforce the award. The district court upheld the award. It rejected the employer's position that the arbitrator exceeded his authority by ordering back pay and reinstatement beyond the contract's expiration date. The court pointed out that it was the employer who delayed the grievance procedure by refusing to arbitrate initially. If the employer had complied with the grievance procedure at the outset, the employees could have been reinstated before the contract expired. The court concluded that the employer "cannot now complain of

---

[57] Decision and Award of Milton H. Schmidt in the Matter of Enterprise Wheel and Car Corp. and United Steelworkers of America, October 21, 1957, included in the Appendix to the Brief of Appellee, Enterprise Wheel and Car Corp. v. United Steelworkers of America, No. 538 (October Term 1959).

[58] *Id.* at 23.

the nearly 23 months of back pay awarded the employees who were improperly discharged."[59]

The court of appeals disagreed with the lower court about the mootness issue. The appellate court reasoned that once the contract expired, the employees could have been discharged at any time for any reason. On this basis, it concluded that as of April 4, 1957, the men lost the right to reinstatement or damages. The court of appeals therefore modified the judgment to eliminate reinstatement rights or any damage recovery for lost wages after the contract period.[60]

The Trilogy Cases in the Supreme Court

The Goldberg–Feller Legal Strategy

Goldberg and Feller had been watching all three cases as they worked their way through the lower courts because they posed questions left open by *Lincoln Mills.* In the middle of 1959, as the courts of appeals decisions came down, they developed a strategy to have the three cases heard together in the Supreme Court. In May 1959, the Sixth Circuit decided *American Manufacturing.* The Fourth Circuit decision in *Enterprise* was issued on June 16, 1959, and in July 1959, the Fifth Circuit decided *Warrior & Gulf.* As Feller later explained, "We now had three cases involving arbitration. All three involved the Steelworkers Union and we had lost all three. The question was how to maneuver the cases so that we would have what eventually came out to be the *Steelworkers Trilogy.*"[61] They decided to apply for certiorari review in a sequence that would maximize their chances to have all three cases taken up by the higher court.

In their view, *American Manufacturing* presented the simplest issue of the three—whether a court could refuse to order arbitration on the ground that a grievance was frivolous. Accordingly, they filed a petition for a writ of certiorari in *American Manufacturing* first, on August 28, 1959. Their petition emphasized that the case was important to resolve ambiguities left by *Lincoln Mills.*

Feller reasoned that getting the Court to grant certiorari in *Warrior & Gulf* was more complicated because the arbitration clause in that case exempted matters that were "strictly a function of management," invit-

---

59 168 F.Supp. 308, 313 (S.D. W.Va. 1958).

60 269 F.2d 327, 331 (4th Cir. 1959). The court of appeals also found that the award was incomplete because the precise cost of the ten-day penalties was not calculated for each of the eleven grievants. It ordered the parties back to arbitration to calculate the precise damage amounts.

61 David E. Feller, *How the Trilogy Was Made*, Proc. of the 47th Ann. Mtg., Nat'l Acad. of Arbitrators 329, 341 (1995).

ing a court to look at the underlying facts to determine the scope of the clause. He and his colleagues knew that the Supreme Court is generally reluctant to grant review in such fact-bound cases.[62] So on September 30, 1959, they filed a petition for a writ of certiorari in *Warrior & Gulf*, arguing that *Warrior & Gulf* presented the same problem as *American Manufacturing*, for which a certiorari petition was then currently pending. They wrote:

> In both cases, the essential question is the same: to what extent, if any, should a federal court, when asked to compel arbitration of a union's claim that an employer has violated a collective bargaining agreement, enter into an examination of the merits of that claim before directing that it be settled in the forum which the parties have specifically chosen to settle such claims.[63]

The Court granted certiorari in *American Manufacturing* on November 9. Getting the Court to grant review in *Enterprise* was even more problematic than the other two because, on the merits, the lower court's position was reasonable. There was logic as well as considerable precedent for the proposition that once a collective agreement expires, employees can be fired at any time and thus cannot be reinstated by an arbitrator. Goldberg and his associates applied for certiorari review in *Enterprise* on November 23. In their petition for review in *Enterprise*, the union lawyers pointed out that the issue there was closely related to the issue in *American Manufacturing,* in which certiorari had been already granted, and to the issue in *Warrior & Gulf,* in which a certiorari petition was pending. They argued that the question in all three cases was important to the "development of a sound body of federal law relating to grievance arbitration, as contemplated in *Textile Workers v. Lincoln Mills*, [because all three cases] raise the very fundamental question of the extent to which a court should concern itself with issues which the parties have agreed should be resolved through arbitration."[64]

The Supreme Court granted certiorari in *Warrior & Gulf* on December 7, and in *Enterprise* on January 11, 1960. By tying the issues in the three cases together, Goldberg and Feller succeeded in getting the Supreme Court to take all three. The Court set the three cases for argument on the same day.

---

62 *Id.*

63 Petition for a Writ of Certiorari at 9, United Steelworkers of America v. Warrior & Gulf Navigation Co., No. 443 (October Term 1959) (filed Sept. 30, 1959).

64 Petition for a Writ of Certiorari at 9, United Steelworkers of America v. Enterprise Wheel & Car Corp., No. 538 (October Term 1959) (filed Nov. 23, 1959).

THE BRIEFS OF THE PARTIES

Goldberg, together with Feller, Bredhoff and a new associate, Jerry Anker, wrote a single brief to present their arguments in all three cases. They argued that federal labor law policy requires courts to respect arbitration and refrain from reviewing the merits of a case when parties have agreed to settle their disputes in arbitration. They explained that the principle of deference to arbitration means that courts should not review the merits either before an arbitration hearing is held, when asked to enforce a promise to arbitrate, or after an arbitration award is issued. The union attorneys avoided discussing whether collective bargaining agreements created a usage, an agency or third-party beneficiary relationship. Instead they asserted that a collective agreement is not properly described as a contract at all, but "more nearly resembles a statute ... [that provides] a standard to govern future conduct."[65] They emphasized that a collective bargaining agreement is intended to apply to unanticipated situations, so that, like a statute, it often speaks in general terms which must then be applied in specific situations. But they also stated that a collective bargaining agreement is more than merely a statute: "[I]t is a complete code of standards to govern the employment relationship." As they explained,

> It provides not only the benefits which the employees will be entitled to and the rules for their distribution but also, by negative implication, what benefits they are not entitled to receive.... The agreement is fixed for the term and it therefore confers on management the right to take any action with respect to matters except as limited by the agreement. It contains, as it were, a Tenth Amendment.

The union lawyers' brief applied its analysis of the nature of collective bargaining agreements to the cases at hand by arguing that "the application of this code is as much a part of the collective bargaining process as is the negotiation of the code itself." To apply a collective bargaining agreement to a particular dispute, they maintained, requires " 'creative' interpretation" of a sort that is unfamiliar to judges in contract cases. "Grievance arbitration," they claimed,

> has its own body of jurisprudence, which is familiar to both labor and management.... Courts are by and large unfamiliar with this institution. It is not necessary that they become familiar with it, but it is necessary that they respect it and defer to it if it is to continue to operate effectively as Congress intended it should, as a peaceful method of resolving industrial disputes.

---

65 Brief for the Petitioner at 35, United Steelworkers of America v. American Manufacturing Co., et al., Nos. 360, 443, and 538 (October Term 1959).

They also maintained that arbitrators have the appropriate tools to understand not only the contractual language but the underlying nature and function of collective bargaining. In light of the special qualifications and methodology of the arbitrator, courts should order arbitration of all disputes, not merely those that the courts find to be meritorious. "[T]he role of the courts in enforcing grievance arbitration is simply to determine whether the union seeking arbitration is claiming that the employer violated the agreement. If that is the claim it is arbitrable."

In their specific discussion of *American Manufacturing*, they claimed that the lower court had incorrectly interpreted the contract and the evidence when it found that Sparks was unable to return to work. They presented their own construction of the contract and evidence to show that the court had gotten it wrong. Then they argued that the case was a "perfect illustration of the inability of courts to make a correct preliminary judgment on the merits of a grievance, and the absolute necessity of holding parties to their obligation to arbitrate all disputes concerning the proper interpretation and application of the agreement."

In their discussion of *Warrior & Gulf,* Goldberg and his associates criticized the lower court for using bargaining history and company practice to interpret the scope of the arbitration clause. They claimed that the court had improperly delved into the merits of the grievance. They also engaged in a detailed discussion of the contract to show that the clause precluding arbitration of issues that were "strictly a function of management" could only be understood in light of other clauses in the agreement, and hence should be interpreted not by a court but by an arbitrator.

When they got to the *Enterprise* case, their approach was a little different. There they argued that judicial review of arbitral awards should adopt the approach taken in commercial arbitration—that arbitral awards cannot be reviewed for errors or law or fact. They conceded that courts could reverse "decisions in which the arbitrator exceeds his jurisdiction, or where fraud, bribery, or some other flaw in the arbitration process itself can be demonstrated," but otherwise courts should not review arbitral awards on the merits.[66]

The three defendants chose not to submit a single unified brief. Instead, they each submitted a brief in their respective case. American Manufacturing's brief argued that Congress, in enacting § 301, had

[66] In their brief, Goldberg and his associates also argued that the expiration of a collective agreement should not prevent the enforcement of the award, because otherwise management would be able to postpone settlement of all grievances until after the agreements expired, undermining the role of grievance arbitration to promote peaceful collective bargaining. Brief for the Petitioner, United Steelworkers of America v. American Manufacturing Co., etc., Nos. 360, 443, and 538 (October Term 1959).

entrusted determination of breach of contract suits between labor and management to the district courts, not to arbitrators. Further, it maintained, Congress did not intend to make the courts "a mere dumb waiter to convey an alleged grievance, regardless of its evident baseless nature, to an arbitrator."[67] It presented authority from case law and scholarly commentary to the effect that a court should not order arbitration for a claim that is frivolous and patently baseless. The company brief did not join issue with the union argument about the inherent nature of the collective bargaining agreement or the role of arbitration in the labor-management relationship.

Warrior & Gulf's lawyers also argued that § 301 requires courts to scrutinize arbitration clauses, not merely to enforce them by rote. They called upon the Court to reject the union's "abstract principle of blind acceptance to the absolute autonomy of arbitration." Their brief stressed the evidence presented in the district court hearing indicating that: (1) the contract did not limit the company's right to contract out work; (2) the company had engaged in that practice throughout its existence; and (3) the union had tried without success on several occasions to negotiate for a contractual limitation on the company's right to contract out.[68] Because the issue of contracting out was, they contended, a function of management under the parties' agreement, the decision of the court of appeals denying arbitration should be upheld.

The lawyers for Enterprise Wheel urged the Court not to discard contract law principles altogether in interpreting collective bargaining agreements. They argued that "many legal doctrines are based on time-tested notions of fairness and sound public policy.... [Accordingly] in deciding the scope of the arbitrator—that is whether an obligation is within or without the context of the contract—the uniqueness of the industrial complex has no controlling force."[69] In this case, they asserted, the arbitrator had improperly modified the contract by "erroneously granting the eleven grievants back pay and reinstatement on a theory that they had employment security rights continuing even beyond the expiration of the collective bargaining contract." Because the contract had expired by the time of the arbitral hearing, and no new one was ever negotiated, the grievants were only able to recover monetary compensation from the time they were discharged to the date the contract expired.

[67] Brief for the Respondent at 13, United Steelworkers of America v. American Manufacturing Co., No. 360 (October Term 1959).

[68] Brief for Respondent Warrior & Gulf Navigation Co., at 22–24, United Steelworkers of America v. Warrior & Gulf Navigation Co., No. 443 (October Term 1959).

[69] Brief for the Respondent Enterprise Wheel and Car Corporation, United Steelworkers of America v. Enterprise Wheel and Car Corporation at 21–25, No. 538 (October Term 1959).

"All rights of the grievants arose from the contract and they were guaranteed protection from discharge without cause only until April 4, 1957."[70] The brief presented considerable case support for its argument that an arbitrator cannot award back pay or reinstatement beyond contract termination.

The Oral Argument

Oral argument for the three cases in the *Trilogy* was set for April 27 and 28, 1960. It was an unusual argument because each side was granted one hour for oral argument for each case—a total of three hours for each side. Goldberg was ill at the time, so David Feller argued *American Manufacturing* and *Warrior & Gulf* for the union and Elliot Bredhoff argued *Enterprise Wheel*. As Feller described it many year later, "With three hours . . . I had the opportunity, probably never to be repeated, given the Court's current manner of scheduling arguments, to really attempt to educate the Court on the nature of the arbitration process."[71]

Feller began his *American Manufacturing* argument by stating that the three cases all posed the question of the appropriate role of courts in enforcing arbitration agreements. All three involved grievances of a type that are heard every day and collective bargaining agreements that were normal in most respects. Yet, he said, "the decisions in these cases will have an impact on the practice of arbitration all over the country."[72] After presenting the facts, he criticized the lower courts for addressing the merits of Sparks' grievance. Feller asserted that when there is a broad arbitration clause, the court should only decide (1) if there is a question as to the meaning of the contract; and (2) if the employer has refused to arbitrate it.

Throughout his argument, Feller emphasized that there was an essential difference between commercial and labor arbitration. In commercial arbitration, parties devise a private court in place of a public court to decide their dispute, and if they do not arbitrate, they will litigate. Not so in labor arbitration. With labor disputes, parties who do not arbitrate will strike because, as Feller explained, historically unions have not looked to the courts to adjudicate their disputes. Justice Frankfurter intervened to inject the idea that in labor arbitration, unlike in commercial matters, arbitration is the apex of an entire structure governing industrial relations. Feller endorsed this view, stating that the

---

[70] *Id.* at 32.

[71] David E. Feller, *How the Trilogy Was Made*, Proc. of the 47th Ann. Mtg., Nat'l Acad. of Arbitrators 329, 344 (1995).

[72] This description of the oral argument and the quotations in this section are taken from the audio tapes of the Supreme Court oral argument of the three cases.

collective bargaining agreement is more than a contract. It is a code to govern the parties' relationship.

Justice Whitaker asked Feller whether parties had to submit to arbitration an issue they had not agreed to arbitrate. Feller said they did not; that courts should determine arbitrability and only require arbitration of that which the parties had agreed to arbitrate. However, Feller emphasized, if a court says a dispute is not arbitrable and if there is an applicable no-strike clause, the union would have no recourse. Thus, he admonished:

> [W]hen parties have agreed to arbitrate all questions of interpretation, and have also agreed to an absolute no-strike clause, barring the relief that the union would have otherwise had, in that case the court should construe the question [of the scope of] arbitration precisely as they say it, and as a matter of fact, if there are any doubts, they should give the broadest possible scope to the arbitrate clause.... [T]he consequence of saying it is not arbitrable is not that it is litigible [sic], but [that] this controversy is one in which the employer wins because the union has given up the right to strike.

Neither the justices nor opposing counsel pursued Feller's claim that the union would have no recourse if there were a no-strike clause and a grievance was held not arbitrable. No one raised the possibility that a union then could sue the employer for breach of contract on the merits under § 301. Rather, all accepted Feller's formulation, expressed earlier by Justice Douglas in *Lincoln Mills,* that for a union the *only* alternative to arbitration was a strike.

John Carriger, arguing for the American Manufacturing Company, did not contest any of Feller's arguments about the role of arbitration in labor disputes. Rather, he asserted that courts were obliged to weed out cases for arbitration where there was no issue to decide. Here, he said, the grievance was baseless because the grievant had admitted he was twenty-five percent disabled and could not do the job and the company had no work for a disabled man. In the pleadings, the union had presented no affidavit or other evidence that Sparks could do the job, so there was no evidence at all to establish his claim. Thus, according to Carriger, there was nothing to arbitrate.

In rebuttal, Feller succinctly summarized the differences between the parties. He said, "The company argues that a plaintiff who asks a court to enforce an agreement to arbitrate has to produce evidence on the merits—i.e., a prima facie case on the merits. We think that is wrong. A court is enforcing an agreement to arbitrate, not the seniority provision of the contract."

Immediately thereafter, the Court heard *Warrior & Gulf.* Feller began by conceding that this case was more difficult than *American*

Manufacturing because there was an "unusual arbitration agreement." Here there was a clause that precluded arbitration for items that were "strictly a function of management." Feller explained that in all grievances the parties dispute whether management has acted within its rightful authority. The clause at issue, he maintained, did not remove all such disputes from arbitration. Rather, it removed from the arbitration process only those disputes in which the union does not claim that management is limited by the agreement. Justice Whitaker pointed out, and Feller agreed, that in most grievances, management claims it was not restricted and the union claims it was restricted, either by the express or implicit terms of the agreement. The fact that a collective agreement contains implied as well as express clauses means that a court cannot know from the text itself whether an agreement restricts management. At this point, no one pressed Feller about the role of extrinsic evidence in determining arbitrability, although that became an issue later in the instant and the following case.

Feller devoted much of his *Warrior & Gulf* argument to trying to establish that the district court overstepped its legitimate role when it looked at extrinsic evidence about whether the contract permitted the company to contract out work. He said the district court should only have construed the arbitration provision. In response to a question by Justice Brennan about whether the history of contracting out at the company was relevant to the interpretation of the arbitration clause, Feller said it was not. He conceded that if the history of contracting out were introduced to show that it was part of the discussions of the exclusion in the arbitration clause itself, then it would be relevant, but that was not the limited purpose for which the evidence had been offered in this case. The district court, in Feller's view, was entitled to consider the history of the arbitration clause in order to interpret the scope of the promise to arbitrate, but the court should not interpret or consider the history of other substantive provisions of the contract—that was the task of the arbitrator. "In the guise of deciding arbitrability, a court should not actually decide what are management's rights to contract out or how they are limited."

Toward the end of the argument, Justice Stewart raised a hypothetical that several justices returned to in the next case. Justice Stewart asked whether a worker's claim for a \$4-an-hour wage would be arbitrable if the contract set a pay rate of \$3. Feller responded that if the claim were that it would be only fair to pay \$4, then it would not be arbitrable. But if the claim was that, under the contract, \$3 means \$4, Feller said, "Yes, it's a question of interpretation of the agreement."

Samuel Lang, arguing for Warrior & Gulf, began with the proposition that in collective bargaining negotiations, "a union is striving to take and a company is striving to hold." In this case, he said, the company had, without complaint by the union, engaged in contracting out throughout its eighteen years of existence. The union had tried on several occasions in contract negotiations to limit management's right to contract out, but had repeatedly failed. Additionally, the parties had negotiated an arbitration agreement that exempted matters "strictly a function of management" from the promise to arbitrate. Thus, Lang maintained, the parties by their past practice, negotiating history, and express contract had exempted contracting out grievances from the arbitration clause. Justice Frankfurter asked if the claim would be arbitrable if the union had not attempted to negotiate a no-contracting out clause in the past. He further asked how, in such a case, a court would know whether an issue was within management's rights. Lang responded that in such a case, "we wouldn't have a chance." Frankfurter next asked, "Is that because the court would have to decide what the management rights clause means?" Lang agreed that when there was no bargaining history to rely on, if a court denied arbitration, it was necessarily giving an interpretation of the management rights clause. Lang concluded by affirming that the institution of arbitration was highly desirable but that the court must retain power to decide arbitrability on the basis of the "real situation between the parties."

The following day, the Court heard arguments in *Enterprise Wheel & Car*. Elliot Bredhoff, representing the union, argued that a court, when asked to enforce an arbitral award, should look only at whether an arbitrator applied the contract, not whether the arbitrator was *correct* in his application. He contended that the court of appeals had erred when it refused to enforce the reinstatement provisions of the arbitration award and when it denied back pay beyond the contract's expiration.

Justice Frankfurter pursued Justice Stewart's hypothetical from the day before, in which a worker claimed that he should be paid $4 an hour even though the contract specified his rate as $3. Frankfurter asked whether extrinsic evidence—such as evidence that the parties had agreed that "$3" means "$4"—would be admissible on the question of arbitrability. Bredhoff said it would not. Chief Justice Warren then asked if they meant that if a grievant claims his case arises under the contract, no matter what the contract actually says, that it must go to arbitration. Bredhoff said yes. The Chief Justice responded, "Now I'm totally confused about all three cases." Bredhoff attempted to explain that "when an employee alleges claims of a violation of the contract, then he's entitled to have it go to arbitration." Justice Brennan attempted to clarify the union's position, stating that a grievant must show two things to have his case go to arbitration. First, he must show that the grievance arises under the contract, and second, that it is within the arbitration clause. Parol evidence can only be admitted about the negotiation of the arbitration clause itself. Bredhoff acceded to Brennan's characterization.

Justice Whitaker objected that with careful phrasing, a union could prevent review by a court of all issues of arbitrability. Bredhoff did not respond, but instead reserved time for rebuttal and sat down.

Representing Enterprise Wheel, William Beatty argued that the arbitral award was enforceable for the period before the collective agreement was in existence, but not for the period after its expiration. He asserted that this position, endorsed by the court of appeals, separated the valid and invalid portions of the arbitral award, thereby preserving the award. Justice Harlan then asked whether an arbitrator can decide whether an agreement authorizes an award after contract expiration. Beatty responded that an arbitrator is limited to things within the scope of his authority, and that the court must decide what is within the scope of the arbitrator's authority. Frankfurter asked whether an arbitrator has the power to determine what an ambiguous situation means if it is a permissible reading of the contract. He further suggested that "If the language used, plus whatever relevant material may be introduced from without, permits a construction, which if it had been spelled out would have been spelled out that way," then the arbitrator is exercising authority he is permitted to exercise. Beatty disagreed, asserting that the contract here was for one year, and that was the parties' bargain. Beatty said that all rights stem from the contract, and this one expired on April 4, 1957, so that there should be no remedy beyond that date.

David Feller gave a brief rebuttal, focusing primarily on the use of extrinsic evidence to decide questions of arbitrability. Returning to *Warrior & Gulf,* he argued that there the extrinsic evidence did not bear on the meaning of the arbitration clause, but only on the meaning of the management rights clause. He conceded, in response to further questions from the Court, that extrinsic evidence going to the meaning of the arbitration clause would be relevant and might be admissible. He concluded by stressing that courts have an important but narrow role in deciding issues of arbitrability. The court must decide if a claim arises under an agreement. If so, the merits must be left to the arbitrator.

Justice Douglas' Views on Self-Regulation

Feller and Bredhoff were not arguing to a blank slate. Justice Douglas, although silent during the argument, had written the opinion in *Lincoln Mills* that had adopted much of their reasoning. Further, Douglas had strong views about the importance of self-regulation and arbitration that grew out of his work at the Securities and Exchange Commission (SEC) in the 1930's. Douglas was the third Chairman of the SEC, serving from 1937–1939. Faced with the job of regulating an industry hostile to any kind of external regulation, he developed a vision of industry self-regulation.[73] As Douglas told a congressional committee in 1936:

> My philosophy was and is that the national securities exchanges should be so organized as to be able to take on the job of policing their members so that it would be unnecessary for the Government to interfere with that business.... Government would keep the shotgun, so to speak, behind the door, loaded, well oiled, cleaned, ready for use but with the hope it would never have to be used.[74]

As Chairman, Douglas called upon the New York Stock Exchange to reorganize so that it could effectively police itself. In 1938, the SEC approved the change it made, deferring to industry rule-making rather than imposing external standards of conduct. Similarly, in the over-the-counter securities market, Douglas encouraged dealers and brokers to organize into voluntary organizations that could engage in self-regulation. As a result, the National Association of Securities Dealers was formed. Douglas delegated to it the tasks of standard-setting, policing its members, and disciplining violators. Thus when Douglas was presented with the union's arguments in the Steelworkers' cases twenty years later, he was already a believer in the advantages of self-regulation and an advocate of judicial deference to internal governance systems established by voluntary associations.[75]

The Supreme Court Decisions

The decisions in the three cases of the *Steelworkers' Trilogy* were issued on June 20, 1960. The union won all three. In three broad and sweeping decisions, Justice Douglas, writing for the majority, adopted many of the arguments in the union's brief and redefined the framework for collective bargaining in the United States. The decisions made arbitration, not courts, the central institution for the enforcement of collective bargaining agreements. Douglas also established the principle of extreme judicial deference to private arbitration—a level of deference that was until then unheard of. The decisions also defined the collective bargaining agreement as a code of governance, an instrument of self-regulation, by which unions and management jointly engage in governance of the workplace and in which courts refrain from interference.

In *United Steelworkers of America v. American Manufacturing*, the Court ordered the company to arbitrate Sparks' grievance. In reaching

---

73 For a detailed discussion of Justice Douglas' views and actions supporting self-regulation at the SEC, see Katherine V.W. Stone, *Rustic Justice: Community and Coercion Under the Federal Arbitration Act*, 77 N.C. L. Rev. 931, 999–1001 (1999).

74 William O. Douglas, *Democracy and Finance* 82 (1940).

75 *See* Joel Seligman, *The Transformation of Wall Street: A History of the Securities and Exchange Commission and Modern Corporate Finance* (rev. ed. 1995).

this conclusion, Douglas adopted the union's position that a promise to arbitrate contained in a collective bargaining agreement is enforceable without regard to the court's view of the merits of the underlying grievance.[76] Douglas wrote that "the agreement is to submit all grievances to arbitration, not merely those that a court may deem to be meritorious." He further proclaimed that when asked to order a party to arbitrate, a court's role is "confined to ascertaining whether the party seeking arbitration is making a claim which on its face is governed by the contract." Douglas also adopted the union attorneys' characterization of the role of arbitration in the unionized workplace, stating:

> In the context of the plant or industry the grievance may assume proportions of which judges are ignorant.... The question is not whether in the mind of the court there is equity in the claim. Arbitration is a stabilizing influence only as it serves as a vehicle for handling any and all disputes that arise under the agreement.

In *United Steelworkers of America v. Warrior & Gulf*, the Court ordered the company to arbitrate the contracting out grievance.[77] In that opinion, Douglas discussed in detail the nature of the collective bargaining agreement. Echoing the union lawyers' arguments, Douglas wrote that labor arbitration was not subject to the restrictive rules that courts imposed on commercial arbitration:

> In the commercial case, arbitration is the substitute for litigation. Here arbitration is the substitute for industrial strife. Since arbitration of labor disputes has quite different functions from arbitration under an ordinary commercial agreement, the hostility evinced by courts toward arbitration of commercial agreements has no place here. For arbitration of labor disputes under collective bargaining agreements is part and parcel of the collective bargaining process itself.

Douglas also addressed the controversy about the essential nature of the collective bargaining agreement. He wrote, "It is more than a contract; it is a generalized code to govern a myriad of cases which the draftsmen cannot wholly anticipate. The collective agreement covers the whole employment relationship. It calls into being a new common law—the common law of a particular industry or of a particular plant." Douglas thus rejected contractual analogies and instead characterized collective bargaining as "a system of industrial self-government," using language remarkably similar to that in the union's brief. Douglas went on to clarify the central role of arbitration in that system:

---

[76] 363 U.S. 564 (1960).

[77] 363 U.S. 574 (1960).

> [T]he grievance machinery under a collective bargaining agreement is at the very heart of the system of industrial self-government. Arbitration is the means of solving the unforeseeable by molding a system of private law for all the problems which may arise and to provide for their solution in a way which will generally accord with the variant needs and desires of the parties. The processing of disputes through the grievance machinery is actually a vehicle by which meaning and content are given to the collective bargaining agreement.

In *Warrior & Gulf*, Justice Douglas even went beyond what the union had advocated in calling for courts to defer to arbitration. Acknowledging that arbitration could not be ordered unless parties had consented to arbitrate, he adopted a revolutionary approach to ascertaining the existence of consent. He stated:

> An order to arbitrate the particular grievance should not be denied unless it may be said with positive assurance that the arbitration clause is not susceptible of an interpretation that covers the asserted dispute. *Doubts should be resolved in favor of coverage.*[78]

This principle, known as the "presumption of arbitrability," puts the judiciary in the position of promoting labor arbitration. In this case, Douglas employed the presumption to find that the arbitration clause's exclusion of items that were "strictly a function of management" was too vague to demonstrate that the negotiators intended to preclude arbitration of disputes about contracting out. He eschewed consideration of the merits in interpreting the clause and criticized the lower court for using evidence about bargaining history in its construction of the arbitration clause.[79] Thus Douglas adopted a presumption of arbitrability in order to keep courts from interpreting collective bargaining agreements when deciding arbitrability.

Only three other justices agreed with Douglas' presumption of arbitrability. Justice Black took no part in the case and Frankfurter, Harlan and Brennan wrote a concurrence in which they refused to apply such a presumption. Instead, they reached their conclusion that the case was arbitrable by applying rules of construction to discern that the parties had not intended to limit the arbitrator's jurisdiction.

Justice Whitaker dissented. He cited evidence in the record that the employer had engaged in contracting out for nineteen years to which the union had acquiesced. He also noted that the union had tried and failed

---

[78] *Id.* at 582–83. (emphasis supplied).

[79] In *Warrior & Gulf*, Douglas directed a court to "view with suspicion an attempt to persuade it to become entangled in the construction of the substantive provisions of a labor agreement."

on several occasions to limit the employer's right to contract out. This, Whitaker asserted, demonstrated that far from consenting to arbitrate contracting out disputes, the company viewed contracting out as "strictly a function of management" and exempt from an obligation to arbitrate. Justice Whitaker was also highly critical of the newly-announced presumption, describing it as an unwarranted departure from the principle that arbitration must rest on consent of the parties.

In *United Steelworkers of America v. Enterprise Wheel and Car Corp.*, Justice Douglas held that the arbitrator's award should be enforced.[80] He announced the principle that an arbitral award should be enforced regardless of the court's view of the merits of the dispute. He set the standard of judicial review of arbitral awards as follows:

> [A]n arbitrator is confined to interpretation and application of the collective bargaining agreement; he does not sit to dispense his own brand of industrial justice. He may of course look for guidance from many sources, yet his award is legitimate only so long as it draws its essence from the collective bargaining agreement.

In that case, Douglas concluded that even though the arbitrator ordered back pay and reinstatement after contract expiration, the award could have been based on an interpretation of the contract and hence it should be enforced.

Douglas also addressed an issue, not discussed in the briefs of the parties, of whether to enforce an award when it was unclear whether it drew "its essence from the collective bargaining agreement" or from an external source. In the *Enterprise* arbitration, the arbitrator had stated that the grievants were entitled to reinstatement and back pay after the contract expired because "they were protected by the law from . . . termination of their employment without good cause." Not only was this an incorrect statement of the law for at-will employees, it also was, standing alone, evidence that the arbitrator based his decision not on the agreement but upon external law. Douglas avoided that difficulty by holding that the award could have been based upon both an interpretation of external law and an interpretation of the collective agreement, and thus the source of the ruling's "essence" was ambiguous. He said:

> A mere ambiguity in the opinion accompanying an award, which permits the inference that the arbitrator may have exceeded his authority, is not a reason for refusing to enforce the award. Arbitrators have no obligation to the court to give their reasons for an award. To require opinions free of ambiguity may lead arbitrators to play it safe by writing no supporting opinions.

With this language, Douglas created a second pro-arbitration presumption—the presumption that arbitral awards "draw their essence"

---

[80] 363 U.S. 593 (1960).

from the agreement unless there is clear manifest evidence to the contrary. This presumption operates to give arbitral awards a substantial shield from judicial scrutiny.[81]

The Immediate Impact and Continuing Importance of the Trilogy

Although the decisions in the *Steelworkers' Trilogy* were a major victory for the CIO and the Steelworkers' Union, the decisions garnered little attention in the labor movement or the general public when issued. A small item appeared in the Steelworkers' own publication, but otherwise they were not lauded in either the popular or union press. The individuals personally involved in the cases had favorable outcomes. The grievances in *American Manufacturing* and *Warrior & Gulf* went to arbitration and in both cases the union won. Sparks was reinstated and the Warrior & Gulf workers returned to their jobs. In *Enterprise Wheel,* the union had still not achieved a new contract by the time the Court enforced the arbitral award. Subsequently, the union went on strike, the company hired replacements, the union was decertified, and most of the union members were never rehired. Ironically, the eleven employees whom the arbitrator had ordered reinstated—those whose reinstatement rights triggered the judicial battle in the first place—unlike their coworkers, ultimately kept their jobs by virtue of the Supreme Court's decision in the *Trilogy.*[82]

The limited public attention paid to the *Trilogy* decisions at the time they were rendered is understandable because the issue of which forum should decide workplace disputes—a court or arbitration—is an abstract issue that lacks immediacy to most people. It was an issue that mattered most to labor law professionals, who saw it as important for reinforcing union power in the workplace. It was also important to professional arbitrators, who saw the decision as affirming their central role in the industrial relations regime. Ultimately, the decisions were of primary importance to the developing shape of labor law.[83]

---

81 Some scholars have argued that it does not go far enough in shielding arbitration from judicial review. *See, e.g.*, David E. Feller, *Labor Arbitration: Past, Present, and Future: Taft and Hartley Vindicated: The Curious History of Review of Labor Arbitration Awards*, 19 Berkeley J. Emp. & Lab. L. 296, 302–06 (1998). In 1967, David Feller left his law practice in Washington to become a law professor at the University of California, Berkeley. He also served as a labor arbitrator until his death in 2003. *See also* Theodore J. St. Antoine, *Judicial Review of Labor Arbitration Awards: A Second Look at* Enterprise Wheel *and Its Progeny,* 75 Mich. L. Rev. 1137 (1977).

82 David E. Feller, *How the Trilogy Was Made*, Proc. of the 47th Ann. Mtg., Nat'l Acad. of Arbitrators 329, 344 (1995).

83 *See also id.* at 344–45 (Feller suggesting that the litigation strategy that he and Goldberg pursued in *Lincoln Mills* and the *Steelworkers' Trilogy* may have benefitted the labor law profession, including himself, more than it benefitted the "real clients").

The impact of the *Steelworkers' Trilogy* went far beyond the results in the three cases. The *Trilogy* established the enforceability of collective bargaining agreements and drew the boundary between courts and arbitration. The doctrines they announced—the "essence test" for upholding arbitral awards, the presumption of arbitrability, and the principle that courts should look only at the facial nature of the dispute in deciding whether to enforce arbitration agreements—gave labor arbitration a unique status within the legal order. As a result of the *Trilogy*, arbitration became a near-universal feature of collective agreements, and the self-regulating system of collective bargaining worked well in most cases. The *Trilogy*'s framework gave unions the clout to enforce just cause clauses and other employee shop floor protections. The volume of arbitration cases, already high before 1960, continued to expand and less than one percent of arbitral decisions were challenged in court.[84] With unions seeming to prevail in a majority of discipline cases, the *Trilogy* brought union workers considerable job security and other contractual protections.

The *Trilogy*'s governmental theory of the collective bargaining agreement also affected organized labor's position in the larger community. The analogy of the workplace to a mini-democracy gave the labor movement a new mantle of respectability in the public mind. This mantle paid off in real terms: In strike situations, the public was loath to cross picket lines and the unemployed were loath to accept jobs as replacements. This increased public esteem strengthened the labor movement.

The *Trilogy* also served to bolster the prestige and legitimacy of unions in the eyes of their members. It made unions into gatekeepers with the power to decide which cases would be arbitrated and how they should be handled. Unions at the same time gained an inexpensive, quick, and effective mechanism to enforce collective bargaining agreements, and those they represented gained an opportunity to have grievances heard in a relatively unthreatening and informal setting. For several decades after the decisions, strong unions flourished under the grievance and arbitration system facilitated by the *Trilogy*. Unions were able to enforce their collective agreements in arbitration and thus were able to construct a functioning system of workplace self-regulation.[85]

---

[84] Stephen L. Hayford, *The Coming Third Era of Labor Arbitration*, 48 Arb. J. 8 (Sept. 1993).

[85] Lower federal courts have not always been willing to grant arbitral awards the extreme deference that the *Trilogy* mandated. The Supreme Court has revisited the issue several times, reversing lower courts when they have set aside arbitral awards. *See* Major League Baseball Players Ass'n v. Garvey, 532 U.S. 504 (2001) (error for court of appeals to overturn an arbitrator's credibility determination); United Paperworkers Int'l Union v. Misco, Inc., 484 U.S. 29 (1987) (courts do not sit to hear claims of factual or legal error by

However, the gatekeeper role that the *Trilogy* assigned to unions proved to be both a boon and a liability. Because courts refused to review the results of arbitration decisions on the merits, unions had a special responsibility to handle grievances fairly and without bias. This responsibility became a legally enforceable obligation known as the duty of fair representation, or DFR.[86] The duty of fair representation became the mechanism by which the judiciary policed union actions in handling grievances and conducting arbitrations. Since the *Trilogy* was decided, many workers have sued their unions, claiming that a union official mishandled their grievance or arbitration hearings. Courts have scrutinized union actions carefully and debated whether negligence or gross incompetence is sufficient to impose liability.[87] Sam Gompers' fears that judicial enforcement of collective agreements would invite courts into internal unions affairs turned out to be prescient. One effect of the *Trilogy* decisions, combined with the DFR, has been for courts to examine union actions, evaluate union effectiveness, and at times impose crushing financial liability.[88]

Another consequence of the *Trilogy* was to remove labor concerns from the public arena. Arbitration, by its nature, is private and outside the public eye. Thus the *Trilogy* fostered development of a private body of law for each workplace, internal to the workplace and removed from public view. Henceforth, the enforcement of collective bargaining agreements and the disposition of individual grievances became invisible to the public at large.

---

arbitrators and should not overturn "improvident, even silly, fact-finding" by an arbitrator). *See also* Eastern Associated Coal Corp. v. United Mine Workers, 531 U.S. 57 (2000) (court of appeals erred in overturning arbitral award on ground of public policy).

[86] The duty of fair representation (DFR) was first imposed in a case concerning racially discriminatory practices by a railroad union. Steele v. Louisville & Nashville Ry. Co., 323 U.S. 192 (1944). (Chapter Two of *Labor Law Stories* focuses on the *Steele* case.) The DFR was applied to the NLRA in a non-racial case in 1953. Ford Motor Co. v. Huffman, 345 U.S. 330 (1953). Initially the DFR was used to police union actions in negotiating contracts, but in Humphrey v. Moore, 375 U.S. 335 (1964), the Supreme Court applied the DFR to a union's actions in handling a grievance.

[87] For many years, the courts of appeals were divided over whether simple negligence by a union violated the duty of fair representation, or whether gross negligence was required. *Compare* Camancho v. Ritz–Carlton Water Tower, 786 F.2d 242 (7th Cir. 1986) (holding that intentional activity or recklessness violates the duty of fair representation, but not mere carelessness) *with* Hines v. Anchor Motor Freight, Inc., 424 U.S. 554 (1976) (upholding *arguendo* a court of appeals decision that union negligence violated its duty of fair representation). In 1990, in United Steelworkers v. Rawson, 495 U.S. 362 (1990), the Supreme Court settled the question by holding that union negligence, without more, is not a violation of the duty of fair representation.

[88] On union financial liability for breach of duty of fair representation in the handling of grievances, see Bowen v. United States Postal Service, 459 U.S. 212 (1983); Vaca v. Sipes, 386 U.S. 171 (1967).

Labor's high standing in public opinion began to wane by the late 1960's as a result of a number of factors. Several high-profile stories of labor corruption in the popular press began to turn public opinion away from labor. At the same time, other social causes such as the civil rights movements and the anti-Vietnam War movement, captured the hearts and minds of the liberal intelligentsia. By 1970, the labor movement found itself isolated from the rest of American society.[89]

The *Trilogy*'s private regime of self-regulation contributed to the labor movement's isolation. Isolation was not new to the labor movement. As mentioned above, American unions had long eschewed state involvement in union affairs. Over a hundred years ago the AFL embraced a philosophy of voluntarism and developed a set of practices known as business unionism that involved seeking contractual rather than political gains. But the result of the *Trilogy* was to reinforce that isolationist tendency rather than promote an alternative vision that brought labor's concerns into the public arena and fostered alliances with other social groups. Professor Stephen Befort recently articulated the problem with union's self-regulatory path:

> Composed mostly of craft workers, the AFL concentrated on a policy of "business unionism" that sought not to replace capitalism but to share in its gains. Even during the heady years of the New Deal era, organized labor focused on bettering the lot of its members through collective bargaining rather than attempting to craft a new social and economic landscape through political activism. Business unionism fit America's lack of class-consciousness, but it came with a price. American unions today are relatively unpopular and isolated. Many Americans view unions as just another self-serving, special interest group. And having gone it alone when times were good, American unions lack the strong support of allied social partners that many of their European counterparts receive. The insular attitude of American unions also has interfered with their ability to attract members from a new generation of workers.[90]

Thus, while the *Trilogy* gave unions considerable power and legitimacy for a long time, it also imposed some long-term costs.

---

[89] *See* Derek Curtis Bok & John Thomas Dunlop, *Labor and the American Community* 15–19 (1970). *See also* Thomas A. Kochan, *How American Workers View Unions*, Monthly Lab. Rev., Apr. 1979, at 24 (reporting that a majority of Americans hold unions in low esteem); Thomas Edsall, *The New Politics of Inequality* 173 (1984) (attributing erosion of public support for unions to highly publicized disclosures of illegal behavior by some labor officials).

[90] Stephen F. Befort, *Labor and Employment Law at the Millennium: A Historical Review and Critical Assessment*, 43 B.C. L. Rev. 351 (2002).

The *Trilogy*'s extremely deferential approach toward arbitration subsequently altered the law of commercial arbitration. As we saw, the union's task in arguing the *Trilogy* was to distinguish labor arbitration from commercial arbitration so that courts would not apply to labor arbitration the restrictive doctrines they applied to commercial arbitration. Commercial arbitration was governed by the Federal Arbitration Act,[91] a 1925 statute that had been narrowly construed by the courts. However, in 1983, more than twenty years after the *Trilogy* was decided, the Supreme Court applied the *Trilogy* doctrines to commercial arbitration. In *Moses H. Cone Memorial Hospital v. Mercury Construction Corp.,* the Supreme Court declared that there was a "liberal federal policy favoring arbitration" and stated that courts should favor arbitration in determining which disputes fall within a promise to arbitrate.[92] It adopted a presumption of arbitrability, lifting Douglas' language from *Warrior & Gulf.* In *Moses H. Cone,* the Court stated, "[Q]uestions of arbitrability must be addressed with a healthy regard for the federal policy favoring arbitration.... The [Federal] Arbitration Act establishes that, as a matter of federal law, any doubts concerning the scope of arbitrable issues should be resolved in favor of arbitration, whether the problem at hand is the construction of the contract language itself or an allegation of waiver, delay, or a like defense to arbitrability." Since then, courts have borrowed other arbitration doctrines from the labor context and applied them to arbitration under the FAA.[93]

In 1985, in *Mitsubishi Motors Corp. v. Soler Chrysler–Plymouth, Inc.,* the Supreme Court relied on the presumption of arbitrability under the Federal Arbitration Act to hold that an ordinary arbitration clause will be interpreted to apply not merely to contractual disputes, but also to statutory claims. In *Mitsubishi,* the Court applied the FAA to claims arising under the Sherman Antitrust Act.[94] Six years later, the Supreme Court applied the same reasoning to the nonunion employment setting.

---

[91] 9 U.S.C. § 1 et seq.

[92] 460 U.S. 1 (1983)

[93] For example, in Nolde Bros. v. Local No. 358, Bakery Workers, 430 U.S. 243 (1977), the Supreme Court extended *Enterprise* to hold that an arbitration clause applied to a dispute that arose after the collective bargaining agreement expired and the company had closed its plant. *Nolde* has been used as authority to extend arbitration clauses beyond their expiration dates in commercial arbitration settings. *See* Sweet Dreams Unlimited, Inc. v. Dial–A–Mattress, 1 F.3d 639, 643 (7th Cir. 1993) (applying reasoning of *Nolde* to an FAA case). *But see* Litton Financial Printing Div. v. NLRB, 501 U.S. 190 (1991) (limiting the reach of *Nolde* in post-termination disputes). *See generally* Katherine V.W. Stone, *Rustic Justice: Community and Coercion Under the Federal Arbitration Act,* 77 N.C. L. Rev. 931 (1999).

[94] Mitsubishi Motors Corp. v. Soler Chrysler–Plymouth, Inc., 473 U.S. 614 (1985). *See also* Shearson/American Express, Inc. v. McMahon, 482 U.S. 220 (1987) (holding asserted

In *Gilmer v. Interstate/Johnson Lane Corp.*, the Supreme Court held that an employee's claim of age discrimination was subject to arbitration so long as the prospective arbitration proceeding was adequate to vindicate the employee's statutory rights.[95] Since then, many nonunion workers have been forced to arbitrate their employment law claims, losing their rights to a judicial forum, yet lacking the assistance of a union in designing and administering the alternative tribunal.[96]

Conclusion

Thus the law has come full circle. What began in the *Trilogy* as a special set of rules for labor arbitration has become generalized into rules governing all arbitration, including those in the nonunion workplace. While some differences between arbitration under § 301 and under the Federal Arbitration Act remain,[97] the two bodies of law are quickly converging.[98] Ironically, at the same time that arbitration has expanded into other fields, its use in collective bargaining has contracted due to the dramatic decline in unionism since the 1980's. The *Trilogy,* however, remains a major union achievement that conferred legitimacy on the use of alternative fora and opened up a world of informal, accessible, inexpensive tribunals to resolve many kinds of disputes. Whether these tribunals will become a tool for individuals to obtain justice, or whether they will be used by the powerful to disenfranchise the many, is a question that has not yet been resolved.[99]

---

claims under 1934 Securities Act and Racketeer Influenced and Corrupt Organizations Act (RICO) to be subject to arbitration clause).

[95] 500 U.S. 20 (1991).

[96] Many scholars have criticized the use of arbitration in the nonunion workplace for resting on dubious consent, failing to provide due process, truncating statutes of limitations, raising burdens of proof, and limiting remedies available to nonunion workers. *See, e.g.*, Jean Sternlight, *Rethinking the Constitutionality of the Supreme Court's Preference for Binding Arbitration,* 72 Tul. L. Rev. 1 (1977); Katherine V.W. Stone, *Mandatory Arbitration of Individual Employment Rights: The Yellow Dog Contract of the 1990s*, 73 Denv. U. L. Rev. 1017 (1996); Joseph R. Grodin, *Arbitration of Employment Discrimination Claims: Doctrine and Policy in the Wake of* Gilmer, 14 Hofstra Lab. & Emp. L.J. 1 (1996); David S. Schwartz, *Enforcing Small Print to Protect Big Business: Employee and Consumer Rights Claims in an Age of Compelled Arbitration*, 1997 Wis. L. Rev. 33.

[97] The primary respect in which commercial and labor arbitration differ today lies in the standard of review. The standard of review for labor arbitration is the essence test of *Enterprise*, discussed above. The standard of review for arbitration under the Federal Arbitration Act varies somewhat from circuit to circuit, but is usually said to be "manifest disregard of the law." *See* Katherine V.W. Stone, *Arbitration Law* 497–528 (2003).

[98] *See, e.g.*, First Options of Chicago, Inc. v. Kaplan, 514 U.S. 938, 942–44 (1995) (conflating § 301 cases and FAA cases).

[99] *See* Katherine V.W. Stone, *Rustic Justice: Community and Coercion Under the Federal Arbitration Act*, 77 N.C. L. Rev. 931 (1999).

*

5

Laura J. Cooper and Dennis R. Nolan

The Story of *NLRB v. Gissel Packing*: The Practical Limits of Paternalism

How did an unfair labor practice claim deemed utterly meritless by the attorneys who investigated it receive unanimous affirmation in the United States Supreme Court? Why did an attorney for the National Labor Relations Board advance a position that contradicted Board precedent and the Board's own brief, then deny to the Court that his position represented any change? Why did a company lawyer argue his case before the high court without informing it that his client had gone out of business and the case against it was moot? How was it that a Supreme Court decision that purported to define both when an employer would have to bargain with a union that had never won an election and the rights of employer free speech in representation election campaigns end up, as a practical matter, defining neither? The Supreme Court's opinion doesn't raise any of these questions, let alone answer them. To answer them, we need to take a deeper look at the story of *NLRB v. Gissel Packing Company.*[1]

In *Gissel Packing*, the Supreme Court held that an employer could be ordered to bargain with a union that had never won a representation election if the union had obtained authorization cards signed by a majority of bargaining unit members authorizing the union to be their bargaining representative and the employer had committed outrageous and pervasive unfair labor practices that had made impossible the holding of a fair election. The Court also held that employer campaign speech to employees predicting a union's effects on its business would be deemed a threat and thus an unfair labor practice unless the prediction

---

[1] 395 U.S. 575 (1969). ("Gissel" rhymes with "whistle.")

was based on "objective fact" and was used to convey the employer's belief "as to demonstrably probable consequences beyond his control."

The decision known as *Gissel Packing* actually arose from four unrelated cases. Three of the cases came from the Fourth Circuit which heard argument on the cases on the same day and disposed of them together, six months later, with a one-page per curiam opinion in each. In *Gissel*, the union never sought an election; in *Heck's* a requested election was never held; and in *General Steel* an election won by the employer was set aside by the Board because of the employer's unfair labor practices. In each, the Fourth Circuit upheld the Board's findings that the employers had committed unfair labor practices but, relying on circuit precedent, found that the employers' unfair labor practices did not bar them from asserting a good faith doubt about the union's majority status. The Fourth Circuit said that authorization cards were so inherently unreliable as indicators of employee desires for unionization that employers—even those that interfered with the representation process through serious unfair labor practices—could not be ordered to bargain on the basis of a card majority.[2]

The Supreme Court's *Gissel* decision resolves these Fourth Circuit cases along with a First Circuit case that raised not only the bargaining order issue posed by the Fourth Circuit cases, but also the additional question of the limits of employer election speech. In *NLRB v. The Sinclair Company*,[3] the First Circuit agreed with the Board that Sinclair's statements, suggesting that unionization could result in plant closing or work transfer and employee job loss, were unfair labor practices. Unlike the Fourth Circuit, the First Circuit upheld the Board's bargaining order, finding that authorization cards were a sufficiently reliable indicator of employee support to form the basis of a bargaining order when the employer had no good faith doubt of the union's majority status. To avoid unduly complicating the story, we will focus in this chapter largely on the *Sinclair* case since it alone gave rise to both of the issues resolved by the Supreme Court in *Gissel*.

Factual Background

The *Sinclair* case arose from an organizing campaign commenced in 1965 by Local 404 of the Teamsters Union[4] at The Sinclair Company's facility at 60 Appleton Street in Holyoke, Massachusetts. Holyoke was

---

[2] NLRB v. Gissel Packing Co., 398 F.2d 336 (4th Cir. 1968); NLRB v. Heck's, Inc., 398 F.2d 337 (4th Cir. 1968); General Steel Products, Inc. v. NLRB, 398 F.2d 339 (4th Cir. 1968).

[3] 397 F.2d 157 (1st Cir. 1968).

[4] In 1968, the Teamsters Union was the largest union in the U.S. with over 1.7 million members. *BNA Labor Relations Yearbook* 501 (1970).

the first planned industrial community in the country,[5] developed in the early nineteenth century by cotton-industry industrialists from New England who constructed a dam on the Connecticut River to take advantage of the inexhaustible supply of clean water, the power of the falls and the flat land adjacent to the river. These features were attractive not only for the manufacture of cotton, but also for the manufacture of fine writing papers that used cotton rags and water to make a slurry. By 1890 there were twenty-five paper mills in Holyoke, giving it the name of "Paper City." Other companies grew up in the area to supply the paper industry, including foundries and machine shops.[6]

Unions emerged in Holyoke almost as soon as the founding of the paper industry and their fortunes rose and fell together. In the twentieth century the industry suffered from competition from areas of the country newly able to manufacture fine paper from wood instead of cotton, and later from the lower wages available in the southern U.S. and, years later, in Asia. The Holyoke factories, bordered on two sides by canals, could not expand to take advantage of more efficient manufacturing designs that required greater flexibility in routing work flow.

In the late 1950's, industry decline forced both corporate and union mergers. In 1959, the AFL–CIO approved the merger of the United Papermakers and Paperworkers Union with the American Wire Weavers Protective Association (AWWPA) that had represented workers who manufactured wire cloth used in paper-making machines. Starting in 1963, a wave of mill closings decimated much of the Holyoke paper industry.[7]

The Sinclair Company was founded in 1925 by Peter S. Sinclair to manufacture and repair dandy rolls, wire-covered cylinders used in the manufacture of paper.[8] During the Depression, Sinclair took over a failing company and its product lines of other paper industry machinery and moved its operation to the failing company's plant on Appleton Street. In the early 1950's, the sons of the founder were managing the company. Sinclair's wire weavers were then represented by the AWWPA and labor negotiations were conducted on a national basis with approximately twelve similar companies.[9]

---

[5] Craig P. Della Penna, *Holyoke* 7 (1997).

[6] Wyatt E. Harper, *The Story of Holyoke* (1973); Whiting Paper Company, *How Paper is Made at the Whiting Paper Company and a Brief Sketch of the Paper Industry* (1943).

[7] William F. Hartford, *Working People of Holyoke: Class and Ethnicity in a Massachusetts Mill Town, 1850–1960* (1990); James A. Gross, *The Making and Shaping of Unionism in the Pulp and Paper Industry*, 5 Lab. Hist. 183 (1964).

[8] A dandy roll imprints the paper with its watermark or imposes a patterned surface on the paper. For example, a plain wire mesh makes wove paper.

[9] Wyatt E. Harper, *The Story of Holyoke* 224 (1973).

In June 1952, the AWWPA struck Sinclair. The strike lasted until September when the company reopened the plant, without a union contract, offering employment terms consistent with the company's final contract offer to the union. Thereafter, until the 1965 organizing campaign by the Teamsters Union, the wire weavers at Sinclair were not represented by any union. In 1962, one of the founder's sons, David H. Sinclair, who had been in the military during the 1952 strike, became President. In July 1964, The Lindsay Wire Weaving Company of Cleveland, Ohio acquired the stock of The Sinclair Company which then became a division of Lindsay. Following the acquisition by Lindsay, David H. Sinclair remained as President of Sinclair.[10]

The 1965 Organizing Campaign

In early July 1965, two Sinclair wire weavers, Richard Bougie and Gary Brunault, contacted Robert Williams, President of the Wire Weavers Trade Division of the International Brotherhood of Teamsters. Brunault had worked at Sinclair since before the strike, Bougie started there afterwards. Williams talked to them about organizing the shop and told them that he would need to have thirty percent of the employees sign up in order to get an election. The employees gave Williams a list of names of the Sinclair wire weavers.[11] On July 3, 1965, Williams wrote the wire weavers expressing the desire of the Teamsters to represent them and telling them that the Teamsters represented the employees at Lindsay's Ohio facility and at four other major wire weaving firms in the country.

Williams enclosed with each letter a blank authorization card on which employees could indicate their desire to be represented by the Teamsters.[12] In the summer and fall of 1965, fourteen men worked in Sinclair's wire weaving department, most of whom had been members of the AWWPA and participated in the 1952 strike. By July 9, 1965, eleven wire weavers had signed Teamsters authorization cards. About as many employees came personally to David H. Sinclair to tell him about the Teamsters' mailing and show him what they had received from the union.

---

[10] Testimony of David H. Sinclair, Appendix at 92–93, U.S. Supreme Court, The Sinclair Company v. National Labor Relations Board, October Term 1968, No. 585.

[11] Affidavits of Richard Bougie and Gary Brunault (December 20, 1965), and Memorandum of NLRB Region One Attorney George F. McInerny (June 3, 1966), NLRB Case File, The Sinclair Company, 1–CA–5266, The National Archives, College Park, Maryland.

[12] This account of the organizing campaign, except as otherwise indicated, is drawn from the testimony and exhibits from the hearing before the NLRB Trial Examiner contained in the Appendix in the Supreme Court to The Sinclair Company v. National Labor Relations Board, October Term 1968, No. 585.

Knowing that the organizing campaign had begun in the wire weavers department, Sinclair spoke to the employees there in the third week of July. He told them he would be more blunt than in other departmental meetings because he "figured it started here." He said that he was disappointed that this group of employees, who had had a "prior bad experience" with the AWWPA, were again thinking about union representation. He asserted that the company had been having financial problems for many years and stated that he didn't want to be back to a situation where it was presented with demands it couldn't meet and therefore face a strike as it had in 1952. Sinclair told them Lindsay Wire didn't really need the Sinclair plant as a supplier of wire cloth. He said Lindsay expected a profit from Sinclair and that Lindsay would not "pour money in if they had no return."[13]

Sinclair said he didn't have much respect for the Teamsters Union and didn't want to deal with it. He said the 1952 strike had nearly put the company out of business and that it had, ever since, "been running on thin ice." He expressed disappointment that employees hadn't learned the lessons of the past. He told the wire weavers that their advanced age, specialized craft skills and limited education would make it difficult for them to find another job.

On August 17, 1965, Calvin L. McCoy, a lawyer who represented Teamsters Local 859 in Cleveland, Ohio, telephoned V. Jay Einhart, a lawyer with the Cleveland firm of Stanley, Smoyer and Schwartz, demanding that Sinclair recognize the Teamsters Union. Although the Stanley firm didn't represent Sinclair when the request was made, it did represent Sinclair's parent company, Lindsay Wire, in its labor relations with the Teamsters at an Ohio plant.

The Stanley law firm had specialized in labor law even before passage of the Wagner Act. Its founder, Welles Stanley, had made the transition in the early twentieth century from handling animal cruelty cases for the Humane Society to handling labor cases for employers because both specialities then required expertise in injunctions. Passage of the Norris–LaGuardia Act in 1932, which substantially limited the ability of employers to obtain injunctions against unions, nearly put Stanley out of business. A few years later, though, the NLRA created something of a boom for the tiny firm.[14] By the mid–1960's the Stanley firm had four partners and two associates. Despite its small size, the

[13] Sinclair acknowledged he might have said something about Lindsay not wanting to pour money down a "rat hole."

[14] The description of the history of the Stanley firm comes largely from a Telephone Interview with Gregory P. Szuter, January 22, 2004. (Szuter was a member of the Stanley law firm in the 1970's.)

firm had a nationwide management-side labor practice and its attorneys had already argued two cases in the U.S. Supreme Court.[15]

After the Stanley firm received the Teamsters' demand for recognition for the Sinclair employees, David H. Sinclair retained the firm to represent his company. Attorney Einhart wrote to McCoy that Sinclair would not recognize the Teamsters. In a letter dated August 20, 1965, Einhart told McCoy that Sinclair was refusing recognition because it had a good faith doubt of the union's majority status, it considered authorization cards an unreliable indication of employee support, and it had questions about the appropriate bargaining unit. Over the next three months, the Teamsters kept redefining the bargaining unit in which it was seeking representation. In August it wanted to represent the eighty-seven production and maintenance employees; in September just the fourteen employees in the wire weaving department; and in October the larger production and maintenance unit. Sinclair responded to each union demand for recognition with a letter refusing to recognize the Teamsters, each time citing the same reasons in its initial refusal letter. By the time of Sinclair's third denial, the union had filed a representation petition with Region One of the National Labor Relations Board, seeking an election at Sinclair in a unit of wire weavers and apprentices.

On November 2nd, David H. Sinclair met with Union Local President Carmin P. Napoli at the Howard Johnson's in Holyoke and signed a consent election agreement for a representation election. Disagreement about the appropriate bargaining unit continued through November. As a result, some of Sinclair's election communications to employees were distributed to all employees and some went only to the wire weavers. Sinclair's entire election campaign was conducted in accordance with attorney Einhart's instructions. Einhart prepared all of the literature distributed and he reviewed David H. Sinclair's speeches and discussions with workers. Einhart prepared a list of "do's and don't's" for Sinclair's supervisors and went over the list with them personally.[16]

Sinclair's Communications

Sinclair's communications to employees about the forthcoming representation election started on the day he signed the election agreement and continued until the day before the election, ultimately held on December 9th in a unit including only wire weavers. Sinclair's first letter

---

[15] Harry E. Smoyer had successfully represented the employer in NLRB v. Sands Mfg. Co., 306 U.S. 332 (1939). Eugene B. Schwartz successfully represented Ranco, Inc., one of the employers in the cases consolidated in the Supreme Court as NLRB v. Babcock & Wilcox Co., 351 U.S. 105 (1956).

[16] Memorandum from NLRB Region One Attorney George F. McInerny to the File, January 5, 1966. NLRB Case File, The Sinclair Company, 1–CA–5266, The National Archives, College Park, Maryland.

to employees provided a list of questions and answers and explained that employees who signed authorization cards still had the right to vote against the union. The letter included the following paragraph:

> [B]ecause of financial conditions the Sinclair plant has been on "thin ice." We are still on "thin ice," and it just doesn't make sense for us to meet unreasonable Union demands which will result in further losses and eventually the necessity of closing the plant.

He asked employees to consider their vote carefully because it might "have a great effect on the future of all of us."

Just three days later Sinclair wrote again to his employees. He emphasized that to be profitable the Holyoke facility needed to upgrade its machinery to make a wider wire cloth then in demand, but that since Lindsay had no ties with Holyoke it would make its investment decisions based on where it could earn the most profit. He said, "I know that the Teamsters Union promises you a lot, but what can they deliver except pressure—the threat of a strike?" He said that while Lindsay might not care about a strike, he personally wanted to continue to live in Holyoke. He said, "I have pride in the Sinclair family name and would like to see the plant, modernized, expanded and prosper."

In mid-November Sinclair sent employees a flyer that called the Teamsters a "strike-happy outfit." One cartoon in the flyer showed a boarded-up Sinclair plant, its flag at half-mast, with the caption, "The 'closedest' closed shop in Town" and another was of an employee with empty pockets, out of work because of the Teamsters.

On November 22nd, Sinclair supplied each employee with a copy of a book by Robert F. Kennedy, *The Enemy Within*, that reported on corruption and criminal activities of Teamsters Union officials. Kennedy had gathered the information while Chief Counsel to the Senate Select

Committee on Improper Activities in the Labor or Management Field, known popularly as the McClellan Committee. Sinclair encouraged the wire weavers to read this information "from a man who really knows."

A week later, Sinclair placed a notice for employees on the plant bulletin board. A cartoon pictured a graveyard with headstones for area companies that had closed. The Teamsters were pictured digging a grave for Sinclair and a sour-faced Teamsters "Hood," complete with cigar, was delivering a headstone for the Sinclair Company in a wheelbarrow as Sinclair employees stood at the grave. The flyer encouraged employees to visit a dozen factories in the area, five of which were pictured, where companies had closed. The notice attributed the plant closings to unions that had restricted production, increased costs and conducted "bloodletting strikes."

The Sinclair Company

Let's Look At The Record

The next day, Sinclair sent another letter in question-and-answer format to the wire weavers. It described how much more vulnerable to a strike the Sinclair plant was now, as a part of Lindsay Wire, than it had been when it was independent in 1952. He said all the Teamsters could do for the employees would be to make big demands that the company could not meet and to call the employees out on strike. Sinclair encouraged employees to talk to their families about whether they could afford a prolonged strike. Sinclair's December 1st letter focused on "racketeering and hoodlum domination and control" of the Teamsters Union. He said that if the wire weavers paid dues to the Teamsters the funds would be used to defend Teamster officials in criminal court.

At 1:30 p.m. on December 8th, a little more than twenty-four hours before the representation election, David H. Sinclair again spoke to the employees in the wire weaving department. He invited night-shift employees to come in early to hear the speech. This time he spoke from fourteen note cards that repeated the themes he had addressed previously in the campaign. He emphasized the importance and secrecy of the employees' vote. He reminded the employees that they had Senator Kennedy's book about Teamster corruption and racketeering. He noted that Lindsay Wire was concerned about profits and had alternative sources for wire manufacture. He said, "I want my job. I suppose you want yours." He noted how difficult it would be for these employees, because of their age and narrow range of skills, to find new jobs. He said he was "deadly serious" and "deeply concerned." Sinclair closed with these words, "To you and your dependents this is one of the most important elections in which you will ever vote."

The election in the unit of wire weavers was held the next day, December 9, 1965. Six employees voted in favor of representation by the Teamsters and seven voted against.

Prior Proceedings

Proceedings in the Region and the Office of Appeals

The case that ultimately yielded a unanimously pro-union decision in the U.S. Supreme Court had surprisingly inauspicious beginnings in the NLRB regional office. Indeed, for about six months, the regional office vigorously defended its assessment that the union's claims were entirely without merit.

On December 14th, 1965, Caesar C. Guazzo, a New York City attorney representing the union, filed unfair labor practice charges and objections to the election with NLRB Region One in Boston. Guazzo asserted that Sinclair's election speeches and literature violated § 8(a)(1) of the National Labor Relations Act and that Sinclair had violated § 8(a)(5) by refusing to bargain with the Teamsters.[17] The election objections asked that the results of the December 9th election be set

[17] Section 8(a)(1) makes it an unfair labor practice for an employer to interfere with employee rights defined in § 7 of the NLRA including the right to self-organization and the

aside because Sinclair's pre-election conduct interfered with the ability of the employees to exercise free choice.[18] At the NLRB Regional Office, the matter was assigned to NLRB attorney George F. McInerny who obtained affidavits from Bougie and Brunault, the two wire weavers who had initiated the organizing campaign. McInerny also met with David H. Sinclair and his attorney Einhart.[19] McInerny's investigation concluded that "the Company's conduct during the election campaign was highly sophisticated and based in large measure upon recent Decisions of the board with respect to campaign literature and conduct of supervisors." He didn't think the communications constituted an unfair labor practice or required setting aside the election. In mid-January, McInerny's supervisors agreed and dismissed both the unfair labor practice charges and overruled the union's election objections.

That would have been the end of the story but for the fact that the union challenged both regional decisions with officials in different branches of the NLRB in Washington, D.C. The Region's refusal to hold a hearing on the objections to the election was overruled by the National Labor Relations Board on March 8, 1966, in part because it felt that the Region's informal investigation "had not probed deeply enough." At the same time, the union's challenge to the Region's dismissal of its unfair labor practice charges was pending in the Office of Appeals, a section of the agency under the authority of the Board's independent General Counsel rather than under the Board itself.

Since it would now be necessary to hold a hearing on the election objections anyway, Irving H. Herman, the Director of the Office of

right to form, join and assist labor organizations. Section 8(a)(5) makes it an unfair labor practice for an employer "to refuse to bargain collectively with the representatives of his employees...." 29 U.S.C. §§ 158(a)(1), 158(a)(3) and 158(a)(5) (2000).

The unfair labor practice charge also alleged that the employer had discharged Raymond C. Shyloski, a "floor boy" in the wire weaving department, the day after the election, in violation of § 8(a)(3) that makes it unlawful for an employer "by discrimination in regard to hire or tenure of employment to ... discourage membership in any labor organization." The NLRB Regional Office later dismissed this charge when it concluded that the employer had fired him after an investigation of vending machine thefts revealed that Shyloski had omitted from his employment application "an extensive criminal record including convictions for breaking and entering." Final Report and Recommendation, George F. McInerny to Acting Regional Director Ernest Modern, January 13, 1966.

[18] While an employer's commission of an unfair labor practice during the period between the filing of an election petition and an election ordinarily will result in setting aside the results of an election lost by a union, even conduct that does not rise to the level of an unfair labor practice may warrant setting aside an election. General Shoe Corp., 77 NLRB 124 (1948).

[19] Except where otherwise stated, this account of the handling of the Teamsters' unfair labor practice charges by the NLRB's regional office in Boston and its Office of Appeals in Washington, D.C., is drawn from documents in the NLRB Case File of The Sinclair Company, 1–CA–5266, The National Archives, College Park, Maryland.

Appeals, asked the Region to reconsider its decision to dismiss the unfair labor practice charges. The Region was particularly reluctant to issue an 8(a)(5) complaint because its reinvestigation concluded that employees had signed cards to get an election and the employer had a legitimate doubt about whether the union's proposed bargaining unit was appropriate in view of the uncertainty about whether it would cover all production and maintenance employees or only the wire weavers. The Region reported to Washington that the cards would not support a bargaining order and even if the 8(a)(1) charge were sustained it was not serious enough for a bargaining order remedy under recent Board case law.[20] When the Region still declined to issue the 8(a)(5) complaint, on July 1, 1966, Board General Counsel Arnold Ordman officially sustained the union's appeal, requiring the Regional Director to include the 8(a)(5) allegation in the Region's complaint.[21]

Thus, on July 22, 1966, six months after the Regional Office had first concluded that the union's objections to the election and its unfair labor practice charges were without merit, the Region issued its complaint alleging that Sinclair had violated both 8(a)(1) by its pre-election speeches, letters and pamphlets and 8(a)(5) by its refusal to bargain when the company lacked a good faith doubt of the union's majority status.

Proceedings Before the Trial Examiner

The union's objections to the election were consolidated with the unfair labor practice complaint for hearing before NLRB Trial Examiner Louis Libbin in Springfield, Massachusetts on October 4 and 5, 1966. The General Counsel's case began with brief testimony from several wire weavers to establish the circumstances under which each had signed an

---

[20] The Region cited Harvard Coated Products Co., 156 NLRB 162 (1965) and Clearmont's Inc., 154 NLRB 1397 (1965), two cases in which the Board had overruled Trial Examiners and held that 8(a)(1) violations were insufficiently serious to demonstrate a violation of 8(a)(5).

[21] Even within the Office of Appeals there was recognition of the case's weakness. A June 23, 1966, staff report from an attorney identified only as Shanklin to the Office's Appeals Committee noted the absence of any direct evidence of a threat to move or close the plant, but reluctantly recommended sustaining the appeal on the basis of the cartoon of the "closed shop" because it appeared in the context of "such a vigorous anti-union campaign," the cards were clear, and the union lost by only one vote. Most significantly, the memorandum assumed that Sinclair's "factual assertions" in the leaflet were accurate "since the Union, although urging that they are misleading, does not specifically challenge their accuracy." Attorneys in the Region maintained their doubts about the case even after being told to issue the complaint, writing in a memo that the case's weakness made it difficult to draft a credible complaint. They thought that the employer's carefully crafted campaign literature made it difficult to allege that the employer had ever actually threatened to close the plant.

authorization card. Most of the hearing was devoted to the testimony of David H. Sinclair. The Board attorney had Sinclair describe the organizing campaign and Sinclair's employee communications. Sinclair said that he based his belief that a majority of the employees did not want the Teamsters on his personal feeling because he had known the wire weavers for a long time. When asked about the photographs of closed factories in the campaign literature, he admitted that he had no evidence that unions had caused any of the plant closings. Sinclair acknowledged that he had no information suggesting that any of the officials of Local 404 were involved in the sorts of racketeering described in the Kennedy book or that there was any hoodlumism connected with that Local. Nor, he admitted, had the Local ever made any bargaining demands to him. Sinclair testified that the company had "made a small profit" in fiscal year 1965. On cross-examination Sinclair said that in his experience when the AWWPA had represented the wire weavers it had made unreasonable bargaining demands. He said that all of the closed companies he had listed in his flyers had been unionized firms.

Trial Examiner Libbin issued his decision on January 12, 1967. Libbin found that Sinclair's communications collectively conveyed to employees the message that:

> if they selected this Union as their bargaining representative, a strike would be inevitable because the Union would make excessive demands which [Sinclair] would refuse to meet, that a strike would lead to the closing of the plant or the transfer of the weaving production to Lindsay's other facilities, and that the wire weavers would then lose their jobs and find it difficult to get other jobs because of their age and limited craft skills.[22]

Libbin found that these communications violated § 8(a)(1). The violation, he concluded, also interfered with the conduct of a fair election and therefore warranted setting aside the election results. He further found that Sinclair's refusal to bargain with the Teamsters was not based on any good faith doubt. Relying on the Board's *Joy Silk* doctrine,[23] he said that the employer's unfair labor practice gave rise to an inference that its refusal to bargain was not based on any good faith doubt of the union's majority status, but rather by a "desire to gain time within which to dissipate that majority status." Libbin recommended that Sinclair be ordered to recognize and bargain with Teamsters Local 404.

The NLRB's Decision and Enforcement Proceedings in the First Circuit

On May 2, 1967, NLRB Members Gerald A. Brown and Howard Jenkins, Jr., and Board Chairman Frank W. McCulloch issued a brief order adopting the Trial Examiner's order as the order of the Board. For

[22] The Sinclair Co., 164 NLRB 261, 266 (1967) (Trial Examiner's Decision).

[23] Joy Silk Mills, Inc. v. NLRB, 185 F.2d 732, 737, 741 (D.C. Cir. 1950).

reasons largely unrelated to the merits of the order, the Board's decision received an amount of national public attention rare for decisions of the NLRB. In the Trial Examiner's decision, adopted by the Board, Libbin had included in his factual findings a single sentence stating that Sinclair had distributed a copy of Robert F. Kennedy's book, *The Enemy Within*, to its employees. In Libbin's conclusions of law, without any further specific mention of the book, he had stated that the employer's pre-election communications were, as a totality, unlawful. The May 22, 1967, issue of *NAM Reports*, the newsletter of the National Association of Manufacturers, under the headline, "NLRB Overrules Jefferson, Bans Bobby Kennedy's Book," included an article describing the *Sinclair* decision and quoting the sentence about the book from the Trial Examiner's decision.[24] The newsletter item was picked up by the *Wall Street Journal*. Its editorial on May 25, 1967, concluded: "Thus another name was added to the NLRB's blacklist of books. This sort of censorship is not only an abridgment of the employer's freedom of speech but also a blunt insult to [employee] intelligence."

These publications produced a number of protest letters from people across the country written to the NLRB, as well as letters sent to members of the U.S. Senate and House of Representatives and forwarded to the NLRB for response. Ironically, one of the letters was forwarded to the NLRB from Senator Robert F. Kennedy.[25] In response to these complaints, on June 16, 1967, the Board took the unusual step of issuing an Order Supplementing Decision and Order to add a footnote. It stated that the Board did not understand the Trial Examiner to have found distribution of *The Enemy Within* part of the totality of the employer's conduct found to be unlawful and that, in any case, the Board itself would not find such distribution unlawful either in itself or in context.[26]

In October 1967, Lindsay Wire sold its shares of The Sinclair Company back to David H. Sinclair who became the company's sole owner.

---

[24] The reference to "Jefferson" in the article's title was to a quotation from Thomas Jefferson that was printed on a title page of *The Enemy Within*, "I have sworn upon the altar of God, eternal hostility against every form of tyranny over the mind of man."

[25] Miscellaneous letters and responses thereto from John C. Truesdale, NLRB Associate Executive Secretary, May 27–28, 1967, NLRB Case File. In one, a history professor at Oberlin College asked for a list of other books the NLRB had censored. Truesdale replied that the NLRB had never found any book to be an unfair labor practice.

[26] The Sinclair Co., 164 NLRB 261, 261 n.1 (1967). Interestingly, although the Board's footnote says that it is negating an assertion from "Respondent" (that is, Sinclair) that Libbin's totality of the circumstances included distribution of the Kennedy book, the Sinclair Company in its petition to the Supreme Court said that neither Sinclair nor any party to the case requested the clarifying order. Petition for a Writ of Certiorari at 13, 78, U.S. Supreme Court, The Sinclair Company v. National Labor Relations Board, October Term 1968, No. 585.

The NLRB submitted a petition for enforcement of its order in the United States Court of Appeals for the First Circuit. The First Circuit, on July 3, 1968, issued its opinion enforcing the Board's order. The court dismissed Sinclair's arguments that its statements were mere information and that it had made no untrue statements. Citing cases from other circuits, the court explained the governing law as this:

> Conveyance of the employer's belief, even though sincere, that unionization will or may result in the closing of the plant is not a statement of fact unless, which is most improbable, the eventuality of closing is capable of proof. The employer's prediction must be in terms of demonstrable "economic consequences."[27]

The court said that assessment of whether a particular speech was coercive was essentially for the specialized expertise of the Board. It found substantial evidence supporting the Board's findings of coercion. The First Circuit did not address the possible relevance to the speech issue of either § 8(c) of the National Labor Relations Act[28] or the First Amendment to the U.S. Constitution.

With regard to the appropriateness of a bargaining order, Sinclair argued that it had a good faith doubt of the union's majority status, that authorization cards are inherently unreliable, and that it had questioned the appropriateness of the bargaining unit. The court rejected these arguments, saying that Sinclair had consented to an election in this bargaining unit, that it had made no effort to determine the validity of the cards and that it had instead insisted on an election only as a means to gain time to dissipate the union's majority. The court noted that it had previously rejected the argument that cards were inherently unreliable. It held that representative status could be demonstrated by means other than a representation election.

Proceedings in the Supreme Court

On September 28, 1968, Edward J. Simerka and his partner Eugene B. Schwartz from the Cleveland firm of Stanley, Smoyer and Schwartz filed in the U.S. Supreme Court a petition for certiorari in *The Sinclair Company v. NLRB*. Sinclair's attorneys urged the Supreme Court to grant the writ because the First Circuit's holding was inconsistent with decisions of other circuits, including the Fourth, that had rejected

---

[27] 397 F.2d at 160. The court cited Surprenant Mfg. Co. v. NLRB, 341 F.2d 756, 761 (6th Cir. 1965).

[28] "The expressing of any views, argument, or opinion, or the dissemination thereof, whether in written printed, graphic, or visual form, shall not constitute or be evidence of an unfair labor practice under any of the provisions of this Act, if such expression contains no threat of reprisal or force or promise of benefit." NLRA, § 8(c), 29 U.S.C. § 158(c) (2000).

authorization cards and held secret ballot elections to be the only lawful means to establish representative status. They further argued that both the Board and the First Circuit had ignored Sinclair's arguments based on the First Amendment and § 8(c) of the NLRA. Petitioners cited conflicts among the circuits and within the Board itself about the scope of free speech protections for representation campaign communications. They said such questions of constitutional law could not be left to the Board's expertise nor reviewed under the deferential substantial evidence test.

On December 16, 1968, the U.S. Supreme Court granted Sinclair's petition for certiorari and ordered that the case be set for oral argument immediately following oral arguments in the three Fourth Circuit cases that had held that an order to bargain could not be based upon a showing of majority support demonstrated by authorization cards, the cases consolidated under the name *NLRB v. Gissel Packing Company*.[29]

THE SUPREME COURT BRIEFS

The Authorization Card Issue

The oral argument before the Supreme Court took some surprising turns. In order to understand the significance of what happened, one first needs to know what the Board told the Court about the relevant law in its briefs in *Sinclair* and the *Gissel* cases. That in turn requires a brief explanation of pre-*Gissel* authorities regarding authorization cards.

Although Board-conducted bargaining unit elections have been the most common method for determining union representation issues, neither the Wagner Act nor the Taft–Hartley Act expressly required an election to impose a bargaining obligation on an employer. Section 9(a) states only that the exclusive bargaining representative must be "designated or selected for the purposes of collective bargaining by the majority of the employees in a unit appropriate for such purposes." Before the Taft–Hartley Act, § 9(c) provided that when a representation question arose the Board was to provide for a hearing "and may take a secret ballot of employees, or utilize any other suitable method to ascertain such representatives." The most common alternative method used by the Board during the Wagner Act's first four years was a card check—a review of authorization cards signed by members of the bargaining unit. From 1939 on, however, the Board usually relied on elections.

While not mandating an election in all cases, the 1947 Taft–Hartley Act eliminated express permission for the Board's use of "any other

[29] Sinclair Company v. NLRB, 393 U.S. 997 (1968); NLRB v. Gissel Packing Co., 395 U.S. 575 (1969). See the second page of this chapter for a brief description of the Fourth Circuit cases.

suitable method," made an election the exclusive route for Board *certification* of an exclusive representative, and in other respects demonstrated a strong preference for elections. Nevertheless, Taft–Hartley did not expressly *prohibit* the Board from requiring an employer to recognize a union as its employees' bargaining representative in the absence of a Board election and certification. The Board's *Joy Silk*[30] doctrine defined when a union could achieve exclusive representative status in the absence of an election. That doctrine held that an employer could refuse to bargain with a union that claimed an authorization card majority only if it had a "good faith doubt" about the union's claimed majority status. With such a doubt, the employer could insist that the union establish its majority through a representation election. Without it, the employer would violate § 8(a)(5) if it refused to bargain with a union claiming to represent a majority of bargaining unit employees.

Joy Silk placed the burden of proving good faith doubt on the employer. An employer's failure to come forward with valid grounds for doubt would prevent finding good faith. More importantly, even if the employer provided some valid grounds for doubting the union's majority, the Board could still use the employer's independent unfair labor practices to find a lack of good faith. An employer's failure to demonstrate its good faith doubt would therefore lead to an order requiring it to bargain with the union even absent an election or, in some cases, even if the union had lost an election.

The only significant modification of the *Joy Silk* doctrine before *Gissel* occurred in 1966. In *Aaron Brothers*,[31] the Board shifted the burden of proof to the General Counsel to demonstrate the employer's bad faith, "in the light of all the relevant facts of the case, including any unlawful conduct of the employer, the sequence of events, and the time lapse between the refusal and the unlawful conduct." The General Counsel could make the required showing by demonstrating that the employer engaged in "substantial unfair labor practices calculated to dissipate union support" or in "a course of conduct which does not constitute an unfair labor practice" (*e.g.*, repudiating a previously-agreed card check).[32] The significance of the change was that an employer would not violate § 8(a)(5) solely because it refused to rely on authorization cards; it need not even advance any reasons for rejecting the bargaining demand. Good faith, in other words, was still the touchstone but the General Counsel had to prove its absence.

---

30 85 NLRB 1263 (1949), *enf'd*, 185 F.2d 732 (D.C. Cir. 1950).

31 158 NLRB 1077 (1966).

32 *Id.* at 1079.

That was the state of the law on authorization cards when the *Gissel* cases reached the Supreme Court. So clear was the law, in fact, that the Board's brief in the three *Gissel* cases stated the *Aaron Brothers* rule almost perfunctorily.[33] The Board's brief in *Sinclair* was even more succinct. It contained a single citation to the *Aaron Brothers* rule,[34] after which it simply rejected the employer's challenges to authorization cards and applied the established doctrine to the facts of the case. In short, the Board assumed without debate that an employer could refuse a card-based claim of majority status only if it had a good-faith doubt. Neither of the Board's briefs contained any suggestion that the Board had abandoned or weakened the good-faith requirement. The Board's apparent confidence in its precedent is a bit surprising, because several appellate courts had expressed dissatisfaction with the Board's standards even before the *Gissel* litigation.

The confident tone of the Board's brief, however, belied the fundamental disquiet of its authors. Thomas E. Silfen, the initial author of the Board's brief, sent his father a copy of the *Gissel* brief just after it was printed. In the letter enclosed with the brief, Silfen explained his thinking about the case. He described the theory that authorization cards would have to be a basis for recognition in cases in which employers engaged in such "flagrant coercive conduct" that a fair election became impossible. Silfen then said that "unfortunately" the Board had not followed that theory, but rather had relied on the employer's subjective motivation under its "good faith doubt" test. Silfen's letter to his father, with prescience, concluded:

> In our brief, we try to save the day by blurring the difference between these two theories. Thus, we argue that the test of whether an employer is in good faith is whether he has committed unfair labor practices which make impossible a fair election. This is a tortured theory and will cause great difficulty before the Court.[35]

The employers, on the other hand, unaware of the unspoken anxiety underlying the Board's position, had the difficult task of challenging a twenty-year-old doctrine.[36] Surprisingly, even though three of the employers had presented their cases to the Fourth Circuit at the same time

[33] Brief of the Appellant (NLRB) in *Gissel*, *Heck's*, and *General Steel* at 22–23. The NLRB submitted its own brief in those cases.

[34] Brief of the Respondent (NLRB) in *Sinclair* at 31.

[35] Letter from Thomas E. Silfen to Morton Silfen, late February 1969.

[36] The only union to participate independently in this litigation, Food Store Employees Local No. 347, which sought to represent certain Gissel Packing employees, asked the Court to allow an employer to reject a card-based majority only if it immediately filed its own petition for an election. The union wanted to force the reluctant employer to file a petition because union-filed petitions were vulnerable to more procedural delays.

and all four appeared before the Supreme Court on the same day, none consulted with any of the others when preparing their briefs and oral arguments. Nevertheless, they made essentially the same arguments, differing mainly in points of emphasis.

Their chief rhetorical weapon was an assertion that, because authorization cards were inherently unreliable, an election was the only way to determine majority status. Authorization cards, they noted, were obtained by the union in circumstances that could include misrepresentation and pressure. For those reasons, the Board itself and several courts of appeals had described authorization cards as "notoriously unreliable."[37] From that premise, the employers argued that the Taft–Hartley Act's deletion of statutory language permitting determination of majority status by "any other suitable method" could only mean that "certification through a Board election would be the only procedure to be followed when an unrecognized union claimed that it represented employees." In other words, the *employer* had a statutory right to demand an election regardless of its own conduct.[38]

The Free Speech Issue

The parties' briefs made clear that both sides regarded the free speech issue, raised only in *Sinclair*, as the more difficult legal question. The application of First Amendment principles to labor disputes has always been troublesome. Before the mid-twentieth century, courts often restricted labor unions' expression. Apart from some measure of anti-union bias, this reflected the generally narrow view of the First Amendment common at the time. Even after judicial broadening of First Amendment protections in other contexts, courts continued to apply stricter limitations on unions, particularly with regard to picketing and boycotts. After Congress passed the Wagner Act, courts were just as unsympathetic to employer claims of First Amendment protection.

From the passage of the Wagner Act to adoption of the Taft–Hartley amendments, the Board scarcely recognized that employers had any right to comment during election campaigns. In fact, its early decisions treated most negative employer comments as a violation of employee organizational rights. For the most part, courts enforced these Board rulings. Board restriction of employer speech was one of Congress' main concerns in drafting the 1947 amendments. The result was a new § 8(c):

> The expressing of any views, argument, or opinion, or the dissemination thereof, whether in written, printed, graphic, or visual form, shall not constitute or be evidence of an unfair labor practice under

[37] Sunbeam Corp., 99 NLRB 546, 550 (1952).

[38] *E.g.*, Brief for the Petitioner in *Sinclair* at 75. The other three employers made essentially the same arguments.

> any of the provisions of this Act, if such expression contains no threat of reprisal or promise of benefit.

Just three years before it decided *Gissel*, the Supreme Court had recognized that the purpose of § 8(c) was "to encourage free debate on issues dividing labor and management," and held that speech cases are

> to be considered "against the background of a profound . . . commitment to the principle that debate . . . should be uninhibited, robust, and wide-open, and that it may well include vehement, caustic, and sometimes unpleasantly sharp attacks."[39]

It would have been reasonable for Sinclair to expect serious consideration of its claims to freedom of speech since, by the time of the case, federal courts had significantly broadened such protections. Nevertheless, the Board's treatment of the free speech issue in *Sinclair*, both by the Trial Examiner and the Board itself, was merely cursory. The First Circuit's decision enforcing the Board opinion was little better. Neither the agency nor the court gave much attention to the question of how § 8(c) or the Supreme Court's First Amendment jurisprudence might limit the Board's control of employer speech.

Sinclair's brief, ninety-five pages long with eighty-five footnotes and references to scores of cases, did its best to convince the Supreme Court that a major issue of free speech lay among the rather mundane facts of the case. At great length, Sinclair reminded the Court that the Board's ruling effectively limited an employer's ability to speak with its employees about the possible consequences of unionization. Its particular target was the Board's "totality" doctrine, which allowed the Board to punish an employer for the cumulative effect of individually unobjectionable statements. Sinclair noted that the First Circuit "failed to make the required independent review of the entire record to determine whether the Board's order constituted an invasion of constitutional freedoms."[40] Sinclair asserted that the First Circuit had unquestioningly accepted the Board's conclusions, relying on the Board's expertise in labor relations rather than measuring the employer's actual words against the Constitution and the statute.

Sinclair's brief examined the individual statements cited by the Trial Examiner, explaining that each was privileged, accurate, or at least a fair statement of opinion. Sinclair had informed employees, apparently correctly, of the near-bankruptcy caused by the 1952 strike; of the company's weak financial condition; of its relative lack of importance to its new owner, Lindsay; of the Teamsters' expected demands; of the well-documented record of Teamsters corruption; and of the economic risks of

---

39 Linn v. United Plant Guard Workers of America, 383 U.S. 53, 62 (1966) (internal citation omitted).

40 Brief for the Petitioner in *Sinclair* at 49.

strikes. The cartoons used to dramatize its arguments were also protected by § 8(c) and by the Constitution, the company argued. The brief noted that most if not all of the cartoons, including the "graveyard" and "closedest shop in town" ones, had been used by other employers and had even received Board approval.[41]

The Board's brief built a much more elaborate foundation for the Board's decision on the speech question than the Board's opinion itself did. It also dealt with one item the Board had ignored—§ 8(c).

Knowing that Sinclair's brief had parsed the employer's individual sentences and found them reasonable, the Board's brief led off with its strongest argument. It asserted that in determining whether employer communications constituted a threat, "it is necessary to look beyond the bare words and evaluate their impact upon employees in the context in which they are used." Thus an employer's "predictions" can in fact "convey a threat of reprisal." Even "innocuous" words can be coercive "by reliance on the surrounding circumstances."[42]

Having prepared the Court to look beyond Sinclair's "bare words," the Board's brief next explained that § 8(c)'s reference to "threat" must be read in context: "Section 8(c) was never intended to permit sophisticated employers to circumvent the Act's prohibition against coercion of their employees' choice by couching their threats in a particular way." Nothing in the Board's test for coercion is likely to deter an employer from making known its views on unionization. Moreover, the Board asserted, the importance of context makes it critical for a "reviewing court" to recognize "the Board's competence in the first instance to weigh the significance of the raw facts of conduct and to draw from them an informed judgment as to the ultimate fact."[43] In short, only the Board possesses the expertise to distinguish the innocuous from the illegal.

The Board's brief then examined Sinclair's "predictions" and concluded that the Board's special "competence" allowed it to regard the combination of statements as an implied threat to close the plant if the union won the election. "The employees would be likely to interpret Sinclair's remarks as really intended to express an intention on the part of the Company to adopt an intransigent attitude toward the Union's demands, no matter what they were, and thus force the Union to strike."[44] In repeatedly warning that the parent corporation could trans-

---

[41] *Id.* at 64, citing an unreported Board decision, I. F. Manufacturing Co., Case No. 8–RC–3374 (1959).

[42] Brief for the Respondent in *Sinclair* at 13–16.

[43] *Id.* at 19.

[44] The Board's characterization of Sinclair's "intention" is powerful, but note that none of the remarks quoted by the Board actually suggests an "intransigent attitude" toward the Union's demands, "no matter what they are."

fer work elsewhere in the event of a strike, the employees would also recognize that "Sinclair was speaking of matters within management's control." These, the Board concluded, were not permissible expressions of "views and opinion" protected by § 8(c), but rather threats of reprisal prohibited by § 8(a)(1).

The Board also emphasized President Sinclair's admission that he had no knowledge that any of the companies in the "graveyard" had closed because of strikes or unreasonable union demands. While the Board's brief did not go so far as to say that employers were limited to making accurate factual assertions, it left the impression that lack of proof made an employer's predictions questionable if not *ipso facto* illegal. This was a subtle but critical reversal of the usual burden in restriction-of-speech cases: the Board had not shown that the cartoon's implication was *false*; instead, it faulted the employer for not proving its implication *true*.

There is one surprising omission from the Board's brief. Even though petitioner Sinclair had claimed constitutional protection for its communications, the Board's brief did not even mention the First Amendment! Administrative agencies normally don't consider the constitutionality of the laws they apply, but on appeal they do have to face such issues. It is impossible to know, given the brief's total silence on the question, why the Board chose entirely to ignore the Constitution.[45] What is most astonishing is that despite Sinclair's lengthy, detailed, and passionate explication of the First Amendment argument, the Board's lack of concern about constitutional implications would be echoed in the opinion of the Supreme Court itself.

The Lawyers at the Supreme Court

Edward J. Simerka, who argued in the U.S. Supreme Court on behalf of Sinclair, was forty-seven years old. A Harvard Law School graduate and former World War II prisoner of war, he was considered a "true scholar" by his partners at the Stanley firm.[46] One said that, for Simerka, "holidays were times you could take off to write briefs."[47]

---

[45] Perhaps the Board just expected the apparent "labor exception" to the First Amendment to apply despite the broadening of speech protections in other contexts. Or perhaps it believed the constitutional and statutory protections were congruent, so that words violating the statute were constitutionally unprotected. Or it may have believed that Congress' power under the Commerce Clause to protect employee organizational rights trumped any employer constitutional claims. Or the Board may have assumed that employees' statutory rights were of equal weight with employers' constitutional rights.

[46] Telephone Interview with Tim Wood (former member of the Stanley law firm), January 22, 2004.

[47] Telephone Interview with Gregory P. Szuter (former member of the Stanley law firm), January 22, 2004.

Simerka would never go to lunch with his colleagues, instead using the time to read labor law advance sheets reporting new decisions.

Simerka's partner, Eugene B. Schwartz, joined him in the writing of the petition for certiorari and the brief on behalf of The Sinclair Company. Schwartz was a Jewish Hungarian immigrant who had achieved academic distinction in college and law school in Cleveland while supporting himself renting suits and tuxedos and doing dry cleaning at the Commodore Dress Suit Rental Co. Unlike his partner Simerka, Schwartz was a "cigar-chomping, ball of fire," and an aggressive negotiator on behalf of management. Schwartz was at his best surrounded by a crowd listening to his dramatic retelling of stories from his combative dealings with unions in the early days of the National Labor Relations Act.[48]

The task of representing the National Labor Relations Board in the Supreme Court was divided between the Board's General Counsel and the office of the Solicitor General of the United States that handles most Supreme Court cases on behalf of the federal government. Since there were to be two oral arguments, one for the consolidated cases from the Fourth Circuit raising only the bargaining order issue and one for the *Sinclair* case raising both that issue and the free speech issue, the NLRB and the Solicitor's office divided the tasks of briefing and argument, with the NLRB handling the Fourth Circuit cases and the Solicitor's office presenting the government's case in *Sinclair*.

At the NLRB, the tasks were further divided within the office of the Associate General Counsel with Assistant General Counsel Norton Come supervising the brief writing and Associate General Counsel Dominick L. Manoli doing the oral argument. Norton Come was a native of Chicago and a graduate of the University of Chicago and its law school. He first came to Washington as a government lawyer for the Office of Price Administration during World War II and joined the NLRB in 1948. Between 1958 and 1987 he argued fifty-six cases in the U.S. Supreme Court on behalf of the agency.[49]

Come asked Thomas E. Silfen, a young lawyer substituting for Come's usual assistant who was then on maternity leave, to draft the Board's brief for the Fourth Circuit cases.[50] Associate General Counsel Dominick L. Manoli, assigned to present the oral argument, was born in

48 Telephone Interviews with Tim Wood and Gregory P. Szuter, January 22, 2004.

49 Obituary of Norton Come, Wash. Post, Mar. 19, 2002, 2002 WL 15846287. Until a month before his death, at age 82 in 2002, Come was still writing briefs for the NLRB, with "the aid of a walker and a nurse." The week Come died the Solicitor General's Office submitted to the Supreme Court a brief on which Come had consulted. *Id.*

50 Telephone Interview with Thomas E. Silfen, February 12, 2004.

Italy and educated at Harvard College and Harvard Law School. From 1941 to 1971 he represented the NLRB in enforcement litigation in the courts of appeals and the Supreme Court.[51] Between his first certiorari petition in 1945 and his last oral argument in 1971, Manoli's name appeared on 646 documents filed in the Supreme Court. Like Norton Come, Manoli for decades articulated the Board's position in the Supreme Court cases that defined American labor law.

Lawrence G. Wallace represented the NLRB in the Supreme Court in the *Sinclair* case. Then in his late thirties, Wallace was educated at Syracuse University and Columbia University Law School. As Editor-in-Chief of the Columbia Law Review he edited the student note of Ruth Bader Ginsburg, before whom he later argued cases when she was appointed an Associate Justice of the Supreme Court. Wallace clerked for U.S. Supreme Court Justice Hugo L. Black, engaged briefly in private practice in Washington, and taught public law courses at Duke University before joining the Solicitor General's Office in January 1968. In a career extending to January 2003, he argued an extraordinary 157 cases before the high court. His oral argument in *Sinclair*, however, was only his second or third such argument.[52] Wallace represented the federal government through the terms of nine Solicitors General and eight Presidents. Upon his retirement he was described as the "quintessential civil servant, interested more in being true to the Supreme Court and to the law than in mouthing the policy agenda of his politically appointed superiors."[53]

The Oral Arguments

The Fourth Circuit Cases

Because the focus of *Sinclair* was on the free speech issue unique to that case, we must look to the oral argument in the three Fourth Circuit cases to understand the Supreme Court's resolution of the authorization card issue. Recall that the state of the law at the time was clear: An employer's refusal to recognize a union's card-based majority would violate § 8(a)(5) only if the General Counsel could demonstrate that the employer's refusal was not made in good faith. The General Counsel

---

[51] Obituary of Dominick L. Manoli, Wash. Post, July 26, 1980.

[52] Telephone Interview with Lawrence G. Wallace, January 22, 2004.

[53] Tony Mauro, *High Court Farewell: The Supreme Court's Most Prolific Arguer During the 20th Century Reminisces About Ways the Institution Has Changed*, American Lawyer, May 14, 2003. Notably, Wallace once included a footnote in his brief to explain that he personally disagreed with the position of the government, in that case a contention that institutions discriminating on the basis of race were nevertheless entitled to tax-exempt status. Brief of the United States n. * at 1, October Term 1981, Docket Nos. 81–1 and 81–3 (Mar. 3, 1982), Bob Jones University v. United States, 461 U.S. 574 (1983).

could do that by showing that the employer committed substantial unfair labor practices tending to dissipate the union's majority or engaged in some other course of conduct that demonstrated its lack of good faith.

Good faith was still the critical test; the only thing that had changed since *Joy Silk* was that the General Counsel now had to prove the absence of good faith. The Board's brief writers, the four charged employers, the sole union participant, and the groups that submitted amicus briefs all used *Aaron Brothers* as the starting place for their written arguments. With one possible exception, all of the attorneys naturally assumed the oral arguments would track the written.

The one possible exception was Dominick Manoli, the lawyer representing the Board in the Fourth Circuit cases. Representing the petitioner in those cases, Manoli was first to argue.[54] He began with a description of the current law, going back thirty years, requiring employers to bargain when the union could show majority support in authorization cards and "the employer did not have a good faith doubt of the union's majority status." He continued:

> And the employer's concurrent misconduct at the time that he refused to bargain with the union on the basis of those cards ... demonstrates that he is refusing to bargain with the union, not because of any [asserted] doubt of the union's majority status, but in order to gain time, in order to dissipate the union strength and avoid bargaining at all.

A few minutes into his argument, however, Manoli dropped a bomb. In response to a justice's question about when an employer may insist on an election, Manoli stated:

> A ... the Board has said this—the employer may say, "I don't like cards. I don't wish to rely upon cards and I do insist that you go to an election...."
>
> Q That may not get him—the union may just file [8(a)(5)] charges on him then?
>
> A The Board—the General Counsel will not issue a complaint in that kind of a situation where the employer says to the union I don't wish to rely upon cards.
>
> Q I don't care how many cards you have got, I just don't like them. He can get an election then?
>
> A That is right.
>
> Q That is what the position of the Board is?

54 Except where otherwise noted, this description of the oral argument is based on the official transcript.

A That is right. As long as he does not misbehave.

Thus Manoli asserted that good faith was irrelevant so long as the employer did not commit serious unfair labor practices. That was not the *Aaron Brothers* approach, of course. If he were enunciating the Board's previous rulings, he should have said that the employer could reject a card-based bargaining demand *unless the General Counsel could prove that its denial was not in good faith*. Instead, Manoli effectively stated that the employer could refuse recognition *regardless of its good or bad faith*.

The Court immediately spotted the change: "It certainly doesn't emerge from your briefs in this case," commented one justice. "I hope they did," Manoli replied. When asked whether this was always the Board's practice, Manoli answered, "No, your honor, I think the Board has changed that." He added,

> But it has not been a recent change really, your Honor. I think that this began some time in the early 60's. At one time the Board would take the position . . . it was not enough for him to say I don't like the cards. He had to have—or not enough for him to say that I have a good faith doubt in your majority status—he also had to have some objective evidence which supported his good faith doubt.

In the midst of his next sentence, Manoli was interrupted by another question asking where the Board articulated the position announced by Manoli. He answered, "I think you have to take the Aaron Brothers case which is cited in our brief."

There was much more of the same. In response to questions from a very skeptical Court, Manoli repeatedly asserted that the employer could simply demand an election—and more significantly, that the Board had so held in *Aaron Brothers* and in other cases from "the early 60's." Pushed by one justice, he stated the point even more extremely:

Q . . . Assume the union representatives come to than [sic] employer and present some cards to him and say here we have a majority and the employer looks at him and says well, it certainly appears you have a majority and I have no question about the cards and it looks to me like you have a majority of the workers with you.

But I want an election.

A The Board will permit him to go to an election as long as he does not misbehave.

Another justice pointed out that Manoli's description of the Board's position was "a considerably different thing than you have in the brief" and asked if he was sure he wanted the Court to accept his statement. Manoli said simply, "Yes, that is right."

Despite Manoli's assertion that he was merely articulating a long-standing Board policy, he clearly was not, as many in the courtroom immediately recognized. The justices' comments reflect that understanding. The Board lawyer who drafted its brief recalled a "gasp in the courtroom" and a "sense of excitement" when Manoli abandoned the good faith test.[55]

Other counsel were just as astonished. The next advocate, Albert Gore representing the Food Store Employees, began with this extraordinary statement:

> I am in the anomolous [sic] position of having come to this court to argue a case in conjunction with the Board with some slight differences and now in the position of having to take the position almost diametrical to that which has been argued today.
>
> The statement of Board counsel in respect to the response of respective questions of your Honors do not, in my view, suggest the rule that the Board is now following, nor do they suggest the rule that the law lays down.

Gore's argument was interrupted by a lunch break. Gore may have spoken to Manoli during the break, for he resumed his argument by saying, "Perhaps I was a bit presumptuous to suggest what the Board's position is of today.... Unquestionably Mr. Manoli is in a better position to suggest what the Board's position is as of today than I." One justice immediately interjected, "How about yesterday?," to which Gore could only answer "Yes, yesterday's position I thought I understood."

Frederick Holroyd, counsel for Heck's, was just as surprised. When asked about his view of the Board's position as stated by Manoli, he told the Court, "Well, I am going to ask for a printing of the record in that regard from his remarks in presenting that to the next trial examiner that I have because that is certainly news to me." For the most part, though, respondents' counsel contented themselves with arguing that their clients did nothing wrong and that in any event authorization cards were too unreliable to form the basis for a bargaining order.

Other observers were also struck by Manoli's words. Union representatives, who immediately realized that abandoning the good faith test would make it harder to get bargaining orders, were outraged. One Board lawyer recalled that at the break between arguments "The union

---

55 Telephone Interview with Thomas E. Silfen, February 12, 2004. Another young Board lawyer present at the argument, Robert Giannasi, now Chief Administrative Law Judge for the Board, has a similar memory. Board lawyers thought Manoli had "given away the store" but Giannasi now regards Manoli's argument as a "tactical tour de force" because it offered a simple objective standard to replace the cumbersome good faith doubt test. Telephone Interview with Robert Giannasi, February 12, 2004.

people were climbing the walls. I remember chaos. They were all upset."[56]

There was one further oddity about the oral argument that was unrelated to the Board's policy. One of the respondents, Gissel Packing Company, a small family-owned pork producer, had closed its business and liquidated its assets prior to oral argument, making the case against it moot. Article III of the Constitution precludes the Court from hearing cases that have become moot. The matter is taken so seriously at the Court that lawyers are obligated to inform the Court of facts that might cause mootness even if the lawyers believe that the case is not in fact moot. Gissel's counsel, John E. Jenkins, Jr., did not, however, inform either the Court or opposing counsel. Although he no longer had a client to pay for his time, Jenkins was determined to present the oral argument both because he wanted the experience of arguing before the high court and because he thought his presence there would help defend Fourth Circuit precedent favorable to his other food-industry clients.[57] As there were other cases then pending before the Court that raised the same issue as *Gissel*, had Jenkins acknowledged the mootness of his case, the issue would still have been heard and decided in the same way, but we would not today call them "Gissel bargaining orders."

Sinclair

By comparison with the Fourth Circuit cases, oral argument in *Sinclair* was routine. Simerka, representing the petitioner, stuck close to his brief, describing and defending each of the employer's communications and objecting that the Board's "totality" approach violated both the First Amendment and § 8(c). He only addressed the bargaining order issue near the end of his time. Simerka capitalized on Manoli's argument by noting that "the question of good faith is really irrelevant and that the Board said so itself in this case."

Lawrence Wallace of the Solicitor General's office spoke for the Board. He too understandably concentrated on the 8(a)(1) question, beginning with a discussion of § 8(c). Just before the Court recessed for the day, one justice asked him if the statute merely paralleled the First Amendment. Surprisingly, Wallace replied that § 8(c) "goes further," and distinguished a Supreme Court case earlier in the term that found "inherent coercion" in a recommendation by Texaco to its dealers in favor of a particular brand of tires; "certainly the Labor Board would not go this far in the case of 8(c)." Shortly thereafter the Court recessed for the day.

---

56 Telephone Interview with Thomas E. Silfen, February 12, 2004.

57 Telephone Interview with John E. Jenkins, Jr., February 23, 2004.

Returning the next day, Wallace began by admitting that Sinclair had not made any blatant, unequivocal threats but defended the Board's "totality" approach. He said the issue was whether

> an employer who has carefully avoided the utterance of any specific, overt threat, has nevertheless intimidated his employees by getting the message across in the totality of what is said that there is a real threat of company reprisal if they should select the union.

To emphasize the vulnerability of employees to implied threats by their employers, Wallace cited a statement by Judge Hays of the Second Circuit warning that judges may not appreciate "the insecurities of workers who are not so fortunately situated."[58] He then argued that Sinclair's superficially nonthreatening communications "were likely to have had a coercive effect" because the employees' skills had become technologically outmoded. Skillfully weaving the employer's words into the context of the 1952 strike and the economic pressures on the paper machine industry, Wallace argued that the Board could find the employees' free choice "undermined by an implied threat." Concluding his argument on the speech issue after a justice asked if he might address the authorization card question, Wallace warned that a ruling in favor of

---

[58] In preparing his oral argument for the Supreme Court, Wallace was unsure of whether the justices would be offended by an argument that judges, with life tenure, might have difficulty appreciating the job insecurity of ordinary workers. Ultimately he decided to make that point. Telephone Interview with Lawrence G. Wallace, January 22, 2004.

While Wallace's assumption about justices' limited understanding of the lives of ordinary workers might have been true of some justices, it was not true of the Chief Justice. Wallace was apparently unaware of Warren's intimate personal knowledge of workers' lives and their economic vulnerability. Despite Warren's patrician appearance, he was the son of a Norwegian immigrant who worked for the Southern Pacific Railroad in California for more than thirty years. For a time Warren's father was forced to leave his family to work for a different railroad ninety miles away after he was blacklisted for participation in a strike. Warren himself worked for the Southern Pacific every summer and Christmas vacation from the time he was fifteen until he finished law school. Warren gave the last major address of his third campaign for governor at a union hall where he emphasized both his family history in the workforce and his gubernatorial accomplishments benefitting workers. Speaking of himself and his father, he said, "Both he and I have worked twelve hours a day, six days a week, at twenty-five cents an hour." Ed Cray, *Chief Justice: A Biography of Earl Warren* 213–214, 214 (1997). At age fifteen he also became a charter member of a musicians union local when, as a high school clarinet player, he was recruited to play in the town band that performed on ceremonial occasions and at Saturday night summer concerts. Earl Warren, *The Memoirs of Earl Warren* 12–29 (1977). Indeed, as a Supreme Court justice, he remained an honorary union member and twice recused himself from participation in pending cases involving that union, the American Federation of Musicians. American Federation of Musicians v. Wittstein, 379 U.S. 171 (1964) (upholding the union's procedure for voting to increase membership dues); American Federation of Musicians v. Carroll, 391 U.S. 99 (1968) (union practices did not violate anti-trust laws). *See also* Bernard Schwartz, *Super Chief: Earl Warren and His Supreme Court—A Judicial Biography* 715 (1983).

Sinclair could "convert this record into a script which thereafter could be used by employers with impunity to intimidate their employees."

When Wallace finally reached the card issue, he noted that the union had obtained cards from eleven of the fourteen bargaining unit employees and that "the authenticity of these cards is no longer disputed." He managed to tie the cards back to the implied threat, asserting that the union's loss in the election after obtaining so many cards and after the employer's "coercive power during the election campaign" permitted the Board to infer that the employer's refusal to bargain "was motivated not by good faith doubt as to the union's majority status, but motivated primarily by a desire to try, by wrongful means, to dissipate that majority." Even in the absence of an 8(a)(5) violation, he told the Court, "the bargaining order would have been an appropriate remedy for an 8(a)(1) violation."

The Manoli Puzzle

Dominick Manoli's death in 1980 leaves us without access to the most authoritative answer to the question of why he told the Supreme Court that the Board was no longer using good faith as the test of an employer's obligation to bargain, yet at the same time saying that the Board's position had not changed.

He was certainly right that the Board had not changed the law since its *Aaron Brothers* decision. Apart from its largely unused rulemaking authority, the Board can only change the law by decisions rendered by its Board members. The Board issued no new decisions on the good faith issue between the time of the Board's brief, which relied on *Aaron Brothers*, and its oral argument in *Gissel*. But Manoli was certainly wrong in asserting that the Board was no longer using the good faith test. It is quite extraordinary that a career attorney for the National Labor Relations Board who had been arguing cases in the Supreme Court for more than a decade would inform the justices that the Board was employing a legal rule that it had in fact never adopted. Why would he have done that?

Of the two possible explanations, mistake or deliberate misstatement, the latter appears, surprisingly, to be the more likely answer. Such a critical mistake would be inconsistent with Manoli's skill and experience. Manoli's years at the Board put him at the center of articulating the fine points of Board legal doctrine. His responsibilities included reviewing the hundreds of briefs filed annually by Board attorneys in the circuit courts and the U.S. Supreme Court. He was known as a careful and detailed reader of legal arguments. One attorney who wrote Board appellate briefs said that he considered Manoli's approval of a brief a more important measure of its quality than even affirmation by the court.[59]

The more likely explanation is that Manoli, as a zealous advocate, crafted his own statement of Board law in order to make it possible for the Court to rule in the Board's favor.[60] Knowing, however, that the General Counsel had no power to change Board law, he tried to persuade the Court that this more acceptable legal doctrine was the Board's and not his own. Manoli obviously recognized the tension between these two objectives, but in his preparation for oral argument he was unable to devise a better way of handling the dilemma.

There is considerable evidence that Manoli knew that the Board still adhered to its *Joy Silk* doctrine and he was well aware of its problematic nature. A good personal friend of Manoli's at the Board was Melvin J. Welles, then chief counsel to Board Member Sam Zagoria. At a conference at the University of Georgia Law School in November 1968, months before the *Gissel* oral argument, Welles presented a paper that recommended that the Board abandon *Joy Silk* and its reliance on good faith and instead adopt a simpler rule. Welles' recommended doctrine was precisely the one stated by Manoli in his argument, that "a bargaining order issue only as a remedy for unfair labor practices."[61] Manoli had read Welles' paper and liked it.[62] Welles' article was blunt in its criticisms of *Joy Silk*. He said it "does not provide a feasible or logical solution, emphasizes form over substance, and establishes a 'motive' test where none is warranted."[63]

The difficulty of defending *Joy Silk* before the Supreme Court had also been impressed on Manoli as he prepared for his oral argument in *Gissel*. Board attorney Thomas E. Silfen, who had written the first draft of the Board's brief in *Gissel*, was present on a day shortly before the oral argument when Norton Come did a mock argument with Manoli. In the practice session, Manoli was presented with a hypothetical of an employer who hadn't committed any unfair labor practices and who also had no doubt about the validity of the authorization cards. The hypo-

59 Telephone Interview with Robert Giannasi, February 12, 2004.

60 An appellate government attorney has considerable opportunities for creative lawyering in defending an agency's action. For example, the lawyer can offer additional justifications for the agency's action or construe its precedents narrowly. There is no doubt, though, that the line of permissible advocacy is crossed when a lawyer asserts as a fact that the agency no longer follows a precedent it has not abandoned.

61 Melvin J. Welles, *The Obligation to Bargain on the Basis of a Card Majority*, 3 Ga. L. Rev. 349, 357 (1969).

62 Telephone Interview with Melvin J. Welles, January 29, 2004.

63 3 Ga. L. Rev. at 356.

thetical employer told the union he wouldn't recognize the union solely on the basis of authorization cards and wanted an election. The lawyer pretending to be a Supreme Court justice asked Manoli whether this employer would have committed an unfair labor practice. Manoli replied that this wasn't an unfair labor practice. The mock justice then reminded Manoli that in the hypothetical the employer had no good faith doubt. According to Silfen, Manoli "was left speechless, without a good answer."[64]

Manoli could see that this application of the Board's good faith doubt test would be impossible to defend, but he and the other Board attorneys preparing him for the argument believed strongly that the agency's vital policies before the Court in *Gissel* needed to prevail. Most importantly, the Board needed the Court to permit reliance on authorization cards when an employer's serious unfair labor practices made a fair election impossible. If, in the Board's view, the unfair labor practices automatically showed bad faith, was it possible for Manoli to say that the doctrine had evolved to the point that the bad faith label was unnecessary to the analysis and unfair labor practices alone warranted the bargaining order? Silfen left the preparation session unsure of how Manoli would handle the hypothetical should it be asked of him in oral argument. Silfen, however, believed that if the Court pressed Manoli on the good faith doctrine and it stood between the Board and victory, Manoli was ready to say that subjective motivation was no longer the touchstone.

As a representative of the General Counsel, Manoli surely knew that he could not personally create Board law. How could he tell the Court not to worry about *Joy Silk*, even though the Board, alone having that power, had never made such a decision? Maybe Manoli's seemingly confused oral argument was more deliberate than it appeared. Perhaps he articulated the theory he believed critical to a successful outcome (that good or bad faith was not relevant) while holding to a necessary (and truthful) insistence that the Board had not abandoned *Joy Silk*. He may have thought befuddling the Court an acceptable tactic if it let them conclude, without Manoli's expressly saying it, that the Board had abandoned *Joy Silk*. With *Joy Silk* gone and its most indefensible application off the table, the Court would be more likely to accept the use of authorization cards where it really mattered to the Board, in those cases with the most serious unfair labor practices.

Manoli apparently had rejected as unpersuasive a simpler possible answer to the hypothetical question of the right of an employer who had not committed any unfair labor practices to have an election even if it had no good faith doubt of the validity of the cards. While he could

[64] Telephone Interview with Thomas E. Silfen, February 12, 2004.

simply have answered by saying that issue was not before the Court because all four employers had been found guilty of serious unfair labor practices, that reply might not have satisfied the justices. Manoli must have assumed that the Court would be unlikely to accept the validity of cards in the context of serious unfair labor practices if it feared that the Board might also rely upon them in situations where fair elections were possible.

The Supreme Court Decision

Despite the Board's internal divisions and the problems caused by Manoli's oral argument, a unanimous Supreme Court affirmed the Board's decisions in all four cases. In the process it affirmed the First Circuit decision and remanded the Fourth Circuit cases for further proceedings.

The 1968–69 Term of the Supreme Court was the last term of the Warren Court. Chief Justice Earl Warren was to retire on June 23, 1969. Prior to the *Gissel* oral argument, one of Warren's four law clerks, C. Boyden Gray (who later was White House Counsel to President George H. W. Bush), had written a forty-seven page bench memorandum and an additional five-page supplemental memorandum analyzing the issues in the Fourth Circuit cases. As a result of Gray's extensive involvement with the case prior to argument, Warren selected him to draft the opinion deciding *Sinclair,* together with the Fourth Circuit cases, under the name of *Gissel Packing*. Gray worked on *Gissel* while other clerks in Warren's chambers were intensely focused on another case, considered much more important. It, like *Gissel,* was to be decided on June 16, 1969, the very last day that Justice Warren issued opinions before his retirement the following week.[65]

The Authorization Card Issue

After a lengthy description of the facts and arguments, the Court's opinion turned to the question common to all the cases, the use of authorization cards. It began by accepting, as the Board's, Manoli's description of "its current practice" that an employer need not grant a card-based recognition demand "unless he has knowledge independently that the union has a majority." If, however, the employer commits "independent and substantial unfair labor practices disruptive of election conditions," the Board may issue a bargaining order as a remedy, provided the union did not obtain the cards by misrepresentation or coercion. Although the Board previously used a good faith test, the Court commented, "the Board announced at oral argument that it had virtual-

[65] That case was Powell v. McCormack, 395 U.S. 486 (1969), an important constitutional case in which the Supreme Court held that the House of Representatives had acted unconstitutionally in refusing to seat an elected Representative.

ly abandoned the *Joy Silk* doctrine altogether." As a result, an employer can now insist on an election, "regardless of his subjective motivation" so long as he avoids misconduct; "he need give no affirmative reasons for rejecting a recognition request."

The first legal question addressed by the Court was whether a union can ever establish a bargaining obligation other than by a Board election. The Court concluded that the Taft–Hartley Act did not change relevant law. It permits the Board to order an employer to recognize a union, but a union can obtain the extra benefits provided by Board *certification* only through an election.

The next question was whether authorization cards are too unreliable ever to be used to establish majority status. Authorization cards, the Court concluded, are not as reliable as an election but "where an employer engages in conduct disruptive of the election process, cards may be the most effective—perhaps the only—way of assuring employee choice." The Court approved the Board's *Cumberland Shoe*[66] doctrine for assessing the validity of cards when challenged by the employer. The *Cumberland Shoe* doctrine holds that if the cards unambiguously authorize the union to bargain for the employee, as they did in these four cases,[67]

> employees should be bound by the clear language of what they sign unless that language is deliberately and clearly canceled by a union adherent with words calculated to direct the signer to disregard and forget the language above his signature.

The final question regarding authorization cards was the propriety of a bargaining order as a remedy for a refusal to bargain where the employer committed serious unfair labor practices "which have made the holding of a fair election unlikely or which have in fact undermined a union's majority and caused an election to be set aside." The Court emphasized that whether the usual cease-and-desist order could eliminate the effects of the unfair labor practices on employee choice "is for the Board and not the courts ... based on its expert estimate as to the effects on the election process."

The Court distinguished three types of unfair labor practices calling for different rules:

I. The first category consists of "exceptional" cases marked by "outrageous" and "pervasive" unfair labor practices. As even the Fourth Circuit recognized, if the coercive effects of such

---

66 144 NLRB 1268 (1963).

67 The Court did not rule on the conflicting approaches used by various courts of appeals with regard to "dual-purpose" cards that authorize the union both to bargain on behalf of the employee and to seek an election.

unfair labor practices cannot be eliminated by traditional remedies with the result that "a fair and reliable election cannot be had," a bargaining order is appropriate even "without the need of inquiry into majority status."

II. The second category involves "less pervasive practices which nonetheless still have the tendency to undermine majority strength and impede the election process." A bargaining order is within the Board's power in such a case "where there is also a showing that at one point the union had a majority." In choosing a remedy in Category II cases, the Board may consider "the extensiveness of an employer's unfair practices in terms of their past effect on election conditions and the likelihood of their recurrence in the future."

III. The third category involves "minor or less extensive unfair labor practices, which, because of their minimal impact on the election machinery, will not sustain a bargaining order."

In *Sinclair*, the Board found (and the First Circuit did not dispute) that the company's threats of reprisal were so coercive that they fell into the first category, so that a bargaining order was necessary as a remedy even in the absence of an 8(a)(5) violation. In the other three cases, the Board did not decide whether a bargaining order was a remedial necessity or whether a new election would be the most reliable test of employee wishes. The Court therefore remanded those three cases to the Board "for proper findings."

The Free Speech Issue

Turning to the issue that was unique to *Sinclair*, the Court discussed the constitutional issue the Board and the First Circuit virtually ignored. It did so, however, in puzzling manner. Implicitly rejecting the statement by government counsel that 8(c) was broader than the First Amendment, the Court equated the two authorities: Section 8(c), it held, "merely implements the First Amendment" by requiring that the employer's expressions would not be evidence of an unfair labor practice provided they contain no threat of reprisal or promise of benefit. In evaluating an employer's statements, the Board and the courts should take into account the economic dependence of the employees on the employer and their "necessary tendency . . . to pick up intended implications" of the employer "that might be more readily dismissed by a more disinterested ear." The Court signaled its intention to limit free speech rights in labor representation cases by distinguishing those disputes from political elections:

> [W]hat is basically at stake is the establishment of a nonpermanent, limited relationship between the employer, his economically depen-

> dent employee and his union agent, not the election of legislators or the enactment of legislation whereby that relationship is ultimately defined and where the independent voter may be freer to listen more objectively and employers as a class freer to talk.[68]

The Court thus began its treatment of the speech question by equating statutory and constitutional rights. Without citing any authority for its proposition, the Court stated that "an employer's rights cannot outweigh the equal rights of the employees to associate freely, as those rights are embodied in § 7 and protected by § 8(a)(1) and the proviso to § 8(c)." To put it differently, the employees' *statutory* rights are equal to the employer's *First Amendment* rights. By granting employees a statutory right to organize, Congress could therefore limit an employer's constitutional rights.

The Court next discussed the particular type of speech involved in *Sinclair*—the employer's predictions about the consequences of unionization. Because predictions are by their nature unprovable, they are at bottom opinions. In virtually all other contexts (leaving aside obscenity and defamation), the First Amendment protects even those expressions of opinion that listeners find offensive, irrational, or flagrantly wrong. A legislature may impose reasonable restrictions on the time, place, or manner of the speech, but none of those factors was involved in *Sinclair*. The Constitution may not protect threats, however, and the Board did find Sinclair's communications threatening. The surprising part of the Court's opinion is not that it independently found the speech threatening, but rather that it granted an administrative agency such wide latitude to do so. Moreover, the Court went out of its way to limit just what employers might say. The Court recognized the employer's right to "make a prediction as to the precise effects he believes unionization will have on his company" only to impose a severe limitation on that right: "In such a case, however, the prediction *must be carefully phrased on the basis of objective fact* to convey an employer's belief *as to demonstrably probable consequences* beyond his control."[69] If the point were not already clear, the Court drove it home later in the paragraph, agreeing with the First Circuit's statement that

---

[68] 395 U.S. at 617–18. The only authority cited for the proposition that employers' speech may be limited in labor cases was New York Times v. Sullivan, 376 U.S. 254 (1964), a defamation case that had nothing to do with a union representation campaign.

[69] 395 U.S. at 618 (emphasis added). Citing Textile Workers v. Darlington Mfg. Co., 380 U.S. 263 (1965), the Court also allowed the employer to "convey a management decision already arrived at to close the plant in case of unionization." *Darlington* made clear that such a decision, and presumably communication of such a decision, would be permissible only if the employer were to go completely out of business rather than merely closing a portion of its business.

> conveyance of the employer's belief, *even though sincere*, that unionization will or may result in the closing of the plant is not a statement of fact unless, which is most improbable, the eventuality of closing is capable of proof. (Emphasis added.)

The Warren Court's crabbed interpretation of the First Amendment here is likely unique. In no other situation would a speaker lose constitutional protection simply because predictions were not "carefully phrased on the basis of objective fact" or did not convey a belief as to "demonstrably probable consequences beyond his control." In no other situation would a speaker be subject to legal sanctions for conveying a sincere belief in economic consequences unless its prediction is a "statement of fact" which is "capable of proof."

Sinclair argued that the line between "permitted predictions" and "proscribed threats" was "too vague to stand up under traditional First Amendment analysis" and that "the Board's discretion to curtail free speech rights is correspondingly too uncontrolled." A Court that in other contexts would not permit legal regulations that created a "chilling effect" on free speech issued this response in its penultimate paragraph:

> But an employer, who has control over that relationship and therefore knows it best, cannot be heard to complain that he is without an adequate guide for his behavior. He can easily make his views known without engaging in " 'brinkmanship' " when it becomes all too easy to "overstep and tumble [over] the brink." At the very least he can avoid coercive speech simply by avoiding conscious overstatements he has reason to believe will mislead his employees.[70]

Moreover, the Court granted the Board unusually broad discretion to evaluate the true meaning and likely effect of words that in themselves would not be problematic. It rejected without significant discussion Sinclair's complaints that the Board's "totality" doctrine effectively prohibited protected speech. It also warned reviewing courts not to substitute their own interpretation of an employer's communications for that of the Board.

The problem the Court faced should not be forgotten. Employers do have power to take away jobs and employees are likely to view even facially neutral statements suspiciously. When balancing that concern against the employer's freedom of speech, the Court could have opted either to protect the "uninhibited, robust, and wide-open" debate it praised in *Linn* or to protect employees from arguments that might frighten them. Either choice entailed some risks. In *Sinclair* the Court chose the latter option. At bottom, it accepted the Board's paternalistic conclusion that employees are unable to distinguish predictions from

---

[70] 395 U.S. at 620 (internal citation omitted).

threats or to discount exaggerations. Under this view of employees as vulnerable and unsophisticated, it follows that the Board must protect them by forbidding employers to express their fears or beliefs about the negative consequences of unionization. That such a rule might keep employees from hearing potentially meritorious (or at least plausible) arguments did not seem to occur to the Board or the Court.

The Court's opinion on the free speech issue, different from its own First Amendment jurisprudence in other situations, was all the more puzzling because it had a much simpler and more direct way of affirming the Board. It could just have found that threats of reprisal were not constitutionally protected and affirmed the Board's findings that Sinclair's communications were threats. Such a holding might not neatly fit the facts of the case—even considering the employer's influence over the employees, Sinclair's statements and cartoons should fall within the realm of permissible debate about an economic decision of interest to both parties—but at least it would not have relegated speech in labor representation cases to a constitutionally inferior position.

The Immediate Impact of Gissel Packing

For all the resources expended in litigating the four *Gissel* cases, the Supreme Court's decision was ultimately futile. Even though the Board won on every point before the Supreme Court, none of the unions involved managed to establish a lasting bargaining relationship.

SINCLAIR

Despite the Supreme Court's enforcement of the Board's order that Sinclair bargain collectively with the Teamsters as the representative of the wire weavers, there is no evidence that any bargaining ever occurred.[71] On July 21, 1969, David H. Sinclair notified the Compliance Officer for NLRB Region One that he had signed and posted the Board's Notice to All Employees stating that Sinclair would not threaten employees with plant closings or other economic reprisals and that it would, upon request, recognize and bargain with the Teamsters as the representative of journeymen wire weavers at its Holyoke plant. On August 27, 1969, Local 404 President Napoli did contact the company, but apparently nothing came of it. The union made no further contacts and never asked to bargain.

On October 31, 1969, four of the only five wire weavers remaining at the plant who had been involved in the 1965 organizing effort notified the Compliance Officer that Local 404's Business Representative Gordon

[71] This account of the events following the Supreme Court's decision is drawn from documents in the NLRB Case File, The Sinclair Company, 1–CA–5266, The National Archives, College Park, Maryland.

Morris had advised them that their "chances of successfully bargaining would be in vain" since their ability to obtain support from newer employees in the department was "nil." The four employees asked to be "released from any and all affiliations with the Teamsters' Union." The employees' letter apparently led to the filing of a decertification petition, which the Board dismissed. Napoli wrote a letter to the Board on December 19, 1969, disclaiming interest in the bargaining unit, but then asked that the disclaimer be held in abeyance until the union had a final chance in January to consult the employees about their desires with regard to Teamsters representation.

On January 30, 1970, a Board agent spoke with Business Representative Morris who said it was "clear that employees now making up the unit do not want the Union and would not support it." The Agent wrote a note to the file, "The Union is disclaiming any interest in representing these employees any longer and agree that the case should be closed, though [Morris] said it was regrettable that the case ended up this way." On February 3, 1970, Regional Director Albert J. Hoban wrote a letter to Sinclair's attorney Edward J. Simeka informing him that, since the employer had complied with the Board's order, the case of *The Sinclair Company* was now closed.

The Fourth Circuit Cases

Although some of the unions involved in the Fourth Circuit cases were more successful, none achieved a lasting bargaining relationship. As earlier noted, the Gissel Packing Company had gone out of business even before oral argument, so its employees never engaged in collective bargaining.

At General Steel, after two more Board decisions and another from the Fourth Circuit, the Board decided in 1972 that subsequent changes in ownership and management at the company warranted an election rather than a bargaining order. Although the union won the election at General Steel, by 1976 the employees filed for its decertification, the union disclaimed interest and the bargaining relationship ended.

Two unions had sought to organize the employees at Heck's. The Teamsters gained bargaining rights after the Board on remand reissued its bargaining order, but later abandoned its effort to represent employees there. The Food Store Employees, affiliated with the Amalgamated Meat Cutters, did for a time represent employees at seven Heck's grocery stores. Within a few years, however, Heck's opened more modern stores that drew business away from the older unionized stores and then closed the unionized stores.

Despite the Supreme Court's optimistic expectation in *Gissel* that bargaining orders could produce stable bargaining relationships in workplaces where employers had committed the most serious unfair labor practices, the doctrine proved largely ineffective. The disappointing outcomes in these four cases were frequently repeated as the Board sought, in later cases, what now came to be called "Gissel bargaining orders."

Linden Lumber

The hypothetical question feared by Dominick Manoli in his preparation for oral argument in *Gissel* finally reached the Supreme Court a few years later in *Linden Lumber Div., Summer & Co. v. NLRB*:[72] Would the Board ever require an employer who committed no unfair labor practices to recognize a union on the basis of an authorization card majority? As we have seen, the Board had not abandoned *Joy Silk*'s good faith doubt requirement when Manoli told the Supreme Court that it had. Nevertheless, by the time of *Linden Lumber*, the Board had come to embrace Manoli's doctrine as its own. Carefully choosing its words to describe what had occurred in *Gissel*, the Board in *Linden Lumber* said "We decline, in summary, to reenter the 'good-faith' thicket of *Joy Silk*, ... which we announced to the Supreme Court in *Gissel* we had 'virtually abandoned ... altogether.' "[73]

In a 5–4 decision, the Supreme Court approved the Board's policy. Manoli's position thus became the law of the land five years after he announced that it already was. The Board would decline any inquiry into the employer's state of mind and would instead require the union to prove its status in a Board election unless the employer committed serious unfair labor practices.

The Continuing Importance of Gissel Packing Today

The Supreme Court in *Gissel* articulated a vision of how organizational campaigns should be conducted and a vision of the remedies that should be available should their guidelines be transgressed. In the nearly four decades since its *Gissel Packing* decision, the Supreme Court has not revisited either of its holdings. One might therefore expect that those holdings would today define lower federal court jurisprudence regarding when bargaining orders can be based on authorization cards and when employers' predictions will be considered unlawful threats. That, however, has not been the case.

The Authorization Card Issue

The Supreme Court in *Gissel* viewed the bargaining order remedy as routine and directed lower courts to give special deference to the NLRB's

---

[72] 419 U.S. 301 (1974).

[73] Linden Lumber Div., Sumner & Co., 190 NLRB 718, 721 (1971).

judgment of when bargaining orders would be appropriate. The Court said that even when lesser remedies might be successful, the Board should nevertheless issue bargaining orders if, "on balance," the bargaining order would better protect employee desires. The Court minimized the significance of bargaining orders by saying that there was "nothing permanent in a bargaining order" because employees could later decertify the union if they no longer wanted its representation. The Court specifically rejected the prediction of the Fourth Circuit that "in the great majority of cases, a cease and desist order with the posting of appropriate notices" would be a sufficient remedy for unfair labor practices. Instead the Court emphasized that, because of the NLRB's "fund of knowledge and expertise," its remedial decisionmaking must be given "special respect."[74]

The Court's specific handling of the four cases before it in *Gissel* graphically illustrated its understanding of these precepts. The three cases from the Fourth Circuit had been assessed by the Board and the appellate court under the Board's *Joy Silk* doctrine, and thus did not decide whether the employers' unfair labor practices had rendered fair elections impossible. The employers asked the Supreme Court itself to make the assessment and conclude that fair elections were possible. The Court rejected that suggestion, denied that the assessment could be made by the Fourth Circuit, and remanded the cases to the Board for its remedial determination. In *Sinclair* the Board had not challenged the Trial Examiner's conclusory determination that the unfair labor practices were so serious that a bargaining order would have been necessary even if the employer had had a good faith doubt of the union's majority status. Neither the Board nor the Trial Examiner had stated that a fair election would be impossible or why it might be. The Supreme Court nevertheless simply affirmed the Board's decision. The Court indicated that the Board was free to assess when bargaining orders were appropriate, that the Board was not required to detail its full reasoning in each case, and that the Board was entitled to substantial deference from the reviewing court.[75]

While some circuit courts have generally followed Supreme Court guidance on the standards for enforcement of bargaining orders, others have greeted the Board's bargaining orders with overt hostility and the imposition of new requirements never envisioned by the high court.[76] A

---

[74] 395 U.S. at 612–15.

[75] *Id.* at 615–16.

[76] For example, the Court of Appeals for the District of Columbia, which hears a disproportionate share of the *Gissel* bargaining order cases, acknowledges that it has "long viewed them with suspicion." Lee Lumber & Bldg. Material Corp. v. NLRB, 117 F.3d 1454, 1461 (D.C. Cir. 1997).

study of judicial enforcement of 108 Board bargaining orders issued between 1979 and 1982 found that the average enforcement rate in the courts of appeals was 70.4%. While some circuits with only a few such cases enforced all of the bargaining orders, the Second Circuit enforced only 45.5% and the Seventh Circuit enforced a tiny twenty-five percent.[77] The authors of the study, Professors Terry A. Bethel and Catherine A. Melfi, found that "rather than deferring to the Board, courts are making their own assessment of the impact of employer conduct."

Bethel and Melfi identified three broad categories of reasons that courts had given for denying enforcement of Board bargaining orders, none of which were grounded in the Supreme Court's *Gissel* opinion. First, courts most often criticized the Board for not articulating generally-applicable detailed standards for the issuance of bargaining orders and for not identifying specific factors warranting issuance in a particular case. Second, despite the Supreme Court's insistence on administrative deference, courts sometimes just disagreed with the Board's findings of unfair labor practices or with the Board's conclusion that a bargaining order was appropriate. Third, courts sometimes found that during the several years that typically pass between the commission of unfair labor practices and judicial review, workplace circumstances had changed in ways that suggested that a fair election could now be held.[78]

The unwillingness of courts to enforce Board bargaining orders may have affected the Board's willingness to award them. While during the years studied by Bethel and Melfi, 1979–82, the Board issued an average of forty-four bargaining orders per year, more recently, between 1987 and 1996, the Board issued an average of only 9.7 such orders annually. The Board's enforcement success rate in the courts of appeals has also declined. Of twenty NLRB bargaining orders reviewed in the appellate courts in fiscal years 1994–1996, only fifty percent were enforced. Attorney Peter J. Leff, who reported these statistics, catalogued additional tests that each circuit had articulated, creating barriers to enforcement never suggested by the Supreme Court in *Gissel*.[79] For example, some circuits have suggested that there is a presumption against enforcement of a bargaining order in the absence of "hallmark" violations that

[77] Terry A. Bethel & Catherine Melfi, *Judicial Enforcement of N.L.R.B. Bargaining Orders: What Influences the Courts?*, 22 U.C. Davis L. Rev. 139, 161–62 (1988).

[78] *Id.* at 142. Changes in circumstances include such things as turnover of employees, changes in management, and the mere passage of time.

[79] Peter J. Leff, *Failing to Give the Board Its Due: The Lack of Deference Afforded by the Appellate Courts in* Gissel *Bargaining Order Cases*, 18 Lab. Law. 93 (2002). *See also* Gil A. Abramson, *The Uncertain Fate of* Gissel *Bargaining Orders in the Circuit Courts of Appeal*, 18 Lab. Law. 121 (2002).

include completed actions such as plant closures and employee discharges.[80]

In response to the difficulty of securing enforcement of its bargaining orders, the General Counsel of the NLRB has limited the circumstances in which its attorneys will seek bargaining orders. In 1999, the General Counsel issued a memorandum to its regional offices providing guidelines for seeking *Gissel* orders.[81] Ironically, the General Counsel acknowledged that the Board was having difficulty in securing enforcement of bargaining orders involving threats of plant closure, the very issue involved in *Sinclair*, because some appellate courts were unwilling to accept the Board's assessment that mere threats should be considered hallmark violations. The General Counsel continues to require regional offices to seek direction from the Office of Advice before issuing a complaint seeking a *Gissel* bargaining order in cases in which the only violations alleged are of § 8(a)(1) of the Act (typically threats and promises).

As a means to address the problem of the courts' unwillingness to enforce bargaining orders because of the passage of time and changes in circumstances, the Board has considered making greater use of its injunctive authority under § 10(j) of the NLRA. If bargaining orders can be obtained by injunction in district courts soon after a Board investigation, employers are unable to argue that time has dissipated the taint of unfair labor practices. For that reason, the Board's General Counsels have required that, before issuing a complaint seeking a *Gissel* order, attorneys in the regional offices first notify the Board's Injunction Litigation Branch and recommend whether interim injunctive relief should be sought.[82] The process, however, has not yielded a significant number of injunctions. The General Counsel's most recent statement on 10(j) activity, covering the second half of 2003, reported that the Board sought only two interim *Gissel* bargaining orders and obtained just one.[83]

---

80 See, for example, NLRB v. Jamaica Towing Co., 632 F.2d 208 (2d Cir. 1980). Even when cases include "hallmark" violations, courts exercise independent judgment about the propriety of a bargaining order. The Bethel and Melfi study found that in cases involving the hallmark violation of discriminatory discharge, courts enforced only 74.6% of the bargaining orders, just modestly higher than the overall enforcement rate of 70.4%. Terry A. Bethel & Catherine Melfi, *Judicial Enforcement of N.L.R.B. Bargaining Orders: What Influences the Courts?* 22 U.C. Davis L. Rev. 139, 172 (1988).

81 NLRB, General Counsel Memorandum GC 99–8, Guideline Memorandum Concerning Gissel (Nov. 10, 1998), 1999 WL 33313998.

82 *Id.*; NLRB, General Counsel Memorandum GC 01–03, Report on Utilization of 10(j) Injunction Proceedings: Mar. 3, 1998 through Jan. 15, 2001 (Feb. 5, 2001), 2001 WL 988354.

83 NLRB, Report of the General Counsel (Apr. 5, 2004), <www.nlrb.gov>.

Scholars who have studied the difficulties encountered by the Board in enforcement of its *Gissel* bargaining orders have speculated about why the appellate courts have been reluctant to give the Board the remedial deference the Supreme Court directed. Most fundamentally, although the Supreme Court in *Gissel* minimized the seriousness of any interference with employee free choice on the ground that it was temporary, the lower courts continue to be troubled that employees, even temporarily, lose the right to express their views on union representation in a secret ballot election.[84] The Court's paternalistic view that the Board can better determine employees' desires than the employees themselves has not been accepted by the lower courts. Further, without overtly challenging the Supreme Court's factual premise underlying *Gissel* that a union with an authorization card bare majority would have won an election in the absence of serious unfair labor practices, courts have been acting in such a way as to manifest their disbelief. Professors Bethel and Melfi found that courts enforced only about sixty percent of the bargaining orders in which unions had authorization cards from fifty to sixty percent of the employees, but eighty-nine percent of the cases in which unions had cards from more than ninety percent of the employees.[85]

The appellate judges' apparent doubts about the predictive value of authorization cards are supported by the empirical work of Professor Laura Cooper. She tested the fundamental assumption of *Gissel* that, in the absence of serious unfair labor practices, a union that had a card majority would have won the election. Professor Cooper's study of 760 NLRB elections found that when unions had cards from between fifty and sixty percent of employees, circumstances under which the unions would have been eligible for a *Gissel* bargaining order had there been serious unfair labor practices, unions won only 40.9% of elections. Even those unions that presented cards from more than ninety percent of the employees won only 65.7% of elections.[86]

---

[84] See, for example, Overnite Transp. Co. v. NLRB, 280 F.3d 417 (4th Cir. 2002); Traction Wholesale Center Co. v. NLRB, 216 F.3d 92 (D.C.Cir. 2000); and HarperCollins v. NLRB, 79 F.3d 1324 (2d Cir. 1996).

[85] Terry A. Bethel & Catherine Melfi, *Judicial Enforcement of NLRB Bargaining Orders: What Influences the Courts?*, 22 U.C. Davis L. Rev. 139, 170 (1988). A similar pattern was found in a smaller sample of decisions. Laura Cooper, *Authorization Cards and Union Representation Election Outcome: An Empirical Assessment of the Assumption Underlying the Supreme Court's* Gissel *Decision*, 79 Nw.U.L.Rev. 87, 100 (1984).

[86] Laura Cooper, *Authorization Cards and Union Representation Election Outcome: An Empirical Assessment of the Assumption Underlying the Supreme Court's* Gissel *Decision*, 79 Nw.U.L.Rev. 87, 118 (1984). Another empirical study also undermines the theory of *Gissel*. Interviews with more than 1200 union voters in thirty-one representation elections revealed that potential union voters were more likely than company voters to perceive unlawful employer campaigning but that such campaigning did not influence employees to

Judicial rejections of bargaining orders on grounds inconsistent with the Supreme Court's opinion are one measure of the extent to which *Gissel* has failed to achieve its objectives. Another measure is the extent to which *Gissel* bargaining orders have actually resulted in bargaining relationships and collective bargaining agreements. Professors Bethel and Melfi also examined the efficacy of *Gissel* bargaining orders. In more than forty percent of the bargaining order cases they studied unions never bargained at all with employers. Unions were able to obtain contracts in only about twenty percent of the cases.[87]

The Supreme Court's opinion in *Gissel* expressed the belief that sometimes ordinary Board remedies will be so inadequate to combat serious unfair labor practices that a bargaining order is the appropriate resolution. Subsequent events, however, have revealed that such bargaining orders are, as a practical matter, largely unattainable. Unions can only obtain bargaining orders by overcoming a series of significant obstacles. They must obtain authorization cards from a majority of employees under such circumstances that the Board and a court will consider the cards valid[88] and both the Board and the court must confirm that the bargaining unit in which the union established its majority was indeed an appropriate unit. There must be evidence of commission of unfair labor practices satisfactory to both the Board and the court and both must conclude that the unfair labor practices were sufficiently serious to preclude the holding of a fair election. Moreover, a court must find that the Board adequately explained its rationale for issuance of a bargaining order and conclude that circumstances had not changed in the intervening years so as to make a fair election now possible. Even if all of these hurdles are overcome, the union will only have an opportunity to bargain after years of litigation and it will then have just one chance in five of actually obtaining an initial collective bargaining agreement.

The Free Speech Issue

Had the Board and lower courts taken the Supreme Court's words at face value, modern representation campaigns would be remarkably one-sided. Unions could promise the moon if selected as the bargaining

---

vote against union representation. Julius G. Getman, Stephen B. Goldberg & Jeanne B. Herman, *Union Representation Elections: Law and Reality* 121–24 (1976).

87 Terry A. Bethel & Catherine Melfi, *The Failure of* Gissel *Bargaining Orders*, 14 Hofstra Lab. L.J. 423, 438 (1997). In contrast, unions that won representation rights in an election achieved first contracts seventy-seven percent of the time. *Id.*

88 If an employer is able to commit unfair labor practices so early in a union's organizational campaign that the union is precluded from obtaining cards from a majority of the employees, no bargaining order remedy will be available. Gourmet Foods, Inc., 270 NLRB 578 (1984). In a 2–1 decision, the NLRB recently reaffirmed *Gourmet Foods*. First Legal Support Services, LLC, 342 NLRB No. 29, 2004 WL 1509036 (2004).

representative but employers might not be allowed to comment on the potentially negative impact of unionization on profitability, on the risks of strikes, or on the negative experiences of other unionized firms, let alone "predict" what might happen in the immediate workplace. For good or ill, neither the Board nor the lower courts followed that path. Instead, prodded by academic criticism of the holding in *Sinclair*[89] and eager to reconcile election campaign speech with other applications of the First Amendment, they have gradually afforded employers much wider protection than the Supreme Court granted the Sinclair Company. Perhaps to avoid the appearance of overruling the Supreme Court, they often do so after quoting the very statements from *Gissel* that would apparently direct them to find the challenged communications illegal.

The Board's post-*Gissel* speech decisions have not always been clear or consistent. They are necessarily fact-specific, but even so, the distinctions drawn by the Board are sometimes very fine indeed. After an initial series of decisions banning employer predictions,[90] many of which were overturned on appeal, the Board began to exhibit some uncertainty, reaching disparate conclusions in the face of similar statements.[91]

In recent years, however, the Board has hesitated to challenge the sort of speech used by Sinclair. Consider this example of the extent of the Board's current tolerance for employer predictions. In *Manhattan Crowne Plaza Town Park Hotel Corp.*,[92] a panel majority declined to overturn an election, let alone issue a bargaining order, even though the employer distributed a memorandum containing these paragraphs referring to a negotiation dispute at two other Manhattan hotels:

> Yesterday afternoon, after 1 year of negotiating in good faith with the Brotherhood of Security Personnel, Officers and Guard

[89] *See, e.g.,* Ian M. Adams & Richard L. Wyatt, Jr., *Free Speech and Administrative Agency Deference: Section 8(c) and the National Labor Relations Board—An Expostulation on Preserving the First Amendment*, 22 J. Contemp. L. 19 (1996); Julius Getman, *Symposium: Directions in Labor Law—Concern for the Dignity of the Worker: Labor Law and Free Speech: The Curious Policy of Limited Expression*, 43 Md. L. Rev. 4 (1984); Beth Z. Margulies, NLRB v. Gissel Packing Co.: *A Standard Without a Following,* 22 Willamette L. Rev. 459 (1986); Note, *Employer Free Speech During Representation Elections*, 35 S.C. L. Rev. 617 (1984); and Paul D. Snitzer, *Employer Free Speech—The Emergence of a Conflict Between the Board and the Circuits*, 11 Lab. Law. 247 (1995).

[90] *See* Ian M. Adams & Richard L. Wyatt, Jr., *Free Speech and Administrative Agency Deference: Section 8(c) and the National Labor Relations Board—An Expostulation on Preserving the First Amendment*, 22 J. Contemp. L. 19, 32–34 (1996).

[91] *Compare* Action Mining, 318 NLRB 652 (1995) (no violation), *with* Reeves Brothers, Inc., 320 NLRB 1082 (1996) (violation). *See also* Robert A. Gorman & Matthew W. Finkin, *Basic Text on Labor Law: Unionization and Collective Bargaining* § 7.10 (2d ed. 2004) (cataloging which recurrent employer communications are considered by the Board to be implied threats).

[92] 341 NLRB No. 90, 2004 WL 940788 (2004).

> Union without reaching a settlement, the company submitted its final offer to the union. The union rejected that offer, and the company promptly broke off negotiations, contracted with an outside security guard company to provide security services for the hotels, and fired the in-house security personnel.
>
> So, in the final analysis, the majority who voted for this union (as well as the minority who voted against it) gained NOTHING, and LOST EVERYTHING! They lost all their medical benefits, their 401K plans, and most importantly, they lost their jobs!
>
> Each set of negotiations is different, however, keep in mind from a wage and benefit perspective, you guys have one of the best employment situations in the industry. In addition, you did not have to pay anyone weekly dues to get this package. Why would you pay someone for the possibility of losing this arrangement?

In form, the Crowne Plaza's memorandum was quite similar to Sinclair's rhetoric. It used a local example to imply that the union would demand so much in bargaining that the employer would have no choice but to cut jobs. The Regional Director found a clear implication in the memorandum that similar job losses were possible if the union won the election at Crowne Plaza. The Board reversed, quoting *Gissel* but focusing instead on the "concrete" nature of the employer's example and the employer's cautious statement that "each set of negotiations is different."

The appellate courts, too, have had mixed responses to the *Gissel* holding. A few have read *Gissel* literally.[93] Most courts, though, particularly in recent years, have been unwilling to give the Board much room to ban employer speech. The most influential decision on the issue is Judge Richard Posner's in *NLRB v. Village IX*.[94] The employer gave a speech to employees containing these comments:

> Unions do not work in restaurants.... The balance is not here.... If the Union exists at Shenanigans, Shenanigans will fail. That is it in a nutshell.... I won't be here if there is a Union within this particular restaurant. I am not making a threat. I am making a statement of fact.... I respect anyone who wants to join the Union if that in essence is a workable place and can afford to pay Union wages. We can't in the restaurant business ...
>
> Shenanigans can possibly exist with labor problems for a period of time. But in the long run we won't make it. The cancer will eat us up, and we will fall by the wayside. And if you walk into this place five years down the road, if there is a Union in here, then I

93 See, for example, Allegheny Ludlum Corp. v. NLRB, 104 F.3d 1354 (D.C. Cir. 1997) (Sinclair-like cartoon viewed as implicit threat).

94 723 F.2d 1360 (7th Cir. 1983).

> guarantee you it won't be a restaurant. I don't know what it will be. But wherever you people will be working in this town, in Decatur, it will not be in a Union restaurant. It will be in a non-Union restaurant. . . .

The Board, not surprisingly, found the speech coercive.

The court of appeals reversed, noting the thin line between predictions and threats: the speech, Judge Posner wrote, "offered a competent if extremely informal analysis of likely economic consequences of unionization in a highly competitive market in which most companies are not unionized—the restaurant market in Decatur." Referring to the Supreme Court's assertion that employers could only make provable predictions, Judge Posner offered this fig leaf:

> But [he] provided objective support for his prediction of the consequences of unionizing Shenanigans by pointing to the competitive nature of the restaurant business and to the fact that only one restaurant in Decatur was unionized and it was doing badly. More was not required in the circumstances; we do not read *Gissel* to require the employer to develop detailed advance substantiation in the manner of the Federal Trade Commission . . . at least for predictions founded on common sense and general experience.

The court of appeals took a much less paternalistic view of union election voters than did the *Gissel* Court, stating that they should be able to hear both sides: "To forbid expression of that opinion would not serve the interests of Shenanigans' employees, for unionization might in fact hurt rather than help them in the long run."[95] The D.C. Circuit has followed Judge Posner in being similarly tolerant of employer predictions. For example, it found no unfair labor practice when an employer said that with wage increases "there'd be no way that the shop could continue to go," concluding that a small company should not be required to offer technical substantiation on common-sense predictions.[96]

---

[95] *Cf.* Julius Getman, *Symposium: Directions in Labor Law—Concern for the Dignity of the Worker: Labor Law and Free Speech: The Curious Policy of Limited Expression*, 43 Md. L. Rev. 4 (1984). Professor Getman argues that *Gissel* rests on four assumptions that he believes are "counterfactual": that employees are attentive to and easily coerced by employer statements; that union representation decisions merit less constitutional protection than political elections; that employers can adequately state their cases against unionization under the *Sinclair* rules; and that the Board's expertise allows it to determine which employer conduct will have such lasting impact as to require a bargaining order. He notes that after *Gissel*, employers cannot address the potential negative consequences of unionization "without coming close to the brink." That, he argues, ignores the employees' interests, because *Gissel* "assumes employee ignorance which it is unlawful to correct." *Id.* at 9–10.

[96] Somerset Welding & Steel, Inc. v. NLRB, 987 F.2d 777 (D.C. Cir. 1993). *See also* Crown Cork and Seal Co. v. NLRB, 36 F.3d 1130 (D.C. Cir. 1994) (wage increases could endanger employer's competitive position).

In very general terms, the Board and courts seem to be moving the line between permitted and prohibited statements. The Supreme Court in *Gissel* drew the line between statements of fact (permitted) and unprovable predictions (prohibited). Cases like *Manhattan Crowne Plaza*, and *Village IX* draw it between predictions (which by their nature are unprovable and therefore generally permitted) and overt threats of retaliation (which of course are prohibited). Moving the line that far now protects communications like those used by Sinclair and brings the law of free speech in union campaigns closer to the law of free speech in other contexts. Doing so also has the effect of making the *Gissel* holding on the definition of threats virtually irrelevant.

Conclusion

The bargaining order and free speech issues in *Gissel* posed difficult choices for the Supreme Court between the rights and interests of employers and employees. The Court chose, for each of these issues, the more paternalistic alternative. Employees who had experienced serious employer unfair labor practices would be represented by a union even if, had they been given the opportunity to vote, they would have voted against such representation. Employees who might be too naive to understand the self-interest behind an employer's prediction of the future negative effects of unionization on its business would never hear such opinions. Initially these holdings seemed to represent significant victories for unions.

It didn't work out that way. The Court's vision proved to have practical limitations and lower courts refused to enforce many bargaining orders and many findings of unfair labor practices arising from employer predictions. With encouragement from these courts, employers learned how to convey their messages more subtly but with equal effect. The Supreme Court believed that a bargaining order would deter serious unfair labor practices or, where that failed, would provide employees with the protections of collective bargaining. That vision ignored the many practical obstacles to its implementation. Employers who were willing to violate the law to prevent union recognition found new ways to achieve their objective. They could begin illegal conduct so early as to prevent the union from ever obtaining a card majority. They could restructure their businesses to make the union's proposed bargaining unit inappropriate. They could keep litigating until changed circumstances or the passage of time made a bargaining order no longer necessary. And even if all of that failed, they could engage in hard bargaining until the union abandoned hopes of an agreement, knowing from the start that the union lacked sufficient employee support to strike.

In short, the union victories were ephemeral. Within two decades, *Gissel* was little more than an irritation to employers and a symbol of disappointed hopes to unions. Despite the ultimate failure of *Gissel* to achieve its objectives, it nevertheless directed the policymakers' attention to two of the most difficult questions in labor law: how to remedy the most flagrant unfair labor practices and whether and how government should regulate employer communications to economically-dependent workers.

*

6

Calvin William Sharpe, Marion G. Crain and Reuel E. Schiller

The Story of *Emporium Capwell*: Civil Rights, Collective Action, and the Constraints of Union Power

Early Christmas shoppers arriving at the San Francisco Emporium department store on November 9, 1968, were greeted by an unusual sight. Rather than passing quietly through the retailer's neo-classical façade into waiting arms of perfume-toting cosmetics sales personnel, consumers encountered a group of the Emporium's employees: "young black men dressed in black leather jackets and wearing Black Panther pins."[1] The protesters distributed handbills urging shoppers not to patronize the store. The handbills read:

* * BEWARE * * ** BEWARE * * ** BEWARE * *
EMPORIUM SHOPPERS
"BOYCOTT IS ON" "BOYCOTT IS ON" "BOYCOTT IS ON"

---

[1] *Crowd Welcomes Santa To Emporium,* S.F. Examiner & Chron., Nov. 10, 1968, at B11. The United States Supreme Court laid out the facts surrounding the protest in its opinion, Emporium Capwell Co. v. Western Addition Community Organization, 420 U.S. 50 (1975). Considerably more detail can be found in the factual appendix submitted to the Court. Appendix at 50, United States Supreme Court, Emporium Capwell Company v. Western Addition Community Organization, October Term 1973, Nos. 696 & 830. [hereinafter "Appendix"]. This chapter incorporates material previously published in Reuel E. Schiller, *The Emporium Capwell Case: Race, Labor, and the Crisis of Post–War Liberalism,* 25 Berkeley J. Lab. & Empl. L. 129 (2004). This material is reprinted with the Journal's kind permission.

For years at The Emporium black, brown, yellow and red people have worked at the lowest jobs, at the lowest levels. Time and time again we have seen intelligent, hard working brothers and sisters denied promotions and respect.

The Emporium is a 20th Century colonial plantation. The brothers and sisters are being treated the same way as our brothers are being treated in the slave mines of Africa.

Whenever the racist pig at The Emporium injures or harms a black sister or brother, they injure and insult all black people. THE EMPORIUM MUST PAY FOR THESE INSULTS. Therefore, we encourage all of our people to take their money out of this racist store, until black people have full employment and are promoted justly throughout The Emporium.

We welcome the support of our brothers and sisters from the churches, unions, sororities, fraternities, social clubs, Afro–American Institute, Black Panther Party, W.A.C.O. and the Poor Peoples Institute.

Printed for the People—By the People of:

THE WESTERN ADDITION COMMUNITY ORGANIZATION

(W.A.C.O.)[2]

All in all, the boycott was an unremarkable event. Although several heated exchanges occurred between consumers and the leafleteers, mainstream media largely ignored it in favor of coverage of Santa Claus' first appearance of the season and the "Santacade" parade, held the same day. The local African–American newspaper, the *Sun-Reporter*, did cover the boycott—on page five—but only after the Emporium fired the participating workers a week later.[3] The boycott itself petered out after only two Saturdays of leafleting. The fact of the matter was that a small, peaceful civil rights protest in San Francisco at the end of 1968 was simply not newsworthy. It was competing with news of the closely fought 1968 presidential election (among Hubert Humphrey, Richard Nixon, and George Wallace), and its aftermath. Similarly, the events surrounding the contemporaneous student strike and violence at San Francisco State University over adoption of a Black Studies program captured the attention of those concerned with racial protest.

Nevertheless, the conflict among the Emporium, its African–American employees, and, as we shall see, Department Store Employees' Union, Local 1100, generated a trail of litigation that illustrated the

[2] Appendix at 107.

[3] *Racism Charges Against The Emporium—Massive Boycott Planned for Saturday*, Sun–Rep., Nov. 16, 1968, at 5.

conflict between the civil rights movement and the labor movement over the meaning of racial and economic equality, and established the legal framework for resolving the conflict. The specifics of the dispute were quite simple. Could African–American union members bargain directly with their employer over job assignments and promotions, even if satisfying their demands would undermine the seniority provisions of the collective bargaining agreement the Union had negotiated on behalf of all workers? Not surprisingly, Local 1100 had a different answer than did several of its African–American members. The Union and the black workers agreed that the Emporium had engaged in racial discrimination. They disagreed about how best to remedy it.

Social and Legal Background

The confrontation at the Emporium was emblematic of the political unrest and racial tensions that characterized the 1960's. That decade saw the eruption of frustrations over the problems of African–American unemployment and segregation that were the persistent economic legacy of slavery. For African–Americans, the industrial mobilization that accompanied World War II brought job opportunities and relief from poverty and racial segregation in housing and education. During the 1940's, Southern black workers flocked to the North and West in search of high-paying jobs in war industries. When the war ended, so did the temporary surge in prosperity of black migrant families. The situation was exacerbated by a general decline in manufacturing as wartime production levels dropped.

Segregation in the workplace returned with a vengeance. As the "last hired, first fired," black workers who had moved into higher-paying, skilled jobs were displaced by white workers returning from the war; union-negotiated seniority provisions in collective bargaining agreements operated to protect white workers' jobs. Many labor unions were complicit in the re-segregation of black workers. Most unions prohibited blacks from becoming union members, and until the Taft–Hartley Amendments in 1947, the closed shop operated to push blacks out of union jobs, reducing the labor supply, preserving high-paying and skilled jobs for whites, and raising the (white) union wage. Some unions admitted blacks to membership but confined them to segregated "auxiliary" unions complete with racially segregated seniority lists limiting promotion opportunities. This reluctant embrace was designed to prevent employers from using blacks as strikebreakers.[4]

[4] *See* Daniel Crowe, *Prophets of Rage: The Black Freedom Struggle in San Francisco, 1945–1969,* 1–2, 4–5, 122–59 (2000); Albert S. Broussard, *Black San Francisco: The Struggle for Racial Equality in the West, 1900–1954* 48 (1993); Robert Weisbrot, *Freedom Bound: A History of America's Civil Rights Movement* 7, 155 (1990); Philip S. Foner,

Yet segregation itself was not the only evil—with segregation came poverty. By 1960, only fifteen percent of all black workers (compared with forty-four percent of all white workers) held professional, managerial, clerical or sales positions, and nearly half of all black families lived below the federal poverty line. The median black family income was fifty-five percent of white family income. The rate of unemployment for black adults increased steadily between the 1940's and the 1960's, by which time it was more than twice the rate for whites.[5] The sentiments of the urban Northern black underclass were summed up by a black picketer's sign at New York's City Hall in 1963, which proclaimed "I'd eat at your lunch counter—if only I had a job."[6]

By the 1960's, widespread unemployment, stalled efforts at school desegregation and the unrest associated with the segregation of African-Americans into urban ghettos percolated into calls for direct action to effect change. Prior to the 1960's, the most influential civil rights organization had been the National Association for the Advancement of Colored People (NAACP). The NAACP was committed to racial integration and its efforts focused on furthering change inside existing institutions, using the law as leverage. The NAACP eschewed direct action protests, preferring the courts and city hall for its activities. Change was slow, however, and the nonviolent direct action tactics popularized by Dr. Martin Luther King, Jr. in the South soon captured the moral center of the movement. The Congress of Racial Equality (CORE) and the Student Nonviolent Coordinating Committee (SNCC) gained strength. Both organizations pursued direct action strategies, including sit-ins, picket lines, boycotts, and marches. CORE mounted boycotts against employment discrimination at Woolworth's, Kress, Hink's, Montgomery Ward, J.C. Penney's, Macy's, and Sears department stores, all of which had overwhelmingly white retail sales forces, with the few blacks in the store clustered in low-paying janitorial or cafeteria work.[7]

Organized Labor and the Black Worker 1619–1981 64–66 (1982); Herbert Hill, *Black Labor and the American Legal System: Race, Work, and the Law* 185–208 (1977).

[5] African-American unemployment was twenty percent higher than white unemployment in 1940; seventy-one percent higher in 1953; and 112 percent higher by 1963. Daniel Crowe, *Prophets of Rage: The Black Freedom Struggle in San Francisco, 1945–1969* 56 (2000); Robert Weisbrot, *Freedom Bound: A History of America's Civil Rights Movement* 155 (1990).

[6] Robert Weisbrot, *Freedom Bound: A History of America's Civil Rights Movement* 154 (1990).

[7] For excellent histories of the civil rights movement, see Gary Gerstle, *American Crucible: Race and Nation in the Twentieth Century* (2001); Taylor Branch, *Pillar of Fire: America During the King Years, 1963–1965* (1998); Harvard Sitkoff, *The Struggle for Black Equality, 1954–1992* (2d ed. 1993); Taylor Branch, *Parting the Waters: America During the*

More radical organizations soon gained a foothold. Frustrated by the ineffectiveness of both conventional legal and political strategies and nonviolent direct action to alter the conditions of life for the black poor, black nationalists began to advocate revolution against the established order. Black nationalism—especially popular among young, unemployed, low-income blacks—appealed to black pride and urged blacks to organize themselves independently from whites, to build a power base in their own community to be able to speak from a position of strength in combating racism. The Black Power slogan emerged, and was soon endorsed by SNCC and CORE. Indeed, the former expelled its white members in 1966. Similarly, the Black Panther Party for Self–Defense arose in 1966 from a poverty program office in Oakland, California. The Panthers blended black nationalist ideologies with socialist thought in a revolutionary message. They developed a ten-point platform defining the meaning of Black Power in concrete terms and demanding change across a broad range of issues, including employment, housing, educational and police-community concerns.[8]

Black nationalism intensified following the assassination of King in April 1968. King had traveled to Memphis, Tennessee to support the demands of 1300 striking black sanitation workers for a living wage. King, still committed to racially inclusive nonviolent political action, marched with the sanitation workers and urged the civil rights movement to turn its efforts toward economic justice. To King's dismay, the demonstration quickly turned into a riot as young black militants shouting "Black Power" began smashing store windows and looting. The National Guard was called to control the riot. King was assassinated at a Memphis hotel on April 4, 1968. Urban riots in major cities followed, as some blacks vented their rage in what was, for some, the first sign of any unity or allegiance to King's movement.[9]

King Years, 1954–1963 (1988). For studies that focus on the civil rights movement in the Bay Area, see Robert O. Self, *American Babylon: Race and the Struggle for Post–War Oakland* (2003); Daniel Crowe, *Prophets of Rage: The Black Freedom Struggle in San Francisco, 1945–1969* 4, 122–26 (2000).

[8] *See* Robert O. Self, *American Babylon: Race and the Struggle for Post–War Oakland* 217–55 (2003); Gary Gerstle, *American Crucible: Race and Nation in the Twentieth Century* 295–310 (2001); Daniel Crowe, *Prophets of Rage: The Black Freedom Struggle in San Francisco, 1945–1969* 4–5, 86, 122–26, 214, 217–19 (2000); Harvard Sitkoff, *The Struggle for Black Equality, 1954–1992* 195–205 (2d ed. 1993); Herbert H. Haines, *Black Radicals and the Civil Rights Mainstream, 1954–1970* 63–64 (1988).

[9] Gary Gerstle, *American Crucible: Race and Nation in the Twentieth Century* 274–80 (2001); Maurice Isserman & Michael Kazin, *America Divided: The Civil War of the 1960s* 225–28 (2000); Harvard Sitkoff, *The Struggle for Black Equality, 1954–1992* 207–09 (2d ed. 1993); Herbert H. Haines, *Black Radicals and the Civil Rights Mainstream, 1954–1970* 58 (1988).

The alliance between the civil rights movement and the labor movement that King had tried to nurture proved fragile. Until the 1960's, the basic philosophy of both the civil rights movement and the law was to replace racial prejudice and discrimination with reason and neutrality through integration. By the mid–1960's, the civil rights movement sought to stretch this vision to include freedom from poverty as a basic civil right. However, to many, the integrationist strategy seemed inadequate to the challenge of altering the economic structure that entrenched disparities of wealth and social status along racial lines. Black nationalists promoted racial pride and race consciousness—leveraged with direct group action—as an alternative basis of power. Thus, at its most radical, the civil rights movement posed a challenge to the racialized economic order, one that most liberal reformers, including white-controlled labor unions, were loath to embrace.

Factual Background

The events that led to the Emporium boycott and, eventually, to the United States Supreme Court, began in December 1967. At the end of that month, the San Francisco Retailers' Council signed a collective bargaining agreement with Local 1100, covering employees at the Emporium's Market Street location.[10] The Union had represented Emporium workers since 1937, but the 1967 contract was the first one in which the Union had been able to extract a union security provision from the Retailers' Council.[11] Previously, many workers whom the Union represented were not union members. While they enjoyed the benefits of the Union's contract with the Emporium, they did not pay dues. Beginning in January 1968, the new contract required all employees to become dues-paying members or lose their jobs.

Consequently, beginning in 1968, Local 1100 saw a significant increase in its membership. Much of that increase came from African–American workers who were segregated in the "non-selling" areas of the department store, in particular the "Stock and Marking" areas.[12] The union responded to this influx of new members by holding a meeting in April 1968 to identify their concerns. The workers generated a list of complaints, the most significant of which was that the Emporium discriminated against its minority employees. Despite the availability of

---

[10] This account of the factual background, except as otherwise indicated, is drawn from the Appendix.

[11] Interview with Walter Johnson, Secretary–Treasurer of Local 1100 in 1968, San Francisco, Cal., June 6, 2002. [Hereinafter "Johnson interview."]

[12] At this time, few San Francisco businesses had black employees in public service or sales positions. *See* Daniel Crowe, *Prophets of Rage: The Black Freedom Struggle in San Francisco, 1945–1969* 4–5, 54, 122–59 (2000).

numerous supervisory and managerial positions, the Emporium failed to promote qualified African–American workers. Additionally, the Union's new members alleged that minority workers were profoundly underrepresented in the selling areas of the Emporium, where employees earned commissions in addition to wages. The most desirable departments—high-commission selling areas such as home electronics and furniture—were completely devoid of African–American, Asian, or Latino employees.

After the meeting, Local 1100's Secretary–Treasurer Walter Johnson drew up a list of complaints. The allegations of racial discrimination concerned him the most. Johnson forwarded a report to the Retailers' Council by mid-April in which he concluded that "the general situation at the Emporium could become an explosive one" unless the racial discrimination claims were redressed. Johnson subsequently met with officials from the Emporium who agreed to "look into the matter." Over the course of the spring and summer, however, the Emporium took no action. Meanwhile, Johnson had several additional meetings with the employees. By September 3, Johnson and the employees decided to demand arbitration of their claims. Johnson told the workers that processing individual claims of discrimination might take some time, but urged them to follow through since "they would not only be helping themselves, but [the] other people involved. . . ." Several employees provided compelling testimony that was recorded by a stenographer. For example, one worker, James Joseph Hollins, testified that he was told not to come on the main selling floor, and was later denied a position as a temporary supervisor because his hair was styled in an Afro.

On September 4, Johnson sent a letter to the Retailers' Council requesting a meeting of the Adjustment Board to adjudicate the grievances. In particular, Local 1100 accused the Emporium of violating Section 21(E) of the collective bargaining agreement, which provided that "[n]o person shall be discriminated against in regard to hire, tenure of employment or job status by reason of race, color, creed, national origin, age or sex." A hearing before the Adjustment Board was scheduled for October 16th.

Each of the meetings in the spring and summer of 1968 was attended by Hollins as well as several other African–American stock clerks at the Emporium: Thomas Hawkins, Ronald Epps, Carlton Washington, and Russell Young. Indeed, in his letter to the Retailers' Council, Johnson singled out the Emporium's failure to promote Young, despite his skills and seniority, as an example of its discriminatory activities. On October 16th, as the arbitration was scheduled to begin, Hollins, Hawkins, Epps, and Washington announced they would not participate, and walked out of the arbitration. Speaking for the group, Hollins rejected the Union's strategy of processing individual grievances. "We didn't feel like the meeting was really representing us because they wanted to take our case as an individual thing and we were fighting it as a whole." Hollins wanted "some basic change that would benefit the treatment of all minority people." Beyond the demand for respect and equal treatment, it is unclear what sort of change he had in mind, though the Union believed that it involved some sort of direct negotiations between the Emporium and its African–American employees with respect to promotions. Indeed, Hollins stated that the president of the Emporium should meet with the aggrieved workers to discuss the problem of racial discrimination at the store. Over the next few days, Hollins, Hawkins, Epps, and Washington attempted to meet with the Emporium's president, only to be rebuffed.

The previous summer, Hollins and Hawkins had suggested that the Union picket the Emporium or organize a boycott to protest the retailer's discriminatory practices. The Union had rejected their requests, telling them that it was prohibited from doing so by the collective bargaining agreement's no-strike clause. Walter Johnson explained that individuals were free to do whatever they wanted but that the Union preferred to proceed without "drama" and to use "orderly legal procedures." Having abandoned such "orderly procedures" by walking out of the October 16th hearing, the African–American workers turned to the more "dramatic" actions that the Union had eschewed.

Though Local 1100 was unwilling to assist Hollins and Hawkins with the boycott, the two were not without institutional support. One of Hollins' and Hawkins' friends and coworkers at the Emporium was the son of a Western Addition community organizer named Mary Rogers.[13] Rogers was one of the leaders of the Western Addition Community Organization (WACO). Created in 1967 by local community organizers, WACO's *raison d'être* was to resist the federal redevelopment programs that were destroying housing stock and displacing the residents of the Western Addition, the predominantly African–American neighborhood to the west of San Francisco's civic center. Nonetheless, WACO's Constitution also provided that the organization would concern itself with other areas of "social justice and human dignity," including employment practices.[14] Accordingly, WACO agreed to lend its name and resources to Hollins' and Hawkins' undertaking.

A week after they walked out of the arbitration hearing, Hollins and Hawkins, along with Rogers, held a press conference in front of the *Sun-Reporter* building in the Western Addition. Hollins read to the assembled news media the handbill calling for the boycott. He then announced his

---

13 Interview with Kenneth Hecht, attorney at the Employment Law Center in 1968, San Francisco, Cal., Mar. 21, 2001.

14 "Western Addition Community Organization Information Fact Sheet Number 1," page 1, Box 6, Folder 69 "Miscellaneous" San Francisco History Center, Data Center Collection (San Francisco Public Library, San Francisco, Cal.).

intention to distribute the handbill in front of the Emporium until the company's president agreed to discuss with them the working conditions of African–American workers. "I've been working at the Emporium for two years," he said, "and I've never been treated with respect. . . . There are many members of minority groups with similar experiences. We can't see buying in a store where the black employees and other non-white workers are insulted, degraded, and denied a chance for advancement that white employees get."[15]

Hawkins and Hollins did not limit their accusations of racism to the Emporium. Both felt genuinely wronged by Local 1100 for failing to improve minority working conditions and refusing to endorse the boycott.[16] During the spring and summer of 1968 they had put their faith in the Union. By fall they felt betrayed by what they saw as the Union's unresponsiveness and its conservative approach to the Emporium's discriminatory practices.[17] In a "Briefing on Conditions" that Hawkins and Hollins prepared shortly before the boycott, they described the Union's decision to pursue individual grievances as a "con game" and a "smoke screen" by which the Union was trying to "break down the group."[18] "The Union," they wrote, "was itself covering up for the racist Emporium."

The leafleting commenced the following Saturday, November 2. That day a rather dismayed Walter Johnson tried one last time to convince Hollins and Hawkins to pursue arbitration instead: "I informed Mr. Hollins that I thought the only way to resolve the matter was through arbitration. I didn't want to see them get fired." Johnson pointed out that since he, as the secretary-treasurer of the Union, had never had the opportunity to talk to the Emporium's president, he doubted that Hollins would have much luck setting up a meeting. Johnson's final plea fell on deaf ears. Plaintively, he admitted that "[i]t was sort of a one way conversation."

The next week, the Emporium's labor relations manager warned Hollins and Hawkins that should they continue leafleting, they would be fired. "There are ample legal remedies to correct any discrimination you may claim to exist," read a letter they received upon arriving at work the following Monday. "Therefore, we view your activities as a deliberate and unjustified attempt to injure your employer." Despite this warning,

---

[15] Quoted in Anne Ross, *Racism at The Emporium*, Sun–Rep., Oct. 26, 1968, at 2.

[16] *Racism Charges Against the Emporium—Massive Boycott Planned for Saturday*, Sun–Rep., Nov. 19, 1968, at 5.

[17] Interview with Kenneth Hecht, Mar. 21, 2001.

[18] This document is anonymous and undated. However, both Hollins and Hawkins refer to it in their testimony and state that they conducted the survey upon which it was based after the press conference but before the boycott.

the leafleting resumed the next weekend. When Hollins and Hawkins returned to work on Monday, November 11, they were dismissed.

In the following weeks WACO and other Bay Area civil rights organizations attempted, without much success, to promote the boycott.[19] Additionally, Mary Rogers contacted Kenneth Hecht, an attorney at San Francisco Legal Aid's Employment Law Center, whom she knew from WACO's legal battles with the city over redevelopment, to explore Hawkins' and Hollins' legal options.[20] Hecht, who had worked at the NLRB's regional office in San Francisco before joining the Employment Law Center, agreed to take the case. On November 19, he filed charges with the Board's regional office, accusing the Emporium of violating the National Labor Relations Act when it dismissed Hawkins and Hollins. This was the first step in litigation that would end, over six years later, in the United States Supreme Court.

The dispute between WACO and Local 1100 was not the first time that civil rights leaders and San Francisco labor unions had clashed over issues involving structural remedies for racial discrimination. Unions' enthusiastic endorsement of anti-discrimination principles was tempered by their steadfast resistance to affirmative action-type remedies with the potential to affect adversely their members' seniority rights. In 1966, for example, the Hotel Workers' Union succeeded in having an arbitrator nullify an agreement between civil rights groups and the San Francisco Hotel Employers' Association.[21] The unions alleged that the agreement, which was signed after four months of protests about the hotels' discriminatory hiring and promotion practices, would require hotels to promote African–American workers even if doing so violated the seniority provisions of a collective bargaining agreement.[22] Similarly, the San Francisco Labor Council and several Bay Area unions conditioned their support for a proposed city anti-discrimination ordinance containing affirmative action provisions on passage of an amendment to ensure that it would not undermine the seniority provisions of collective bargaining agreements or bypass union hiring halls.[23]

These disputes severely strained relations between San Francisco union leaders and civil rights advocates. Wilfred Ussery, CORE's nation-

---

19 *Racism Charges Against The Emporium—Massive Boycott Planned for Saturday*, Sun–Rep., Nov. 16, 1968, at 5; Marion Fay, *WACO Files Racism Charges Against the Emporium*, Sun–Rep., Nov. 23, 1968, at 4.

20 Interview with Kenneth Hecht, Mar. 21, 2001.

21 *Hotel Employers Association*, 47 Lab. Arb. Awards (CCH) 873 (Nov. 17, 1966).

22 Local Joint Executive Board of Culinary Workers, *Jobs and Hotels, "A Rational and Orderly Way to Better Understanding,"* S.F. Chron., Dec. 5, 1966, at 16.

23 *See* San Francisco, Cal. Draft Ordinance to Amend Administrative Code Chapter 12 to allow the San Francisco Human Rights Commission to Monitor City Contracted Hiring.

al chairman, accused the unions of being "in a more reactionary position than the employers" by seeking to "protect[] jobs for whites" at the expense of the victims of racial discrimination.[24] Members of the San Francisco Labor Council reacted angrily to such statements. This was a classic case of divide-and-conquer, labor leaders asserted. The Chamber of Commerce had long resisted equal employment opportunity legislation. Now it had suddenly and cynically become a champion of civil rights, accusing unions of purposely attempting to undermine black employment as a way of furthering its own interest: to "cut the pay, stretch the hours, and wreck job conditions" of workers, both black and white.[25] San Francisco unions asserted that their efforts redounded to the benefit of *all* workers by preserving the sanctity of collectively-bargained contracts guaranteeing high wages and job security.

Indeed, from a national perspective, San Francisco unions were quite progressive on racial issues. The San Francisco Labor Council repeatedly emphasized its support of the civil rights movement and equal employment opportunity. It enthusiastically endorsed the Civil Rights Act of 1964 and forcefully condemned the violence of Southern law enforcement against civil rights workers.[26] Similarly, it fought to preserve job training programs aimed primarily at minority communities.[27] The Council's member unions represented more than 30,000 African-Americans and, according to the San Francisco Human Rights Commission, over thirteen percent of the workers in union apprenticeship programs in the city were black, the highest percentage in the entire state.[28]

Local 1100's racial attitudes were typical of Bay Area unions. Local 1100's promotional materials proudly displayed a multicultural union,

---

San Francisco City Archives, Records of the Board of Supervisors, File 188–66, Statement of SFBTC, p. 5; Statement of ILWU, p. 1; George W. Johns to AFL–CIO Union Delegates, p. 4 (July 1, 1966); *see also* Official Bulletin of the San Francisco Labor Council, Aug. 24, 1966, at 1; Official Bulletin of the San Francisco Labor Council, Oct. 26, 1966, at 1.

[24] Quoted in Harry Johanesen, *Hotel Bias Ruling is Under Fire*, S.F. Examiner, Nov. 24, 1966, at 4.

[25] Paid Advertisement, Local Joint Executive Board of Culinary Workers, *Jobs and Hotels, "A Rational and Orderly Way to Better Understanding,"* S.F. Chron., Dec. 5, 1966, at 16. *See also Hotel Pact "Attack on the Union Shop" Labor Leader Says*, S.F. Examiner, Dec. 5, 1966, at 9.

[26] "Civil Rights," Official Bulletin San Francisco Labor Council, Vol. 14, No. 20 (Dec. 18, 1963) at 1; "The Shame of Selma," Official Bulletin San Francisco Labor Council, Vol. 16, No. 7 (Mar. 17, 1965) at 1.

[27] "Job Training Threatened," *Official Bulletin San Francisco Labor Council*, Vol. 17, No. 11 (Sept. 21, 1966) at 1.

[28] *Official Bulletin San Francisco Labor Council Bulletin*, Vol. 14, No. 20, (Nov. 18, 1963), unpaginated, third page. Human Rights Commission, Press Release, San Francisco

replete with pictures of African–American, Asian–American, and Latino members.[29] Walter Johnson hired the Union's first African–American business agents and placed a number of black workers on its negotiating committees.[30] Furthermore, the Local had established a "Minority Advisory Panel," charged with maintaining lines of communication between black workers and the union's leadership and critiquing union and employer policies that were perceived as antithetical to the interests of minority workers.[31] Johnson himself explained that the reason the union preferred to utilize the grievance and arbitration procedures to challenge race discrimination was in order to obtain some "long lasting effect."

Nevertheless, by the time the NLRB's Trial Examiner heard WACO's case against the Emporium in the spring of 1969, it was clear that San Francisco unions' commitment to equal employment opportunity did not encompass affirmative action programs that might undermine seniority provisions of labor contracts. Unions were reaching the limit of their racial liberalism, a limit that was defined, in a very real sense, by the seniority provisions of the contracts they negotiated. In the absence of increasing employment opportunities that might avoid a direct conflict between the interests of black and white workers, African–American job equality would only come at the expense of white union members, a price that unions were not willing to pay.[32]

Prior Proceedings

WACO's case rested on the question of whether Hawkins and Hollins had been fired for activity protected by § 7 of the Act. If the discharges were deemed to interfere with § 7 rights, the Emporium would have committed an unfair labor practice in violation of § 8(a)(1), and Hawkins and Hollins would be entitled to reinstatement and back pay.[33] As it prepared to take the case before the Board, WACO's lawyers

---

Labor Council Papers, Correspondence Series 3, Box 26, "Human Rights Commission" folder, San Francisco State University, Labor Archives & Research Center (San Francisco, Cal.).

[29] "Meet Local 1100" (pamphlet); "When Lightning Strikes" (poster). David F. Selvin Collection, Box 18, Folder 8, San Francisco State University, Labor Archives & Research Center (San Francisco, Cal.).

[30] *Id.* Interview with Walter Johnson, June 6, 2002.

[31] "Enough?," "Problem Hit on Other Fronts," *Local 1100 Report*, unpaginated, fourth page, Selvin Collection, Box 18, Folder 5; Walter Johnson Interview.

[32] *See* Official Bulletin San Francisco Labor Council, Vol. 14, No. 20, unpaginated, second and third page.

[33] Section 7 of the NLRA provides in relevant part, "Employees shall have the right to self-organization, to form, join, or assist labor organizations, to bargain collectively through

considered alternatives available under existing law. Legal tools to pressure white-dominated unions to consider minority workers' claims of discrimination were relatively limited.[34] Once a union had attained majority status in a workplace, the labor law doctrines of majority rule and exclusivity constrained minority employees to work within the grievance system established by the collective bargaining agreement. In order to protect workers against divide-and-conquer strategies that employers might use to undermine their collective power, the National Labor Relations Act prohibited employers from bargaining with individual workers once a majority of workers in an appropriate bargaining unit had selected a representative. Thus, the interests of the individual workers were submerged into the collective interests of workers in the unit. The union spoke with one voice on behalf of all the workers, even those who might have voted against the union. If the employer and the union entered into a collective agreement, the contract superseded all individual employment contracts.[35] Section 9(a) of the Act did contain a proviso authorizing individual workers to address their grievances to the employer directly, but it did not authorize bargaining. Thus, once the majority of the workers had selected a union, workers who bargained without the union's approval would be engaging in an unprotected activity, and could be disciplined or discharged without violating the Act.

In an effort to ameliorate the potentially harsh effects of the majority rule and exclusivity doctrines, the Supreme Court had interpreted the Act as imposing on unions a duty of fair representation to all members of the bargaining unit. The duty placed the union in a fiduciary-like relationship with the workers it served as bargaining

representatives of their own choosing, and to engage in other concerted activities for the purpose of collective bargaining or other mutual aid or protection." Section 8(a)(1) makes it an unfair labor practice for an employer "to interfere with, restrain, or coerce employees in the exercise of rights guaranteed in section 7."

34 Title VII of the Civil Rights Act of 1964 was available to remedy discrimination, but practitioners of the day believed that direct action through concerted activity protected under § 7 and enforced by proceedings before the Labor Board was faster and more expeditious than administrative and court proceedings under Title VII. *See* Herbert Hill, *Black Labor and the American Legal System: Race, Work, and the Law* 41–51 (1977); William B. Gould, *Black Workers in White Unions: Job Discrimination in the United States* 259–67 (1977). Drawing upon his earlier experience as an attorney at the NLRB, Ken Hecht also believed that the Board's processes offered the best chance for relief.

35 *See* Medo Photo Supply Corp. v. NLRB, 321 U.S. 678, 684 (1944); J.I. Case Co. v. NLRB, 321 U.S. 332, 337 (1944); *see also* Mark Barenberg, *The Political Economy of the Wagner Act: Power, Symbol, and Workplace Cooperation,* 106 Harv. L. Rev. 1379, 1452–53 (1993) (discussing history of the Act's majority rule and exclusivity provisions). For a detailed history of the drafting and passage of the Wagner Act as well as its aftermath, see Melvin Dubofsky, *The State and Labor in Modern America* 107–67 (1994); Peter H. Irons, *The New Deal Lawyers* 226–89 (1982); James A. Gross, *The Making of the National Labor Relations Board* 130–230 (1974).

agent, both in the negotiation of the labor contract and in its administration. Imposition of the duty laid to rest any concerns about the constitutionality of the labor statutes. Since labor laws preclude minority members from choosing their own representative or bargaining individually with their employers, and since Congress conferred on the bargaining representative "powers comparable to those possessed by a legislative body both to create and restrict the rights of those whom it represents," unions were obligated to represent all members of the unit fairly and in good faith, without hostile discrimination toward any.[36] The duty was narrowly construed, however, in order to provide maximum flexibility to unions in balancing the interests of workers they represented.[37]

In this instance, the union's conduct did not seem to rise to the level of a breach of the duty of fair representation. Local 1100 appeared genuinely concerned about the problem of race discrimination at the Emporium. The disagreement between the union and African-American workers was over tactics, not the goal itself. The union was ready and willing to press the workers' individual grievances forward through arbitration; it was the workers' refusal to participate that had derailed the process. Thus, the union's conduct simply did not rise to the level of arbitrary, discriminatory, or bad faith action. Although sufficient to discharge its duty of fair representation, its action was not enough to satisfy the African-American workers' demands—yet the principle of exclusivity prevented the workers from going directly to the employer to negotiate.

WACO thus had three choices. It could argue that Hollins and Hawkins were not seeking to pressure the Emporium into "bargaining" with them, and try to fit their action into the § 9(a) proviso permitting the presentation of personal grievances. On that theory, their activities would be deemed protected and their discharges would violate § 8(a)(1). This line of argument was ultimately preferred by some of WACO's amici—most notably, the NAACP and Local 1100. They viewed Hollins' and Hawkins' protest as simply pressing a very forceful grievance. No dramatic change in labor law was required to find their activities protected; all that was required was an expansive reading of § 9(a)'s proviso.[38] Alternatively, WACO could seek to expand the union's duty of

---

36 Steele v. Louisville & Nashville R.R. Co., 323 U.S. 192, 200–04 (1944) (imposing duty of fair representation in contract negotiation under the Railway Labor Act); *see also* Ford Motor Co. v. Huffman, 345 U.S. 330, 337 (1953) (imposing duty in contract negotiation under the National Labor Relations Act); Vaca v. Sipes, 386 U.S. 171, 177–83 (1967) (imposing duty in contract administration). Chapter Two of *Labor Law Stories* focuses on the history of the *Steele* case.

37 *See* Michael J. Goldberg, *The Duty of Fair Representation: What the Courts Do in Fact,* 34 Buff. L. Rev. 89, 91 (1985).

38 *See* Brief of Local 1100 at 13–14; Brief of NAACP at 4–6; Brief of WACO at 6–34.

fair representation to encompass Local 1100's conduct. WACO's lawyers did not choose this option, perhaps because the duty's boundaries seemed so clearly to require intentional, hostile conduct.[39] Finally, WACO could ask the Board to limit the doctrine of exclusivity, creating an exception for workers who were attempting to remedy race discrimination. With the recent enactment of Title VII of the Civil Rights Act of 1964 as evidence of the strong national policy favoring anti-discrimination, this option seemed more likely to succeed than the effort to expand the duty of fair representation. Others among WACO's eventual allies, including the EEOC, the Urban League, and the Southern Christian Leadership Conference, favored this strategy. They believed that if the primary goal of national labor policy was to eliminate race discrimination, this goal should trump the principle of exclusivity. The right to protest and remedy race discrimination in the workplace was simply too important to leave to union enforcement.[40]

WACO chose to argue in the alternative. First, WACO contended that the workers were not seeking to bargain with the Emporium. Instead, they sought to present grievances as they believed they were permitted to do under § 9(a), and hence the boycott was protected.[41] Alternatively, even if their actions were not protected under § 9(a), WACO asked the Board to create an exception to the exclusivity principle for worker efforts to combat race discrimination. At some point, WACO asserted, the doctrine of exclusivity had to yield to the broader national policy of anti-discrimination. Traditional labor arbitration had "insurmountable institutional deficiencies ... in dealing with minority claims."[42] Accordingly, minority workers should be allowed to pursue remedies for workplace discrimination outside of collective bargaining agreement procedures.

The Emporium, for its part, disputed WACO's factual assertions. It argued that Local 1100 was acting in a manner reasonably calculated to redress the grievances of the African-American workers, and was doing so in good faith. Hawkins and Hollins were seeking to bargain directly

---

[39] Looking back on the case from a distance of more than thirty years, WACO's attorneys do not remember why they decided against making a duty of fair representation claim. Interview with Kenneth Hecht, Mar. 21, 2001.

[40] Brief of EEOC before the D.C. Circuit at 17, 22–23; Joint Brief of the Urban League and the Southern Christian Leadership Conference at 18; Brief of WACO at 46 n.49, 51–58.

[41] Brief of WACO at 26–34, Reply Brief of WACO before the D.C. Circuit at 48; WACO, oral argument 35–37.

[42] Brief of WACO at 56. These deficiencies included the fact that arbitrators were selected by the employer and the union, each of which might have caused or tolerated the discrimination or have interests in its continuity. In addition, the arbitrator's authority emanated from the collective bargaining agreement, not from Title VII, and arbitrators were therefore "ill-equipped to implement extra-contractual rights." *Id.* at 57.

with Emporium's management, and thus their conduct was unprotected. Moreover, Title VII's legislative history made it clear that Congress had not intended to affect rights created by the NLRA. Aggrieved workers could pursue discrimination claims through the mechanisms established under Title VII, or by filing duty of fair representation claims against their unions, rather than through direct bargaining with employers.[43] The Emporium, later joined by the AFL–CIO as an amicus, defended the principle of exclusivity, arguing that it was the foundation of workers' collective power and suggesting that any dilution would risk balkanization of the labor force. Moreover, the stability of grievance arbitration and collective bargaining itself as mechanisms to insure labor peace would be threatened if workers could opt out of the system and independently employ economic weapons.[44]

WACO's arguments clearly asked for innovation by the Board and the reviewing courts. To require an exception to the principle of exclusivity and thereby authorize collective activity independent of the union was a novel interpretation of the NLRA and a creative attempt to blend its statutory mandate with that of Title VII. Nevertheless, the position of WACO and its allies was hardly unsupportable. Indeed, at the time the NLRB brought the case in November 1968, the idea of carving out an exception to the principle of exclusive representation may have seemed like the logical next step in the Board's burgeoning civil rights-oriented jurisprudence.

The Board's decisions during the 1960's were fully cognizant of political and legal pressures that the civil rights movement and its political allies were placing on public policy and government institutions. The Board, aided no doubt by President Kennedy's appointment of its first African–American member, Howard Jenkins, in 1963, began to incorporate an understanding of racial divisions in the American labor market into its decisions. In 1962 the Board started ordering new representation elections when management or unions made appeals to racial prejudice.[45] Similarly, in 1964 the Board held that racial discrimination by unions was an unfair labor practice and was thus within the Board's jurisdiction to remedy.[46]

---

43 Brief of the NLRB at 29–31; Brief of AFL–CIO at 18–20.

44 Brief of the NLRB at 17–26; Brief of the Emporium at 10–11, 14–15, 23–25; Brief of AFL–CIO at 4–7.

45 Sewell Manufacturing, 138 NLRB 66 (1962).

46 Indep. Metal Workers, Local No. 1, 147 NLRB 1573 (1964); Locals 1367 & 1368, ILA, 148 NLRB 897 (1964), *enforced*, 368 F.2d 1010 (5th Cir. 1966).

Perhaps the most encouraging precedent for WACO was the Board's 1967 decision, *Tanner Motor Livery*.[47] *Tanner* involved the dismissal of two white workers, Abramson and Dorbin, for pressuring their employer, Tanner, a Santa Monica cab company, to hire its first African-American driver. Although Tanner's drivers were unionized, Abramson and Dorbin directly tried to persuade the company to integrate its workforce, without involving the union. Shortly after picketing Tanner's office both drivers were fired. The Board held that the dismissals violated the NLRA. Concerted activities protesting racially discriminatory hiring practices were clearly protected under the Act.[48] So long as the workers "were not acting in derogation of their established bargaining agent" their actions did not violate the exclusivity principle.[49] Indeed, the Board held that Abramson and Dorbin's actions could not have undermined the union's interests because it would have been unlawful, under the duty of fair representation, for the union to oppose the elimination of Tanner's discriminatory hiring practices.[50]

Thus, by spring 1969, when WACO, the Emporium, and the NLRB attorneys argued their cases before a NLRB Trial Examiner in San Francisco, the Board seemed ready to take the next step. *Tanner* held that collective action promoting equal employment opportunity, taken without consulting the union, was protected activity if it did not undermine lawful union objectives. The only difference for WACO and its allies was that, in their case, Hawkins' and Hollins' actions arguably did conflict with the union's lawful goal of combating Emporium's discrimination through grievance arbitration procedures. What WACO had to do was convince the Board that the NLRA had to be construed to recognize what for WACO was labor relations reality: that labor unions could not be expected to represent the interests of minority workers.

The first round of litigation, before the NLRB's Trial Examiner, did not turn out well for WACO.[51] In October 1969, Trial Examiner William Spencer held that Hawkins' and Hollins' picketing was not protected by the NLRA. This was the case because these actions had the effect of

---

[47] 166 NLRB 551 (1967). *Tanner* was first heard by the Board in 1964. 148 NLRB 1402 (1964). The Ninth Circuit reviewed the case and remanded to the Board for a more detailed opinion. 349 F.2d 1 (9th Cir. 1965). This was the opinion released in 1967. Two years later, the Ninth Circuit refused to enforce the Board's 1967 opinion. 419 F.2d 216 (9th Cir. 1969).

[48] 148 NLRB at 1403.

[49] 166 NLRB at 551.

[50] *Id.* at 551–552. There was no allegation that Title VII was violated because the incidents at issue all occurred before its passage.

[51] This account of the proceedings before the Trial Examiner and the Board, and all quotations, are taken from their respective decisions in The Emporium, 192 NLRB 173 (1971), unless otherwise stated.

circumventing Local 1100. The union repeatedly urged them to use the contract's grievance arbitration machinery, yet they refused. In doing so, Spencer held, they prevented the Union from fighting the racial discrimination that it acknowledged existed. Furthermore, it was clear that the Hollins' and Hawkins' desire to meet with management sprang not simply from a desire to air their grievances. Instead, the boycott attempted to force the Emporium to "bargain with the picketing employees for the entire group of minority employees." There was no doubt in Spencer's mind that such an objective was not allowed by the Act. By trying to deal directly with the Emporium, Hollins and Hawkins "seriously undermine[d]" the Union, thereby infringing the right of employees to be represented by a bargaining agent of their choosing. They also placed the Emporium in the untenable position of "attempting to placate self-designated representatives of minority groups" while trying to satisfy the conflicting demands of the Union as required by the collective bargaining agreement.

The General Counsel and WACO filed exceptions to the Trial Examiner's decision, which also sparked a response among groups interested in the case. Local 1100, the NAACP and the EEOC all filed *amici curiae* briefs. The case was also argued orally on January 4, 1971. Following oral argument, the Board majority adopted the Trial Examiner's findings, conclusions, and recommendations. Members Gerald Brown and Howard Jenkins dissented. Brown adopted WACO's more conservative argument. "There is not a scintilla of proof that the picketing employees wanted discussions leading to agreements on new conditions of employment, or even a modification of existing ones." Hollins and Hawkins, Brown reasoned, "simply wanted to call attention to their situation." Accordingly, since they did not wish to bargain with the Emporium, their actions could not be construed as an attempt to undermine union strength. They were simply grieving. Indeed, in Brown's opinion, they were not even doing that. They were letting off steam.

Jenkins met head-on the tension between the Act's exclusivity principle and racial discrimination. The exclusivity principle, read in light of the duty of fair representation, Title VII, and the U.S. Constitution, simply could not justify allowing Hollins and Hawkins to be fired. An individual employee's right to combat his employer's discriminatory practices had to trump the NLRA's exclusivity concerns. Otherwise, the Board "places itself in the position of participating in and aiding and abetting the continuance of those phases of racial discrimination which the Union elected not to try to remedy." Jenkins was willing to follow the Ninth Circuit's holding in *Tanner*. Workers first had to ask the union to address their complaints of racial discrimination. However, having done that, if they were not satisfied with the union's response, the Act should protect any additional action they might wish to take.

Having lost before the Board, WACO turned its attention to the federal court of appeals. The Act allows parties dissatisfied with the Board's disposition of a case to appeal its decision to a federal appeals court in either the District of Columbia or in the circuit where the unfair labor practice was alleged to have taken place—in this case, the Ninth Circuit. Choosing between these two was easy for WACO. Eighteen months earlier, the Ninth Circuit had refused to enforce the Board's ruling in *Tanner Motor Livery*.[52] By contrast, the D.C. Circuit enjoyed a reputation as one of the most liberal in the country, particularly on civil rights issues.[53] Moreover, the D.C. Circuit had recently indicated its willingness to read the NLRA broadly, incorporating the anti-discrimination policy of Title VII into traditional labor law doctrines. In *United Packinghouse, Food, and Allied Workers v. NLRB,*[54] the D.C. Circuit had permitted a labor union to bring an 8(a)(3) claim against an employer group on the basis of racial discrimination rather than discrimination predicated on the exercise of § 7 rights. This case suggested that the D.C. Circuit was willing to read the NLRA creatively in light of changing national priorities and thus bolstered WACO's argument that the recently articulated national policy of anti-discrimination in employment must trump the exclusivity principle.

Indeed, the D.C. Circuit confirmed its earlier inclination. While the D.C. Circuit's June 1973 opinion was not an unadulterated victory for WACO, it did reverse the Board and sought to adapt the NLRA to Title VII's anti-discrimination principle.[55] The case was heard by an eclectic panel: Judge George MacKinnon, Judge Spotswood Robinson, and Judge Charles Wyzanski (a senior judge of the U.S. District Court of Massachusetts, sitting by designation). MacKinnon was a Republican who had been elected to Congress in 1946 and had served on the House Labor Committee when it worked on the Taft–Hartley Amendments. As a United States Attorney he had spearheaded the investigation of some of the most famous labor racketeering cases of the era, including the investigation of James Hoffa. Despite his reputation in some circles as a staunch conservative (he was particularly skeptical about the efficacy of labor unions and the NLRB),[56] he was moderate on some issues, includ-

---

[52] 166 NLRB 551 (1967), *enforcement denied,* 419 F.2d 216 (9th Cir. 1969).

[53] Christopher P. Banks, *Judicial Politics in the D.C. Circuit Court* 23–26 (1999).

[54] 416 F.2d 1126 (D.C. Cir. 1969).

[55] Western Addition Community Org. v. NLRB, 485 F.2d 917 (D.C. Cir. 1973).

[56] Interview with Patrick Hardin, Feb. 15, 2004 (Chief Legal Counsel to the NLRB, 1970–71); *see* <http://www.mnhs.org/library/findaids/00108.html> (visited May 18, 2004)

ing race discrimination, and thus could be unpredictable.[57] Robinson, the first African–American appointed to the D.C. Circuit, had been a well-known civil rights litigator with the NAACP Legal Defense and Education Fund before he came on the bench; he had worked on the brief with Thurgood Marshall in *Brown v. Board of Education*.[58] Wyzanski was a self-described judicial activist.[59] As the Labor Department's Solicitor in 1935, he had been involved in drafting the Wagner Act and he defended the Act's constitutionality before the Supreme Court two years later.[60] Despite this background, Wyzanski's support for the Act was never unalloyed. From the very beginning, he had feared that the Act could be used by unions to pressure and coerce workers.[61]

The D.C. Circuit's opinion, authored by MacKinnon, acknowledged the tension between the NLRA's exclusivity principle and national labor policy prohibiting race discrimination in cases where dissident minority workers sought to address complaints about racial discrimination directly to the employer.[62] It then distinguished concerted action challenging racial discrimination from concerted action challenging other working conditions. Protests against racial discrimination enjoyed a unique status under the NLRA because the prohibition on race discrimination emanated from Title VII and not simply from the collective agreement. Therefore, national labor policy would not allow the union to oppose employees' protests against race discrimination.[63] Nonetheless, the employees' demand for bargaining[64] did undermine the collective bargaining and grievance process. Indeed, by refusing to cooperate with the union the

(biography of George E. MacKinnon and inventory of his papers at the Minnesota Historical Society).

57 Interview with Professor Charles C. Craver, Feb. 25, 2004. Professor Craver served as a clerk to Judge MacKinnon during the period when the D.C. Circuit had the *Emporium Capwell* case before it, but did not work on the case because he was committed to practice with one of the law firms involved after his clerkship ended.

58 Interview with Professor Charles C. Craver, Feb. 25, 2004.

59 *See* Charles E. Wyzanski, Jr., *An Activist Judge: Mea Maxima Culpa: Apologia Vita Mea,*7 Ga. L. Rev. 202 (1973); Charles E. Wyzanski, Jr., *Whereas—A Judge's Premises* (1965); *see generally In Memoriam: Charles E. Wyzanski, Jr.*, 100 Harv. L. Rev. 705 (1987).

60 *See* Peter H. Irons, *The New Deal Lawyers* 230, 280–89 (1982).

61 *Id.* at 320.

62 Western Addition Community Organization v. NLRB, 485 F.2d 917 (D.C. Cir. 1973).

63 According to the court, "the law does not give the union an option to tolerate *some* racial discrimination, but declares that *all* racial discrimination in employment is illegal." 485 F.2d at 928.

64 The court accepted the Board's finding that the workers had sought to bargain with the employer rather than to "talk" or "discuss" the situation, so that the § 9(a) proviso did not apply. *See id.*, 485 F.2d at 929 n.34.

African–American workers had rendered the union's strategy of processing individual grievances "essentially ineffective." Accordingly, even when racial issues were at stake, the court opined that workers should be required to submit the disputes to the union before resorting to concerted action; otherwise, the utility of contractual grievance and arbitration machinery as a means to resolve labor disputes would be undermined. The court adopted a test which required workers seeking to remedy race discrimination to submit their disputes to their union before engaging in concerted action. In ensuing § 7 cases challenging employer discipline or discharge, the NLRB should inquire "whether the union was actually remedying the discrimination to the *fullest extent possible, by the most expedient and efficacious means.*" If the union's efforts failed to meet this "high standard," the employees' independent concerted action would be protected.

Here, the workers had presented their claims to the union, and the union and the workers were not in disagreement about whether racial discrimination had occurred—their conflict was only about the means to challenge racial discriminatory practices.[65] Thus, the potential for undermining union efficacy was minimal, and the union's choice of method should not preclude dissidents with reasonable grounds from pursuing a different strategy. The court nevertheless remanded the case to the Board so that it might consider whether the picketing lost its protection because it was disloyal. The court apparently believed that the disparaging and intemperate leaflet language might provide an independent justification for discharge under the doctrine established in *NLRB v. Local Union No. 1229 (Jefferson Standard).*[66]

Judge Wyzanski dissented.[67] He would have gone further than the majority. At the core of his opinion was his disagreement with the majority's effort to minimize the conflict of interest between the union and the African–American dissidents, and its painstaking efforts to enunciate a test that would harmonize the NLRA and Title VII. Wyzanski would have found "unequivocally" that the Emporium's discharge of Hollins and Hawkins violated § 7; the majority's efforts to avoid the central clash of interests were "exercises in futility or postponement." An exception to the exclusivity doctrine for racial protests was constitu-

---

[65] The court noted that there was no evidence in the record of bad faith on the part of the union, and thus no suggestion that it had breached its duty of fair representation.

[66] 346 U.S. 464 (1953). Neither the Board nor the Trial Examiner had resolved the question, though it had been discussed below at length by the Trial Examiner.

[67] In narrow terms, he disagreed with the idea of a broad remand for consideration of disloyalty—he saw no evidence of utterances that rose to this level, and the Board itself had not ruled on this basis. Wyzanski believed that a narrow remand with a directive to grant appropriate relief was appropriate.

tionally required. In his view, unless an exception to the exclusivity doctrine for discriminatory challenges were permitted, cloaking the majority representative with the power to thwart a minority group's claim of racial discrimination would violate due process, risk perpetuating the consequences of slavery, and make a mockery of democracy. Judge Wyzanski did not find it surprising that the union's stance on challenging racially discriminatory policies at the Emporium would differ from the black workers' position. Union leaders beholden to a white majority for their continued appointment would understandably wish to protect their political power by guarding the interests of white workers. Moreover, hiring and promotions were a zero-sum game: to hire or promote black workers meant that some white workers would not be hired or promoted. Thus, Wyzanski reasoned, "[e]ven if we assume that the whites are tolerant, nay generous, their short-term interest is in conflict with the short-term interest of the non-whites." Mincing no words, Wyzanski's conclusion, written entirely in capital letters, leapt off the normally staid pages of the Federal Reporter:

> TO LEAVE NON–WHITES AT THE MERCY OF WHITES IN THE PRESENTATION OF NON–WHITE CLAIMS ... WOULD BE A MOCKERY OF DEMOCRACY.... IN PRESENTING NON–WHITE ISSUES NON–WHITES CANNOT, AGAINST THEIR WILL, BE RELEGATED TO WHITE SPOKESMEN, MIMICKING BLACK MEN. THE DAY OF THE MINSTREL SHOW IS OVER.

Both the Board and the Emporium asked the Supreme Court to overturn the D.C. Circuit's decision. Considering the breadth of the D.C. Circuit's opinion and the inflammatory nature of Wyzanski's rhetoric, WACO's attorneys were not surprised. Nor were they particularly sanguine about their chances before the Court.[68] Nevertheless, an opinion the Court had handed down in the interim, *Alexander v. Gardner–Denver Co.*,[69] gave WACO some cause for optimism.

Gardner-Denver was the Supreme Court's first significant case dealing with the interplay between the NLRA and Title VII. In a unanimous decision authored by Justice Powell, the Court ruled that an employee whose union had pursued arbitration of a race discrimination claim under a collective bargaining agreement was not barred from bringing suit in court on the same claim under Title VII. Because contractual rights were conferred collectively and could be exercised or relinquished

---

[68] Interview with Kenneth Hecht, Mar. 21, 2001. Hecht's younger assistant on the case, Edward Steinman, was more optimistic than Hecht. Both men thought they would get the votes of Justices Brennan, Marshall, and Douglas. Steinman though it was possible that two others might vote with these three liberal justices, particularly since Nixon's appointees, as of 1975, had been reading Title VII fairly broadly.

[69] 415 U.S. 36 (1974).

by the union for the good of the majority, arbitration processes were not suited to the vindication of Title VII's ban on discrimination, which was absolute in its protection of individual freedom from discrimination. An individual's Title VII rights could "form no part of the collective-bargaining process," including the continuation of bargaining under the arbitration and grievance provisions of the labor contract. The foundation had been laid for analytical separation of individual claims of race discrimination and collective rights controlled by unions.

The Supreme Court Decision

Clearly the Court was ready to consider the interplay between civil rights and labor rights. On February 19, 1974, the same day that it decided *Gardner-Denver*, the Supreme Court granted the Emporium and NLRB petitions for certiorari.[70]

The arguments made before the Court in *Emporium* were predictable, echoing the claims the parties had made below. According to the Emporium, the Board, and their amici (the AFL–CIO, the National Association of Manufacturers, and the National Retail Merchants Association), the D.C. Circuit's decision would create industrial chaos. It frustrated one of the central purposes of the NLRA, channeling disputes into contractually agreed-upon grievance and arbitration procedures. It required employers to make promises to dissidents that were inconsistent with the collectively-bargained contracts. Furthermore, how was an employer to know whether the union satisfied the standard articulated by Judge MacKinnon? How was an employer to know which subgroups were allowed to ignore the exclusivity principle and which were not? Additionally, the decision undermined the NLRA's other main goal: equalizing bargaining power. A shop floor balkanized into racial subgroups could never attain the type of unity needed to counterbalance employer strength at the bargaining table.

WACO and its amici (NAACP, CORE, SCLC, and Local 1100) also made familiar arguments. First, they repeated their claim that Hawkins and Hollins were simply grieving and that their actions were protected by § 9(a). They then argued that even if Hollins and Hawkins were trying to bargain, the dictates of Title VII limited the union's right of exclusivity. In instances when racial discrimination was at issue, anti-discrimination principles trumped § 9(a). Indeed, from WACO and its allies' perspective, their case was perfectly analogous to *Gardner-Denver*. Title VII was Congress' declaration that race was different. Unions could bargain away many rights, but not those articulated in Title VII. Similarly, exclusive representation might normally dictate that the will of the union majority trump the desires of individual workers—but only

---

[70] 415 U.S. 913 (1974).

when those individual workers' desires were related to issues other than combating racial discrimination. With respect to that issue, Congress had spoken loudly and clearly. Congress had created a right to combat racial discrimination individually (or as a racial group) that could not be bargained away by a union.[71]

The Supreme Court, however, was not convinced. Justice Marshall, the Supreme Court's first African–American Justice, authored an opinion from which only Justice Douglas dissented, overturning the D.C. Circuit.[72] It is hard to imagine that Chief Justice Burger's decision to assign the case to Marshall was an accident. Marshall was a long-time opponent of racial discrimination as counsel to the NAACP.[73] He directed the NAACP Legal Defense and Education Fund, Inc. from 1939 to 1961, winning such landmark cases as *Brown v. Board of Education*[74] and *Sweatt v. Painter*.[75] The charter of what came to be known as the Inc. Fund made clear the organization's purpose to "render free legal aid to [African–Americans] who suffer legal injustice because of their race or color and cannot afford to employ legal assistance."[76] Also, Marshall's informal statements while a member of the Supreme Court reflect his continuing concern about the problem of racism.[77] Thus, Marshall's assignment to write the *Emporium Capwell* decision demonstrated the Court's sensitivity to minority interests.[78]

The Court declined WACO's invitation to disturb the Board's finding that Hawkins and Hollins were attempting to bargain rather than present a grievance. However, in a footnote, it did seek to clarify the operation of the proviso by suggesting that Hollins and Hawkins would not have been protected even if they had been attempting to file a

---

71 For citation to *Gardner-Denver* articulating these principles, *see* Joint Brief of the Urban League/Southern Christian Leadership Conference at 16–18, 20–21, 25–26, 34; Brief of WACO at 21–22, 25, 41–42.

72 *See* Emporium Capwell Co. v. Western Addition Community Org., 420 U.S. 50 (1975).

73 *See* Gary Peller, *Race Consciousness,* 1990 Duke L.J. 758, 760 (discussing tension between integrationism and black nationalism in the civil rights movement, and noting Marshall's key role as an advocate for integration).

74 347 U.S. 483 (1954).

75 339 U.S. 629 (1950).

76 Michael D. Davis & Hunter R. Clark, *Thurgood Marshall: Warrior at the Bar, Rebel on the Bench* 108 (1992).

77 *See* Carl T. Rowan, *Dream Makers, Dream Breakers: The World of Justice Thurgood Marshall* 388–99 (1993) (where Marshall discusses his own continuing sensitivity to the issue of racism).

78 Interview with former Deputy Solicitor General Lawrence G. Wallace, Feb. 6, 2004.

grievance. Specifically, the Court said that the proviso "permit[ted] employees to present grievances and ... authorize[d] the employer to entertain them without opening itself to liability." The Court added that the Act did not protect grievance filing by "making it an unfair labor practice for an employer to refuse to entertain" a grievance or authorizing economic coercion in support of the grievance.

Having set aside this issue, the Court focused on whether their efforts to engage in separate bargaining were protected. In setting the stage for its ruling, the Court set forth the guarantees contained in § 7 of the Act. The opinion then characterized those rights as follows:

> These are, for the most part, collective rights, rights to act in concert with one's fellow employees; they are protected not for their own sake but as an instrument of the national labor policy of minimizing industrial strife "by encouraging the practice and procedure of collective bargaining."

The Court then elaborated upon the centrality of majority rule in fostering collective bargaining, saying that Congress established a "regime of majority rule" in order to "secure to all members of the unit the benefits of their collective strength and bargaining power ... in full awareness that the superior strength of some individuals or groups might be subordinated to the interest of the majority."

Marshall hastened to point out that the broad power vested in the majority representative does not "authorize a tyranny of the majority over minority interests." He wrote that bargaining unit determination, union democracy provisions guaranteeing member free speech, and the duty of fair representation served to protect minority rights. Marshall embraced the prominence of anti-discrimination principles in national labor policy and the need to construe the NLRA in the context of this policy, but rejected the argument that separate bargaining was the way to eliminate discrimination. Instead, Marshall used the facts of this case—the agreement's prohibition of discrimination, the existence of an arbitration procedure to reach an orderly determination of discrimination, and the effectiveness of adverse arbitration awards in curbing discriminatory practices—to demonstrate the superiority of exclusive bargaining in achieving this goal. He contrasted the effectiveness of exclusive bargaining, which uses the contractual grievance arbitration procedure, with the ineffectiveness of separate bargaining. In his view, separate bargaining left an employer unable to respond adequately to the competing claims of minority groups and allowed it to manipulate claims against the interests of those groups. Indeed, the Court suggested that minority groups would be doomed to dividing and further subdividing themselves "along racial and other lines" or clashing with the collective bargaining representative in ways that would make the "likelihood of making headway against discriminatory practices ... minimal."

The Court then took on the D.C. Circuit's claim that minority bargaining would not have a significant impact on the union. Here the Court distinguished "the substantive right to be free of racial discrimination" and the procedures under the NLRA for securing those rights. Even where the employer agrees to incorporate its statutory obligation not to discriminate into the collective bargaining agreement, it still has a legitimate interest in not bargaining on several fronts, said the Court. Similarly, even though the union cannot lawfully negotiate a discriminatory regime, it still has an interest in the power of presenting a united front. The Court viewed these interests as protected by the exclusivity principle. Finally, the Court dismissed claims based on the greater efficiency of Board procedures as more appropriately directed to Congress.

It is tempting to speculate that this decision was a difficult one for Marshall, pitting, as it did, the rights of African-American workers against the power of labor unions and the dictates of the NLRA. Yet there is no indication in either Marshall's papers or in the currently available papers of the other justices who sat on the Court that Marshall found the *Emporium Capwell* opinion to be particularly troubling. Indeed, such speculations are based on a misunderstanding of Marshall's beliefs about which tactics were most effective in procuring civil rights for African-Americans. Throughout his career Marshall expressed discomfort with even non-violent direct action by civil rights protestors.[79] He was openly hostile to Black Power and was deeply dismayed by the Civil Rights Movement's turn away from integrationism in the late 1960's.[80] Though Marshall has earned a reputation as a judicial activist, he also exhibited a competing sensitivity to his obligation as a jurist to exercise judicial restraint.[81] Considering that fact, it is hard to imagine

---

[79] Juan Williams, *Thurgood Marshall: American Revolutionary* 247 (1998); Howard Ball, *A Defiant Life: Thurgood Marshall and the Persistence of Racism in America* 155, 209 (1998).

[80] Juan Williams, *Thurgood Marshall: American Revolutionary* 343, 359 (1998); Carl T. Rowan, *Dream Makers, Dream Breakers: The World of Justice Thurgood Marshall* 298, 356, 365, 433 (1993); Michael D. Davis & Hunter R. Clark, *Thurgood Marshall: Warrior at the Bar, Rebel on the Bench* 249–51 (1992).

[81] Rowan at 390 (containing an account of Marshall's statement: "When you take an oath to hand out justice, you in your own mind have to take any prejudice you have, or predilection that you might have, and push it back, out of your mind until after you decide the case, and then go back and pick it up, if you want."). *See also* Calvin William Sharpe, *"Judging in Good Faith"—Seeing Justice Marshall's Legacy Through a Labor Case*, 26 Ariz. St. L. J. 479 (1994); Elena Kagan & Cass Sunstein, *"Remembering ATM,"* 30 Occasional Papers of the Law School of the University of Chicago 5 (1993).

him engaging in an expansive reading of the NLRA in order to promote a type of civil rights activism of which he did not approve. Indeed, the type of moderate, legalistic reform of the workplace that Local 1100 was engaging in was exactly the type of reform that appealed to Marshall's lawyerly sentiments.[82]

The same could not be said of Douglas' dissent, which was more sympathetic to the plight of the dissident workers. He argued that Hawkins and Hollins eschewed the duty of fair representation and Title VII claims because each was "fraught with obstacles." He observed that the issue of racial discrimination in employment is a proper subject of concerted activity protected by § 7. Douglas also acknowledged the principle of exclusive representation embodied in § 9 of the Act, but drawing upon *Gardner-Denver*, argued that the union could not demand exclusive control in the area of racial discrimination. Capturing this balance, Douglas said:

> The law should facilitate the involvement of unions in the quest for racial equality in employment, but it should not make the individual a prisoner of the union. While employees may reasonably be required to approach the union first, as a kind of "exhaustion" requirement before resorting to economic protest . . . , they should not be under continued inhibition when it becomes apparent that the union response is inadequate.

Though Douglas' opinion might have provided some small solace, the Supreme Court's opinion marked the end of the line for Hollins and Hawkins. The National Labor Relations Act would not provide a remedy. As it turned out, however, the Emporium won the battle but lost the war. Hecht and his colleagues at the Employment Law Center eventually brought a Title VII suit against the Emporium. The Emporium settled the case in the early 1980's.[83]

The Immediate Impact of Emporium Capwell

Practitioners and legal scholars of the day took a keen interest in the interplay between the NLRA and Title VII. Some defended the exclusivity principle.[84] Others were critical of the Court's resolution of

[82] Mark Tushnet, *The Legitimation of the Administrative State: Some Aspects of the Work of Thurgood Marshall*, 5 Studies in Am. Pol. Devel. 94, 103–06 (1991).

[83] The case was settled for a seven-figure sum. The employees received a pittance; most of the recovery was attorneys' fees. Hawkins, one of the discharged workers, was among the plaintiffs and received a small amount of money from the settlement. Walter Johnson recalls the amount as in the neighborhood of $2500. Interviews with Hecht, Johnson.

[84] *See, e.g.,* Averill G. Marcus, *The Emporium Case—A Dissenting Opinion,* 26 Lab. L.J. 270, 275–76 (1975) (criticizing D.C. Circuit opinion for creating an ambiguous standard and a "potentially chaotic" remedy since Title VII has potential application to almost all

the tension, believing that the decision would undermine labor power in the long run.[85] Professor George Schatzski authored a provocative and influential article advocating the abolition of majority rule and exclusivity provisions.[86] Others focused on the potential harm to minority workers wrought by the Court's decision.[87] Professor William Gould, a prominent African–American labor law scholar of the era who later served as Chair of the NLRB, defended the D.C. Circuit's opinion that racial disputes stood on a "special plateau."[88]

The academic debate over the political and policy tensions of *Emporium Capwell* continues. Some critique the decision as preempting a diversity in the labor movement that would better address the special

---

aspects of the employer-employee relationship, including pension plans, job bidding systems, severance plans, and seniority systems); Charles B. Craver, *Minority Action versus Union Exclusivity: The Need to Harmonize NLRA and Title VII Policies,* 26 Hastings L.J. 1, 52–55 (1974) (defending the exclusivity principle and proposing that minority protests be protected only when the union in fact violates the duty of fair representation).

[85] *See* Norman L. Cantor, *Dissident Worker Action, After The Emporium,* 29 Rutgers L. Rev. 35 (1975) (worrying that the decision could be read as withdrawing statutory protection for a wide range of concerted activities by dissident workers even in the absence of a demand for bargaining, and urging a narrow reading); Staughton Lynd, *The Right to Engage in Concerted Activity After Union Recognition: A Study of Legislative History,* 50 Ind. L.J. 720, 722–26 (1975) (interpreting *Emporium Capwell* as establishing that concerted activity otherwise protected under § 7 becomes unprotected because of the presence of a recognized union).

[86] *See* George Schatzski, *Majority Rule, Exclusive Representation, and the Interests of Individual Workers: Should Exclusivity Be Abolished?,* 123 U. Pa. L. Rev. 897 (1975).

[87] *See, e.g.,* Eileen Silverstein, *Union Decisions on Collective Bargaining Goals: A Proposal for Interest Group Participation,* 77 Mich. L. Rev. 1485 (1979) (assessing consequences of unions' virtually unrestrained authority to establish bargaining priorities and to reconcile conflicts of interest among workers in the unit, and urging the formation of internal union structures designed to ensure representation for minority interests).

[88] For this proposition, Gould cited Steele v. Louisville & Nashville R.R., 323 U.S. 192 (1944) (imposing duty of fair representation upon union in race discrimination action under the Railway Labor Act); Brown v. Bd. of Education, 347 U.S. 483 (1954) (striking down "separate but equal" doctrine in public education and ordering school desegregation); and New Negro Alliance v. Sanitary Grocery Co., 303 U.S. 552 (1938) (interpreting the Norris–LaGuardia Act to except racial labor disputes from injunctions). Professor Gould argued that the stark conflict of interests between the protesting black dissidents and the white union majority, viewed against a backdrop of union discrimination against minorities, necessitated placing the burden upon the union to show that it was doing its utmost to eradicate race discrimination. Racial walkouts should be presumed protected under § 7 even where they were disruptive of the bargaining process unless the union could meet this standard—a standard more rigorous than that established by the duty of fair representation cases. *See* William B. Gould, *Racial Protest and Self–Help Under Taft–Hartley,* 29 Arb. J. 161, 169–71 (1974); *see also* William B. Gould, *Black Workers in White Unions: Job Discrimination in the United States* 259–67 (1977).

concerns of women and minorities.[89] Within this critique, some have built upon Schatzski's thinking, arguing that exclusivity prevents unions from responding effectively to minority interests and the current challenges for organized labor.[90] Others focus more narrowly on the scope of exclusivity, arguing that non-majority or "members only" representation recognize the need for legislative reform to implement such programs.[91] On the other side, scholars support the Supreme Court's rationale, arguing that class solidarity holds the most promise for advancing the interests of white and minority workers and seeking to reconcile solidarity and diversity interests.[92]

---

[89] *See, e.g.,* Elizabeth M. Iglesias, *Structures of Subordination: Women of Color at the Intersection of Title VII and the NLRA*, 28 Harv. C.R.-C.L. L.Rev. 395 (1993) (criticizing the fragmentation of Title VII and NLRA analysis in *Emporium Capwell* as contributing to the maintenance of race and gender subordination in the American workplace); Marion Crain & Ken Matheny, *"Labor's Divided Ranks": Privilege and the United Front Ideology*, 84 Cornell L. Rev. 1542 (1999) (criticizing *Emporium Capwell* as preventing women and minorities from collectively challenging gender and race discrimination in an organized workplace and exclusivity and majority rule more generally as inhibiting unions from effectively representing gender and racially diverse workforces); Marion Crain, *Women, Labor Unions, and Hostile Work Environment Sexual Harassment: The Untold Story*, 4 Tex. J. Women & L. 9 (1995) (noting *Emporium Capwell* as a potential barrier to proposal for identity caucuses to pressure male-dominated unions to better serve the interests of women in collective bargaining and arbitration, particularly in the context of sexual harassment).

[90] *See* George Schatzski, *Majority Rule, Exclusive Representation, and the Interests of Individual Workers: Should Exclusivity Be Abolished?*, 123 U. Pa. L. Rev. 897 (1975). *See, e.g.,* Richard R. Carlson, *The Origin and Future of Exclusive Representation in American Labor Law*, 30 Duq. L. Rev. 779 (1992) (extolling the promise of nonexclusive representation while acknowledging the necessity of exclusivity to effective collective bargaining and the impediments of exclusivity to employee organization) and Matthew W. Finkin, *The Road Not Taken: Some Thoughts On Nonmajority Employee Representation*, 69 Chi–Kent L. Rev. 195 (1993) (expanding upon Professor Schatzski's "prescient" article, making arguments for the workability and timeliness of "members only" representation informed by the historical debates and experience of the Wagner Act).

[91] *See* Richard R. Carlson, *The Origin and Future of Exclusive Representation in American Labor Law*, 30 Duq. L. Rev. 866–67 (1992) (suggesting amendments to 8(a)(2) and 9(a)); Matthew W. Finkin, *The Road Not Taken: Some Thoughts On Nonmajority Employee Representation*, 69 Chi–Kent L. Rev. 205–06 (1993) (proposing amendments to §§ 9(a) and 8(a)(5) of Act).

[92] *See* Calvin William Sharpe, *"Judging In Good Faith"—Seeing Justice Marshall's Legacy Through a Labor Case*, 26 Ariz. St. L.J. 479 (1994) (applauding Justice Marshall's decision in *Emporium Capwell* as exemplary of "judging in good faith"); Martha R. Mahoney, *Constructing Solidarity: Interest and White Workers*, 2 U. Pa. J. Lab. & Emp. L. 747 (2000) (characterizing proposals for eliminating majority rule and exclusivity as posing high risks for labor solidarity and advocating the recognition of shared goals for whites and minorities based on equality and the support of minorities) and Molly S. McUsic & Michael

The substantial scholarly response to the Supreme Court's decision has not been matched outside of the halls of academe. The media coverage of *Emporium* was minimal. The Court's decision did focus some attention on the labor movement's failure adequately to represent the interests of black workers. In the 1970's, the Ford Foundation donated money to not-for-profit organizations with programs dedicated to training and certifying black trade unionists to assume leadership positions, particularly as shop stewards and business agents.[93] However, proposals for labor law reform that surfaced in subsequent years made no attempt to create exceptions to the principle of exclusivity. Indeed, the major package of labor law reforms considered by Congress in 1977 (and enthusiastically endorsed by the NAACP) said nary a word about exclusivity, focusing instead on improving the Board's efficiency, making union organizing easier, and increasing penalties for employers who committed unfair labor practices.[94]

Thus, *Emporium Capwell* was not a catalyst for political or legal reform. To the contrary, it was instead a symbol of the paralyzing political crisis that American liberalism found itself mired in at the beginning of the 1970's as it sought to accommodate its constituents' disparate visions of what economic equality and social fairness entailed. To scholars studying the 1960's and 1970's, this conflict is quite familiar. The clashes between civil rights groups and labor unions in San Francisco were emblematic of the fragmentation of the Democratic Party and of post-war liberalism generally. Historians have demonstrated that the unusual combination of interest groups that kept the Democratic Party in power between 1932 and 1968 collapsed at the end of the 1960's.[95] Franklin Roosevelt, these historians argue, was able to forge a potent but unstable coalition of Southerners, ethnic Catholics and Jews, union members and other blue-collar workers, coastal intellectuals, and African-Americans. The power of this coalition ensured that Democrats won

---

Selmi, *Postmodern Unions: Identity Politics in the Workplace*, 82 Iowa L. Rev. 1339 (1997) (proposing a return to cosmopolitanism in the workplace).

93 Interview with Professor William Gould, Feb. 6, 2004; Interview with Professor Steven Diamond, Feb. 5, 2004.

94 *See* H.R. 8410, 95th Cong., 1st Sess. (1977) and S. 1883 95th Cong., 1st Sess. (1977). For civil rights organizations' support of this legislation see Hearings Before the Subcomm. on Labor of the Comm. on Human Resources on S. 1883, Labor Reform Act of 1977, 95 Cong. 602–37; and Hearings Before the Subcomm. on Labor–Management Relations of the Comm. on Education and Labor on H.R. 8410, Labor Reform Act of 1977, 95 Cong. 320–37.

95 For the rise of the New Deal Coalition see William E. Leuchtenberg, *Franklin D. Roosevelt and the New Deal, 1932–1940* 184–96 (1963); Anthony J. Badger, *The New Deal: The Depression Years, 1933–1940* 245–60 (1989). For African–Americans' place within that coalition, see Harvard Sitkoff, *A New Deal for Blacks. The Emergence of Civil Rights as a National Issue: The Depression Decade* 84–101 (1978).

seven of the nine presidential elections during this period and dominated Congress as well.

By the late 1960's, this coalition had begun to fragment.[96] White Southerners began their defection to the Republican Party. Lower middle-class, white, ethnic voters flirted with candidates such as George Wallace and Richard Nixon and then committed themselves wholeheartedly to Ronald Reagan. Similarly, more affluent middle-class voters from ethnic and cultural backgrounds who had traditionally voted Democratic abandoned the party in increasing numbers throughout the 1970's.

Emporium Capwell demonstrates the way in which the woes of the Democratic Party paralleled those of the labor movement. To explain contemporary liberalism's difficulties sociologist Jonathan Rieder has focused on what he has called "the structural limits of racial reform in America."[97] Put simply, the rise of contentious issues involving race (black pride, affirmative action, and busing, for example) fragmented the Democratic Party. On the one hand, many white Democrats felt that their party had been captured by African–Americans who were implementing policies that disadvantaged whites. On the other hand, African–Americans believed that the Democrats were unwilling to take the steps necessary to guarantee the emergence of genuine racial equality in the United States. The Democratic Party's white ethnic constituency supported desegregated schooling but not busing. It supported equal employment opportunity but not affirmative action. In essence, these whites had reached the limits of their tolerance for the demands of the civil rights movement.

Scholars who study the 1960's have catalogued a number of signature events illustrating the limits of racial reform including the Mississippi Freedom Democrats' conflict with Democratic Party regulars in Atlantic City in 1964; the expulsion of whites from the Student Non–Violent Coordinating Committee in 1966; and the conflict between African–American parents and white teachers in the Ocean Hill–Browns-

---

[96] Allen J. Matusow, *The Unraveling of America: A History of Liberalism in the 1960s* 395–440 (1984); David Farber, *The Age of Great Dreams: America in the 1960s* 90–116, 190–211 (1994); Maurice Isserman & Michael Kazin, *America Divided: The Civil War of the 1960s* 286–88 (2000).

[97] Jonathan Rieder, *The Rise of the Silent Majority, in The Rise and Fall of the New Deal Order*, 1930–1980 (Steve Fraser & Gary Gerstle eds., 1989); Maurice Isserman & Michael Kazin, *America Divided: The Civil War of the 1960s* 272–73 (2000); Gary Gerstle, *American Crucible: Race and Nation in the Twentieth Century* 290–92, 309, 343 (2001); E.J. Dionne, Jr., *Why Americans Hate Politics* 78–79, 82–86, 89–94 (1991); William E. Nelson, *The Legalist Reformation: Law, Politics and Ideology in New York*, 1920–1980 282–84 (2001).

ville neighborhood of Brooklyn in 1967.[98] The conflict between WACO and Local 1100 is hardly on the scale of these events. Indeed, it fits more easily into the less epic narratives about how the normal fabric of the lives of individual Americans was stretched and twisted by the political and ideological conflicts of the day.[99] The lawyers for WACO struggled mightily to shape old laws to accommodate the problems of race Americans had finally decided to address. For a moment, it seemed as if the legal system might evidence more flexibility than the political system. Ultimately, however, the old legal order, like the old political order, simply could not solve the problems that plagued liberalism in the late 1960's and early 1970's. The *Emporium Capwell* case was thus a legal confirmation of that which, by 1975, was already quite apparent: American liberalism was having a difficult time accommodating its commitment to racial egalitarianism with the desires of its traditional working-class white constituency.

The Continuing Importance of Emporium Capwell Today

What impact has *Emporium Capwell* had on the interpretation of § 9(a) of the Act? As a pivotal case dealing with a core principle of the statute, a sea change in the law of exclusivity would not have been surprising. However, the actual effect of the decision on the development of the law seems to have been more wide than deep.

The legal implications of *Emporium Capwell* have been seen in cases involving a range of issues from attempts by grievants to use privately retained counsel in arbitration,[100] to the legality of excluding player agents from bargaining over salaries in professional sports.[101] However,

---

98 Maurice Isserman & Michael Kazin, *America Divided: The Civil War of the 1960s* 172–75 (2000); Gary Gerstle, *American Crucible: Race and Nation in the Twentieth Century* 269–70, 286–95, 303–04, 328, 331 (2001); Jerald E. Podair, *The Strike that Changed New York: Blacks, Whites, and the Ocean Hill–Brownsville Crisis* (2002).

99 *See, for example,* Lillian B. Rubin, *Families on the Fault Line: America's Working Class Speaks about the Family, the Economy, Race, and Ethnicity* (1994); Jonathan Kaufman, *Broken Alliance: The Turbulent Times Between Blacks and Jews in America* (1995); Jonathan Rieder, *Canarsie: The Jews and Italians of Brooklyn Against Liberalism* (1985); Samuel J. Freedman, *The Inheritance: How Three Families and the American Political Majority Moved from Left to Right,* (1998); Ronald P. Formasano, *Boston Against Busing: Race, Class, and Ethnicity in the 1960s and 1970s* (1991).

100 *See* Castelli v. Douglas Aircraft Co., 752 F.2d 1480, 1484 (9th Cir. 1985) (issue arose in context of duty of fair representation suit) and Avery Allen Baxter v. United Paperworkers International Union, Local 7370, 140 F.3d 745 (8th Cir. 1998) (like *Castelli,* shows exclusivity under § 9(a) as a defense to duty of fair representation claim in private representation cases.)

101 *See* Thomas M. Collins v. NBPA, 850 F.Supp. 1468 (D. Colo. 1991) (pointing out that § 9 of the Act and *Emporium Capwell* provide the basis for the NBPA's regulation,

the recurring issue of greatest import has concerned wildcat strikes. Before *Emporium Capwell* the majority of circuits had held dissident concerted activity to be unprotected.[102] Bucking this trend was *NLRB v. RC Can*,[103] where the court held protected a quickie strike by a small group of employees, because it sought to support the union's position in negotiations with the employer. The protection persisted "so long, of course, as the means used do not involve a disagreement with, repudiation or criticism of a policy or decision previously taken by the union."[104] Some courts that had found wildcat activity unprotected nevertheless suggested that some circumstances might warrant protection.[105] Ironically, *Emporium Capwell* seems to have reversed the trend, with courts finding unauthorized wildcat activity protected unless it is an attempt to bargain with the employer or it undermines the effectiveness of the union or collective bargaining.[106] In the absence of an attempt to bargain, general dissatisfaction with the union, lack of union authorization, lack of prior contact, and even working at cross-purposes with the union may

certification, and exclusion of nonqualifying agents from representing NBA players except on terms sanctioned by the union).

102 *See, e.g.*, NLRB v. Draper Corp., 145 F.2d 199 (4th Cir. 1944) (wildcat strike to pressure the employer in the face of what the union saw as stalling tactics by the employer); Harnischfeger Corp. v. NLRB, 207 F.2d 575, 578 (7th Cir. 1953) (where a small group of "discontented employees undertook by a work stoppage or strike movement to take charge of and direct the actions of their chosen bargaining representative"); Robert Gorman, *Basic Text on Labor Law* 311 (1976) ("wildcat concerted activities are unprotected and render the participants susceptible to discharge").

103 328 F.2d 974 (5th Cir. 1964).

104 328 F.2d at 979.

105 *See, e.g.*, NLRB v. Shop Rite Foods, 430 F.2d 786, 791 (5th Cir. 1970) (noting that minority concerted activity outside of union processes might be protected even though an agreement is in force).

106 *See, e.g.*, NLRB v. Bridgeport Ambulance Service, 966 F.2d 725 (2d Cir. 1992) (goal was to protest working conditions and unfairness and not to bargain); Richardson Paint Company v. NLRB, 574 F.2d 1195 (5th Cir. 1978) (an employee's gathering of signatures on a petition against a layoff was protected); East Chicago Rehabilitation Center Inc. v. NLRB, 710 F.2d 397 (7th Cir. 1983) (walkout to protest discontinuation of paid lunch break off premises protected); United Cable Television Corp. and Freight Checkers, Clerical Workers and Helpers, Teamsters Local 856, 299 NLRB 138, 142 (1990) (charging party's letter advocating higher wages deemed to be consistent with the union's goals and announcing the following test: "[D]issident activity 'which is in support of, and does not seek to usurp or replace the certified bargaining representative' is protected if it is 'more nearly in support of the things which the union is trying to accomplish.' "). *But see* NLRB v. Architectural Research Corp., 748 F.2d 1121 (6th Cir. 1984) (where the persistent complaints of two employees about the elimination of a paid afternoon break negotiated by the union and management after being advised by the union and management that the matter should be resolved through the union were deemed unprotected).

not alone be a sufficient showing of an undermining effect.[107] On the other hand, efforts to by-pass the union, attacks on the union, and ignoring union advice are likely to establish such a showing.[108]

Courts have said little about the scope of the § 9(a) proviso since the decision in *Emporium Capwell*. The *Emporium* Court's discussion of the proviso created ambiguity. While it is clear the Court interpreted the Act not to protect employees who seek through the use of economic coercion to insist upon the filing of a grievance, it is not clear that the mere filing of a grievance is unprotected activity that subjects an employee to discharge. The Court was explicit that the employer does not commit an unfair labor practice simply by refusing to entertain the grievance. However, the opinion does not address retaliatory discharge. To read § 9(a) to allow an employer to retaliate against an employee who files a grievance would seem to fly in the face of well-settled Supreme Court precedent finding § 7 protection where the grievance filing concerns a right contained in the collective bargaining agreement.[109] On the other hand, it is possible to read the Court's disavowal of a right to file a grievance as also depriving the filer of a remedy for the employer's retaliation. The Court addressed the issue in response to Emporium's assumption that to conclude Hollins and Hawkins were filing a grievance would have entailed a conclusion that they could not be discharged. The Court called this view a "misapprehension," even though the Court discussed only whether the 9(a) proviso allowed the employer to refuse to entertain the grievance, not whether the employer could fire the grievant in retaliation.

Cases decided since *Emporium Capwell* have not cleared up this ambiguity. The Sixth Circuit addressed the relationship between § 7 protected concerted activity and the § 9(a) proviso in *Aro, Inc. v. National Labor Relations Board*.[110] In that case an employer refused to rehire a temporary janitorial employee in retaliation for her post-termination complaints about the employer's having terminated two other employees and herself. *Aro* predated the Supreme Court's acceptance of the "*Interboro* doctrine," which grants § 7 protection to individual assertion of rights grounded in collective bargaining agreements. In that

107 *See* NLRB v. Bridgeport Ambulance Service, 966 F.2d 725 (2d Cir. 1992).

108 *See, e.g.*, NLRB v. Architectural Research Corp., 748 F.2d 1121 (6th Cir. 1984).

109 It is an unfair labor practice under § 8(a)(1) of the Act to discharge an employee for protected concerted activity. *See also* NLRB v. City Disposal Systems Inc., 465 U.S. 822 (1984) (affirming the Board's "*Interboro* doctrine," protecting "an individual's assertion of a right grounded in a collective-bargaining agreement" as concerted activity). Of course, the result would be different if the agreement waived the employee's right to file a grievance.

110 596 F.23d 713 (6th Cir. 1979).

case the Sixth Circuit joined two circuits declining to follow the doctrine, and refused to enforce the Board's order finding that the employee had engaged in protected concerted activity by lodging the post-termination complaints.

Interestingly, the Board relied upon the § 9(a) proviso to argue "that Congress intended to establish an affirmative right to complain for individual employees at least as broad as the doctrine enunciated in *Interboro*." Moreover, according to the court, the Board's position was an illegitimate effort to graft § 7 protection onto § 9(a). In rejecting this argument, the Sixth Circuit reiterated the scope of the 9(a) proviso as set forth in *Emporium Capwell* and said, "nothing in Section 9(a) expands the definition of concerted action in Section 7, nor does it serve to define Section 7 rights by illustration." Then, noting that the proviso "may amount to an exception to the concerted action requirement of Section 7, and not a statement of its scope," the court concluded that the language of the § 9(a) proviso did not control its determination of what constituted concerted activity under § 7.[111] Unfortunately, this decision leaves intact the ambiguity created in *Emporium Capwell* about the scope of the § 9(a) proviso.

Conclusion

Quite apart from the impact of *Emporium Capwell* on the development of the law of exclusivity, the larger policy questions remain. How should the tension be resolved between protecting union power to advance economic interests and furthering racial justice goals under Title VII of the Civil Rights Act? Does *Emporium Capwell* strike the right balance?

On one hand, preserving unions' monopoly power over the labor market through defense of the exclusivity principle has enhanced their ability to secure improved compensation and benefits for all unionized workers, regardless of race.[112] As Justice Marshall recognized, exclusivity is vital to counteract the high potential for "strife and deadlock" in the context of competing demands by groups of workers on the employer's limited resources.[113] Exclusivity ensures that the union presents a united front at the bargaining table, making union strike threats more credible and employer concessions in bargaining more likely.[114] Minority workers

---

111 *Id.*

112 *See* Martha R. Mahoney, *Constructing Solidarity: Interest and White Workers,* 2 U. Pa. J. Lab. & Emp. L. 747, 748, 762 (2000).

113 *See* Calvin William Sharpe, *"Judging in Good Faith"—Seeing Justice Marshall's Legacy Through a Labor Case,* 26 Ariz. St. L.J. 479, 488 (1994).

114 *See* Richard B. Freeman & James L. Medoff, *What Do Unions Do?* 143–45 (1984); *but see* Matthew W. Finkin, *The Road Not Taken: Some Thoughts on Nonmajority*

stand to gain the most from union membership and collective bargaining. Indeed, African–American workers have enjoyed disproportionately greater benefits from union membership than workers in general.[115] Exclusivity also prevents employers from capitalizing on racial divisions in the workforce and thereby undermining union solidarity. Finally, exclusivity is efficient for employers. It avoids the necessity of dealing with a multiplicity of smaller sub-groups of workers with competing demands. Under exclusivity, the union—rather than the employer—resolves the conflicts of interest between groups of workers internally.

On the other hand, the story of *Emporium Capwell* itself reveals the inherent potential of union power to neglect and even disserve the interests of minority constituencies with limited recourse available under labor law through duty of fair representation claims. As the *Emporium Capwell* protestors recognized, race discrimination is a group injury and group action may offer the only truly effective remedy. Ironically, because concerted activity is protected under § 7 when there is no exclusive representative (i.e., in a nonunion context),[116] one possible interpretation of *Emporium Capwell* is that minorities in nonunion workforces may have more freedom to engage in concerted action to oppose discrimination than minorities in unionized workforces.[117] Historical outsiders to the union movement might thus be encouraged to form their own identity-based workplace action groups in preference to unionizing, or to turn to government agencies, private attorneys and the courts for redress rather than forming unions and invoking the power of collective action.[118] Is this desirable? What effect might this have on labor strength and solidarity?[119] Is this the result the Court intended?

Employee Representation, 69 Chi.-Kent L. Rev. 195, 201 (1993) (analyzing significance of strike weapon in contemporary era).

115 Unionized African–American workers earn forty-five percent more than nonunionized African–Americans. By contrast, labor economists believe that the wage premium for all unionized workers is between ten and twenty percent. Executive Summary, Labor Day 1999: Futurework: Trends and Challenges for Work in the 21st Century, A Report of the United States Department of Labor, Alexis M. Herman, Secretary, *reprinted* at Daily Lab. Rep. (BNA) No. 170, Sept. 2, 1999; *see also* Marion Crain, *Colorblind Unionism,* 49 UCLA L. Rev. 1313, 1315–17 (2002).

116 *See* NLRB v. Washington Aluminum Co., 370 U.S. 9, 14–16 (1962).

117 *See* Marion Crain & Ken Matheny, *"Labor's Divided Ranks" Privilege and the United Front Ideology,* 84 Cornell L. Rev. 1542, 1562 (1999).

118 *See* Marion Crain & Ken Matheny, *Labor's Identity Crisis,* 89 Cal. L. Rev. 1767, 1769 (2001).

119 *See generally* Nelson Lichtenstein, *State of the Union: A Century of American Labor* 174–75, 260–76 (2002) (describing debilitating consequences for labor union strength of clash between labor solidarity and rights consciousness); Karl E. Klare, *The Quest for Industrial Democracy and the Struggle Against Racism: Perspectives from Labor Law and*

At the same time, however, exclusivity need not necessarily preclude the exercise of minority voice *within* unions.[120] It may, for example, promote dissident activity within the union aimed at making unions more responsive to the needs of minority constituencies, while simultaneously preserving the bargaining power of the overall bargaining unit. The pressure of dissident internal activity also creates an opportunity for unions to heighten their mediatory roles and promote a dialogue among constituent groups that may empower both the groups and the larger union.[121] The AFL–CIO has embraced many worker caucuses organized around identity and brought them within its umbrella of affiliated organizations, including the Coalition of Black Trade Unionists, the A. Philip Randolph Institute, the Labor Council on Latin American Advancement, and the Coalition of Labor Union Women (all in existence since the 1970's), as well as the more recently-formed National Organization for Working Women, 9 To 5, the Asian Pacific American Labor Alliance, and Pride At Work.[122] These caucuses function as avenues for the promotion of minority voice within the union structure and press unions to respond to issues of concern to minority constituencies.

The *Emporium* Court relied upon Title VII and its enforcement scheme as the appropriate remedy for complaints of racial discrimination that were not redressed within the union context. This approach was consistent with the Court's earlier decision in *Alexander v. Gardner–Denver Co.*, preserving employees' individual rights to bring claims in court to vindicate Title VII's guarantee of freedom from race discrimination. This resolution of the tension between the two statutory schemes preserved the exclusivity principle without undermining the goals of Title VII.[123] But was there a price to be paid for the potential creation of a two-track system—the NLRA as the protective mechanism

---

Civil Rights Law, 61 Or. L. Rev. 157, 162 (1982) (criticizing unions for failing to make the eradication of racism a central goal).

[120] For proposals aimed at furthering internal union democracy within the confines of majority rule, see Elizabeth M. Iglesias, *Structures of Subordination: Women of Color at the Intersection of Title VII and the NLRA. NOT!,* 28 Harv. C.R.-C.L. L.Rev. 395 (1993); Eileen Silverstein, *Union Decisions on Collective Bargaining Goals: A Proposal for Interest Group Participation,* 77 Mich. L. Rev. 1485 (1979).

[121] *See* Molly S. McUsic & Michael Selmi, *Postmodern Unions: Identity Politics in the Workplace,* 82 Iowa L. Rev. 1339, 1368–72 (1997).

[122] On the role of identity caucuses in the labor movement more generally, see Ruben J. Garcia, *New Voices At Work: Race and Gender Identity Caucuses in the U.S. Labor Movement,* 54 Hastings L.J. 79 (2002); Michael J. Yelnofsky, *Title VII, Mediation and Collective Action,* 1999 U. Ill. L. Rev. 583; Alan Hyde, *Employee Caucus: A Key Institution in the Emerging System of Employment Law,* 69 Chi.-Kent L. Rev. 149 (1993).

[123] *See* Calvin William Sharpe, *"Judging in Good Faith"—Seeing Justice Marshall's Legacy Through a Labor Case,* 26 Ariz. St. L.J. 479, 492 (1994).

for majoritarian economic interests and Title VII as the tool for advancing individuals' racial justice concerns? Might such a system, for example, encourage courts to conceptualize race discrimination as an individual rather than a collective harm, ultimately undermining union power to address it? One recent case suggests this possibility. In *Air Line Pilots Association, International v. Northwest Airlines, Inc.*,[124] newly-hired pilot trainees were asked to sign individual employment contracts with the employer in which they agreed to binding arbitration of any statutory employment discrimination claims that might arise. The union challenged this practice, arguing that the employer must bargain with the union over the issue rather than approach individual employees directly. The D.C. Circuit ruled that while an individual employee may waive her statutory rights in exchange for the employer's agreement to furnish binding arbitration, the union may not. Since the union could not legally agree to the provision the employer sought to have the workers sign, the topic was not a mandatory subject of bargaining.[125] Thus, the employer was free to deal directly with the employees over the arbitration of statutory discrimination claims.[126] Did the *Emporium* Court intend to sever anti-discrimination agendas from union agendas at law, leaving minority workers to stand alone against the employer in negotiating redress for racial discrimination? Is *Air Line Pilots Association* simply wrongly decided, or does it reveal an underlying flaw in the two-track system sanctioned by the *Emporium* Court's reasoning?

One way to assess the Court's resolution of the competing interests is to consider the alternative. What might the landscape look like if exclusivity were not the rule? Majority rule and exclusivity are unique to the American and Canadian labor law regimes. Other forms of worker organization and vehicles for democratic governance prevail in most economically advanced democracies.[127] What, if any, correlation might

---

[124] 199 F.3d 477 (D.C. Cir. 1999), *judgment reinstated on reh'g en banc,* 211 F.3d 1312 (D.C. Cir.), *cert. denied,* 531 U.S. 1011 (2000).

[125] *But see* Wright v. Universal Maritime Service Corp., 525 U.S. 70 (1998). In that case an employer argued that Gilmer v. Interstate/Johnson Lane Corp., 500 U.S. 20 (1991), had sufficiently undermined *Gardner-Denver* that a union could waive an employee's right to a judicial forum. The Court did not reach the question of enforceability of a union waiver, because the union had not clearly and unmistakably waived the right.

[126] 199 F.3d at 484, 486.

[127] *See generally Comparative Labour Law and Industrial Relations in Industrialized Market Economies* (Roger Blanpain ed., 8th ed. 2004) (describing forms of worker representation in many countries including Belgium, Australia, France, the United Kingdom, Switzerland, Hungary, Germany, Italy, Israel, the Netherlands, and the United States). Japanese labor law requires employers to bargain with any union representing at least two people; multiple unionism is common. *See* Karl J. Duff, *Japanese and American Labor Law: Structural Similarities and Substantive Differences,* 9 Emp. Rel. L.J. 629, 633 (1984).

this bear to the fact that nearly all of these countries enjoy higher union density than does the United States? Are there differences between these countries and the United States that justify a legally mandated united front in the United States? What is the most significant justification for maintaining exclusivity in the modern era?

While *Emporium Capwell* raised these larger policy questions, it did not resolve them. Rather, the Court made a narrow, doctrinal choice that, unlike the D.C. Circuit's majority opinion, did not purport to reconcile the exclusivity doctrine of the NLRA with the antidiscrimination principles of Title VII. The Court, it seems, has done no better than contemporary liberalism at resolving the tensions between equal employment opportunity and majoritarian unionism. Since the questions related to this issue continue to have vitality, the effect of the *Emporium Capwell* decision may simply be to defer them to another day and, perhaps, another forum.

*

7

Alan Hyde

The Story of *First National Maintenance Corp. v. NLRB*: Eliminating Bargaining for Low–Wage Service Workers

The maintenance workers at a Brooklyn nursing home voted to be represented by a union. As a consequence, within four months they were on the streets. They had no union, no jobs, and no right to bump or transfer into another job. From this sad story, the United States Supreme Court would, four years later, fashion a narrative of rights and freedom. Not the rights and freedom of the workers, whose very names have been lost to history. Rather, the maintenance contractor who employed them turned out to be free, to have the right, not to meet at all with their union, nor any substantive obligation to them, and the same was true of the nursing home itself.

The case was *First National Maintenance Corp. v. National Labor Relations Board* (*FNM*).[1] Every student of labor law reads it, for it clearly established the existence of a category of managerial decisions which are too important to be bargained with a union. "We conclude that the harm likely to be done to an employer's need to operate freely in deciding whether to shut down part of its business purely for economic reasons outweighs the incremental benefit that might be gained through the union's participation in making the decision, and we hold that the decision itself is *not* part of § 8(d)'s 'terms and conditions,' over which Congress has mandated bargaining."[2]

---

[1] 452 U.S. 666 (1981).

[2] 452 U.S. at 686 (emphasis original; two footnotes omitted).

Over two decades earlier, the Supreme Court had accepted the Board's rule that subjects of bargaining could be classed as mandatory, permissive, or illegal. This distinction is not found in the statute itself. On the contrary, as the Supreme Court later noted in the *FNM* opinion, the House of Representatives in the 1947 debates over the Taft–Hartley amendments to the NLRA had voted down a proposed list of subjects of bargaining.[3]

The distinction between mandatory and permissive subjects of bargaining was first made by the Board, rather casually, as a new way of analyzing bargaining table conduct that the Board believed prevented the reaching of agreement. As part of its interpretation of the statutory duty to bargain in good faith, the Board had long examined the substance of employer bargaining proposals as evidence of the employer's good faith. In the 1950's, some courts of appeals questioned this analysis as inconsistent with Section 8(d), added to the NLRA in the Taft–Hartley amendments,[4] particularly as interpreted by the Supreme Court.[5] The Board's response, adopting the suggestion of one court of appeals, was to divide bargaining subjects into those that might be insisted on, and others that might merely be proposed.[6] The Supreme Court accepted this analysis in the very case that adopted it, *NLRB v. Wooster Division of Borg–Warner Corporation*. Curiously, neither party in the Supreme Court challenged the division of bargaining subjects itself.[7] There though the employer was found to be in bad faith by tying

---

3 452 U.S. at 675 n.14.

4 Section 8(d), 29 U.S.C. § 158(d), states in part that the statutory obligation to bargain "does not compel either party to agree to a proposal or require the making of a concession."

5 NLRB v. American Nat. Ins. Co., 343 U.S. 395 (1952) held, reversing the Board, that an employer was privileged to bargain for a broad "management rights" clause that would reserve to itself freedom of action during the life of the collective agreement.

6 *Borg–Warner* was the first case to find an employer guilty of bad faith bargaining because of its insistence on permissive subjects of bargaining. Earlier cases had examined employer substantive bargaining proposals only as evidence of overall bad faith, e.g., Jasper Blackburn Prods. Corp., 21 NLRB 1240 (1940) (employer-dominated shop committee); Allis–Chalmers Mfg. Co., 106 NLRB 939 (1953) (insistence on contract ratification tantamount to bypassing union), *enforcement denied*, 213 F.2d 374 (7th Cir. 1954). In the latter case, the court of appeals held, reversing the Board, that any party might insist on any "statutory" bargaining subject. In *Borg–Warner*, the Board adopted this rule. The facts of *Borg-Warner* were identical to *Allis–Chalmers*: an employer insisting in negotiations that a union agree to submit last proposals for membership ratification before holding a strike vote. General Counsel had expressly not challenged the employer's overall bad faith. The Board majority asserted: "[W]e ... believe that the Respondent's liability under Section 8(a)(5) turns not upon its good faith, but rather upon the legal question of whether the proposals are obligatory subjects of collective bargaining." 113 NLRB 1288, 1291 (1955).

7 356 U.S. 342 (1958). The Board, of course, defended the division of bargaining subjects into mandatory and permissive. Dean St. Antoine reported that counsel for the

up negotiations in trivial issues, and it was these trivial issues that were found, for that reason, to be permissive subjects of bargaining.

First National Maintenance is different, for it found that some decisions are too important to be mandatory subjects of bargaining. The existence of such a category had been accepted in an earlier Supreme Court concurrence in *Fibreboard Paper Products Corporation v. NLRB*[8] and indeed by the Board itself.[9] *First National Maintenance*, however, was the first time the Supreme Court held that certain management decisions or prerogatives, because of their importance to management and lack of amenability for bargaining, could be undertaken unilaterally, without bargaining with the union. Since then the Supreme Court has decided no further cases in this area, so the category defined in *First National Maintenance*, and the method employed for determining its boundaries, remain authoritative.

Yet the Supreme Court's opinion has brought no clarity to this corner of law. The opinion is universally criticized for vagueness and internal inconsistency. While subsequent cases in the Board and lower courts cite *First National Maintenance* as the authoritative Supreme Court case, no case really attempts to employ its analysis, and it is impossible to find a subsequent case that one is confident would have been decided differently had *First National Maintenance* never existed. We shall see that this is largely because the Supreme Court was induced to decide a kind of hypothetical case, carefully constructed to represent an appealing limitation on the category of mandatory subjects of bargaining. The facts that the Supreme Court decided have never arisen again. Indeed, they were not the actual facts of the case itself. Finally, the Court's opinion combined the rather different analyses of two different justices, without clear indication of their relationship. The important recent developments in bargaining structures for low-wage

---

company "seriously considered" attacking this division, arguing that the duty to bargain in good faith attached to any subject about which any party wanted to bargain. This would have won the case for his client. Instead, however, on orders from his client, he accepted the division and argued only, and ineffectually, that his client's specific demands were in good faith. The company, showing considerably more foresight than the Board or the unions, realized that an expansive definition of mandatory subjects of bargaining would ultimately increase union power. Theodore J. St. Antoine, *Legal Barriers to Worker Participation in Management Decision–Making*, 58 Tul. L.Rev. 1301, 1305 n.25 (1984).

[8] 379 U.S. 203, 246 (1964) (Stewart, J., concurring) ("An enterprise may decide to invest in labor-saving machinery. Another may resolve to liquidate its assets and go out of business. Nothing the Court holds today should be understood as imposing a duty to bargain collectively regarding such management decisions, which lie at the core on entrepreneurial control.").

[9] General Motors Corp., 191 NLRB 951 (1971), *review denied sub nom.* International Union, United Automobile Workers v. NLRB, 470 F.2d 422 (D.C. Cir. 1972).

service workers take place entirely outside the framework of *First National Maintenance*.

Factual Background

The Supreme Court decided a case of an employer that eliminated a portion of its operations by terminating a contract with a particular customer, an economic decision turning not at all on labor costs and completely free of anti-union hostility, a case only preserved as a legal matter because the employer refused to meet with the union at all. Could such a case ever have existed?

First National Maintenance Corporation, its lawyer later told the Supreme Court, began doing the maintenance work at Greenpark Care Center around early March 1976.[10] It is impossible now to reconstruct who did the maintenance work before, or how FNM came to be chosen. FNM's lawyer, Sanford E. Pollack, thought the work might previously have been done by Greenpark's own employees.[11]

Despite its grandiose name, FNM was a relatively small, local operation run by three childhood friends. Leonard Marsh handled the union matters and testified at the Board hearing. He was forty-four years old in the spring of 1977 and had previously worked as a garment worker, egg dealer, and window washer before his current business ventures.[12] His partner Hyman Golden was married to Marsh's sister. A third partner and friend was Arnold Greenberg, whose father had run a delicatessen on the lower east side of Manhattan that Greenberg had converted into a health food store in 1972. The partners in the maintenance company also ran (out of the same warehouse) a company distributing fruit to health food stores, Unadulterated Food Products, Inc., and, sometime by 1978, had begun to manufacture carbonated apple juice under their own name.[13] A businessman who visited their warehouse a decade later in 1989 found three quarreling partners in a chaotic and shabby warehouse; despite instructions to hold calls, their meeting was interrupted six times.[14]

FNM, according to Pollack, had no general objection to labor unions. Most of their employees were represented by unions. When they did

---

10 Transcript of Supreme Court Oral Argument at 4 ("We had some 17 months covered by the entire period of operation in the particular facility which is affected.").

11 Telephone Interview with Sanford E. Pollack, May 12, 2004.

12 Harry Berkowitz, *Annoyed, Frustrated (and Very Rich)*, Newsday, Nov. 25, 1996, at C8.

13 Jon Pessah, *Kid Pals Strike it Rich*, Newsday, Nov. 3, 1994, at A37.

14 Mark H. McCormack, *It Sometimes Pays to Hook Up with a Startup*, [Cleveland] Plain Dealer, Apr. 4, 1995, at C3.

maintenance work at factories and cafeterias, their workers were covered by a "me too" contract with whatever union represented the production workers. The partners felt differently, however, about District 1199, the union representing hospital and health care workers nationally. While nominally a district of the old Retail, Wholesale, and Department Store Union (RWD), it dwarfed its parent.[15] Its founders such as Leon Davis, still in charge in 1977, were strongly left-wing.[16] Pollack counseled his clients that 1199 was a "difficult, militant" union that they should not let into their company.

While Pollack represented FNM during 1199's successful representation campaign in March 1977, today he remembers little about the campaign itself. Unhappy as FNM's owners were about the prospect of a victory by 1199, they saw no realistic prospect of defeating the union at a Board election. The maintenance workers worked alongside Greenpark workers who were already represented by 1199, and anyway "1199 usually won elections, at least at that time." So FNM did not campaign against 1199. It had a different plan for avoiding that union, one that would have been hurt by an open display of animus to 1199. Local 1199 won the union election at FNM in March 1977.

FNM used crude tactics to avoid 1199 at another nursing home. At Haven Manor, in Far Rockaway, when FNM began doing maintenance work in 1974, 1199 tried to organize its employees. FNM instead recognized Local 690, Amalgamated Workers Union of America, a notorious sweetheart union, over the opposition of the employees who later responded by voting to deauthorize Local 690's union shop. FNM nevertheless extended the Amalgamated Workers Union collective bargaining agreement when 1199 filed an election petition in 1978.[17] The Board later held the extension to violate NLRA § 8(a)(2), since the Amalgamated Workers Union did not represent a majority of Haven Manor employees; the Administrative Law Judge expressed doubts that it existed as a union at all.[18]

---

[15] It is now part of the Service Employees International Union (SEIU).

[16] Leon Fink & Brian Greenberg, *Upheaval in the Quiet Zone: A History of Hospital Workers' Union, Local 1199* 17–27 (1989). Davis retired as president in December 1981, *id.* at 210.

[17] For more on the Amalgamated Workers Union, see Priore v. Nelson, 626 F.2d 211 (2d Cir. 1980) (denying parole to former president of AWUA Local 690); U.S. v. Sanfillipo, 48 Lab.Cas. ¶ 18635 (E.D.N.Y. 1963) (criminal conviction of AWUA officers for labor kickbacks).

[18] First National Maintenance Corp., 254 NLRB 289, *enforced*, 681 F.2d 802 (2d Cir. 1981) (mem.). The Board decision in this case was issued in January 1981 but was not called to the attention of the Supreme Court, which treated FNM throughout as a company without animus toward 1199.

Greenpark offered FNM an easier, yet still risky, way of avoiding 1199. It would not be necessary to contract with a sweetheart union. FNM could simply cancel the underlying maintenance contract, which permitted either party to terminate it on thirty days' notice. The contract was not a lucrative one, even for little FNM. It netted only a $250 weekly management fee after Greenpark paid FNM's payroll costs. Marsh testified at the Board hearing that FNM was losing money at Greenpark. It is not easy to see how this could be true if Greenpark was paying all payroll costs. However, no doubt FNM was making little money and was happy enough to say goodbye to Greenpark as a customer.

The victory for 1199 in the March union election made FNM's financial situation more acute. FNM asked Greenpark administrator Simon Pelman if Greenpark could pay more money. FNM anticipated having to increase wages to its newly-unionized employees, but Pelman did not think that New York State would reimburse him for any additional payments to FNM, and refused to raise them.[19]

But while the union victory made FNM's departure from Greenpark more imperative, it also created legal complications. FNM faced a difficult choice. It could have told 1199 of its plans to drop Greenpark as a customer and bargained to impasse over that decision. Or it could have kept 1199 in the dark and announced the decision to leave Greenpark only on the day of implementing it. Each path had advantages and risks. To understand these, we must discuss the state of the duty to bargain in 1977.

Legal Background

Must a unionized employer bargain with the union before eliminating jobs? This question, which the *First National Maintenance* case was supposed to answer (and did not), was if anything even more difficult to answer in 1977. The premise of the Supreme Court's grant of certiorari was that neither the Board nor the courts of appeals had been consistent in these cases, and that premise, at least, was quite correct.

As we have seen, the legal concept of permissive subjects of bargaining was invented by the Board in 1955, almost casually, as a new way of limiting some bargaining-table conduct, insistence on unacceptable proposals, that the Board had long seen as detrimental to reaching agreement.[20] In 1961, however, the same concept became, simultaneously and

---

[19] Telephone Interview with Simon Pelman, April 16, 2004. Pelman was still employed at Greenpark in 2004.

[20] *See, e.g.*, Local 164, Painters, 126 NLRB 997 (1960) (employer performance bonds and worker residency requirements are not mandatory subjects of bargaining; union violates § 8(b)(3) in insisting on them).

by definition, the limit of management's power to act unilaterally.[21] Consider how this works in either of two clear, polar cases, involving management decisions that clearly are, or clearly are not, mandatory subjects of bargaining.

Consider first something that is clearly a mandatory subject of bargaining, such as wages or hours, mentioned in the statute since 1947.[22] An employer whose employees are represented by a union is no longer free to raise (or lower) wages unilaterally and would commit an unfair labor practice in doing so. The employer must first make its proposal to the union, and bargain to impasse, before it is free to act unilaterally. It need not bargain until the union's agreement is achieved—that is, there is no requirement of codetermination—and the union cannot block the unilateral change, or prolong negotiations once impasse has been reached.[23]

By contrast, consider a clearly permissive subject of bargaining, in the original, too-trivial-to-tie-up-negotiations-over sense, such as employer performance bonds. One might first question why a trivial issue, insistence on which constituted the negotiating party's lack of good faith, must automatically be an issue over which the employer retains unilateral freedom of action. Why shouldn't that trivial issue nevertheless be taken to the union if the context shows it was not a pretext for avoiding a collective bargaining agreement? A reasoned discussion of this issue cannot be found among NLRB decisions. The Board seems simply to have assumed that any issue not a mandatory subject of bargaining is

[21] Fibreboard Paper Prods. Corp., 130 NLRB 1558 (1961), *reversed on reconsideration*, 138 NLRB 550 (1962). The earlier decision held that subcontracting was not a "term and condition" of employment, and therefore management need not bargain, and was free to act unilaterally. The decision does not employ the terms "mandatory" or "permissive" subject of bargaining. It was also reconsidered, and reversed, the following year, and it was the latter decision, holding that the employer did indeed have to bargain, that was ultimately enforced by the Supreme Court. The earlier *Fibreboard* decision, soon reversed, is the first NLRB decision equating management's privilege not to bargain with its privilege to act unilaterally.

[22] In that year, as part of the Taft–Hartley amendments to the NLRA, Congress added the following definitional section, § 8(d), to the Act:

> For the purposes of this section, to bargain collectively is the performance of the mutual obligation of the employer and the representative of the employees to meet at reasonable times and confer in good faith with respect to wages, hours, and other terms and conditions of employment, or the negotiation of an agreement, or any question arising thereunder, and the execution of a written contract incorporating any agreement reached if requested by either party, but such obligation does not compel either party to agree to a proposal or require the making of a concession....

29 U.S.C. § 158(d) (2000).

[23] NLRB v. Katz, 369 U.S. 736 (1962).

automatically an issue on which management may act unilaterally. The Supreme Court did not actually decide this point until 1971.[24]

As we have seen, the concept of nonmandatory or permissive subjects of bargaining was created to permit Board regulation of bargaining-table conduct. Once it is equated with the limits of unilateral action, that is, not meeting with the union at all, the concept reduces the statutory duty to bargain below the level that had previously been suggested as the minimum. During the 1950's, discussions about the scope of the duty to bargain, following the most influential article, distinguished between a minimal approach, under which that duty merely reinforced the statutory obligation to recognize the union, and a broader approach, under which the duty ruled out certain bargaining table conduct.[25] The Board's concept of nonmandatory subjects of bargaining turns this distinction on its head. Under the rule equating permissive subjects of bargaining with management unilateral action, management need not even recognize the union's existence on those issues. Permissive subjects of bargaining are alibis for not recognizing the union at all. Not recognizing the union at all, and being excused for doing so, reduces the scope of the statutory duty below what had previously been thought to be the minimum, that is, reinforcing union recognition. *FNM* would eventually illustrate this well.

Must the employer meet with the union before it eliminates jobs? In the twenty-five years or so before the Supreme Court's decision in *First National Maintenance*, the Board usually held that employers had to bargain about decisions that resulted in job elimination. However, the Board never held squarely that such decisions were presumptively bargainable. It just typically found them bargainable.[26] The Board made exceptions to this normal practice in some cases in which it found the employer's decision to involve managerial prerogative, capital investment or disinvestment, or basic changes in its business. The Board never defined these terms or explained how they would be traded off against

---

[24] Allied Chemical and Alkali Workers Local 1 v. Pittsburgh Plate Glass Co., 404 U.S. 157 (1971) (employer's unilateral changes to health insurance benefits for already-retired employees are not an unfair labor practice since permissive subject of bargaining; § 8(d) procedures for modifying collective agreements are limited to mandatory subjects of bargaining). The *Borg-Warner* decision is not authority for this point. The permissive subject of bargaining there, over which the employer tied up negotiations, was the union's procedure for calling strikes. This was plainly an internal union issue over which the employer had no unilateral, or any other, freedom of action.

[25] Archibald Cox & John T. Dunlop, *Regulation of Collective Bargaining By the National Labor Relations Board*, 63 Harv. L.Rev. 389 (1950) (advocating limiting the scope of § 8(a)(5) to refusals to recognize the union).

[26] The most frequently-cited Board case was Ozark Trailers, Inc., 161 NLRB 561 (1966) (closing one plant).

other values that might favor bargaining, such as the impact of such decisions on employees, or the value of informing unions so as to permit meaningful bargaining.[27] The Board's requirement of bargaining over some subcontracting decisions had been upheld by the Supreme Court, but in an opinion that cautioned that it was not even requiring bargaining over all subcontracting, and invoked a medley of factors supporting the decision to require bargaining in the case at hand.[28] Courts of appeals frequently denied enforcement to Board orders requiring bargaining over job elimination, but did not converge on any alternative analysis.[29]

This unclear state of the law will obviously be most relevant when our story reaches the Supreme Court. But for now, consider its implications for FNM, and its lawyer, in the spring of 1977. As we know, FNM decided to drop Greenpark as a customer and lay off all thirty-five maintenance workers there. Ultimately they did not pay for this decision, except in litigation costs. However, at the time they made it, it was a risky one. There were no reported cases dealing with an employer that decided to eliminate jobs by termination of a particular contract. This decision could easily be characterized either as a mandatory or as a permissive subject of bargaining. Arguments in favor of calling it mandatory included the fact that the Board normally required bargaining over management decisions that resulted in job loss; that this decision involved no capital investment or disinvestment or change in corporate structure; that labor costs were essentially the only component of FNM's operation; that 1199 was newly-certified (giving the entire decision a flavor of union avoidance); and that FNM was resisting that union, not only at Greenpark, but also at Haven Manor. Arguments in favor of calling it permissive included the fact that the Board had never held

27 Particularly puzzling was General Motors Corp., 191 NLRB 951 (1971), *review denied*, 470 F.2d 422 (D.C. Cir. 1972), in which the Board refused to require bargaining over a corporate decision to sell certain unionized divisions to what would become independent contractors who would then contract the same services to the company. Other frequently-cited decisions in which the Board had refused to require bargaining over management decisions that eliminated jobs were Summit Tooling Co., 195 NLRB 479 (1972) (closing subsidiary) and National Car Rental System, Inc., 252 NLRB 159 (1980) (closing one location and moving work twenty miles away with clear antiunion animus; duty to bargain only about effects of decision, not decision itself), *enforced as to effects bargaining*, 672 F.2d 1182 (3d Cir. 1982). The Board never satisfactorily explained the criteria that excepted these cases from its general preference to require bargaining.

28 Fibreboard Paper Products Corp. v. NLRB, 379 U.S. 203 (1964) (invoking the construction of the statutory phrase "terms and conditions of employment", industrial practice, salience of labor costs in the decision, and the employer's "freedom to manage the business").

29 As an attorney in the NLRB's branch of appellate courts litigation in 1975–76, several times I briefed cases in which the Board had required bargaining over decisions to eliminate jobs. All the attorneys in the branch were then keenly aware that Board decisions were not reconcilable, either on their facts or on the method of analysis.

choice of customer to be a mandatory subject of bargaining; that FNM's dissatisfaction with Greenpark was ostensibly over the size of its management fee; and that FNM had no record of anti-union animus at Greenpark (though it did at Haven Manor).

In this circumstance, many employers would have chosen to avoid legal proceedings. They would have made an appointment with the union and informed it that they were not making enough money at Greenpark and had decided to drop it as a client. They would have expressed a willingness to listen to what the union had to say, but would have stressed that the dispute was entirely about management fees, not labor costs. The negotiations would not have been complicated. Impasse might well be reached in an hour or two. At that point, this hypothetical employer would have discharged its statutory duty to bargain, which, you will recall, does not involve an obligation to reach agreement with the union or give the union any rights to block management action after impasse.

FNM did not pursue this path. Instead, it refused to meet with 1199 at all. Two days before the expiration of its contract with Greenpark, it informed the employees (not the union) that they would be dismissed. Doing this risked a Board finding that FNM was guilty of failure to bargain in good faith. In that case, FNM would normally be liable for back pay for all terminated employees, from the date of their termination until they found alternative employment. Indeed, the Board eventually did find that FNM had violated its duty to bargain and awarded just such back pay, and its order was enforced in the court of appeals. Only the intervention of the Supreme Court, something that could surely not have been predicted in 1977, saved FNM from a large backpay order that it might have avoided by a few hours of meeting with the union. Why did FNM take the risky path of not meeting with the union at all?

Sanford Pollack counseled his client FNM to accept the risky path. First, Pollack was confident that FNM would not be required to bargain. "Nobody can tell me that I have to stay in business if I'm losing money." He figured that the Board would find FNM in violation of the duty to bargain, but that the Second Circuit would deny enforcement.[30]

Second, he did not find the alternative of bargaining to impasse attractive. "I practiced for forty-five years and can't tell you what impasse is. You never know where a case on impasse goes." "I would much rather not talk at all. That way, you control the litigation. Trying to bargain to impasse makes your fate not your own to control." "There

30 Telephone Interview with Sanford E. Pollack, May 12, 2004.

are cases where the union has been on the street for three weeks and the Board says impasse wasn't reached.''[31]

Third, Greenpark's own employees were also represented by 1199. As soon as the union was told that FNM was withdrawing, a picket line would have been established that several hundred nursing home employees would have refused to cross.

Finally, however, and far from least, FNM's owners wanted absolutely nothing to do with 1199, which they were fighting vigorously (indeed, illegally) at another location. Had FNM talked to 1199 at all, the union's chief demand would have been to permit the workers doing maintenance at Greenpark to transfer to other FNM locations. Pollack compared this with ''letting a virus loose in the company. We didn't want militant people to infect the other locations.'' Avoiding ''letting a virus loose'' was, Pollack said, well worth back pay for thirty-five employees, the worst that could happen if they lost the NLRB case.

So FNM informed Greenpark that it would not be renewing their contract, and withdrew from Greenpark without ever meeting with 1199.

Prior Proceedings

The unfair labor practice trial before the Board's Administrative Law Judge, on July 5, 1978, gave no hint that the case would assume any importance.

The General Counsel was represented by Stephen Appell from the Board's Brooklyn regional office. Appell, today an NLRB attorney in Manhattan, recalls only two witnesses testifying at the hearing. Edward Wecker, a union vice-president, described FNM's complete refusal to bargain with 1199. Leonard Marsh, testifying for the company, explained that FNM was losing money at Greenpark, could not persuade Greenpark to raise the management fee, and exercised its right not to renew the contract.[32]

Appell remembers that the trial was over by lunch. The General Counsel did nothing to challenge Marsh's story. Despite the fact that the Haven Manor representation, union shop deauthorization, and unfair labor practice cases were being handled contemporaneously in the same Board office, the General Counsel did not try to use information from that case to prove FNM's animus toward 1199. Nor did it call Greenpark administrator Simon Pelman who might have explained then, as he did in 2004, that FNM's purported reliance on the level of the management fee was more realistically a concern about demands for increased wages

---

[31] *Id.*

[32] Telephone Interview with Stephen Appell, February 29, 2004.

from the newly recognized union.[33] Indeed, at no level of the case did anyone challenge the naive assumption that an employer, whose employees had just voted to unionize, would be concerned only about its management fee, not its labor costs. Appel saw no reason to have any of the maintenance workers testify.

The Administrative Law Judge to whom the case was assigned died shortly after the hearing, and the case was assigned to Judge Thomas A. Ricci for decision on the record. Judge Ricci took a strong dislike to FNM's Leonard Marsh:

> Asked how many other nursing homes his Company services, Leonard Marsh, an officer of Respondent and one-third owner, answered "I would venture to guess between two and four." It was an evasive answer, unless Respondent's overall operations are so extensive that the secretary-treasurer cannot keep in mind how many are of a particular type.[34]

Judge Ricci found that FNM's complete refusal to meet with 1199 was "a very clear unfair labor practice." He did not distinguish FNM's obligation to bargain about the *effects* of its decision on its employees from its obligation to bargain about the *decision* itself, partly because it had done neither. He considered the cases in which the Board had held certain core managerial financial decisions to lie outside mandatory bargaining:

> If ever there was a business in which taking on, finishing, or discontinuing this or that particular job is no more than a regular and usual method of running its affairs, it is this Respondent's overall activity. There was no capital involved when it decided to terminate the Greenpark job. The closing of this one spot in no sense altered the nature of its business, nor did it substantially affect its total size.[35]

The Administrative Law Judge ordered FNM to bargain with 1199 over both its decision to eliminate its Greenpark operation and the effects of that decision on employees. He also ordered FNM to pay back pay to those employees, from their 1977 termination until agreement was reached. Six months later, without analysis, a panel of the full Board adopted his order, broadening the remedies to include a preferential hiring list for the FNM Greenpark workers—exactly what FNM most wanted to avoid—and an extension of the union's certification.

---

[33] Telephone Interview with Simon Pelman, April 16, 2004.

[34] 242 NLRB 462, 464 (1979).

[35] 242 NLRB at 464.

The Board's decision didn't surprise Pollack but the subsequent decision of the court of appeals did. At the oral argument before the appellate court, William Stewart, for most of his career the only African–American attorney handling appellate litigation on behalf of the Board, represented the agency.[36] By the time of the argument in the court of appeals, Pollack had stipulated that FNM had a duty to bargain over the effects on the employees of its departure from Greenpark. Pollack delayed the actual bargaining over effects until after that court's decision "to make sure that it wouldn't turn into bargaining about anything else."[37]

The Second Circuit, in an opinion by the highly-respected district judge Morris Lasker, sitting by designation, enforced the Board's order.[38] As a result of Pollack's stipulation, the court of appeals dealt only with FNM's obligation to bargain over the decision itself. The court noted the conflict, since *Fibreboard*, between the Board's typical orders to bargain over decisions resulting in job loss, and the reluctance of the appellate courts to enforce such orders. Deciding that a *per se* rule was inappropriate in an area in which the Supreme Court (in *Fibreboard*) had expressly counseled consideration of many factors, the court followed a recent decision of the Third Circuit to state, more clearly than the Board ever had, that a presumption existed that any "partial closing" decision was a mandatory subject of bargaining.[39] It would therefore lie with employers

36 Stewart died in 2004. Obituary, Wash. Post, Feb. 19, 2004, at B6; N.Y. Times, Mar. 8, 2004, at A17. He was a Phi Beta Kappa graduate of Indiana University, and Coif graduate of its law school, who served successively as a lieutenant in the Army, Board attorney, director of labor relations and employment opportunity for a private company, and Board attorney again, ending his career as chief counsel to then-Chair William J. Gould IV. I knew Stewart; he was always the epitome of calm and reason.

It is not clear who argued on behalf of FNM at the Second Circuit. It was either Pollack or his Associate Stuart Kirshenbaum; both recall having done the argument. Interview with Stuart Kirshenbaum, April 22, 2004.

37 Telephone Interview with Sanford E. Pollack, May 12, 2004.

38 627 F.2d 596 (2d Cir. 1980).

39 Brockway Motor Trucks v. NLRB, 582 F.2d 720 (3d Cir. 1978). This opinion was carefully studied throughout the *FNM* litigation. In a lengthy and scholarly opinion by Judge Arlin Adams, the court reviewed numerous decisions analyzing whether particular closing decisions were mandatory subjects of bargaining. (A footnote, 582 F.2d at 722 n.1, cites Rousseau, Philip Selznick, Judith Shklar, and Roberto Unger.) The court concluded that employer decisions to close portions of their operations were presumptively mandatory subjects of bargaining, but that particular economic circumstances had to be examined in each case to determine whether particular employer interests, such as a need for speed, made particular decisions not mandatory subjects of bargaining. Since that analysis had not been done, it denied enforcement to the Board's order but permitted the Board to hold additional hearings.

to bring forth evidence "that the purposes of the statute would not be furthered by imposition of a duty to bargain."

> Without an attempt to enumerate all those instances in which the presumption may be rebutted, a few examples may be noted for purposes of illustration. The employer might overcome the presumption by demonstrating that bargaining over the decision would be futile, since the purposes of the statute would not be served by ordering the parties to bargain when it is clear that the employer's decision cannot be changed. Other relevant considerations would be that the closing was due to emergency financial circumstances, or that the custom of the industry, shown by the absence of such an obligation from typical collective bargaining agreements, is not to bargain over such decisions. The presumption might also be rebutted if it could be demonstrated that forcing the employer to bargain would endanger the vitality of the entire business, so that the purposes of the statute would not be furthered by mandating bargaining to benefit some employees to the potential detriment of the remainder. This might be a particularly significant point if the number to be laid off was small and the number of the remainder was large.[40]

The court held that FNM had failed to demonstrate any of these factors, or any other that might excuse its total failure to bargain. Judge Amalya Kearse dissented, briefly, stating that "the respondent's decision in this case to conserve its capital by closing a losing operation was a matter of fundamental entrepreneurial discretion and was not 'suitable for resolution within the collective bargaining framework.' "[41]

Pollack's gamble had seemingly failed. FNM was probably not particularly troubled by a back pay remedy, or an order to bargain with 1199 that could probably be limited to the effects of its decision, nor about a small amount of severance pay. But the company now faced exactly what it had most wanted to avoid—an order requiring it to give former Greenpark maintenance employees hiring preference at its other operations. Pollack had gambled that the court of appeals would save him, but it did not. A petition for certiorari seemed unrealistic. The company was too small for such expenses, and Pollack had never taken a case to the Supreme Court.

The Supreme Court Decision

But, of course, the case did go to the Supreme Court. Someone at the U.S. Chamber of Commerce read the court of appeals decision and

[40] 627 F.2d at 601–02.

[41] 627 F.2d at 604 (quoting *Fibreboard*).

realized that *FNM* was an ideal case for asking the Supreme Court to limit *Fibreboard*. The Chamber asked Marvin E. Frankel, then recently retired as a federal judge and head of the labor law group at the New York law firm of Proskauer Rose Goetz & Mendelsohn, to handle the case in the Supreme Court. Although Proskauer firm attorneys' names appear only on the brief submitted by the Chamber as an *amicus curiae*, they in fact prepared the petition for certiorari and both the principal and reply briefs for petitioner FNM.[42]

Why was this issue important to the Chamber? Many law professors have expressed skepticism about the importance of the definition of mandatory subjects of bargaining generally.[43] David Feller, for example, claimed that the legal distinction between mandatory and permissive subjects is "unimportant," an "academic discussion." The distinction "is only important when an unwary employer who doesn't know that something is a mandatory subject of bargaining takes unilateral action." But the distinction "makes little difference in the outcome of bargaining or the degree to which employees exercise control at the workplace," because "careful" unions may always strike over a mandatory subject.[44]

Proskauer partner Saul Kramer was amused at hearing the academic controversy and explained the Chamber's quite practical interest. "The Chamber did not spend all that money on a theoretical issue." Any management decision that is a mandatory subject of bargaining, such as the subcontracting in *Fibreboard*, "moves up the time when you have to bargain." The decision must be announced to the union early enough to permit what the Board calls "meaningful bargaining." It cannot be announced, as FNM's decision was, on the morning it was implemented. Management normally does not want to announce downsizing decisions in advance. Once such a decision is announced, there are possibilities of sabotage. "You have a period when everything goes crazy in your place, or at least there is a possibility of that, and nobody wants that in management." After announcement of a downsizing decision, production will decline, partly from union slowdowns, partly from "people looking for other jobs." The union will demand information, and this can delay or burden negotiations.[45] The *FNM* case itself shows that, on the issue of the importance of the definition of mandatory subjects of bargaining, Kramer was right and Feller was wrong. A narrow definition of manda-

---

[42] Telephone Interview with Proskauer partner Saul Kramer, May 11, 2004. Frankel died in 2002 (a month after his last argument in the Supreme Court).

[43] Thomas C. Kohler, *Distinctions Without Differences: Effects Bargaining in Light of* First National Maintenance, 5 Indus. Rel. L.J. 402, 421 (1983).

[44] David Feller, *Response (to Colloquium: The Labor Movement at the Crossroads)*, 11 NYU Rev. L. & Soc. Change 136, 136–39 (1982–83).

[45] Telephone Interview with Proskauer partner Saul Kramer, May 11, 2004.

tory subject of bargaining gives an employer a device to avoid union recognition; it also permits the employer to control the information available to the union and thus its capacity for economic action.

Thus, it was "an important issue for the Chamber" to seek to get the Supreme Court to adopt the *Fibreboard* concurrence and squarely find a category of important managerial prerogatives that were, for that reason, permissive subjects of bargaining. Why did *FNM* look like the case in which to pose the issue? Chamber attorney Kramer explained, "This was a very clean case" since the facts showed that FNM was "losing money." FNM terminating Greenpark was, Kramer said, "ostensibly" about its management fee, not labor costs. And the record in this case revealed no animus against 1199.[46]

The briefs prepared at the Proskauer firm carefully and accurately depicted the state of the law: the question about the scope of *Fibreboard*, the conflicts between the Board and courts of appeals. The *amicus* brief for the Chamber mainly discussed the implications of *Darlington*, a case privileging some decisions to close operations against a complaint of unlawful discrimination under § 8(a)(3).[47] These briefs did not, however, address the issue that would soon divide the Supreme Court: what should the test be for identifying mandatory subjects of bargaining? Nor would the Court get help on this issue from the other briefs. The Board's brief argued that the Board always weighs multiple factors, including the impact on management, in determining mandatory subjects of bargaining, and that *FNM* did not differ from the Board's usual approach. The AFL–CIO also appeared *amicus curiae*, filing a totally ineffectual brief, that was to play little role in the Supreme Court's analysis, arguing that an old Railway Labor Act case had actually decided that partial closings were mandatory subjects of bargaining.[48] Its brief offered no alternative way of analyzing mandatory-subject-of-bargaining cases or, more fundamentally, challenging the analytic framework. The AFL–CIO's apparent inability in this brief to imagine an alternative vision of labor law,

---

[46] *Id.*

[47] Textile Workers Union v. Darlington Mfg. Co., 380 U.S. 263 (1965) (partial closing of operations motivated by antiunion animus violates § 8(a)(3) only when motivation is to chill unionism in remaining operations of that employer). The later Supreme Court opinion in *FNM* did not address the implications of *Darlington*.

[48] Order of Railroad Telegraphers v. Chicago & N. W. R. Co., 362 U.S. 330 (1960) (Norris–La Guardia Act deprives federal court of jurisdiction to enjoin strike of railroad union in protest of closing and consolidation of operations). The Supreme Court opinion dismissed the case in a footnote at the end of the opinion, 452 U.S. at 686 n.23: "The mandatory scope of bargaining under the Railway Labor Act and the extent of the prohibition against injunctive relief contained in Norris–LaGuardia are not coextensive with the National Labor Relations Act and the Board's jurisdiction over unfair labor practices."

different than that advanced by management, was unfortunately characteristic of AFL–CIO Supreme Court briefs in the postwar period; there is an interesting article waiting to be written about those briefs.

At oral argument, on April 21, 1981, Pollack represented FNM. Both he and Kramer agree that the Chamber, which was paying Pollack's and Proskauer's fees, offered Pollack money—Pollack claims $50,000—to let Judge Frankel argue the case. Pollack refused. It was his case, after all. Pollack still speaks of the day with pride. It was, he said, the most exciting thing he ever did. His son was there for the argument, and Pollack remembers how proud he felt before his son, and also how sad he felt that he would never do anything so exciting again.[49]

The Board was represented by its Deputy Associate General Counsel Norton Come who, between 1958 and 1987, argued fifty-six cases in the U.S. Supreme Court on behalf of the agency.[50] By 1981, Come was only sixty-one years old but seemed much older, at least to me at that time. Never a brilliant oralist, he was thought, during the time I served the Board, to be trusted and respected by the justices for his memory of what the Board had decided. As was his custom, he wore formal attire to the argument in *FNM*.

Most of the Court's questions for Pollack concerned practical questions such as what happened to the terminated workers (he didn't know), what had been the results of the bargaining over the effects of FNM's decision (some severance pay), and was there a successor employer (yes, the nursing home itself). Pollack was asked a hypothetical about an employer relocating work from one closed factory to a new factory, and responded that this was no different from *Fibreboard* and would therefore be a mandatory subject of bargaining.[51]

Come faced tough questioning to determine the Board's position. What about a decision to cease operations entirely because of "hassle constantly with the union"? Come: "I don't know that the Board has had that case but I would point out that there are cases that suggest that the Board would find that there might not be an obligation in that situation." What about a flat decision to go out of business because the owner wanted to retire? "The Board would be unlikely to find a bargaining obligation in that sort of a situation. But that is poles apart

---

[49] Telephone interview, Sanford E. Pollack, May 12, 2004.

[50] Obituary of Norton Come, Wash. Post, Mar. 19, 2002, 2002 WL 15846287.

[51] "Question [Chief Justice Burger]: Are you saying that if Ford simultaneously opened a new plant in Hamburg, Germany, employing substantially the same number of people, that would be a subject of mandatory bargaining? MR. POLLACK: Yes, Your Honor. I believe that that is correct. I believe that because of that set of circumstances the employer still remains the employer. The work is being done by a replacement group. Now, that's really what Fibreboard said." Transcript of Oral Argument at 13–14.

from the situation that we have here and the situation that we have in many of the termination cases." "Mr. Come, why is it poles apart? What is the difference between that case—maybe the man is a little older, but still, on the economic decision, he'd rather spend his money in Florida than where he was. And here [FNM] the man decides he doesn't want to spend his operation in this particular location."

> Well, I think that Judge Adams in the *Brockway* case summed it up better than I can when he pointed out that a decision to close down can be motivated by a variety of considerations. On some considerations, the union is not a very helpful interlocutor. On others, it may very well be, and what we're talking about here is that the end result is a termination of employment, a termination of the jobs of the employees.[52]

As Justice Brennan said later at conference, "Poor Come!"[53] The conference revealed a majority in favor of reversing the court of appeals and denying enforcement to the Board order. The opinion was assigned to Justice Blackmun.

The drafting of the opinion may be traced in Justice Blackmun's papers in the Library of Congress. The crucial issue became the correct method for determining which management decisions were mandatory subjects of bargaining. On this issue of method, the Court received no assistance from any of the briefs. It emerged that there were two distinct approaches within the majority. Justice Blackmun, joined by Justice Stevens, favored a multi-factor balancing test. Justice Powell, apparently speaking for Chief Justice Burger and Justices Stewart and Rehnquist, favored some categorical definitions of decisions that would not be mandatory subjects of bargaining and would not be subject to balancing. The Court's eventual published opinion combined these two perspectives, not particularly happily.

Blackmun's first draft was circulated on June 1, more than five weeks after the oral argument and close to the end of the term. While it found that FNM did not have to bargain over its decision to cease operations at Greenpark, and seems familiar to anyone acquainted with the eventual opinion of the Court, it contained three features that proved controversial among his brethren. First, it called for a balancing test, under which the determination of mandatory subjects of bargaining required analysis of neutral interests in bargaining, management's interest in avoiding it, and any public interest, and characterized *Fibreboard* as having employed such a balancing test.[54] Second, it seemed to state

---

52 Transcript of Oral Argument at 22.

53 Blackmun Papers, Library of Congress.

54 "[B]argaining over management decisions that have a substantial impact on the continued availability of employment should be required only if the benefit, for labor-

that decisions turning on labor costs would normally be subject to bargaining. "Only in the rare event that *labor costs* are the motivating factor behind a reduction in operations should an employer be required first to negotiate with the union over a decision to close part of its business."[55] Third, it refused to define any managerial prerogatives that would clearly escape bargaining and not even be subject to the general balancing test. "[D]ifferences between management and labor over issues that might be resolved through collective negotiation should not be excluded arbitrarily out of deference to a fixed concept of 'managerial prerogatives.' "[56]

The next day, June 2, both Justices Stevens and Powell sent memoranda to Blackmun and the conference. Stevens objected only to the language on labor costs. He thought that labor costs were not a "rare" factor in reductions in operations but rather "a significant factor in most such reductions." He also thought that the importance of labor costs in reductions in operations was not a reason for the law to compel bargaining in cases in which management had chosen not to.[57]

Justice Powell's objections were much deeper. He objected to the quoted language above on labor costs and managerial prerogatives, but, rather than suggest specific alternatives, voiced deeper objections:

> I fully agree with the result you reach in this case, but I do not subscribe to a balancing approach when the issue is the discontinuance of a losing portion of a business operation.... I view the problem of partial closings somewhat differently. I share the view that Potter [Stewart] expressed in [his concurrence in *Fibreboard*] that § 8(d) of the Act describes a "limited area subject to the duty of collective bargaining," and that excluded from this area are "managerial decisions which lie at the heart of entrepreneurial control." ... It seems to me that a balancing test is not appropriate in this context. If a partial closing is a mandatory subject of bargaining, I suppose the union could strike in support of its wishes at all the employer's plants. Companies thus may be forced to keep a losing plant open for fear of strikes at profitable plants elsewhere. I cannot ascribe to Congress an intention so severely to constrict managerial freedom—particularly since the employees' interests should be ade-

management relations and the collective bargaining process, outweighs the burden placed on the conduct of the business. The Court in *Fibreboard* implicitly performed this balancing...." June 1 draft at 17–18, Blackmun Papers, Library of Congress.

55 June 1 draft at 28, Blackmun Papers, Library of Congress (emphasis original). The draft also has similar language at 20.

56 *Id.* at 17.

57 Justice John Paul Stevens to Justice Blackmun, June 2, 1981, Blackmun Papers.

> quately protected by management's duty to bargain over the *effects* of the closing.
>
> In sum, I cannot join your opinion as it is now written. Unless another Justice wishes to write, I probably will write an opinion concurring in the result.[58]

The next day, Susan G. Lahne, law clerk to Justice Blackmun, met with Paul Cane, Jr., law clerk to Justice Powell, to learn more about Justice Powell's objections and what it might take to gain his assent to the opinion. Although it was unusual for law clerks for different justices to meet to draft opinions, they did in this instance. Cane recently explained, "Unlike the impression given by *The Brethren*, cases are rarely decided by law clerks cobbling. The process of drafting an opinion is mostly on paper and transparent. This case was an exception to that. As the notes indicate, Susan Lahne and I did talk quite a bit. We would go into the interior courtyards of the Court building and argue."[59]

Justice Blackmun had already agreed with Justice Stevens to delete the language on labor costs.[60] Justice Powell objected to it, also, for reasons that did not appear in his memo to the Court. He felt that it was all too easy for any union, after the fact, to assert that any management decision might have been avoided, given hypothetical reductions in labor costs to which the union never in fact would have agreed.[61] This objection, in turn, was just a specific example of Justice Powell's more general objection to Justice Blackmun's draft. Powell thought the opinion must identify certain managerial decisions, that, categorically, would not be subject to bargaining. The decisions had to be identified with a fairly "bright line" so that the Board would never even begin proceedings, what former law clerk Cane described as a "summary judgment"-type test. Powell's problem with balancing tests was not the concept of considering many factors, but with the vagueness of a test that always depended on retrospective construction of negotiations that never happened. Lahne reported to Justice Blackmun:

> Encouraging news: I spoke with Justice Powell's clerk, Paul Cane, again this afternoon and he informed me that he spoke briefly with

---

[58] Letter, Justice Lewis F. Powell, Jr. to Justice Blackmun, June 2, 2004, Blackmun Papers, Library of Congress (emphasis original).

[59] Telephone Interview with Paul Cane, Jr., May 4, 2004. Cane now practices management-side labor and employment law in San Francisco. Cane's reference is to Bob Woodward & Scott Armstrong, *The Brethren: Inside the Supreme Court* (1979). Lahne is now a pension law specialist at the U.S. Department of Labor; she declined to be interviewed.

[60] SGL (Susan G. Lahne) to Justice Blackmun, June 2, 1981, Blackmun Papers.

[61] Telephone Interview, Paul Cane, Jr., May 4, 2004.

> Justice Powell this morning. He confirmed that the disagreement is over the "bright line" as to partial closings, not the rest of the analysis, and he intends to go over the opinion this afternoon and make concrete suggestions for our consideration. Justice Powell is eager to avoid writing separately, if possible.[62]

Lahne had earlier that day telephoned the other chambers. She reported that Powell spoke at least for Chief Justice Burger and Justices Stewart and Rehnquist. Justice White had not committed himself and if he joined Powell they would constitute their own majority. Lahne, presumably reflecting the views of Justice Blackmun, was most eager to retain a majority for "the larger idea, expressed in section II, that management decisions should be bargainable when to require bargaining would advance the purposes of the NLRA" and therefore felt, given the head count, that it might be necessary to adopt a brighter line for managerial prerogatives and a corresponding limitation on the Board's control.

It appears from Lahne's memoranda to Justice Blackmun that common ground proved elusive. Both sides were proceeding without any anchor in the statute itself or the Board's interpretation of it. Lahne pointed out that Cane had no statutory basis for a category of managerial prerogative, let alone one defined by a bright line. Cane pointed out that Lahne had no statutory basis for a balancing test. Both were correct, since the statute does not even provide for classifying subjects of bargaining. On June 4, Lahne was pessimistic in a memo to Justice Blackmun:

> I had a fairly long talk with Justice Powell's clerk, Paul Cane, concerning [*FNM*]. It does not look all that hopeful, but there is a small chance that we may be able to change the opinion enough to convince Powell without gutting it entirely.
>
> It appears that his preferred approach would have been simply to adopt Justice Stewart's concurrence in *Fibreboard* and to distinguish the facts of that case. To him, there *is* an area of "managerial prerogatives" that is fixed and immutable and that Congress did not intend to require bargaining about. He also believes that this decision to close part of a business falls within that removed area. His clerk, however, could not supply *any* reasoning to back that conclusion up with. It seems simply a given that certain management decisions are beyond "terms and conditions of employment."
>
> Thus, Justice Powell would prefer that we not only draw a bright line in section III, but also revise section II to remove the suggestion that we are doing any "balancing" of the good to collective bargaining against the harm to the employer. I do not think I am willing to

---

[62] SGL (Susan G. Lahne) to Justice Blackmun, June 3, 1981, Blackmun Papers.

go all this way. Because Justice Powell has no alternative analysis to offer, I continue to think my analysis is preferable to no analysis at all. However, it is possible, according to his clerk, that if we muffle the language a little in section II and get rid of certain sentences that are particularly troubling to Justice Powell, he may be willing to join.

What I would propose is the following. I will attempt a redraft of sections II and III, trying to remove what is especially troubling to Justice Powell without doing away with all analysis and drawing a bright line as to partial closings. If Justice Powell finds it acceptable, we will have won. If Justice Powell does not agree, I would propose circulating a modified draft to try to draw votes from Justice White, Justice Marshall, and the Chief. Perhaps also Rehnquist. I do not propose abandoning the analysis I have adopted. Of course, I stand willing to do your bidding in this matter.[63]

Lahne made very few changes in the draft. She took out the two sentences to which Justice Powell had particularly objected, the language on "labor costs" and the sentence casting doubt on a "fixed concept of 'managerial prerogative.' " The latter sentence had been preceded by a footnote, numbered 18 in both the June 1 draft and the final opinion, listing cases gradually expanding the number of issues found subject to bargaining. The new draft retained that list of cases, but now described mandatory subjects of bargaining as having "changed" rather than "increased." The footnote was now preceded by: "Congress did not explicitly state what issues of mutual concern to unions and management it intended to exclude from mandatory bargaining." This sentence has always baffled readers of the opinion since it begs the important question: Congress in fact did not explicitly state that it intended to exclude *any* subjects from bargaining, and in fact rejected proposals to do just that. Lahne also added a quotation from Justice Stewart's *Fibreboard* concurrence.

At the same time, Lahne made two language changes that arguably moved the opinion away from Justice Powell's wishes. At note 14 she had written that in 1947 Congress refused to define or limit the words "wages, hours, and other terms and conditions of employment" "for it recognized the need for flexibility and for change and growth." The latter quoted phrase became, "for it did not intend to deprive the Board of the power further to define those terms in light of specific industrial practices." Secondly, Lahne changed the opening words of section III B of the opinion, discussing the specific facts of *FNM*. It had initially said, "In order to give guidance in the application of this analysis." As revised it became, "In order to illustrate the limits of our holding." In other

63 SGL (Susan G. Lahne) to Justice Blackmun, June 4, 1981, Blackmun Papers.

words, the second draft made clear both the Board's power (as it reversed the Board) and the limited scope of its holding.

The new opinion was circulated on June 9, along with a memorandum from Justice Blackmun which Lahne had drafted:

> I am not persuaded that I should modify the opinion to eliminate or replace the *analysis* on which it is based: that deciding whether decisions of this type, *i.e.*, decisions that have such a direct and immediate impact on jobs, should be mandatory subjects of bargaining depends on a consideration of the purposes behind the enactment of the NLRA and Taft–Hartley, which include principally the removal of industrial conflict from the sphere of overt clashes to the arena of collective bargaining supervised by the NLRB.
>
> I readily concede that Congress did not intend to bring within the mandatory subjects of bargaining *all* employment decisions. I have found nothing, however, to suggest that Congress, in passing these two acts, had in mind a clear list of subjects, even as to management decisions, that were immune from bargaining. Surely, there is nothing in the statute itself to suggest that Congress contemplated a fixed set of "managerial prerogatives" that it intended to immunize, and I have seen nothing to this effect in the legislative history. Congress intended not to require bargaining over what fell outside "wages, hours, and terms and conditions of employment," but it left further definition of those terms to the parties, the NLRB, and the courts. A conclusion that Congress itself excluded specific subjects, among them these partial closing decisions, also would substantially undermine much precedent in the Board and the lower courts, which have approved, with this Court's acquiescence, a widening sphere of mandatory subjects of bargaining, whether we like to acknowledge it or not. Thus, I think we must look elsewhere for the limiting definition.
>
> Although I agree with it, Lewis's statement that "[d]ecisions as to partial closings are solely managerial ... because they determine the basic scope of the enterprise" seems to me to be only a conclusion, which, if not supported by some more basic analysis, will provide no guidance to lower courts. Looking to whether a management decision involves a "basic" shift in operations or a "major" reallocation of capital, as most of the Courts of Appeals have done, results in essentially ad hoc distinctions. The line between "major" and "minor" and "basic" and "non-basic" becomes simply a matter of opinion, dependent on whether one favors management or labor interests. For instance, I do not perceive that the decision in this case was intrinsically any more "basic" than the subcontracting decision in *Fibreboard*. First National Maintenance apparently rou-

> tinely entered into and terminated these maintenance agreements with its customers. This was its regular manner of conducting business, and it must have resulted in employees' routinely losing their jobs. Thus, the termination of the Greenpark contract did not involve a basic shift of direction or a fundamental alteration of the company's size or shape. If anything, the subcontracting decision in *Fibreboard*, which was unprecedented and a major alteration of the way the plant was run, was a more "fundamental" change in the way the company allocated capital and shaped the enterprise.
>
> I think that the implicit basis for Lewis's conclusion is that requiring bargaining over this type of management decision would be just too burdensome for the employer. This in fact is the core of my analysis, and it contains nothing startling or even novel. The Court in *Fibreboard* explicitly considered the type of factors that I discussed in the opinion and concluded: "To hold, as the Board has done, that contracting out is a mandatory subject of collective bargaining would promote the fundamental purpose of the Act by bringing a problem of vital concern to labor and management within the framework established by Congress as most conducive to industrial peace." 379 U.S., at 211. I had not thought that the Court now wanted to overrule *Fibreboard* or to confine it to its facts, and I attempted merely to apply its analysis. My consideration of the factors present in partial closing decisions leads me to conclude that bargaining over these decisions will not incrementally improve the collective bargaining process, but in fact will have detrimental effects on the employer, thus weakening the likelihood that bargaining will reduce industrial tensions.
>
> This is as far as I can go. I hope that it will prove to be acceptable; if not, perhaps the case should be reassigned or be put over for reargument in the Fall.[64]

Ultimately, a majority of the Court, now including Justice White, agreed to sign Justice Blackmun's revised opinion. Former law clerk Paul Cane could only speculate why the other justices agreed to the revised opinion, since it differed little from the June 1 version. The new draft did include some modest changes that other justices would have viewed as positive. It was the end of the term. Reargument is a major affront. Justice Powell had wanted more reliance on Justice Stewart's *Fibreboard* concurrence, but it is referenced. If (for example) Justice Stewart or Rehnquist had already joined or was known to be about to, Justice Powell would no longer have had any negotiating leverage and the game would have been over. Cane doesn't remember whether any

---

[64] Justice Harry A. Blackmun, Memorandum to the Conference, June 9, 1981, Blackmun Papers.

other justice would have signed the revised opinion without Justice Powell. A final possibility, intriguing but speculative, is that Justice Powell read the following paragraph, present in both the June 1 and final drafts, to adopt some of the "bright line," categorical definitions of decisions outside bargaining that he had sought:

> [M]anagement may have great need for speed, flexibility, and secrecy in meeting business opportunities and exigencies. It may face significant tax or securities consequences that hinge on confidentiality, the timing of a plant closing, or a reorganization of the corporate structure. The publicity incident to the normal process of bargaining may injure the possibility of a successful transition or increase the economic damage to the business. The employer also may have no feasible alternative to the closing, and even good-faith bargaining over it may be both futile and cause the employer additional loss.[65]

Many readers of the opinion have been puzzled by this paragraph. "*[N]one* of these interests was implicated in this case. . . ."[66] Perhaps Justice Powell, or others, read this as the list of "bright lines" he sought, that would clearly exclude some decisions from bargaining, or even balancing, while others read them as factors that instead would, when present, enter into the balance. As we shall see, subsequent cases have not clearly adopted either position.

The Immediate Impact of First National Maintenance

The Impact of the Decision on Bargaining Practices

The Supreme Court had decided a hypothetical, carefully selected by the Chamber of Commerce as its best opportunity to establish a set of managerial prerogatives, bargainable only if management chooses. That hypothetical is the management decision that results in the elimination of jobs but: (1) is based entirely on economic considerations, (2) turns not at all on labor costs, and (3) reflects no animus toward the union. Indeed, such a hypothetical must have existed as a hypothetical long before it became the *FNM* case, much as photographs, which we naively imagine to portray reality, show subjects and compositions that existed already as paintings before photographic subjects, or even photography, even existed.[67] Law professors must have put just this hypothetical to students, in the years following *Fibreboard*, to show how that case implicitly defined a new category of permissive subjects of bargaining.

[65] 452 U.S. at 682–83 (footnotes omitted).

[66] James B. Atleson, *Values and Assumptions in American Labor Law* 134 (1983) (emphasis in original).

[67] Peter Galassi, *Before Photography: Painting and the Invention of Photography* (1981).

The realization of such a hypothetical case must be very rare, if it exists at all. Developments in law and industrial practice following *FNM* have not revealed one clear example. It is not hard to see why. An employer with harmonious union relations, that anticipates future relations with that union, has no reason to disguise a necessary economic downsizing decision. The union will be unlikely to be able to avert the decision, but—if the decision really turns on unavoidable economic factors—the union will normally accept the decision and may be able to help implement it in the most painless way, particularly since the union retains the right to bargain about the effects of the decision. Consequently, as we shall see in the next section, employers who keep the union in the dark about downsizing decisions almost always are either planning to do the same work at a different location, or are trying to undercut or eliminate the union, or are trying to avoid bargaining about clearly bargainable issues, or, frequently, all of the above. These practical realities are more likely than the decision in *FNM* to guide employer conduct.

But did the *FNM* decision influence management behavior in a symbolic way? In the same year as the *FNM* decision, the new President, Ronald Reagan, hired replacements for striking air traffic controllers. It is often alleged that this incident emboldened private employers to hire strike replacements more frequently than previously, although in truth the existence of this increase is not easy to demonstrate, let alone its cause.[68] Did *FNM* have such a symbolic impact, emboldening managers to make unilateral changes without bargaining? The decision coincided with a recession that was particularly severe in heavy industry, commonly unionized, in the Great Lakes region. "Plant closings" and "deindustrialization" were extensively studied in the 1980's, and their causes debated from various political perspectives. Some plant closings were negotiated with labor unions, and some were not. There is no scholarly or polemical literature, from any perspective, suggesting that management showed any decreased tendency after 1981 to bargain with unions about plant closings.[69]

---

[68] There are no data series that directly observe the hiring of strike replacements. U.S. General Accounting Office, *Labor–Management Relations: Strikes and the Use of Permanent Replacements in the 1970s and 1980s* (1991) surveys management and labor respondents. Michael LeRoy, *Regulating Employer Use of Permanent Striker Replacements: Empirical Analysis of NLRA and RLA Strikes 1935–1991*, 16 Berkeley J. Emp. & Lab. L. 169 (1995) surveys reported legal decisions. Both suggest increased use of strike replacements in the 1980's, possibly beginning earlier.

[69] *See* William J. Baumol, Alan S. Blinder & Edward N. Wolff, *Downsizing in America: Reality, Causes, and Consequences* (2003); Barry Bluestone & Bennett Harrison, *The Deindustrialization of America: Plant Closings, Community Abandonment, and the Dismantling of Basic Industry* (1982); Gordon L. Clark, *Unions and Communities Under Siege: American Communities and the Crisis of Organized Labor* (1989); Gilda Haas &

THE IMPACT OF THE DECISION ON THE LAW

All reported real-world cases of management downsizing, without informing its union, involve some combination of relocation of work to another location, desire to save labor costs, or antiunion animus. The application of *FNM* to any of these cases remains unclear. A review of subsequent decisions demonstrates that *FNM* did not clearly change the law. It is impossible to find a single post-*FNM* case that one is confident would have come out differently had *FNM* never existed.

Certainly *FNM* did not change the way any lawyer involved in such a case would gather or present evidence. Before *FNM*, lawyers for charging parties, and the General Counsel, seeking to demonstrate that a decision was bargainable, emphasized the elimination of jobs, the lack of fundamental change in the company's operations, and any hints of antiunion animus in the record. Lawyers for employers emphasized the fundamental change in company operations; the economic necessity of downsizing; and any special factors suggesting that bargaining would have been futile (such as the company's need for speed or secrecy). These are precisely the factors that remain relevant after *FNM*.

Nor has *FNM*'s methodology, the multifactor balancing test that considers the interests of the public and the employer, been influential.[70] There do not appear to be any cases that adopt it. The Board, however, has continued to be inconsistent, sometimes approaching mandatory subjects of bargaining as the application of rules and sometimes emphasizing factors idiosyncratic to particular cases. Whatever approach the Board takes, some court of appeals will disagree with it. All sides will cite *FNM*.

Subcontracting decisions, like *Fibreboard*, show the Board at its most rule-like. The Board holds that management must bargain about decisions to subcontract that merely substitute one group of workers for another. At least where such decisions have "nothing to do with change in the 'scope and direction' of its business," *FNM*'s concerns with protecting the "core of entrepreneurial control" do not come into play,

---

Plant Closures Project, *Plant Closures: Myths, Realities and Responses* (1985); Richard B. McKenzie, *Fugitive Industry: The Economics and Politics of Deindustrialization* (1984); Francis A. O'Connell, *Plant Closings: Worker Rights, Management Rights, and the Law* (1986); Lawrence E. Rothstein, *Plant Closings: Power, Politics, and Workers* (1986); Wayne R. Wendling, *The Plant Closure Policy Dilemma: Labor, Law, and Bargaining* (1984); *Plant Closings: Public or Private Choices?* (Richard B. McKenzie ed. 1984); *Plant Closing Legislation* (Antone Aboud ed. 1984).

[70] ". . . in view of an employer's need for unencumbered decisionmaking, bargaining over management decisions that have a substantial impact on the continued availability of employment should be required only if the benefit, for labor-management relations and the collective-bargaining process, outweighs the burden placed on the conduct of the business." 452 U.S. at 679.

and no balancing is necessary.[71] The D.C. Circuit has approved this analysis, at least for subcontracting decisions plainly turning on labor costs. The opinion is skeptical of the Supreme Court's opinion in *FNM,* noting that its three-prong division of management decisions, and economic analysis, make little sense.[72] That court has also approved a flat rule mandating bargaining for the decision to transfer work from unionized workers to managers.[73] On the other hand, the Third Circuit reads *FNM* to require a balancing of factors before the Board orders bargaining even of subcontracting decisions.[74] As we know from Justice Blackmun's papers, this is surely an incorrect reading of *FNM*, in which all the justices who wrote memoranda rhetorically expressed fidelity to *Fibreboard* and disclaimed any desire, as Justice Blackmun put it, "to overrule *Fibreboard* or confine it to its facts."[75]

Relocation decisions, in which work is transferred from a unionized location to another (typically nonunion), are analyzed differently.[76] The Board in *Dubuque Packing Company* articulated a balancing approach which the D.C. Circuit accepted.[77] The Board's approach though is not the freewheeling balancing of *FNM* with its consideration of all the "interests" of each side and the public.

> Initially, the burden is on the General Counsel to establish that the employer's decision involved a relocation of unit work unaccompanied by a basic change in the nature of the employer's operation. If the General Counsel successfully carries his burden in this regard, he will have established prima facie that the employer's relocation decision is a mandatory subject of bargaining. At this juncture, the employer may produce evidence rebutting the prima facie case by establishing that the work performed at the new location varies significantly from the work performed at the former plant, establishing that the work performed at the former plant is to be discontinued entirely and not moved to the new location, or establishing that the employer's decision involves a change in the scope and direction

[71] Mid–State Ready Mix, Div. of Torrington Industries, 307 NLRB 809 (1992).

[72] Rock–Tenn Co. v. NLRB, 101 F.3d 1441 (D.C. Cir. 1996).

[73] Regal Cinemas, Inc. v. NLRB, 317 F.3d 300 (D.C. Cir. 2003).

[74] Furniture Renters of America, Inc. v. NLRB, 36 F.3d 1240 (3d Cir. 1994).

[75] Justice Harry A. Blackmun, Memorandum to the Conference, June 9, 1981, Blackmun Papers.

[76] Recall that at the oral argument in *FNM*, the Supreme Court put a hypothetical about relocation to FNM's counsel, who responded that this would be a mandatory subject of bargaining.

[77] Dubuque Packing Co., 303 NLRB 386 (1991), *enforced sub nom.* United Food & Commercial Workers Int'l. U., Local 15–A v. NLRB, 1 F.3d 24 (D.C. Cir. 1993).

> of the enterprise. Alternatively, the employer may proffer a defense to show by a preponderance of the evidence: (1) that labor costs (direct and/or indirect) were not a factor in the decision or (2) that even if labor costs were a factor in the decision, the union could not have offered labor cost concessions that could have changed the employer's decision to relocate.[78]

The Fourth Circuit though has rejected the approach of *Dubuque Packing*, holding that an employer has no duty to bargain at all about a decision to close anything, even if work is then transferred to a new plant.[79]

FNM has failed to appear in other contexts in which one might have expected citation to it. The Board once distinguished it as "a situation where control over the employer's decision rested with a third party."[80] If this fact is material to the holding of *FNM*, the case has little application at all. Even its author managed to forget it. Six years after *FNM*, Justice Blackmun again wrote for the Court, in a case finding a dyeing business, formed by former officers and customers of a failed unionized company, to have succeeded to its predecessor's bargaining obligation when it hired a workforce comprised mainly of employees of the predecessor. "[D]espite the Union's desire to participate in the transition between employers, it was left entirely in the dark about petitioner's acquisition."[81] Justice Blackmun had forgotten why that was.

There are few academic defenders of the *FNM* opinion, particularly its balancing approach. Most recent academic discussions of mandatory subjects of bargaining attempt to redefine the category with bright-line tests, drawn either from antitrust law,[82] or from a self-described economic approach under which some management decisions, based on subject matter, are stipulated to be efficient (ergo not bargainable), whilst others are termed opportunistic.[83] This scholarship has exerted no influence over actual cases, as we have seen. The concept of efficiency does not fit

---

78 *Id.*

79 Dorsey Trailers, Inc. v. NLRB, 233 F.3d 831 (4th Cir. 2000).

80 Collateral Control Corp., 288 NLRB 308, 309 n.4 (1988).

81 Fall River Dyeing & Finishing Corp. v. NLRB, 482 U.S. 27, 39 n.6 (1987).

82 Michael C. Harper, *Leveling the Road from* Borg–Warner *to* First National Maintenance*: The Scope of Mandatory Bargaining*, 68 Va. L.Rev. 1447 (1982).

83 Michael L. Wachter & George M. Cohen, *The Law and Economics of Collective Bargaining: An Introduction and Application to Problems of Subcontracting, Partial Closure, and Relocation*, 136 U. Pa. L.Rev. 1349 (1988); Armen A. Alchian, *Decision Sharing and Expropriable Specific Quasi–Rents: A Theory of First National Maintenance v. NLRB*, 1 Sup. Ct. Econ. Rev. 235 (1982).

the duty to bargain in good faith. All else being equal, it is more efficient to replace five unionized workers with three, or five nonunionized workers, or five workers in China. In the absence of a duty to bargain, however, the replaced workers bear all the costs of this decision. The distribution of those costs is obviously a distributional question that is not captured by any concept of efficiency.

Over two decades after *FNM*, it remains as difficult as ever to predict whether any particular instance of downsizing is a mandatory subject of bargaining. The Supreme Court was induced to decide a hypothetical case, and there are few, if any, real cases that resemble it.

Larger instances of job elimination are, since 1998, governed by the Worker Adjustment Retraining and Notification (WARN) Act, requiring (to oversimplify) firms with at least one hundred employees to give sixty days' notice of decisions causing job loss for at least fifty employees.[84] Ironically, the very reason that motivated the Chamber of Commerce to take *FNM* to the Supreme Court—to give employers the right not to inform their unions of impending downsizing—afforded some protection by *FNM*, is now largely lost with WARN. One would expect that today unions with WARN notice of imminent downsizing are often able to extend their right to bargain about the effects of the decision to bargaining about the decision itself, but there are so far no behavioral studies that document such a development.

The Impact of the Decision on First National Maintenance and its Lawyer

First National Maintenance Corporation no longer exists under that name. Its partners, Marsh, Golden and Greenberg, soon pursued other business interests. Their carbonated apple juice, sold under the name Snapple, was not a success. The next Snapple product, bottled iced tea, was. Snapple went public in 1992 and was soon thereafter sold to Quaker Oats (it has been sold several times since). Gradually, the founders left the company as very wealthy men. Hyman Golden as late as 1996 helped his sons run an office cleaning company, "a successor to one of the businesses the Snapple founders used to own."[85] Arnold Greenberg and Leonard Marsh, looking back on their careers, offer these "tips for entrepreneurs": "Hire the best people you can afford and pay them as much as you can afford. Don't be cheap when it comes to hiring the best people because they will get a better job elsewhere. Don't be afraid to pay what you might think is an exorbitant amount to get the best people. Give your key employees a piece of the business because they'll work

[84] 29 U.S.C. §§ 2101–2109 (2000).

[85] Harry Berkowitz, *Annoyed, Frustrated (and Very Rich)*, Newsday, Nov. 25, 1996, at C8.

harder. They're not only making themselves rich; they'll make you rich.''[86]

Sanford Pollack was right. His Supreme Court argument was indeed his proudest moment. Nine years later, he persuaded a Teamster pension fund of which he was counsel to deposit $30 million with Prudential Securities, which then kicked back over $100,000 to Pollack. Two years after that, he arranged for the destruction of his Florida vacation house by arson, and then removed $9.3 million from the same Teamster pension fund. He pleaded guilty to some of these (and other counts), was convicted of others, and served several years in prison.[87] Not every lawyer would have advised FNM in 1977 to risk back pay by refusing to bargain with 1199 at all. But Pollack, as we know, was a risk taker.

Conclusion

In the same spring of 1977, a different group of maintenance workers, at a condominium complex a few hundred miles from Brooklyn, worked for a maintenance contractor and were represented by a union. The maintenance contractor, like FNM, withdrew from the building. When the dust settled, the Labor Board held that the owner of the condominium buildings was their employer, with a duty to bargain with their union.[88] While there are a number of factual distinctions between this case and *FNM*, the principal distinction is Lake Ontario. These maintenance workers worked in Toronto; their labor board was the Ontario Labour Relations Board; and their case is the fountainhead of that aspect of modern Canadian labor law that often, though by no means always, finds the owner of the building to be the legal employer of maintenance employees working under a contractor.[89]

Generalization about who is the employer in Canadian labor law is difficult. Provincial labor boards and courts, like courts in the U.S. determining who is the employer, utilize a multi-factored approach that

---

[86] Harry Berkowitz, *Annoyed, Frustrated (and Very Rich)*, Newsday, Nov. 25, 1996, at C8.

[87] United States v. Pollack, 91 F.3d 331 (2d Cir. 1996) (appeal of conviction); Pollack v. Hobbs, 98 F.Supp.2d 287 (E.D.N.Y. 2000) (denying motion to vacate conviction), *aff'd*, 8 Fed. Appx. 37 (2d Cir. 2001) (mem.); Local 875 IBT Pension Fund v. Pollack, 992 F.Supp. 545 (E.D.N.Y. 1998) (civil suit); In re Pollack, 640 N.Y.S.2d 790 (App.Div. 1996) (disbarment); St. Paul Fire & Marine Insurance v. Horowitz & Pollack P.C., Supreme Court, New York County, NYLJ, Feb. 13, 1998, at 24 (available on LEXIS, New York Law Journal database) (malpractice insurance void because of Pollack's material misrepresentations). All have different information about Pollack.

[88] Labourers' International Union of North America Local 183 v. York Condominium Corp. No. 46, 1977 OLRB Rep. Oct. 645.

[89] These two paragraphs derive from an unpublished seminar paper by David A. Wright, Agency Workers and Collective Bargaining Law in Canada (2000).

resists generalization across cases. Indeed, the Supreme Court of Canada has insisted on such a multi-factor approach.[90] However, it is not unusual for this multi-factor analysis to result in a finding that the owner of a building is the employer of the maintenance workers, either jointly, or nominally, employed by a contractor.[91] U.S. readers will find particularly ironic that this jurisprudence stems from a case, like *FNM* but with sharply different results, arising from the 1977 decision of a maintenance contractor to withdraw from serving a building.

If a case like *FNM* arose today, advocates and decisionmakers would be armed with several concepts and categories not in common use in 1977. First, we would understand that the case involves the "working poor," "low-wage service workers," whose jobs are growing numerically, while their wages never rise above poverty level and provide no other benefits.[92] We would understand how employment of maintenance workers by independent contractors is related to their poverty. Maintenance workers employed by contractors earn less than maintenance workers employed directly, despite equal educational attainment; are half as likely to be unionized and about a third as likely to have health insurance; and are more heavily female, African–American, Latino and Latina.[93] We would know how bargaining unit rules, secondary boycott law, and other aspects of labor law frustrate collective bargaining for low-wage maintenance workers, particularly those working for contractors.[94] We would know how successful union organization among janitors often involves lawful public pressure on the building owner who is the ultimate consumer of their services, for example in the Justice for Janitors campaigns of the Service Employees International Union.[95]

---

90 Pointe–Claire (City) v. Quebec (Labour Court), [1997] 1 S.C.R. 1015 (dictum).

91 1 Jeffrey Sack, Q.C., C. Michael Mitchell, & Sandy Price, *Ontario Labour Relations Board Law and Practice* §§ 2.6–2.12 (3d ed. 1997).

92 *See, e.g.*, Barbara Ehrenreich, *Nickel and Dimed: On (Not) Getting By in America* (2001); Katherine S. Newman, *No Shame in My Game: The Working Poor in the Inner City* (1999); David K. Shipler, *The Working Poor: Invisible in America* (2004); Beth Shulman, *The Betrayal of Work* (2003).

93 Arindrajit Dube & Ethan Kaplan, *Outsourcing, Wages, and Benefits: Empirical Evidence from the Service Sector*, paper presented at the American Economics Association Annual Meeting, Washington, D.C., January 5, 2003.

94 Howard Wial, *The Emerging Organizational Structure of Unionism in Low–Wage Services*, 45 Rutgers L.Rev. 671 (1993); Alan Hyde, *Who Speaks for the Working Poor?: A Preliminary Look at the Emerging Tetralogy of Representation of Low–Wage Service Workers*, 13 Corn. J. L. & Pub. Policy 599 (2004).

95 Howard Wial, *The Emerging Organizational Structure of Unionism in Low–Wage Services*, 45 Rutgers L.Rev. 671, 693–98 (1993); Christopher L. Erickson, Catherine Fisk, Ruth Milkman, Daniel J.B. Mitchell, & Kent Wong, Justice for Janitors in Los Angeles and Beyond: A New Form of Unionism in the 21st Century? *in The Changing Role of Unions:*

Today, if the maintenance workers at Greenpark worked under the supervision of Greenpark supervisors and alongside Greenpark employees—we do not know whether this was true in 1977—District 1199, union for those other employees, might seek to accrete them into the Greenpark unit, on the theory that they were jointly employed by Greenpark and FNM and shared a community of interest with Greenpark employees.[96]

It is only a matter of time before a union seeking to represent maintenance employees will claim, Canadian-style, that their employer, either individually or jointly, is the owner of the building that they maintain. It is not possible to predict how the Board will deal with this claim. In employment statutes other than the NLRA, for which federal courts are more free to make policy, courts have greatly expanded the concept of "employer" and "joint employment" in the past three years. Courts in the Second Circuit, where *FNM* arose, have found that garment workers are jointly employed by a labor contractor and the garment manufacturer who is the ultimate purchaser of their services;[97] delivery personnel for supermarkets are jointly employed by those markets and the contractors who supply their labor, despite attempts to characterize them as independent contractors;[98] and recipients of public assistance, required to work without pay on city maintenance jobs as a condition of receiving welfare grants, are employees of the city, protected by civil rights[99] and labor standards law.[100] Finding maintenance workers to be jointly employed by a maintenance contractor and a building owner would avoid the absurd result of *FNM*, in which the contractor didn't have to bargain because its choice of customers was a managerial

New Forms of Representation (Phanindra V. Wunnava, ed.) (2004); Jesús Martínez Saldaña, *At the Periphery of Democracy: The Binational Politics of Mexican Immigrants in Silicon Valley* (Ph.D. dissert., University of California, Berkeley, Ethnic Studies, 1993).

[96] M.B. Sturgis, Inc., 331 NLRB 1298 (2000); *overruled by,* H.S. Care LLC, 343 NLRB No. 76, 176 LRRM 1033 (2004).; see particularly the companion *Jeffboat* case, involving a similar accretion. The Board has changed its policies in this area many times.

[97] Ling Nan Zheng v. Liberty Apparel Co., Inc., 355 F.3d 61 (2d Cir. 2003) (FLSA); Liu v. Donna Karan International, Inc., 2001 WL 8595 (S.D.N.Y. 2001); (FLSA and state wage law).

[98] Ansoumana v. Gristede's Operating Corp., 255 F.Supp.2d 184 (S.D.N.Y. 2003) (FLSA and state wage law).

[99] United States v. City of New York, 359 F.3d 83 (2d Cir. 2004) (recipients of public assistance working without pay in Work Experience Program are statutory employees protected by Title VII against sexual harassment). Note that Title VII, like the NLRA, uses a common law test to determine who is an employer.

[100] Stone v. McGowan, 308 F.Supp.2d 79 (N.D.N.Y. 2004) (recipient of public assistance working in Work Experience Program is statutory employee who must be paid minimum wage).

prerogative, while the building owner didn't have to bargain because it hired through a contractor.

There will never again be a case like *First National Maintenance.* But, then again, there never was.

8

Robert B. Moberly

The Story of *Electromation*: Are Employee Participation Programs a Competitive Necessity or a Wolf in Sheep's Clothing?

How did Electromation, a small Indiana company that established employee committees, become the vehicle for a national struggle between competing visions of worker participation and company unions, involving the National Labor Relations Board, the federal courts, Congress, and the President of the United States? When the Teamsters Union lost an election and an Administrative Law Judge found that Electromation committed a seemingly routine violation of the National Labor Relations Act, why and how did the Board select this case for a national debate, much to the surprise of the parties involved? After the union won a second election and the parties negotiated a collective bargaining agreement, why did the law firm representing Electromation continue appealing the matter to the Board and the U.S. Court of Appeals on a *pro bono* basis? When the company lost at the Board and court of appeals, why did Electromation and its law firm *not* appeal such an important case to the U.S. Supreme Court?

In *Electromation, Inc.*,[1] the National Labor Relations Board held that employee participation committees at Electromation constituted a "labor organization" as defined by § 2(5)[2] of the National Labor Relations Act,[3] and that the company dominated and interfered with the

---

1 309 NLRB 990 (2000).

2 29 U.S.C. § 152(5) (2000).

3 National Labor Relations Act of 1935, 29 U.S.C. §§ 151–69 (2000) [hereinafter NLRA].

formation and administration of this labor organization in violation of § 8(a)(2).[4] Unions objected to these committees on the grounds that they dealt with conditions of work, and that employer involvement with the committees interfered with employees' rights to independent representation and collective bargaining. Many American companies attacked this decision, advocating employee involvement in workplace decisionmaking to improve productivity, quality, efficiency, and global competitiveness. The debate spawned by this decision called into question the adversarial labor-management model allegedly contemplated by the NLRA, and the suitability of such a model for today's global economy.[5]

Social and Legal Background

The Rise of Company Unions

At the turn of the century, a number of reformers and progressive employers attempted to bring worker democracy to industry. During World War I, the federal government provided impetus to this movement by encouraging employee representation committees; experimentation with such committees continued after the war. Some employee representation committees "were intended to involve employees in the enterprise and to give them the sense of having an interest in its success," and others "were plainly intended to keep unions out" but "whether a well-intentioned system of meaningful employee participation, or a device to create an employer-controlled sham of a labor union, both became fixed with the label of 'company union.' "[6]

The establishment of company unions was further accelerated by the adoption of the National Industrial Recovery Act in 1933. Section 7(a) created the right of employee representation, and many employers "dominated the 'employee representatives' by instigating their creation, shaping the rules of organization and operation, influencing policy by having company representatives in official positions, inducing or requiring employees to join the organization, controlling its pursestrings and giving it special privileges within the plant (such as facilities and time for solicitation and meetings)."[7] Of the company unions in existence in 1935, three-fifths had been organized since 1933, and company unions grew at a faster rate than trade unions.[8] John L. Lewis, President of the

---

[4] 29 U.S.C. § 158(a)(2) (2000).

[5] *See* A.B. Cochran, *We Participate, They Decide: The Real Stakes In Revising Section 8(a)(2) of the National Labor Relations Act*, 16 Berkeley J. Emp. & Lab. L. 458 (1995).

[6] Archibald Cox, Derek Curtis Box, Robert A. Gorman & Matthew W. Finkin, *Labor Law; Cases and Materials* 193 (13th ed. 2001).

[7] Robert Gorman & Matthew Finkin, *Labor Law—Basic Text* 257 (2d ed. 2004).

[8] Archibald Cox, Derek Curtis Box, Robert A. Gorman & Matthew W. Finkin, *Labor Law: Cases and Materials* 193 (13th ed. 2001).

United Mine Workers of America, voiced his concern over the proliferation of company unions in testimony before the Senate on the bill that later became the NLRA:

> [C]ompany unions . . . [are] not unions in fact, but mere makeshifts and hollow mockeries deceptive in themselves and intended to divert the energies of the workers from their own self-protection to the protection of the corporation which employs them.[9]

THE NLRA: §§ 8(a)(2) AND 2(5)

Senator Robert F. Wagner of New York, for whom the NLRA was named, was the primary sponsor and drafter of the 1935 Act. Senator Wagner sought to ban company unions, commonly perceived as sham unions.[10] The proposed ban emerged as "the most important substantive issue in the political fight over the drafting and passage of the Wagner act."[11] Senator Wagner thought that "the greatest obstacles to collective bargaining are employer-dominated unions, which have multiplied with amazing rapidity."[12] He noted "the company union is generally initiated by the employer; it exists by his sufferance; its decision[s] are subject to his unimpeachable veto."[13] Such a union, he argued, "makes a sham of equal bargaining power." Wagner further explained:

> [O]nly representatives who are not subservient to the employer with whom they deal can act freely in the interest of employees. . . . For these reasons, the very first step toward genuine collective bargaining is the abolition of the employer-dominated union as an agency for dealing with grievances, labor disputes, wages, rules or hours of employment.[14]

To accomplish the abolition of the employer-dominated union, 8(a)(2) makes it an unfair labor practice for employers to "dominate or interfere with the formation or administration of any labor organization or contribute financial or other support to it."[15] The Senate report on the

---

[9] 1 *Legislative History of the National Labor Relations Act 1935,* 173 (1949).

[10] *See* Mark Barenberg, *The Political Economics of the Wagner Act: Power, Symbol, and Workplace Cooperation*, 106 Harv. L. Rev. 1379, 1386 (1993); *see also* David H. Brody, *The Future of Labor-Management Cooperative Efforts Under Section 8(a)(2) of the National Labor Relations Act*, 41 Vand. L. Rev. 545, 554–55 (1988).

[11] Mark Barenberg, *The Political Economics of the Wagner Act: Power, Symbol, and Workplace Cooperation*, 106 Harv. L. Rev. 1379, 1386 (1993).

[12] 1 *Legislative History of the National Labor Relations Act 1935,* 15–16 (1949).

[13] Robert F. Wagner, *Company Unions: A Vast Industrial Issue*, N.Y. Times, Mar. 11, 1934, § 9, at 1.

[14] 1 *Legislative History of the National Labor Relations Act 1935,* 15–16 (1949).

[15] 29 U.S.C. § 158(a)(2) (2000).

Act stated:

> The so-called "company-union" features of the bill are designed to prevent interference by employers with organizations of their workers that serve or might serve as collective bargaining agencies. Such interferences exist when employers actively participate in framing the constitution or bylaws of labor organizations; or when ... changes in the structure of the organization cannot be made without the consent of the employer. It exists when they participate in the internal management ... of a labor organization or when they supervise the agenda or procedure of meetings.... The committee feels justified ... in outlawing financial or other support as a form of unfair pressure. It seems clear that an organization or a representative or agent paid by the employer for representing employees cannot command ... the full confidence of such employees. And friendly labor relations depend upon absolute confidence on the part of each side in those who represent it.[16]

Section 2(5) broadly defines a "labor organization" as:

> any organization of any kind, or any agency or employee representation committee or plan, in which employees participate and which exists for the purpose, in whole or in part, of dealing with employers concerning grievances, labor disputes, wages, rates of pay, hours of employment, or conditions of work.[17]

Professor Edwin Witte of the University of Wisconsin, a prominent labor economist of the time, was influential in securing this broad definition of "labor organization." He wanted to include the most prevalent form of company-dominated union, the employee representation committee, including those committees that merely "deal" or "adjust."[18]

This broad interpretation was reinforced by early Board and Supreme Court cases. In *Pennsylvania Greyhound Lines*,[19] the very first NLRB case in 1935, the Board found that an organization violated § 2(5) because it "was entirely the creation of management, which planned it, sponsored it, and foisted it on employees who had never requested it, and ... the organization's functions were described to it by management."[20]

16 S. Rep. No. 74–573, 104th Cong., 2d Sess., at 9–11 (1935).

17 29 U.S.C. § 152(5) (2000).

18 *See generally,* Mark Barenberg, *The Political Economics of the Wagner Act: Power, Symbol, and Workplace Cooperation*, 106 Harv. L. Rev. 1379 (1993) (establishing the intention of the framers to create a broad definition of "labor organization").

19 Pennsylvania Greyhound Lines, 1 NLRB 1 (1935), *enforced in part*, 91 F.2d 178 (3d Cir. 1937), *rev'd,* 303 U.S. 261 (1938).

20 Electromation, Inc., 309 NLRB 990 (1992), *citing* 1 NLRB at 13–14.

In *Newport News Shipbuilding Co.*,[21] the Supreme Court found an employee representation plan to be unlawful even though it had been in effect for several years with employee approval. The Court said that employer motive and employee satisfaction are not pertinent, and that regardless of how innocuous the company's actions appeared, company-dominated organizations could not be allowed if the Wagner Act's goal of promoting collective bargaining was to succeed.

In the landmark *Cabot Carbon Co.* case, the Supreme Court broadly defined "dealing with" in § 2(5), holding that the term is more inclusive than the term "bargaining with."[22] The Court considered a broad definition of "labor organization" as necessary to protect the independence of employee organizations, and found:

> It is therefore as plain as words can express that these Committees existed, at least in part, for the purpose of dealing with employees concerning grievances.... This alone brings them within the statutory definition of a labor organization.

Cabot Carbon also affirmed a two-step process for the Board to follow: First, is the employee committee a "labor organization" within the meaning of 2(5)? Second, if so, did the employer dominate, interfere with and support the labor organization in violation of 8(a)(2)?[23]

In 1947, Congress debated the scope of 8(a)(2) when considering the Taft–Hartley amendments to the Wagner Act. A House proposal would have allowed employers to form and maintain a committee of employees, and discuss matters of mutual interest with the committee, if the employees did not have a bargaining representative.[24] The Senate, however, only authorized individual employees and employers to deal directly with each other over grievances.[25] Congress adopted the Senate version as 9(a). The House proposal was rejected, according to the conference report, because it permitted the employer to meet with groups of employees, as opposed to the Senate version which only permitted the employer to respond to individual grievances.[26]

In the 1980's, the Sixth Circuit Court of Appeals seemed to open the door for committees as "communication" devices between employees and management, and for committees whose members do not serve as

---

[21] NLRB v. Newport News Shipbuilding Co., 308 U.S. 241 (1939).

[22] NLRB v. Cabot Carbon Co., 360 U.S. 203, 210–12 (1959).

[23] *Id.* at 209.

[24] 1 *Legislative History of the National Labor Relations Act 1935,* 324 (1949).

[25] *Id.* at 545.

[26] *Id.* at 505, 549.

representatives of other employees. In *Airstream, Inc. v. NLRB*,[27] the court held that an employee committee did *not* constitute a "labor organization," but instead functioned as a means of communication between employees and management. In *NLRB v. Streamway Division of Scott and Fetzer Co.*,[28] the same court had held that the employee committee was not a "labor organization" because committee members acted as individuals rather than employee representatives. The court quoted an earlier opinion by Judge John Minor Wisdom:

> [A]n inflexible attitude of hostility toward employee committees defeats the Act. It erects an iron curtain between employer and employees, penetrable only by the bargaining agent of a certified union, if there is one, preventing the development of a decent, honest, constructive relationship between management and labor.... There is nothing in *Cabot Carbon*, or in the Labor Management Act, or in any other law that makes it wrong for an employer "to work together" with employees for the welfare of all.[29]

Rise of Employee Participation Programs (EPPs) and Potential conflict with 8(a)(2)

Since at least the late 1970's, employers, unions and other interested parties have paid considerable attention to the development of employee participation and labor-management cooperation programs. Such programs seek to increase the contributions and morale of employees, and to promote greater worker satisfaction, productivity, quality and efficiency. Management sometimes introduces such programs unilaterally; in other instances, the programs emerge through collective bargaining.[30] These participation programs have taken a variety of forms, including workers on company boards of directors, worker ownership, quality-of-worklife programs, quality circles, productivity gain-sharing and profit-sharing. To some extent, Japanese and German models of cooperative labor-management relations have influenced American business.[31] "During the past 20 years employee involvement has emerged as the most drastic development in human resource management. One reason is that worker involvement has become a key method of improving American

---

[27] 877 F.2d 1291 (6th Cir. 1989).

[28] 691 F.2d 288 (6th Cir. 1982).

[29] *Id.* at 292, *quoting* NLRB v. Walton Mfg. Co., 289 F.2d 177 (5th Cir. 1961).

[30] Robert B. Moberly, *The Worker Participation Conundrum: Does Prohibiting Employer–Assisted Labor Organizations Prevent Labor–Management Cooperation*?, 69 Wash. L. Rev. 331 (1994).

[31] *See, e.g.*, Marley S. Weiss, *Innovations in Collective Bargaining: Nummi—Driven to Excellence,* 13 Hofstra Lab. L.J. 433 (1996); Robert B. Moberly, *New Directions in Worker Participation and Collective Bargaining,* 87 W. Va. L. Rev. 765, 766 (1985).

competitiveness."[32] "More than 80 percent of the largest employers in the U.S.—nearly 30,000 employers—have implemented some form of EP [employee participation] program."[33]

There are at least three views with respect to § 8(a)(2) and employee participation programs (EPPs).

(1) Some EPP proponents argue that Congress should amend or repeal § 8(a)(2), given its origins in an outdated adversarial relationship between labor and management. They maintain that the modern global economy necessitates labor-management cooperation and therefore cooperative programs should be unrestrained. These advocates reject the notion that employers would use such programs for reasons other than simply increasing employee satisfaction and, ultimately, productivity.[34]

(2) Alternatively, those who oppose amending § 8(a)(2) remain skeptical or critical of EPPs. They do not deny that § 8(a)(2) created adversarial relationships between labor and management, and in fact advocate such relationships. They reject cooperative programs, regardless of their restrictions, because they view cooperative programs simply as management usurpation of employee collective bargaining power.[35]

(3) A third view is that EPPs can be beneficial and ought to be encouraged, but that § 8(a)(2) remains a vital protection against employer interference with union organization and collective bargaining. This view disputes the contention that Congress intended to promote adver-

---

[32] Teamwork for Employees and Management, S. Rep. No. 104–259, 104th Cong., 2d Sess. (1995).

[33] K. Bruce Stickler & Patricia L. Mehler, *Employee Participation Programs After* Electromation*: They're Worth The Risk!,* 2 Annals Health L. 55, 55 (1993), *citing* Letter from Congressman Steve Gunderson (R.-Wis.) to the Members of the House of Representatives (Mar. 1, 1993) (on file with the Loyola University [Chicago] Institute for Health Law). A Forbes magazine article also cites a 30,000 figure. Janet Novack, *Make Them All Form Unions*, Forbes, May 11, 1992, at 174.

[34] *See, e.g.,* John W. Bowers, *Section 8(a)(2) and Participative Management: An Argument for Judicial and Legislative Change in a Modern Workplace,* 26 Val. U. L. Rev. 525 (1992); Shaun G. Clarke, Note, *Rethinking the Adversarial Model in Labor Relations: An Argument for Repeal of Section 8(a)(2),* 96 Yale L.J. 2021 (1987); Arnold E. Perl, *Employee Involvement Groups: The Outcry over the NLRB's* Electromation *Decision,* 44 Lab. L.J. 195 (1993); Note, *Collective Bargaining as an Industrial System: An Argument Against Judicial Revision of Section 8(a)(2) of the National Labor Relations Act,* 96 Harv. L. Rev. 1662 (1983).

[35] *See, e.g.,* Owen E. Herrnstadt, *Why Some Unions Hesitate to Participate in Labor–Management Cooperation Programs,* 8 Lab. Law. 71 (1992); Thomas C. Kohler, *Models of Worker Participation: The Uncertain Significance of Section 8(a)(2),* 27 B.C. L. Rev. 499 (1986); Wilson McLeod, *Labor-Management Cooperation: Competing Visions and Labor's Challenge,* 12 Indus. Rel. L.J. 233 (1990).

sarialism. Advocates of the third view argue that Congress sought to promote cooperation through collective bargaining.[36]

Although EPPs come in many shapes and sizes, they share the underlying purpose of addressing economic or human workplace issues. Economic issues include productivity, product quality, machine efficiency, and material usage. Human issues include job security, training, opportunity for advancement, and worker dignity. Effective EPPs address both economic and human areas to obtain maximum program benefits.[37]

Despite these important goals, a conflict arises when an EPP involves employers and employees discussing "conditions of work"; under these circumstances the employee committee may be considered a "labor organization." An employee group may be considered a "labor organization," as defined under § 2(5) of the NLRA, when (1) employees participate in the group, (2) there is employee "representation," (3) the group exists for the purpose of dealing with the employer, and (4) the subject of the "dealing" concerns grievances, labor disputes, wages, rates of pay, hours of employment, or conditions of work. Section 8(a)(2) protects such a labor organization from employer interference or domination in its formation or administration. Depending on the structure and function of the EPP, its very existence, however lofty its objectives, may be unlawful under the NLRA. The task for the NLRB in its *Electromation* decision was to explain and apply these statutory terms while at the same time trying to mediate these fundamentally conflicting perspectives on employee involvement.

Factual Background

Electromation was a small manufacturer of electrical components for the automobile industry and power equipment manufacturers. It was a subsidiary of American Electronic Components, a privately-held corporation formed in 1985. At the time this dispute arose in 1989, the Company employed about 200 workers, mostly women, in Elkhart, Indiana. Electromation has been bought and sold since the events discussed here, and currently is operating as American Electronic Components.

During the last five months of 1988, Electromation lost "almost a half a million dollars."[38] American Electronic Components became con-

---

[36] Robert B. Moberly, *The Worker Participation Conundrum: Does Prohibiting Employer–Assisted Labor Organizations Prevent Labor–Management Cooperation*?, 69 Wash. L. Rev. 331 (1994).

[37] Amicus Brief for Labor Policy Association at 7, Electromation, Inc., 309 NLRB 990 (1992) (No. 25–CA–19818).

[38] Official Report of Proceeding Before the NLRB at 275, Electromation, Inc., 309 NLRB 990 (1992) (No. 25–CA–19818) (Testimony of John Howard). This account of the events of the *Electromation* case is drawn from the Transcript unless otherwise stated.

cerned with this poor financial performance, and John Howard was appointed president in November 1988. Mr. Howard, an Ohio native with a master's degree in engineering from the Massachusetts Institute of Technology,[39] worked for General Motors for twenty years. Prior to his appointment as President of Electromation, he served as Vice President of Manufacturing and Chief Operating Officer of American Electronic Components.

Mr. Howard introduced numerous ideas to improve productivity and cut costs. One of the significant costs was a program established by Electromation's former president to discourage absenteeism that cost "well over $20,000 a month." Howard believed that "part of the losing money problem was an absentee bonus program that was put in place that did absolutely nothing to improve absenteeism." Another cost-cutting idea concerned general wage increases scheduled for the coming year. Company executives decided to restructure the attendance bonus, cancel the wage increases, and instead distribute Christmas bonuses based on employees' length of service.

Howard announced the benefit changes during the company Christmas party on December 23, 1988. He distributed notices detailing major changes to the attendance program and cancelling the wage increases for the coming year. He perceived that employees at the party appeared satisfied with the benefit changes and excited to receive the length-of-service cash bonus.[40] The plant closed over the holiday week and reopened on January 2, 1989. After returning to work, many employees expressed second thoughts about the benefit changes. "Recognizing the impact of the changes in the attendance policy, and the lack of a pay increase, [they] indicated to management their unhappiness with management."[41] Sixty-eight employees submitted a petition asking for reconsideration of the attendance policy.

On January 10, 1989, Howard called a supervisors' meeting to discuss the employees' concerns. At this meeting the company decided to identify sources of employee dissatisfaction and possible solutions. The previous company president had sometimes created employee-management committees for such functions. The company now scheduled a meeting with eight employees, six of whom were chosen at random and two who requested to join, as well as four management members, including Howard. The group discussed several issues, including "over-

---

[39] Information in this paragraph about Mr. Howard was obtained from an obituary and news article in the Hartford Courant, dated February 2, 2002, on file with the author. Howard remained as President until 1997.

[40] Tr. 282 (Testimony of John Howard).

[41] Electromation, Inc., 309 NLRB 990, 1016 (1992) (No. 25–CA–19818) (Administrative Law Judge Decision and Report) [hereinafter referred to as ALJ Decision].

time, tardiness, wages, bonuses, attendance, bereavement leave, sick leave, and incentive pay."

After the employee meeting, Howard and plant supervisors decided that management "possibly made a mistake in judgment in December in deciding what we ought to do," and that "the best course of action would be to involve the employees in coming up with solutions to these issues." The company scheduled another meeting for January 18 between the same group of eight employees and management representatives. At this meeting, management presented to the employees the idea of pursuing "action committees," comprised of up to six employees and one or two management representatives, to address five areas of general concern: absenteeism/infractions, no-smoking policy, communication network, pay progression for premium positions, and the attendance bonus program. Howard explained to the employees that the action committees:

> would meet and try to come up with ways to resolve these problems; and if they came up with solutions that were, that we believed were within budget concerns and that they generally felt would be acceptable to the employees, that we would implement those suggestions, or proposals, or whatever you want to call them.[42]

Initially, employees did not react positively to the action committees idea, desiring instead to return to the old attendance and wage increase plan. However, after management explained Electromation's financial situation and the need for change, the employees, in Howard's view, "began to understand that that was far better than leaving things as they were" and eventually agreed.[43]

The company posted volunteer sign-up sheets for employees interested in serving on action committees. Employee Benefits Manager Loretta Dickey took charge of the action committee program. Ms. Dickey, a graduate of Bethel College with a B.S. in Human Resource Management, had been working in human resources since 1987.[44]

Electromation management limited each action committee to six employees. No employee was permitted to serve on more than one committee. Management asked two employees who signed up for more than one committee to choose only one. After determining committee membership, the company posted a memorandum to "All Electromation Employees" that named committee members, noted that committees

---

[42] Tr. 301 (Testimony of John Howard).

[43] Tr. 302 (Testimony of John Howard).

[44] Telephone Interview with Loretta Dickey, and biography provided by Ms. Dickey via e-mail, on August 2, 2004. She currently serves as Vice–President of Global Human Resources for Trico Products Corporation at its corporate office in Rochester Hills, Michigan.

would serve in a representative capacity, and urged all employees to contribute by providing input to the representatives.[45]

The committees met in the company's conference room in late January and early February, and thereafter scheduled weekly meetings. The company paid employee committee members for their time spent on committee work, and supplied writing materials and calculators. Hourly employees, salaried employees and supervisors served on the committees. The company controller participated in the Attendance Bonus Committee; a senior engineer joined the Communication Network Committee; a line supervisor served on the Absenteeism Committee; and another line supervisor worked with the Pay Progression for Premium Positions Committee. As coordinator, Dickey attended meetings of all committees. She believed that the committees worked well together, the employees were interested, and committee members gathered useful information, especially about the practices of other companies that could be used at Electromation.[46] "There was a lot of discussion, everyone joined in, and there were no complaints even from the employee witnesses in this case about the conduct of the meetings."[47]

Prior Proceedings

On February 15, 1989, Local Union No. 1049 of the International Brotherhood of Teamsters, Chauffeurs, Warehousemen and Helpers of America, filed a petition with the NLRB for an election at Electromation. Howard consulted with Attorney Dan Rudy, Chair of the Labor Law Department of Barnes & Thornburg, the largest law firm in Indiana.[48]

According to Howard, "Once we were served with the petition for election, we were advised that if we continued these employee participation meetings . . . they could be construed as unfair labor practices."[49] Howard informed company management of the union campaign and announced that management would not be able to meet with the action committees during the campaign. Howard also stated that the committees could meet after the election. The next week, Dickey advised committee members that they would suspend meeting with management, but she said they could continue to meet individually if they wished. All action committees stopped meeting except two that continued to meet on paid time on company property.

---

[45] General Counsel's Ex. 2.

[46] Telephone Interview with Loretta Dickey, August 2, 2004.

[47] ALJ Decision, 309 NLRB at 1017.

[48] *Id.*, and Telephone Interview with Dan Rudy, July 30, 2004. Rudy is retired and living in Florida, but still serves as counsel to the firm.

[49] Tr. 307.

The company and union stipulated to an election in a bargaining unit comprised of all production and maintenance employees, including all quality control employees, tool room employees, warehousemen and truck drivers. The Board conducted an election on March 31, 1989, and the union lost by a vote of ninety-five to eighty-two. Jimmy Skipper, President of Local 1049 and the primary union organizer, attributed the loss to the company appointment of committees and related promises. Skipper claimed that the company knew about the organizing efforts before establishing the committees, despite findings to the contrary by the ALJ, as noted below. Skipper contends that the company witnesses lied to the ALJ on this question, and that the company "put roadblocks at every turn" leading up to the election.[50]

The union filed objections to the election with the Board, and also filed charges alleging that Electromation's activities constituted unfair labor practices in violation of §§ 8(a)(1) and (2) of the NLRA.[51] The union specifically alleged that Electromation interrogated employees, threatened plant closure, and dominated and assisted the action committees, all in violation of §§ 8(a)(1) and (2). The Board consolidated the election objections with the unfair labor practice proceeding, and on October 2, 1989, Administrative Law Judge George F. McInerny conducted a hearing in the Elkhart municipal building. Jimmy Skipper appeared on behalf of the union, and Walter Steele, an attorney from the Board's Indianapolis office, appeared on behalf of the Board's General Counsel. Two attorneys from Barnes & Thornburg appeared on behalf of Electromation, with attorney Kathleen Brickley taking the lead.[52]

On April 5, 1990, McInerny issued a recommended Decision and Order. The decision held that Electromation did not threaten or interrogate employees in violation of § 8(a)(1), finding that witness testimony supporting these specific allegations to be imprecise, vague and unreliable. "There is no evidence in the record that the Company knew of this [union] activity before receiving the demand for recognition, or the petition, sometime in the week of February 13–17."[53]

On the central issue of the legality of the committees, the ALJ found the action committees to be labor organizations as defined by § 2(5) of the NLRA. He said that Electromation's lack of knowledge of the union

---

[50] Telephone Interview with Jimmy Skipper, July 29, 2004.

[51] Section 8(a)(1) declares that "It shall be an unfair labor practice for an employer to interfere with, restrain, or coerce employees in the exercise of the rights guaranteed in section 157." Section 157 is § 7.

[52] Telephone Interview with Kathleen Brickley, August 2, 2004. Ms. Brickley today is a partner at Barnes & Thornburg, specializing in labor and employment law.

[53] ALJ Decision, 309 NLRB at 1018.

activities did not "alter the legal effects of [the] Company's actions." The ALJ further found that the company dominated the action committees in violation of §§ 8(a)(1) and (2) by structuring, organizing and directing meetings, providing use of company property, supplying committees with necessary supplies, and paying committee members for their time. Section 8(a)(2), the ALJ said, was not concerned with employer motive, but rather was designed to remedy the "inherent injury to the rights of employees to bargain collectively through representatives of their own choosing."

The ALJ set aside the election, ordered a new election, and ordered the company to cease and desist from dominating, assisting, or otherwise supporting the action committees at its Elkhart plant. On May 25, 1990, the company filed exceptions to the ALJ decision. The proceeding immediately was transferred to the Board in Washington, D.C.

Under the NLRA, a union is entitled to seek another election one year after losing a previous election. On June 19, 1990, more than one year after its March 1989 loss, the Teamsters filed a petition for a second election. About one month later, on July 13, 1990, the Union filed a "Motion to Sever Cases and to Withdraw Objections to the Election ... in order to permit another Board-conducted election." The Board granted the motion on August 1, 1990, thereby severing the objections case from the unfair labor practice case, and continuing the unfair labor practice case before the Board.[54]

The parties stipulated to the second election, to be conducted on September 14, 1990, and the union continued to organize Electromation's employees.[55] Jimmy Skipper, President of Local 1049 in Elkhart, again led the effort. However, he sought the assistance of Local 364, based in South Bend, Indiana, and the two locals worked together. According to Skipper, the union thought it had a better chance because the company had hired employees from another plant that closed down, many of whom were members of the Teamsters Union. Skipper met with the employees every week, and handbilled at least once a week. These efforts met with success, although the election was close. The Union won by a vote of sixty-one to fifty-six. After the election, Local 1049 merged into Local 364.

The company and union then entered into a "dual track" process: bargaining and the appeal of the unfair labor practice charges.[56] Attorney

[54] The Board order is on file with the author.

[55] Information in this paragraph was provided by Jimmy Skipper, former President of Local 1049, in a telephone interview on July 29, 2004.

[56] Information in this and the next paragraph, unless otherwise noted, is based on telephone interviews with company attorney Dan Rudy on July 29, 2004; Local 1049

Dan Rudy negotiated for the company, and Local 364 President Bobby Warnock, Jr., negotiated for the union. The company did not pressure the union to withdraw the pending unfair labor practice charges. Rudy could see no purpose in delaying bargaining; even if the company won on the unfair labor practice charges, it would have to bargain because the union had already won the second election.

At this point no outside groups of either employers or unions were involved in the litigation or negotiations. Rudy characterized the collective bargaining process as normal for a first contract; there were "no hard feelings or yelling." He recollects that the parties reached agreement without much difficulty. In April 1991, the parties signed their first collective bargaining agreement, effective from January 1, 1991, to December 31, 1993. The employees received wage increases rather than lump-sum bonuses, and neither the initial nor succeeding contracts contained provisions for employee committees.[57] Rudy noted that the labor contract "covered almost all of the issues which were to be addressed by the action committees."[58]

The Union regretted that the first contract did not contain a provision for binding arbitration of grievances. In congressional testimony the Teamsters' General Counsel stated:

> Because the Union lacked bargaining power, Chief Steward Berna Price reports that eventually the rank-and-file negotiation committee on which she participated accepted a contract which fell short of their hopes.... The depth of management's aversion to any real employee involvement in workplace decisions ... was evidenced by its steadfast refusal to include a standard arbitration requirement that unresolved grievances be decided by a neutral third party.[59]

In October 1993, before the first contract expired, a decertification petition was filed. The Union prevailed in the subsequent election,[60] and "the next round of bargaining was much more successful."[61] The parties

President Jimmy Skipper on July 29, 2004; and Local 364 President Bobby Warnock, Jr., on October 8, 2004.

57 The collective bargaining agreements from 1991through 2007 are on file with the author.

58 Jeff Kurowski, *NLRB Says Electromation Violated Labor Law,* S. Bend Trib., Dec. 19, 1992, at A6.

59 Judith A. Scott, testimony before the Subcomm. on Employer–Employee Rel., Comm. on Econ. and Educ. Opportunities, U.S. House of Representatives, Feb. 8, 1995, at 7, on file with the author.

60 The Board certification, dated February 11, 1994, is on file with the author.

61 Judith A. Scott, testimony before the Subcomm. on Employer–Employee Rel., Comm. on Econ. and Educ. Opportunities, U.S. House of Representatives, Feb. 8, 1995, at 8, on file with the author.

signed an agreement effective from January 1, 1994, through 1996. This and subsequent agreements contained a provision for binding arbitration of grievances. The parties have continued to enter into collective bargaining agreements, with the most recent effective from 2004 through 2007. The current Business Agent for Local 364, Robert Warnock III, states that the parties now enjoy a "pretty good rapport and working relationship."[62]

The National Labor Relations Board and Court of Appeals Decisions

About a month after the parties entered into their first collective bargaining agreement, the NLRB dropped a bombshell. In May 1991, more than a year after the ALJ decision, the Board took the unusual step of scheduling oral arguments, stating that the case "raised important 8(a)(2) issues."[63] A contemporary news account set the stage:

> ELKHART, Ind.—Eighteen minutes outside the RV capital of the world, the Electromation factory stands like an uninvited guest in cornfields gone wild with grass. From behind its high corrugated walls come solenoids and relays for the auto and marine industries, and an unexpected struggle for the soul of American labor law. Neither the plant bosses nor the women running coil winders could possibly have foreseen the notoriety visited upon this corner of nowhere since the National Labor Relations Board (NLRB) transformed a mundane complaint against the company into a public meditation on worker-management cooperation.... The principals regarded the case as garden variety; nobody would have wasted a dime betting that the board would do what it next did.[64]

Neither party requested oral arguments; the Board order "came out of the blue."[65] Both parties asked about avoiding oral argument to avoid the expense, without success.

The NLRB scheduled oral arguments for September 5, 1991, and the notice of hearing framed these issues: "(1) At what point does an employee committee lose its protection as a communication device and become a labor organization? (2) What conduct of an employer constitutes domination or interference with the employee committee?"[66]

---

[62] Telephone Interview with Robert Warnock III on July 29, 2004.

[63] 309 NLRB 990, 990 (1992).

[64] Diane Katz, *Labor Pains in Indiana,* Det. News, Aug. 30, 1992, D, at 1.

[65] Information in this paragraph, aside from the newspaper account, was provided by Attorney Kathleen Brickley in a telephone interview on August 2, 2004.

[66] 309 NLRB 990 (1992).

The fact that neither party requested oral arguments, and that both parties sought to avoid them, raises the interesting question as to how and why the Board picked this case for special consideration. At that time, the Board was comprised of three Republicans and two Democrats, with Chair James Stephens (1985–95), a Republican former congressional counsel, its most senior member.[67] Democratic-appointee Mary Cracraft (1986–91) served on the Board when it considered whether to set oral argument in *Electromation*, but her term expired before the Board decision.[68] Democrat Dennis Devaney (1988–94) had represented employer interests in private law practice before his appointment by President Ronald Reagan.[69] Republican Board Member Clifford Oviatt (1989–93) had been a partner in Washington, D.C., law firms representing management before his appointment by President George H. W. Bush.[70] Republican John Raudabaugh (1990–93) had represented employers in an Atlanta law firm prior to joining the NLRB.[71]

According to Member Raudabaugh, he noticed the case and insisted to the other Board members that it be scheduled for oral arguments.[72] At the time, he was familiar with literature on Japanese management styles, and with a 1986 Department of Labor study that discussed a possible conflict between 8(a)(2) and similar forms of labor-management cooperation in American companies.[73] Board member Oviatt and Chair Stephens were opposed to oral argument, but Raudabaugh, Devaney and Cracraft supported the idea. Raudabaugh thought that the NLRA possi-

67 Stephens worked as a judicial law clerk and as labor counsel to House and Senate committees before President Reagan appointed him to the NLRB. After leaving the Board, he served as Deputy Executive Director for the Office of Compliance in the U.S. Congress, and in 2002 President Bush appointed him to the Occupational Safety and Health Review Commission.

68 Cracraft clerked for the Missouri Supreme Court, and then worked for the NLRB as a field attorney in Region 17 and in private practice. When her term expired in 1991, she worked in the NLRB Solicitor's Office and then became an administrative law judge for the Board, where she serves today in San Francisco.

69 Devaney had represented brewery and food associations. Since leaving the NLRB he has practiced and taught law and served as a member of the U.S. International Trade Commission. In 2004 he was engaged in management-side labor practice with a large Michigan law firm.

70 Prior to appointment to the NLRB, Oviatt, in addition to being an attorney, had been a U.S. Marine decorated for combat valor and a Red Sox minor league baseball player.

71 Raudabaugh, in 2004, represents management clients at the large Detroit-based law firm of Butzel Long.

72 Information in this paragraph is based on a telephone interview with John Raudabaugh on July 30, 2004.

73 *See* Stephen I. Schlossberg & Steven M. Fetter, *U.S. Labor Law and the Future of Labor-Management Cooperation* (1986).

bly did not accommodate these methods, but he thought they should. He also thought that the statute should be interpreted flexibly, and that the legality of labor-management committees was a major issue in the workplace. He "wanted to make it a big deal, and to bring it to the attention of Congress and the public." It was a "calculated event from the get-go from me to bring attention to the issue." Dennis Devaney confirmed the split among Board members, and agreed that Raudabaugh played a strong role in persuading the Board to set the case for oral argument.[74]

The Board members engaged in considerable debate among themselves, including thirteen interoffice memoranda, relating to the grant of oral argument. The NLRB denied this author's request to obtain these memoranda under the Freedom of Information Act on the ground that they "are privileged from disclosure under FOIA."[75]

Oral Arguments and Briefs

On the day of the Board hearing, reporters from around the country and other observers packed the hearing room. Bulbs were flashing and there was standing room only. National press coverage included a page-one story in the *National Law Journal* under the headline "Case Holds Key to U.S. Competitiveness."[76]

The company, the union, the NLRB General Counsel, and numerous amici curiae were represented in oral arguments and briefs before the Board. Eight organizations participated as amici curiae supporting management's position, including the U.S. Chamber of Commerce and the National Association of Manufacturers. Amici supporting the union included the AFL–CIO, a union, and, most unusually, an individual law professor, Charles J. Morris, Professor Emeritus at Southern Methodist University School of Law, editor of a major labor law treatise.

Professor Morris' involvement began when he learned of the scheduled *Electromation* argument while visiting NLRB General Counsel Jerry M. Hunter on another matter.[77] At Morris' request, the Board granted him permission as an individual to file an amicus brief and

---

[74] Telephone Interview with Dennis Devaney on September 10, 2004. Mary Cracraft declined to comment on the Board's decision to request oral argument. E-mail from Mary Cracraft on September 14, 2002, on file with the author. Attempts to reach James Stephens were unsuccessful.

[75] Letter from Jacqueline A. Young, NLRB Freedom of Information Officer, September 24, 2004.

[76] Randall Samborn, *Case Holds Key to U.S. Competitiveness,* Nat'l L.J., Apr. 6, 1992, at 1.

[77] Information in this paragraph is from a telephone interview with Professor Morris on November 16, 2004.

participate in oral argument. Professor Morris believes this was the only time in the Board's history that it afforded such a role to an individual, rather than to an organization. Professor Morris was able to make a more fact-specific argument than other amici because he had obtained copies of briefs and the ALJ hearing transcript from a "mole" in the NLRB. Looking back on the experience, Morris thought it demonstrated that a law professor could be just as, if not more, effective in influencing decisions as an "activist" than as an author of law review articles. The Board seemed to give special deference to Professor Morris, twice extending his allotted time to obtain his opinion on various questions. At the end of the hearing, Member Raudabaugh approached Professor Morris with a copy of his book and asked him to autograph it. In the view of another participant in the argument, the Board was not nearly as deferential toward other amici, including two former NLRB members, Robert Hunter and Don Zimmerman, who were representing management clients.

Arguing for the Board's General Counsel was an attorney with the NLRB's Region 25 office in Indianapolis, Rik Lineback.[78] Lineback received no directives from the agency for handling the case.[79] He was told only to "go look at Board law" and base his brief and oral argument on what he found. Lineback recalls that Professor Morris expressed concern that the General Counsel would "punt" the case, but eventually was pleased with Lineback's briefs and arguments.

Teamsters staff attorney James Wallington was assigned to the *Electromation* case after the ALJ decision, when the local union asked the international union to participate.[80] The union, in its argument, could point to the subsequent events at Electromation to show that the NLRA was working as intended. As a result of the second election, the union became the certified representative of the employees and had successfully negotiated a collective bargaining agreement with Electromation. While employer associations wanted this case to raise the issues of quality circles and labor-management committees, the union saw the case as an attempt to revive company unions.[81]

---

[78] NLRB press release R–2527 (Apr. 23, 2004), on file with the author. Lineback is an Indiana native and Army veteran. He was later promoted to several supervisory positions in the NLRB regional office and in 2004 became the Regional Director of Region 25.

[79] Information in this paragraph is from a telephone interview with Rik Lineback on August 5, 2004.

[80] Wallington enforced coal safety regulations and represented unions in West Virginia before becoming a Teamsters staff attorney. Since 1992 he has practiced union-side labor law in private practice in Washington, D.C.

[81] Information in this paragraph is from a telephone interview with James Wallington on August 13, 2004.

The company's lead counsel was Kathleen Brickley, who had represented the company at the ALJ hearing. Prior to arguments, she had received offers of assistance from attorneys and employer associations all over the country.[82] One of the employer associations provided an opportunity for her to present a mock argument before experienced labor lawyers in Washington.

In their briefs and oral arguments, the parties addressed the following primary issues: (1) Did the action committees at Electromation qualify as labor organizations under § 2(5) of the NLRA, and (2) If so, did Electromation dominate or interfere with the action committees in violation of § 8(a)(2) of the NLRA?

1. *Did the action committees at Electromation qualify as labor organizations under § 2(5) of the NLRA?*

Relying primarily on *Airstream* and *Scott & Fetzer,* the two Sixth Circuit cases discussed above, Electromation argued that the company-selected volunteers served as individual employees rather than representatives of the employees, since the employees had not formally selected representatives. Electromation contended that it acted lawfully to allow "valid employee expressions of concern in a fair, progressive fashion designed to enhance communication and creativity."[83]

The Board's General Counsel and the Union asserted that the action committees constituted a "labor organization" as defined by § 2(5) of the NLRA. They argued that the action committees easily met the § 2(5) definition of a labor organization because it was an agency or employee representation plan in which employees participated. Pointing to *Cabot Carbon,*[84] they also contended that the Electromation committees were unlawfully "dealing with" the employer on "grievances, labor disputes, wages, rates of pay, hours of employment, or conditions of work" under § 2(5) when they discussed absenteeism, pay progression, and the attendance bonus program. Lineback and Wallington also criticized, factually distinguished and offered precedent contrary to the Sixth Circuit's *Airstream* and *Streamway* cases upon which Electromation relied. Both lawyers noted that the action committees in those cases were found to exist only for communication purposes, as opposed to Electromation's express purpose of addressing five specified areas and developing recommendations for management.

82 Information in this paragraph is from a telephone interview with Kathleen Brickley on August 2, 2004.

83 Brief for Respondent at 26, Electromation, Inc., 309 NLRB 990 (1992) (No. 25–CA–19818).

84 360 U.S. 203 (1959).

2. *If the action committees qualified as labor organizations, did Electromation dominate or interfere with them in violation of § 8(a)(2) of the NLRA?*

Electromation relied upon courts of appeals cases holding that § 8(a)(2) required "actual" domination of an employee committee, and contended that Electromation's action committees represented only a potential for, rather than the reality of, domination. Electromation cited cases holding that employees' subjective view determines the existence of employer domination or interference with employee freedom of choice. Because employees expressed satisfaction with the action committees, it argued, no domination occurred. Finally, Electromation cited precedent that considered employer intent and asserted that Electromation never intended to stymie the founding of the union.

Lineback and Wallington cited cases contrary to Electromation's "potential domination" and "intent" arguments. They asserted that the test to determine domination is straightforward under §§ 8(a)(2) and 2(5), and that the facts of each case determine violations. Finally, these lawyers argued that there was substantial evidence of domination since Electromation controlled the selection process, ultimately determined the discussion topics, provided meeting rooms and work materials, paid committee members, and placed at least one supervisor or manager on each committee.

As amicus for the Union, Professor Morris' submission included a speech about *Electromation*, asserting that organized industry was attempting to have the Board give new language to the NLRA. He argued:

> Notwithstanding the absence of anti-union motive, the mere recognition and existence of the "action committees," which had been created by the employer in good faith but without consent of the majority of bargaining unit employees, interfered with the employees' right to select a labor organization of their own choosing.

Ellis Boal, counsel for amicus Labor Education and Research Project, a non-profit organization committed to revitalizing American labor,[85] quoted a familiar law school refrain to describe Electromation's position: "If you are weak on the facts, argue the law. If you are weak on the law, argue the facts. If you are weak on both, argue policy." Boal added that "what [employers] really want is new policy set through sweeping dictum." Boal further asserted that the elements of a § 8(a)(2) violation do not require scienter, "actual" domination, or employee subjective belief of employer control. Boal, citing articles and studies, also argued that the benefits of EPPs themselves are questionable, and that the risk to employee rights outweighs any possible value of EPPs.

---

[85] *See* Brief for Labor Education and Research Project at 1.

The amicus briefs supporting Electromation focused on cases that considered "scienter" in determining violations of § 8(a)(2), as well as factual distinctions in Electromation. They urged the Board to exercise its discretion in deciding sound labor policy, in light of (1) industry practices and beliefs, (2) the success of EPPs in contributing to a successful American economy, and (3) federal policy favoring labor-management cooperation. Representing the U.S. Chamber of Commerce, attorney Arnold Perl from Memphis attempted to differentiate modern employee participation plans from sham unions:

> In-house unions ... of the 1930's were totally different. When we look today at quality circles ... we're dealing now with a situation ... where there is no longer an adversarial model.... Today ... the interest of employers and employees is inseparable ... the committees that we're talking about here ... [are] part of an essential business strategy to make a company stronger, more secure, more competitive.[86]

The Board's Decision

On December 16, 1992, the four-member Board, all appointed by Republican presidents, held that the action committees constituted labor organizations within the meaning of § 2(5), and that Electromation dominated and interfered with the committees in violation of § 8(a)(2). Chair Stephens and Members Devaney and Oviatt signed the majority opinion. Devaney and Oviatt filed separate concurring opinions, as did Raudabaugh, who did not join the majority opinion.

The Board was careful not to condemn all EPPs:

> These findings rest on the totality of the record evidence, and they are not intended to suggest that employee committees formed under other circumstances for other purposes would necessarily be deemed "labor organizations" or that employer actions like some of those at issue here would necessarily be found, in isolation or in other contexts, to constitute unlawful support, interference, or domination.[87]

As an introduction to its analysis, the Board noted that statutory language alone was not sufficient to determine whether the statute applied to particular facts. Accordingly, the Board examined legislative history to determine the kinds of activity Congress intended to prohibit. In the Board's view, the legislative history revealed that prohibiting company-dominated labor organizations was critical to Senator Wagner's goal of eliminating industrial strife by encouraging collective bargaining.

---

[86] Transcript of oral argument, at 80–81.

[87] Electromation, Inc., 309 NLRB 990, 990 (1992).

Senator Wagner wanted to include not only those groups that were highly organized, such as labor unions, but also those groups that were only loosely organized representation committees (a prevalent form of company union at the time). He defined the term "labor organization" broadly in order to eliminate employer-dominated unions, and avoid creating a loophole that could eviscerate the entire Act.

Utilizing legislative history, the Board identified the type of employer conduct that Congress intended § 8(a)(2) to prohibit, and highlighted revisions to the Wagner bill as it made its way through the legislative process. The original proposal prohibited any type of employer involvement. A later version substituted the words "dominate or interfere with the formation or administration" for "initiate, participate in, supervise, or influence." According to the Board, Congress changed this language to acknowledge the positive nature of employer-employee interaction that promoted industrial peace. Yet Congress maintained fairly strict limits on employer involvement because of the belief that most employer involvement fatally threatened the employee group's independence. The Board concluded that by prohibiting domination, interference, or assistance, Congress intended to provide broad assurance that employee groups representing employee interests would be free to act independently of employers.

The Board next considered step one of the two-pronged inquiry established in *Cabot Carbon*: whether Electromation's action committees were labor organizations under § 2(5). With legislative history and judicial precedent in mind, the Board defined a labor organization as a group in which (1) employees participate, (2) that exists, at least in part, for the purpose of "dealing" with employers, and (3) whose dealings concerned "conditions of work" or other statutory subjects. Further, if the organization had as a purpose the representation of employees, it would meet the statutory definition of "employee representation committee plan" under 2(5).[88] Actual bilateral negotiation was not a prerequisite for an employee committee to be deemed a labor organization. Rather, if an employee committee merely discussed and then made proposals or requests on any of the topics specifically mentioned in 2(5) ("grievances, labor disputes, wages, rates of pay, hours of employment, or conditions of work"), it was deemed a labor organization. However, the Board acknowledged that some unilateral mechanisms do not constitute "dealing with," including suggestion boxes, brainstorming groups

[88] The majority opinion, because it found that the employee members of the action committees acted in a representational capacity, expressly declined to determine whether an employee group could ever be found to constitute a labor organization without a finding that it acted as a representative of employees. The majority noted that Member Devaney, who separately concurred, would have reached that issue. Devaney concluded that representation is necessary for a group to be a labor organization within the meaning of § 2(5).

and other information exchanges. "Dealing with" contemplates a bilateral mechanism involving proposals from the employee committee concerning statutory subjects, coupled with real or apparent consideration of those proposals by management. The organization escapes the "dealing with" label if it is limited to performing essentially a managerial or adjudicative function, such as deciding employees' complaints without dealing or interacting with the employer.

Applying these principles to the facts of this case, the Board classified Electromation's action committees as labor organizations, based on four findings. First, employees participated in the group. Second, the committees were actively "dealing with" management by sending proposals to management for consideration. Third, the subject matter of the dealing, including treatment of employee absenteeism, bonuses and other monetary incentives, clearly concerned conditions of employment. Fourth, the employees acted in a representational capacity, since part of their assignment was to talk with other employees regarding solutions that would satisfy the employees as a whole.

The Board concluded that the action committees functioned solely to address employee dissatisfaction by creating a bilateral process to reach bilateral solutions on the basis of employee proposals. The company did not limit the purpose of the action committees to achieving quality or efficiency, and did not design the committees solely as a communication device. Thus the majority opinion did not address the question of whether an employer-initiated committee existing solely for quality, efficiency, or communication purposes may constitute a labor organization under § 2(5).[89]

Moving to step two of its analysis, whether Electromation dominated or interfered with the action committees in violation of 8(a)(2), the Board again relied on the Supreme Court's decision in *Cabot Carbon*:[90]

> Thus, the Board's cases following *Cabot Carbon* reflect the view that when the impetus behind the formation of an organization of employees emanates from an employer and the organization has no effective existence independent of the employer's active involvement, a finding of domination is appropriate if the purpose of the organization is to deal with the employer concerning conditions of employment.

[89] However, the concurring opinions of members Devaney and Oviatt clearly did not view such committees as labor organizations. Member Oviatt unequivocally noted "[t]he statute does not forbid direct communication between the employer and its employees to address and solve significant productivity and efficiency problems in the workplace."

[90] 360 U.S. 203 (1959), *cited in* 309 NLRB at 996.

Applying these standards to Electromation's action committees, the Board found domination and interference. Electromation formed and unilaterally directed the action committees, determined their composition, appointed management representatives to them, and paid committee members for their activities on company time. The Board concluded that:

> [T]his case presents a situation where an employer alters conditions of employment and, as a result, is confronted with a work force that is discontented with its new employment environment. The employer responds to that discontent by devising and imposing on the employees an organized Committee mechanism composed of managers and employees instructed to "represent" fellow employees. The purpose of the Action Committees was, as the record demonstrates, not to enable management and employees to cooperate to improve "quality" or "efficiency," but to create in employees the impression that their disagreements with management had been resolved bilaterally. By creating the Action Committees the Respondent imposed on employees its own unilateral form of bargaining or dealing and thereby violated Section 8(a)(2) and (1) as alleged.

The four Board members made considerable efforts to develop one unanimous opinion without concurring or dissenting opinions, so as to provide significant guidance on the use of employee committees.[91] However, the efforts were not completely successful, as Devaney, Oviatt and Raudabaugh wrote concurring opinions. Devaney has written elsewhere that "the concurring opinions emphasize that each of the Board members draws the outside boundaries of legality differently, but the collection of views clearly illustrates that there is significant latitude for lawful cooperative programs."[92] His concurring opinion stated that significant opportunity remains under § 8(a)(2) for employers to implement programs involving employees in the workplace; that the legislative history of the Wagner Act showed no concern for employer-initiated programs relating to managerial issues such as quality, productivity and efficiency; that the Supreme Court had not dealt with employer programs limited to managerial issues such as safety and efficiency; and that prior Board precedent allowed a broad range of lawful communications between employers and employees. Devaney also discussed the "representation" issue not addressed by the majority, stating that he would not be inclined to find labor organization status unless the group acted as a representative of other employees, and that if a committee was an agent of the employer it is evidence that the committee lacked a

---

91 Telephone Interview with Dennis Devaney on September 10, 2004.

92 Dennis M. Devaney, *Much Ado About Section 8(a)(2): The NLRB and Workplace Cooperation after* Electromation *and* Du Pont, 23 Stetson L. Rev. 39, 44 (1993).

representational purpose. Finally, he stated that he would not be inclined to find that the employer's solicitation of ideas from an employee group constituted "dealing with" that group.

Member Oviatt also emphasized the degree to which labor-management communication has been found to be compatible with 8(a)(2). He noted that the conduct in *Electromation* was "garden variety 8(a)(2) conduct," but nonetheless expressed approval for a wide spectrum of worker participation programs such as quality circles, quality-of-work programs, joint problem-solving structures that engage management and employees in finding ways to improve operations, and committees established to improve communications between management and employees. Oviatt identified the critical question as "whether the entity is created with any purpose to deal with 'grievances, labor disputes, wages, rates of pay, hours of employment, or conditions of work.' " He also observed that the Board has upheld self-regulating employee teams with unilateral power over job duties.

Member Raudabaugh advocated a new test to determine violations of 8(a)(2). He contended that reinterpretation of § 8(a)(2) was justified and necessary, given the major changes in federal policy and the labor world since passage of the Wagner Act; that the Wagner Act's underlying theory of adversarial struggle between labor and management was inconsistent with today's cooperative labor relations; and that the 1947 Taft–Hartley amendments to the Wagner Act created a more level playing field: "In short, Taft–Hartley emphasized (1) employee free choice rather than governmental encouragement of unionism; and (2) the encouragement of peaceful methods for resolving labor-management disputes rather than strikes and lockouts." Raudabaugh further asserted that contemporary legislative intent can be determined by more recent laws that foster labor-management cooperation, such as the National Productivity and Quality of Working Life Act of 1975 and the Labor Management Cooperation Act of 1978. In proposing a new test for evaluating EPPs under § 8(a)(2), Raudabaugh contended that his view was "not a rejection of collective bargaining and the underlying adversarial model but a recognition of changed statutory language making room for a variety of choices for shaping workplace relations with employee free choice charting the way."

Under Raudabaugh's proposed test, the following factors would be determinative:

> (1) the extent of the employer's involvement in the structure and operation of the committees; (2) whether the employees, from an objective standpoint, reasonably perceive the EPP as a substitute for full collective bargaining through a traditional union; (3) whether employees have been assured of their Section 7 rights to choose to

be represented by a traditional union under a system of full collective bargaining, and (4) the employer's motives in establishing the EPP.

Applying these four factors, Raudabaugh found that Electromation violated § 8(a)(2). He observed that Electromation controlled the formation, structure and organization of the action committees; that discussion focused around employee grievances; and that members of the action committees were reasonably perceived as representatives for the employees as a whole.

In summary, the Board held that representative employee participation groups that deal with management on conditions of employment are unlawful when established and dominated by management. The concurring opinions, however, emphasized the legality of, and support for, a variety of cooperative programs.

The Court of Appeals Decision

The Seventh Circuit Court of Appeals heard Electromation's petition to set aside the order of the NLRB in September 1993. As the company had already entered into a collective bargaining agreement with the union and did not wish to bear the cost of appeal, Ms. Brickley's law firm handled the case on a *pro bono* basis because of the importance of the issues.[93] Her colleague Brian J. Martin presented the oral argument on behalf of Electromation.

Linda Dreeben, then a supervisory attorney in the NLRB Appellate Court Branch, represented the agency.[94] Knowing that the Board regarded *Electromation* as a "big issue" at the time, she had requested the opportunity to work on the case.[95] Gary Witlen, Director of Legal Services for the International Brotherhood of Teamsters in Washington, presented the union's argument. According to Witlen, at one point in the oral argument the company's attorney told the court that the Board's *Electromation* decision was not the way Senator Wagner wanted the Act to be interpreted. Judge Hubert L. Will, who also authored the opinion of the court, responded "young man, I was on Senator Wagner's staff, and that is exactly the way he intended the Act to be interpreted."[96]

---

[93] Telephone Interview with Loretta Dickey on August 2, 2004.

[94] Dreeben joined the NLRB Appellate Court Branch upon graduation from law school and since 2000 has been the Deputy Branch Chief of the Appellate Court Branch. Her career includes appearances on behalf of the Board in eleven of the twelve circuit courts. Biographical information provided by e-mail from Linda Dreeben to the author on August 22, 2004.

[95] Telephone Interviews with Linda Dreeben on August 13 and August 27, 2004.

[96] Telephone Interview with Gary Witlen on July 29, 2004. Judge Will was a district judge for the Northern District of Illinois, sitting on the court of appeals by designation. He

Although the oral arguments took place in a low-key setting,[97] they received media attention. The *Chicago Tribune* noted that "the future of labor-management committees nationwide is now in the hands of a federal appeals court panel in Chicago, say manufacturing and business interests."[98]

A year later, on September 15, 1994, the court affirmed the Board's decision, concluding:

> [T]he principal distinction between an independent labor organization and an employer-dominated organization lies in the unfettered power of the independent organization to determine its own actions. . . . The Electromation action committees, which were wholly created by the employer, whose continued existence depended upon the employer, and whose functions were essentially determined by the employer, lacked the independence of action and free choice guaranteed by Section 7. This is not to suggest that Howard and the other management representatives were anti-union or had devious intentions in proposing the creation of the committees. But, even assuming they acted from good intentions, their procedure in establishing the committees, their control of the subject matters to be considered or excluded, their membership and participation on the committees, and their financial support of the committees all combined to make the committees labor organizations dominated by the employer in violation of the Act.[99]

In addition, however, the court made the following observation about the legitimacy of employee participation programs:

> [T]his case does not foreclose the lawful use of legitimate employee participation organization, especially those which are independent, which do not function in a representational capacity, and which focus solely on increasing company productivity, efficiency, and quality control, in appropriate settings. We agree with amici that the loss of these programs would not only be injurious to United States companies' ability to compete globally, but also that it would deprive employees of valuable mechanisms by which they can assist in the formation of a healthy and productive work environment. It is clear

---

served on Senator Wagner's staff in 1939. He was appointed to the bench by President Kennedy in 1961, assumed senior status in 1979, and served until his death in 1995.

97 Telephone Interview with Kathleen Brickley on August 2, 2004.

98 William Grady, *Court Weighs Labor–Management Groups,* Chi. Trib., Sept. 28, 1993, Sec. 3, at 1.

99 Electromation v. NLRB, 35 F.3d 1148, 1170–71 (7th Cir. 1994).

that today, in many cases, the interests of the employer and employee are not mutually exclusive.[100]

Electromation did not attempt to appeal this decision to the Supreme Court. According to its attorneys, the decision was not appealed because interested employer representatives decided instead to pursue legislative relief,[101] as further discussed below.

The Immediate Impact and Continuing Importance of Electromation

Both before and after *Electromation*, a flood of academic, legal, labor relations and media commentators discussed the case and its implications. Business and union representatives expressed strong reactions to the decision. The President of the Labor Policy Association, a public policy advocacy organization representing corporate America in governmental human resource policy,[102] stated that the *Electromation* decision placed "companies and their workers in a real bind." He explained that:

> They either continue workplace cooperation and live in fear of NLRB action against them, or they revert to the traditional form of labor-management relations in which employees only do what they are told. Yet, taking the latter course means that employees not only lose their autonomy, but their jobs are placed at risk because the company loses its competitive edge.[103]

The *Wall Street Journal* called the Board a "quality circle buster" that spent "its time patrolling the industrial landscape in search of anything that looks even vaguely like a 'company union.' " In contrast, Teamster President Ron Carey opined that "this ruling exposes management-dominated quality of work life programs for what they are: attempts to pit worker against worker and undermine workers' rights."[104] Views on the impact and significance of *Electromation* were highly diverse: "An NLRB Ruling on Labor–Management Panels Alarms Employers"[105], "Impact of Electromation Case Overrated NLRB's Devaney

---

[100] *Id.* at 1157.

[101] Telephone Interviews with Dan Rudy, on July 30, 2004, and Kathleen Brickley on August 2, 2004.

[102] *See* Brief for Labor Policy Association at 1. *See also* <www.hrpolicy.org/lpa/index.asp>.

[103] Jeffrey C. McGuiness, in *":Action Committees" Are Not Lawful "Communication Devices" But Employer–Dominated Labor Organizations, NLRB Holds*, 141 Lab. Rel. Rep. (BNA) 513 (Dec. 28, 1992).

[104] *Id.*

[105] *An NLRB Ruling on Labor–Management Panels Alarms Employers*, Wall St. J., Dec 29, 1992, at A1.

Says,"[106] "NLRB Muddies Regulatory Waters."[107]

Perhaps the media attention was prompted by the Board's activities suggesting that it would significantly reevaluate past interpretations of 8(a)(2).[108] The Board held oral arguments (rarely used), accepted amicus briefs, and reopened the record after conclusion of the oral arguments to accept additional amicus briefs. Board members made public statements while the case was still pending. Member Raudabaugh was reported as saying "I've been studying [the *Electromation* case], and studying it, and studying it because it's been made into a major deal"; member Devaney was quoted as saying "[The *Electromation* decision] is not out because it's a very difficult and complex issue, it will have a tremendous impact."[109]

Proposals to Modify 8(a)(2)

The TEAM Act and the Dunlop Commission

Three months after the Board's decision in *Electromation*, Wisconsin Republican Congressman Steve Gunderson and Kansas Republican Senator Nancy Kassebaum introduced the Teamwork for Employee and Managers (TEAM) Act of 1993.[110] Representative Gunderson asserted that EPPs were necessary for the survival of American business in the competitive global environment; that EPPs were widely appreciated across the United States; and that the Board's interpretation of § 8(a)(2) reflected turbulent labor relations of the 1930's, not the labor market of the 1990's.[111] The TEAM Act proposed the following qualifications to § 8(a)(2):

> Provided further, that it shall not constitute or be evidence of an unfair labor practice under this paragraph for any employer to establish, assist, maintain or participate in any organization or entity of any kind, in which employees participate to address matters of mutual interest, including issues of quality, productivity and efficiency, and which does not have, claim or seek authority to

---

[106] *Impact of* Electromation *Case Overrated NLRB's Devaney Says*, Daily Lab. Rep. (BNA) No. 15, at 1 (Jan. 26, 1993).

[107] Steve Gunderson, *NLRB Muddies Regulatory Waters*, Wall St. J., Feb. 1, 1993, at A10.

[108] Rafael Gely, *Where Are We Now?: Life After* Electromation, 15 Hofstra Lab. & Emp. L.J. 45, 45 (1997).

[109] *Id.*, and sources cited therein.

[110] H.R. 1529 and S. 669, 103rd Cong. (1993).

[111] *See* Statement by Rep. Gunderson and text of Teamwork for Employee and Managers Act, Daily Lab. Rep. (BNA) No. 20 at D-5 (Jan. 31, 1995).

> negotiate or enter into collective bargaining agreements with the employer or to amend existing collective bargaining agreements between the employer and any labor organization.[112]

The TEAM Act's stated purpose was to

> (1) protect legitimate employee involvement programs against governmental interference; (2) preserve existing protections against deceptive, coercive employer practices; and (3) permit legitimate employee involvement structures where workers may discuss issues involving terms and conditions of employment, to continue to evolve and proliferate.[113]

In March 1993, during the same time period as legislative efforts for the TEAM Act, the Clinton Administration, in response to *Electromation* and the Republican TEAM initiative,[114] appointed the Commission on the Future of Worker–Management Relations, chaired by John T. Dunlop, professor emeritus at Harvard and former Labor Secretary during the Ford Administration. The Administration charged the Commission to evaluate the current legal labor framework and bargaining procedures, as well as provide proposals to affect workplace productivity, employee participation, and labor-management cooperation positively. The Commission conducted numerous national hearings, sought and received a variety of studies, articles and viewpoints from business and labor groups, professional organizations, and individuals, and examined relevant agency complaints, investigations, cases and litigation. It issued a Fact Finding Report in May 1994 and a Final Report in December 1994.[115] Among other issues, the Commission considered *Electromation* and § 8(a)(2). The Commission concluded that § 8(a)(2) should be retained, but that Congress should "clarify" its meaning to ensure that EPPs would not be unlawful "where discussion of working conditions is incidental to the broad purposes of these programs," the employer's purpose is not to frustrate employee efforts to obtain independent representation, and employees are protected from retaliation for communicating their views and seeking outside expertise.[116]

---

112 H.R. 1529, 103rd Cong. (1993).

113 S. 669, 103rd Cong. (1993).

114 *See* Arthur J. Lewis, *Symposium: Current Critical Issues In Labor and Employment Law: Company Sponsored Employee Involvement: A Union Perspective*, 40 St. Louis L.J. 119 (1996).

115 U.S. Depts. of Labor and Commerce, Commission on the Future of Worker–Management Relations, Fact Finding Report (May 1994) and Report and Recommendations (Dec. 1994).

116 U.S. Depts. of Labor and Commerce, Commission on the Future of Worker–Management Relations, Report and Recommendations 8–9 (Dec. 1994).

The Dunlop Commission reports did not slow congressional efforts to adopt the TEAM Act, despite strong political disagreements over its provisions. Employer groups favored the Act, but unions considered it to be nothing more than a stilted attempt by the management lobby to dilute employees' rights and legalize a return of company unions of the 1930's.[117] In the November 1994 elections, Republicans gained control of the Senate and the House of Representatives, thereby changing the political dynamics considerably. Both houses subsequently passed the TEAM Act in votes split largely along party lines. The Senate passed the Act in September 1995 by a vote of fifty-three to forty-six, with fifty-one affirmative votes coming from Republicans and forty-five negative votes from Democrats.[118] The House of Representatives passed the Act in July 1996, by a vote of 221 to 202, with 206 affirmative votes by Republicans and 179 negative votes by Democrats.[119] However, President Clinton, owing a large political debt to organized labor, vetoed the bill,[120] stating:

> This legislation, rather than promoting genuine teamwork, would undermine the system of collective bargaining that has served this country so well for many decades. It would do this by allowing employers to establish company unions where no union currently exists and permitting company-dominated unions where employees are in the process of determining whether to be represented by a union. Rather than encouraging true workplace cooperation, this bill would abolish protections that ensure independent and democratic representation in the workplace.[121]

Electromation's Progeny

In May 1993, just six months after its *Electromation* decision, the Board decided *E.I. DuPont de Nemours & Co.*[122] The Board affirmed an ALJ's holding that six safety committees and one fitness committee were labor organizations under 2(5), and that the company dominated the formation and administration of the committees in violation of 8(a)(2). The Board offered additional rationale for the ALJ's decision to "provide

---

117 *See* Arthur J. Lewis, *Symposium: Current Critical Issues In Labor and Employment Law: Company Sponsored Employee Involvement: A Union Perspective*, 40 St. Louis L.J. 119 (1996).

118 *See* <www.senate.gov>.

119 *See* <www.clerk.house.gov>.

120 H.R. 743, 104th Cong. (1996).

121 54 Cong. Q. Wkly. 32 (Aug. 10, 1996). A summary of attempts to amend 8(a)(2) is contained in Charles Morris, *Will There Be a New Direction for American Industrial Relations?—A Hard Look at the TEAM Bill, The Sawyer Substitute Bill, and the Employee Involvement Bill,* 47 Lab. L.J. 89 (1996).

122 311 NLRB 893 (1993).

guidance for those seeking to implement lawful cooperative programs between employees and management.''[123]

DuPont was *Electromation*'s unionized sister case. The Chemical Workers Association had represented the clerical, production and maintenance employees at DuPont's plant in Deep Water, New Jersey, for about fifty years. In 1984, DuPont began experimenting with cooperative programs. The company established a number of committees that included management as well as bargaining unit employees. Making decisions by consensus, employees and management discussed conditions of work such as safety and incentive awards, and benefits, including employee picnic areas and jogging tracks. In June 1990, the Union filed unfair labor practice charges contending that the committees functioned as company-dominated labor organizations, and that the Company unlawfully bypassed the Union in dealing with them. The Board issued consolidated complaints in April 1991, and the case was tried in June 1991. The company denied that the committees dealt with it as representatives of the employees, contending that the committees functioned only as a management vehicle to enhance safety through communication or ''similar management functions.''

In considering the first-step question of whether the *DuPont* committees were ''labor organizations'' within the meaning of 8(a)(2), the Board concentrated on the ''dealing with'' issue. Again relying on the Supreme Court's holding in *Cabot Carbon,* the Board stated that ''dealing with'' ''involves only a bilateral mechanism between two parties.''[124] The Board added that a

> bilateral mechanism ordinarily entails a pattern or practice in which a group of employees, over time, makes proposals to management, management responds to these proposals by acceptance or rejection by word or deed, and compromise is not required. If the evidence establishes such a pattern or practice, or that the group exists for a purpose of following such a pattern or practice, the element of dealing is present. However if there are only isolated instances in which the group makes ad hoc proposals to management followed by a management response of acceptance or rejection by word or deed, the element of dealing is missing.

The Board suggested several safe havens that would not meet this definition of ''dealing with,'' including brainstorming sessions, suggestion boxes, information gathering committees, and committees that plan educational seminars. The opinion further noted:

---

[123] *Id.*

[124] *Id.* at 894, *citing Electromation* at n.21.

> The mere presence, however, of management members on a committee would not necessarily result in a finding that the committee deals with the employer within the meaning of Section 2(5). For example, there would be no "dealing with" management if the committee were governed by majority decision-making, management representatives were in the minority, and the committee had the power to decide matters for itself, rather than simply make proposals to management. Similarly, there would be no "dealing" if management representatives participated on the committee as observers or facilitators without the right to vote on committee proposals.

The DuPont committees, said the Board, went too far because management representatives interacted with employee committee members under rules of consensus decisionmaking, and could reject employee proposals. Therefore, the committees were "dealing with" the employer within the meaning of § 2(5).

In the second step of the Board's two-pronged analysis, the Board found that management "dominated" the administration of these committees within the meaning of 8(a)(2). As noted above, management retained veto power over any committee action because decisions were by consensus. In addition, a management member served as either the leader or the resource person for each committee, and therefore played a key role in establishing agendas and conducting meetings. Management also controlled how many employees could serve on the committee, and which employee volunteers would be selected if there were an excess number of volunteers. The employees had no voice in determining any aspect of the composition, structure, or operation of the committees. Moreover, management could change or abolish any of the committees at will. The Board held that these procedures constituted company domination over the administration of the committees in violation of § 8(a)(2).

Member Devaney joined the majority, but again, as in *Electromation*, wrote a concurring opinion. He emphasized that the company attempted to freeze the union out of areas in which it had vital and legal interests, such as health, safety, bonuses, and grievances. He found that the company manipulated the employee committees "to weaken and undermine the employees' freely chosen exclusive bargaining agent." This behavior contrasted with certain safety meetings that the Board found to be lawful because employees were encouraged to raise their own issues and propose their own ideas while "bargainable" issues were tabled. Devaney attempted to use the company's conduct in the two employee participation settings to "outline the boundaries of lawful activity under section 8(a)(2)."[125]

[125] Dennis M. Devaney, *Much Ado About Section 8(a)(2): The NLRB and Workplace Cooperation after* Electromation *and* Du Pont, 23 Stetson L. Rev. 39, 48 (1993).

> Section 8(a)(2) should not create obstacles for employers wishing to implement such plans—as long as such programs do not impair employees' free choice of a bargaining representative. Section 8(a)(2) does not ban agenda-setting, establishing or dissolving committees, or mixing managers and statutory employees on a committee. It does, however, outlaw manipulating such committees so that they appear to be agents and representatives of employees when in fact they are not.

Board decisions subsequent to *Electromation* and *DuPont* have reaffirmed their holdings while providing additional guidance for employers. The Board has made clear that a single incident of "dealing with" would not make an otherwise lawful committee illegal.[126] It has upheld the legality of groups limited to communication of operational concerns, such as safety, quality and efficiency, on the ground they were not "labor organizations"[127] and permitted a committee limited to reviewing and filtering employee suggestions for management consideration.[128] More recently, the Board found lawful committees that included management and employees, had substantial authority, and made managerial decisions by consensus vote.[129]

Electromation, DuPont and their progeny continue to curtail employer domination of representative employee groups. However, contrary to the critical views of *Electromation* discussed above, these cases do not outlaw most existing employee participation programs aimed at productivity and efficiency. Rather, the opinions support such programs when limited to productivity, quality and efficiency, or when negotiated through collective bargaining. Worker participation programs remain a vital part of American industry today,[130] and continue unabated as long as they address product quality, productivity, or matters such as customer relations, rather than working conditions.[131] A study by James Rundle

---

126 Vons Grocery Co., 320 NLRB 53 (1995).

127 Simmons Industries, Inc., 321 NLRB 228 (1996).

128 EFCO Corp., 327 NLRB 372 (1998).

129 Crown Cork & Seal Co., 334 NLRB 699 (2001).

130 *See, e.g.*, Note, *Cooperation or Co-optation: When Does a Union Become Employer–Dominated Under Section 8(a)(2) of the National Labor Relations Act?,* 100 Colum. L. Rev. 1022 (2000); Michael H. LeRoy, *Employee Participation in the New Millennium: Redefining a Labor Organization Under Section 8(a)(2) of the NLRA*, 72 S. Cal. L. Rev. 1651 (1999); Michael H. LeRoy, *"Dealing With" Employee Involvement in Nonunion Workplaces: Empirical Research Implications for the TEAM Act and* Electromation, 73 Notre Dame L. Rev. 31 (1997); Marley S. Weiss, *Innovations in Collective Bargaining: Nummi—Driven to Excellence,* 13 Hofstra Lab. L.J. 433 (1996).

131 *See, e.g.,* H. Victoria Hedian, *The Implications of* Crown Cork & Seal Co. *For Employee Involvement Committees as "Labor Organizations" Under the Wagner Act: What*

of Cornell University found that during the previous twenty-two years the NLRB issued only fifty-eight decisions ordering the disbanding of employee committees under 8(a)(2). In fifty-six of the fifty-eight cases, the committees were established during organizing drives or by employers who committed other unfair labor practices. Rundle stated that "There is absolutely no evidence that the NLRB has ever, in the past 22 years, disestablished a committee of the type employers say they must have to be competitive."[132]

Edward B. Miller, a well-known management attorney who served as Chair of the Board during the Nixon administration, made the following comments after the *Electromation* decision:

> It is indeed possible to have effective [employee participation] programs in both union and non-union companies without the necessity of any change in current law.... While I represent management, I do not kid myself.... If section 8(a)(2) were to be repealed, I have no doubt that in not too many months or years sham company unions would again recur.[133]

Conclusion

Professors Harper, Estreicher and Flynn have concluded that "Section 8(a)(2) has largely eliminated collective bargaining with company unions."[134] The courts and NLRB now rarely hear cases in which the employer has established a company union of the sort addressed by early cases such as *Greyhound, Newport News* and *Cabot Carbon*. Professor Stanley Henderson documented this phenomenon:

> There has ... been a sharp decline in blatant employer abuses, and thus in overall 8(a)(2) charges. In 1993, for example, only 4.2 percent of the 24,000 unfair labor practice cases against employers included allegations of 8(a)(2) violation. In fiscal 1998, just 2.3 percent of the 23,600 8(a) filings against employers involved 8(a)(2). Such charges accounted for approximately 20 percent of the complaint proceedings against employers during the years immediately following passage of the Wagner Act.[135]

Constitutes "Dealing With" Pursuant to Section 2(5) of the Act Since Electromation, Inc.?, 18 Lab. Law. 235 (2002).

132 James Rundle, *The Debate Over the Ban on Employer-Dominated Labor Organizations: What is the Evidence?, in Restoring the Promise of American Labor Law* 173 (1994)

133 *Former NLRB Chairman Miller Calls Electromation Problem "Myth,"* Daily Lab. Rep. (BNA) No. 201, at A-5 (Oct. 20, 1993).

134 Michael Harper, Samuel Estreicher & Joan Flynn, *Labor Law* 259 (5th ed. 2003).

135 Stanley Henderson, *Labor Law* 235–36 (2001) (internal citations omitted).

Similarly, in fiscal year 2003, 2.3 percent of the 21,765 8(a) filings against employers involved 8(a)(2).[136] Perhaps even more importantly, of almost 12,000 cases in which remedial action was taken, only six cases involved 8(a)(2).[137] Of course, such statistics do not measure instances in which employers have established employee representation programs in violation of *Electromation* that remain unseen by the NLRB because of the absence of union organizing efforts at those workplaces.

The longstanding concern over company unions has not become moot. While typically less overt, employee participation programs raise the same concerns about employer domination or interference that § 8(a)(2) was intended to counter. In this sense, the NLRB in *Electromation* addressed a conundrum. It did not want unnecessarily to disadvantage American industry in a changing global economic environment, nor did it want employers to exploit the use of employee participation programs and circumvent § 8(a)(2) simply by proclaiming the need for American competitiveness. The Board successfully resolved this conundrum by establishing criteria that allow companies to establish needed EPPs without infringing on employee rights.

Interestingly, the union, Board and management representatives who argued *Electromation* agree that the case has had an impact, in that 8(a)(2) complaints are few and employers have not had undue difficulty operating within *Electromation*'s perimeters. Teamsters' attorneys Wallington and Witlen, as well as NLRB attorneys Lineback and Dreeben, report that 8(a)(2) cases are now extremely rare. Witlen saw the United Parcel Service abandon an effort to establish committees independent of the collective bargaining structure in the wake of the Board decisions. Kathleen Brickley, who represented Electromation, concluded that the case had an impact, especially upon larger companies, which made appropriate changes to comply with the law.[138] As Professor Henderson stressed, "8(a)(2) is no obstacle to a wide range of efforts to elicit employee participation or experimentation with tactics aimed at achieving greater cooperation."[139]

In the late 1980's and early 1990's there seemed to be a loud and unanimous cry from American employers that 8(a)(2), a little piece of New Deal legislation, had to be repealed or substantially modified to permit American companies to compete in the emerging global economy.

---

136 68 NLRB Ann. Rep. 126 (2003).

137 *Id.* at 133.

138 Telephone Interviews with James Wallington on August 13, 2004 and Gary Witlen, July 29, 2004; Interviews with Rik Lineback on August 5, 2004; with Linda Dreeben on August 13, 2004; with Kathleen Brickley on August 2, 2004.

139 Stanley Henderson, *Labor Law (Teacher's Manual)* 47 (2001)

Although powerful efforts were amassed to challenge 8(a)(2) at the NLRB, in the U.S. Congress and in the courts, they all failed. Despite their failure, the prediction that the provision would impair American economic competitiveness has been proven wrong. In 2004, American workers, constituting five percent of the global workforce, were producing thirty percent of the world's output. Japanese workers are only seventy-four percent as productive as Americans and European workers are only eighty-four percent as productive.[140] American productivity has risen at an annual rate roughly twice that of Europe since the mid–1990's.[141]

With 8(a)(2) in place, as interpreted in *Electromation*, non-union employers, as a practical matter, remain free to establish employee representation plans. Even unlawful plans are not likely to be challenged in the absence of a union organizing drive, and even if challenged, at most the employer risks a Board order to disestablish the committee. In those situations where a union seeks to organize such a workplace and views the committees as an impediment to its organizational effort, *Electromation* allows the union to seek Board assistance to remove the barrier. Senator Wagner's 8(a)(2) has survived the crucible and demonstrated its continuing wisdom in the twenty-first century.

---

140 Mark J. Perry, *Labor Day*, Milwaukee J. Sentinel, Sept. 5, 2004, at 6J.

141 Christopher, Rhoads, *U.S., EU Productivity Gap is Widening*, Wall. St. J., Jan. 19, 2004, at A2.

*

9

Marley S. Weiss

Kentucky River at the Intersection of Professional and Supervisory Status: Fertile Delta or Bermuda Triangle?

Introduction

On January 27, 1997, the Kentucky State District Council of Carpenters, AFL–CIO, petitioned Region Nine of the National Labor Relations Board (NLRB) for a representation election at the Caney Creek Rehabilitation Complex. Caney Creek was a psychiatric rehabilitation facility, owned and operated by Kentucky River Community Care, Inc. (KRCC), a non-profit organization. The union sought to represent all employees except guards, clerical and administrative employees, and supervisors, who are excluded by § 2(11) of the National Labor Relations Act (NLRA) from its protections.[1] The union's most important strategic consideration was to ensure that the rehabilitation counselors, borderline professional employees, were included in the bargaining unit. These workers strongly supported the unionization effort. Rehabilitation counselor Glenn Moore was doing the lion's share of organizing the workplace from within.[2] In the union's view, the rehabilitation counselors and

[1] Petition, Ky. River Cmty. Care, Inc., NLRB Case No. 9–RC–16837.

[2] The description in this chapter of the union's perspective is based on a telephone interview with Carpenters Union counsel Thomas J. Schulz, October 1, 2004 and a telephone interview with Carpenters Union Supreme Court counsel, AFL–CIO Associate General Counsel Craig Becker, December 17, 2004. The description of AFL–CIO advocacy from the mid–1990's onwards is based on the telephone interview with Becker, as well as a telephone interview with AFL–CIO Associate General Counsel Jim Coppess, December 17,

nurses working at Caney Creek were non-supervisory professional employees whose right to join unions is explicitly protected by § 2(12) of the NLRA.

There were three strategic prongs to the employer's response, two legal and one practical: (1) try to avoid having any election at all by claiming to be exempt from the National Labor Relations Act (NLRA); (2) try to exclude as many workers as possible from the bargaining unit, particularly pro-union voters such as Glenn Moore and his rehabilitation counselor coworkers, by claiming that they were supervisors; (3) try to defeat the union in the election. Initially, KRCC failed on all three fronts. Following established NLRB case law, the Regional Director ruled against all of KRCC's arguments. The union won an overwhelming victory at the polls, even though the employer fired Moore and other union activists during the campaign.

The Sixth Circuit, however, in which KRCC was located, had harshly criticized NLRB formulations of the fundamental distinction between non-supervisory health care professionals and supervisors holding professional credentials who exercise significant discretion and authority over subordinates in personnel matters. Nevertheless, in the appellate court, the employer only prevailed to the extent of excluding the six registered nurses (RNs) from the overall bargaining unit. KRCC was unable to overturn the certification as to the other ninety-five percent of the workforce. The union would have happily declared victory, and begun bargaining. The employer would have accepted its modest partial victory, and pursued passive resistance at the bargaining table. Exclusion of six RNs from a 100 employee unit was not critical to either side. The NLRB petitioned for certiorari, despite the risk of an adverse outcome. However, the NLRB lost the case and did not get the legal clarity it sought. Rather, in *NLRB v. Kentucky River Community Care,* the Supreme Court rejected the Board's rule that professionals are not supervisors if the only form of authority they exercise is to use judgment based on their professional training in directing less skilled coworkers in the delivery of services, pursuant to standards set by the employer. Although the Court rejected the NLRB's rule, it did not articulate one of its own and did little to clarify the very uncertain line between professional

2004. The description of the employer's perspective is based upon telephone interviews with Kentucky River's lawyers, George J. Miller on December 17, 2004, and Michael W. Hawkins on January 13, 2005. The description of the NLRB's perspective is based on a telephone interview with former General Counsel Fred Feinstein, December 16, 2004; a telephone interview with former General Counsel Leonard R. Page, February 16, 2004; an interview with former Member Sarah M. Fox in Silver Spring, Maryland, August 28, 2004; a telephone interview with former Member Fox, December 17, 2004; an interview with former Member John E. Higgins, Jr. in Silver Spring, Maryland, August 28, 2004; and a telephone interview with Associate General Counsel John H. Ferguson, December 17, 2004.

employees who provide some direction to non-professional subordinates, and supervisors who are also professionals.[3]

This chapter will tell the story of how the Supreme Court arrived at its construction of § 2(11) in a ruling which opened up as many questions as it resolved, on the basis of facts barely related to the adjudicated legal issues. It will consider future interpretation of § 2(11) and the *Kentucky River* decision's impact upon the broad structure of organizing and bargaining under the NLRA. It also will describe the NLRB's clear victory on the question of the burden of proof. This sleeper issue, to which other litigants paid little attention, may have significant consequences for all of the exclusions from NLRA coverage.

Social and Legal Background

Kentucky River merged two streams of social and legal history: the branch differentiating between rank and file and supervisory workers, and the tributary on NLRA applicability to the health care industry. This chapter next will review the antecedents of today's issues, first, in the Wagner Act treatment of craft and industrial supervisors, next, in the adoption of the Taft–Hartley amendments, and then, in the checkered sequence of NLRA coverage and exclusion of health care employers. The two streams combined in a 1994 case about the supervisory status of nursing home charge nurses, *NLRB v. Health Care & Retirement Corp. of America (HCR)*, discussion of which will follow. *HCR* sets the stage for *Kentucky River*, which will be considered thereafter.

The Battle Over Unionization of Supervisors

How § 2(11) Came To Be: (1) Wagner Act Treatment of Foremen's Unionization

Initially, the Wagner Act did not explicitly exempt supervisors from the statutory definition of employees protected by the Act. The rise and fall of unions of foremen is a fascinating story, which led directly to enactment of the Taft–Hartley amendments that deprived supervisors of the right to unionize while protecting the right of professionals to do so.[4] The maritime, metal, building and printing trades of the American

[3] NLRB v. Ky. River Cmty. Care, Inc., 532 U.S. 706 (2001).

[4] This history of the treatment of supervisors prior to adoption of the Taft–Hartley Act draws upon the following contemporary sources: Ernest Dale, *The American Foreman Unionizes*, 19 J. Bus. U. Chi. 25 (Jan. 1946); Walter L. Daykin, *The Status of Supervisory Employees under the National Labor Relations Act*, 29 Iowa L. Rev. 297 (1944); David Levinson, *Foremen's Unions and the Law*, 1950 Wis. L. Rev. 79; Herbert R. Northrup, *Unionization of Foremen*, 21 Harv. Bus. Rev. 496 (1943); Russell A. Smith, *Labor Law—Some Developments During the Past Five Years (A Service for Returning Veterans)*, 44 Mich. L. Rev. 1089, 1109–12 (1946); Comment, *Rights of Supervisory Employees to Collective Bargaining under the National Labor Relations Act*, 55 Yale L.J. 754 (1946);

Federation of Labor (AFL) had long included all members of the occupation, regardless of managerial level. This tradition continued after enactment of the 1935 Wagner Act. In the 1930's and early 1940's, the recently-founded Congress of Industrial Organizations (CIO) organized factory-wide "production and maintenance" units in mass production, the growth sector of industry. Union membership quintupled from three million to fifteen million between 1935 and 1947.[5] As unions won collective bargaining agreements improving wages and working conditions of factory workers, however, front-line supervisors found that their own position had deteriorated compared to their subordinates. This led in the early 1940's to large-scale unionization by manufacturing foremen. Unionization threatened to shift the allegiance of foremen to the working class, depriving employers of loyal front-line agents and potentially impairing operational efficiency. Manufacturing firms depended on their foremen to enforce discipline and productivity in harsh, unsafe, repetitive assembly line jobs. Union-based loyalty to the interests of the workers could subvert the supervisor's enforcement of policies aimed at extracting increased productivity and discipline. Unionized foremen also might strike with the rank and file, or honor their picket lines.

Under the Wagner Act, placement of supervisors in the NLRA scheme arose in three different contexts: (1) whether a foreman's anti-union conduct could be imputed to the employer for purposes of establishing employer liability for unfair labor practices (ULPs); (2) protection of foremen as employees against employer anti-union discrimination; and (3) foremen's organizing and bargaining rights. Although the statutory text has been amended, the problem of the treatment of supervisors continues to arise today in each of these distinct settings. As a matter of statutory construction, the Board had to decide whether the foremen fell under the § 2(2) definition of "employer," the § 2(3) definition of "employee," or both at once, in each of the three contexts. The Wagner Act definition of "employer" in § 2(2) expansively provided: "The term 'employer' includes any person acting in the interest of an employer, directly or indirectly." The § 2(3) definition of "employee" in the Wagner Act was either extremely broad or else vague and was, in any event, circular; it simply stated that: "The term 'employee' shall include any employee."

Note, *The Status of Supervisory Personnel under the NLRA*, 59 Harv. L. Rev. 606 (1946); Martin Bordon, Note, *Labor Law: Right of Supervisory Employees to Bargain Collectively Under Provisions of the National Labor Relations Act*, 34 Cal. L. Rev. 245 (1946); Edwin R. Fischer, Note, *Problem of the Propriety of a Foreman's Union*, 34 Geo. L.J. 89 (1946); Note, *Collective Bargaining By Supervisory Employees Under the Wagner Act*, 13 U. Chi. L. Rev. 332 (1946). *See also* Joseph E. Moore, *The National Labor Relations Board and Supervisors*, 21 Lab. L.J. 195 (1970).

[5] *See, e.g.*, David Brody, *Workers in Industrial America: Essays on the Twentieth Century Struggle* 157 (2d ed. 1993).

Acts of first-level supervisors were consistently treated as binding the employer for ULP purposes, so long as no issue of foremen's unionization was on the horizon.[6] Thus, if a foreman made an anti-union statement, the law would impute the statement to the employer, and the employer might be liable for a ULP. When the foremen acted in their own collective interests, however, or contrary to instructions from higher management, and in the interests of rank and file workers, their actions were not attributed to management under § 2(2). On the contrary, when foremen claimed to be victims of employer discrimination based on their own union activities, they were held to be protected as § 2(3) "employees." The dual role theory prevailed:

> There is no inconsistency [between Sections 2(2) and 2(3)].... A foreman, in his relation to his employer, is an employee, while in his relation to the laborers under him he is the representative of the employer and within the definition of Section 2(2) of the Act. Nothing in the Act excepts foremen from its benefits nor from protection against discrimination nor unfair labor practices of the master.[7]

The clarity of the dual role approach, however, evaporated when it came to determining collective bargaining units under § 9. In early cases involving craft unions which had traditionally included supervisors, they were deemed statutory "employees" entitled to organize. Absent such a history, however, the Board excluded supervisors from bargaining units of ordinary workers.[8] The Board vacillated over certification of separate units of foremen in manufacturing. In 1942, in *Union Collieries Coal Co.*,[9] the NLRB held that foremen were § 2(3) employees, with the right to organize and bargain. Member Reilly dissented, stressing that unionized foremen could both deprive employees of the free choice of union representative, either in the interest of the foremen themselves or in their employer's interest, and also deprive the company of the foremen's full loyalty in disciplining and supervising subordinates. Six months later, in *Maryland Drydock Co.*,[10] Member Reilly wrote for a new NLRB majority, and held against further certification of foremen's bargaining units. Without resolving the question whether foremen were entirely excluded from the definition of employee in § 2(3), the Board asserted

---

6 *See, e.g.*, Int'l Ass'n of Machinists v. NLRB, 311 U.S. 72, 79–80 (1940); H.J. Heinz Co. v. NLRB, 311 U.S. 514, 518–21 (1941); NLRB v. Link-Belt Co., 311 U.S. 584, 598–99 (1941).

7 NLRB v. Skinner & Kennedy Stationery Co., 113 F.2d 667, 671 (8th Cir. 1940).

8 *See* Walter L. Daykin, *The Status of Supervisory Employees Under the National Labor Relations Act*, 29 Iowa L. Rev. 297, 301, 311–13, 317–19 (1944) (collecting cases).

9 41 NLRB 961 (1942); 44 NLRB 165 (1942) (supp. op.).

10 49 NLRB 733 (1943).

that it had wide discretion under § 9 to determine that an appropriate bargaining unit could not include supervisors, except in industries where pre-Wagner Act traditions supported unionization. For a brief period, the Board attempted to hold that supervisors were "employees" protected against anti-union reprisals by their employer but that they could not unionize under § 9.[11] However, it proved difficult to sustain the position that foremen were full-fledged "employees" against whom ULP violations of §§ 8(1), 8(3), and 8(4) could be committed, yet they had no § 7 rights to organize under NLRB § 9 auspices, and employers could not violate § 8(5) by refusing to bargain with foremen's unions. Shortly thereafter, in *Packard Motor Car Co.*,[12] one Board member reversed his position, and the Board restored the right of low-level supervisors to organize in a separate unit.

Mass production employers did not acquiesce in the new approach. Packard itself refused to comply, and the Board successfully petitioned for enforcement in the Court of Appeals. The Supreme Court affirmed, accepting the dual status theory, reasoning that the Board had correctly held that the plain language of § 2(3) dictated treating foremen as "employees" with respect to their own terms and conditions of employment, with full rights, including organizing and bargaining. In dissent, Justice Douglas rejected the dual status concept, noting the employer's dilemma when "[a]n act of a foreman, if attributed to the management, constitutes an unfair labor practice; the same act may be part of the foreman's activity as an employee. In that event the employer can only interfere at his peril." The Wagner Act was intended, he reasoned, to protect "the right of free association—the right to bargain collectively—by the great mass of workers, not by those who were in authority over them and enforcing oppressive industrial policies."[13] Contemporaneously with *Packard*, the Board and the Court had broadly defined "employee" in two other, related contexts: plant guards and independent contractors.[14] All three issues—treatment of foremen, contractors, and plant security staff—were regarded by corporations as unduly expanding their

---

[11] Soss Mfg. Co., 56 NLRB 348 (1944).

[12] Packard Motor Car Co., 61 NLRB 4 (1945) (separate unit represented by independent union). *See also* Packard Motor Car Co., 64 NLRB 1212 (1945) (rejecting employer's challenge to certification on ground of union affiliation with rank and file union); L.A. Young Spring & Wire Corp., 65 NLRB 298 (1946) (unit of higher levels of supervisors); Jones & Laughlin Steel Corp., 66 NLRB 386 (1946) (one union representing two separate units).

[13] Packard Motor Car Co. v. NLRB, 330 U.S. 485, 489–92 (1947); *id.* at 497, 499 (Douglas, J., dissenting).

[14] NLRB v. Jones & Laughlin Steel Corp., 331 U.S. 416 (1947) (plant guards); NLRB v. E.C. Atkins & Co., 331 U.S. 398 (1947) (plant guards); NLRB v. Hearst Publ'ns, Inc., 322 U.S. 111 (1944) (independent contractors).

duty to bargain collectively and disrupting their ability to operate efficiently.

How § 2(11) Came To Be: (2) Congress Reacts by Enacting the Taft–Hartley Amendments

By the end of World War II, the labor relations tide had turned.[15] Although wartime efforts to prevent unionization of foremen, including the Smith bills of 1943, had failed for lack of support, in 1946 the Republicans took control of Congress and adopted an omnibus overhaul of the NLRA (known as the Case bill) that excluded most foremen from organizing rights. The bill passed Congress, but was vetoed by President Truman; Congress lacked the votes to override.[16] The next year, Congress adopted the Taft–Hartley Act. President Truman vetoed this bill as well, but this time, Congress overrode the veto. The foremen's union drives, especially a strike of the Foremen's Association of America while congressional debate was in progress, provided pivotal impetus for Congress' adoption of the overlapping set of provisions on employee and supervisory status.

The Taft–Hartley Act neither adopted the Smith bill approach of outright prohibition against foremen organizing, nor the two-tier approach of the Case bill, which would have preserved bargaining rights only for foremen in industries with a pre-NLRA history of unionized foremen. Instead, the law eliminated supervisors from *all* NLRA rights, by excluding them from the § 2(3) definition of covered "employee." Employers were free to "prohibit supervisors from [union] membership because Congress believed that granting supervisors a protected right to join a union [would] be 'inconsistent with the policy of Congress to assure workers freedom from domination or control by their supervisors' and 'inconsistent with our policy to protect the rights of employers.' "[17]

---

[15] On Taft–Hartley Act history, in addition to historical sources already cited, this chapter draws upon David Brody, *Workers in Industrial America: Essays on the Twentieth Century Struggle* (2d ed. 1993); James A. Gross, *The Reshaping of the National Labor Relations Board: National Labor Policy in Transition, 1937–1947* (1981); R. Alton Lee, *Truman and Taft–Hartley: A Question of Mandate* (1966); Harry A. Millis & Emily Clark Brown, *From the Wagner Act to Taft–Hartley: A Study of National Labor Policy and Labor Relations* (1950); and Christopher L. Tomlins, *The State and the Unions: Labor Relations, Law, and the Organized Labor Movement in America, 1880–1960* (1985), as well as NLRB, *Legislative History of the Labor Management Relations Act, 1947* (Reprint ed. 1985) [hereinafter *Legis. Hist.*].

[16] The Smith bills were H.R. 2239, 78th Cong. (1943) and H.R. 1996, 78th Cong. (1943). The Case bill was H.R. 4908, 79th Cong. (1946). *See* H.R. Rep. No. 80–245, at 8, 17 (1947), *reprinted in* 1 *Legis. Hist.* at 299, 308. President Truman's veto message is reprinted at 1946 U.S.Code Cong. Serv. 1686.

[17] NLRB v. Int'l Bhd. of Elec. Workers, Local 340, 481 U.S. 573, 593 n.17 (1987) (quoting H.R. Rep. No. 80–245, at 14 (1947), *reprinted in* 1 *Legis. Hist.* at 305).

At the same time, a new § 14(a) disclaimed any prohibition against "voluntary" collective bargaining for supervisors. Where employers and unions with supervisor members found it in their mutual interest, they could bargain collectively, albeit outside NLRB auspices. This avoided any contention that the law violated the asserted constitutional rights of supervisors to organize.[18]

The Taft–Hartley framers were eager to address the conflicting obligations Wagner Act dual role case law had imposed upon employers. In fact, Taft–Hartley solved some of these problems twice over. Besides excluding supervisors in § 2(3), Congress insulated from union pressure the employer's control over those of its supervisors permitted by the employer pursuant to § 14(a) to have union representation. In § 8(b)(1)(B), Congress limited union disciplinary pressures upon unionized supervisors aimed at influencing the supervisors' representation of management's position in responding to employee grievances, and restricted union pressures aimed at management's selection of supervisors to handle grievances or perform collective bargaining-related functions. Congress narrowed § 2(2) to cut back the range of workers whose acts could be imputed to the employer as to alleged ULPs. The definition of employer was changed from "any person acting in the interest of an employer" to "any person acting as an agent of an employer."

At the heart of Taft–Hartley was its response to business outrage at the expansive construction of the term "employee." Congress amended the § 2(3) definition to exclude both "supervisors" and "independent contractors." New, cross-referenced definitions were inserted in § 2, legislatively overruling the Supreme Court. At the same time, Congress rejected employer efforts to exclude professional employees and plant security staff, two groups employers had analogized to supervisors, based on management's need for their undivided loyalty as well as their different class allegiance and higher status compared to laborers. Congress did not adopt the Smith bill formulation for supervisory exclusion, which would have barred from unionizing "any individual employed in a bona fide executive, administrative, professional, or supervisory capacity."[19] Instead, Congress inserted a definition of "professional" in § 2(12) and amended the representation provisions of § 9 to provide that professional and non-professional employees could not be combined in a single bargaining unit unless a majority of the professionals voted in favor of inclusion. After Taft–Hartley, outside of fields with a pre-NLRA tradi-

---

18 Comment, *Rights of Supervisory Employees to Collective Bargaining under the National Labor Relations Act*, 55 Yale L.J. 754, 766 (1946) (relying upon Tex. & New Orleans R.R. v. Bhd. of Ry. & S.S. Clerks, 281 U.S. 548 (1930) and Gompers v. Bucks Stove & Range Co., 221 U.S. 418 (1911)).

19 H.R. 1996, 78th Cong. (1943). *See also* H.R. 2239, 78th Cong., § 4 (1943).

tion of union representation of foremen, few businesses "voluntarily" allowed their foremen to join rank and file bargaining units or to organize separately. Rather, they addressed the sources of foremen's discontent by upgrading front-line supervisors and making them feel more a part of management. The Foremen's Association of America rapidly withered away.

The statutory exclusion of supervisors has provided a whole new arena for litigation-related delays. The amendment presumed that a bright line could be drawn between supervisory and non-supervisory staff. It also presupposed that the organization of jobs and allocation of supervisory functions would not be altered by management with an eye to labor law consequences. These assumptions, however, had been debunked by commentators well before enactment of Taft–Hartley.[20] The 1947 redefinition of "employee" encouraged employers to label even low-level workers as supervisors and to reorganize job responsibilities for reasons unrelated to economic performance simply to maximize statutory exclusions. More recently, that definition has rewarded litigation seeking to broaden the definition of supervisor within newer forms of work organization, excluding expanding categories of workers. These developments have been especially evident among professionals in the health care industry. Before considering precisely who is a "supervisor" in light of Taft–Hartley, however, we first review NLRA coverage and exclusion of health care, which has strongly influenced interpretation of § 2(11).

Belated NLRA Coverage of Health Care and Its Consequences for Organizing

Exclusion, and Re–Inclusion of Health Care Institutions Under the NLRA

Eliminating supervisors and independent contractors was not the only way Congress changed NLRA coverage in Taft–Hartley. The original Wagner Act covered health care employers, but the 1947 legislation excluded most of the industry. It amended the § 2(2) definition of "employer" to exempt non-profit hospitals.[21] It was not until the Health Care Amendments Act of 1974[22] that coverage was restored for all private sector health care employers. Section 2(14) was added, defining "health care institution." Special restrictions on strikes against health

---

[20] For example, Comment, *Rights of Supervisory Employees to Collective Bargaining Under the National Labor Relations Act,* 55 Yale L.J. 754, 770–71 (1946).

[21] Section 2(2) excluded "any corporation or association operating a hospital if no part of the net earnings inures to the benefit of any private shareholder or individual." Pub. L. No. 80–101, § 101, 61 Stat. 136 (1947).

[22] Pub. L. No. 93–360, 88 Stat. 395 (1974).

care employers were imposed. Congress recognized that "the needs of patients in health care institutions required special consideration"—essentially, greater protection against disruption of patient care in the course of labor disputes.[23] Subsequent cases regarding solicitation and distribution of union literature likewise have recognized this priority.[24] Strikes interrupting the delivery of health care were a major impetus behind restoration of NLRA coverage. Congressional testimony indicated that ninety-five percent of strikes in non-profit hospitals had been recognitional. Resuming NLRA coverage was expected to reduce recognitional strikes by providing NLRB machinery for establishing enforceable union representation rights. The special rules regulating health care industry work stoppages were intended to encourage peaceful resolution of disputes over new agreements. Congress also hoped that collective bargaining would improve wages and benefits in the industry, and lead to better-qualified workers and higher standards of patient care.[25]

By the time the health care amendments had been adopted, however, the labor relations climate among employers, legislatures, courts, and the NLRB was less favorable to collective bargaining, compared to earlier decades, and more delay was to ensue. Seventeen years of litigation over appropriate units in health care institutions followed adoption of the 1974 amendments, dampening union organizing, especially among RNs and other professionals.[26] Health care is unusual in having a heavy composition of diverse state-licensed professionals, each with a scope of practice and professional responsibility governed by state law, and with highly distinct professional identities. Many technical occupations are likewise state-regulated. The patient-care occupations are arranged in a strict education-based status hierarchy, with doctors on top, registered nurses, technologists, and other professionals below them, LPNs, technicians, and other technical employees underneath them, and nurses aides and other service employees at the bottom.[27] Eventually, the NLRB held

---

[23] S. Rep. No. 93–766, at 3 (1974). The provisions are NLRA §§ 2(14), 8(d), 8(g); LMRA § 213.

[24] *See* NLRB v. Baptist Hosp., Inc., 442 U.S. 773 (1979); Beth Israel Hosp. v. NLRB, 437 U.S. 483 (1978).

[25] *See* H.R. Rep. No. 93–1051, at 4 (1974); S. Rep. No. 93–766, at 3 (1974). *See also Beth Israel Hosp.*, 437 U.S. at 497–98 & nn. 14–15 and legislative sources cited therein.

[26] The discussion regarding appropriate bargaining units in health care facilities is based on the the Supreme Court opinion in the rulemaking case, Am. Hosp. Ass'n v. NLRB, 499 U.S. 606 (1991), the underlying rulemaking proceedings, 52 Fed. Reg. 25,142 (July 2, 1987) (Notice of Proposed Rulemaking) (hereinafter NPR I); 53 Fed. Reg. 33,900 (Sept. 1, 1988) (Second Notice of Proposed Rulemaking) (hereinafter NPR II); 54 Fed. Reg. 16,336 (Apr. 21, 1989) (Final Rule), *codified at* 29 CFR § 103.30 (2004).

[27] *See, e.g.*, David R. Kochery & George Strauss, *The Nonprofit Hospital and the Union*, 9 Buff. L. Rev. 255, 265 (1960).

its first-ever formal rulemaking proceeding to regularize appropriate health care bargaining units. The Board found that "organizing and initial bargaining among health care workers has historically been by occupationally homogeneous units," and adopted a rule for acute care hospitals that put registered nurses, physicians, technical employees, skilled maintenance employees, business office clerical employees, guards, and all other nonprofessional employees each in separate units. Nursing homes, rehabilitative hospitals, and psychiatric hospitals, however, were excluded from the rule; bargaining units in these types of facilities remain subject to determination through adjudication.[28] Only after the 1991 Supreme Court decision upheld the rule did organizing in the industry, especially among RNs and other professionals, begin to pick up speed.[29] It was thus not until the 1990's that a large volume of cases arose regarding the supervisory status of health care professionals.

Who is a Supervisor: The Law Before Health Care & Retirement Corp.

In the interim, some aspects of the interpretation of § 2(11) became settled. Disputes over supervisory status arise in dozens of cases annually.[30] The 1947 amendments altered § 2(3), defining "employee" as excluding "any individual employed as a supervisor," and inserted a new § 2(11), defining a "supervisor" as:

> [A]ny individual having authority, in the interest of the employer, to hire, transfer, suspend, lay off, recall, promote, discharge, assign, reward, or discipline other employees, or responsibly to direct them, or to adjust their grievances, or effectively to recommend such action, if in connection with the foregoing the exercise of such authority is not of a merely routine or clerical nature, but requires the use of independent judgment.

Section 2(11) has been parsed into a three-part test. To be a supervisor: (1) a worker must possess one or more of the twelve types of personnel authority listed in § 2(11); (2) the worker must exercise that authority "in the interest of the employer," rather than anyone else; and (3) the worker's exercise of that authority must "require the use of independent judgment" rather than be of "a merely routine or clerical nature." Because the § 2(11) list is written in the disjunctive, possession of even one type of authority will render the worker a statutory supervisor. The legislative history indicates that Congress was aiming squarely

---

28 29 C.F.R. § 103.30(a),(f),(2),(g); NPR II, 53 Fed. Reg. at 33,910; Final Rule, 54 Fed. Reg. at 16,346, 16,347–48.

29 Am. Hosp. Ass'n v. NLRB, 499 U.S. 606 (1991).

30 For numbers in the 1970's, see Note, *The NLRB and Supervisory Status: An Explanation of Inconsistent Results*, 94 Harv. L. Rev. 1713, 1713 (1981). The numbers today are, if anything, greater.

at excluding foremen in drawing the § 2(11) line between employees and supervisors. Congress sought to differentiate between "straw bosses, leadmen, set-up men, and other minor supervisory employees, on the one hand, and the supervisor vested with such genuine management prerogatives as the right to hire or fire, discipline, or make effective recommendations with respect to such action."[31] Drawing this line has proven easier said than done, even in the industrial workplace with its conventional, hierarchical chain of command. In settings deviating from that model, the task has been vexing indeed.

Forms of authority to make tangible personnel changes are most readily adjudicable. If the putative supervisor has a record of hiring, suspending, laying off, recalling, promoting, discharging, conferring pay increases or other rewards, or disciplining employees, the individual will be held to be a supervisor. However, neither a job title, such as "foreman" or "supervisor," nor a paper job description establishes supervisory status. Some evidence that the individual actually possesses the authority is necessary. If a worker has held a position for several years without exercising supervisory authority, the credibility of a job description purporting to confer it is undermined. If the worker attempts to exercise the authority but is rebuffed by higher management, the claim of supervisory status is negated. "Effectively recommend" is interpreted to mean the marginal supervisor's recommendations are usually followed without independent investigation. The Board rejects as lacking probative value conclusory testimony about authority nominally conferred upon workers holding a particular job title without specifics establishing its actuality. Some courts of appeals, however, more readily accept such general statements as probative.

The Board does not deem supervisory authority to include intermediate personnel functions such as investigation and reporting of incidents, or evaluation of coworkers' job performance without recommendations regarding discipline, promotion, or pay increase, and without reward or punishment as a direct consequence. Even oral disciplinary warnings are held by the Board to be too weak to constitute § 2(11) disciplinary authority, unless they may lead to tangible personnel consequences. Neither "evaluate," "investigate," nor "report" appears on the § 2(11) list. On the contrary, the Taft–Hartley conference committee compromise embraced the Senate language for supervisory status and rejected the House version, which would have deemed supervisory those job classifications involving investigative or evaluative functions such as claims investigators.[32] Although some circuits have deferred to the Board's interpretation, others have rejected it, holding marginal or

[31] S. Rep. No. 80–105, 4, (1947) *reprinted in* 1 *Legis. Hist.* at 167–68.

[32] H.R. 3020, 80th Cong., § 2(12), (1947), *reprinted in* 1 *Legis. Hist.* at 167–68.

intermediate forms of personnel authority sufficient to render a worker a statutory supervisor. The courts often disagree with the Board's crediting of facts or drawing of inferences in this area, sometimes making it difficult to discern whether the circuit court has applied a different standard for § 2(11) status, or merely decided that the Board's factfinding was unsupported by substantial evidence, the standard for appellate review.

Directing work and assigning tasks, divorced from other forms of § 2(11) authority, have posed the greatest problem. The Board has never fully resolved whether "assignment" is limited to assigning individual workers to shifts, departments, and job classifications, or whether it also reaches assigning individual tasks to a worker. The syntax and context of § 2(11) suggests the former, leaving task assignment to be addressed under the "responsibly direct" rubric. Board treatment of responsible direction is even murkier. Many years ago, the Board adopted a narrow construction of "responsibly to direct" based on its understanding of general legislative intent in 1947. This analysis was promptly rejected by the Sixth Circuit in favor of a broad, dictionary definition, later accepted in several other circuits: "To be responsible is to be answerable for the discharge of a duty or obligation."[33] The NLRB has avoided rather than resolved the issue, determining supervisory status, insofar as possible, without relying on "responsible direction." Failing that, it has interpreted "responsible direction" only as modified by "independent judgment," in a single package, leaning heavily on the "independent judgment" element to avoid interpreting "responsible." "Responsible direction" has been problematic in industrial cases, and even more so in professional employment.

Rather than excluding professionals, the Taft–Hartley Act in § 9(b)(1) treated them specially as to bargaining unit placement. It also added § 2(12), defining "professional employee" as an employee engaged in "predominantly intellectual and varied" work "involving the consistent exercise of discretion and judgment" and "requiring knowledge of an advanced type in a field of science or learning customarily acquired by a prolonged course of specialized intellectual instruction and study in an institution of higher learning or a hospital." The task in cases alleging a professional to be a statutory supervisor is thus to differentiate between the exercise of "independent judgment" in the performance of personnel functions listed in § 2(11) as supervisory attributes, on the one hand, and the exercise of professional "discretion and judgment" in the performance of professional work described in § 2(12)(a)(ii), on the other. In addition, that § 2(12) also defines a professional to include new profes-

[33] Ohio Power Co. v. NLRB, 176 F.2d 385, 387, (1949) *denying enforcement of* 80 NLRB 1334 (1948).

sional school graduates who are completing their qualification for professional credentials by "working under the supervision of a professional person," seems to contemplate professional employees overseeing the work performance of trainees. This is in tension with the inclusion of "responsibly to direct" in the list of § 2(11) forms of authority which render a worker a supervisor. Placing emphasis on "responsibly," and requiring that the supervisor be above the supposed subordinate in a reporting hierarchy could reconcile the two provisions, and would fit well with the 1947 Congress' central focus on foremen and those above them in the hierarchy when it enacted § 2(11). It would be at odds, however, with the Sixth Circuit's interpretation of "responsibly direct," at least outside the professional employee context.

The great majority of disputed supervisory status cases before the 1980's involved employees in occupations such as shop foreman, plant superintendent, and store manager, which are subject to unregulated employer discretion as to job title and content. The factual inquiry as to whether at a particular facility, a person holding the title "foreman" actually possesses the requisite authority under § 2(11) has always had to be conducted separately in every case. As a general rule, the NLRB leaned in favor of a narrow construction of each aspect of supervisory authority. A broad interpretation of § 2(11) might advantage an employer seeking to exclude a borderline supervisor from collective bargaining, or to avoid a ULP charge for discriminating because of the putative supervisor's union sympathies. However, it might advantage a union seeking to exclude the anti-union, borderline supervisor's vote in a representation election, or in imputing the marginal supervisor's anti-union interference to the employer in a different ULP case.

It was not until professionals began organizing on a larger scale that construction of § 2(11) became tied consistently to NLRA treatment of particular categories of workers. Educational, licensure, and regulatory requirements, especially in the health care industry, have standardized elements of many professional and technical job descriptions. In these occupations, although union and employer interests remain subject to *ad hoc* considerations favoring labeling a particular worker an "employee" or a "supervisor," the two sides also take into account systemic considerations, with unions favoring the employee label, and employers favoring the supervisor label for many professionals. It is no coincidence that the two Supreme Court cases construing the elements of § 2(11) arise in the context of professional health care employees.

Health Care & Retirement Corporation: Dry Run for *Kentucky River*

Starting in the mid–1970's, the Supreme Court decided three cases, each by a 5–4 vote, involving NLRB categorical exclusions from the definition of employee in which the Court emphasized that the "employer is entitled to the undivided loyalty of its representatives."[34] In each, the Court construed aspects of § 2(11) or § 2(12), or both, in order to decide these other issues. First, in 1974, in *NLRB v. Bell Aerospace Company*,[35] the Court created an implied exclusion from § 2(3) employee status for all managerial employees, rejecting the NLRB's narrower exclusion of only those managers involved in labor relations decisionmaking. The Court concluded that despite its silence in Taft–Hartley, and its narrow, express exclusion of supervisors in § 2(11), "Congress intended to exclude from the protections of the Act all employees properly classified as 'managerial.'" The Court endorsed older NLRB case law excluding on that basis " 'executives who formulate and effectuate management policies by expressing and making operative decisions of their employer.' "[36] Second, the Court in 1980 in *NLRB v. Yeshiva University* applied the managerial exclusion to the collegial, collective decisionmaking powers of a university faculty over curriculum, grading policies, teaching methods, and matriculation standards. The Court reasoned, "the faculty determines . . . the product to be produced, the terms upon which it will be offered, and the customers who will be served," concluding that "it is difficult to imagine decisions more managerial than these."[37] However, the next year, the Court backed away from its trend toward broad, implied exclusions from coverage. In *NLRB v. Hendricks County Rural Electric Membership Corp.*,[38] the Court upheld the NLRB's longstanding exclusion from bargaining units of those employees with access to confidential labor relations information, while not excluding workers whose jobs made them privy to non-labor-relations confidential business information.

All three cases relied on legislative history; the plain language of § 2(3) entitles any employee not specifically excluded to the protections of the statute. In each of the three, the § 2(12) treatment of professionals played a role in the analysis. In both *Bell Aerospace* and *Yeshiva*, the Court went to great pains to make clear that it did not intend the judicially-implied managerial exclusion to eviscerate Congress' express inclusion of professionals. The *Yeshiva* Court cited approvingly NLRB decisions in which professionals working as project captains of teams of professionals were "deemed employees despite substantial planning responsibility and authority to direct and evaluate team members," including one case involving nurses. *Yeshiva* also pointed for support to the

---

34 NLRB v. Yeshiva Univ., 444 U.S. 672, 682 (1980).

35 416 U.S. 267 (1974).

36 *Id.* at 275, 286 (quoting Palace Laundry Dry Cleaning Corp., 75 NLRB 320, 323 n.4 (1947)).

37 444 U.S. at 686.

38 454 U.S. 170 (1981).

fact that "[i]n the health care context, the Board asks in each case whether the decisions alleged to be managerial or supervisory are 'incidental to' or 'in addition to' the treatment of patients, a test Congress expressly approved in 1974" in adopting the health care amendments to the NLRA.[39]

In *Hendricks County*, to support limitation of the implied confidential employee exclusion to workers with direct access to secret labor-relations related materials, the Court relied on the Taft–Hartley conference committee's rejection of the House bill's broad definition of "supervisor," which would have encompassed a wide range of confidential employees as well as professionals. The conference committee adopted instead the Senate version, which "confined the definition of supervisor to individuals generally regarded as foremen and employees of like or higher rank." The Court also pointed to § 2(12), covering such professionals as " 'legal, engineering, scientific and medical personnel together with their junior professional assistants,' . . . almost all [of whom] would likely be privy to confidential business information. . . . It would . . . be extraordinary to read an implied exclusion for confidential employees into the statute that would swallow up . . . the professional-employee inclusion."[40]

Commentators after *Bell Aerospace* and *Yeshiva* were apprehensive that doctrinal developments were creating a slippery slope which might eviscerate statutory coverage of professionals.[41] The Board, however, perhaps lulled into complacency by the Court's reasoning supporting preservation of professional employee coverage, continued to follow its line of health care cases, finding supervisory status when the health care professional's exercise of authority over a less highly educated coworker was "in addition to" as opposed to "incidental to" patient care. The Sixth Circuit was particularly vehement in rejecting the Board's interpretation in nursing cases. The NLRB successfully petitioned for certiorari in one, *NLRB v. Health Care & Retirement Corp. of America (HCR).*[42]

---

[39] 444 U.S. at 690 & n.30.

[40] *Hendricks County*, 454 U.S. at 184 n.15, 184–85 (quoting 93 Cong. Rec. 6442 (1947) (remarks of Senator Taft) and quoting H.R. Conf. Rep. No. 80–510, at 36 (1947)).

[41] *See, e.g.*, Matthew W. Finkin, *The Supervisory Status of Professional Employees*, 45 Fordham L. Rev. 805 (1977); Marina Angel, *Professionals and Unionization*, 66 Minn. L. Rev. 383 (1982); David M. Rabban, *Distinguishing Excluded Managers from Covered Professionals Under the NLRA*, 89 Colum. L. Rev. 1775 (1989); Marion Crain, *Building Solidarity Through Expansion of NLRA Coverage: A Blueprint for Worker Empowerment*, 74 Minn. L. Rev. 953, 972–73 (1990).

[42] 511 U.S. 571 (1994). Facts of the case which go beyond those reported in the Supreme Court opinion are taken from the decision of the NLRB Administrative Law Judge, 306 NLRB 63, 68 (1992).

Health Care & Retirement Corporation had been charged with disciplining four LPNs in retaliation for their concerted activities. If they were supervisors, the discipline could not have violated the Act. The nursing home's nursing department was headed by a director and assistant director, two § 2(11) supervisors. Reporting to them were about ten nurses, some of whom were RNs and others LPNs, plus about fifty nurses aides. Both types of nurses were assigned the same duties, an approach common in nursing homes. The Court therefore examined the case as though the LPNs were professional rather than technical employees.

The Board had defended the case before the Supreme Court on the basis of the agency's rule that when "the nurses' direction of other employees is carried out in the exercise of professional judgment and is incidental to the treatment of patients," it is not "in the interest of the employer," and hence does not constitute § 2(11) authority. Justice Kennedy's opinion for the 5–4 majority of the Court rejected the NLRB's use of the third § 2(11) prong, "in the interest of the employer," to differentiate between professional task delegation to and oversight of less skilled workers, on the one hand, and general responsible direction of subordinates by a superior, on the other. The *HCR* Court rejected the Board's "incidental to patient care" gloss on "in the interest of the employer" not only as being contrary to the plain meaning of the phrase, which the Court emphatically claimed was unambiguous, but also as contravening the broad interpretation the 1947 *Packard* Court placed on the phrase as it appeared in the Wagner Act § 2(2) definition of employer. The Court also criticized the Board's interpretation of "in the interest of the employer" as, in effect, reading "responsibly to direct" out of the Act as to nurses, and castigated the Board for creating an interpretation of "in the interest of the employer" unique for a profession or industry.

Whatever the weaknesses of the Court's analysis in terms of syntax and history, the Board's distinction between discretionary actions based on professional norms and those based on personnel authority delegated by the employer was too heavy a load to place on the phrase "in the interest of the employer" standing alone. The NLRB's point would have been stronger had it been based on the legislative policies and compromises embodied in the Taft–Hartley Act as a whole, and the entirety of § 2(11) in particular. Before the Supreme Court, however, the Board had boxed itself in, formally limiting itself to interpretation of "in the interest of the employer," rather than arguing on all three bases—in the interest, independent judgment, and responsible direction—alternatively, or construed together.

For the NLRB, the *HCR* opinion provided contradictory messages. The Court emphasized that its opinion addressed only the "in the interest of the employer'' phrase, and no other portion of § 2(11). Because the Court distinguished similar reasoning in other professional employee cases as relying on the ''independent judgment'' phrase rather than the ''in the interest'' phrase of § 2(11), it was easy for the Board to read *HCR* as leaving open the interpretation of ''independent judgment'' and of each of the twelve listed forms of supervisory authority, including ''responsibly to direct.'' Moreover, although the Court claimed that ''in the interest of the employer'' is clear and unambiguous, it conceded that ''independent judgment'' and ''responsibly to direct'' are ambiguous, entailing judicial deference to the NLRB's reasonable construction of these terms.

Despite these assurances, however, *HCR* also contained many warning flags for the Board. Portions of the opinion assume an expansive meaning for ''independent judgment,'' ''assign,'' and ''responsibly to direct.'' In characterizing the facts regarding the nurses' job, the Court's conclusory description more closely resembles the employer's and the Sixth Circuit's version than it does the NLRB's carefully detailed rendition, despite the statutory requirement that the Board's findings of fact be conclusive on the courts so long as they are supported by substantial evidence.

Soon after *HCR* was decided, the NLRB General Counsel advocated taking the Court at its word on limiting the holding to interpretation of ''in the interest of the employer.'' His approach was a two-legged one, depending simultaneously on construction of ''independent judgment,'' the other phrase of limitation in § 2(11), and on construction, rather than fact-specific application, of the ambiguous terms among the list of twelve forms of supervisory authority, particularly ''assign,'' and ''responsibly to direct.''[43] The NLRB then decided a hospital case, *Providence Hospital* and a nursing home case, *Ten Broeck Commons*,[44] which only partially followed the course urged by the General Counsel. The Board took at face value the Court's pronouncements limiting the *HCR* holding to ''in the interest of the employer.'' However, the Board rejected the General Counsel's two-legged approach, also strenuously urged upon it by the AFL–CIO, and chose instead to stand only on one leg, construction of ''independent judgment.'' The Board held that nurses' direction and assignment of tasks to less-educated and less-trained nurses, nursing assistants and aides is ''merely routine,'' and does not reflect § 2(11) ''independent judgment,'' so long as the decisionmaking is sufficiently

---

[43] *See, e.g.,* Cascade Care Ctr., 1995 NLRB GCM LEXIS 90 (Nov. 7, 1995); Wesley Willows, 1994 NLRB GCM LEXIS 83 (Nov. 17, 1994); Villa Elizabeth, Inc., 1995 NLRB GCM LEXIS 95 (Mar. 10, 1995); North Oakland Med. Ctrs., 1995 NLRB GCM LEXIS 96 (Mar. 8, 1995).

[44] Providence Hosp., 320 NLRB 717 (1996); Nymed, Inc., d/b/a/ Ten Broeck Commons, 320 NLRB 806 (1996).

cabined by directives from the employer or by professional norms. The Board said it was applying its "traditional analysis for determining the supervisory status of employees in other occupations," in an effort to comply with the *HCR* Court's holding that the Act does not distinguish professional employees from others in the § 2(11) definition of supervisor.

The Board Members, General Counsel and staff were keenly aware that § 2(11) was headed back to the Supreme Court. Guidelines were issued instructing the regions to follow the *Providence Hospital* and *Ten Broeck Commons* "independent judgment" rubric in all cases.[45] The circuits fragmented, some deferring to the NLRB's statutory interpretation and factfinding, others skeptical but moderate in tone, and the Fourth and Sixth extremely hostile.[46] The Sixth Circuit declared the Board's new analysis "disingenuous," a manipulative shell game to support the Board's continuing to treat cases exactly as it had previously. What the Board regarded as an invitation from the Supreme Court to devise a new rubric to support similar results, some of the circuit courts, especially the Sixth, saw as the Court's warning shot across the agency's bow. The NLRB staff did not want legal developments to turn on the chance decision of an employer to seek certiorari, or on the calculated decision of an employer group to target a case for Supreme Court review. They scrutinized circuit court rulings, looking for a clean case with an adverse appellate decision based on minimal indicia of supervisory status. Such a case would afford an appealing vehicle for the agency to return to the Court with the Board's new § 2(11) analysis. In *Kentucky River*, the NLRB believed that it had found one.[47]

Factual Background

The organizing drive in *Kentucky River* had some distinctive aspects, but none which would have led the participants to anticipate their case going to the Supreme Court.[48] In the fall of 1996, Glenn Moore ap-

[45] Telephone Interview with NLRB Associate General Counsel John H. Ferguson, December 17, 2004.

[46] *See, e.g.*, NLRB v. GranCare, Inc., 170 F.3d 662 (7th Cir. 1999) (*en banc*) (deferential); Passavant Ret. & Health Ctr. v. NLRB, 149 F.3d 243 (3d Cir. 1998) (intermediate); Beverly Enters., Va., Inc. v. NLRB, 165 F.3d 290 (4th Cir. 1999) (*en banc*) (hostile); Caremore, Inc. v. NLRB, 129 F.3d 365 (6th Cir. 1997) (same).

[47] Telephone Interview with former Member Fox, December 17, 2004; Telephone Interview with NLRB Associate General Counsel Ferguson, December 17, 2004; Telephone Interview with former NLRB General Counsel Feinstein, December 16, 2004.

[48] The factual background is derived from telephone interviews with Schulz and Miller, October 1, 2004 and December 17, 2004, and from the NLRB Region Nine file in Kentucky River Community Care, Inc., NLRB Case No. 9–RC–16837, and the Region Nine file in Kentucky River Community Care, Inc., NLRB Case No. 9–CA–34926. Excluding portions as

proached the Kentucky State District Council of Carpenters about organizing the employees at KRCC's Caney Creek psychiatric rehabilitation and long-term care facility. The union's director of organizing, Lawrence Hujo, tried to talk Moore into approaching some other union. The Carpenters Union primarily represents skilled trades workers at construction sites, not professional and technical employees at health care facilities. Moore, however, had decided that he and his fellow employees really needed a union. He had asked around among his political and union contacts, seeking the best union in the area, and was repeatedly told that the Carpenters Union "would treat you right." Moore continued to press the Carpenters to organize at Caney Creek.

Because of Moore's persistence and enthusiasm, the Carpenters Union reconsidered. His web of connections and support at Caney Creek had already halfway organized the workforce. Once the Carpenters Union undertook the campaign, it put its full effort into it. The campaign rapidly moved from initial organizing to amassing enough support to demand employer recognition and file the election petition with the NLRB. Major issues in the campaign included the difficult job conditions, low pay, and control over scheduling and staffing. Arbitrary exercise of management discretion over pay increases was a particularly festering irritation for those workers who were not in their supervisors' social clique since the unit coordinators and nursing coordinator had almost unfettered discretion in performance evaluations that determined pay increases. After organizing for a little over a month, on January 22, 1997, union organizer Hujo wrote to KRCC demanding recognition. When the employer refused, on January 27, Hujo filed the union's petition with the NLRB Region Nine office in Cincinnati, Ohio. The estimated eighty-six employee unit included the six RNs, the twenty rehabilitation counselors, as well as the single licensed practical nurse then on the payroll, the forty rehabilitation assistants, a few recreation assistants, and some kitchen, service and maintenance workers. The union submitted as its showing of interest union authorization cards signed by about eighty percent of the proposed bargaining unit.

Because Moore was the key in-facility organizer, the rehabilitation counselors were the heart of the union's support and the crucial strategic factor shaping the bargaining unit requested in the petition. There was no question of the union seeking to represent the rehabilitation

---

to which privilege was asserted, the files were provided to the author by the NLRB pursuant to a series of requests submitted under the Freedom of Information Act. Some documents are reprinted in the appendix section of the Petition for a Writ of Certiorari, Kentucky River Community Care, Inc., *available at* <http://supreme.lp.findlaw.com/supreme_court/docket/2000/febdocket.html> [hereinafter Petition for a Writ of Certiorari] and excerpts from the transcript and exhibits in the representation proceeding are reprinted in the Joint Appendix (J.A.), available on microfiche.

assistants, recreation assistants, and LPNs alone, in a technical employee unit. The union was unsure whether the rehabilitation counselors would properly be characterized as professionals in any event. As union in-house counsel Tom Schulz put it, the union "bluffed" the issue, simply asking for a single, all non-supervisory, non-guard bargaining unit. KRCC counsel did not focus on it. The RNs, unlike the rehabilitation counselors, were not essential to the union, even though some were among the union's strongest supporters. Being in the Sixth Circuit, where *HCR* had been decided before it went to the Supreme Court, union counsel was aware that the RNs were likely to be challenged as supervisory. They were included in the unit, not only because they were union supporters, but also as a "diversionary tactic, if need be, to trade-off and get the rest" of the workers, said Schulz.

The union's petition blindsided management, which had had little awareness of the organizing campaign until it received Hujo's formal demand for recognition. Management retained counsel George J. Miller only at that point. Miller, an experienced labor lawyer, was a partner in the Lexington, Kentucky office of the 200-attorney, Louisville-based law firm of Wyatt, Tarrant & Combs. KRCC responded to the petition first, by claiming to be exempt from the Act; and second, by trying to exclude as supervisors both the RNs and the rehabilitation counselors, in effect arguing that its entire professional employee complement fell outside the protections of the NLRA. The first argument contended that KRCC, a non-profit corporation, was operating in lieu of a state government-created body, with authority contractually delegated to it by the state and with its discretion in personnel matters so heavily constrained by its contract with the state that it should be deemed a governmental unit. Miller later explained, "If we won on the first issue, the case was over. If we won on the second issue, we would have carved those people out of the unit and made them available to use in campaigning against the union." Employers commonly resort to a third, fallback strategy if pre-election legal strategies fail: trying to defeat the union in the election, through legal means such as captive audience speeches and campaign literature, or through tactics of dubious legality, such as promises of benefits if employees vote against the union, "predictions" that job loss will ensue if the union wins, or firing of leading union supporters ostensibly for disciplinary reasons. KRCC's election campaign efforts fit this pattern, but they were insufficient to derail the pro-union majority.

Prior Proceedings

Proceedings Before the NLRB: The Representation Proceeding

The representation case was assigned to Natalie Morton of the NLRB Region Nine office. She verified the union's "showing of interest," and in a pre-hearing conference call, unsuccessfully tried to persuade the parties to consent to an election in an agreed-upon bargaining unit. In February 1997, Morton presided over a pre-election hearing in the Perry County Courthouse in Hazard, Kentucky, which lasted a total of about nine hours. Although regional staff members preside over representation case hearings, the regional directors issue quasi-adjudicatory decisions resolving disputed matters on the basis of the record created in the hearing. On February 21, 1997, Region Nine Regional Director Richard L. Ahearn issued his Decision and Direction of Election, finding KRCC to be covered by the Act, and finding both the registered nurses and the rehabilitation counselors to be "professional employees" and not "supervisors" under the Act.

The Caney Creek complex was headed by administrator Leonard Echols, who reported directly to KRCC CEO Louise Howell. Reporting to Echols were the assistant administrator, the nursing coordinator, and unit coordinator Mark Stone, as well as a second unit coordinator whose position was then vacant, with Echols himself filling in in the interim. These positions were stipulated to be § 2(11) supervisors. The facility is divided into four identical twenty-bed units, each staffed by five rehabilitation coordinators and ten rehabilitation assistants. Each of the two unit coordinators was in charge of two of the four units. Each unit coordinator thus had thirty subordinates: ten rehabilitation coordinators and twenty rehabilitation assistants. In each unit, four of the five rehabilitation coordinators worked the day shift, while one worked a swing shift, covering the afternoon half of the day shift, and early evening portion of the evening shift. The ten rehabilitation assistants per unit were divided up among all three shifts, although more assistants worked the day shift to handle many of the activities and training programs for residents.

The employer contended that the rehabilitation counselors directed the work of the rehabilitation assistants with sufficient independent judgment and discretion to be § 2(11) supervisors. The Regional Director found, however, that the rehabilitation counselors "do not have the authority to hire, fire, discipline, promote, or evaluate employees and any assignment or direction which they may give other employees is routine."[49] The Regional Director followed *Providence Hospital* and *Ten Broeck Commons* in determining that mere authority to coordinate the work of others is not sufficient independent judgment to satisfy § 2(11), and that mere formulation of treatment plans fulfilled by other employees is not a form of § 2(11) authority at all. He distinguished *HCR* as limited to the "in the interest of the employer" analysis. He bolstered his conclusion by noting that under KRCC's analysis, there would be an

[49] Decision and Direction of Election at 7, *reprinted in* Petition for a Writ of Certiorari, 35a, 49a.

unrealistic 1:2 ratio of supervisor rehabilitation counselors to subordinate rehabilitation assistants.

The employer's claim of supervisory status for RNs was artfully bolstered by conflation of two separate bases for arguing about their supervisory status: their regular role as nurses and their role as building supervisors when management was away from the premises. Nursing coordinator Alicia Cook had authority over all nurses. Fully staffed, the facility employed six RNs and three LPNs, but as of the hearing only one LPN was on the payroll. The nurses were the only trained medical personnel in the facility at most times; the doctor and psychiatrist were independent contractors on the premises a few hours per week. The six RNs were assigned two to a shift, rotating across all seven days per week, to ensure 24/7 coverage. Each RN worked about four weekend shifts per month. The primary role of the RN was to provide direct medical services to the residents, and to document medical treatment and changes in medical condition of residents, acting under the instructions of the resident's physician or psychiatrist. She either herself administered all doctor-ordered medication or was responsible for documenting its administration by an LPN. She also cooperated with the rehabilitation counselor in development and revision of individual resident treatment plans, with regard to the medical aspects of those plans. She was not in the line of supervision or regular direction of either rehabilitation counselors or rehabilitation assistants. The employer's own treatment in its formal job descriptions of supervisor-subordinate reporting relationships, its employment handbook references to supervisors' role in performance evaluation, pay increases, and grievance procedures, as well as the verbal usage throughout the testimony of KRCC's management witnesses, consistently labeled only the unit coordinators and nursing coordinator as supervisors. Both the rehabilitation assistant job description and the rehabilitation counselor job description showed these workers as reporting to the unit coordinator as their supervisor, not to the RN, or for that matter, the rehabilitation counselor. The employer did not offer into evidence the job description of either the RN or the LPN position.

The employer's argument rested on two very thin bases to claim the RNs responsibly directed other workers, exercising independent judgment, in their regular job duties: they had to ensure proper LPN administration of medication when an LPN was on duty simultaneously with the RN, and they occasionally requested help from a rehabilitation assistant in dealing with an unruly resident. If the RNs were all supervisors over the single LPN, the supervisor-to-subordinate ratio would have been a ridiculous 6:1; even with a full three LPN complement, it would still have been 2:1. Moreover, Registered Nurse Alice

Anderson testified that the RNs and LPNs had a relationship of equality at the facility.

The stronger aspect of KRCC's contention that the RNs were supervisors rested on their role as "building supervisor" when none of the stipulated § 2(11) supervisors were on the premises at night and on weekends. The details of this role, however, were hotly contested. The union offered what it contended was the only officially disseminated description of the special duties added to the RN position when the RN served as building supervisor. The memorandum indicated that the main role of the building supervisor was to buffer the off-duty, on-call manager from unnecessary telephone calls, and also to make sure minimum staffing requirements were met on each unit. If unexpected absences or weather emergencies reduced the ratio of staff to residents below unit minimums pre-set by management, the building supervisor was to obtain additional staff to restore the minimum ratio. Solving the staff ratio problem could be done by moving a rehabilitation assistant from a unit with excess staff to the short-staffed unit for the duration of the shift; or, absent extra staff, the building supervisor could ask someone to stay over from the departing shift; failing that, she could call someone in to work who would otherwise be off duty.

The employer offered two additional memos documenting beefed-up authority for the building supervisor, but testimony failed clearly to establish whether the memos were ever distributed to employees. These memos increased the authority and responsibility of the building supervisor by placing her in charge of the entire facility and giving her the duty to check staffing levels every day when she came on duty, authorizing her to require, rather than merely request, the affected staff member to switch units, work overtime, or report to work, and instructing her to "write up" anyone who refused her instruction. One manager testified that the building supervisor not only could require staff to work longer or come in from home to meet minimum ratio requirements, but that she also had the discretion to increase the staffing level above the pre-set minimum if problems arose with residents on a unit during a particular shift. This witness also testified that the building supervisor had authority to send home from work a worker who was intoxicated or otherwise misbehaving, and only thereafter contact the employee's regular supervisor, although she conceded that this had never occurred. This evidence conflicted with Nurse Anderson's testimony that such actions would have exceeded the scope of her authority, and that she would first have contacted the on-call administrator for instructions prior to taking any action. The only time Anderson had failed to get advance approval from the on-call supervisor before asking an employee to stay over to meet pre-set ratios, she had been reprimanded by unit coordinator Mark Stone, the on-call manager, and the other employee was sent home early so that KRCC would not have to pay overtime. The employer's own witness, Caney Creek's top manager, Echols, corroborated Anderson's testimony that as building supervisor, the RN could only request, and not require other workers to stay over or come in to work on a day off, and that in calling in employees during inclement weather, they simply resorted to the list of local employees provided by management. Testimony that there was no formal handover of authority when the last administrator left the building for the day, and that when two RNs were on duty at once, they decided among themselves which one should fill the role, further bolstered the union's depiction of the modest, informal nature of the building supervisor role.

The Regional Director, after noting that the employer had the burden of proof on § 2(11) status, concluded that even when serving as building supervisors the RNs were not statutory supervisors. At most, he found, they could request coworkers, such as LPNs and rehabilitation assistants, to perform tasks routinely part of the coworkers' job description, and, as building supervisors, in accordance with pre-set policies about staffing ratios, could ask workers to remain on the job after the end of their shift or could call in volunteers. He specifically found the building supervisor RNs "do not have any authority . . . to compel an employee to stay over or come in to fill a vacancy under threat of discipline."[50] The functions, he held, are too routine to qualify as independent judgment for purposes of § 2(11). The Regional Director ordered that the election be held in two separate voting groups, one composed of the non-professionals, and the other composed of the professional employees, *i.e.*, the RNs and the rehabilitation counselors. He further held each of these two separate bargaining units, as well as the combined unit, appropriate. The votes of the professional group were to be counted at the outset. If a majority voted for inclusion in the overall unit, then its votes on whether to have the Carpenters as bargaining representative would be counted together with the votes of the non-professional employees, and a majority of the total votes cast by the workforce would be required for the union to prevail; otherwise each group's votes for or against unionization would be counted separately.

On March 6, 1997, the employer filed a request for review of the Regional Director's decision with the NLRB in Washington. To obtain this discretionary review, the requester must show "compelling reasons." On March 21, 1997, a panel composed of NLRB Chairman William B. Gould, IV, plus Members Sarah M. Fox and John E. Higgins, Jr. issued a one-sentence order, denying the request "as it raised no substantial issues warranting review." The panel viewed both the RN

[50] Decision and Direction of Election at 8, *reprinted in* Petition for a Writ of Certiorari, at 35a, 51a.

and rehabilitation counselor issues as routine applications of the NLRB's recent decisions in *Providence Hospital* and *Ten Broeck Commons.*[51]

The election campaign took place while the request for review was pending in March 1997. The union's campaign at the outset highlighted the same festering issues that originally had led Glenn Moore to approach the Carpenters Union. On February 26, 1997, however, management suspended Moore, and on March 13, fired him. Several other union activists also were discharged in the course of the campaign. The union filed a series of ULP charges, challenging not only the allegedly discriminatory discipline and discharge practices, but also claiming that the employer had offered a new discounted vacation package to employees, had discriminated in permitting employee posting of anti- as opposed to pro-union literature, had threatened the loss of business and jobs if employees voted for the union, and had threatened that it would refuse to negotiate anyway if employees voted in the union. The union also included a request to proceed, so that the charges would not block the election timetable.[52] The discharged workers also filed for unemployment compensation. When the employer contested their claims, Tom Schulz represented them for free, and the employees all won their benefits by establishing that KRCC's anti-union animus rather than employee misconduct was the reason for their discharge. Anti-union firings sometimes deflate support for a union seeking to organize a workforce. At Caney Creek, however, Moore and some of the others became martyrs to the union cause, solidifying employee support for union representation.

The election was conducted and the ballots were counted. A 15–4 majority of the professional group was tallied as having voted for inclusion in the combined bargaining unit. The ballots of all employees were then counted together. Of approximately ninety-six eligible voters, ninety-one actually had attempted to vote. Fifty-six employees voted for the union, twenty-nine voted against, with six casting challenged ballots. Because the number of challenged votes was too small to affect the outcome of the election, the results were certified without those ballots being opened.

Proceedings Before the NLRB: The Technical Refusal to Bargain

Armed with the certification, on April 24, 1997, the Carpenters Union wrote to KRCC, requesting that it commence collective bargaining. KRCC counsel Miller replied that the employer "declines to recognize or bargain with the union, for the purpose of testing the Regional Director's certification of the union." On May 20, the union filed an

---

51 Interview with former Member Sarah M. Fox, Silver Spring, Maryland, August 28, 2004.

52 Kentucky River Community Care, Inc., NLRB Charge No. 9–CA–34653–3.

unfair labor practice charge, initiating a "technical refusal to bargain case," in which the employer's refusal to bargain with the union provides the procedural vehicle for the employer to obtain federal appellate court review of the underlying representation proceeding, which is not otherwise reviewable. The NLRB issued a formal complaint, KRCC filed an answer, and in rapid order, the General Counsel moved for summary judgment, the case was transferred to the Board in Washington, and an opportunity was provided for KRCC to file a response. On July 10, 1997, the same three-member panel that had previously rejected the employer's request for review in the representation proceeding issued the NLRB Decision and Order in the ULP case.[53] It granted summary judgment, holding that the employer's admitted refusal to recognize and bargain with the union violated § 8(a)(5) and § 8(a)(1).

Proceedings in the Court of Appeals

On July 15, 1997 Region Nine Director Ahearn wrote to Miller to advise that he was recommending commencement of proceedings to enforce the NLRB's order. Two days later, Miller filed a petition for review of the order with the Sixth Circuit.[54] A week after that, however, KRCC changed counsel. Michael W. Hawkins and Cheryl E. Bruner, of the Cincinnati law firm of Dinsmore & Shohl, took over as counsel for KRCC. Hawkins, with decades of experience handling NLRA matters, would represent the employer in both the Sixth Circuit and in the Supreme Court. The NLRB, in the meantime, had cross-applied for enforcement and the union had moved to intervene, which the charging party in a ULP proceeding may do as a matter of right.

Despite the change in counsel, the employer made similar arguments before the circuit court that it had made during the representation proceeding. The lion's share of KRCC's briefs was devoted to the political subdivision argument, with only short sections contending, alternatively, that RNs and rehabilitation counselors were statutory supervisors. They relied heavily on the authority conferred in the two contested building supervisor memos, treating them as undisputed fact even though the Regional Director had failed to credit them as having been implemented. Hawkins artfully utilized prior cases in which the

---

[53] 323 NLRB No. 209 (1997), *reprinted in* Petition for a Writ of Certiorari at 26a.

[54] The description of proceedings in the Sixth Circuit Court of Appeals in Case No. 97–5885/97–5983 is taken from telephone interviews with Thomas Schulz, October 1, 2004, George Miller, December 17, 2004, and Michael Hawkins, January 13, 2005, the court's docket sheet in the case, *reprinted at* J.A. 3–4, as well as the briefs and papers submitted by the parties, and the judgment of the court. These portions of the appellate court file were provided by the NLRB pursuant to a Freedom of Information Act request. The judgment of the Sixth Circuit and the order denying the employer's suggestion for rehearing en banc are reprinted in Petition for a Writ of Certiorari at 61a and 64a.

Sixth Circuit had found nursing home charge nurses to be supervisors and reversed NLRB decisions. His brief reiterated the Sixth Circuit's own protestation that the Board "has steadfastly failed to apply" Sixth Circuit precedent in nurse supervisor cases, and characterized the KRCC case as yet "another situation where the NLRB has ignored the Sixth Circuit."[55] KRCC also briefly discussed another Sixth Circuit precedent, *NLRB v. Beacon Light Christian Nursing Home*, noting parenthetically that that case states that the NLRB "always has the burden of coming forward with evidence showing that the employees are not supervisors in bargaining unit determinations."[56] The thrust of the KRCC briefs was to induce the circuit court to analogize the building supervisor RNs, as well as the rehabilitation counselors, to charge nurses, whom a series of Sixth Circuit cases had found to be supervisors because they regularly delegate patient care tasks to nurses aides.

The NLRB brief framed the issue quite differently—whether substantial evidence supported the Board's finding that the rehabilitation counselors and the registered nurses were not supervisors.[57] The brief documented evidence substantiating the Regional Director's factfinding about the RNs' authority and noted the conflicting evidence about dissemination of the pivotal building supervisor memoranda. The brief succumbed to the temptation to rely on NLRB case law holding that RNs delegating patient care tasks to LPNs and aides constitutes "routine" performance of the RNs' professional duties, not "responsible direction" of less skilled employees "in the exercise of independent judgment." Although the brief distinguished adverse Sixth Circuit authority on nurse supervisors on the grounds that the nurses in those cases had disciplinary, overtime assignment, and pay-related evaluation responsibilities, the brief also suggested that those cases were inconsistent with the NLRB's new approach because they relied on a different phrase in § 2(11). This strategy might have prompted the circuit court to bridle at the agency's resistance to following circuit court case law. The brief also implicitly seemed to accept the employer's overstatement of the degree to which RNs supervised other employees in administering medication and delivering care; the Board's brief merely asserted that that responsibility was "simply an aspect of their performance of their professional

---

[55] Brief of Petitioner/Cross–Respondent Kentucky River Community Care, Inc. at 46 [hereinafter KRCC Brief] (quoting Health Care & Ret. Corp. v. NLRB, 987 F.2d 1256, 1260 (6th Cir. 1993), *aff'd*, 511 U.S. 571 (1994)). *See also* Reply Brief of Petitioner/Cross–Respondent Kentucky River Community Care, Inc., at 19 [hereinafter KRCC Reply Brief] (citing Caremore, Inc. v. NLRB, 129 F.3d 365 (6th Cir. 1997)).

[56] 825 F.2d 1076, 1080 (6th Cir. 1987), cited in KRCC Brief at 39 and in KRCC Reply Brief at 12.

[57] Brief for the NLRB, at 3–4.

duties.'' The agency's brief made no mention of the burden of proof issue.

The Sixth Circuit heard oral argument on November 5, 1998. Michael Hawkins argued for KRCC, Daniel J. Michalski argued on behalf of the NLRB, and Tom Schulz argued for the union. Almost a year later, the court issued a split decision.[58] The majority overturned the holding that the RNs were covered employees, while enforcing the remainder of the NLRB order directing the employer to recognize and bargain with the union on behalf of the non-professional employees and the rehabilitation counselors. KRCC succeeded in its strategy of mobilizing the court's festering irritation with the Board for exercising its right to adhere to the agency's own interpretation of the Act, contrary to that adopted by the circuit. After castigating the Board for placing the burden of proof of supervisory status on the employer, the court found that the RNs had, as to administration of medication, authority to responsibly direct in the exercise of independent judgment the LPNs, who had become three in number based on a non-factual assertion in the KRCC brief. As building supervisor, the court found, the RNs were the highest ranking staff member on the premises, with authority to ''seek additional employees in the event of a staffing shortage, move employees between units as needed, and . . . write up employees who do not cooperate with staffing assignments.'' The latter finding, without evidentiary explanation, ignored the contrary evidence credited by the Regional Director. The majority had rejected the Board's construction of ''independent judgment'' as contrary to circuit precedent and as unworthy of judicial deference because the agency, according to the court, applied it manipulatively. Applying Sixth Circuit case law, the court held that these forms of authority were sufficient to render the RNs § 2(11) supervisors. Dissenting as to the nurses, Judge Nathaniel R. Jones would have deferred to the Board's factfinding, which he found had substantial support on the record as a whole.

The Supreme Court Decision

On May 12, 2000, the government petitioned the Supreme Court for certiorari.[59] The decision to seek certiorari was hotly debated within the

58 193 F.3d 444, 454 (6th Cir. 1999).

59 The description of proceedings in the Supreme Court is based upon telephone interviews with Hawkins, Schulz, Carpenters Union Supreme Court counsel and AFL–CIO Associate General Counsel Becker, AFL–CIO Associate General Counsel Coppess, former Member Fox, former NLRB General Counsel Feinstein, former NLRB General Counsel Page, and NLRB Associate General Counsel Ferguson, as well as the Supreme Court docket sheet, and the briefs and other filings in NLRB v. Kentucky River Community Care, Inc., Supreme Court Case No. 98–1815. The docket sheet and joint appendix are available on microfilm. The transcript of the oral argument and the NLRB's briefs are available at

NLRB. The agency has sought certiorari in very few cases over the past twenty years. At almost the same time as it decided *Kentucky River*, the same Sixth Circuit panel decided another nurse supervisor case, *Integrated Health Services of Michigan, at Riverbend, Inc. v. NLRB*,[60] a nursing home case in which Judge Jones had filed a concurrence. The government could have sought certiorari in either of these cases, or in one from another circuit, or awaited a better case from the Sixth.

Kentucky River was in several respects an atypical nurse supervisory status case, making the choice of it for Supreme Court review an odd one. The case is set in a psychiatric facility rather than the more typical hospital or nursing home. As the employer had unsuccessfully argued before the Sixth Circuit, the relationship of the rehabilitation counselors to the rehabilitation assistants somewhat paralleled that of the RN or LPN to nurses aides or certified nursing assistants in the hospital or nursing home. The RNs at Caney Creek, by contrast, exercised little authority to responsibly direct others in the performance of patient care tasks, and there were no nurses aides. Despite a modicum of evidence about the RNs directing an LPN in the administration of medications, the weight of the circuit court's conclusion that the *Kentucky River* RNs were supervisors was based on their building supervisor role, a role almost wholly independent of their professional skills and judgment. If the employer had not been required to have an RN on duty at all times, it might well have designated one of the rehabilitation assistants on each shift to the role, which would have altered the complexion of the supervisory status argument. The building supervisor role, moreover, gave the employer the strong practical argument in favor of supervisory status that when serving as building supervisor, the RNs were the highest ranking staff member in the facility, and they filled this role for long periods of time each week.

The General Counsel and the Board nevertheless concluded that *Kentucky River* was the best case available. They wanted a case from the Sixth Circuit because of its explicit attitude of non-deference to the factfinding and statutory interpretation of the Board and because it was the only circuit rejecting the NLRB's allocation of the burden of proof. As between the two Sixth Circuit decisions, *Kentucky River* presented the better case for review. *Integrated Health Services* did not present cleanly the "independent judgment" issue in the context of responsible direction; there was too much evidence of disciplinary authority. A Supreme Court decision upholding the Board's position would not have changed the result in *Integrated Health Services*, precluding satisfaction

---

<http://supreme.lp.findlaw.com/supreme_court/docket/2000/febdocket.html>. The remaining briefs of the parties and of *amicus curiae* are available on Lexis and Westlaw.

60 191 F.3d 703 (6th Cir. 1999).

of Supreme Court certiorari criteria. In *Kentucky River*, had the Court accepted the Board's § 2(11) independent judgment analysis along with its allocation of the burden of proof, the RNs would not have been deemed supervisors. The Jones dissent in *Kentucky River* was another plus since it enhanced the credibility of the Board's case before the Supreme Court.

The tenor of Sixth Circuit case law also militated against waiting in hopes of a more perfect certiorari vehicle. As NLRB General Counsel Feinstein put it, the Sixth Circuit had invited employers to forum shop. Major nursing home chains always have a location in the Sixth Circuit, and therefore have the right to file their petitions for review of adverse NLRB ULP decisions in that circuit, no matter the location of the nursing home where the case arose. The effect was to give nearly nationwide effect to the case law of that one circuit, contrary to that of the Board. As Judge Jones had opined in his concurring opinion in *Integrated Health Services*, the circuit had "become so entrenched in our disagreements with the Board regarding the construction of § 2(11) that, as a practical matter, we have made it impossible for nurses to form bargaining units at nursing homes."[61] The General Counsel and the Board Members felt it imperative to obtain a Supreme Court ruling on the construction of "independent judgment" in the health care industry as well as on the allocation of the burden of proof of supervisory status.

Those most actively involved in the decision thought the Board would win in the Supreme Court. Others in the agency, however, were more pessimistic, as were AFL–CIO lawyers who had been working with union counsel on many nurse supervisor cases at the circuit court level. Nevertheless, the General Counsel and the Board urged the Solicitor General, who had the final decision, to seek certiorari in *Kentucky River*, and the Solicitor General did so.

The Board sought Supreme Court review on three questions: (1) the Board's construction of "independent judgment" in § 2(11) as not encompassing "an employee's exercise of ordinary professional or technical judgment in directing less-skilled employees to deliver services in accordance with employer-specified standards"; (2) the propriety of the NLRB's allocation of the burden of proof to the party alleging an individual to be a supervisor, whether in a representation proceeding or a ULP case; and (3) whether in applying its interpretation of § 2(11) "independent judgment" and its allocation of the burden of proof, the NLRB reasonably found the RNs to be employees rather than supervisors. The Carpenters Union had not joined in the petition, or responded to it, because it could not afford to take the case to the Supreme Court. However, once the Board had petitioned, to the delight of the Carpen-

---

[61] *Id.* at 713 (Jones, J. concurring).

ters, the AFL–CIO stepped in. Its lawyers wrote the Carpenters Union's response in support of granting certiorari and later, wrote the brief on the merits. The AFL–CIO had a much broader interest in the case than the Carpenters Union, because of the impact of the nurses issue on many AFL–CIO affiliate unions. KRCC counsel Hawkins also opposed certiorari. He accused the NLRB of picking on a small, poor employer as a weak opposing litigant in choosing the case for certiorari. Hawkins later explained that his client had not wished to expend its meager resources on Supreme Court litigation. On September 26, 2000, the Court granted the writ.

The NLRB's main brief was largely divorced from the evidence. Most of the brief was devoted to arguing that in light of *HCR*, "independent judgment" was ambiguous, hence the Board's interpretation was entitled to deference because it was rational and consistent with the Act. The Board presented the *Providence Hospital* analysis as its controlling interpretation of "independent judgment": "an employee does not exercise the 'independent judgment' that triggers supervisory status ... when the employee exercises ordinary professional or technical judgment in directing less-skilled employees to deliver services in accordance with employer-specified standards." The Regional Director's decision on the Kentucky River RNs was erroneously characterized as flowing straightforwardly from application of that test, and many of the facts were rearranged to fit more appropriately within the schema of professional direction of less skilled employees. The RNs were said to "work with and occasionally direct less-skilled employees to deliver services in accordance with the employer-specified standards expressed in the treatment plans," a neat application of the *Providence Hospital* rule to a hypothetical Caney Creek which differed significantly from the one portrayed in the representation proceeding. The treatment plans at Caney Creek were overwhelmingly aimed at mental and social rehabilitation programs designed by the rehabilitation counselors, and performed by them and by the rehabilitation assistants; the nurses' role in connection with the treatment plans was almost entirely limited to medication monitoring and administration, under physician guidance. Any direction regarding performance of the treatment plans was done by the rehabilitation counselors, whose employee status was no longer at issue. The NLRB briefs also overstated the nurses' working relationship with the rehabilitation assistants: "the RNs perform hands-on medical treatment and give limited direction to other members of their teams, based on their experience and special competence, pursuant to the requirements of the residents' treatment plans."[62] The Caney Creek RNs had no teams.

[62] Reply Brief for the NLRB, at 9–10. *See also* Brief for the NLRB at 5.

The NLRB's briefs handled the facts very poorly, at several key points accepting the employer's or the Sixth Circuit's version rather than the conflicting evidence upon which the Regional Director had relied. For example, in the NLRB's brief, there were three LPNs working at Caney Creek, "the RNs and LPNs provide medical services to residents throughout the [residential] units," and "two RNs and one LPN generally work on each of the three shifts, . . . although occasionally only one RN works on the third shift." Aside from the fact that, as of the hearing, only one LPN position was filled, this text made it sound as though at all times, two RNs and one LPN were on duty together. Instead, they were spread across seven days a week of the particular shift, so that usually only two out of the three nurses would be on the job at the same time; with only one LPN on the payroll as of the hearing, most of the time, the RNs each worked alone. When part of the supervisory status claim is that the RNs supervised the LPNs in administering medications, it is important that most of the time each RN worked there was no LPN on duty to "responsibly direct." The NLRB briefs confused the several building supervisor memos, citing as authoritative one that the Regional Director did not find to have been disseminated. This was compounded by the brief then weakly stating that there was no evidence that any building supervisor had actually exercised the authority conferred by that memo to "write up" a worker refusing to work overtime in the event of staff shortage. In fact, as noted above, Nurse Anderson had been reprimanded the only time she ever kept a worker over without prior management authorization.

The employer's brief treated the facts conclusorily "found" by the Sixth Circuit, as well as those repeated from its Sixth Circuit brief, as though they were uncontradicted in the record, and again leaned heavily on the lack of any other supervisor on the premises during building supervisor hours. It persuasively picked up on a view the *HCR* majority had expressed in connection with "in the interest of the employer": KRCC argued that the Board's effort to separate out professional judgment from independent judgment would have the effect of precluding a finding of supervisory status whenever the supervisory authority was exercised on the basis of the individual's professional training and expertise, unless it involved a change in the employee's status such as promotion, discipline or discharge. KRCC argued that under the Board's construction of "independent judgment," all professionals would be employees, and none would be supervisors, no matter how much managerial and personnel authority they exercised over other workers. In its reply brief, the Board reversed the argument, contending that on KRCC's construction, all professionals would be supervisors, and none would be covered employees.

KRCC made a fall-back argument which the NLRB did not parallel. KRCC argued that even under the NLRB's construction of "independent judgment," the RNs were supervisors, but it relied for this point on evidence that had been contested and not credited by the Regional Director, particularly the building supervisor memoranda. The NLRB, on the other hand, did not bother to argue that, if the agency's analysis of "independent judgment" were rejected by the Court, the record was nevertheless sufficient to support the Regional Director's conclusion that they lacked supervisory status. With better marshalling of the record, the Board could have argued that the RNs' direction of LPNs and rehabilitation assistants was *de minimis*, as was their discretion when operating within the building supervisor role, falling far below any threshold for "responsible direction," as well as "independent judgment."

The union briefs partially compensated for the deficiencies of the NLRB briefs by meticulously detailing the evidence, linking the facts in the record with the Board's entitlement to deferential review on its factfinding, and point by point, highlighting the many liberties the KRCC brief took in its characterization of the evidence. The union briefs also provided greater clarity than the Board's about the distinction the NLRB drew between occupational discretion and judgment, on the one hand, and supervisory independent judgment, on the other. The former, the union explained, is the judgment a professional, technical or skilled employee must exercise in carrying out her own work responsibilities. If one imagines a highly skilled worker performing an assignment without any assistance from another worker, judgment the highly skilled worker exercises is of necessity professional or occupational rather than supervisory, since there are no personnel functions involved. The latter is discretion in the decision about delegating particular tasks to less skilled workers, or about the selection of one particular worker rather than another to perform a given task.

At the oral argument on February 21, 2001, Deputy Solicitor General Lawrence G. Wallace argued first, on behalf of the NLRB, and Michael W. Hawkins argued on behalf of the employer. The NLRB did not split time with the union intervenor. Early in the argument, one of the justices successfully pressed Wallace to concede that the case was limited to construction of "independent judgment," and did not include interpretation of "responsibly to direct." Wallace focused his presentation almost entirely on the Board's "independent judgment" test distinguishing "professional judgment," a distinction several justices found confusing if not incoherent. When asked questions about key facts, he became confused, and vacillated. Several times in the argument Wallace failed to make clear to the justices the strongest facts in the record that supported the Board's conclusions and the places in which the Sixth Circuit had misstated the record or rejected the Board's factual findings even though supported by substantial evidence. KRCC counsel Hawkins pressed hard on the danger to institutionalized patients if the highest level employee on duty for ten hours at night was not a supervisor with undivided loyalty to the employer. There was no discussion at all during the argument about the burden of proof issue. The NLRB and union attorneys at the argument left discouraged about the chances of a favorable opinion; Hawkins and employer attorneys left elated.

Hawkins later remarked on how abstract and policy-oriented the Court's focus was during oral argument. The Carpenters Union counsel Schulz expressed a similar view, and also was trenchantly critical of Wallace's performance. In Schulz's recollection, Wallace had been

> so totally focused on whether the Board had the right "independent judgment" standard, he never clearly argued that assuming the Board was right, the employer had the burden of proof, and the employer never proved supervisory status. Also, he failed to hone in on the three key documents, [the three RN building supervisor exhibits,] and that the Sixth Circuit in effect had overturned a reasonable Board ruling on credibility as to whether the later ones were real and actually in effect despite conflicting testimony. The test of substantial evidence on the record as a whole should have forced reversal of the Sixth Circuit on the RNs even if the Court had remanded the case under a new standard. In addition, Wallace should have argued the fallback position that the employer never proved the supervisory status of the RNs under any standard. After all, they were really arguing about ordinary supervisory authority with respect to the building supervisor role, not anything unique to professionals.

On May 29, 2001, the Supreme Court rendered a 5–4 decision in *Kentucky River*.[63] The majority, in an opinion by Justice Scalia, rejected the NLRB's new formulation for § 2(11) status, although it unanimously affirmed the Board's allocation of the burden of proof to the party claiming that the worker is a supervisor. The Court conceded, on the basis of its reasoning in *HCR*, that the term "independent judgment" was indeed ambiguous, hence the NLRB was entitled to judicial deference in its construction, so long as it was rational and consistent with the statute. However, according to the Court, the Board's interpretation was neither, hence it was "unlawful."

The predicate for the Court's analysis was its reasoning about the nature of the ambiguity in the term "independent judgment." The Board's formula for independent judgment, and its brief outlining its

[63] 532 U.S. 706 (2001). All quotes in this and following paragraphs are from the opinion.

interpretation, had straddled the question of whether the agency was arguing about a distinction based on quality or quantity; in effect, it was arguing for both. The NLRB used "independent judgment" to differentiate between direction of coworkers based on professional or technical judgment, as opposed to judgment based on personnel factors, while also including a quantitative aspect, based on how broad a range of discretion was conferred upon the putative supervisor. The Supreme Court, however, held that "independent judgment," particularly as distinguished in § 2(11) from "activity routine or clerical in nature" was ambiguous as to the minimum degree or scope of discretion required to render the judgment "independent" rather than "routine," but that the phrase left no room for differentiation based on the nature, quality, or source of the judgment. Introduction of differentiation based on the nature of the judgment as professional or technical inserted a "categorical exclusion" into statutory text whose plain meaning suggests only one of degree rather than kind. Moreover, much as it had in *HCR*, the *Kentucky River* Court feared this distinction would permit the Board to deem to be covered employees many workers exercising broad human resources discretion over coworkers, asking "[w]hat supervisory judgment worth exercising . . . does not rest on 'professional or technical skill or experience?' "

In addition, as the Court understood it, the Board's "independent judgment" analysis was effectively limited to "responsibly to direct." The Court was particularly impatient with this error in statutory construction. It regarded the Board, in developing its formulation, as having ignored the Court's teaching in *HCR*, that "in the interest" required a construction applicable to all twelve § 2(11) supervisory functions, a syntax-based analysis just as relevant to "independent judgment." The Court accused the Board once again, as in *HCR*, of having in effect "read the responsible direction portion of § 2(11) out of the statute in nurse cases." The Court characterized the Board's interpretation of the interrelation of § 2(11) and § 2(12) as an argument that the § 2(12) policy of coverage of professionals supports the "categorical exclusion of professional judgments" from "independent judgment." Such an interpretation of "independent judgment" restricted to its use to limit "responsible direction," the majority concluded, "contradict[s] both the text and structure of the statute, . . . as well [as] the rule of [*HCR*] that the test for supervisory status applies no differently to professionals than to other employees."[64]

The majority rejected the Board's construction of "independent judgment" but not its underlying policy-based reasoning that the express

[64] *Id.* at 715, 717, 720–21 (quoting NLRB v. Health Care & Ret. Corp. of Am., 511 U.S. 571, 579–80 (1994)).

inclusion of professionals in § 2(12) supported interpretation of § 2(11) so as to avoid their wholesale elimination as supervisors. Similarly, the Court did not dispute the propriety of the Board's reliance on Taft–Hartley Act legislative history emphasizing Congress' intent only to exclude "true supervisors" with "genuine management authority" but not "minor supervisors." Conceding that "the Board is entitled to judge [the soundness of its labor policy] without our constant second-guessing," the Court reasoned that "[t]he problem with the argument is not with the soundness of its labor policy . . . [but] that the policy cannot be given effect through this statutory text." The majority suggested that the Board instead might be able to limit the scope of the supervisory exclusion in responsible direction cases by "distinguishing employees who direct the manner of others' performance of discrete tasks from employees who direct other employees, as § [2(11)] requires," noting that some NLRB case law had already drawn that distinction. Because the Board had "carefully insisted that the proper interpretation of 'responsibly to direct' [was] not at issue," however, the Court declined to consider this alternative.

The NLRB did win a victory on its other major issue. The Court unanimously held that the Sixth Circuit erred in not deferring to the Board's allocation of the burden of proof. Allocating the burden, both in representation cases and in ULPs, to the party advocating a special exclusion from a statutory prohibition, the Court reasoned, follows the general rule of statutory construction. In addition, it is easier to demonstrate that an employee has one of the twelve § 2(11) supervisory functions than to disprove that the employee has any of the twelve. The Court also rejected the employer's and the Sixth Circuit's position that in technical § 8(a)(5) cases the NLRB General Counsel nevertheless should bear the burden of proof because the validity of the bargaining unit is an element of the case. Disproving supervisory status, the Court held, is not an element of the ULP. Rather, the General Counsel must only prove that the unit was properly certified, which it was unless the *employer* successfully bore its original burden of proof, in the earlier representation proceeding, of the supervisory status of the RNs.

One might have expected the Court to remand the case to the Sixth Circuit for reconsideration under the correct burden of proof, but it did not. The Board's error in construing "independent judgment" prevented the Court from enforcing the NLRB order as to the RNs, and the Court held that it could not enforce the agency's order by substituting a legal standard of its own devising, which the Board had in any event not asked the Court to do. Thus far, the reasoning is uncontroversial. The decision goes on, however, to point out that under similar conditions in *HCR*, the Court simply affirmed the judgment of the circuit court, and "since neither party has suggested that [*HCR*'s] method for determining the propriety of a remand should not apply here, we take the same course." The affirmance of the circuit court left its judgment standing, meaning the employer was ordered to bargain as to the wall-to-wall bargaining unit, excluding the RNs. Both KRCC counsel Hawkins and Union counsel Schulz found this portion of the Court's reasoning mystifying.

The *Kentucky River* majority opinion was almost entirely divorced from the facts of the case. The Supreme Court quotes the lower court's opinion as though it accurately described the facts in stating "that the Board had erred by classifying 'the practice of a nurse supervising a nurse's aide in administering patient care' as 'routine [simply] because the nurses have the ability to direct patient care by virtue of their training and expertise, not because of their connection with management.' "[65] Of course, there were no nurses aides at Caney Creek, so the nurses could not have been supervisors in directing employees who did not exist. Elsewhere, the Court characterized the Board's interpretation of "independent judgment" as "[t]he only basis asserted by the Board, before the Court of Appeals and here, for rejecting respondent's proof of supervisory status with respect to directing patient care." Yet the reasoning below turned very little on RN direction of patient care, as opposed to their building supervisor role, a role nearly totally divorced from the professional judgment aspect of the NLRB's "independent judgment" analysis. This error, as well as the Court's failure to remand the case, shows that it handled the case as though it were simply reviewing an NLRB rule adopted through a rulemaking process. The Court ignored the fact that this was a case in which the effect of its holding was to deprive six registered nurses of rights as employees under the NLRA, when what it should have done was to remand the case to have their employee status litigated under a properly allocated burden of proof. All nine justices found that the court of appeals misallocated the burden of proof. Had the case been remanded to fix that error, the results for the RNs might have been different.

Justice Stevens, joined by Justices Souter, Ginsburg, and Breyer, dissented on the holding regarding RN status. The dissenters insisted that the § 2(11) terms "independent judgment" and "responsibly to direct" are "quintessential examples of terms that the expert agency should be allowed to interpret in light of the policies animating the statute." The NLRB's reading, asserted Justice Stevens, provided a definition of supervisor that, unlike the majority's, would not completely eliminate the coverage of professionals. The dissent defended the Board's distinction between the judgment that nurses exercise when asking others to take a patient's temperature and the judgment that nurses

---

[65] *Id.* at 710 (quoting 193 F.3d 444, 453 (6th Cir. 1999)).

exercise when they discipline others. In the dissent's view, the Board was correct in concluding that the exercise of independent judgment should mean one thing when it modified the ambiguous term "responsibly to direct" and something else when it modified the unambiguous terms in the other § 2(11) supervisory functions, such as "promote" or "discharge." The Board's reading was correct because only the term "responsibly to direct" was ambiguous and only it was "capable of swallowing" the statutory inclusion of professionals "if not narrowly construed." The dissent also pointed out the irony of the majority's conclusion that the RNs, who had no subordinates, were supervisors while leaving untouched the Board's conclusion that the rehabilitation counselors, who did routinely direct activities of the rehabilitation assistants, were not supervisors. Finally, the dissent maintained that since the Court had unanimously concluded that the Sixth Circuit had applied the wrong burden of proof, it should not have affirmed the lower court's judgment, but instead remanded for the lower court to apply the correct standard.

The majority's main holding effectively sends the NLRB back to the drawing board to interpret § 2(11). The decision leaves the Board with only four clear guidelines for its future construction of § 2(11) "independent judgment." First, it cannot use that phrase to differentiate based on the nature or quality of the judgment. Second, it can set a reasonable threshold or minimum quantity, degree or scope of discretion as requisite for the judgment to be "independent." Third, the Court accepted the tail end of the NLRB's *Providence Hospital* formulation; "the degree of judgment ... may be reduced below the statutory threshold by detailed orders and regulations issued by the employer."[66] Fourth, the Board should carefully ensure that the interpretation it places on "independent judgment" applies identically, across-the-board, to all twelve forms of § 2(11) supervisory authority. Apart from these points, however, the decision shines a hazy light on a possible interpretation of "responsibly to direct" as requiring more than assignment of discrete tasks.

HCR has ruled out "in the interest of the employer" as a means to resolve the tension between professional and supervisory status. *Kentucky River* has ruled out the use of "independent judgment" in terms of the qualitative nature of the judgment, or its source in professional, technical or skilled craft knowledge rather than personnel management. The Court has, however, left open the prospect of a minimum threshold of discretion in managing other workers being required, as well as the possibility of interpretation of "responsibly to direct" and "assign" which might accomplish much the same accommodation of coverage of professional employees as the Board's earlier formula for "in the interest of the employer" and "independent judgment." On the other hand,

[66] *Id.* at 713–14.

similar dicta in *Yeshiva* lured the Board onto the rocks in *HCR* and similar dicta in *HCR* led the Board to run aground in *Kentucky River*. This new invitation holds great promise of sending the NLRB over Niagara Falls in a barrel, taking with it the NLRA rights of professionals and perhaps also many technical and skilled trades employees.

The Immediate Impact of NLRB v. Kentucky River

The decision in *Kentucky River* had important consequences—for the Caney Creek employees, for nurses around the country seeking to organize, and for those with union representation attempting to continue collective bargaining. The ripples have rapidly spread to other professions, as well as to borderline supervisors in manufacturing and service industries. Most directly, the end of the story for the parties in *Kentucky River* is that, except for the RNs, the employees finally won their bargaining rights.[67] Although the Supreme Court litigation delayed the commencement of bargaining for about two years, it is unclear to what extent this additional delay altered the course of contract negotiations. It is doubtful whether the decision to exclude the RNs from the unit has made much difference, since their inclusion would have only very modestly increased the union's bargaining leverage with the employer. Ironically, the failure to remand, although depriving the union of the chance to argue that the employer failed to carry its burden of proving the RNs to be supervisors under a revamped NLRB standard for "independent judgment," benefitted the rest of the unit. It moved the case to closure, with an order to bargain covering ninety-five percent of the requested positions for the bargaining unit. The employer then abandoned its open resistance to union representation. The war for entrenchment of the union as bargaining agent, and negotiation and implementation of a collective bargaining agreement, on the other hand, continues. As of early 2005, no labor contract had been reached, and the prospects for one have become increasingly remote.

The § 8(a)(3) charges regarding the discharge of Glenn Moore and a few other workers during the election campaign dragged on throughout the litigation up to the Supreme Court and thereafter. The cases were all settled in the end. Moore won a substantial settlement, but had to agree to waive reinstatement. For a while Moore went to work for his father, then he drifted around for a period and moved on. Moore's departure, as well as a large layoff and turnover among the workforce, has contributed to the erosion of the union's support at Caney Creek. Some of the rehabilitation counselors spearheaded a failed effort at decertification a year or two after the employer commenced bargaining with the Carpenters. The union has found itself trapped in a no man's land, in which the

[67] Telephone Interview with union counsel Thomas Schulz, October 1, 2004; Telephone Interview with KRCC counsel Michael Hawkins, January 13, 2005.

opponents of union representation lack sufficient support to decertify, but the union lacks enough hard core support to exert serious economic pressure on KRCC through a strike, picket line, or other job action that might bring labor contract talks to a conclusion. Exacerbating the union's weakness is the reluctance of the rehabilitation assistants and counselors to take any job action that might jeopardize patient care and progress. Dinsmore & Shohl continued to handle the contract negotiations for the employer for about a year after the Supreme Court decision. Since then, KRCC CEO Dr. Louise Howell and other in-house staff have handled the employer's negotiations, although from time to time, they continue to consult Hawkins. Schulz regards Dr. Howell as a "tough negotiator."

The Continuing Importance of Kentucky River Today

The broader story of NLRB construction of § 2(11) likewise has not reached closure. The aftermath at the NLRB might best be described as "deja vu all over again." On July 23, 2003, a Board now composed predominantly of Bush administration appointees issued a notice inviting the filing of briefs by parties and interested amici in three representation cases, *Oakwood Healthcare, Inc.*, *Beverly Enterprises–Minnesota, Inc. (Golden Crest Healthcare Center)*, and *Croft Metals, Inc.*[68] These cases, one involving a hospital, one a nursing home, and one a manufacturing plant, are to be the vehicle through which the Board will attempt, yet again, to resolve how to interpret § 2(11), this time within the constraints of *Kentucky River*. Major employer organizations, the AFL–CIO and many major unions filed briefs, as did the NLRB General Counsel.[69] A General Counsel Memorandum instructs regional staff, both in handling ULP cases and when presiding in representation cases, to ensure a full factual record on these issues.[70]

The Board's notice invites suggestions about the gamut of post-*Kentucky River* issues. Following directly from the Supreme Court's reasoning, it asks where to set the minimum "degree" or "scope of

68 Notice and Invitation to File Briefs, Oakwood Healthcare, Inc., NLRB Case No. 7–RC–22141; Beverly Enterprises–Minnesota, Inc., d/b/a Golden Crest Healthcare Ctr., Cases 18–RC–16415, 18–RC–16416; Croft Metals, Inc., Case 15–RC–8393, July 25, 2003, <www.nlrb.gov/nlrb/press/releases/kyriver.pdf>.

69 Brief of the General Counsel, Oakwood Healthcare, Inc., NLRB Case No. 7–RC–22141; Beverly Enterprises–Minnesota, Inc., d/b/a Golden Crest Healthcare Ctr., Cases 18–RC–16415, 18–RC–16416; Croft Metals, Inc., Case 15–RC–8393, *reprinted as attachment to* Evidentiary Guidelines for Determining Supervisory Status, GC Memorandum OM 04–09, Oct. 31, 2003, *available at* <http://www.nlrb.gov/nlrb/shared_files/ommemo/ommemo>.

70 Evidentiary Guidelines for Determining Supervisory Status, GC Memorandum OM 04–09, Oct. 31, 2003, *available at* <http://www.nlrb.gov/nlrb/shared_files/ommemo/ommemo>.

discretion" for § 2(11) "independent judgment"; how to define "responsibly," in "responsibly to direct"; how to differentiate or address the overlap between "assign" and "direct," and how one can intelligibly distinguish between directing other employees and directing the manner in which others perform discrete tasks. The notice also requests views on additional fundamental issues of statutory construction, including how to resolve the tension between § 2(11)'s exclusion of supervisors and § 2(12)'s inclusion of professionals, whether a viable distinction can be drawn between § 2(11) "independent judgment" and § 2(12) "discretion and judgment," and whether there are identifiable functions which can serve as points of demarcation to differentiate, in Congress' words, between true supervisors possessing "genuine management prerogatives," and "minor supervisory employees." In reconciling the supervisory exclusion with the professional inclusion, the notice specifically asks, "[d]oes the Act contemplate a situation in which an entire group of professional workers may be deemed supervisors, based on their role with respect to less-skilled workers?" In addition, responders are asked to address an employer's ability to rotate, alternate, or divide up supervisory functions among its workforce, so as to exclude the great majority of workers as statutory supervisors, or to devolve those functions to collective decisionmaking by self-regulating work teams. The final question seeks advice on the extent to which the Board should continue to take into account in supervisory status determinations the so-called "secondary indicia" such as ratio of supervisors to subordinates and proportion of time spent performing rank and file work by putative supervisors. These indicators are labeled "secondary" because they do not appear in the text of § 2(11), yet they have functioned as powerful markers, or as the General Counsel's brief suggested, "circumstantial evidence" regarding the actual allocation of authority within a workplace, an important brake on manipulation of job content by employers to exclude many ordinary workers as supervisors.

In the meantime, *Kentucky River* has sharply affected union organizing and collective bargaining, especially among nurses and other health care workers. Employers have been emboldened to seek to exclude from NLRB rights entire existing as well as proposed bargaining units of staff nurses, sometimes on grounds of their professional task delegation to nursing aides or technicians and sometimes on the basis that the nurses rotate through or occasionally serve as substitutes in the position of charge nurse. One health care employer has deemed guard leaders working with two or three other guards to be supervisors and an automotive parts manufacturer has challenged as supervisory the team leaders of its self-directed production teams.[71] Aided by the *Kentucky*

[71] Decision and Direction of Election, Providence Everett Med. Ctr., Case 19–RC–14157 (Nov. 29, 2001) (leader security guards); Decision and Direction of Election, Borg Warner

River holding that the proponent of supervisory status bears the burden of proving it, unions continue to win favorable regional director decisions in about nine out of ten representation cases in which the employer seeks to exclude hospital or nursing home nurses as § 2(11) supervisors. However, since *Kentucky River*, employers have been filing requests for review in many of these cases. As of December 2004, one AFL–CIO lawyer estimated that there were over thirty pending before the NLRB, awaiting disposition of *Oakwood* and *Golden Crest*, in addition to those before the courts of appeals.

Kentucky River precludes the Board from interpreting "independent judgment" to differentiate based on the quality or nature of the judgment, but invites the Board to define the term by setting a minimum threshold of discretion which it would require the putative supervisor to have in the performance of at least one § 2(11) function before it would attach the "independent judgment" label. It also suggests that one permissible construction that might reconcile § 2(11) with the coverage of professionals in § 2(12) would be to treat direction of discrete tasks as insufficient to qualify as "responsible direction," requiring instead that the worker "responsibly direct" other employees in their overall work. This has reopened, rather than settled, the issue of where and how to draw the line between "employees" and "supervisors," putting into question nearly all established Board case law on all but the most clear-cut bosses, on the one hand, and laborers, on the other. At the least, it will entail a change in the Board's analytical methodology, if not a change in outcomes. Moreover, because the Court has insisted that the Board may not devise a construction of § 2(11) that explicitly treats professionals differently from other employees, future cases construing § 2(11) will affect not only professionals and technicals, but also skilled trades workers directing apprentices and helpers, and leaders and machine set-up employees directing production employees.

When Taft–Hartley was enacted, it is highly improbable that Congress had any idea that its last-minute addition of "responsibly to

(Morse Tec, Inc.), (Case 17–RC–12183) (May 21, 2003) (team leaders of self-directed work teams); Decision and Direction of Election, HMR of Maryland, LLC, Case 5–RC–15444 (Sept. 13, 2002) (entire proposed RN and LPN bargaining unit, where nurses rotated through charge nurse positions); Decision and Direction of Election, Gordon Health Ventures, 6–RC–12195 (Mar. 25, 2003) (entire six RN and LPN bargaining unit on grounds that they served as shift supervisor/charge nurses with authority over the nursing assistants); Decision and Direction of Election, Hosp. Gen. Menonita, Inc., Case 9–RC–17602 (Feb. 21, 2002) (all eighty members of proposed RN staff nurse bargaining unit because of role utilizing technicians, LPNs and service personnel in patient care); Decision and Order, Integrated Health Servs., Inc., Case 6–UC–445 (Dec. 19, 2002) (petition for clarification of ten-year-old all-LPN bargaining unit effectively to eliminate entire unit based on LPNs' role directing CNAs). All these decisions are available at <http://www.nlrb.gov/nlrb/legal/decisions>.

direct" to the list of twelve § 2(11) functions might lead to interpretation of the supervisory exclusion as encompassing most professionals, expressly covered in § 2(12) and § 9(b)(1), or the many skilled trades workers who delegate and oversee work of trainees, given special bargaining unit rights in § 9(b)(2). When the statute is read as a whole, such an interpretation would undermine effectuation of several provisions. It is clear from the legislative history that Congress had in mind foremen charged with running entire departments or production lines. The reports, statements, and speeches rarely refer to "supervisors," but rather, most of the time, to "foremen." This is consistent with the statement of Senator Flanders, who in proposing the insertion of "responsibly to direct" on the Senate floor said he merely wanted to ensure that even where a personnel department ignored the foremen's recommendations on discipline or pay increases too often for them to satisfy the § 2(11) requirement that they be "effective recommendations," a foreman with authority and control to run an operation would still be a statutory supervisor. Had Congress thought that provisions of the bill effectively would repeal NLRA coverage for ordinary skilled trades workers, because they delegate tasks to helpers and apprentices, the political forces of the day, particularly the AFL craft union affiliates, probably would have marshaled enough votes in Congress to block Taft–Hartley, or at least they would have prevented the override of President Truman's veto. It is only when the pieces of § 2(11)—"responsibly to direct" and the other listed forms of authority, "in the interest of the employer," and "independent judgment"—are dissected separately, extracted from their statutory and historical context, that one can conclude the contrary.

AFL–CIO Associate General Counsel Craig Becker, now filing briefs in the post-*Kentucky River* NLRB and court of appeals cases, summarized the situation: "As a legal matter it has been an interesting exercise. There is a strong argument based on the legislative history that Congress did not intend this group of workers to be excluded. However, the statutory language does not lend itself to an easy effectuation of this intent and the Board's choice of means to effectuate that intent, moving first from 'in the interest of the employer,' shifting then to 'independent judgment,' was not necessarily the best possible."[72]

It remains to be seen whether yet another interpretative move under § 2(11) will suffice to reconcile the statutory command favoring inclusion of professionals with the command to exclude "true supervisors" to ensure employers the undivided loyalty of their representatives. There is a substantial risk of yet another replay of *HCR* and *Kentucky River*, whether the Board interprets "responsible direction" so as to

[72] Telephone Interview with Craig Becker, December 17, 2004.

exclude direction of *ad hoc* tasks, or shifts to an interpretation of "independent judgment" setting a fairly high quantum of discretion as a threshold, or both. Moreover, whatever formula is adopted by the Board, it is likely to influence personnel practices in areas starting with the health care industry, but spreading far afield. Labor lawyers, industrial relations practitioners, and personnel specialists will no doubt rethink how they organize work and allocate functions, with an eye toward influencing legal consequences.

In the center of this picture of broader labor relations consequences is the plight of nurses, doctors, and other health care workers, and the undoing of the congressional intent behind the 1974 health care amendments that brought the industry under NLRA jurisdiction. The Supreme Court in *HCR* found the legislative history of these amendments to have no value in interpreting § 2(11) because that provision had been enacted by Congress twenty-seven years earlier. Nevertheless, the 1974 Congress clearly thought it was covering employee RNs, LPNs, MDs, and other health care professional and technical employees who, because of their specialized jobs, routinely delegate tasks to less-skilled workers. Had it believed otherwise, Congress might well have amended the definition of employee in the statute to cover them specifically, as the American Nurses Association had in fact requested. In 1974, the NLRA was amended because recognition strikes were disrupting health care and because low pay and poor working conditions for unorganized workers were driving the brightest and most talented out of the field. As it becomes progressively harder for nurses to organize, their pay and conditions worsen and the nursing shortage continues to grow—exactly the problems for the industry and for patients that Congress sought to avoid. In its reasoning in both *HCR* and *Kentucky River*, the Supreme Court tacitly assumes that by excluding such professional and technical workers from the protections of the Act, the employer will have their "undivided loyalty" because they will lose the statutory right to organize and bargain collectively. Depriving them of the right to organize does not guarantee their loyalty, and it does not prevent them from taking collective action—it merely moves the activity outside the regulation of the NLRA, restoring the status quo ante 1974. A new wave of recognition strikes for excluded "supervisor" nurses in hospitals and nursing homes could be the ultimate undoing of the goals of the 1974 legislation.

Conclusion

Unlike the typical NLRA organizing campaign story, in which the employer's allegedly unfair labor practices or objectionable campaign activities take center stage, the *Kentucky River* story has focused on structural issues of bargaining unit composition. The bargaining unit is both an election district and a grouping for economic pressure tactics in the heat of collective bargaining. The inclusion or exclusion from the protections of the Act of professional workers at the boundary line of supervisory authority affects both elections and the union's collective bargaining power. For the workers involved in *Kentucky River*, the union, the employer, and their trial counsel, the case was one focused on factual issues determining who would be included in the bargaining unit, hence whether the union would win the election and, ultimately, whether it could pressure the employer into a collective bargaining agreement. For the agency's lawyers, however, particularly at the appellate and Supreme Court level, as well as for the AFL–CIO, the *Kentucky River* story was mainly about technical legal issues and NLRB agency policy: the correct formula for interpreting the supervisor definition while preserving the right to organize and bargain for ordinary professional employees. For employers such as KRCC, the issue was how to ensure that the employer retains control over those workers representing it in directing subordinates.

For scholars of labor law and industrial relations, the focus is different still. *Kentucky River* flows through core structural questions about the Act. It compels reexamination of questions regarding which types of workers have rights of freedom of association and collective bargaining and how large a percentage of the workforce can be excluded from statutory coverage without rendering § 7 a hollow promise. In the early days of the Wagner Act, the foremen's unionization drives triggered a battle between those on the bottom and those on the top over the loyalties of those in the middle. In transmuted form, the battle continues today for the hearts and minds—and NLRA status—of workers who use skill and education to exercise judgment but who have little control over coworkers. In the modern workplace, with flattened managerial hierarchies, and with managerial authority pushed downward to the lowest possible level and distributed as widely as possible, a broad construction of the § 2(11) factors could render nearly everyone a supervisor excluded from employee status under the Act. Congress, the Board, and the courts have struggled with where to draw the line since the earliest days of the NLRA. They no doubt will continue to do so in an ever-growing volume of cases triggered by new forms of work organization in the Bermuda Triangle established at the intersection of *HCR* and *Kentucky River*.

10

Catherine L. Fisk and Michael J. Wishnie

The Story of *Hoffman Plastic Compounds, Inc. v. NLRB*: Labor Rights Without Remedies for Undocumented Immigrants

Are there two sets of rules for the twenty-first century workplace, one for citizens and legal immigrants and the other for the millions of undocumented workers in the United States? Are the employers of those undocumented workers free to ignore the mandates of the National Labor Relations Act, Title VII of the Civil Rights Act of 1964, the Fair Labor Standards Act, the Occupational Safety and Health Act, and other federal and state labor and employment laws, without fear of ordinary liability?

To an immigration lawyer, familiar with immigration law's "plenary power doctrine" and the notion of an ascending scale of rights that privileges legal immigrants over undocumented ones, the intuitive answer might be, "of course; there are frequently different rules for immigrants and citizens, and for legal immigrants and the undocumented."[1] Undocumented workers are non-citizens who are neither lawful permanent residents nor have an immigration status authorizing them to work in the U.S. and thus have fewer legal rights. To a labor lawyer, familiar with labor law's embrace of collective action and private rights enforcement to achieve public deterrence, the instinctive response

[1] *See, e.g.*, Johnson v. Eisentrager, 339 U.S. 763, 770–71 (1950) ("The alien, to whom the United States has been traditionally hospitable, has been accorded a generous and ascending scale of rights as he increases his identity with our society."); Mathews v. Diaz, 426 U.S. 67 (1976) (approving discrimination in public benefits eligibility between citizens and permanent residents).

might be, "of course not; there are no statutory exceptions to labor law coverage based on immigration status, and the fate of all workers depends on the treatment of each." *Hoffman Plastic Compounds, Inc. v. NLRB* is a tale of the efforts of unions, employers, civil rights advocates, legislatures, executive branch agencies, and ultimately the Supreme Court to reconcile the immigration and labor statutory schemes, to make sense of the sometimes contradictory legislative impulses these twin regimes manifest, and to develop a framework for the humane and effective regulation of both borders and markets.[2]

In important ways, laws regulating U.S. borders and labor markets share a common ancestry that traces to early colonial rules on slavery, the slave trade, and indentured servants. Although modern lawyers are accustomed to thinking of "labor law" and "immigration law" as wildly disparate, proposals for mammoth new guestworker programs, "earned" legalization, and a new paradigm for U.S.-Mexico relations reflect the deep connections between these two bodies of law. This common heritage is apparent as well in the competing political pressures embodied in both schemes—at times and in places protectionist, nativist, bigoted, and designed to favor the interests of management; at other times and in other places open, non-discriminatory, universalist, and designed to favor the interests of working people.

In *Hoffman Plastic Compounds v. NLRB* five justices of the U.S. Supreme Court viewed the labor and immigration laws as fundamentally at odds with one another. The majority held that an employer who unlawfully discharges a worker for union organizing is immune from ordinary labor law liability for backpay if the worker lacks work authorization under immigration law and the employer learns of the worker's status only after the illegal discharge. Four justices viewed the labor and immigration laws as fundamentally in harmony. In dissent, they would have allowed the National Labor Relations Board to enforce its backpay award, notwithstanding an immigration law that prohibited employers from knowingly hiring or employing unauthorized workers.

Hoffman will not be the last word on labor rights for immigrants and labor obligations for their employers. It remains to be seen whether the decision helps spur broader legislative reform, strengthening the right to organize for all workers and thereby reducing an incentive for outlaw employers to prefer undocumented employees, or whether it instead promotes an already-flourishing underground economy and thereby stokes the demand for illegal immigration.

---

[2] 535 U.S. 137 (2002). One author of this chapter, Michael Wishnie, participated in the *Hoffman* case at the Supreme Court and has been involved in legislative efforts to respond to it. Some references later in this chapter to the *Hoffman* litigation strategy and legislative responses to the Court's decision are drawn from his knowledge.

Social Background

The *Hoffman* case was litigated over thirteen years amidst three important social and legislative developments. One occurred in the labor movement, one in Congress, and one in the population as a whole.

First, by the time the Supreme Court decided *Hoffman* in 2002, the union movement had significantly withered, representing only approximately 8.5% of private-sector, non-agricultural employees. This was a fraction of union density in the post-World War II era and a figure so low as to raise fundamental questions about the capacity of unions to protect the interests of working people. To labor advocates this decline was especially discouraging because John Sweeney had assumed the leadership of the AFL–CIO in the mid–1990's with a pledge to reinvigorate moribund organizing campaigns. Organized labor appeared largely unable to attract enough new members or to win elections in numbers substantial enough to halt, if not reverse, a decades-long decline.

Perhaps not coincidentally, through the 1990's and into the new century, organized labor's attitudes toward immigration continued to reflect, in large measure, traditional fears that immigrants would work for lower wages than long-time residents and thus drive down wages. There were important exceptions to this attitude, such as successful organizing drives targeting high-immigrant industries initiated by unions such as the service employees' union (SEIU) and the hotel and restaurant employees' union (HERE), the AFL–CIO Executive Council's adoption of a pro-immigrant resolution in February 2000, and the Immigrant Worker Freedom Ride of 2003.[3] It was also true that labor organizers increasingly found low-wage immigrant workers more receptive to unionization drives, despite the risk of deportation, than low-wage American workers, and a number of unions came to perceive organizing immigrants as essential to their success.[4] Nevertheless, concerned about the impact on wage levels of large numbers of new workers, and perhaps reflecting a residual nativism, important voices within the labor movement remained unpersuaded of the wisdom of legalizing undocumented workers and repealing the employment verifi-

---

[3] Among the important organizing initiatives targeting immigrant-intensive industries were SEIU's Justice for Janitors campaign, HERE's hotel industry campaigns in Las Vegas and elsewhere, and health care worker drives in California and New York. The AFL–CIO's February 2000 Executive Council statement, which advocates legalization measures and "replacing" the I–9 employment verification system that was at issue in *Hoffman*, is available at <http://www.aflcio.org/aboutaflcio/ecouncil/ec0216200b.cfm>. In 1986, the AFL–CIO had supported adoption of the same system.

[4] Telephone Interview with Muzaffar Chishti, Senior Policy Analyst, Migration Policy Institute and former Director, UNITE Immigration Project, June 3, 2004.

cation system that the AFL–CIO had endorsed when enacted by Congress in 1986.[5]

Second, in the 1990's, as *Hoffman* worked its way through the NLRB and the courts, Congress enacted and President Clinton signed three major anti-immigrant laws. The legislation slashed the public benefits eligibility of millions of indigent immigrants and their families, mandated detention and deportation for tens of thousands of permanent residents, and restricted traditional forms of deportation relief such as political asylum.[6] The human consequences of these bills were dramatic. The draconian Welfare Act of 1996, for instance, sought to achieve nearly one-half of its estimated savings through elimination of benefits for immigrants, even though far fewer than half of welfare recipients were non-citizens.[7] And the number of permanent residents deported for minor past criminal convictions rose significantly, separating tens of thousands of long-time residents from their families, jobs, and communities.[8] The net effect of these laws was also significantly to increase the risk for immigrant workers of participating in a union organizing drive. For undocumented workers, deportation in the event of a retaliatory employer call to the INS became more certain, and for legal immigrants, the availability of a social safety net—public benefits—in the event of a retaliatory discharge became far less likely. The trend towards ever-more punitive immigration laws continued following the terrorist attacks of September 11, 2001, although perhaps paradoxically, the USA PATRIOT Act, Homeland Security Act, and other major post-September 11 legislation have effected less sweeping changes to the immigration statutes than did the 1996 laws.

Third, despite the indifference of some in the labor movement towards immigrants, and despite the adoption of numerous harsh stat-

[5] Immigration Reform and Control Act of 1986, Pub. L. No. 99–603, § 101(a)(1), 100 Stat. 3359 (Nov. 6, 1986), *codified at* 8 U.S.C. § 1324a (2000).

[6] These laws were the Antiterrorism and Effective Death Penalty Act of 1996, Pub. L. No. 104–132, Title IV, 110 Stat. 1214; Personal Responsibility and Work Opportunity Reconciliation Act of 1996, Pub. L. No. 104–193, §§ 400–451, 110 Stat. 2105; and the Illegal Immigration Reform and Immigrant Responsibility Act of 1996, Pub. L. No. 104–208, Division C, 110 Stat. 3009–546.

[7] The Congressional Budget Office estimated that $23.7 billion of the anticipated $53.4 billion in federal savings from the 1996 welfare law would be attributable to the anti-immigrant measures. Cong. Budget Office, Federal Budgetary Implications of the Personal Responsibility and Work Opportunity Reconciliation Act of 1996, at 3 tbl. 2 (1996). Congress did subsequently restore some benefits. *See, e.g.*, Balanced Budget Act of 1997, Pub. L. No. 105–33, 111 Stat. 251 (restoring Supplemental Security Income benefits for some legal immigrants).

[8] In 1986, the INS removed fewer than 2,000 immigrants because of past criminal convictions, a figure that rose to approximately 71,000 persons with criminal convictions removed in 2002. 2002 *Yearbook of Immigration Statistics*, 176–77 & tbl 46 (Oct. 2003).

utes in the 1980's and 1990's, the number of noncitizens in the country increased substantially. From 1970 to 2000, the foreign-born population in the United States tripled, to 28.4 million persons.[9] While record figures in absolute terms, as percentages of the overall population, they are not: in 2000, 10.4 percent of the population was foreign-born, the highest proportion since 1930, but from 1860 to 1930, the percentage of foreign-born was higher still. The increase in the non-citizen population was more dramatic, however, rising from 3.5 million in 1970 to 17.8 million in 2000. Data on the undocumented population are notoriously imprecise, but estimates have risen from approximately five million persons in the mid–1990's to perhaps ten million in 2004.[10]

Nationwide, a large and crucial segment of the workforce is undocumented. Driven by a remarkable ninety-six percent labor-force participation rate for undocumented men, there are approximately six million undocumented immigrant workers, representing five percent of the total workforce (including four percent of the urban workforce and forty-eight percent of the agricultural workforce).[11] An employer group estimated in 2001 that immigrants (both legal and undocumented) contribute $1 trillion per year to the Gross Domestic Product and account for twelve percent of total hours worked in the U.S. Not surprisingly, undocumented workers are concentrated in some of the lowest-paying and most dangerous jobs in the country.

By the time the events giving rise to *Hoffman Plastic* occurred, the effect of immigration on the California workforce had been dramatic. In many of the state's industries, including manufacturing, construction, and service work, wages and working conditions had deteriorated after employers eliminated or weakened unions in the 1970's and native

---

9 The data in this paragraph are from U.S. Census Bureau, Profile of the Foreign–Born Population in the United States: 2000, at 3, 8, 9, Figure 1–1, 20, Table 7–1 (Dec. 2001). "Foreign born" refers to persons who are not U.S. citizens at birth, and includes those who have become U.S. citizens through naturalization and those who remain non-citizens, including lawful and undocumented immigrants.

10 The INS estimated the undocumented population to be five million persons as of October 1996 and seven million as of January 2000, U.S. INS, Estimates of the Unauthorized Immigrant Population Residing in the United States: 1990–2000 (2003), but other demographers have concluded the total undocumented population may be closer to eleven million. *See* Jeffrey S. Passel, Randy Capps, & Michael Fix, *Undocumented Immigrants: Facts and Figures* (2004) (estimating undocumented population at 9.3 million); Cindy Rodriguez, *Census Bolsters Theory Illegal Immigrants Undercounted*, Boston Globe, Mar. 20, 2001, at A4 (noting estimates ranging from six to eleven million persons).

11 The data in this paragraph are from Jeffrey S. Passel, Randy Capps, & Michael Fix, *Undocumented Immigrant: Facts and Figures* 1–2 (2004); Orrin Bair, *Undocumented Workers and the NLRA: Hoffman Plastic Compounds and Beyond*, 19 Lab. Law. 153, 160 (2003) (citing *How Many Undocumented: The Numbers Behind the U.S.-Mexico Migration Talk*, PEW Hispanic Center 3 (May 21, 2002)).

workers were increasingly replaced by immigrants. Nearly one-fourth of the state's population was foreign-born (compared to one-tenth in the United States as a whole). Foreign-born Latinos constituted seventeen percent of California's total workforce, and forty-two percent of its factory operatives, one-half of its laborers, and over one-third of its service workers.[12] The dominance of Latino workers was especially apparent in Southern California, where the Hoffman Plastic plant is located.

The greater Los Angeles area has a substantial amount of light manufacturing.[13] Most of it is concentrated in an old industrial area, the Alameda Corridor, which lies between downtown Los Angeles and the ports of Long Beach and Los Angeles. Less than ten percent of the manufacturing jobs are unionized and a majority of the workers are Latino. Many workers live in Alameda Corridor communities, thus creating the possibility of using community and religious organizations, kinship bonds, and neighborhood and ethnic ties as well as workplace solidarity to forge a union.[14]

Legal Background

The legal background to the *Hoffman* case reflected some of these social developments as well. The NLRB had taken the position since at least the late 1970's that undocumented immigrants were "employees" covered by the National Labor Relations Act.[15] As employees, undocumented workers who were fired for union organizing would be entitled to the full range of remedies under the NLRA. The Board normally orders reinstatement and backpay from the date of discharge until the date of reinstatement, issues a cease-and-desist order proscribing similar misconduct in the future, and orders the employer to post a notice announcing the Board's decision and promising to abide by it. The NLRB requires employees to mitigate damages by seeking interim employment. Therefore, a backpay award may be reduced by wages an employee earned in interim employment or, if the employee failed to make reasonable efforts to find employment, by the amount he or she would have earned. Eligibility for backpay depends on the employee being available

[12] David Lopez & Cynthia Feliciano, *Who Does What? California's Emerging Plural Labor Force, in Organizing Immigrants* (Ruth Milkman ed. 2000).

[13] Marla Dickerson, *L.A. County Leads U.S. in Factory Jobs,* L.A. Times, Jan. 21, 2004, at C2.

[14] Hector L. Delgado, *The Los Angeles Manufacturing Action Project: An Opportunity Squandered? in Organizing Immigrants* (Ruth Milkman ed. 2000).

[15] *See, e.g.*, Duke City Lumber Co., 251 NLRB 53 (1980); Apollo Tire Co., 236 NLRB 1627 (1978), *enf'd,* 604 F.2d 1180 (9th Cir. 1979); Amay's Bakery & Noodle Co., 227 NLRB 214 (1976); Hasa Chemical, Inc., 235 NLRB 903 (1978).

for work, and, therefore, a backpay award will be reduced for any period during which the employee is unavailable for work, as for example, when she or he is in jail or out of the area of the employer's operations. The Board will not order reinstatement if the employee engaged in misconduct so egregious as to make him or her unfit for reinstatement, or if the employer shows that at some point after the unlawful discharge the employee would have been terminated in any event. Interest will be computed on a backpay award.[16]

In 1984 in *Sure-Tan v. NLRB*, 1984, the Supreme Court endorsed the view that undocumented workers are "employees" within the meaning of the NLRA.[17] In *Sure–Tan*, an employer contacted the INS shortly after his employees voted in a union. The INS visited the factory and investigated the immigration status of all Spanish-speaking employees. The INS arrested five and, by the end of the day, all were on a bus ultimately bound for Mexico. The Board found that the employer, with full knowledge that they were undocumented, invited the raid solely because the employees supported the union. The Board ordered reinstatement with backpay, leaving for the compliance hearing the question whether the deported workers were available for work, a requirement for backpay eligibility. On review, the court of appeals held that six months was a reasonable period to believe the discriminatees would have been employed absent the employer's unfair labor practice and modified the Board's order to award a minimum of six months' backpay.

The Supreme Court upheld the Board's conclusion that undocumented immigrants are statutorily protected as employees under the NLRA. The Court explained: "Application of the NLRA helps to assure that the wages and employment conditions of lawful residents are not adversely affected by the competition of illegal alien employees who are not subject to the standard terms of employment." But the Court reversed the court of appeals' mandatory minimum backpay award as too speculative. Recognizing that the discharged employees would receive no backpay because they were deported the very day they were fired, the Court nevertheless rejected the contention that the Board has the power to order minimum backpay regardless of an employee's particular circumstances. Specifically, the Court was concerned that enforcing the Board's backpay award could undermine "the objective of deterring unauthorized immigration that is embodied in the [immigration statutes]." Thus, in providing directions for remand, the Court stated that remedies "must be conditioned upon the employees' legal readmittance to the United States" and that "in computing backpay, the employees

---

16 On general NLRB remedies in unlawful discharge cases, see 2 Patrick Hardin & John E. Higgins, Jr., *The Developing Labor Law* 2521–29 (4th ed. 2001).

17 467 U.S. 883 (1984).

must be deemed 'unavailable' for work (and the accrual of backpay tolled) during any period when they were not lawfully entitled to be present and employed in the United States."

At the time *Sure–Tan* was decided, it was not unlawful for an undocumented immigrant to be hired or to work in the United States; under the immigration laws, all that was prohibited was entering without inspection or remaining beyond the term of one's visa. Seizing on this point, as well as the Supreme Court's attention to the physical unavailability of the workers in *Sure-Tan*, the first court of appeals to consider the backpay eligibility of undocumented workers who remained in the country after discharge determined that such workers were in fact eligible.[18]

Two years after the *Sure–Tan* decision, however, and only months after the Ninth Circuit had held that workers in this country were eligible for backpay regardless of their immigration status, Congress enacted the Immigration Reform and Control Act of 1986 (IRCA). IRCA embodied a bargain struck between legislators who favored increased immigration enforcement and those who favored a legalization program. The bill's two key provisions were, first, a one-time amnesty for those who could demonstrate continuous residency since 1982, and second, "employer sanctions", which for the first time prohibited employers from knowingly hiring or employing "unauthorized workers."[19] Employer organizations such as the U.S. Chamber of Commerce opposed the employer sanctions provisions as a costly, burdensome, and inefficient strategy to compel the private sector to enforce public immigration laws. The AFL–CIO, on the other hand, endorsed employer sanctions in the hope they would reduce wage competition by deterring employment of undocumented immigrants.

The 1986 law defined "unauthorized alien" as a non-citizen who was not, at the time of employment, either a lawful permanent resident or authorized to work—in other words, undocumented immigrants, whether they have overstayed a visa or entered the country without inspection, as well as those persons holding non-immigrant visas that did not allow employment.[20] IRCA did not create penalties for unauthorized workers who accepted employment; instead, Congress chose a scheme of civil and criminal penalties for *employers* who knowingly hire or employ

[18] Local 512, Warehouse and Office Workers' Union v. NLRB (Felbro), 795 F.2d 705 (9th Cir. 1986) (wrongfully discharged undocumented worker who remains in country eligible for backpay).

[19] *See* 8 U.S.C. § 1324a(a)(1) (2000).

[20] 8 U.S.C. § 1324a(h)(3) (2000) (defining "unauthorized alien" for purposes of employer sanctions). Many visas, including those for tourists and some students, do not carry work authorization.

unauthorized workers. This was a deliberate legislative choice that grew out of many years of congressional studies and commissions and the recognition that Congress could not hope to influence the supply of undocumented workers—the wage discrepancies between the United States and Mexico were just too great—but it could hope, through regulation, to dampen employer demand.[21] The "employer sanctions" regime thus obligates employers to check the work authorization status of all new employees within three days of hire by completing an INS Form I–9, indicating that the employee is either a U.S. citizen or an immigrant authorized to work in this country. Employers must retain their completed I–9s and make them available to immigration agents for inspection upon request.[22] Finally, when Congress enacted IRCA, it recognized that employers would need time to adjust to the law's new requirements. Accordingly, it provided for a slow phase-in, in which the Attorney General was to issue no fines to employers in the first six months after IRCA's enactment nor for a first employer offense committed in a subsequent grace period of twelve months, or up to June 1, 1988.

After IRCA made it unlawful to hire undocumented workers, employers sought to revisit the question whether undocumented workers were protected by the NLRA, as *Sure-Tan* had held. The first wave of post-IRCA cases involved conduct that occurred before IRCA went into effect. Courts uniformly concluded that undocumented workers were statutory employees, and moreover, that if they remained present in the country after a wrongful discharge, they were eligible for backpay.[23] As cases involving post-IRCA conduct began to reach the courts, the Seventh Circuit concluded that undocumented workers were ineligible for backpay, thus raising questions about the continuing viability of the contrary view asserted by the Second and Ninth Circuits before IRCA had gone into effect.[24]

---

21 *See* Brief *Amici Curiae* of ACLU et al., No. 00–1595, 2001 WL 1631648 (discussing legislative history, including congressional acknowledgment that legislation might influence employer behavior but could not overcome wage differentials motivating employee migration).

22 In addition to prohibiting the knowing employment of unauthorized workers, in 1986 Congress adopted provisions barring employers from engaging in discriminatory I–9 practices based on national origin or citizenship status, 8 U.S.C. § 1324b, and later added provisions barring immigrants from tendering false documents in satisfaction of the I–9 obligation, *id.* § 1324c.

23 *See* Rios v. Enterprise Ass'n Steamfitters Local 638, 860 F.2d 1168, 1172–72 & n.2 (2d Cir. 1988); *see also* EEOC v. Hacienda Hotel, 881 F.2d 1504, 1517 (9th Cir. 1989) (same as to backpay under Title VII for pre-IRCA conduct).

24 *Compare* Del Rey Tortilleria, Inc. v. NLRB, 976 F.2d 1115 (7th Cir. 1992) (undocumented workers who remain in the country ineligible for back pay) *with* Rios v. Enterprise Ass'n Steamfitters Local 638, 860 F.2d 1168, 1172–72 & n.2 (2d Cir. 1988) (undocumented

The NLRB attempted to reconcile the divergent courts of appeals opinions. In its lengthy decision in *A.P.R.A. Fuel Oil Buyers Group*, it reaffirmed the view that undocumented immigrants are employees protected by the NLRA and rejected the argument that immigration status was a flat bar to backpay. The Board held that undocumented workers were entitled to the same remedies as other employees so long as the remedies did not require the employer to violate IRCA.[25] Thus, the employer could be ordered to reinstate employees so long as at the time of reinstatement the employees could present verification that their immigration status enabled them to work in the U.S. The Board held that an employer could be ordered to provide backpay from the date of discharge until either the date of reinstatement or the date when the employee failed to produce evidence of eligibility to work in the U.S. In later cases, the Board made clear that the backpay would be tolled as of the date the employer learned that the employee was not legally permitted to work in the U.S. It was against this background that *Hoffman Plastic* arose.

Factual Background

In May 1988, not long after IRCA went into effect and prior to the expiration of IRCA's "first offense" grace period for employers, a man whose real name may have been Samuel Perez applied for a job under the name Jose Castro at Hoffman Plastic Compounds factory in Panorama, California.[26] He spoke little English and so someone helped him fill out the six-page application form. On the form, he answered "Yes" to the question "Are you prevented from lawfully becoming employed in this country because of visa or immigration status?" At some point in the application process, he also completed the I–9 Form establishing that his immigration status permitted him lawfully to work. In that connection, Castro presented a birth certificate stating he was born in El Paso, Texas, a California ID card with his name and photograph, and a Social Security card in his name. Reflecting on this discrepancy in the file, the

---

workers eligible for backpay); EEOC v. Hacienda Hotel, 881 F.2d 1504, 1517 (9th Cir. 1989) (same). In a *sui generis* Title VII case, the Fourth Circuit adopted the Seventh Circuit's approach, arguably deepening the split. *See* Egbuna v. Time–Life Libraries, Inc., 153 F.3d 184 (4th Cir. 1998) (*en banc*) (per curiam) (temporarily unauthorized worker refused reinstatement after resignation cannot state claim under Title VII, implying undocumented workers not covered by Title VII).

[25] 320 NLRB 408 (1995).

[26] Except where indicated otherwise, this account of Castro's employment at Hoffman Plastic Compounds and subsequent events is drawn from testimony of Castro, his niece, and other witnesses at the backpay hearing before the Administrative Law Judge in Los Angeles on March 4–5, 1993 and June 14, 1993. In the Matter of Hoffman Plastic Compounds, Inc. and Casimiro Arauz, Case No. 21–CA–26630, National Labor Relations Board.

NLRB lawyer who litigated the case suspected that a Hoffman Plastic office employee looked at the application and explained to Castro that he could not be hired until he produced a birth certificate, picture ID, and Social Security card and that Castro went away and came back with the requested documents.[27] Or maybe it was simply that Castro did not understand the question when the application was translated and filled out on his behalf. In any event, Castro was hired and went to work at the factory. While working there he lived in the home of his niece, sleeping on the living room couch.

Hoffman Plastic Compounds, a family-owned firm, produces a type of plastic, polyvinylchloride (PVC) pellets, on order for firms that use PVC to make pharmaceutical, construction, and household products. Its laboratory employees develop formulae to suit specific customer needs. The production employees then operate compounding machines that mix and cook the ingredients according to the formula, and extruding machines that press the PVC into pellets. Shipping employees bag, store, and ship the pellets to customers. Jose Castro worked as a production employee, operating compounding and extruding machines.

Shortly before Christmas 1988, the United Rubber, Cork, Linoleum and Plastic Workers of America, AFL–CIO, began to organize the plant. Dionisio Gonzalez, a union organizer, visited the plant frequently and gave authorization cards to employees to distribute to co-workers. Castro was one of the employees who passed out cards. In January 1989, after supervisors learned of the organizing drive and unlawfully interrogated employees about their union activity, nine employees were laid off. One of them was Castro.

One might wonder why Jose Castro, an undocumented minimum-wage worker who had no home of his own and who had so much to lose, took the risk of speaking up for the union. According to Peter Tovar, the NLRB Regional Attorney who handled the case, Castro had been considered a good, hard-working employee and he was not a leader of the union organizing drive. He was just in the wrong place at the wrong time. To the extent that he did actively support the union, we can only speculate about his reasons. Scholars who studied union organizing campaigns in Southern California in the 1980's and 1990's found little fear. Some workers said that if they were deported they would simply come back. Others said that the possibility of INS raids seemed remote. Some Mexican and Central American immigrants had had positive experiences of unionism in their home countries and believed that, in contrast to the death threats leveled against union organizers by right-wing groups in Central America, in the U.S. the worst thing that could happen would be

---

27 Telephone Interview with NLRB Region 21 Regional Attorney Peter Tovar, January 21, 2004.

that they would lose a low-wage job and be deported home to family.[28] Some undocumented workers vow to reenter the U.S., even as they are being deported to their home countries, because the conditions are so dire at home.[29]

According to Hoffman's lawyer, Ryan McCortney, the organizing drive failed and the union withdrew the election petition a few days before the date of the election. To his knowledge, there have been no other efforts to unionize the plant, which remains nonunion. Many of the employees who were fired for union activity were reinstated, although some were later terminated, according to McCortney, for other reasons.[30]

Prior Proceedings

One of the laid-off employees, Casimiro Arauz, filed an unfair labor practice charge. In April 1990, over a year after the layoffs, an ALJ for the NLRB held a hearing on the complaint. The employees testified that the supervisors had told employees that the union was "cabron" (which the ALJ rather delicately described as "an expression in Spanish which meant 'bad' or 'something not good' ") and that they "could get into trouble if management found out about [their] passing out union cards." Ron Hoffman, the company owner, denied that union activity had anything to do with the layoffs, insisting that they were due to a decline in orders, and further that employees were selected for layoff based on a combination of seniority, disciplinary record, and skills. The ALJ found that the plant hired employees during the time the union employees had been fired and required existing employees to work overtime to keep up production. The ALJ found that the evidence was in conflict about whether Hoffman had laid off employees to rid itself of the union or for lack of work or some combination of the two. In any event, however, the ALJ found that Hoffman had selected employees for layoff based on their union activity because all of the union adherents were laid off and

---

[28] Ruth Milkman, *Introduction, in Organizing Immigrants* at 8–9 (Ruth Milkman ed. 2000). By contrast, for those who have traveled greater distances and at greater cost, such as undocumented Chinese immigrants who may incur upwards of $50,000 in debt to the "snakeheads" who smuggle them, with family members liable in the event of default, the consequences of deportation can be far more dire. *See* Peter Kwong, *Forbidden Workers: Illegal Chinese Immigrants and American Labor* (1997). Similarly, with the increased militarization of the U.S.-Mexico border since September 11, the prospects of illegal reentry following deportation have dimmed, and the possibility of removal has become more frightening to many Mexican and Central American immigrants.

[29] Chris Kraul, *Illegal Immigrants Receive a One-Way Ticket to Mexico,* L.A. Times, July 13, 2004.

[30] Telephone Interview with Ryan McCortney, January 16, 2004.

because supervisors had interrogated them about their support for the union.[31]

Both the General Counsel and the employer filed exceptions, which is the process by which a party appeals an ALJ decision to the Board. In January 1992, the Board issued a decision that largely upheld the ALJ's findings and conclusions, except it found that one of the nine employees would have been laid off regardless of his union activity.[32] Eventually, the other fired employees settled their charges with Hoffman, and their immigration status never became an issue.[33]

In June 1993, an ALJ conducted a compliance hearing to determine the amount of backpay owed to Castro. Hoffman's lawyer, Ryan McCortney, was a relatively young lawyer at the time of the compliance hearing. He had graduated from the University of Southern California Law School in 1987 and worked in the Los Angeles office of the Sheppard Mullin law firm since graduation. He claimed later that he had no idea at the start of the hearing that Castro might be undocumented but hit upon the possibility entirely by accident based on something Castro blurted out at the hearing.[34] Castro had missed an earlier compliance hearing and McCortney inquired about his absence. According to McCortney, Peter Tovar, the Regional Attorney, replied that Castro was in jail in Texas. Thinking that the jail time would toll the backpay award, McCortney hired a private investigator to figure out where he was in jail and how long he had been there. The private investigator faxed Castro's birth certificate to the jail. McCortney was surprised when informed that there was no one by that name in the jail. Suspecting that the birth certificate was faked, the investigator went to the hospital where Castro had been born and learned that the certificate was valid. Rejecting the possibility that Castro was undocumented, McCortney then asked for a background check on Castro to see whether he had been in jail at other times that would toll the backpay period. The check revealed two things: one, that Castro had a trucker's license, which led McCortney to believe that he easily could have mitigated his lost wages, and two, that he had briefly been in jail in Los Angeles County. Armed with this information, McCortney went to the compliance hearing intending to use the information to impeach Castro's credibility about his mitigation efforts.

McCortney spent quite a bit of the first part of the hearing trying to establish where Castro had lived in the four years since his layoff.

---

[31] Hoffman Plastic Compounds, Inc., 306 NLRB 100 (1992).

[32] *Id.*

[33] Petitioner's Brief at 3 n.1.

[34] Telephone Interview with Ryan McCortney, January 16, 2004.

McCortney sought to show that Castro had either not been in California, and thus unavailable for work at the Hoffman plant and ineligible for backpay, or that he had not made adequate efforts to find work. In addition, there was some dispute about whether Castro had received a letter from Hoffman offering him reinstatement (which would also toll the backpay award). Castro, testifying through a translator, said that he had been employed at a variety of irregular and low-paying jobs as a gardener, carpenter's assistant, and mechanic's assistant since being fired from Hoffman and that he had spent six or seven months in El Paso. McCortney inquired why he had missed earlier compliance hearings. Castro answered that he had missed one because he was in jail for four days for drinking in public. The hearing recessed briefly for a sidebar discussion about whether McCortney could inquire further about the jail time.

McCortney thought Castro's testimony about his mitigation efforts was evasive and he began to wonder whether he had the right Jose Castro. The Los Angeles County jail records contained a description of Castro which mentioned tattoos on his arms. When the hearing reconvened, McCortney asked: "Mr. Castro, do you have a California driver's license?" Castro answered no. McCortney later recalled that he suspected at this point that he had the wrong Jose Castro. McCortney then said, abruptly, and incomprehensibly if one were relying only on the transcript to follow the thread of the action: "If he rolls up his sleeves on his arms, that's the end of it. I mean, if he doesn't have any tattoos, then it's not the person." The ALJ asked Castro whether he had any tattoos on his arms. Castro did not. "Okay, that's not him," said McCortney. McCortney later recalled that he crumpled up the birth certificate and threw it in the wastebasket as a dramatic demonstration that this was the wrong person. The record simply indicates that the hearing resumed with more questions about interim earnings and efforts at mitigation.

Tovar's theory for why Castro had not worked constantly since being laid off in 1989 was that Castro had so little education he had difficulty finding jobs.[35] Thus, on cross-examination, Tovar asked how much education he had received, and Castro replied that he had only two years of formal education while a young child in Mexico. That made no sense to McCortney—why would someone born and raised in Texas have left school in the second grade? It was not until Castro said he had attended school in Mexico that it occurred to McCortney that Castro had borrowed the birth certificate because he was not a legal immigrant. On redirect, McCortney asked how many years of education he had, and Castro again said two. McCortney then asked why he had stated on his employment application that he had eight years of education, and Castro

---

[35] Telephone Interview with Peter Tovar, January 21, 2004.

replied, "So that I could obtain work." McCortney continued, "Now, you were born in El Paso, Texas, correct?" "No, I am Mexican," responded Castro. "You're not a citizen of the United States?" "No." Over the objection of Tovar, the Regional Attorney, the ALJ permitted McCortney to ask Castro whether he had documents permitting him to work in the United States. Castro said he had the birth certificate but admitted that he had borrowed it from a friend so he could get a job.

A few weeks after the compliance hearing, McCortney wrote the Regional Director to argue Castro was ineligible for backpay because he was not authorized to work. Peter Tovar, relying on the Board's interpretation of *Sure–Tan,* took the position that backpay was not tolled unless or until the INS issued a deportation order, so McCortney threatened to report Castro to the INS unless Tovar stipulated that Castro was an undocumented alien who had not been legally present in the United States since before he was hired at Hoffman Plastic. The Regional Director refused to make such a stipulation, and then sought guidance from the Division of Advice. In August 1993 the General Counsel issued an Advice Memorandum concluding that Castro was indeed entitled to reinstatement and backpay.[36]

At that time, the case law of the NLRB and the Ninth Circuit held that undocumented workers could be awarded backpay and reinstatement, although some of the cases predated the enactment of IRCA. Yet the ALJ rejected this authority and held that Castro was ineligible for backpay. The ALJ distinguished the Board's 1992 decision in *A.P.R.A Fuel Oil Buyers Group*, which had ordered reinstatement of two undocumented workers, because in that case the employer knew of the employees' undocumented status at the time of hire. He distinguished the Ninth Circuit decision in *EEOC v. Hacienda Hotel*, which awarded backpay under Title VII to undocumented workers, because their claims arose prior to IRCA's effective date.[37] And he did not cite the Ninth Circuit's decision in *Local 512 Warehouse and Office Workers' Union v. NLRB (Felbro, Inc.)*, which held that undocumented workers were entitled to backpay under the NLRA, albeit also involving pre-IRCA misconduct.[38] Rather, the ALJ followed the Seventh Circuit's decision in *Del Rey Tortilleria v. NLRB*, which held that undocumented workers were not entitled to backpay after IRCA.[39]

McCortney was thrilled that the ALJ had rejected the Board position from *A.P.R.A. Fuel* which made immigration status irrelevant to a

---

36 Advice Memorandum to Region Twenty-One (Aug. 31, 1993).

37 881 F.2d 1504, 1517 (9th Cir. 1989).

38 795 F.2d 705, 722 (9th Cir. 1986).

39 976 F.2d 1115 (7th Cir. 1992).

backpay award.[40] He thought it a vindication of his view that it would be unfair to award backpay to an employee who could not legally have been hired and could not legally mitigate damages by seeking interim employment. In his view, making Castro eligible for backpay would result in an unjust windfall. Peter Tovar, of course, saw the matter differently. In his view, it was simply unrealistic to think that undocumented immigrants would sit around rather than mitigate damages. He said: "They are here to work and they do work. Castro reported to us every job he had after being fired from Hoffman, and we discounted the backpay request to reflect all his interim earnings. There was no unfairness to the employer."[41]

The Regional Director filed exceptions in December 1993. In response, McCortney argued to the Board that Castro had misled Hoffman Plastic by presenting false documents, had misled the NLRB by failing to testify truthfully at the compliance hearing (having lied about his name), and could not legally have been hired by Hoffman in the first instance.[42] By the time the case reached the Supreme Court McCortney had come to characterize his client as entirely "innocent," without knowledge of Castro's undocumented status, and thus as an employer who did not need an NLRA backpay award to deter further hiring of undocumented workers.[43] In the post-hearing brief, however, McCortney did not take such a strong position. There was no evidence in the record as to whether Hoffman Plastic had knowingly hired other undocumented workers, knew of Castro's immigration status, or had a company policy against hiring undocumented workers, except the information on the employment application and the I–9 Form. The most that McCortney could argue was that the evidence about Castro's immigration status on his employment application and I–9 Form conflicted, and that it was unnecessary to show that Hoffman had a policy against hiring undocumented workers in order to eliminate its backpay liability because the law prohibited hiring them.

There followed an unexplained five-year delay in the case. Interestingly, William B. Gould, IV, a Stanford law professor who became Chair of the NLRB in December 1994, did not recall *Hoffman Plastic* as being the "big case" on the issue of the rights of undocumented workers.[44]

---

[40] Telephone Interview with Ryan McCortney, January 16, 2004.

[41] Telephone Interview with Peter Tovar, January 21, 2004.

[42] Answering Brief of Respondent to the Exceptions and Brief of the Counsel for the General Counsel. Case No. 21–CA–26630 (Jan. 30, 1994).

[43] Transcript of Oral Argument, 2002 U.S. Trans Lexis 11 at 14; Petitioner's Reply Brief at 12.

[44] Telephone Interview with William B. Gould, IV, January 21, 2004.

Rather, the big case on that issue was the second decision in *A.P.R.A. Fuel Oil Buyers Group* which was issued in December 1995 while the *Hoffman* decision was pending.[45] In *A.P.R.A.*, four members of the Board (Gould, Browning, Cohen, and Truesdale) exhaustively considered how to reconcile the NLRA's remedial provisions with the IRCA prohibition on the employment of unauthorized immigrants. The majority of the Board concluded that the major purpose of IRCA was to deter the employment of undocumented workers and that providing full NLRA remedies was consistent with this purpose:

> [T]he appeal of undocumented workers to employers is that aliens will often accept wages and conditions of employment considered unconscionable in this country. A ready supply of individuals willing to work for substandard wages in unsafe workplaces, with unregulated hours and no rights of redress, enables the unscrupulous employers that depend on illegal aliens to turn away Americans and legally working alien applicants who hesitate to accept the same conditions. In addition, the continuous threat of replacement with powerless and desperate undocumented workers would certainly chill the American and authorized alien workers' exercise of their Section 7 rights.[46]

Thus, the Board concluded in *A.P.R.A Fuel* that granting NLRA remedies was consistent with, and indeed necessary to, achieve the goals of IRCA. The Board noted that the employer knew from the time it first hired the workers that they were undocumented and thus that backpay was appropriate because they would have remained employed but for their union activity and the employer's illegal retaliation for it. The Board ordered the employer to provide backpay from the dates of discharge up to the date of reinstatement or the date the workers failed to produce evidence required by IRCA of an immigration status authorizing them to work.[47] The Board pointed out in a footnote that an employer ordinarily would be permitted to cut off backpay liability by proving that the employees had engaged in conduct that would have led the employer to discharge them. In *A.P.R.A.*, though, because the employer knew they were undocumented at the time of hiring it was precluded from alleging that it would have terminated them on that basis.[48] Two members dissented in part: Browning because the decision did not do enough to protect the undocumented workers, and Cohen because it did too much.

---

[45] 320 NLRB 408 (1995).

[46] A.P.R.A. Fuel Oil Buyers Group, Inc., 320 NLRB 408, 414 (1995).

[47] *Id.* at 416.

[48] *Id.* at 416 n.44.

By September 1998, when the Board finally issued its decision on Castro's entitlement to backpay, Board membership had changed. Cohen, Browning, and Truesdale were gone. Fox, Liebman and Hurtgen, who replaced them, seemed to have a slightly different view of remedies for undocumented workers. They followed the decision in *A.P.R.A.* and concluded that undocumented workers are entitled to some backpay. But they found a significant difference between *Hoffman* and *A.P.R.A.*, in that in *A.P.R.A.* the employer clearly knew the employees were undocumented when it hired them, and the evidence about whether Hoffman knew Castro was undocumented was, at most, conflicting. The Board stated:

> [T]he record supports the Respondent's contention that it would not have offered Castro initial employment had it known of his unauthorized immigration status. In this connection, the record shows, and the judge found, that the Respondent attempted to comply with IRCA when it hired Castro, and that the Respondent did not learn until the backpay hearing that Castro used fraudulent identification in applying for employment.[49]

The Board noted in a footnote that Castro answered "yes" to the question on the application whether his immigration status prevented him from lawfully becoming employed. But the Board rejected the contention that this showed that Hoffman knew of Castro's status "because the record clearly shows that the Respondent only hired Castro after he had supplied, as the Respondent required, documents that appeared to be genuine and relate to the person presenting them." Therefore, the Board ordered that Hoffman's backpay liability terminate effective June 14, 1993, the date of the hearing at which Castro confessed to being undocumented. The Board thus determined that Castro was entitled to $66,951 in backpay plus interest for the four and a half years from when he was fired in January 1989 until the June 1993 compliance hearing.

There is no reason in the record why the Board took five years to rule on the case. McCortney said that some well-placed sources told him that the Board deliberately sat on the case waiting for Board membership to change.[50] Chairman Gould did not remember any such efforts, though he did recall members of the Board delaying release of the decision for some time as they disagreed about how to handle it. He remembered *Hoffman* as a somewhat controversial decision, and in fact drafted an opinion in the case (which was never issued) in which he disagreed with other members of the Board about whether Hoffman

---

[49] Hoffman Plastic Compounds, Inc., 326 NLRB 1060 (1998).

[50] Telephone Interview with Ryan McCortney, January 16, 2004.

knew of Castro's immigration status.[51] That unpublished dispute about Hoffman's knowledge was the last time the issue was raised; for the rest of the litigation, McCortney insisted without challenge that his client did not know Castro was undocumented and would not have hired him if it had.[52]

It is unclear whether political controversy was the sole or principal cause of the delay in issuing the opinion. Nor is it clear what prompted the Board to reject Chairman Gould's view that Hoffman was not an innocent employer whose backpay liability should be terminated. It is clear, however, that the years the case was pending at the Board were extremely contentious times, especially after Republicans gained the majority in the House of Representatives in 1994. Congressional subcommittees conducted unprecedented oversight hearings at which they interrogated Chairman Gould about particular Board decisions and policies with which they disagreed, and threatened to reduce the Board's appropriations.[53] Gould recalled that some Board members or staff feared that extending statutory rights to undocumented immigrants would be very controversial.[54]

McCortney informed company owner Ron Hoffman of the costs and benefits of petitioning for review of the Board decision. Although advised that the costs would be high and the chance of winning uncertain, Hoffman wanted to fight on. When Regional Attorney Tovar insisted that if Hoffman refused to pay the award the Region would seek enforcement in the Ninth Circuit, McCortney decided to act. He knew that the law was not favorable in the Ninth Circuit and that the Act allows a "person aggrieved" by a Board order to seek judicial review in the circuit court of appeals where the dispute arose or in the D.C. Circuit. He filed a petition for review in the D.C. Circuit that same day, in order to beat the NLRB to the courthouse.

McCortney's belief that the D.C. Circuit would be a hospitable venue turned out to be wrong. The AFL–CIO filed a forceful amicus brief in support of the Board and Marsha Berzon, then one of the nation's leading labor and employment attorneys and soon to be confirmed by the Senate as a member of the U.S. Court of Appeals for the Ninth Circuit,

---

51 Telephone Interview with William B. Gould, IV, March 3, 2004.

52 One amicus brief to the Supreme Court opened with a reminder that "Hoffman does not contest that one of the illegally laid-off workers had indicated on his employment application that he was not authorized to work in the United States." Brief *Amici Curiae* of Employers and Employer Organizations at 7. But the reviewing courts were necessarily bound by the factual finding that Hoffman was unaware of Castro's status.

53 These events are recounted in William B. Gould, IV, *Labored Relations* (2000).

54 Telephone Interviews with William B. Gould, IV, January 21, 2004 and March 3, 2004.

participated in oral argument on behalf of *amici*. Berzon was a skilled and experienced appellate advocate, and as one member of the panel later recalled, she did a superb job presenting the case for enforcement.[55]

The D.C. Circuit panel, in a majority opinion by Judge David Tatel, noted a number of points that had been largely overlooked by others.[56] The opinion canvassed the history and structure of IRCA and the various relevant NLRB doctrines on remedies. Judge Tatel observed that at the time Castro applied for a job, IRCA did not prohibit using another's birth certificate or documents to obtain employment. Thus, in the majority's view, the issue was not a comparative judgment of Castro's misconduct in securing the job versus Hoffman's misconduct in firing him. Rather, it was whether Castro's immigration status rendered him ineligible for backpay. As to that, the majority concluded, Congress' intention was plain that there should be "expanded enforcement of existing labor standards and practices in order to deter the employment of unauthorized aliens and to remove the economic incentives for employers to exploit and use such aliens."[57] The majority also emphasized that IRCA "does not make it unlawful for an *alien* to work; it makes it unlawful for an *employer* to hire 'an alien knowing the alien is ... unauthorized.' Having now discovered Castro's unauthorized status, Hoffman can no longer employ him lawfully. But at the time Hoffman hired Castro, it complied with IRCA, and from that date until it learned he is unauthorized, nothing prohibited his continued employment." The Board's limitation of the backpay award to the period of Castro's lawful availability for employment complied with IRCA and was consistent with both labor and immigration policy.[58]

The majority opinion also dealt with the sentence in *Sure–Tan* stating that "in computing backpay, the employees must be deemed

[55] Telephone Interview with the Honorable David S. Tatel, June 8, 2004. Berzon's San Francisco firm, Altshuler, Berzon, Nussbaum, Berzon & Rubin, had particular expertise in these issues. Another member of the firm, Michael Rubin, had successfully litigated several of the leading post-*Sure–Tan* cases, including Patel v. Quality Inn South, 846 F.2d 700 (11th Cir. 1988) (undocumented worker is employee for purposes of Fair Labor Standards Act and may sue for unpaid wages and liquidated damages) and Local 512, Warehouse and Office Workers' Union v. NLRB (Felbro), 795 F.2d 705 (9th Cir. 1986) (wrongfully discharged undocumented worker who remains in country eligible for backpay). Earlier the same year Berzon argued *Hoffman*, the firm had also unsuccessfully petitioned for certiorari in Egbuna v. Time–Life Libraries, Inc., 153 F.3d 184 (4th Cir. 1998) (*en banc*) (per curiam) (temporarily unauthorized worker refused reinstatement after resignation cannot state claim under Title VII, implying undocumented workers not covered by Title VII).

[56] Hoffman Plastic Compounds, Inc. v. NLRB, 208 F.3d 229 (D.C. Cir. 2000).

[57] *Id.* at 240 (quoting Pub.L. No. 99–603 § 111(d), 100 Stat. 3359 (1986)).

[58] *Id.* at 243 (quoting 8 U.S.C. § 1324a(a)(1)(A) (1986)).

'unavailable' for work (and the accrual of backpay therefore tolled) during any period when they were not lawfully entitled to be present and employed in the United States." In the majority's view, that sentence was *dicta,* because the *Sure–Tan* employees were not physically present in the United States at the time; the sentence was designed to respond to the Board's lump-sum award of six months' backpay for deported workers, which was not tailored to their actual circumstances. Judge Tatel also read the *Sure–Tan* sentence in context as indicating approval of the Seventh Circuit's having limited its backpay award so as to avoid creating an incentive for the employees to reenter the country unlawfully to claim backpay.

Judge David Sentelle dissented. In his view, the case was quite simple. Since Hoffman could not lawfully employ Castro, the company was immune from ordinary backpay liability for wrongful discharge. Were it not for the Supreme Court's decision in *Sure–Tan,* which granted undocumented workers statutory rights, Judge Sentelle "would hold that by no theory of law or equity could the federal government compel an employer to employ an illegal alien to do nothing and pay him for doing nothing when it could not lawfully employ him to work and pay him for working."[59] Judge Sentelle's opinion set forth his view that the *Sure–Tan* sentence regarding employees "deemed 'unavailable' for work ... during any period when they were not lawfully entitled to be present and employed in the United States" definitively foreclosed Castro's claim.[60]

McCortney and his client then had another choice to make. A petition for rehearing en banc would be a long shot—the D.C. Circuit grants rehearing en banc in only a handful of cases each year. But McCortney had heard that dissenting Judge Sentelle was a friend and hunting companion of Justice Antonin Scalia and, thus, was an influential voice within the court of appeals. So Hoffman gave the go-ahead.[61]

The D.C. Circuit agreed to re-hear the case en banc, a strong sign that a majority of the ten active judges considered the panel decision to have been wrongly decided.[62] James Coppess of the AFL–CIO Office of

---

[59] *Id.* at 253.

[60] *Id.* at 254 (quoting *Sure–Tan*, 467 U.S. at 903).

[61] Telephone Interview with Ryan McCortney, January 16, 2004.

[62] 2000 WL 985015, 164 L.R.R.M. (BNA) 2814 (D.C. Cir.2000). Of the ten judges who voted on the petition for rehearing, only nine took part in the argument and decision. Judge Silberman assumed senior status between the time of the *en banc* argument and the date of the *en banc* decision, and accordingly participated in the decision, but Judge Merrick Garland took no part in the argument or decision. 237 F.3d 639, 640 n.* (D.C. Cir. 2001) (*en banc*).

General Counsel, an advocate widely respected by the members of the D.C. Circuit, participated in argument on behalf of the amici.[63]

To the surprise of prognosticators, the *en banc* court denied Hoffman's petition for review and enforced the Board's award, in a 5–4 decision which saw two prominent conservative judges join three of the court's more progressive members in the majority.[64] The majority opinion, again written by Tatel, largely repeated the analysis of the panel opinion, and the dissents by Sentelle and Ginsburg largely repeated Sentelle's earlier argument that the *Sure–Tan* sentence controlled.

The Supreme Court Decision

Supreme Court Proceedings

Hoffman filed a petition for certiorari in the Supreme Court in the spring of 2001. McCortney thought it was another long shot. His brief argued that the D.C. Circuit's decision was in conflict with *Sure–Tan* and that the Supreme Court's intervention was necessary to resolve a "severe" circuit split.[65] In opposition, the Board argued that the D.C. Circuit opinion was fully consistent with *Sure–Tan*, that no circuit split existed since the Board's decision in *A.P.R.A. Fuel Oil Buyers Group* had addressed the divergent approaches of the Seventh and Ninth Circuits, and that in any event this case was a poor vehicle to resolve any uncertainties about the best interpretation of *Sure–Tan*. Foreshadowing a note of defensiveness that would later reappear in the government's brief on the merits, the Board repeatedly stressed that this case, in which the employer was unaware of Castro's status at the time of hire, differed from the knowing employer in *A.P.R.A.* and most other such cases, and was therefore "atypical" of the remedial settings in which the Board had ordered backpay to undocumented immigrants.[66] As in Hoffman's petition, the Board's opposition contained only passing reference to immigration law other than IRCA.

And then came the attacks of September 11, 2001. McCortney thought it made all the difference. Although a "cert memo" analyzing whether the Court should grant the writ of certiorari would have been produced over the summer by a law clerk in one of the eight chambers

---

[63] Telephone Interview with the Honorable David S. Tatel, June 8, 2004. Marsha Berzon had been sworn in as a member of the Ninth Circuit months before the *en banc* argument.

[64] Hoffman Plastic Compounds, Inc. v. NLRB, 237 F.3d 639 (D.C. Cir. 2001).

[65] The petition for certiorari failed to note the Fourth Circuit's decision in *Egbuna* but did contend a split existed between the Seventh and the D.C., Second, and Ninth Circuits. Petition for Certiorari, U.S. No. 00–1595, 2001 WL 34091948 (filed Apr. 16, 2001).

[66] Brief for the NLRB in Opposition, 2001 WL 34090274, at *23 (June 16, 2001).

participating in the Justices' cert pool (which shared the task of analyzing all cases filed), recommending a disposition of the petition, and a justice may well have selected the case to nominate for discussion well before September 11, the attacks and their aftermath may have influenced the Court's consideration in conference. McCortney recalled that the Court granted the cert petition two weeks to the day after September 11.

In preparing his brief on the merits and for oral argument, McCortney thought a lot about whether and how to raise the link between lax immigration enforcement and terrorism. He ultimately decided he did not need to. One day when he had called the Court to ask a question about the briefing schedule, the clerk's office inexplicably did not answer. He learned when the clerk returned his call the following Monday that the Court had been evacuated because a letter containing anthrax had been mailed to the Court. (No evidence was ever made public indicating that an immigrant was responsible for the anthrax, but the popular perception at the time was that there may have been a connection to foreign terrorists.) The clerk explained that he was working out of his van, which was parked on the street near the Court building. McCortney concluded he did not need to mention the security issues posed by illegal immigration—the justices had had personal experience with the threat of terrorism. The most McCortney thought he needed to do at argument was to mention categories of visas that would allow people to be in the U.S. but not to work, and thus would render even legal visitors ineligible for backpay. The example he chose was student visas, because people had told him that they associated the reference to student visas with the men who flew the planes into the World Trade Center.[67]

The NLRB's brief on the merits also avoided direct reference to the events of September 11, but it continued in some ways the cautious approach of the opposition to certiorari. Paul Wolfson, Assistant to the Solicitor General, who argued the case for the Board in the Supreme Court, later recalled that the INS had some discomfort with the position of the Board. He said, however, that the INS accepted the proposition that border enforcement alone could not stop undocumented immigrants from entering the country in search of work and it endorsed further efforts to reduce the employment magnet. Unlike review of other agency actions, however, where the Solicitor General's office might sometimes facilitate internal discussions with the challenged agency that could lead to slightly different agency decisions—and a more legally defensible position—the Solicitor General's office must defend the decisions of the Board as they are issued. The reason is that the NLRB, unlike other

---

[67] Telephone Interview with Ryan McCortney, January 16, 2004.

agencies, renders decisions in an adjudicative process that, like a judicial proceeding, is confidential until the decision is made; there is no opportunity for involvement of lawyers from the Department of Justice or the Solicitor General's Office to craft decisions with likely Supreme Court litigation in mind. This left Wolfson unsure that *Hoffman* was winnable. He was concerned that the Court would treat the case as obviously controlled by *Sure–Tan* and dismiss the Board's opinion as practically frivolous, resting on a factual distinction of no legal moment—the continued physical presence of the worker after discharge. In its merits brief, the Board thus spent nearly the first half of its argument presenting a detailed discussion of the *Sure–Tan* case. Only later did the Board address the remedial purposes of the NLRA, the goals of IRCA, and the ways in which the backpay award to Castro was consistent with both. Mitigation was treated in a paragraph, on the penultimate page of argument.[68]

Meanwhile, soon after the Supreme Court granted certiorari, attorneys for the AFL–CIO, civil rights groups, and others began working to coordinate the preparation of amicus briefs. It was quickly agreed that the AFL–CIO and its outside counsel would approach the case from a labor law perspective, including a close analysis of the *Sure–Tan* case and an emphasis on the tradition of deference to the Board's broad remedial authority. The ACLU would analyze the case from an immigration law perspective, including an exhaustive examination of the legislative origins of IRCA, to argue that Congress did not intend IRCA to alter the outcome in *Sure–Tan,* nor to limit labor law remedies. The ACLU would argue that IRCA made only more evident Congress' intent that undocumented workers be eligible for backpay. Several civil rights advocacy organizations would organize a "Brandeis brief" collecting stories of exploitation of immigrants in the workplace. Finally, the attorneys agreed that two less common briefs would be useful, one by state attorneys general emphasizing that, whatever the outcome in *Hoffman*, state labor, employment, workers' compensation, tort, contract, and insurance law must be left undisturbed. Last, if possible, would be a brief on behalf of mainstream employers frustrated by unfair competition from outlaw shops that violated labor and immigration laws. All five

[68] Brief for the NLRB, No. 00–1595; Telephone Interview with Paul R.Q. Wolfson, March 1, 2004; Telephone Interview with Bo Cooper, INS General Counsel in 2001–03, July 23, 2004. Notably, neither the Board nor Hoffman nor any of the amici engaged Board precedent addressing the appropriate remedy for wrongful discharge where there is a legal impediment to reinstatement other than immigration status, such as wrongful discharge of underage workers or unlicensed drivers, neither of whom can be re-employed lawfully. *See, e.g.*, NLRB v. Future Ambulette, Inc., 903 F.2d 140 (2d Cir. 1990) (crafting remedy of backpay and conditional reinstatement for wrongfully discharged driver with suspended license).

briefs, including the states'[69] and employer association briefs,[70] were eventually filed.

Tellingly, the U.S. Chamber of Commerce declined to file a brief on either side, which supporters of the Board considered a victory.[71] If McCortney was dismayed by the fact that employer organizations either came in on the other side or stayed out of the case entirely, he did not admit it. He dismissed as "nonsense" the argument that giving backpay would give unethical employers a competitive advantage. When told that his position gained no support from employer or business organizations, Ron Hoffman just said "basically, to hell with them."[72] Nor, despite the immigration law features of the case, did any representative of the immigration bar file briefs.

As oral argument approached, observers considered Justice Kennedy the likely decisive vote. Chief Justice Rehnquist had dissented from the *Sure–Tan* holding that undocumented workers were even statutory "employees" under the NLRA, and together with Justices Scalia and Thomas seemed certain to reject the analysis of the Board and D.C.

---

69 The state attorneys general *amicus* was drafted by labor attorneys in the office of Elliott Spitzer, Attorney General of New York, see 2001 WL 1636790, and other states were recruited to sign on. The New York Attorney General's Office recognized that a substantial number of their labor cases involved immigrant workers, and that an adverse Supreme Court ruling might threaten to undermine not only state labor law regimes but unemployment insurance, workers' compensation, tort, and other laws as well. The eventual signatories to the *amicus* included the attorneys general from three of the states with the highest population of undocumented immigrants (California, New York, and Arizona). Despite last-minute efforts in the week before briefs were due, attorneys working through state labor federations, bar associations, and personal contacts failed to persuade the attorneys general of Florida, Illinois, and Texas to sign on. Telephone Interview with M. Patricia Smith, Assistant Attorney General in Charge of Labor Bureau, Office of the Attorney General of the State of New York, July 21, 2004.

70 While notable for their endorsement of a Board decision favoring an employee, the employer associations applied a traditional economic analysis in arguing that a rule exempting employers of undocumented immigrants from ordinary backpay liability for wrongful discharge was "bad for business" and would allow outlaw shops to compete unfairly with mainstream businesses that honored labor and immigration laws. 2001 WL 1631729. One author of this chapter, Michael Wishnie, was counsel of record for the employer association amicus.

71 Although the September 11 attacks temporarily derailed broad-ranging U.S.-Mexico talks that had been underway all that year, important employer sectors such as the hotel industry and agribusiness continued to hope for an expanded guestworker program and other legislation to increase the number of available immigrant workers. The employers, sensitive to criticism that guestworker programs had historically sanctioned widespread labor exploitation, may not have wished to be seen endorsing an employer's efforts to avoid sanction for the retaliatory discharge of an immigrant involved in a union organizing campaign.

72 Telephone Interview with Ryan McCortney, January 16, 2004.

Circuit. Justice O'Connor, as the author of *Sure–Tan*, was assumed to be hostile to backpay for immigrants and might perceive the Board's decision as an unprincipled effort to limit *Sure–Tan* to its facts. On the other side, Justice Stevens had dissented in *Sure–Tan*, and Justices Ginsburg, Souter, and Breyer had displayed both a willingness to defer to reasonable Board decisions and a sensitivity for immigrants and working people. That left Justice Kennedy who, while a member of the Ninth Circuit, had joined an opinion holding that the NLRA applied to undocumented immigrants, penning a short concurrence that declared, "If the NLRA were inapplicable to workers who are illegal aliens, we would leave helpless the very persons who most need protection from exploitative employer practices...."[73] Although considered generally conservative, Kennedy had at times cast important votes in favor of civil rights and immigrant rights, and he had also supplied a fifth vote to affirm the Board in at least one case in which the justices might have come out differently were they judging the matter in the first instance.[74] Labor and immigration advocates hoped Kennedy's sympathy for the situation of exploited immigrant workers might combine with an understanding of the concerns of law-abiding small businesses about unfair competition to yield a fifth vote.

It was Ryan McCortney's first Supreme Court argument. He had been involved in the case since he was a junior associate, and by the time he stood before the justices he was a partner. A more senior lawyer had argued both times in the D.C. Circuit, but Ryan had told him, at a time when it was just talk, that if the case went to the Supreme Court, he wanted to argue it. So McCortney got his chance. It was a big day in his life—he said everyone expects to be really nervous, but that the morning of the argument he woke "as calm as I've ever been in my life." McCortney invited Wendy Delmendo, a former Sheppard Mullin associate who, while a stay-at-home mother, had drafted the briefs for McCortney, to come to the argument. Going into the argument, McCortney believed the key votes were those of Justices O'Connor and Kennedy.

As counsel for petitioner, McCortney spoke first. When, at the beginning of the argument, Kennedy asked him a friendly question—"And is it correct that when *Sure–Tan* was argued, IRCA ... was being considered by Congress and the Government in its argument told us that if IRCA had been passed, back pay would not be available?"—McCortney

---

[73] NLRB v. Apollo Tire Co., 604 F.2d 1180, 1184 (9th Cir. 1979) (Kennedy, J., concurring).

[74] *See* Romer v. Evans, 517 U.S. 620 (1996) (invalidating anti-gay state initiative); INS v. St. Cyr, 533 U.S. 289 (2001) (interpreting immigration statutes as preserving judicial review of certain removal decisions and not applying retroactively); Holly Farms Corp. v. NLRB, 517 U.S. 392 (1996) (upholding as reasonable Board determination that chicken catchers are NLRA "employees," not exempt agricultural workers).

figured he had Kennedy and needed only O'Connor's vote to win.[75] McCortney's theory was that he had to distinguish his client—who he claimed did not know he had hired an undocumented worker—from employers who did know. He had decided to label his client as the "innocent employer" to distinguish him from "the unscrupulous employer." The problem was that the NLRB's rule, which terminated backpay liability on the date the employer learned the employee was undocumented, might actually treat the employer who knew it hired undocumented workers more favorably than one who did not. As one justice remarked, "It seems to me that's absolutely upside down." McCortney was forced to admit, "that's the problem with the rule, is that it in some ways rewards the unscrupulous employer in *Sure–Tan* and penalizes the innocent employer, as in *Hoffman*." He continued, "If the unscrupulous employer knowingly hires an illegal alien, then whenever some kind of union organizing drive comes along and say gee, we can get rid of them, and we know they're illegal, and we're going to terminate them, then they can report them to the INS right from the outset ... get him deported, and cut off back pay." That prompted the following interchange:

> JUSTICE BREYER: Take an employer who, you know, all he does, he says, I've checked their cards, I've checked their cards, the cards say they're here legally, and he runs some God-awful sweat shop. Now, your theory, there is no remedy under any law against that employer but for a prospective remedy, and so everyone gets one bite at that apple.
>
> JUSTICE SCALIA: Well, he has to pay for the sweat, though, doesn't he?
>
> MR. McCORTNEY: Absolutely.
>
> JUSTICE BREYER: And it's pretty low cost, because he's violating every labor law under the sun.

Wolfson approached the oral argument with different concerns. A skillful and experienced Supreme Court advocate, Wolfson had clerked for Justice Byron White in 1989–90 and spent nearly the entire Clinton Administration in the Solicitor General's Office, handling a number of ERISA, labor, and employment law matters. But Wolfson was apprehensive that the Court would "tear my head off in this case," because the justices might conclude that the Board had impermissibly ignored *Sure–Tan*. The key vote of Justice Kennedy seemed to Wolfson "almost impossible" to secure. Wolfson also recognized that a hostile opinion reversing the D.C. Circuit could sweep more broadly than necessary, endangering cases involving knowing employers, state law regimes, and

[75] The transcript of oral argument is available at 2002 WL 77224.

perhaps the Board's remedial authority generally. Wolfson also knew that when his colleague Edwin Kneedler had argued *Sure–Tan* before the Supreme Court, Kneedler had seemed to concede that, were Congress to prohibit the employment of undocumented workers, those workers would become ineligible for backpay (Wolfson later did not recall any discussion in the Solicitor General's Office of the possibility that Kneedler, who had argued many recent immigration cases before the Court, would take on *Hoffman*).[76]

Despite these concerns, there were some signs during McCortney's argument that not all was lost for Castro and the Board. Justices Scalia and Kennedy had both commented that the Court's *Sure–Tan* opinion did not decide the issues in *Hoffman*— remarks that signaled a majority of the Court might agree with the D.C. Circuit and Board on this crucial threshold point. Yet Wolfson was challenged the moment he rose to speak, unable even to complete the traditional opening, "May it please the Court," before Justice Scalia interrupted. "What was the position of the Immigration and Naturalization Service— ... in this matter when it was told that it—that you're going to argue that courts should pay illegal aliens money that it was unlawful for them to earn? What did the INS say to that?" Wolfson replied, "The INS has agreed with it and accepts it." Scalia retorted, "well, I have no—it explains why we have a massive problem of illegal immigration, if that's how the INS feels about this."[77] Scalia then pushed Wolfson on whether undocumented immigrants should ever be eligible for backpay because they are unable lawfully to mitigate: "If he's smart he'd say, how can I mitigate, it's unlawful for me to get another job.... I can just sit home and eat chocolates and get my back pay."

More devastating than Scalia's barbs, however, was the moment mid-way through Wolfson's argument when Justice Kennedy leaned forward to ask if it would be lawful if a union "knowingly uses an alien for organizing activity." Wolfson answered that under *Sure–Tan* and Board precedent, undocumented immigrants are included in a bargaining unit, but Kennedy pressed the unexpected, and unmistakably hostile, point. "And that doesn't induce illegal immigration? ... Here what

[76] Sure–Tan, Inc. v. NLRB, Transcript of Oral Argument, 1983 Trans Lexis 5, at 47–48 (government statement that if Congress barred employment of undocumented immigrants, the "employment relationship would then become illegal, and for the Board to order the reinstatement of the employee to an illegal relationship and to pay him inconsistent with such a statute would clearly be improper"); Telephone Interview with Paul R.Q. Wolfson, March 1, 2004.

[77] Wolfson recalled that Solicitor General Theodore Olson was dismayed by Scalia's question, because the Solicitor's Office represents both the INS and the NLRB. Wolfson himself thought the inquiry an improper intrusion into the internal deliberations of the executive branch. Telephone Interview with Paul R.Q. Wolfson, March 1, 2004.

you're saying is that a union can, I suppose even knowingly, use illegal aliens on the workforce to organize the employer.... That seems to me completely missing from ... any equitable calculus in your brief. I'm quite puzzled by it." Kennedy's aversion to the very idea of undocumented immigrants participating in a union was an ominous portent and strongly suggested that the Board would lose.

McCortney had expected his "innocent employer" strategy to be successful, but only in the middle of the government's presentation did he feel it had truly delivered the case. Justice O'Connor asked Wolfson, "What [the Board's rule is] doing, though, really is kind of odd, because the result is that back pay awards to illegal workers are likely to be greater than to legal ones under this Board's policy, and that's so odd, and it gives the illegal alien an incentive to try to phony up more documents and to extend for the longest possible time the charade that the worker is here lawfully, and that's surely strongly against the policies of the immigration act at the very least." At this question, McCortney suspected he had the fifth vote he needed.

Overall, Wolfson had wanted to present the case as a *labor* case in which deference to the Board was appropriate, but much of the argument treated it as an *immigration* case arising under IRCA. "I could hear the INS attorneys shifting nervously behind me," Wolfson remembers, during questioning about the Board's authority and expertise in considering IRCA when fashioning a remedial order. The justices' focus on IRCA also served to highlight Castro's wrongdoing in tendering false documents; had the argument centered more on the NLRA, Wolfson would have had more opportunities to discuss Hoffman's own misconduct in discharging Castro for his union activities. In a final reminder that behind the Court's theoretical discussion of national immigration and labor policies exist the lives and experiences of real people, the day after argument Wolfson received a call from the Office of the President of Mexico, offering to assist in locating the man still referred to as Jose Castro.

Many observers of the litigation had predicted before argument that Hoffman would prevail, and the oral presentations seemed to confirm their hunch. Accordingly, the very afternoon of the argument, a small group of labor and immigration advocates met with staff to the Senate Labor Committee and Senate Immigration Subcommittee to begin developing a legislative strategy in the event the Court overturned the Board's order.

The Supreme Court Decision

The Supreme Court reversed the D.C. Circuit, 5–4. Chief Justice Rehnquist wrote the majority opinion, which was joined by Justices

Scalia, Thomas, O'Connor, and Kennedy. Justice Breyer dissented, joined by Justices Stevens, Souter, and Ginsburg.[78] This was the same line-up that had decided many other politically controversial decisions of the Rehnquist Court, including civil rights, voting rights, federalism issues, and the election-determining *Bush v. Gore*.[79]

Chief Justice Rehnquist's opinion began by analogizing employees who work without immigration authorization to employees who are ineligible for reinstatement or backpay because they have "committed serious criminal acts" such as trespass or violence against the employer's property. The Court then noted that in *Sure–Tan* it had held that the Board lacked authority to order reinstatement of employees who had departed for Mexico, even though the employer had violated § 8(a)(1) and § 8(a)(3) by reporting the employees to the INS in retaliation for union activity. Next, the Court distinguished its prior decision in *ABF Freight System, Inc. v. NLRB*, which had held that the Board was not obligated to deny backpay to an employee who gave false testimony in a compliance proceeding.[80] The Court said that perjury, "though serious, was not at all analogous to misconduct that renders an underlying employment relationship illegal."

Then the Court came to the heart of its reasoning—whether a backpay award would undermine "a federal statute or policy outside the Board's competence to administer," namely, the immigration laws. The Court explained that IRCA prohibits employers from hiring undocumented workers, and obligates employers to discharge them upon discovery of the undocumented status. The Court also noted that the Immigration and Nationality Act prohibits non-citizens from using false documents. Repeatedly characterizing Castro's behavior as "criminal"—despite Castro's acknowledgment on his initial employment application that he was unauthorized to work in the United States and the absence of any criminal charge or conviction—the Court went on to explain that awarding backpay "condones and encourages future violations" of immigration law because the eligibility for backpay turns both on remaining (presumably illegally) in the United States and mitigating damages by finding other work (also presumably illegally). Hoffman's own illegal conduct in firing Castro for his union activities was almost absent from the majority opinion. To the question whether denial of backpay would encourage employers who hire unauthorized workers by allowing them to violate labor law with impunity, Rehnquist responded curtly that the cease and desist order and notice posting requirement are "sufficient to effectuate national labor policy." The majority expressly declined to

---

[78] Hoffman Plastic Compounds, Inc. v. NLRB, 535 U.S. 137 (2002).

[79] 531 U.S. 98 (2000).

[80] 510 U.S. 317 (1994).

decide whether awarding backpay to Castro would be impermissibly punitive, inasmuch as undocumented workers "have no entitlement to work in the United States at all," and, therefore, arguably might not be entitled to be paid anything. Notably, Chief Justice Rehnquist's opinion did not attempt to reargue that undocumented workers are not statutory "employees," the point on which he and Justice Powell had dissented in *Sure–Tan*.

In dissent, Justice Breyer began by noting that all agencies of the United States responsible for enforcing immigration and labor policy had concluded that backpay was consistent with immigration policy and, indeed, "helps to deter unlawful activity that *both* labor laws *and* immigration laws seek to prevent." Justice Breyer continued: "Without the possibility of the deterrence that backpay provides," employers might conclude that they could violate the labor laws with impunity. Next, examining the text and history of the INA, Breyer noted that IRCA does not state how violation of its provisions should affect enforcement of other laws, but that the policy underlying IRCA—"to diminish the attractive force of employment, which like a 'magnet' pulls illegal immigrants toward the United States"—is undermined by denial of backpay, which reduces the cost of labor law violations for employers and thus "increases the employer's incentive to find and to hire illegal-alien employees."

Justice Breyer also challenged the majority's analogy to cases in which backpay was denied because of an employee's serious criminal acts. In those cases, Breyer observed, reinstatement and backpay were denied because the employee *responded* to the employer's anti-union conduct with illegal conduct, and it was the employee's illegal conduct that both prompted and justified the employer in firing the employee. Here, in contrast, the employer's anti-union conduct was the firing, and it was neither motivated by nor justified by the employee's own conduct. After all, according to the uncontested factual finding, Hoffman had no idea that Castro was undocumented. Finally, Justice Breyer dismissed the majority's objection that a backpay award would represent "unlawfully earned wages" that could be obtained only through "criminal fraud." The same award "requires an employer who has violated the labor laws to make a meaningful monetary payment" for work that the employer believed the employee could lawfully have earned for work that he would have performed absent the employer's illegal conduct.

Ultimately, the Court confronted a choice. It could wholly exempt a law-breaking employer from all monetary sanction, as Hoffman urged, because the illegally discharged employee happened also to be an unauthorized immigrant. Or the Court could defer to the Board's conclusion and enforce a compromise remedy that awarded Castro less than the traditional make-whole relief of full backpay *and* reinstatement, but more than nothing. At a broader level, the Court faced a choice between reading the labor and immigration laws as contradictory or, as the legislative history of IRCA seemed to indicate, as part of a comprehensive congressional scheme to protect wage levels in the U.S. while diminishing the incentive for outlaw employers to prefer unauthorized immigrants to legal workers. In the majority opinion's only reference to the legislative history of IRCA, a footnote, the opinion dismissed the legislative history as "a single Committee Report from one House of a politically divided Congress." The majority went on to assert that the legislative history showed only that Congress endorsed the *Sure–Tan* holding that undocumented aliens are employees, and said nothing about the Board's authority to award backpay. The majority rejected the possibility that, because Castro had in fact sought and obtained work after Hoffman illegally fired him, the precise operation of the duty to mitigate could be postponed to a future case. Instead, the majority chose a different path, convinced that the NLRA's compensatory and deterrence goals were either fully accomplished through a cease-and-desist order, or could not be reconciled with IRCA, or, more likely, that the NLRA's purposes were simply less important than those of the immigration law's document fraud provisions.

The Supreme Court handed down its opinion in *Hoffman* in March 2002, only two months after the argument. The rapid ruling caught advocates for both sides by surprise. McCortney and his client were delighted; labor and immigrant defense advocates were quick to condemn the decision and vowed to seek a legislative fix. McCortney heard about it on the radio on his way into work and by the time he spoke to his client, Ron Hoffman said: "There are five TV camera trucks in my parking lot. What should I do?" Hoffman insisted the case was less a matter of money than of principle. Indeed, he ultimately paid as much in legal fees ($45,000) as he would have paid in back wages had he simply followed the Board's initial order to offer reinstatement to Jose Castro.[81] By March 2002, if the backpay award going back to 1989 were upheld, the accumulated pay plus interest would have been a considerable sum. Hoffman had told the press after the case was argued that it was unfair that he should be forced to pay backpay to *any* worker whom he fired, regardless of immigration status. "I don't think it's right to pay backpay for anyone who doesn't earn it—whether they are here legally or illegally."[82] Both he and McCortney were upset that the long delays in the appellate process (the Supreme Court decided the case thirteen years after Castro had been fired) meant that the accumulated interest on the backpay award was substantial, and that the number of years for which

---

[81] Steve Toloken, *Supreme Court Hears Hoffman*, Plastics News, Jan. 21, 2002, at 3.

[82] Thomas Maier, *Pitting Labor Against INS Laws*, Newsday, Feb. 19, 2002.

Castro might have been eligible for backpay vastly exceeded the number of months that Castro had worked for Hoffman.

To organizers and workers watching the case, the thirteen-year delay sent an equally troubling message. A wait of more than a decade from termination to final adjudication, even if backpay relief were available, is enough to dissuade many workers from bothering to pursue relief from the Board. Union organizers working in Los Angeles today agree. Lawyers and unions working with the predominantly Latino, and heavily undocumented, low-wage workforce in Southern California believe that the NLRB will do nothing to help protect workers who seek to join unions. They long ago concluded that the Board's processes are worse than useless for winning representation, and recognize that organizing campaigns are won based solely on the union's support among workers and the community, not based on legal protections for union elections. They regard *Hoffman Plastic* as just another nail in the coffin of labor law. As one SEIU organizer said, "the law was bad before, but it's ridiculous now. But the strength of the union doesn't come from the law.... It comes from the power of the members."[83] An SEIU lawyer did not think that undocumented workers were deterred from joining a union by weak NLRA protections.[84]

Wolfson was naturally disappointed by the result but also relieved that the Court had found the case relatively difficult and had split 5–4. He was also consoled that Chief Justice Rehnquist's opinion had not been disdainful of the Board. From the perspective of the Solicitor General's Office, which represents the Board before the Court every Term, preserving the justices' respect for the NLRB is an important goal. *Hoffman Plastic* was an important case, but it was only one of many the Board must defend before the Court. Wolfson felt he had protected the Board's institutional reputation and its claim to deference in future cases.

Whatever the case meant to others, it seemed to have done little for Jose Castro. At the time of the compliance hearing in June 1993, Castro was living and working in Texas. By the time of the Supreme Court argument, according to an NLRB spokesperson, he was living in Mexico.[85] The case did trouble Dionisio Gonzalez, the organizer who first tried to help the Hoffman employees. When interviewed about the decision in

---

[83] Interview with SEIU organizer Leticia Salcedo, September 24, 2003. On the attitudes of Los Angeles union organizers toward the challenges of organizing immigrant workers, see *Organizing Immigrants: The Challenge for Unions in Contemporary California* (Ruth Milkman ed. 2000).

[84] Interview with Monica Guizar, lawyer representing SEIU Local 1877 in Los Angeles, September 26, 2003.

[85] Steve Toloken, *Supreme Court Hears Hoffman*, Plastics News Jan. 21, 2002, at 3.

April 2002, he was working as an organizer for the United Steelworkers. He said: "It makes it real difficult to convince someone to sign a union card.... At Hoffman I told them they were protected under the law. I guess I was wrong."[86]

The Immediate Impact and Continuing Importance of Hoffman Plastic

Not surprisingly, the initial reaction to the decision by labor and immigrant rights advocates was extremely critical. One scholar labeled *Hoffman* as a revival of the infamous Bracero Program, a discredited form of guestworker program that brought 4.6 million Mexicans to the United States for agricultural work between 1946 and 1962 but did so under circumstances that ensured they worked for low wages in poor conditions.[87] Others expressed dismay that the decision had encouraged employers to violate labor laws with impunity.[88] While some of these concerns may be overstated, some employers did seek to take immediate advantage. In New York, a lawyer for an employer who had violated minimum wage laws threatened a group of protesters outside his client's store, citing *Hoffman* and claiming the Supreme Court had ruled "illegal immigrants do not have the same rights as U.S. citizens."[89] Immigrants, perhaps cowed by the reduced protection against retaliation, reported fewer labor violations to the New York Attorney General's Office after the Court's decision.[90] Reflecting the lack of a uniform employer view on the case while it was being litigated, employer responses to the decision were mixed.[91]

The *Hoffman* decision had a number of immediate legal effects. At the Supreme Court, the lawyers and the justices seemed concerned about

---

[86] Nancy Cleeland, *Employers Test Ruling on Immigrants Labor; Some Firms are Trying to Use Supreme Court Decision as Basis for Avoiding Claims Over Workplace Violations*, L.A. Times, Apr. 22, 2002, at C1.

[87] Christopher David Ruiz Cameron, *Borderline Decisions: Hoffman Plastic Compounds, the New Bracero Program, and the Supreme Court's Role in Making Federal Labor Policy*, 51 UCLA L. Rev. 1, 2–4 (2003).

[88] Rebecca Smith & Maria Blanco, *Used and Abused: The Treatment of Undocumented Victims of Labor Law Violations Since Hoffman Plastic Compounds v. NLRB*, 8 Bender's Immigr. Bull. 890 (May 15, 2003).

[89] Ironically, the attorney for the workers, Ben Sachs, had been the principal author of the ACLU's amicus brief in *Hoffman Plastic*, and he was well-positioned to advise his clients on the actual holding of the case.

[90] Telephone interview with M. Patricia Smith, July 21, 2004.

[91] *See, e.g.*, Scott Hauge, *Letter, Court hurts those who play by rules*, S.F. Chron., Apr. 4, 2002 ("small business community is outraged" by Hoffman decision, which is "slap in the face to employers that play by the rules" and unfair "to the employer who is trying to play it straight").

the implications of the ruling for remedies under labor and employment laws other than the NLRA. McCortney had argued that a ruling for Hoffman would affect only backpay for work not performed. Thus, he attempted to draw a line between laws like the Fair Labor Standards Act that require payment of wages for work performed—to which undocumented immigrants would be entitled—and laws like the NLRA and Title VII that provide prospective remedies, such as backpay, for work not performed. Wolfson pointed out in his argument that most states have held that undocumented workers are entitled to workers' compensation benefits even though the benefits compensate in part for wages that were not earned.

The first wave of legal developments after *Hoffman* occurred in executive branch agencies and concerned just this question of remedies. Within months, federal and state agencies began to rescind old regulatory materials and issue new guidance. In general, federal agencies assumed *Hoffman* barred backpay and reinstatement under federal laws, but did not preclude other statutory remedies. The EEOC rescinded its prior directive that undocumented workers are eligible for backpay under Title VII and other federal anti-discrimination statutes, but reaffirmed that undocumented immigrants are statutory "employees" and remain eligible for compensatory and punitive damages.[92] The U.S. Department of Labor acted similarly, declaring that undocumented workers were still covered "employees" under the Fair Labor Standards Act and the Migrant and Seasonal Agricultural Worker Protection Act, and that such workers remained eligible for minimum wage or overtime compensation for work already performed.[93] And the Board itself, in its first post-*Hoffman* decision to touch on these issues, agreed that undocumented workers were eligible for damages for work already performed, where the employer unlawfully reduced employee wages in retaliation for protected activity.[94]

Only one agency explicitly grappled with the case of the "knowing" employer, a distinction that had been crucial to McCortney in crafting his arguments and a case that Justice Breyer in dissent had maintained was not before the Court. Unfortunately for workers, in July 2002 the NLRB General Counsel rejected the arguments of the AFL–CIO and others and concluded that all employers, innocent or knowing, were exempt from backpay liability for the wrongful discharge of undocu-

---

[92] Nancy Montwieler, *EEOC: EEOC Limits Undocumented Workers' Relief Based on Recent Supreme Court Decision*, 126 Daily Lab. Rep. (BNA) at A–2 (July 1, 2002).

[93] U.S. Dep't of Labor, *Fact Sheet #48, Application of U.S. Labor Laws to Immigrant Workers: Effect of* Hoffman Plastics *Decision on Laws Enforced by the Wage and Hour Division* (Aug. 19, 2002).

[94] Tuv Taam Corp., 340 NLRB No. 86, at 4 & n.4, 2003 WL 22295361 (2003).

mented workers.[95] The General Counsel sets enforcement policy for the NLRB, and thus his determination that employers who deliberately hire undocumented workers are exempt from backpay liability was a blow for those in the NLRB's regional offices and in the labor movement who had hoped that the NLRB would take a more limited view of *Hoffman.*

Some state agencies, including in California and Washington, took a different view, concluding that nothing in *Hoffman* preempted state laws allowing backpay, the very remedy at issue in *Hoffman*, to undocumented workers. The Attorney General of New York went no further than the U.S. Department of Labor, agreeing that undocumented workers remained eligible for minimum wage and overtime damages for work already performed, but declining to express a view on backpay, punitive damages, or other state law remedies.[96]

The implications of *Hoffman* have only just begun to be tested in litigation. To date, every federal court to consider the issue has endorsed the view, shared by all agencies, that immigration status is no bar to recovery of damages for work already performed.[97] As to other remedies, workers have succeeded in the earliest cases in pressing points rejected by the federal agencies. For instance, the only court since *Hoffman* to publish an opinion in a case involving a "knowing" employer determined that the employer was not immune from post-discharge liability.[98] And the first federal court of appeals to examine a post-*Hoffman* question rejected the EEOC's assumption that *Hoffman* even applies in Title VII actions. It said: "the overriding national policy against discrimination

---

[95] Memorandum GC 02–06, Procedures and Remedies for Discriminatees Who May be Undocumented Aliens after *Hoffman Plastic Compounds, Inc.* (July 19, 2002), *available* at <www.nlrb.gov/gcmemo/gc02–06.html>.

[96] *See* Cal. Dep't of Indus. Relations, *All California Workers Are Entitled to Workplace Protection* (after *Hoffman* decision, announcing labor agency will seek backpay "without regard to the worker's immigration status"); *Statement of Gary Moore, Wash. State Dep't of Labor and Indus.* (May 21, 2002) (stating that *Hoffman* will not affect availability of remedies under Washington state labor laws); 2003 N.Y. Op. Atty. Gen. No. F3 (*Hoffman* does not bar undocumented worker recovery under state wage and hour law for work already performed).

[97] *See, e.g.,* Liu v. Donna Karan Int'l, Inc., 207 F.Supp.2d 191, 192 (S.D.N.Y. 2002) (immigration status irrelevant to FLSA claims for time actually worked); Topo v. Dhir, 210 F.R.D. 76, 78 (S.D.N.Y. 2002) (same); Flores v. Amigon, 233 F.Supp.2d 462, 463–65 (E.D.N.Y. 2002) (same); Flores v. Albertsons, Inc., No. CV0100515AHM(SHX), 2002 WL 1163623, at *5 (C.D. Cal. 2002) (same); Cortez v. Medina's Landscaping, Inc., No. 00 C 6320, 2002 WL 31175471 (N.D. Ill. Sept. 30, 2002) (same); *see also* Martinez v. Mecca Farms, Inc., 213 F.R.D. 601, 604–05 (S.D. Fla. 2002) (explaining that, under AWPA, farm workers eligible for compensation for work already performed, regardless of immigration status, even after *Hoffman*).

[98] Singh v. Jutla, 214 F.Supp.2d 1056, 1061 (N.D. Cal. 2002). The *Singh* opinion was authored by Judge Charles Breyer, brother of Justice Stephen Breyer.

would seem likely to outweigh any bar against the payment of back wages to unlawful immigrants in Title VII cases. Thus, we seriously doubt that *Hoffman* applies in such actions.''[99] State courts have also generally held since *Hoffman* that the decision does not preclude undocumented immigrants from recovering for lost wages under tort law[100] or in workers' compensation cases.[101]

Courts have also generally barred discovery of immigration status in labor and employment litigation, concluding that compelled disclosure of a worker's status is irrelevant where remedies are available regardless of status and would have an obvious *in terrorem* effect on the willingness of immigrant workers to vindicate labor rights.[102] The NLRB too has concluded that discovery of immigration status is not relevant at the merits stage of an unfair labor practice proceeding and, further, that at the compliance (remedy) proceeding, it is the employer's burden to establish an employee's lack of work authorization to toll the backpay period.[103] Importantly, the Board has already rejected an employer's

---

99 Rivera v. Nibco, 364 F.3d 1057, 1069 (9th Cir. 2004) *petition for cert. filed*, 73 U.S.L.W. 3415 (U.S. Dec. 27, 2004) (No. 04–936).

100 *See, e.g.*, Tyson Foods, Inc. v. Guzman, 116 S.W.3d 233, 242–44 (Tex. App. 2003) (undocumented worker may seek damages for lost wages in negligence action for injuries suffered in forklift collision); Cano v. Mallory Mgmt., 760 N.Y.S.2d 816 (Sup. Ct. Richmond Co. 2003) (same, for injuries caused by electric meter explosion during course of employment); *see also* Madeira v. Affordable Housing Foundation, Inc., 315 F.Supp.2d 504, 506–07 (S.D.N.Y. 2004) (same, for injured construction worker seeking damages under state law). *But see* Sanago v. 200 E. 16th St. Housing Corp., 788 N.Y.S.2d 314 (App. Div. 1st Dept. 2004) (Undocumented worker injured at construction site may recover damages for lost wages only at rate he would have been compensated in home country); Balbuena v. IDR Realty, 787 N.Y.S. 2d 35 (App. Div. 1st Dept. 2004) (same).

101 Rajeh v. Steel City Corp., 2004 Ohio 3211, 2004 WL 1379829 (Ohio App. 7 Dist. June 15, 2004) (undocumented immigrant under order of deportation eligible for Ohio workers' compensation benefits); Correa v. Waymouth Farms, Inc., 664 N.W.2d 324 (Minn. 2003) (undocumented worker eligible for benefits under Minnesota workers' compensation law); Safeharbor Employer Services I, Inc. v. Velazquez, 860 So.2d 984 (Fla. Ct. App. 2003) (same); Cherokee Industries, Inc. v. Alvarez, 84 P.3d 798, 801 (Okla. Civ. App. 2003) (same); Wet Walls, Inc. v. Ledezma, 598 S.E.2d 60 (Ga. App. 2004) (same); *see also* Medellin v. Cashman, 2003 WL 23100186 (Mass. Dept. Ind. Acc. Dec. 23, 2003) (same). *But see* Reinforced Earth Co. v. Workers' Comp. Appeal Bd. (Astudillo), 810 A.2d 99, 108–09 & n.12 (Pa. 2002) (undocumented worker is statutory employee and eligible for medical compensation, but wage-loss benefits may be suspended due to immigration status); Sanchez v. Eagle Alloy Inc., 658 N.W.2d 510, 514–16 (Mich. Ct. App. 2003) (undocumented worker who tenders false documents ineligible for workers' compensation pursuant to state law ''commission of crime'' exception to coverage).

102 Liu v. Donna Karan Int'l Inc., 207 F.Supp.2d 191, 192 (S.D.N.Y. 2002) (barring discovery of immigration status in FLSA litigation); Topo v. Dhir, 210 F.R.D. 76, 78 (S.D.N.Y. 2002) (same, in litigation of FLSA and Alien Tort Claims Act cases).

103 Tuv Taam Corp., 340 NLRB No. 86, 2003 WL 22295361 (2003).

tender of a Social Security Administration "no-match" letter as sufficient to carry this burden.[104]

Labor and immigration advocates have pursued legislation to address the consequences of *Hoffman.* California enacted a law directing that state labor and civil rights remedies, "except any reinstatement remedy prohibited by federal law, are available to all individuals regardless of immigration status."[105] In 2004, Senator Ted Kennedy and others introduced major immigration reform legislation that included a "*Hoffman* fix."[106] It is notable, however, that the *Hoffman* fix was incorporated in a lengthy immigration bill providing for an expanded guestworker program and earned legalization—that is, a bill unlikely to be acted on for several years, as wider debates about comprehensive immigration reform unfold. The *Hoffman* fix provision was not attached to a "must-pass" bill essential to the AFL–CIO's legislative agenda, which suggests that while the measure has the support of the labor movement, it is not today among its highest priorities.

Finally, labor advocates have sought to attack *Hoffman* in international settings. In October 2002, the AFL–CIO and the Confederation of Mexican Workers filed a complaint with the International Labor Organization, alleging that the decision impermissibly infringed on workers' rights to organize, to bargain collectively, and to freedom of association. After reviewing the U.S. government's response, the ILO concluded that "the remedial measures left to the NLRB in cases of illegal dismissals of undocumented workers are inadequate to ensure effective protection against acts of anti-union discrimination" under international law.[107] Advocates also raised objections to the *Hoffman* opinion at the Inter–American Court of Human Rights, where in May 2002 the Government of Mexico had requested an Advisory Opinion whether the *Hoffman* decision was consistent with international human rights law. In 2003,

---

104 "No-match" letters are correspondence from the Social Security Administration to employers identifying discrepancies between SSA records and employer payroll tax filings. No-match letters are frequently used by employers as grounds to conclude particular employees are undocumented. The NLRB rejected an SSA no-match letter as not being "legally cognizable evidence regarding the immigration status" of listed employees. *Id.* at 5 & n.7.

105 Cal. Lab. Code § 1171.5(a) (West 2003); Cal. Civ. Code § 3339(a) (West 2004); Cal. Govt. Code § 7285(a) (West 2004). All three provisions were amended by enactment of Cal. Senate Bill 1818, c. 1071.

106 Safe, Orderly, Legal Visas and Enforcement (SOLVE) Act of 2004, S. 2381 (introduced May 2004), H.R. 4262 (introduced May 2004), § 321 (backpay or other monetary relief for labor or employment violation not to be denied because of employer or employee INA violation).

107 *See* Complaints Against the United States by AFL–CIO and Confederation of Mexican Workers, Case No. 2227, ¶ 610 (2003).

the Inter–American Court advised that under international law, immigrant workers, regardless of their status, were entitled to the same basic labor protections as citizens—including backpay.[108] To date, however, condemnations of U.S. labor policy in international tribunals have produced little change in the U.S.

It is perhaps hardest to measure the impact of *Hoffman* on actual labor organizing campaigns. Pragmatic labor organizers and employers know that even for citizen workers, the Board can rarely provide prompt or meaningful redress in the event of a legal violation. The loss of eligibility for backpay, a partial and delayed remedy at best, may not affect the decision of many undocumented workers whether to participate in a union campaign. The *Hoffman* decision "hinders workers from coming forward, but the real problem is employer sanctions" and the inability to secure reinstatement, observed one long-time labor organizer who, as an undocumented garment worker himself, once received an NLRB backpay award in the pre-IRCA era.[109] Even before *Hoffman*, unauthorized workers faced the risk of job loss and deportation, without possibility of reinstatement.[110] Yet, although undocumented workers were entitled to full NLRA remedies in the mid–1980's, the situation of immigrant workers was not a priority for the mainstream labor movement. Following *Hoffman*, however, the leadership of organized labor, especially those have embraced the cause of undocumented workers, have no choice but to address the reality of non-citizens in the workplace. Labor must confront the fact that there are now two sets of rules for workers, one that provides some remedies and deterrence to protect citizens and legal immigrants, and one that provides no meaningful remedies or protection for undocumented, low-wage workers.

Conclusion

Hoffman did not break new doctrinal or theoretical ground. Nor is it likely to affect labor or immigration jurisprudence generally. Rather than harmonizing the two statutory regimes, the majority concluded that immigration policies, as divined by five justices, trump labor policies. In many ways the opinion appears anachronistic, out of step with a trend toward deeper integration of regional, if not global, labor markets. It is also out of step with emerging norms of international labor law and human rights, as reflected in the critical appraisals issued by the ILO and Inter–American Court.

---

108 Advisory Opinion No. 18, Inter–American Court of Human Rights (Sept. 2003).

109 Telephone Interview with Wing Lam, Executive Director, Chinese Staff & Workers Association, July 22, 2004. *See* Russ Togs, Inc., 253 NLRB 767 (1980).

110 Telephone Interview with Muzaffar Chishti, June 3, 2004.

Nor is the opinion certain to endure. With the U.S. Chamber of Commerce and the AFL–CIO now united in opposition to IRCA's employer sanctions provisions, there is a real prospect that the prohibition on employment of unauthorized immigrants may be lifted before long, perhaps as part of another grand bargain on comprehensive immigration reform. Beyond repeal of employer sanctions, the interest of the business community in expanding guestworker programs, and its growing recognition of the inefficiencies of maintaining a vast transnational underground economy, together with the AFL–CIO's commitment to the cause of undocumented workers, have increased the prospects for broader reforms affecting immigrant workers. Behind the current policy discussions, too, looms the interest of both political parties in cultivating support among Latino voters. And there are national security considerations now as well, which favor creating a path to lawful status that will encourage undocumented immigrants to come forward, "instead of the current situation in which millions of people are unknown, unknown to the law."[111]

But whatever the prospects for eventual reform, in the meantime *Hoffman* seems likely to embolden unscrupulous employers who would hire and exploit unauthorized immigrants, resulting in more unfair competition for businesses that play by the rules, worse conditions of employment for citizens and legal immigrants, and an intensification of the "magnet" effect against which Congress legislated in 1986. For the *Hoffman* majority, Chief Justice Rehnquist wrote reassuringly that immunity from backpay liability "does not mean the employer gets off scot-free,"[112] because employers of undocumented workers remain subject to cease-and-desist orders and notice-posting requirements. To millions of workers in this country like Jose Castro, who labor under a different set of workplace rules, those words are of little comfort.

---

[111] President George W. Bush, New Temporary Worker Program: Remarks on Immigration Policy (Jan. 7, 2004) (transcript available at <http://www.whitehouse.gov/news/releases/2004/01/20040107-3.html>).

[112] 535 U.S. at 152.

Biographies of *Labor Law Stories* Contributors

Laura J. Cooper is the J. Stewart and Mario Thomas McClendon Professor in Law and Alternative Dispute Resolution at the University of Minnesota Law School and has twice taught at Uppsala University in Sweden. She received her B.A. degree from the University of Southern California and her J.D. degree from Indiana University School of Law, Bloomington, both *summa cum laude*. She clerked for Judge John S. Hastings of the United States Court of Appeals for the Seventh Circuit and worked as an attorney for Region Eighteen of the National Labor Relations Board. She currently serves as an arbitrator and mediator of workplace disputes. Her publications include textbooks and historical, analytical and empirical articles on labor law, labor arbitration and workplace dispute resolution. She is the co-author of *ADR in the Workplace* (West, 2d ed. 2005) (with Dennis R. Nolan and Richard A. Bales) and previously explored issues arising from the *Gissel Packing* case in *Authorization Cards and Union Representation Election Outcome: An Empirical Assessment of the Assumption Underlying the Supreme Court's* Gissel *Decision*, 79 Nw. U. L. Rev. 87 (1984). Professor Cooper is the Chair of the Labor Law Group, a non-profit international organization of scholars that has, for more than fifty years, collaboratively written textbooks in labor and employment law. Professor Cooper is Chair of the Legal Affairs Committee of the National Academy of Arbitrators and is the former Chair of the Labor and Employment Law Section of the Association of American Law Schools. She is grateful for the bibliographic assistance of Suzanne Thorpe of the University of Minnesota Law Library and the archival research of Georgetown University Law School student Jonathan Suh in preparation of the chapter on *Gissel Packing*.

Marion Crain is the Paul Eaton Professor of Law and Associate Dean for Faculty Research and Development at the University of North Carolina. She received her B.S. from Cornell University and her J.D. from the UCLA School of Law. A member of the California state bar, she practiced with Latham & Watkins and clerked for Judge Arthur Alarcon of the Ninth Circuit Court of Appeals before joining the faculty at West

Virginia University College of Law in 1986. She has since held permanent or visiting appointments at Duke University, George Washington University, the University of Alabama, the University of Michigan, and the University of Toledo. Professor Crain is the co-author of two textbooks published by Lexis Law Publishing, *Labor Relations Law* (with Theodore St. Antoine and Charles Craver) and *WorkLaw* (with Pauline Kim and Michael Selmi), and numerous law review articles. Professor Crain thanks the University of North Carolina School of Law for research support and Pamela Brown for excellent research assistance.

Kenneth G. Dau-Schmidt is the Willard and Margaret Carr Professor of Labor and Employment Law at Indiana University—Bloomington. He received both his Ph.D. in Economics and his J.D. from the University of Michigan. During law school, Professor Dau-Schmidt worked as a clerk for the United Auto Workers, and after graduation he worked first as the Counsel for the Labor Committee of the Minnesota House of Representatives and then as an Associate with the firm of Previant, Goldberg & Uelman in Milwaukee, Wisconsin. Professor Dau-Schmidt has co-authored or authored several books and numerous articles on labor and employment law and the economic analysis of law including: *Legal Protection of Individual Employees* (3d ed. 2002) (with Matthew W. Finkin, Alvin L. Goldman and Clyde W. Summers); *Labor and Employment Law: Cases and Materials* (3d ed. 2002) (with Robert J. Rabin, Eileen Silverstein and George Schatzki); *Law and Economics Anthology* (1998) (with Thomas S. Ulen); *Employment in the New Age of Trade and Technology: Implications for Labor and Employment Law*, 76 Ind. L.J. 1 (2001); *The Fruits of Our Labors: An Empirical Study of the Distribution of Income and Job Satisfaction Over the Legal Profession*, 49 J. Legal Educ. 342 (1999) (with Kaushik Mukhopadhaya); *Economics and Sociology: The Prospects for an Interdisciplinary Discourse on Law*, 1997 Wis. L. Rev. 389; *A Bargaining Analysis of American Labor Law and the Search for Bargaining Equity and Industrial Peace*, 91 Mich. L. Rev. 419 (1992); and *An Economic Analysis of the Criminal Law as a Preference Shaping Policy*, 1990 Duke L.J. 1. He has been a member of the law faculties at the University of Cincinnati and the University of Wisconsin, and has taught at Christian-Albrechts-Universität (Kiel, Germany), Friedrich-Alexander-Universität (Erlangen, Germany), and Université Panthéon-Assas (Paris II) (Paris, France). Professor Dau-Schmidt thanks Andrea Taylor, Chris Patterson, Carmen Brun and Nancy Brun for very able research assistance in the writing of his chapter. Andrea Taylor did the initial work, locating the attorneys who were interviewed and using her gift of personal charm to elicit their stories. Nancy Brun is a librarian by calling and vocation, and participated in this project for nothing more than the thrill of rummaging through archives. Chris Patterson and Carmen Brun are simply very bright and hard-working research assistants who always make Professor Dau–Schmidt look good by making impossible finds on short notice.

Catherine L. Fisk is Professor of Law at Duke University, where she teaches civil procedure and various labor and employment law courses. She graduated *summa cum laude* from Princeton University and from the law school of the University of California at Berkeley (Boalt Hall). After clerking on the federal court of appeals, she practiced labor law in Washington, D.C., before joining the appellate staff of the civil division of the U.S. Department of Justice. She has previously taught at the University of Wisconsin, Loyola Law School in Los Angeles, UCLA Law School, and the University of Southern California Law School. She has published frequently on union organizing among immigrant janitors, on the role of union lawyers in providing legal representation to individual employees on wage and hour and other individual rights claims, and on a variety of other labor and employment-related topics. Her writings are included in *Organizing Immigrants* (Ruth Milkman, ed. 2000) and in *The Changing Role of Unions: New Forms of Representation* (P.V. Wunnava, ed. 2004). In addition, she has published a series of articles and is currently writing a book on ownership of knowledge in the context of the nineteenth-century employment relationship. Her work has appeared in the Stanford Law Review and the University of Chicago Law Review among other journals. She thanks Paytre Topp, University of Southern California Law School Class of 2005, for her research assistance on the *Hoffman* chapter.

Julius G. Getman is the Earl E. Sheffield Regents Chair in Law at the University of Texas School of Law. He has previously taught at the law schools of Yale University, Stanford University, the University of Chicago, Indiana University—Bloomington and Georgetown University. He has worked as an attorney for the National Labor Relations Board and as an arbitrator, mediator and negotiator. He was previously a member of the Editorial Committee of the Labor Law Group and President of the American Association of University Professors. He has published many articles on labor law and previously explored the issues of *Mackay Radio* in his book, *The Betrayal of Local 14: Paperworkers, Politics and Permanent Replacements* (Cornell 1998). He is also the author of *In the Company of Scholars: The Struggle for the Soul of Higher Education* (Texas, 1992); and co-author of *Union Representation Elections: Law and Reality* (Russell Sage Foundation 1976) and *Labor Relations: The Basic Processes, Law and Practice* (Foundation Press 1988). His most recent book, edited with Ray Marshall, is *The Future of Labor Unions: Organized Labor in the 21st Century* (L.B.J. School of Public Affairs 2004).

Alan Hyde is Professor and Sidney Reitman Scholar at the School of Law, Rutgers, The State University of New Jersey, Newark. He is the author of *Working in Silicon Valley: Economic and Legal Analysis of a High–Velocity Labor Market* (2003), *Bodies of Law* (1997) and the co-author of *Cases and Materials on Labor Law* (2d ed. 1982, with Clyde W. Summers and Harry H. Wellington). He is currently working with Professors Summers and Dau–Schmidt on another labor law textbook, *Cases and Materials on Labor and Employment Law*. He has been a visiting professor at Yale, Columbia, New York University, Cardozo, and the University of Michigan law schools. His current research projects include the game-theoretic analysis of transnational labor standards; design of a North American Free Labor Market; work relations in labor markets with extremely short tenures and rapid turnover, such as Silicon Valley, California; and new global labor markets characterized by extensive transnational outsourcing of production and labor migration. His earlier articles deal with such topics as new modes of employee representation (such as caucuses and nonmajority unions); employee stock ownership; and political models of labor legislation. He lectures frequently on new employment relations, including serving as the key-note speaker at the XII Interamerican Conference of Ministers of Labor, Montréal, October 2002. He is a director of the Association for Union Democracy, Inc., and has represented the organization in litigation. He has also represented the American Civil Liberties Union and its projects in litigation concerning worker privacy and constitutional aspects of worker action. Professor Hyde maintains a personal web page at http://andromeda.rutgers.edu/~hyde/. Alan Hyde thanks Michelle McBrian, Marcus Villanueva, and Helen Walter for research assistance.

Thomas C. Kohler is Concurrent Professor of Law and Philosophy at Boston College. He teaches and writes in the areas of domestic and comparative labor, employment and employment discrimination law. He has published widely on these themes in the United States as well as in French, Japanese and German scholarly journals. Beyond labor and employment law, he teaches and writes on the themes of civil society, personhood, and religion and public life. He serves on the editorial board of the Comparative Labor Law and Policy Journal and is a member of the American Law Institute, the Labor Law Group, the Council on Civil Society, and the Council on Families of the New York-based Institute for American Values. Professor Kohler has held visiting appointments at the University of Texas School of Law and the Graduate School of Business of Columbia University, and served as Fulbright Visiting Professor on the Law Faculty of the University of Frankfurt (Germany). He has lectured widely in the United States, Europe and Asia. He has given the Hugo Sinzheimer Memorial Lecture at the University of Frankfurt and the Japan International Labor Law Foundation Distinguished Lecture at the University of Tokyo Faculty of Law. He has served as an Academic Expert for the Pontifical Academy of the Social Sciences at the Vatican, a member of the International Advisory Committee to the National College of Ireland, and Consultant to the Department of Sociology of the University of Warsaw for the American Council of Learned Societies. Prior to entering teaching, he practiced labor and employment law with a Michigan law firm and served as an attorney with the National Labor Relations Board in Washington, D.C.

Deborah C. Malamud is the An–Bryce Professor of Law at New York University Law School. She received her B.A. from Wesleyan University and her J.D. from the University of Chicago Law School, where she studied labor law with Prof. Bernard Meltzer. She clerked for Judge Louis H. Pollak of the United States District Court for the Eastern District of Pennsylvania, and for Justice Harry A. Blackmun of the United States Supreme Court. She practiced labor and employment law, on the union side, for four years at Bredhoff & Kaiser in Washington, D.C., where her practice included many duty-of-fair-representation cases. She began her career in law teaching in 1992 at the University of Michigan. In 2003, she joined the New York University Law School faculty, where she teaches labor law, employment discrimination, constitutional law, and the administrative and regulatory state. Her research focuses on issues of race and class, both in the contemporary United States and in the New Deal. *Steele v. Louisville & Nashville Railroad* is about all of these things and more, and serves as a reminder of the richness of labor law as a field of study and practice. Professor Malamud has written extensively on class-based affirmative action and on the role of the law in the development of the American understanding of what it means to be middle class. She thanks Eric Arnesen for his pioneering work on black railroad unions, Gretchen Feltes for extraordinary research librarianship, Catherine Fisk for editorial assistance beyond the call of duty, and the staffs of the many archives whose collections are cited in her chapter.

Robert B. Moberly is Professor of Law and Dean Emeritus at the University of Arkansas. Before moving to Arkansas as Dean, he was Trustee Research Fellow and Professor of Law at the University of Florida, where he served as Director of the Institute for Dispute Resolution. Additional appointments have included visiting professorships at the University of Illinois, the University of Louvain (Belgium), and the Polish Academy of Sciences. After receiving his B.S. and J.D. from the University of Wisconsin, Professor Moberly served as a law clerk on the Wisconsin Supreme Court and was a labor attorney in government and private practice. He has written extensively in the areas of labor law and alternative dispute resolution, co-authoring two books and publishing more than thirty articles in law reviews, including Cornell, Florida, Illinois, Washington, and Wisconsin, as well as in scholarly journals such as the Journal of Legal Education. He received the Center for Public

Resources Award for Outstanding ADR scholarship, and was the principal drafter of mediator ethical standards adopted by the Florida Supreme Court. Professor Moberly served as Chair of the Labor Law and Alternative Dispute Resolution sections of the Association of American Law Schools, and was an executive board member of the Labor Law Group and the U.S. Branch of the International Society for Labor Law and Social Security. He is a thirty-year member of the National Academy of Arbitrators and a life member of the Industrial Relations Research Association/Labor and Employment Relations Association. He gratefully acknowledges assistance in the preparation of this article from the University of Arkansas School of Law summer research program; J. David Dixon, third-year law student at the University of Arkansas; and Lynne M. Webb, Professor in Communication, Fulbright College of Arts and Sciences, University of Arkansas.

Dennis R. Nolan is the Webster Professor of Labor Law at the University of South Carolina School of Law. He was educated at Georgetown University and Harvard Law School and received a master's degree in history from the University of Wisconsin—Milwaukee. Professor Nolan practiced labor law with Foley & Lardner in Milwaukee and was Legal Advisor to the Deputy Under Secretary of the Army, working primarily on treaty negotiations. He joined the University of South Carolina law faculty in 1974, where he now teaches a range of labor and employment law courses. He has taught at the University of Washington and George Washington University. Fulbright grants took him on sabbatical leave to University College Galway (Ireland) in 1981–82 and to the University of Otago (New Zealand) in 1989–90. In 1996, he was a Visiting Professor of Law at the University of Sydney (Australia). Professor Nolan has published eight books and forty major articles and chapters on labor law, labor and employment arbitration, and legal history. He has delivered nearly a hundred and fifty papers and lectures, including conferences and lecture tours in Australia, Canada, England, Greece, Ireland, and New Zealand. In addition to his teaching and research, Professor Nolan has maintained an active arbitration and mediation practice since 1976. In October of 2002, President George W. Bush appointed him to the Presidential Board of Inquiry on the Work Stoppage in the West Coast Ports. He thanks Holly Newell of the University of South Carolina, Class of 2004, for her diligent research assistance.

Reuel E. Schiller is a Professor of Law and the Associate Academic Dean at the University of California, Hastings College of the Law. The primary focus of his research is twentieth-century American legal history. He has published several articles on the development of labor law and on the relationship between law and the administrative state since the New Deal. Professor Schiller teaches labor law, employment discrimination, administrative law and American legal history. He is currently at work on a book-length study of the interaction of race, labor, and the law in post-war California. His contribution to this volume was based on *The* Emporium Capwell *Case: Race, Labor Law, and the Crisis of Post–War Liberalism*, 25 Berkeley J. Emp. & Lab. L. 129 (2004). He would like to thank the librarians at the Hastings Law Library, the San Francisco Public Library, and the Labor Archives and Resource Center at San Francisco for their assistance obtaining materials used both in that article and his contribution to *Labor Law Stories*.

Calvin William Sharpe is the John Deaver Drinko—Baker & Hostetler Professor of Law and Director of the Center for the Interdisciplinary Study of Conflict and Dispute Resolution at Case Western Reserve University School of Law. He received his J.D. from Northwestern, his M.A. from Chicago Theological Seminary and B.A. from Clark College. Professor Sharpe was a law clerk to Federal District Judge Hubert L. Will of the Northern District of Illinois, an associate at Cotton, Watt, Jones, King & Bowlus, and a trial attorney for the National Labor Relations Board before entering law teaching. He teaches courses in labor and employment law, including a seminar on labor and employment law issues in the global economy, evidence, and alternative dispute resolution—all subjects addressed in his scholarship. Specifically in labor and employment law, he is the author of the treatise, *Understanding Labor Law* (2d ed. 2005, with Douglas E. Ray and Robert N. Strassfeld). His articles include *Integrity Review of Statutory Arbitration Awards,* 54 Hastings L. J. 311 (2003); *Review of CCMA Arbitral Awards: A Comparative Perspective*, in *Rethinking South African Labour Law in the New Millennium* (2001); *"By Any Means Necessary"—Unprotected Conduct and Decisional Discretion Under the National Labor Relations Act*, 20 Berkeley J. Emp. & Lab. L. (1999); *Seniority* in *Common Law of the Workplace* (1998); *"Judging In Good Faith"—Seeing Justice Marshall's Legacy Through a Labor Case*, 26 Ariz. St. L.J. 479 (1994); and *NLRB Deferral to Grievance–Arbitration: A General Theory*, 48 Ohio St. L. J. 595 (1987). Professor Sharpe has served as advisor to South Africa's post-apartheid Commission for Conciliation Mediation and Arbitration, and he currently serves as Chair of the Amicus Brief Advisory Committee of the National Academy of Arbitrators and member of the Board of Directors for the JUSTPEACE Center for Mediation and Conflict Transformation. Professor Sharpe thanks Robert Hartman for his valuable research assistance on this project.

Katherine Van Wezel Stone is Professor of Law at the UCLA School of Law where she teaches courses in labor law, employment law, comparative labor law, alternative dispute resolution, and contracts. She was previously the Anne Evan Estabrook Professor of Dispute Resolution at the Cornell University School of Industrial and Labor Relations and Professor of Law at the Cornell Law School. She received her B.A. from Harvard University *magna cum laude* and her J.D. from Harvard Law School. Prior to entering law teaching she practiced labor and employment law and civil rights law at the firms of Cohen, Weiss & Simon and Rabinowitz, Boudin & Standard in New York City. Professor Stone has taught at the Benjamin N. Cardozo Law School and has visited at the law schools of Yale University, Stanford University, the University of Chicago and New York University. She has also taught comparative labor law at the Sorbonne University—Paris I and was awarded a Davis Fellowship in the History Department of Princeton University. Professor Stone has published over fifty articles and book chapters in the fields of labor law, employment law, arbitration, and international labor law, including publications in the Yale Law Journal, the Stanford Law Review, the University of Chicago Law Review, and the UCLA Law Review. Her previous work in labor history includes the 1974 article, *The Origin of Job Structures in the Steel Industry*. Her books include *Arbitration Law* (Foundation Press 2002), *Private Justice: The Law of Alternative Dispute Resolution* (Foundation Press 2000), and the *Handbook for Labor Union Women* (1973). Professor Stone's most recent book is *From Widgets to Digits: Employment Regulation for the Changing Workplace* (Cambridge University Press 2004).

Marley S. Weiss is Professor of Law at the University of Maryland School of Law, where she has been a member of the faculty since 1984. She received her B.A. from Barnard College, and her J.D. from Harvard Law School. Professor Weiss has also taught at Eötvös Loránd University Faculty of Law, in Budapest, Hungary, and, in the summer program, at Central European University in Budapest. Before entering law teaching, for ten years she worked, first as Assistant General Counsel and later as Associate General Counsel, for the International Union, UAW. From 1986–1997, she maintained a part-time law practice, primarily handling labor law matters for a small, independent registered nurses' union. Professor Weiss' teaching and research interests encompass all aspects of labor and employment law—domestic, comparative, and international. Her most recent scholarly publication is *Two Steps Forward, One Step Back—Or Vice Versa: Labor Rights Under Free Trade Agreements from NAFTA, Through Jordan, Via Chile, To Latin America and Beyond*, 37 U.S.F. L. Rev. 689 (2003). Professor Weiss wishes to express her gratitude to Neda Morrar for her diligent research assistance which greatly facilitated the writing of the *Kentucky River* chapter.

Michael J. Wishnie is Professor of Clinical Law at New York University School of Law where he co-directs the Immigrant Rights Clinic and the Arthur Garfield Hays Civil Liberties Program. Professor Wishnie's scholarship, litigation, and advocacy have concentrated on immigration, labor and employment, and civil rights issues. Before joining the NYU faculty, Professor Wishnie was a staff attorney at The Legal Aid Society of New York and the ACLU Immigrants' Rights Project. He was a law clerk to Justices Harry A. Blackmun and Stephen G. Breyer of the Supreme Court of the United States and to Judge H. Lee Sarokin of the U.S. Court of Appeals for the Third Circuit. He is a graduate of Yale College and Yale Law School. In *Hoffman*, Professor Wishnie was counsel of record for *amici* business groups in support of the NLRB, edited several other *amicus* briefs, and participated in one of the moot arguments at the Solicitor General's Office. He gratefully acknowledges the financial support of the Filomen D'Agostino and Max E. Greenberg Research Fund at the New York University School of Law for the research and writing of the *Hoffman* chapter.

†